D0030436

How To Read This Guide

ACCESS® FLORENCE & VENICE is arranged so you can see at a glance where you are and what is around you. The numbers next to the entries in the following chapters correspond to the numbers on the maps. The text is color-coded according to the kind of place described:

Restaurants/Clubs: Red

Hotels: Purple | Shops: Orange

Parks/Outdoors: Green | Sights/Culture: Blue

Rating the Restaurants and Hotels

The restaurant star ratings take into account the quality, service, atmosphere, and uniqueness of the restaurant. An expensive restaurant doesn't necessarily ensure an enjoyable evening; a small, relatively unknown spot could have good food, professional service, and a lovely atmosphere. Therefore, on a purely subjective basis, stars are used to judge the overall dining value (see the star ratings at right).

Keep in mind that chefs and owners often change, which sometimes drastically affects the quality of a restaurant. The ratings in this guidebook are based on information available at press time. The price ratings, as categorized at right, apply to restaurants and hotels. These figures describe general price-range relationships among other restaurants and hotels in the area.

The restaurant price ratings are based on the average cost of a three-course meal for one person, excluding tax and tip. Hotel price ratings reflect the base price of a standard room for two people for one night during the peak season.

At press time the exchange rate was about 1.08 euros to $1 US.

Restaurants

★	Good
★★	Very Good
★★★	Excellent
★★★★	Extraordinary Experience
$	The Price Is Right (less than $25)
$$	Reasonable ($25–$45)
$$$	Expensive ($45–$70)
$$$$	Big Bucks ($70 and up)

Hotels

$	The Price Is Right (less than $125)
$$	Reasonable ($125–$175)
$$$	Expensive ($175–$250)
$$$$	Big Bucks ($250 and way up)

Map Key

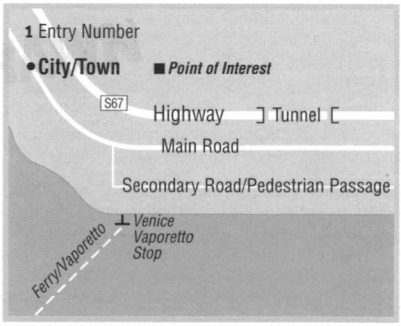

Getting to Italy

Airlines

The airports with the most international arrivals are Rome, Milan, and Genoa. Connections to the other cities in Italy can be made with national airlines like **Air One, Meridiana,** and **ALITALIA** (800/223.5730; www.alitalia.it), which also flies to Florence and Pisa.

You might also consider traveling to London and getting one of the new basic budget airlines. **Ryanair** flies from Stansted to Pisa (00 44 50503 770; www.ryanair.com), as does **British Airways** from Heathrow (00 55 50501 838; www.britishairways.com). **Meridiana** (00 44 199 111 333; www.meridiana.com) flies direct to Florence from London Gatwick. Just one word of warning: The Meridiana web site can be tricky to negotiate, and prices are much higher that the others even if you can get through the maze.

Getting Around Italy

Buses

Two bus services connect most of Italy: **ANAC** (Piazza dell'Esquilino 29, at Via Cavour, Rome, 06/4820531) and **SITA** (Via Santa Caterina da Siena 17r, between Via Luigi Alamanni and Via della Scala, Florence, 055/214721, 055/4782231). See the Orientation chapters of the individual cities for more information.

Driving

Members of the European Economic Community (EEC) can use their countries' driver's licenses in Italy. US citizens can get by with a photo-ID driver's license, but you may want to get an International Driver's Permit from the **American Automobile Association (AAA)** (check your local yellow pages or write to 1000 AAA Dr, Heathrow, FL 32746-5080, 407/444.7000; fax

407/444.7380) to be 100 percent official. Car rental abroad is almost always cheaper when arranged from the US in advance. Emergency service is provided by the **Automobile Club Italiano (ACI)**; simply dial 116 from any phone in the country.

Trains

The Italian state railway is known as **Ferrovie dello Stato**, or **FS**. The fastest train is the *Pendolino,* which links Milan, Florence, and Rome. The other trains, in order of efficiency, are the *EuroCity (EC),* an international train; *InterCity (IC),* its domestic equivalent, which operates between major cities with minimal stops; express (*espresso*), which is considerably slower than the *IC* and *Pendolino*; direct (*diretto*), which stops at most stations; and local (*locale*), which stops at all stations. *EC* and *IC* trains require the payment of a supplement (*supplemento*). A wide variety of special passes is available and deals on train tickets are constantly changing–check with a travel agent about them. Leave plenty of time to buy a ticket at the station, or purchase it in advance from a local travel agency (be sure to specify if you prefer traveling on an *EC* or *IC* train in order to pay for and receive the appropriate supplement; there is a stiff penalty if either the ticket or supplement is purchased on board). Another word of caution: Before boarding the train, be sure to validate your ticket in the machine that's usually located at the head of each track to avoid paying a hefty penalty aboard the train.

A seat reservation (*prenotazione*) is almost always recommended during the busy summer months and is included in the cost of an *EC* or *IC* supplement (it may be optional or obligatory on other trains and will cost extra). Nonsmoking seats are available in both first- and second-class sections, but they disappear extremely quickly, so be sure to reserve them well in advance.

CIT (Compagnia Italiana Turismo), owned by **FS**, has two offices in the US and two in Canada. They can help with rail schedules, passes, and ticket costs:

- 15 W 44th St, 10th Floor, New York, NY 10036 (800/CIT.RAIL, 800/248.8687; 212/730.2400 in New York).
- 6033 W Century Blvd, Los Angeles, CA 90045 (800/CIT.RAIL, 310/338.8616 in Los Angeles).
- 1450 City Councillors, Suite 750, Montreal, Quebec H3A 2E6, Canada (514/845.9101).
- 80 Tiverton Ct, Suite 401, Markham, Ontario L3R OG4, Canada (416/927.7712).

Information is also available from **Rail Europe** (800/4.EURAIL).

Yearly timetables are on sale at newsstands. They are called *In Treno* and are published by Trenitalia. They cost about $2, and cover the north and center of the country in one volume and the south in a separate volume.

City Maps

Individual city maps, collectively called *Tutto Città,* cover extensive ground off the beaten track. Most hotels and bars have a copy on hand. Less detailed maps are readily available at most hotels and all tourist information offices (see individual city Orientations for locations).

FYI

Climate

Northern Italy has a fairly moderate climate, although in recent years wintry conditions have frequently extended well into March and April.

Customs and Immigration

A valid passport is required to enter and leave Italy; no inoculations are needed. Visas are not necessary for visits of fewer than six months (for stays of six months or more, contact the nearest Italian consulate). Those visiting for more than three months are required to register with the local police station once in Italy. Hotels generally ask for your passport on arrival and will take care of this formality for you. If you are not staying in a hotel, you are expected to register yourself each time you change residences, though the Italian authorities are usually fairly lax about enforcing this requirement and few are the visitors who subject themselves to the guaranteed long lines and bureaucratic red tape.

Visitors are allowed to bring in up to 10,000 euros (about $10,000) cash; two still cameras and 10 rolls of film for each; one movie camera and 10 rolls of film for it; one video camera and one cassette for it; 400 cigarettes and 500 grams of cigars or pipe tobacco; and two bottles of wine and one bottle of hard liquor. When bringing in any other special equipment or prescription medicines, be sure to have documentation to back them up. From the US, contact the **US Customs Service** (202/927.6724) about obtaining the proper forms for equipment; a physician can provide a letter about medications.

Check with your local customs service about what may be brought back from Italy.

Drinking

Drinking is so civilized in countries like Italy. It is a genuine part of the culture. There is no minimum age limit, and bars are open daily for business from 8AM. Of course, almost all cafés and pasticcerias also sell alcohol, so there is no sense of having to go to a "drinking" place to drink. The more you know about your chosen tipple, the better. Especially where wine is concerned, Italians like you to be specific. Name your wine, or at least tell the bartender what you like and ask his advice. Drunken behavior is not acceptable here and is seldom seen in Italians. If your longing for a Manhattan or a JD and Coke gets overwhelming, Italy has an increasing number of what are called "American Bars" offering mixed drinks and premium spirits.

Drugs

Italy has stiff penalties for possession of any amount of narcotics.

Etiquette

Italians love titles, the most popular being *dottore* (*dottoressa* for women) for anyone with a university degree. More specific titles good for both sexes are *ingegnere* (engineer), *architetto* (architect), and *avvocato* (attorney). When in doubt, *dottore* or *dottoressa* will take you further than a simple *signore* or *signora*.

Holidays

There are a number of religious and state holidays when everything closes down. Expect massive delays, if not complete lack of services, on:

Capo d'Anno (New Year's Day), 1 January

Befana (Epiphany), 6 January

Pasqua (Easter), 16 April 2006, 8 April 2007

Pasquetta (Easter Monday), 9 April 2007

Liberazione (Liberation Day), 25 April

Festa del Lavoro (Labor Day), 1 May

Ferragosto (Feast of the Assumption), 15 August

Tutti Santi (All Saints' Day), 1 November

Festa della Madonna Immacolata (Feast of the Immaculate Conception), 8 December

Natale (Christmas), 25 December

Santa Stefano (St. Stephen's Day), 26 December

Each city also celebrates the feast day of its patron saint (see individual city Orientations for more information).

Hours

Many state-run museums now have extended hours to lessen the amount of waiting time. They are open Tuesday through Saturday, 9AM-10PM, and Sunday, 9AM-8PM, and close only on such important holidays as Christmas and Easter. City museums and smaller, privately owned or operated museums have confusing and ever-changing schedules. Refer to local listings or ask a hotel concierge or tourist office for a more definitive answer about all museums. See the individual city Orientations for information about dining, bank, and shop hours.

Medical Care

The **International Association for Medical Assistance to Travelers (IAMAT)** provides a list of English-speaking physicians throughout the world as well as a number of useful publications. Membership is free. Sign up by contacting the organization at 417 Center St, Lewiston, NY 14092, 716/754.4883; 40 Regal Rd, Guelph, Ontario N1K 1B5, Canada, 519/836.0102 ext 57; Voirets, 1212 Grand Lance, Geneva, Switzerland; or PO Box 5049, Christchurch 5, New Zealand.

Travelers with special medical needs should check with their doctors about the latest health precautions; in the US, call the **Centers for Disease Control** travel information line (404/639.3311; fax 888/232.3299) for up-to-date information. Your physician can provide generic prescriptions.

In nonemergency situations, ask a hotel concierge or contact the appropriate consulate (see individual city Orientations for listings) for help in finding a doctor or dentist.

Money

On 1 January 2002, the euro became the currency of Italy (including San Marino and Vatican City). It is now the sole currency.

€1 is just slightly less than $1. Making a trip to Europe a much simpler economic prospect for the American traveler, the euro is divided into 100 cents. Coin denominations are 1, 2, 5, 10, 20, and 50 cents and €1 and €2. The notes are €5, €10, €20, €50, €100, €200, and €500. All euro coins will be the same on the side showing their value, but the flip side will have a design peculiar to the country of origin. All coins and notes are legal tender throughout Europe except in Denmark, Sweden, and the UK. For more information there is a web site: www.europa.eu.int/euro.

Currency exchange offices (*cambio*) in airports and train stations sometimes charge exorbitant fees (information about these rates is usually posted, albeit in small print, according to amount changed), but this is so everywhere in the world. If there's no alternative, change only enough to make it through the day. As a general rule, the state-owned travel agency (CIT) and American Express offices offer good rates and fair fees. Money may also be exchanged in travel agencies, banks, and hotels at varying rates and for a fee.

Generally the best deal is to be got by taking money out of an automated teller machine (ATM). ATMs, called *bancomat* in Italian, are commonplace in Florence and Venice. Most are connected to such international networks as CIRRUS and PLUS; machines that accept Visa or MasterCard are also common. Your bank or credit card company can provide additional information about locations in different Italian cities. *Note:* Before leaving home, make sure your PIN (personal identification number) has the number of digits that will be acceptable in Italy.

Most hotels, shops, and restaurants accept major credit cards, but be aware that some credit card companies charge one percent of the transaction amount as a fee for converting foreign currencies. The rate of exchange depends not on the date of purchase but the date the transaction is processed, though the daily fluctuation of rates has generally been marginal in the last few years.

Postal Service

The Italian postal service (*ufficio postale*) is considered the most expensive and least efficient in Europe. Post offices provide mail, telex, telegram, and fax services (except to the US and Canada; to send faxes there, use a hotel or private fax service); use a courier for anything

Mannerist architect Bernardo Buontalenti is credited with creating in 1565 the first gelato, for the court of Francesco I de' Medici.

The Main Events

Traditional festivals are celebrated in most Italian towns in commemoration of local historical or religious events. The most notable in Florence, Venice, Tuscany, and the Veneto are listed here; some draw such large crowds that it's a good idea to make reservations in advance.

January

Epiphany is celebrated on the sixth of the month throughout Italy. In the **Regata delle Befane** in Venice, boats of all sizes are decorated and then rowed by costumed and made-up *befane* (witches) along the **Canal Grande** from **Palazzo Balbi** at **San Tomà** to the *calzagigante* (giant sock) that hangs from the **Ponte di Rialto**.

February

While **Carnevale** officially starts about two weeks before **Ash Wednesday**, Venetians really don't begin festivities until about a week before. Officially revived by the mayor of Venice in the late 1970s, this pre-**Lenten** festival is celebrated with masks and costumes, theatrical entertainment, masked balls, and an air of gaiety and lightheartedness. With crowds topping 100,000, **Piazza San Marco** and the neighboring streets become extremely crowded and noisy, while backstreet routes, restaurants, and hotels remain relatively tranquil. The grand finale includes fireworks over the lagoon on **Shrove Tuesday**. Tuscany's rendition of Carnevale is best experienced in the seaside resort of **Viareggio**, which bursts from its wintertime hibernation for the three Saturdays preceding Shrove Tuesday. On these days, the city's famous parade of floats—featuring papier-mâché images that are satirical commentary on the year's local and international political news—takes place. A fourth and final procession occurs on Shrove Tuesday.

March

El Rogo de la Vecia, Veneto dialect for "the burning of the buffoon," is a bonfire celebration with pagan undertones (overtones, too) held in various towns of the Veneto at the middle of **Lent**. In **Treviso** it's developed into high satire, in which papier-mâché puppets of lawyers, judges, politicians, and celebrities are put on trial in wildly comical proceedings and condemned to execution by burning, which takes place at night over the river. Eating, drinking, and other kinds of merriment accompany the festivities.

April

Scoppio dei Carro, literally "explosion of the cart," takes place at the **Duomo** in Florence on **Easter Sunday** in celebration of a Christian victory during the Crusades, and culminates in a great fireworks display. At High Mass, when the bells announce the Resurrection of Christ, the Cardinal Archbishop of Florence sets off a dove-shaped rocket (with flints said to have been brought back from Jerusalem during the Crusades) that runs along a metal wire into the piazza and into a large cart drawn by white oxen. When the cart explodes, the spectators cheer with joy, taking the event and the flight of the "dove" as a good omen for the future.

Festa di San Marco, on the 25th, is the feast day of Venice's beloved patron saint, when loved ones exchange red roses and a special High Mass is celebrated in the basilica of **San Marco** at 10AM.

May

On **Ascension Thursday**, in May or June, Florentine children celebrate the **Festa del Grillo** by going to **Le Cascine**, a park along the **Arno** at the edge of the center, buying crickets in cages and setting them free.

In mid-May (usually on a Sunday), Venetians of all ages and in all kinds of boats participate in the annual **Vogalonga**, a local regatta second only in popularity and color to the **Regata Storica** (see September, opposite). The regatta starts at 9AM at the **Molo** off Piazza San Marco.

The **Maggio Musicale** takes place in Florence from early May through the end of June. This festival, featuring classical music, dance, and opera, draws renowned performers from all over the world. (For more information, see "Maggio Musicale" on page 24.)

In Venice, the feast of **La Sensa** (the Sunday after Ascension) is a celebration of the marriage of Venice to the Sea. The mayor and assorted VIPs sail out into the lagoon in a copy of the *Bucintoro* (the official barge of the ancient doges) and a laurel wreath is dropped into the water. This is an updated version of an ancient ceremony in which a golden ring was dropped into the sea. The original words of the ceremony translate as "We espouse thee, o sea, in sign of our real and perpetual dominion over thee." Originally (and this ceremony has been on the go from AD 1000) divers would then compete to find the ring. For fairly obvious reasons, that is no longer done.

June

Florence is bathed in medieval splendor during the **Festa di San Giovanni Battista** (Feast of St. John the Baptist) on 24 June honoring its patron protector. The celebration includes a parade of more than 500 Florentines wearing colorful 16th-century costumes, followed by an extremely rough no-holds-barred game of something that resembles soccer, *calcio storico fiorentino*. Three games are actually played—two preliminaries and a final—within two weeks of 24 June. Four teams of 27 people play, each representing the old rival neighborhoods of **San Giovanni**, **Santo Spirito**, **Santa Croce**, and **Santa Maria Novella**.

From June through October, in odd-numbered years, the important **Esposizione Internazionale d'Arte Moderna** (International Exposition of Modern Art), better known as **Biennale d'Arte**, takes place in Venice in a small park beyond the **Riva dei Sette Martiri**.

On the last Sunday in June, Pisan residents line up to take part in a competition (dressed in Renaissance costume, of course) to push a giant leaden cart over the Ponte Vecchio to the other team's side in the Gioco del Ponte. Residents from opposite sides of the Arno river have always been on . . . well, opposite sides—so why stop now?

July

On the third Saturday of July, Venice commemorates the end of a deadly 16th-century plague with **Festa del Redentore** (Feast of the Redeemer). A bridge of pontoons is built across the **Canale della Giudecca**, from the door of the church of the **Redentore** to **Le Zattere**. The church, designed by **Palladio** and built as an offering of thanks for the end of the terrible plague, is open that Saturday and Sunday for visiting and Mass. Boats of all sizes and degrees of luxury (from ports far and near) arrive in the morning, their passengers opening bottles of wine and setting out food, flowers, and lounge chairs. As dusk approaches, celebrants eat, drink, and greet their neighbors. At 11PM the sky explodes for a half hour of spectacular fireworks, followed by the tooting of hundreds of horns. As the frenzy dies down, the great pontoon "bridge" opens, and for the next 24 hours, boats make the trek across the water. Spectators on land crowd the canalside *fondamente* to watch the festivities and then keep San Marco's restaurants busy into the wee hours of the morning.

And of course, in Siena the frantic, 90-second **Palio** race is run around the city center (see page 149).

August

Venice's annual **Mostra Internazionale di Cinematografica** (International Film Festival) is a 10-day festival held on the **Lido** in late August and early September.

In Montepulciano's Bravio delle Botte, after an entire week of serious partying (medieval style) amongst the whole town, teams of two from each of Montepulciano's eight neighborhoods compete in rolling huge barrels up the hill town's steep streets to the piazza at the top.

September

In Venice, on the first Sunday of the month, boat races and a magnificent procession of decorated barges and gondolas filled with Venetians in Renaissance dress highlight the **Regata Storica** (Historic Regatta) on the Canal Grande.

The **Festa delle Rificolone**, on the seventh, is celebrated in Florence with a procession along the Arno and across the **Ponte San Niccolò** with colorful paper lanterns and torches.

Also in Florence is the **Mostra dell'Antiquariato**, a prestigious international antiques fair, held in odd-numbered years in September and October at the **Palazzo Strozzi**.

Tuscany's centuries-old wine culture holds its annual festivities during the **Sagra dell'Uva** (Grape Festival) in **Chianti**'s principal town of **Greve**.

October

On the third Sunday of the month, a marathon starts along the Veneto's **Brenta Canal**. Runners follow the tow paths, passing Palladian villas, and finish the race in the center of Venice at the basilica of **San Marco**. Contact the **Venice Marathon Secretariat** (34 Via Felisati, Mestre, 940644; fax 940349) for more information about competing.

In Montalcino, they celebrate the Sagra del Tordo—the hunting season, basically—by displaying their archery skills, along with huge vats of polenta. All washed down, of course, with Brunello di Montalcino.

November

Venice celebrates the **Festa della Salute** on 21 November, forming a "bridge" of boats from **Santa Maria del Giglio** to **Santa Maria della Salute**.

December

Nine of Venice's churches work together throughout the Advent season to present **Christmas with Art**, a very grand version of the traditional *presepi*, or crèches, in which their artworks featuring imagery of the Nativity are put on display.

The **Feast of the Immaculate Conception** on 8 December is an important holiday everywhere in Italy, but in **Cortona** it is the day of the **Sagra della Caccia Fritta** (fried focaccia festival), when the Umbrian bread is served in every imaginable presentation and poems in its honor are read in the town's main piazza.

Radicchio in Piazza celebrates Treviso's most beloved native, the wonderful purple-and-white radicchio that grows there, on the Tuesday before Christmas, with the city's main square buried in tons of soil and turned into a radicchio garden, and local restaurant menus focusing on this divine lettuce.

LITERARY ITALY

Cradle of more than a few great Italian writers (Dante in Florence, Petrarch from Arezzo), Northern Italy has also had its share of expatriate writers-in-residence. The Brownings doted on Florence and Ruskin on Venice. The following is a sampler of the wealth of literature on these two cities and their surrounding regions.

Florence

The Agony and the Ecstasy by Irving Stone (Doubleday, 1961). This historical novel breathes life into the story of Michelangelo Buonarroti, offering a glimpse into the genius and troubled emotions that fueled one of the greatest artists of all time. It takes the reader through the daily, and often turbulent, life of the High Renaissance in Florence under the powerful Medici family.

The City of Florence by R. W. B. Lewis (Farrar, Strauss, Giroux, 1995). Lewis, a British scholar who called Florence his second home, gives a densely chronicled account of Florentine history from the bitter conflicts of the Guelphs and Ghibellines to his personal experiences as an intelligence officer in World War II.

A Florentine Merchant by Giovanni Caselli (Bedrick, 1986). The daily life of Florence is seen through the eyes of an adolescent Russian slave, Zita, who describes her master's household near the city during the 14th century. Based on the extensive household accounts and letters of Messer Francesco, this title gives great feeling for the period.

The Gardens of Florence (Rizzoli, 1992). This volume is filled with photos of Florence's lush greenery and meticulous lawns, along with text about the unique history (dating from the Renaissance) of each garden and the influential families that lived in the palatial structures surrounded by them.

The House of Medici: Its Rise and Fall by Christopher Hibbert (William Morrow and Company, 1974). Florence's most influential family provided the world with some of its most colorful diplomats, scholars, art patrons, popes, builders, and soldiers. The story begins in Florence during the Renaissance, with Donatello, Fra Angelico, Michelangelo, and Botticelli working for the Medici, and ends there several hundred years later amid decay and dissoluteness.

The Sixteen Pleasures by Robert Hellenga (Delta Fiction, 1989). After the disastrous flood of 4 November 1966, waves of foreigners swept into Florence to help rescue the city and its precious artworks from permanent damage from mud, water, and heating oil. One of these "mud angels," Margot, is a 29-year-old American who comes to see what she can save, including herself.

Tuscany

Under the Tuscan Sun by Frances Mayes (Chronicle Books, 1996). Widely published poet and food and travel writer Mayes spins a wonderful tale of the tastes and pleasures of Tuscany, peppered with an occasional recipe. With a poet's eye, Mayes leads the reader through the joy and frustration of building and restoring an abandoned villa near **Cortona**, embellishing her personal tale with observations about the Tuscan landscape, history, and culture.

Within Tuscany: Reflections on a Time and Place by Matthew Spender (Viking/Penguin, 1993). English sculptor Spender left his native land to explore the region that gave us the Renaissance and some of its legendary artistic heroes. With an artist's sensibility, the author recounts his life in Tuscany, melding history, anecdotes, and personal observations into a cultural profile that guarantees educational and enjoyable armchair travel.

Venice

Acqua Alta by Donna Leon (HarperCollins Publishers, 1996). The fifth in a series featuring police

important. Tobacconists also sell stamps. To receive mail at a post office, have the sender mark it *fermo posta* (c/o the post office or *ufficio postale*) in the city where it will be picked up; there's a small charge for this service.

American Express offices will hold mail for clients without charging a fee. Federal Express and DHL have courier services throughout Italy, but though they strive to meet American standards, they are still working out such bugs as on-time pickup and delivery.

PUBLICATIONS

Such English-language periodicals as the *International Herald Tribune*, the *Financial Times*, *USA Today*, *Time*, *Newsweek*, and *The Economist* are available on newsstands throughout Italy. Once an amenity of only the more expensive hotels, even lower-priced hotels now carry **CNN**, **Skychannel**, and other cable networks. **Radio Vaticano**, the Vatican radio station, periodically broadcasts the news in English.

RESTAURANTS

Most restaurants, including a number of hotel dining rooms, observe a *giorno di riposo,* one closing day per week. Tacked on to restaurant bills are a nominal charge for *pane e coperta* (bread and cover) and a separate service charge. Although most dining is à la carte, some restaurants offer a fixed-price *menù turistico,* a "one from column A, one from column B" affair of two or three courses. It's a good idea to make a reservation, although it is not required in most dining establishments. Lunch is usually served noon-3PM; dinner, 7:30PM-10:30PM.

Commissario Guido Brunetti, this mystery dabbles (as did one of the murdered characters) in stolen artifacts. As always, Brunetti provides a subtle investigation into Venice's sense of mask—things are never as they seem—and offers probing speculations on the residents' remote natures in this city on water where reality and illusion mix in fleeting reflections. Other titles by the author include *Death at La Fenice* (HarperCollins Publishers, 1992), *Death in a Strange Country* (HarperCollins Publishers, 1993), *Dressed for Death* (HarperCollins Publishers, 1994), and *Death and Judgment* (HarperCollins Publishers, 1995).

Across the River and Into the Trees by Ernest Hemingway (Scribner & Sons, 1950; reissued 1978). Colonel Cantwell has come back to Venice to die in what he calls "my town," but his improbable love affair with a young Venetian countess often seems secondary to Hemingway's passion for Venice. In this novel, the writer creates the literary fame of the **Gritti Palace** hotel and **Harry's Bar**—often way stations for today's American pilgrims. With his sensuous feeling for place, Hemingway invites the reader to walk the city's *calli* (streets), where "what you win is the happiness of your eye and heart."

Death in Venice by Thomas Mann (Alfred A. Knopf, Inc., 1928). On a trip to Venice in search of everlasting beauty, Gustav von Aschenbach, a successful author, becomes aware of his decadent tendencies and finally succumbs to a consuming love. The story is full of symbolism, with frequent overtones from Greek literature.

The Grand Canal (Vendome Press, 1993). This photographic and textual survey carries the reader—as if in a gondola—along the famous watercourse, all the while detailing the aesthetic and social history of each building.

The Stones of Venice by John Ruskin (Da Capo Press, 1853; reissued 1985). The author wrote this critique in response to what he feared would be the destruction of medieval Venice through restoration and neglect. Despite Ruskin's contempt for such buildings as the churches of **San Giorgio Maggiore** and **La Salute**, his magnificent account remains a classic, especially admired for the section on "The Nature of the Gothic."

Those Who Walk Away by Patricia Highsmith (Atlantic Monthly Press, 1967; reissued 1988). Ray Garrett convinces the police in Rome that his new bride committed suicide, but his father-in-law, Ed Coleman, believes otherwise. After Coleman's failed attempt at revenge, he heads for Venice; a wounded Ray follows close behind. Their eerie game of cat-and-mouse plays out in the back alleys and narrow canals of Venice.

Miss Garnet's Angel by Sally Vickers (HarperCollins, 2000). A wonderful novel: atmospheric, compelling, and, best of all for the Venice visitor, it creates a perfect little itinerary around Venice in the footsteps of the sweetly melancholic spinster Miss Garnet.

The Veneto

Italian Journey by Johann Wolfgang von Goethe (Penguin Books, 1962). In this fine travelogue about Italy, Goethe includes a description of his jaunt across Northern Italy to Venice. He brings both a poet's sensibility and a scientist's accuracy to his observations and impressions.

Italian Neighbors by Tim Parks (Grove Press, 1992). This perceptive and engaging record of late-20th-century life in Northern Italy was written by a "lapsed Anglo-Saxon." As a long-term resident of Veneto, Parks conveys both the follies and blessings of his adopted home.

Smoking

As of 1 January 2004, smoking in all public places has been outlawed. Large restaurants, hotels, and other establishments are allowed smoking areas, but they must be separated from the main part of the building by doors and have a specified amount of ventilation.

Taxes

Taxes are always included in hotel room rates and the price of meals and merchandise. The EEC levies a sales tax (Value Added Tax, called IVA in Italy) of about 19 percent (much higher for jewelry and other luxury items) on merchandise sold in Italy. Non-EEC visitors can request partial exemption on purchases of €100 or more made in any one store, and any tax paid can be refunded by mail or credited to your credit card. Getting a check refund by mail, however, often takes many weeks and sometimes months. Italian customs officials at refund counters in the major airports before check-in will ask to see a special form filled out by the merchant, an official receipt, and the merchandise.

Telephones

Making local or long-distance telephone calls from your hotel room usually costs at least twice as much as it would on the outside. The least expensive way to phone the US is to call collect and have someone call you back. AT&T calling-card users and those people calling collect can dial 1721011 to be connected to an AT&T operator in the US. MCI users can dial 1721022. Otherwise, go to an office of the **Telecom** phone company (formerly known as **SIP** or **ASST**), and pay cash after the call is made.

There are two kinds of phones in Italy; both offer international direct dialing. All phones accept euro coins or prepaid phone cards freely available at most vendors. When a phone is not working, a red light comes on and the initials "FS" (*fuori servizio*) appear on the screen. A sign posted on the phone reading *guasto* also means out of order.

The other kind of public phone accepts prepaid phone cards in 5,000-, 10,000-, and 15,000-lire amounts. These are sold at many bars and tobacconists (ask for a *scheda telefonica*). After tearing off the perforated corner, insert the card into the metal box on the phone. Many telephones offer both coin and card options, but most of the newer phones accept only the cards. The card decreases in value as it is used; be sure to have a fresh card to slip in before the card in use runs out of money and cuts off the call.

Recorded messages of changed numbers are appearing more and more in English, as well as in Italian. Dial information (12) for a listing.

Time Zone

Florence and Venice are on Greenwich Mean Time plus one hour (six hours ahead of US Eastern Standard Time). Clocks in Italy are set ahead one hour in the spring and back one hour in the fall, to coincide with Daylight Saving Time in the US and elsewhere in Europe. Italian timetables use the 24-hour clock, denoting 3:15PM, for example, as 15.15.

Tipping

In restaurants, the tip (usually about 15 percent) has been included when the words *servizio compreso* or *servizio incluso* appear on the bill, but you may choose to leave a bit more to bring it up to 17 or 18 percent. Otherwise, adding 15 percent is generous and should be greatly appreciated. Italians themselves generally leave an additional 1 to 2 euros per diner on the table. Taxi drivers get 10 percent. Tip porters, hotel maids, and concierges according to the quality of service.

Toilets

There are few public bathrooms in Italy. An air of self-confidence and a good sense of direction will help get you to the facilities available in the more upscale hotels. Otherwise, the price of a coffee or mineral water at the counter will entitle you to ask for *la toiletta* or *il gabinetto* in a coffee bar.

Palazzo Vendramin Calergi, Venice

FLORENCE ORIENTATION

Of all of Italy's glorious tourist destinations, Florence is perhaps the most popular. As the birthplace of the Renaissance, the city has a wealth of artistic and architectural treasures produced during that period. In the **Centro Storico** (Historical Center), behind the harsh stone of the city's numerous churches and patrician palazzi, lie some of the greatest works of art in the Western world. This, after all, is the city of

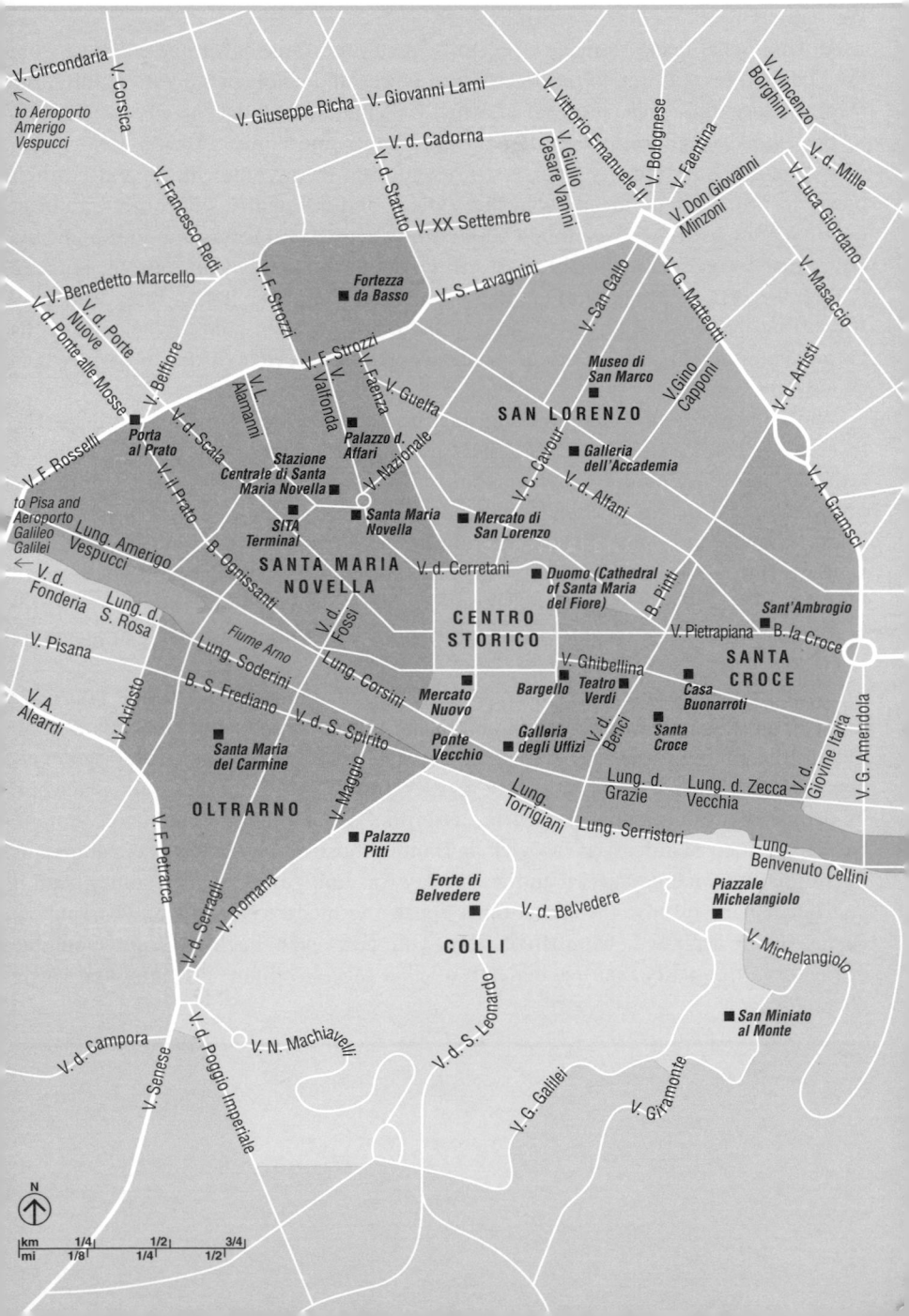

Michelangelo, Botticelli, and Ghirlandaio, and their works are here in profusion—in the **Galleria degli Uffizi** (Uffizi Gallery), **Palazzo Pitti** (Pitti Palace), and **Galleria dell'Accademia**. Some of the buildings themselves are architectural wonders known to every student of the humanities in the world—most notably **Brunelleschi**'s dome for **Santa Maria del Fiore** (the **Duomo**). Renaissance Florence was not just about art and architecture, though; the city also boasted some of the great writers and thinkers of the age, including Dante Alighieri, Petrarch, Boccaccio, Machiavelli, Leonardo da Vinci, and Galileo. Dante's *Divine Comedy* and Machiavelli's *The Prince* are two of Western civilization's classic writings.

Much of what made Florence a preeminent cultural force as Europe emerged from the Middle Ages was due to the wealth and power of a single aristocratic family, the Medici, whose influence (and coat of arms) is visible throughout the city even today. In the 14th through 16th centuries, the merchants and bankers of the Medici clan controlled not only the city's purse strings but also its government. They used their power to install family members in the Vatican and intermarry with other European nobility. They used their wealth to commission architectural works and to support the city's greatest artists. One of the most influential of the family's art patrons, Lorenzo Il Magnifico (1449-1492), put Florence in the forefront of the Italian Renaissance by supporting the work of Botticelli, Ghirlandaio, Filippo Lippi, and Michelangelo. His patronage resulted in such glorious masterpieces as Botticelli's *Spring* and Michelangelo's *David*.

While the glory days may be long past, there is a sense of continuity here. The fashionable courtiers in the city's Renaissance paintings are kin to today's stylishly attired Florentines. Modern-day merchants like Gucci have built international empires that could rival their Renaissance counterparts, and the city offers some of the finest shopping to be found anywhere in Europe. The Florentines' infallible sense of style is evident even in the touristy open-air **Mercato di San Lorenzo** (San Lorenzo Market), where, bypassing the mass-produced dross, the determined shopper can still find accessories and souvenirs of fine quality, made in Italy and for sale at moderate prices.

Florentines have sometimes been faulted for refusing to acknowledge that anything of note happened after the golden age of the Renaissance (or even before, though the site was probably settled by the ancient Etruscans and certainly developed by the Romans). There is, in fact, a reserved self-assurance about the place and its people that might support such an assertion. The Florentine character, though, has been criticized at least as far back as Dante, whose native dialect was adopted as the official Italian language when the country was unified in the last century. And if you listen hard to how the Florentines speak the modern version of *la lingua di Dante*—in an aspirated, countrified way—you may even begin to appreciate the down-to-earth quality that lies beneath all that Machiavellian ceremony and Gucci gloss.

City code is 055 unless otherwise noted. To call Florence from the US, dial 011-39-055, followed by the local number. When calling from inside Italy or within Florence, dial 055 and the local number.

Getting to Florence

Airports

Aeroporto Galileo Galilei

Pisa's **Aeroporto Galileo Galilei** (050/849300) is 85 kilometers (53 miles) from Florence. www.pisa-airport.com

Airport Services

Currency Exchange 050/41288
Customs 050/26280
Ground Transportation 050/44325
Lost Baggage 050/582400
Lost and Found.....050/44325
Police 050/29329
Traveler's Aid 050/582460

Airlines

Air France 284304, 800/237.2747
Alitalia 27888, 800/223.5730
British Airways.....800/247.9297
Lufthansa 1478, 02/588372251, 800/645.3880
Sabena 3371201, 800/955.2000

Getting to and from Aeroporto Galileo Galilei

By Car

To get to Florence from the airport, follow the signs out of the airport to **S67** east. This becomes **Via Baccio da Montelupo** in Florence, and crosses the **Arno** at **Piazza Taddeo Gaddi**. From there, either continue on to the **Piazza della Stazione** or turn right onto **Lungarno Amerigo Vespucci**. An alternative route (though not as scenic) is to take the **A11** autostrada east to Florence, then take **S66** east into the city, and turn right on **Via Francesco Baracca**, which becomes **Via del Ponte alle Mosse** on the opposite side of **Piazza Giacomo Puccini**. At the **Piazzale di Porta al Prato** (you'll see the old medieval entranceway to the city), go left to the Piazza della Stazione or continue and turn left on Lungarno Amerigo Vespucci, which runs along the banks of the Arno River.

Rental Cars

The following rental-car agencies have offices at **Galileo Galilei** airport:

Avis 050/42028, 800/331.1084
Budget 050/42574, 800/472.3325
Europcar.....050/41017, 800/227.3876
Hertz 050/49187, 800/654.3001

By Taxi

Taxi service to and from Florence is extremely expensive (about $170 at press time). The taxi stand is just outside the airport, and the trip takes about an hour.

By Train

Trains in Florence run to and from Pisa airport from Santa Maria Novella station. The direct train runs eight times per day and the last train from the airport is at 8:20PM. You will have to change at Pisa Centrale. Journey takes about one hour.

By Bus

Express coaches run from the airport to the bus station in Florence. Some airlines (Ryanair, for example) have buses coordinated to meet their flights.

Aeroporto Amerigo Vespucci

Service and facilities at Aeroporto Amerigo Vespucci (formerly called Aeroporto Peretola; 306.1300), located 4 kilometers (2.5 miles) from Florence, have greatly improved and expanded and after three months of renovation, the new Florence airport is open. It is gorgeous! The Florentines have spent 11 million euros on new and improved runways and 4.5 million euros on renovating and extending the airport facilities to ensure that coming to Florence and leaving Florence are pleasant experiences. New check-in desks, security check areas, and departure areas allow the airport to handle an ever increasing number of passengers. There are elegant shopping arcades, new bars and restaurants, business areas, chic lounges, and dedicated facilities for the elderly, the young, and passengers with disabilities. The new web site is very helpful: www.aeroporto.firenze.it. Information via e-mail: infoaeroporto@aeroporto.firenze.it

Airport Services

Currency Exchange 315642
Customs 3061610
Information.....3061606
Lost and Found.....308023
Police 317307

Airlines

The local general information number for most European airlines serving Amerigo Vespucci is 30615.

Air France 800/237.2747
Alitalia.....800/223.5730
Lufthansa 800/645.3880

Getting to and from Aeroporto Amerigo Vespucci

By Bus

Bus service to and from Florence's **SITA** terminal (Via Santa Caterina da Siena 17r, between Via Luigi Alamanni and Via della Scala, 214721, 4782231)

operates daily at approximately 45-minute intervals. The trip takes about 15 minutes.

By Car

To get from the airport to the center of Florence, follow the "Centro" signs out of the airport to **A11** east to Florence. Follow signs for **Viale Alessandro Guidoni**, then for "Centro–Viale Circonvalazione." After four stoplights, turn right on **Via Enrico Forlanini** to the roundabout. Bear left onto **Viale Francesco Redi**. At the next large intersection, head right on **Viale Belfiore** and continue toward **Porta al Prato**. Go left to the **Piazza della Stazione**. The rental car agencies can provide a map and more detailed instructions.

Rental Cars

The following rental car agencies have offices at **Aeroporto Amerigo Vespucci**:

Avis 315588
Budget/Maggiore 311256
Europcar.....318609
Hertz.....307370

By Taxi

Taxis to downtown Florence are available outside the airport. The trip takes about 15 minutes.

Bus Station (Long-Distance)

Two private bus companies, **SITA** (see opposite) and **Lazzi** (Piazza della Stazione 4-6, across from the train station), serve the Tuscany region. For information and schedules (in Italian only) for Lazzi, call 166856010, daily from 6AM-10PM.

Train Station (Long-Distance)

Florence's main train station, **Stazione Centrale di Santa Maria Novella** (Piazza della Stazione, 147888088), is right in the center of town. When buying a ticket to Florence, make sure the train stops at that station (also called "Firenze S.M.N.") and not the **Campo di Marte** or **Rifredi** stations, which are in inconvenient locations outside the town center. There's a taxi stand in front of the Santa Maria Novella station. www.trenitalia.com

Getting Around Florence

Bicycles and Mopeds

It's easy to see Florence on foot, but cycling to its sights is an attractive alternative. Many locals have adopted this mode of transport, especially now that most of the Centro Storico is closed to traffic (even mopeds). To rent a bicycle or moped, contact **Alinari** (Via Guelfa 85r, at Via Nazionale, 280500) or **Motorent** (Via San Zanobi 9r, between Via Guelfa and Via XXVII Aprile, 490113). For those who want to get out into the country, **I Bike Italy** (Borgo degli Albizi 11, between Piazza San Pier Maggiore and Via delle Seggiole, 2342371, 561/231.3804 in the US) offers a daylong cycling trip in Tuscany. Included in the price is a 21-speed bike, a helmet, a bilingual guide, lunch, and a stop at a local winery.

Buses

Florence's orange **ATAF** city buses run frequently and efficiently. Bus routes are published in the yellow pages of the telephone directory. Tickets, which are good for one trip or three hours, are available at most newsstands, tobacconists, and bars/cafés, and must be purchased before boarding the bus (get on at the rear door, as the center one is for getting off). Once on the bus, validate the ticket in the orange machine. A special seven-day Carta Arancio permits unlimited travel on all city buses, as well as other buses and trains throughout the province of Florence. This pass can be purchased at the ATAF office at 115 Viale dei Mille (between Via Antonio Pacinotti and Piazza delle Cure, 56501). ATAF also has an information office at the entrance to the Santa Maria Novella train station (5650222). Both offices are open daily.

Driving

Because of the Dantesque rings of traffic zones in Florence, getting around by car is not recommended. An ever-expanding *zona blu* (pedestrian zone) in the Centro Storico is completely closed to nonresident vehicles Monday through Saturday, 7:30AM-6:30PM, and part of Sunday. This can get tricky if your hotel lies within the restricted area, and most of them do. If traffic police stop you in this section, mention the hotel's name and address, show a confirmation (if possible), and they'll wave you on through.

Parking

Street parking is hard to find and towing of illegally parked cars is frequent, costly, and a major hassle. Private and public garages throughout the city often give daily and weekly rates; ask your hotel if it has a deal with one of them. In addition, a multilevel parking lot beneath the train station offers parking possibilities near the center.

Taxis

Cabs are plentiful and drivers pleasant in Florence. You can find them waiting at strategic locations around town (usually in or near the principal squares), or you can call for one by contacting **Radio Taxi** (4242, 4798, 4390) or **Mototaxi** (4386). You may occasionally hail a cab on the street when its "taxi" sign is illuminated. Ask about additional charges for evening, Sunday, and holiday service, and for luggage.

Tours

Half- and full-day tours of the city and nearby Tuscan towns are arranged through **American Express** (Via Dante Alighieri 22r, at Via dei Cerchi, 50981) and **SITA** (see above). **Enjoy Florence** (167/274819 toll-free in Italy) offers an inexpensive three-hour walking tour of the city. Private guides are expensive, but a luxurious way to splurge for history or art buffs; the **Informazione Turistica** booths (see "Visitors' Information Office," page 16) have lists of qualified guides. **Custom Tours in Tuscany** (206 Ivy La, Highland Park, IL 60035, 847/432.1814; fax 847/432.1889) arranges customized historical, food/wine, and shopping tours, daylong walks in Florence, and driving excursions throughout Tuscany.

Phone Book

Emergencies

Ambulance 118
Fire 115
Police Emergency 112
24-hour Medical Service 118394

Visitors' Information

Bus (citywide) 5650222
Taxi 4390, 4499, 4798, 4242
Train 166/105050

Walking

Florence's Centro Storico is small and quite self-contained, and easy to negotiate with the help of a city map. Most principal sites of interest are within walking distance of one another and in the pedestrian-only zones.

FYI

Accommodations

It's a good idea to reserve a hotel ahead of arrival, particularly during the busiest times of year (Easter through June, September through October, and the Christmas holidays). Travelers who arrive without reservations should inquire at the **Informazione Turistica** booth (see "Visitors' Information Office" on page 16) for assistance. Informazione Turistica also runs a hotel information line (282373, 268673).

A pleasant alternative to conventional hotel accommodations is renting an apartment. Suzanne Pitcher (Via Pietro Thouar 2, at Viale della Giovine Italia, 2343354; fax 2347240) and Suzanne B. Cohen & Assoc. (94 Winthrop St, Augusta, ME 04330, 207/622.0743; fax 207/622.1902) are independent real estate agents who rent a vast variety of apartments, farmhouses, and villas by the week or month in Florence and Tuscany.

Addresses

Residence addresses are posted in black numerals on the streets and written as simple numbers; business addresses are posted in red numerals and written as a number followed by an "r" for *rosso* (red). To add to the confusion, these two series of numbers usually do not run in parallel order. For example, Via Sant'Andrea 129 (black) may be found adjacent to Via Sant'Andrea 5r (red). Long-standing plans to make all numerals black have been on hold for some time, as they might make things even more confusing than before.

Climate

Located in a valley on the banks of the Arno River, Florence is hot and humid in summer. The average low temperature in July and August is 65 degrees Fahrenheit; the average high is 87 (often going way into the 90s). Late October and November can be rainy, and winters are cold and damp. The average low temperature in January is 35 degrees, the average high 48. The most ideal weather is in May, June, September, and October.

Months	Average Temperature (°F)
January	45
February	47
March	50
April	60
May	67
June	75
July	80
August	85
September	64
October	63
November	55
December	46

Embassies and Consulates

British Consulate Lungarno Corsini 2
(at Via dei Tornabuoni) 284133

US Consulate Lungarno Amerigo Vespucci 38
(near Via Giuseppe Garibaldi) ..... 2398276; fax 284088

The nearest Australian consulate is in Milan. US and Canadian embassies are located in Rome.

Holidays

In addition to the national holidays (see page 5), Florence shuts down on 24 June to celebrate the feast day of San Giovanni (St. John the Baptist), the city's patron saint.

Hours

As a general rule, shops are open from about 9AM to 1PM and then from 4PM to 7:30PM. Food shops tend to open earlier than that in the morning, and markets operate from around 7AM to noon. Most are closed one or one and a half days a week. However, many of the shops in city centers stay open all day, every day. To further complicate matters, hours vary with the season. And the appearance of *torno subito* (back soon) or *caffè moment* signs is a common occurrence. So the best thing to do is to give a place a try and then come back if it turns out to be closed. Churches tend to be open Monday through Saturday, 7AM-1PM, and sometimes for a short while later in the afternoon. Again, use this as a rule of thumb but check individual times.

Medical Emergencies

Contact the **Tourist Medical Service** (Via Lorenzo Il Magnifico 59, at Via Angelo Poliziano, 475411) in the event of a medical emergency. The phone line is open 24 hours a day and has English-speaking operators to handle incoming calls. Doctors are available at the office Monday through Friday, 11AM-noon and 5-6PM; and Saturday, 11AM-noon. Another 24-hour service that has an ambulance and doctor team is the **Emergenza Sanitaria** (Emergency Medical Service, 1118394). The **Associazione Volontari Ospedalieri** (403126), a volunteer organization, offers free interpreting services for travelers who need medical care.

Money

Banks are open Monday through Friday from about 8:30AM to 1:30PM, and reopen for an hour or so (usually 3:30-4:30) in the afternoon. **American Express** (see "Tours" on page 14) and **Universalturismo** (Via Camillo Cavour 180, between Via Venezia and Viale Giacomo Matteotti, 50391) are also good places to exchange money. Avoid changing large quantities of money at the airports and train stations or at private exchange bureaus around town that charge high commission rates.

Personal Safety

It is remarkably safe to walk the streets of Florence at night. But take elementary precautions—using common sense will outwit most bag, camera, and wallet snatchers. Never carry more than you can afford to lose—i.e., keep your passport and larger amounts of cash in the hotel safe or well concealed in a money purse—and don't leave any valuables (especially those that are visible) in a rented car.

Pharmacies

The following drugstores are open 24 hours:

Farmacia Comunale inside the **Stazione Centrale di Santa Maria Novella** (Piazza della Stazione) 289435

Farmacia Molteni, Via dei Calzaiuoli 7r (at Via Porta Rossa) 289490

All'Insegna del Moro, Piazza San Giovanni (at Via de' Cerretani) 211343

Postal Service

The main post office, **Poste e Telecommunicazioni**, is at Via Pellicceria 3 (between Via Porta Rossa and Via degli Anselmi, 218240, 218204). It's open Monday through Friday, 8:15AM-7PM, and Saturday, 8:15AM-12:30PM.

Publications

English-language listings of cultural events include the monthly *Florence Concierge Information,* available at the better hotels, and *Florence Today,* available at the tourist information office (see "Visitors' Information Office," opposite). *Firenze Avvenimenti* and *Un Ospite a Firenze* ("A Guest in Florence"), two Italian-language publications, are also available at the tourist information office. The local daily newspaper, *La Nazione,* and the national daily, *La Repubblica,* are other good sources of information. The bimonthly, Italian-language *Firenze Spettacolo* is the most comprehensive publication.

Restaurants

Most restaurants close one or two days a week, some for a week or so in August (often the entire month), and from Christmas to New Year's Eve. Lunch can start anytime from noon on, and kitchens tend to close around 2:30-3PM. Dinner usually starts around 7PM. Reservations, while not required, are suggested and may be essential at the most expensive or popular restaurants. Major credit cards are accepted at most of the moderately priced and all of the most expensive restaurants.

Shopping

Florence, Italy's fashion capital in the 1960s, still has some of the most wonderful shopping on the Continent. For designer clothing, head for **Via dei Tornabuoni**, **Via della Vigna Nuova**, **Via dei Calzaiuoli**, or **Via Roma**. Since 1593 the **Ponte Vecchio** has been the destination of choice for gold jewelry (though some former residents have now moved elsewhere in the city). The open-air **Mercato di San Lorenzo** and **Mercato Nuovo** are crowded, colorful, and lively; they are good places to pick up souvenirs, leather and wool goods, and table linens. Be forewarned: The days of bargaining and big discounts are over.

Street Plan

Florence is divided by the Arno River. Most of the major tourist sites are on the right bank, or north side, of the river. From west to east the neighborhoods on the right bank are Santa Maria Novella, Centro Storico, and Santa Croce. The left bank, called Oltrarno (meaning "beyond the Arno"), is home to the Palazzo Pitti and the Giardino di Boboli (Boboli Gardens), but is somewhat less touristy.

Telephones

At the **Telecom Cavour** office (Via Camillo Cavour 21, between Via dei Gori and Via Guelfa, 212910), you can make phone calls using American calling cards or credit cards or paying afterward in cash. It is open daily, 8AM-9:45PM.

Visitors' Information Office

Every visitor's first stop should be the **Informazione Turistica** booth in the train station or at Via Camillo Cavour 1r (between Via dei Gori and Via Guelfa, 290832/3). Both are open Monday through Saturday, 8:15AM-7:15PM, and Sunday, 8:15AM-1:45PM, March through October; Monday through Saturday, 8:15AM-1:45PM the rest of the year. Information is also available from the tourist information office at 29r Borgo Santa Croce (just south of Piazza Santa Croce, 2340444). It's open Monday through Saturday, 8:15AM-7:15PM.

CENTRO STORICO

The old city center of every Italian town is called Centro Storico (literally, historical center), but the term is especially meaningful in Florence. While not the repository of antiquity that Rome is, Florence offers varying and vivid impressions of all periods from its rich history within its small Centro Storico. To begin with, ancient Roman colonials gave many of the streets their grid pattern. Though only a rare column or capital remains from those days, some streets have taken on the names of the Roman buildings that once stood on them—the baths were on **Via delle Terme**, the capitol was on **Via del Campidoglio**. But what is most noticeable in this part of Florence is its medieval aspect. The powerful guilds, predecessors of modern-day unions, were active and influential in governing the city during that period. The enclaves in which their workshops were clustered gave the names to streets you can still find, among them **Via Pellicceria** (furriers), **Via dell'Arte della Lana** (wool makers), and **Via delle Ruote** (wheel makers). **Palazzo Vecchio**, the **Bargello**, the **Ponte Vecchio**, and what remains of the medieval churches and towers evoke the era of Florence's first stirrings as a powerful force in international commerce. That wealth made possible construction of the great **Duomo**—ushering in the Renaissance—and financed the building of imposing private palazzi. In the 17th century, a local version of the Baroque took its place in a few churches alongside the great works of the Renaissance.

The next great building boom happened in the 19th century, when Florence became, albeit briefly, the capital of a newly united Italy. Inspired by Haussmann in Paris, the city fathers strove for a monumental look, knocking down old buildings and replacing them with more grandiose edifices. Finally, the postwar phenomenon of Italian design has brought about some exciting interior spaces in shops right in the center of Florence. And it's all as easy to see as it is enjoyable, now that the Centro Storico is largely a pedestrian zone (though buses, taxis, and vehicles making deliveries or belonging to residents may still enter), just as it was in the centuries before the advent of the automobile.

Though the number of cars and mopeds zooming around the cathedral has been cut back drastically, thus reducing the pollution that has wreaked havoc on the Duomo, the cathedral's full-time team of restorers still have more than enough to keep them busy. The concentration of art and architecture here is the densest in the Western world. Its effect on visitors is so overwhelming that a Florentine psychiatrist coined the term Stendhal syndrome (named after the Grand Tour–era French novelist and Italophile) to describe the dizziness she observed in one bewildered tourist after another.

Fortunately, there are a number of antidotes close at hand. Besides the legacy of Leonardo and Michelangelo, a

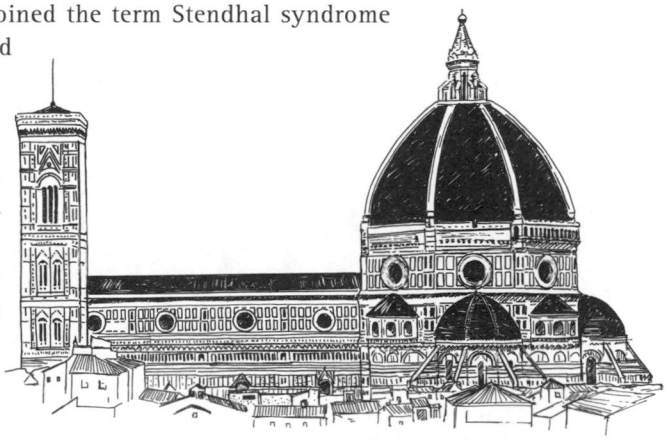

Duomo and Campanile

SAN LORENZO
SANTA MARIA NOVELLA
SANTA CROCE
OLTRARNO
COLLI
V. dell'Alloro
V. d. Conti
V. F. Zannetti
B. S. Lorenzo
V. Martelli
V. Ricasoli
V. d. Pucci
V. M. Bufalini
V. d. Servi
V. d. Cerretani
Piazza Santa Maria Maggiore
V. Teatina
V. d. Boni
V. d. Agli
V. d. Pecori
P. dell'Olio
Piazza San Giovanni
Piazza del Duomo
V. d. Campanile
V. d. Canonica
V. d. Oriuolo
V. d. Corsi
V. d. Campidoglio
V. d. Tosinghi
V. Brunellesci
V. Roma
V. d. Oche
V. d. Bonizzi
V. d. Pescioni
V. d. Vecchietti
V. d. Medici
V. d. Calzaiuoli
V. S. Elisabetta
V. d. Studio
V. d. Proconsolo
V. d. Strozzi
Piazza della Repubblica
V. d. Speziali
V. d. Corso
B. d. Albizi
V. d. Anselmi
V. Orsanmichele
V. d. Tavolini
V. Dante Alighieri
V. S. Margherita
V. d. Presto
V. Cavalieri
V. d. Lamberti
V. d. Cimatori
Via d. Cerchi
V. d. Magazzini
Piazza de Davanzati
V. Porta Rossa
V. Pellicceria
V. Calimala
V. dell'Arte d. Lana
V. d. Condotta
V. Calimaruzza
Piazza San Firenze
V. d. Anguillara
C. Ricasoli
V. d. Bombarde
V. d. Fiordaliso
V. d. Terme
Borgo S. S. Apostoli
C. d. Cornino
C. d. Manetto
V. d. Capaccio
V. Vaccherecciа
Piazza della Signoria
V. d. Gondi
Borgo d. Greci
P. d. Limbo
C. d. Lung. Bene
Lung. Acciaiuoli
Vic. d. Oro
V. Por S. Maria
V. Lambertesca
C. d. Baroncelli
V. d. Ninna
V. d. Corno
V. d. Lagni
V. Vinegia
V. d. Parlascio
V. d. Neri
Vic. Marzio
V. d. Georgofili
Volta d. Girolami
Lung. Archibusieri
Ponte Vecchio
P. d. Uffizi
V. d. Castellani
V. d. C. d'Altafronte
V. d. O. d. Guanto
V. d. Saponai
Piazza dei Giudici
V. d. Mosca
V. d. Vagellai
B. S. Jacopo
V. d. Guicciardini
V. d. Bardi
Fiume Arno
Lung. Gen. A. Diaz
Costa d. S. Giorgio
V. d. Canneto
Costa d. Pozzo
Costa d. Magnoli
Lung. Torrigiani
V. d. Bardi
N
km
mi
1/8
1/16

vital part of Florence's heritage is the commercial skill that helped amass the fortunes of the Medici and other merchant families. So even here in the Centro Storico, things that appeal to the purse and palate are interspersed with things that engage the eye and the mind. Past and present, it's all Florence.

1 Santa Maria Maggiore

One of the oldest churches in Florence (built in the 11th century and reconstructed in the 13th), this one has a plain stone façade like many in the city. High up on its old Romanesque bell tower on the Via de' Cerretani side is a late-Roman bust of a woman. The interior, redesigned by **Bernardo Buontalenti**, contains a number of artworks, most notably a 13th-century painted wood sculpture of the *Madonna and Child* attributed to Coppo di Marcovaldo. ♦ Piazza Santa Maria Maggiore and Via de' Cerretani

2 Fiaschetteria Nuvoli

★★$ Once upon a time, according to historian Giovanni Villani, there were 86 places just like this throughout the city. It must have been wonderful then. This tiny bar is presided over by a charming and gentlemanly *padrone* and offers an impressive selection of equally impressive wines. There are grappas and non-Italian spirits as well. But who would drink them when there is a marvelous Chianti Classico to wash down your crostini or panini? The tiny round rolls stuffed with homemade pâté or porcini mushrooms flavored with truffle are absolutely sublime. Through the back there is an intimate little bottle-lined dining space where all the classic Tuscan specialties are offered. The *ribollita* (a fresh thick vegetable stew) is top notch. ♦ M-Sa, 7AM-9PM. No credit cards accepted. Piazza dell'Olio 15r (between Via de' Pecori and Via de' Cerretani). 2396616

3 Scudieri

You will either like or loathe the location—right on the cobbled piazza surrounding the Duomo—but you will love the pastries. And you have a huge list to choose from that includes the most famous plum cake in Florence and *schiaccata alla fiorentina* (a traditional flat sweet cake dusted with sugar). They also have a window full of the most impressive whole candied fruit you can imagine. ♦ M-Tu, Th-Su, 7:30AM-9PM. Piazza San Giovanni 21r (at Via de' Cerretani). 210733

4 Torrini

This exclusive Florentine jeweler carries such international brands as Rolex, but it is unique for the ultimate souvenir of Florence—a handcrafted reproduction of the florin, with the lily symbol of Florence on one side and the city's patron saint, John the Baptist, on the other. Jacopus Torrini moved to Florence in 1369 and copyrighted the trademark his descendants still use today. ♦ M-F, Sa, morning Mar-Oct; M afternoon, Tu-Sa Nov-Feb. Piazza del Duomo 10r (between Via dei Servi and Via Ricasoli). 2302401

5 Bottega d'Arte Favelli

Florence's finest engravers and chiselers also specialize in signet rings. In addition to etched gold jewelry in Favelli patterns, the crafters here will reproduce practically any design you bring them. ♦ M-F, Sa morning June-Sept; M afternoon, Tu-Sa Oct-May. Piazza del Duomo 16r (between Via dei Servi and Via Ricasoli). 211846

6 San Salvatore al Vescovo

The façade is all that's left of this 13th-century Romanesque church (the rest was remodeled and incorporated into the surrounding **Palazzo Arcivescovile**). Its green-and-white marble matches that of the **Baptistry** and **San Miniato al Monte**. ♦ Piazza dell'Olio (between Via de' Pecori and Via de' Cerretani)

7 Palazzo Arcivescovile (Archbishop's Palace)

The façade of this palace, built 1573-1584 by **Giovanni Antonio Dosio**, was sliced off to enlarge the piazza in 1895. Its interior courtyard leads to the tiny church of **San Salvatore al Vescovo**, built on the site of a Romanesque church and completely frescoed like a pastry from **Scudieri** (see opposite). For a lower-calorie treat, go around the corner to see the Romanesque façade of the original church, which is part of the palazzo wall facing **Piazza dell'Olio**. ♦ Piazza San Giovanni (between Via de' Pecori and Via de' Cerretani)

8 Arciconfraternità della Misericordia

Continuing a Florentine tradition established in 1294 and secured during the plague years of the 14th century, this charitable organization of volunteers from all walks of life tends to the sick and needy free of charge, supported entirely by contributions. To preserve the tradition of anonymity, members cloak themselves in hooded black robes (although today the faces are not covered with hoods), a custom adopted during the plague of 1630. The organization is housed inside the **Palazzo della Misericordia**, where statues of *St. Sebastian* and the *Madonna* by Benedetto da Maiano, as well as a tabernacle by Andrea della Robbia, can be found. Architect **Alfonso Parigi** began work on the structure in 1575 and was later assisted by **Stefano Diletti**. ♦ Piazza del Duomo 19 (at Via dei Calzaiuoli)

9 Duomo (Cathedral of Santa Maria del Fiore)

Though construction of this cathedral began in 1296 following the plans of **Arnolfo di Cambio**, and continued from 1334 under **Giotto** and from 1357 under **Francesco Talenti** and **Lapo Ghini**, **Filippo Brunelleschi**'s dome, constructed in 1436, is what most people notice and remember. Unbelievable as it may seem, Brunelleschi proposed to raise the entire dome without scaffolding. It was raised in sections. Years later, when Michelangelo was commissioned to create the Dome at St. Peter's in Rome, he said, "I'll make it the sister of the Brunelleschi dome—bigger, but no more beautiful." The octagonal, red-tile cupola soars above Florence's *duomo,* or cathedral (pictured on page 17), overwhelming the city and dominating the countryside for miles around.

According to Renaissance chronicler Giorgio Vasari's *Lives of the Artists,* Brunelleschi won the commission to erect a dome on the base of the candy-colored cathedral by challenging his competitors to make an egg stand up on a flat piece of marble. "So an egg was procured and the artists in turn tried to make it stand on end; but they were all unsuccessful," the account goes. "Then Filippo was asked to do so, and taking the egg graciously he cracked its bottom on the marble and made it stay upright. The others complained that they could have done as much, and laughing at them Filippo retorted that they would also have known how to vault the cupola if they had seen his model or plans. And so they resolved that Filippo should be given the task of carrying out the work." Unarguably, it was Filippo's bold feat (the first dome in Italy since the Pantheon, which Brunelleschi studied) that helped usher in the Renaissance.

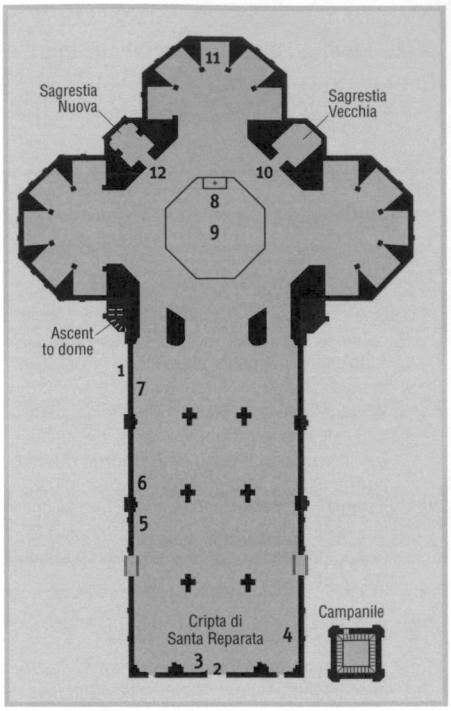

Other greats of the era to have their say about the dome were **Andrea Verrocchio**, who designed the bronze globe and cross for the top of its lantern, and Michelangelo, whose remark that **Baccio d'Agnolo**'s balcony at its base was a "cricket cage" halted construction after only one of its eight sides had been so embellished.

A half-millennium later, the dome is riddled with fissures, some due to age and others because modern restorers filled in holes with concrete, blocking the built-in safeguards for expansion and contraction from temperature changes. No one quite knows what to do about it, but should Humpty Dumpty have a great fall, all the authorities' lasers, plumb lines, and other measuring devices (some 300 of them make it the most closely watched structure in the world) will be there to duly record, if not prevent, the event.

The dome overpowers the confection of Tuscan marble (red from Maremma, white from Carrara, and green from Prato—the colors of the Italian flag), facing the building beneath it. Its original Gothic façade by Arnolfo di Cambio was never completed, and was demolished in 1587. The current neo-Gothic version was put up in the late 19th century as part of the frenzy of construction and destruction when Florence became the capital of the newly united kingdom of Italy.

But the richly ornamented *Porta della Mandorla* [1] (numbers refer to the floor plan above) on the north side, with an

Assumption of the Virgin by Nanni di Banco in its pediment, dates from the late-Gothic period. Much of the rest of the decoration—indoor and outdoor—is now in the **Museo dell'Opera di Santa Maria del Fiore** (see below).

The cathedral is a metaphor for the Florentine character—showy on the outside, austere on the inside—for despite the directive that it be *il più bello che si può* (as beautiful as can be), the interior remains remarkably spartan.

The entrance wall [2] has three stained-glass windows made to the designs of **Lorenzo Ghiberti**, better known for (and represented by) the three-dimensionality of his bronze door reliefs on the **Baptistry** (see page 24); also on the entrance wall is Paolo Uccello's giant clock with the heads of four prophets and the hands going backward. Just to the right is Tino da Camaino's almost minimalist monument to Bishop Antonio d'Orso [3]. In the right aisle, under a bust of Brunelleschi by his adopted son, Buggiano, is the architect's tomb slab [4] found just beneath its current location during the excavation of the **Cripta** (Crypt of Santa Reparata). The earlier church, built on Roman foundations in the fourth or fifth century, occupied the western third of the present cathedral's nave. The entrance to the site, which has Roman early Christian relics as well as Gothic tombs and frescoes, is at the first pillar of the right aisle.

Farther ahead, across the nave in the left aisle, are two equestrian paintings, Andrea del Castagno's tribute to Nicolò da Tolentino [5] and Uccello's homage to Sir John Hawkwood [6]. Presumably commissioned as monumental sculptures, they were instead executed in paint to resemble marble as trompe l'oeil frescoes. Beyond them is a more straightforward, albeit complicated, Florentine subject, Domenico di Michelino's *Dante Explaining the Divine Comedy* [7]. Inside the cupola are restored frescoes of *The Last Judgment* [8] by Vasari and Federico Zuccari. Beneath them is a choir by Bandinelli and a crucifix (over the high altar) [9] by Benedetto de Maiano. The entrance to the **Sagrestia Vecchia** (Old Sacristy) [10], to the right of the altar, is topped by a terra-cotta lunette of the *Ascension* by Luca della Robbia. Della Robbia was also responsible for the two terra-cotta angels in the chapel at the extreme end of the nave [11] (the nave also contains a bronze urn by Ghiberti, which holds the relics of St. Zanobius); for the terra-cotta *Resurrection* above the doors to the **Sagrestia Nuova** (New Sacristy) [12] to the left of the altar; and for the bronze doors themselves, a unique example of his use of this medium. The doors played a significant role on a dark day in Florentine history—the Pazzi Conspiracy. On Sunday, 26 April 1478, a group of assassins led by the Pazzi family (the name means crazies) attempted to seize power from the Medici family by murdering them in the cathedral at the ringing of the bells at the most sacred moment of the Mass. Giuliano died after receiving 29 dagger blows; Lorenzo (aka Il Magnifico, or The Magnificent) fought off his attackers and took shelter behind della Robbia's doors, which slammed shut with a clang that echoed through the enormous space.

The real beauty of the cathedral interior is its expansive space. As a cathedral, it is surpassed in size only by St. Peter's in Rome, St. Paul's in London, and the Duomo in Milan—and it is less cluttered than any of them. If not exactly intimate, at least its empty grandeur is evocative: Above the quiet shuffling of the tourists, it is easy to imagine the Pazzi Conspiracy, or, just a few years later, the fanatic preacher Girolamo Savonarola railing at a packed house for being more worshipful of the ancients than of the saints. Today the crowds gather outdoors in the piazza on Easter Sunday to watch *Lo Scoppio del Carro* (the explosion of the cart), a medieval folk event in which an ornately decorated cart is drawn by white oxen into the piazza. At the Gloria of the Mass, a rocket in the shape of a dove is lit inside at the high altar; then, traveling the length of the church along a wire attached to the cart, the bird sets off a riot of fireworks. The event is meant to recall the days when a flame ignited during the Gloria was then distributed to the townspeople.

The cathedral's enormous size and height provide the perfect opportunity to view some of the world's most famous indoor and outdoor spaces, including 4,000 square feet of restored frescoes by Vasari. The 463-step climb to the top along the catwalks and spiral staircases used by the builders provides close-up views of Brunelleschi's dome-within-a-dome structure, and the lantern offers panoramas of Florence's sea of terra-cotta roofs and monuments in *pietra forte* (strong stone). ♦ Duomo and all attached sights: free. M-W, F, Sa, 10AM-5PM; Th, 10AM-3:30PM; Su, closed during Mass. Crypt (admission charged): M-Sa, 10AM-5PM; Su, closed during Mass. Cupola (admission charged): M-F, 8:30AM-7PM; Sa, 8:30AM-5PM. Piazza del Duomo (between Via dell'Oriuolo and Piazza San Giovanni). 2302885

10 Museo dell' Opera di Santa Maria del Fiore

Also known as the Museo dell'Opera del Duomo, the cathedral was originally named

Santa Maria del Fiore, but now it is known simply as "the Duomo." The *Opera del Duomo* literally means "the work of the Cathedral." A group of men were formed to oversee the maintenance of the Duomo in 1296, and from the early 15th century they were based in a palazzo at Piazza del Duomo No. 9, owned by Cosimo de Medici. This is the palazzo where Michelangelo and Donatello worked on many of the pieces that ended up in the cathedral. Over the decades the more fragile and most precious works of art from the Duomo, the Campanile, and the Baptistry were moved here for safekeeping. In 1891 the doors were opened to the public and the Museo was born. Now, after more restructuring the museum is a wonderful, airy, light-filled space with over five floors including a mezzanine. As you enter, there is a 1:20 scale model of the Duomo as it looked in 1587, before the façade was altered.

In the courtyard beyond the smart, very modern ticket office is an atrium that is home to all eight of **Ghiberti**'s original famed bronze panels from "The Doors of Paradise." They are incredibly beautiful. The doors at the Baptistry today are copies. Here you will also find the *Baptism of Christ* (1502–1525) by Andrea Sansovino. On the same level are rooms devoted to Gothic sculpture from the Baptistry and the Duomo, as well as a huge room full of the original sculptures from the west front of the Duomo, including works by **Arnolfo di Cambio,** the original architect of the cathedral (for example, a *Madonna and Child* and *St. Reparata*). On the mezzanine floor is a much disputed Michelangelo. This wonderfully sad *Pietà* is thought to be a late work, intended for his own tomb and sculpted when the great man was nearly 80. Vasari said that the face of Nicodemus in the group is a self-portrait. Others claim that the work is not by Michelangelo at all. Yet another story tells that Michelangelo was unhappy with the quality of the marble and took hammer and chisel to the left leg and arm of Christ. One can only imagine his confession in church the next day! According to this version, Tiberio Calcagni, a pupil of Michelangelo's, restored the leg and completed the figure of the Madonna. **Donatello**'s glorious cantoria (choir loft), done in 1433 and decorated with a playground of putti (little cherubs), is on the first floor along with another cantoria by Luca della Robbia. Carved in 1431, this is thought to be della Robbia's first major commission. In the same room there are several life-sized figures sculpted by Donatello for the Campanile. There is a story that the figure of the prophet Habakkuk was so lifelike that the sculptor grabbed it and demanded it "speak, speak!" Perhaps Donatello would be less entranced to know that locally the statue is known as *lo Zuccone* (pumpkin head). The other figures in the room include two Sybils and four Prophets attributed to Andrea Pisano and the *Sacrifice of Isaac*, which is also by Donatello but in collaboration with Nanni di Bartolo. More Donatello is next door—a later wooden carving of a tragic-looking Mary Magdalene (1453–1455). In the same room is the beautiful silver altar from the Baptistry, which depicts the life of John the Baptist executed from 1366 to 1480 by a consortium of artists (including Michelozzo, Verrocchio, and Antonio del Pollaiuolo). The other special things to see are the bas-reliefs that came from the Campanile. They form an allegory of the spiritual journey and salvation of humanity through work, art, and spirituality. Luca della Robbia created the last five reliefs between 1437 and 1439. The óthers are older and designed, it is thought, by Giotto and created by Andrea Pisano and son between 1348 and 1350. Elsewhere you will find a beautiful bust of Filippo Brunelleschi by Buggiano, the original drawings by Arnolfo di Cambio of the façade of the Duomo, and a fascinating collection of Brunelleschi memorabilia including his death mask.

The museum has an excellent bookshop selling art books, guides, postcards, and other gifts and collectibles. ♦ Daily, 9AM-7:30PM. Piazza del Duomo 9 (between Via dell'Oriuolo and Via dei Servi). 2398796

Giotto's tower, the lily of Florence blossoming in stone.

—Henry Wadsworth Longfellow

As you leave the Uffizi you are advised first to wait under the loggia until your eyes can take the light and the street life again. . . .

—Hermann Hesse

11 Palazzo Orlandini del Beccuto

This massive palazzo, redesigned in 1679 by **Antonio Maria Ferri** and owned by a succession of noble Florentine families, has housed the local branch of Monte dei Paschi di Siena, the world's oldest bank, since the beginning of this century. The bank has restored the palazzo to something of its original splendor, visible indoors in the terra-cotta floor, white stucco walls, and *pietra serena* (warm-colored stone) details, including the only 15th-century wall fountain in Florence. ♦ M-F. Via de' Pecori 6-8 (between Piazza dell'Olio and Via dei Vecchietti)

12 Raspini

The biggest names in Italian and international clothing and shoe design for the whole well-

A Challenge . . .

For the last six years, December in Florence has held one of the strangest sporting challenges in the calendar: the **Ponte Vecchio Challenge**, organized by the Conte of Florence with the enthusiastic backing of the Italian Golf Association. It is like no other golfing competition. The one and only tee is on the Ponte Vecchio itself. The holes are on three rafts covered in real grass, which float on the River Arno below at distances of 70, 110, and 150 meters from the bridge. The prize money is not inconsiderable, although if you just want to have a go, amateurs get their chance to lose a few dollars worth of balls in the river the day after the tournament proper. For information, go online at www.pontevecchiochallenge.com.

heeled family are here next to the store's own prestigious label of Florentine leather goods. There are three shops in town, but none outside of Florence, so if a well-designed and well-crafted style works with yours, this is the best place to take out your wallet.♦ M-F, Sa morning Mar-Oct; M afternoon, Tu-Sa Nov-Feb. Via Roma 25r (between Via de' Tosinghi and Via de' Pecori). 213077. Also at Via Martelli 5r (at Piazza San Giovanni). 2398336; Via Por Santa Maria 72r (at Via Vacchereccia). 215796

13 Calzoleria Bologna

A very Italian shoe shop. Just wait till you see their take on the classic American cowboy boot. Alongside the multicolored, glittering, figured, bejeweled boots sit a gloriously frivolous selection of sandals and wedgies, girlie party-time shoes, and state-of-the-fashion trainers and loafers. Each new season brings a new wave of color and fun for feet. ♦ Daily. Piazza San Giovanni 13/15r. 290545. www.calzoleriabologna.com

14 Loggia di Santa Maria del Bigallo

The original home of the Misericordia, the loggia by Alberto Arnoldi dates back to 1352-1358. Lost and abandoned children were taken in and housed here until they could be reclaimed by their parents or fostered. The children lived in the upstairs part of the building. The organization occupying the palazzo now still takes care of needy children and also runs a rest home for the aged. The little museum within the loggia contains a limited collection of artworks including Niccolò di Pietro Gerini's painting depicting orphaned children being assigned to their new mothers and Bernardo Daddi's *La Madonna della Misericordia*, which is the earliest known depiction of the city of Florence and in fact shows the Duomo with an incomplete façade. ♦ Museum: Admission. M, 8:30AM-noon; Th, 4PM-6PM. Piazza San Giovanni 1 (at Via dei Calzaiuoli)

15 Campanile

Known locally as *"Il Campanile di Giotto,"* the bell tower was actually a collaborative effort. **Giotto** designed the first story and **Andrea Pisano** and **Francesco Talenti** finished it, creating visual harmony by using the same three colors of marble that cloak the cathedral. (Musical harmony is provided by the bells, named *Grossa, Beona, Completa, Cheirica,* and *Squilla*—Big, Tipsy, Finished, Priestling, and Shrieker.) The ascent by foot up the 414 steps offers views of the city and surroundings, as well as a dumbfounding view of **Brunelleschi**'s dome. If you have a medical condition or are very unfit you are advised not to attempt the climb, as there is no elevator should you need assistance. ♦ Admission. Daily, 8:30AM-7PM (Apr-Sept), 9AM-5:30PM (Oct), 9AM-4:30PM (Nov-Mar). Piazza del Duomo (between Via dell'Oriuolo and Piazza San Giovanni)

16 Old England Stores

Florentines, already mad for local knockoffs of English style, go gaga for the real thing at this shop, stocked with such exotic items as Port, Sherry, biscuits, and a full line of American breakfast cereals, as well as a fine selection of British woolens in the back. Expatriate Anglophones may be seen here during the holidays stocking up on plum pudding and cranberry sauce. ♦ M, 3:30PM-7:30PM; Tu-Sa, 8:30AM-1PM and 3:30PM-7:30PM. Via dei Vecchietti 28r (between Via del Campidoglio and Via de' Pecori). 211933

17 Luisa Via Roma

Florence's most international boutique by far, this is the one place in town you're guaranteed to find Kenzo and Comme des Garçons alongside such Italian sartorial maestros as Dolce & Gabbana and Alberta Ferretti for both sexes. ♦ M-Sa, 10AM-7:30PM; Su, 11AM-7PM. Via Roma 19-21r (between Via de' Tosinghi and Via de' Pecori). 217826

Maggio Musicale

One of Europe's most prestigious music festivals, "Musical May" was started in 1933 and has been an annual event since 1937. Originally performances were held only in May, but today the festivities spill over into June and often into the first week of July as well. Music (with an emphasis on classical), opera, and dance concerts are given in theaters, abbeys, and piazzas all over Florence. Top-rate artists, troupes, and orchestras from all around the world partake in this cultural extravaganza. Closing the festival's run at the end of June are two free gala performances—one music, one dance—on a spectacular stage in **Piazza della Signoria**.

One of the key players in the festival is the **Orchestra del Maggio Musicale**. Now considered one of the leading orchestras in the country, the philharmonic has enjoyed an ever-increasing reputation since its founding in 1928 by Vittorio Gui. The secret to its success lies in the winning combination of world-class conductors and the exceptional musicians who come from Florence and all over the world. Their offerings are so diverse, they seem to deliberately avoid musical chauvinism. Berg and Stravinsky are as likely to be on the program as Rossini and Puccini.

Chief conductor of **Maggio** from 1969 to 1981, Riccardo Muti left a lasting impression for his carefully researched and theatrical interpretations. A parade of guest conductors followed the period of Muti's command, including all the big names: Sawallisch, Giulini, Solti, Chung, Chailly, Ozawa, and Semyon Bychkov, the crowd-pleasing Russian chief guest conductor.

Emerging from this mass of talent is Zubin Mehta, who has been in the chief role since 1985. Mehta, who is known for his tremendously long rehearsals when preparing for a concert, often keeps his musicians overtime in the evenings and on weekends to perfect a piece. The result: The crisp, cohesive orchestra is capable of reaching great emotional intensity. Mehta has also acted as a magnet for young, talented musicians who have come from all parts to seek a coveted position under his baton.

The remainder of the year, the orchestra usually performs during opera and ballet season (September-December) and a winter symphonic season (January-April) at the **Teatro Comunaie**.

To book tickets in advance for the festival from abroad, call 055/211158 or fax 055/2779410. Specific requests by fax will be accepted only if accompanied by exact credit card information. The office is open generally Tuesday through Saturday, 9AM-1PM and 2PM-5PM. No tickets are required for free performances. Ask your hotel concierge for assistance in obtaining last-minute tickets.

18 Battistero di San Giovanni (Baptistry of San Giovanni)

Dante fondly referred to this church dedicated to Florence's patron saint as *"bel San Giovanni"* (beautiful St. John). Florentines once flattered themselves by believing it to be an ancient Roman temple of Mars dating to the fifth century, but although there are classical elements in the decoration of the green-and-white marble façade and authentic Roman columns inside, it dates from much later. The Baptistry is best known for the gilded bronze doors on three of its eight sides. The original doors, now replaced by copies, are gradually being restored (at press time no completion date had been set) and are displayed in the **Museo dell'Opera di Santa Maria del Fiore**. The doors were made in the 14th and 15th centuries, the first such work since the ancients. The south doors (begun in 1330), by **Andrea Pisano**, combine the Gothic style with the neorealism of **Giotto**. The upper 20 panels tell the story of the life of John the Baptist; the lower eight portray the cardinal and theological virtues. The north doors (1403-1424) are by **Lorenzo Ghiberti**, who beat **Brunelleschi** in a famous competition held for them in 1401 (their entries are on display in the **Bargello**). The upper 20 panels depict scenes from the *New Testament* (the artist also cast his self-portrait, the hooded head on the left door); the lower eight panels represent the four evangelists and the four doctors of the church. Artistically the most important, the east doors (1424-1452), also by Ghiberti, were called "The Gates of Paradise" by the usually cryptic Michelangelo. (These doors face the main entrance to the **Duomo**.) The 10 panels illustrate scenes from the *Old Testament* and are surrounded by playful animal motifs and portrait heads (another one of Ghiberti is on the left door, the fourth from the top on the right side, next to a portrait of his son Vittorio).

The vault inside contains mosaics made to the designs of Cimabue and other artists. A marble pavement of the zodiac surrounds the baptismal font, and the hands of Donatello and Michelozzo may be seen in the tomb of Cardinal Baldassare Coscia. ♦ Admission. M-Sa, noon-7PM; Su, 8:30AM-2PM. Piazza San Giovanni (south of Piazza del Duomo and east of Via dei Calzaiuoli)

19 Ricordi

Here you'll find the best selection of records, tapes, CDs, and sheet music in this part of town. The helpful young staff is not above naming that tune for you if it's slipped your mind and you hum a few bars. ♦ M-F, Sa morning Mar-Oct; M afternoon, Tu-F, Sa morning Nov-Feb. Via Brunelleschi 8r (at Via de' Tosinghi). 214104

20 Torre degli Adimali

During the Middle Ages, Florence was filled with towers like this 13th-century example and even higher ones, as can be seen in the Tuscan town of San Gimignano even today. In 1250, however, the Commune passed what amounted to a zoning law requiring that the height of no tower surpass 100 feet and that those exceeding that height be truncated. ♦ Via delle Oche (between Via dello Studio and Via del Campanile)

21 Alessi

A Florentine institution that is part deli, part confectioner's, part wine shop, and part wine bar. The confectionary section has a wide selection of traditional candies, including all those marvelous cakes and pastries Italians eat to celebrate holidays—*pannetone* at Christmas, *pan d'oro* and *colombo* at Easter. The wine bar is small but boasts a classy list of wines by the glass, and they have a mind-boggling selection of exclusive single-malt whiskies. But the real thrill of this place is the cellar. Step down there and you step into a wine wonderland. Wines from every region in Italy are arranged in stacks from floor to ceiling, and they range from simple country wines to the finest and most expensive vintages from the great winemakers of Italy. If you are even a little knowledgeable, this is a great place to spend time browsing. Everything you need to consume anything you might buy, from top-quality drinking and tasting glasses, to bartender sets, to decanters and funnels, is sold here. ♦ M-Sa, 9AM-1PM and 4PM-8PM. Via delle Oche 27-31r (between Via Santa Elisabetta and Via dei Calzaiuoli). 214966

21 Grom

Well, hallelujah! The Centro Storico has got itself a decent gelateria. Actually, Grom is much more than decent. If Michelin gave stars to ice-cream parlors, Grom would have a constellation. This is glorious, gourmet stuff, lovingly handmade in small quantities in the pristine spaces behind the counters by the man who serves you. It is wonderful on many levels. First, the flavors are astounding. The creamy ones are like satin and the fruity ones intensely fruity. Pure frozen flavor bursts. More than just delicious, these ice creams and sorbets are all created from the finest ingredients without a hint of an additive or anything artificial. Ingredients are carefully listed on the wall of this temple to taste. Read the list and marvel. The chocolate comes from Ecuador; the eggs are organic; sorbets are made with organic sugar, San Barnaba mineral water, and fruit like Granny Smiths, blood oranges, Sicilian lemons, and (in season) prickly pear from Calabria, watermelon, and pomegranate. Their hazelnuts are local and their pistachios are de Bronte. Also offered are licorice, coffee, and a rich *marron glacé*. It is a pleasure and a privilege to stand and taste these chilly works of culinary art. I plan to keep going until I have tasted everything. I thoroughly recommend you do too. ♦ Daily, 11AM-11PM. Via delle Oche 25r. 216158. www.grom.it

22 Paperback Exchange

As its name implies, this is the place to trade your English-language paperback book (as well as war stories about your travels in Italy) for one of thousands of well-thumbed volumes. Credit for your book is applied to the already discounted price of your selection. Half of the stock is new, with an emphasis on "Italianistica": Florentine and Italian art, culture, and history. ♦ M-F, 9:30AM-7:30PM; Sa, 10AM-1PM and 3:30-7:30PM. Via delle Oche 4r. 2478154. www.papex.it

23 Arte Creta

Elizabetta di Constanza is Positanese by birth and Tuscan by adoption, but wherever she has been, the sun has obviously inspired her work. Landscapes and bright dancing flowers cover the lovely majolica pieces she makes and fires in her workshop here. The pieces range from little tiles and soap dishes, bowls, cups, and saucers to huge platters. The vibrancy and simplicity of the colors speak of the south, although she says the landscapes are those around her home in Chianti. This is gloriously Italian stuff. Every piece is made and fired, then painted and signed, and finally coated in a lead-free glaze by hand, and so each is unique. ♦ Daily, 10:30AM-7:30PM. Via del Proconsolo 63r. 284341

24 Hotel Brunelleschi

$$$$ Partially housed in a medieval church and a semicircular Byzantine tower, which was once used as a women's prison and now serves as a small museum of archeological finds made when the building was reconstructed, this hotel combines the best of early Christian architecture with the upscale ambience of Postmodern style in its own

Florentine Crafts

Florence has been renowned for its craftsmanship since medieval times. By the 14th century, the eve of the Renaissance, the city was already one of Europe's richest and most powerful free city-states and was officially governed by its merchants' and crafts' guilds. These associations organized everyone from butchers, bakers, and silk spinners to money changers. The Florentines were the first powerful bankers of Europe; they invented the letter of credit and established the first stable international currency—the 13th-century gold florin.

The consummate craftsmanship of these guild members was later elevated to the uncontested level of art when the Medici called upon them to further embellish their royal lifestyles. Master gold- and silversmiths were appointed to set lavish banquet tables, textile merchants draped the court habitués with silk brocades and hand-stitched damasks that rivaled those of the Orient, jewelers adorned nobles' heads and throats with precious stones, and leather artisans custom-saddled regal steeds and shod aristocratic feet.

Today's artisans maintain the same high level of originality, creativity, attention to detail, and, perhaps most important, pride, as did their ancestors half a millennium ago. Many operate third- or fourth-generation family concerns in *botteghe* (small workshops) in the **Oltrarno** neighborhood across the river from the **Duomo**, where age-old methods are often integrated with sophisticated mechanical techniques. Such enterprises, characteristic of Italy in general, form the basic economic structure in Tuscany, where few large industries exist. Shopping in these family-owned stores is a pleasant experience that promises—and delivers—high-quality merchandise.

Traditional artisans, the keepers of the flame of ancient techniques handed down from generation to generation, believe that the splendor of Italy lies in its matchless history; they use their ancestors' skills to prolong the past, reproducing antique objects and styles whose beauty, they feel, contemporary crafters could never achieve. More modern artisans, however, are equally concerned with preserving their crafts. They, too, may claim four or more generations of family experience, but these crafters use a creative spirit to express their talents in novel and contemporary ways. Their imaginative interpretations can be found in everything from such diverse crafts as trompe l'oeil and semiprecious stone inlay to marbleized paper goods.

Although the days of runaway bargains are long gone and anything handcrafted is by definition on the expensive side, there are still some good buys to be found. One Tuscan specialty is leather crafting that combines modern technology with ancient methods of curing, dyeing, and finishing of hides and reptile skins brought in from around the globe. The town of **Santa Croce sull'Arno**, 29 miles from Florence, is devoted almost entirely to tanning leather. The supreme talent of Florence's leather artisan community is the designing, cutting, and sewing of leather articles and garments.

secret little piazza. The 96 rooms are tastefully decorated, some incorporating architectural details from the ancient tower, a few with views of the **Duomo**. The restaurant is open Monday through Saturday for breakfast, lunch, and dinner. ♦ Piazza Santa Elisabetta 3 (off Via Santa Elisabetta, between Via del Corso and Via delle Oche). 27370; fax 219617. www.hotelbrunelleschi.it

25 Zecchi

You'll find the city's best selection of artists' materials here, from paints and brushes to a rainbow of pigments—carmine red made from insects, amber varnish made from fossilized amber, malachite green made exclusively by Zecchi from the mineral, and lapis lazuli imported from Afghanistan. ♦ M-F, Sa morning Mar-Oct; M afternoon, Tu-F, Sa morning Nov-Feb. Via dello Studio 19r (between Via del Corso and Via delle Oche). 211470

26 Valli

The windows of this classic store are always full of the most eye-catching fabrics, figured and hand-printed. Valli has the most delicate and beautiful appliquéd silks you can imagine, beaded and sequined fabrics in zingy entrance-making colors, delicate sheeny satins, and, in one window, frothing, cobweb-fine, gently glimmering lace fabrics made into the kind of bridal gown that almost had me proposing to the next male passer-by. There are fabrics for men's tailoring with names like Ungaro and Zegna stitched into the selvage. The store is happy to recommend dressmakers or tailors to you—the kind who can cut the kind of fabulous clothes that suit these fabulous cloths. ♦ Closed Sunday and Monday morning. Via Strozzi 4r

27 Piazza della Repubblica

The piazza was the site of the ancient Roman forum, which later became the **Mercato Vecchio** (Old Market), bordering on Florence's Jewish ghetto at its north end. Florentines still bemoan the 1887 demolition of what was one of the city's most picturesque piazzas, as seen in displays in the **Museo di Firenze Com'Era** (see page 105), in spite of the plaque on the piazza's grand arch referring to the *secolare squallore* (centuries-long

The finest leather goods are sold at both the deluxe flagship stores of local dynasties, including **Gucci**, **Salvatore Ferragamo**, and such smaller fashionable boutiques as **Cellerini** and **Taddei**. For top-of-the-line leather gloves, **Madova** has the best selection of silk, cashmere, and fur-lined gloves—in all the latest colors, including purple and red. For a lower-priced alternative, visit **Stand No. 21** next to the church of **San Lorenzo** at the **Mercato di San Lorenzo** (San Lorenzo Market). Beware of much of the leather sold in the markets and the knockoff bags displayed on the sidewalks. Many of these are not worth their low price, as they are often made of inferior or imitation leathers and are poorly stitched. Fine gold jewelry—both the refined and traditional works and the bold and extravagant pieces—has also been long synonymous with Florence. Gold is almost always 18 karat, and most of the simple pieces without stones are weighed upon purchase and priced to reflect the daily rates. The **Ponte Vecchio** has been the exclusive domain of goldsmiths and jewelers since 1593. Before this, butchers, greengrocers, blacksmiths, and leather workers were the tenants of the bridge's shops. When the powerful Medici family moved their sumptuous courts to the **Palazzo Pitti** on the southern banks of the **Arno** and began to use the bridge for commuting to the **Palazzo Vecchio**, they were so affronted by the stench of these "vile arts" that the Grand Duke Ferdinando de' Medici issued a decree that all stores on the Ponte Vecchio be restricted to the guild of goldsmiths and jewelers. Ferdinando immediately installed 41 of these more genteel crafters, and collected twice the royal rent to boot! As an alternative to these boutiques, try the big gold market **C.O.I.** a block from the Ponte Vecchio or one of the many smaller shops on neighboring streets.

Marbleized paper is no newcomer on the Florentine artisan scene. It comes in a variety of designs and color schemes, either in sheets or already applied to the outside of writing books, picture frames, desk accessories, and many other items. The technique for decorating the paper comes from the Far East and probably dates back to the invention of paper. Marbleized paper was traditionally used for lining the inside of leather book covers until Enrico Giannini, a fifth-generation crafter in the Oltrarno neighborhood, began to experiment with new designs, colors, and uses for the papers in the 1960s. He still makes every sheet by hand and continues to be a trendsetter for his craft. Today marbleized objects inspired by (or copied from) Giannini can be found on almost every street corner in Florence; they are probably the most sought-after souvenirs in the city. For the most original designs and highest-caliber products, visit either of the two **Giulio Giannini & Figlio** stores. More quality paper can be found at any of the **Il Papiro** stores in **Centro Storico** and **San Lorenzo**. Avoid paper and items to which it is applied that are sold at the open-air markets—the paper is usually photocopied, giving it a tired, opaque look that matches the low-quality cardboard accessories to which it is attached.

squalor) that the restoration claims to have eradicated. The "restoration" actually eradicated 26 ancient streets, 18 little lanes, 341 residential buildings, 451 stores, and 173 warehouses and other buildings, and forced the relocation of 5,822 residents. And we thought only war did that! The visitor may like to conjure up those centuries past while walking in the piazza, surrounded by historical cafés. Going about your business at the post office beneath the classical-style loggia paved in colored marbles along the piazza's western edge, you can wonder whether patrons of Diocletian's baths might have enjoyed similarly imperial diminishing perspectives. (The baths of ancient Roman Florence were, in fact, nearby on Via delle Terme.) On Thursday, the flower market is reminiscent of the piazza's earlier commerce. The piazza's parking lot and taxi rank were recently removed, and the square is now one of the city's prettiest urban spaces. ♦ At Via degli Speziali and Via degli Strozzi, and Via Calimala and Via Roma

On Piazza della Repubblica:

Paszkowski

★$$ One half of one side of the square is taken up by this café restaurant, while the other half is occupied by **Gilli**, under the same management. Paszkowski offers, alongside a mouthwatering menu of coffees, hot chocolates, snacks, pastries, and other delicious waistline thickeners, live music in the summer months. There are plenty of tables outside, and it is a lovely (though pricey) place to spend a summer evening. A full wine list and selection of aperitifs and spirits complements a full menu of meals, ranging from omelettes and pizzas to pasta dishes and a smaller selection of entrées featuring meat and fish. ♦ Tu-Su, 7AM-1:30AM. Piazza della Repubblica 6r (at Via Brunelleschi). 210236

Gilli

★★$$ The most elegant of the piazza's many cafés preserves the glory days from when it moved here in 1910 (there's been a Gilli café in Florence since at least 1733). Stained-glass windows, stucco walls, and marble-top tables are matched by Florence's trendiest cocktails and creamiest *coppa gelato* (the delicious *coppa fiorentina* is concocted out of coffee pudding, chocolate ice cream, and whipped cream). When seating moves outside, these are some of the most coveted tables in the piazza. ♦ M, W-Su, 7:30AM-midnight Mar-Oct; M, W-Su, 7:30AM-9PM Nov-Feb. Piazza della Repubblica 39r (at Via Roma). 2396310

Savoy

$$$$ Though its name was changed from Savoia after Italy's rulers from that royal house were politely requested to abdicate (just as Piazza della Repubblica was changed from Piazza Vittorio Emanuele II), this 101-room hotel retains some of its former glory. Opened in 1896, it is the oldest and most centrally located, if not the grandest, of Florence's luxury hotels and has recently had a makeover by Olga Polizzi. There are 88 bedrooms decked out in chic neutral tones. Olga's sense of humor pays homage to "designer Florence" with prints of shoes throughout the hotel. Most rooms have walk-in wardrobes and all have modern conveniences. There are 14 suites, and many have views over the piazza and the Duomo you could gaze at forever. Two suites have their own steam rooms equipped with chromotherapy and aromatherapy facilities. Should your budget not allow a suite, you can still work out in the hotel gym, which has a breathtaking (difficult if you are on the treadmill) panoramic view over the city. The restaurant—*l'Incontro*—serves dinner, and the more informal bar offers light lunches. ♦ Piazza della Repubblica 7 (at Via Roma). 27351; fax 2735888. www.roccofortehotels.com

Pendini

$$ A recent refurbishment of this 42-room family-run hotel—in operation for more than a century—has left the old-fashioned charm intact. It's still an unrivaled value, considering the simple but spacious guest rooms (large enough to accommodate a cot) and central location on the **Piazza della Repubblica**. On summer nights piazza-side rooms can be too noisy for some, though the new double-paned windows help enormously. In keeping with modern demands, there is free Internet access and e-mail facilities for guests. There's no restaurant. ♦ Via degli Strozzi 2 (at Piazza della Repubblica). 211170; fax 281807. www.florenceitaly.net

La Rinascente

This six-floor emporium is the newest and nicest of the city's growing number of department stores. With marble floors and airy spaces, it is an elegant representation of Italy's well-known chain that specializes in its own exclusive private label of clothes and accessories for men, women, and children. There are also tiny boutiques dedicated to the trends of Ferrè, Zegna, and Versace, but the final destination of most shoppers is the café on the fifth floor with its fantastic views over most of the city. ♦ M-Sa, 9AM-9PM; Su, 10:30AM-8PM. Piazza della Repubblica 1r (at Via degli Speziali). 219113

Giubbe Rosse

★$$ This has to be the most historic of the piazza's cafés, named after the red jackets still worn by the waiters, whose antecedents served Florence's intellectuals a century ago. The atmosphere today is rather more lightweight; the restaurant in the back serves a convincing approximation of American-style breakfast for the homesick. You won't be lulled into thinking you're back in Kansas, though—if you've procured an outdoor table, you'll *know* you're in Firenze. Tuscan standards are served at lunch and dinner. ♦ Daily, 8AM-1AM. Piazza della Repubblica 13-14r (at Via Pellicceria). 212280

Donnini

★$ This is the smallest of the piazza's cafés, although it has its share of smartly white-clothed tables stretching out onto the piazza. It is plainer than the others, but there is something really charming about the clotted cream and green interior with its huge mirror and tiny tables. The coffee is absolutely terrific, the selection of cakes and pastries irresistible. Donnini has a couple of features that make it my favorite. One is the best lemon soda I have drunk in Florence—on tap, it's a strangely murky color but delicious and so refreshing. The other is the mini-sized cakes and pastries from an array of tiny rum babas to petite profiteroles to baby pastry horns filled with *crème patissière*. Donnini is also the most reasonably priced of the cafés. ♦ Daily, until 1AM Mar-Oct; M, W-Su, 7AM-9PM Nov-Feb. Piazza della Repubblica 15r (between Via Calimala and Via Pellicceria). 213694

28 Profumerie Aline

Those who simply can't go on without their favorite European, American, or Japanese brand of cosmetics will most likely find what they are looking for in this *profumeria*. Locals were amused when the American men's cologne Tuscany made its European debut here. ♦ M-F, Sa morning Mar-Oct; M afternoon, Tu-Sa Nov-Feb. Via dei Calzaiuoli 53r (at Via degli Speziali). 215269. Also at Via Vaccherecia 11r (between Piazza della Signoria and Via Por Santa Maria). 294976

29 Santa Margherita in Santa Maria de' Ricci

The façade by **Gherardo Silvani** dates from 1611, but the interior of this elaborately porticoed little church was redone in Baroque style in 1769 by **Zanobi dei Rosso**. The *Madonna de' Ricci* on the altar is a venerated image. The church is an evocative setting for frequent organ concerts. ♦ Via del Corso 10 (between Via dello Studio and Via Santa Elisabetta)

30 Via del Corso

If you have a sense of humor or kitsch you will love this shop. If what you have always wanted was to theme your life around cows, then here you can buy the bathroom scales, cups, lamps, cuddly toys, and cushions. There are light-up Leonardo da Vincis and Beethovens; mad, funny crockery, and toilet brushes shaped like an arrow going into its heart-shaped red holder. A fun shop. And if you have small people in your life, it is a must for gift shopping. ♦ M,1PM-7:30PM; Tu-Su, 10AM-7:30PM. Via del Corso 28r. 213385

31 Palazzo Salviati

Built on the site of the houses of the Portinari family, whose daughter Beatrice captured Dante's heart, today this imposing 16th-century palazzo houses the Banca Toscana. Inside are a 14th-century fresco of the *Madonna and Child with Saints* and 16th-century frescoes by Alessandro Allori, including a lively cycle taken from *The Odyssey*. ♦ M-F. Via del Corso 6 (between Via del Proconsolo and Via dello Studio)

32 Palazzo Nonfinito (Unfinished Palace)

Begun for Alessandro Strozzi in 1593 by **Bernardo Buontalenti**, the palace was never completed to its original scheme. Buontalenti was responsible for the ground floor, **Giovanni Battista Caccini** finished the next two floors to the designs of **Vincenzo Scamozzi**, and **Ludovico Cardi da Cigoli** designed the courtyard. Part of the palazzo houses Italy's first anthropological museum (**Museo Nazionale di Antropologia ed Etnologia**), established in 1869 while Florence was still the capital. These days it might as well be called the "unopened museum," since access to its magnificently musty collection of shrunken heads and the like is more erratic than at any other of Florence's cultural institutions. ♦ Free. Th-Sa, 9AM-1PM. Museum: Admission. W-M, 10AM-noon. Via del Proconsolo 12 (at Borgo degli Albizi). 2396449

33 Hotel Calzaiuoli

$$$ This ultra-central hotel is built on the remains of a medieval tower, its own façade dating back to the 1800s. It was fully renovated in 2003 and the 45 rooms (doubles, twins, and triples) around the lovely central *pietra serena* staircase are rather nice, reasonably spacious, and fully equipped with modern conveniences including satellite TV, Internet, and minibar. Each has a view over the Duomo, the Palazzo Vecchio, or the Uffizi that is really quite special. There is a garage, too (in Florence this is even more special). A quiet wood-paneled bar and reading room and a decorated breakfast room where you can enjoy a buffet breakfast are provided. ♦ Via Calzaiuoli 6 (between Via dei Tavolini and Via del Corso). 212456

34 MA Sfilio

This shop is just a little treasure trove. New and old sparkly things nestle cheek by jowl—jewelry and candlesticks, silver and stones all higgledy-piggledy. Look in the window as you come in to see their great selection of handmade cameos from Naples. M-Sa, 10:30AM-7:30PM. Via del Corso 45r. 214227

35 Albergo Firenze

$ This popular hotel is one of the nicest of the small and inexpensive hostelries in the Centro Storico, following a recent complete renovation. It boasts an excellent location around the corner from Dante's house and smack in the center of everything, and all 57 rooms have brightly tiled baths. Although the hotel no longer caters to a student crowd, prices have been kept low to guarantee a high occupancy rate year-round; be sure to book well in advance. There's no restaurant. ♦ No credit cards accepted. Piazza Donati 4 (at Via del Corso). 214203; fax 212370

36 Taddei

Many leather-goods shops in Florence have dispensed with the "Made in Italy" label altogether. Not so at this third-generation, family-run business, where the taste in impeccably handcrafted leather boxes, frames, and desk accessories is as highly regarded as the craftsmanship. The best quality of calf leather is shaped, then hand-rubbed to achieve a burnished shine in rich, warm colors like burgundy and chocolate. ♦ M-F, Sa morning. Via Santa Margherita 11 (between Via Dante Alighieri and Via del Corso). 2398960

37 Santa Margherita dei Cerchi—Dante's Church

The name of this tiny church is derived from those of St. Margaret of Antioch and the Cerchi family, who were joint patrons of the church from 1353. The first mention of a church on this spot was in 1032. The other name it acquired over the centuries is "Dante's Church." At the high altar is Neri di Bicci's 15th-century work *Madonna Enthroned with St. Lucy, St. Margaret, St. Agnes and St. Catherine of Alexandria*—not exactly pithy, but accurate. The church's main claim to fame is as the putative first meeting place of Dante and his beloved Beatrice. Slightly ironic, then, that this should also be where Dante married Gemma Donati. And even more ironic that both women are buried here. ♦ Via Santa Margherita

38 Cucciolo

Bomboloni—fresh, deep-fried pastries *con crema* (stuffed with custard) or *con marmellata* (filled with jam) and dusted with sugar—are the specialty of this unassuming *pasticceria*, which in turn is always stuffed with appreciative Florentines. ♦ M-Sa, 3PM-9PM. Via del Corso 25r (between Via del Presto and Via Santa Margherita). 287727

39 Palazzo Pazzi-Quaratesi

This rustic 15th-century palazzo was designed by **Giuliano da Maiano** for Jacopo de' Pazzi, who lived here but died up the street at the **Bargello**, where he was hanged in 1478 for his instigative role in the Pazzi Conspiracy. Step inside for a look at the arcaded courtyard. ♦ Via del Proconsolo 10 (at Borgo degli Albizi)

40 Brioni

The medieval palazzo that once housed the Arte della Lana (Wool Guild) is now the splendid setting for the Florence home of the famous Roman tailor, whose classic made-to-measure and ready-to-wear men's clothing adds a bit of conservative theatricality to the rational Florentine silhouette. ♦ M-F, Sa morning July-Aug; M afternoon, Tu-Sa Sept-June. Palagio Arte della Lana, Via Calimala 22r (at Via Orsanmichele). 210646

41 Orsanmichele

Talk about mixed-use architecture! This odd Gothic box, built on the site of the eighth-century garden and oratory of Orto di San Michele (the origin of its name), had an even odder function when it was built in 1337 by **Neri di Fioravante**, **Benci di Cione**, and **Francesco Talenti** (all of whom also worked on the **Duomo**). The ground floor, which had become a covered market, was converted into an oratory; the upstairs housed a communal granary. The ruling Guelph party assigned the decoration of the exterior, begun in the next century, to various guilds.

The edifice combines the essence of much of Florence: the practicality of using a house of worship to store grain, the glorification of mercantilism in the guilds' sponsorship of the decoration, and the early-Renaissance genius of the decoration itself. (Not to mention the city's trick of moving its sculptures around in a gargantuan sleight-of-hand game. Many of the originals are now indoors in museums, with copies in the niches here.) The sculpture in the 14 niches is as follows: Via dei Calzaiuoli side: Ghiberti's *St. John the Baptist for the Calimala* (cloth importers); Verrocchio's *Doubting Thomas,* with medallion by Luca della Robbia above, for the *Mercantazia* (merchants' tribunal); Giambologna's *St. Luke* for the *Giudici e Notai* (judges and notaries). Via Orsanmichele side: Ciuffagni's *St. Peter* for the *Beccai* (butchers); Nanni di Banco's *St. Philip* for the *Conciapelli* (tanners); Nanni di Banco's *Four Crowned Saints,* with medallion by Luca della Robbia above, for the *Maestri di Pietre e Legname* (masons and carpenters); a bronze copy of Donatello's *St. George* (marble original in the **Bargello**) sculpture and relief for the *Corazzai* (armorers). Via dell'Arte della Lana side: Ghiberti's *St. Matthew* for the *Cambio* (bankers); Ghiberti's *St. Stephen* (it replaced the statue by Andrea Pisano now in the **Duomo Museum**) for the *Lana* (wool guild); Nanni di Banco's *St. Eligius* for the *Maniscalchi* (smiths). Via de' Lamberti side: Donatello's *St. Mark* for the *Linaiuoli e Rigattieri* (linen drapers); Niccolò di Piero Lamberti's *St. James the Great* for the *Pellicciai* (furriers); Piero Tedesco's or Niccolò di Piero Lamberti's *Madonna della Rosa,* with medallion by Luca della Robbia above, for the *Medici e Speziali* (doctors and druggists); Baccio da Montelupo's *St. John the Evangelist,* with medallion by Andrea della Robbia above, for the *Setaiuoli e Orafi* (silk merchants and goldsmiths).

The interior, still used as a church, has stained-glass windows based on designs by Lorenzo Monaco and an elaborate 14th-century tabernacle by Andrea Orcagna surrounding a *Madonna* completed by Bernardo Daddi in 1348. For access to the granary, go to the 14th-century **Palagio dell'Arte della Lana** (the exquisite palazzo that once housed the Wool Guild) next door. A connecting bridge, often closed, leads you back to the rooms known as the **Saloni di Orsanmichele**, which offer marvelous views of the heart of Florence. ♦ Free. Daily, 9AM-noon and 4PM-6PM. Closed first and last Monday of each month. Entrances on Via dei Calzaiuoli and Via dell'Arte della Lana (between Via de' Lamberti and Via Orsanmichele)

42 Cantinetta da Verrazzano

★$ This ambitious and immediately successful eating establishment is operated by the Cappellini family, whose Chianti farmland provides this handsome wood-and-marble-decorated wine bar *cum* bread store with its simple and rustic fare. A wood oven constantly churns out heavenly focaccia, which you can buy topped with all manner of deliciousness or have made into a sandwich with one of their excellent hams or salamis or some local cheese. The open-faced sandwich with *sopressata* (a pressed sausage) flavored with chives and freshly grated lemon rind is delicious. There are breads made with soy flour and breads flavored with olives, grissini, cute little rolls, and all manner of little pastries. Eating in is a joy at one of the marble-topped tables (be prepared to share) and the choice of wines would be astonishingly impressive were we not in Tuscany, where it is taken for granted. ♦ Shop, M-Sa, 8AM-9PM; enoteca, 12:30PM-9PM. Via dei Tavolini 18-20r

43 Paoli

★★$$ Vaulted ceilings frescoed in neo-Gothic abandon set the amusingly kitsch scene for "atmospheric" dining in the former storerooms of a 15th-century palazzo. It's a bit a matter of style over substance, though the food is substantial enough, and best appreciated if one happens to be in a Gothic kind of mood, say, having just come from the highly Gothic **Orsanmichele** (see page 30). The basically Tuscan menu offers such dishes as *pollastrino alla griglia* (grilled chicken), supplemented by classic Italian staples such as *tagliatelli al pesto*. They also offer *filetti alla tartara* (steak tartare). ♦ M, W-Su, lunch and dinner. Closed August. Via dei Tavolini 12r (between Via dei Cerchi and Via dei Calzaiuoli). 216215

44 Perchè No!

And why not, indeed, have a morning or midnight ice cream in one of Florence's oldest *gelaterie* (ice-cream parlors)? Myriad flavors of creamy gelati and the mousselike *semifreddi* include *zuppa inglese* (trifle) and *riso* (rice). There are a few stools, but the ritual is to bring the ice cream with you for a stroll through **Piazza della Signoria**. ♦ Daily, 11AM-midnight. Closed Tuesday. No credit cards accepted. Via dei Tavolini 19r (between Via dei Cerchi and Via dei Calzaiuoli). 2398969

45 Tripperia

"A Firenze c'è una trippaia," went a popular love song to a fetching *venditrice* of tripe, a Florentine specialty and a favorite street eat. The delicacy (cow's stomach), stewed in an herb broth, is sold along with *lampredotto,* the fattiest part of the poor beast's intestine, at this spotless stainless-steel outdoor stand. Both are eaten served on waxed paper or in sandwich form, accompanied by the traditional garnish of salt and pepper, ground red pepper, or *salsa verde* (a green sauce of parsley). Blue- and white-collar types alike stop by for a snack of either innard; you may just want to look. The stall has recently been taken over by a new young owner and upgraded. The tripe is just as good! There are similar tripe vendors to be found in other parts of the city—the Mercato Nuovo and Oltrarno, for example. Don't leave Florence without at least trying the stuff . . . it is actually delicious. And you'll definitely want the secret recipe for the *salsa verde*! ♦ M-Sa. No credit cards accepted. In front of Via Dante Alighieri 16 (at Via dei Cerchi). No phone

45 Da Ganino

★★$$ This was one of the first of the younger-generation places in Florence to bring back the tradition of *cucina genuina,* in the sense of unpretentious (an understated sign says simply *Vini e Olii*). It offers a seasonal menu along with such year-round items as *risottino verde* (rice infused with spinach) and other vegetarian dishes, all served in a simple, old-fashioned setting. ♦ M-Sa, lunch and dinner. Piazza dei Cimatori 4r (at Via dei Cerchi). 214125

45 Fratelli Poli

★★$$ This atmospheric, traditional-looking eatery offers a genuinely interesting menu including a carpaccio of goose breast, a variety of dishes for two to share, lots of good vegetarian options (unusual in carnivorous Florence) like *gnocchetti con asparagi e Pecorino*, and the traditional *baccalà* (salt cod) on Fridays. There are tables outside in the tiny Piazza dei Cimatori and a good choice of wines to sip there. ♦ M-Sa, lunch and dinner. Piazza dei Cimatori 2

46 Oratorio dei Buonomini di San Martino

This used to sit beside the ancient church of San Martino del Vescovo (important because it was the parish church of the Donato and Alighieri families). Very little of the original church remains—the portal is now in Via del Canto ala Quarconia. This building was founded by St. Anthony in 1432 and became the seat of the Confraternità Buonomini in 1479. The Confraternità was a group of 12 "good men" who existed to look after the "ashamed destitute"—noblemen and aristocrats who had fallen on hard times but were too proud or genteel to beg. When the Buonomini needed money they used to light a candle over the door, leaving the Italian language with the phrase *"essere ridotto al lumacino"* (to be reduced to a liitle light). The

Oratorio holds an ancient bust of St. Anthony and frescoes from the workshop of Domenico Ghirlandaio, including 10 lunettes depicting *Scenes from the Life of St. Anthony* and the *Works of Mary*. ♦ M-Su, 10AM-noon and 3PM-5PM. Piazza San Martino 2 (at Via Dante Alighieri)

47 Casa e Museo di Dante (Dante House and Museum)

After Dante's death, his brother sold part of his house to the Mardolli family in 1332. Over the years the rest of the house was broken up, renovated, sold, and broken up again. In 1865, on the sixth centenary of his death, the Florentine authorities decided that Dante might not have been the city's favorite son (he called Florence the city of "self-made men and fast-got gain"), but his Divine Comedy had generally been accepted as a work of genius, so it was thought that it might be a good idea to reclaim him for Florence. But it took years of academic research, going through the city records, checking old maps, and doing extensive tests on the stone and walls of the building, before it was recognized as Dante's house, and it is *still* not accepted as such by everyone. In 1911 work began on the recovery and reconstruction, neighboring houses were torn down to make space, and now you can see the result.

While there is definitely something of the "school project" about its contents, just to be inside the house is worth the tiny entrance fee. If you take your reading glasses, it is packed with information not just about Dante, but about Florence and its history. Don't expect any artifacts; you won't find them here. What you *will* find are three floors of immaculately restored stonework, a number of poster-type boards with words and pictures (Italian and English) telling the story of Dante and Beatrice, his muse and lifelong love. On the top floor you'll find a room with reproductions of some of the many artworks that have, over the centuries, been based on *The Divine Comedy*, including a wall-sized hanging with the work in tiny print spread out in columns and a large screen whereon *The Divine Comedy* plays endlessly in words and images—which to some might seem a vision of Hell and to others a vision of Heaven. In the gift shop you can buy books and diaries, little Dante busts, reproduction old Florentine coins, limited-edition stamp collections, and all the rest. ♦ Small admission charge. Tu-Sa, 10AM-5PM; Su, 10AM-1PM. Via Santa Margherita 1 (at Via Dante Alighieri).

The area that includes the Duomo and its Baptistry, today considered the very heart of Florence, stood outside the circuit of city walls until the eighth century. At that time new walls were built to include this grand architecture within the newly fortified town.

Medieval Florence was surrounded by fortified walls—there was nowhere to build except up. As families expanded, one room was built atop the other until some towers stretched as high as 240 feet, comparable to a 10- or 12-floor apartment building!

48 Torre della Castagna

Once the home of the supreme magistrate of the Priori delle Arti guild, this *pietra forte* medieval tower dating to 1282 now houses the Associazione Nazionale Veterani e Reduci Garibaldini, veterans of the Garibaldi campaigns, whose numbers must certainly be dwindling. ♦ Piazza San Martino 1 (at Via Dante Alighieri)

49 Grand Hotel Cavour

$$$ Housed in the renovated 14th-century **Palazzo Strozzi-Ridolfi**, this tasteful contemporary hotel is located smack in the center of town (its small roof garden has a breathtaking 360-degree view of the Centro Storico). The 105-room hostelry preserves an air of quiet—thanks to the double-paned windows—despite its location on a busy street. ♦ Via del Proconsolo 3 (between Via Dante Alighieri and Via del Corso). 282461; fax 218955. www.albergocavour.it

Within the Grand Hotel Cavour:

Angels

The hotel's American bar and restaurant, Angels, is becoming a magnet for young hip Florence. And should you be pining for a good old American brunch to rescue you from all that caffè latte and pastry in the morning, this might be the place to come. Every Sunday from noon until 3PM, pancakes, French toast, eggs every which way, steak, and a great breakfast buffet are served at more-than-reasonable prices. The rest of the menu is pretty impressive too—tagliatelle comes with a pheasant sauce and a beautifully tender beef fillet perfumed with black truffle. The bar does seriously good cocktails and in the early evenings terrific hors d'oeuvres. ♦ Daily, 11AM till late. 3493629859/2398762. www.florenceforfun.org

50 Palazzo delle Poste e Telegrafi

The Renaissance-style post office was built in 1917 by **Rodrigo Sabatini** and **Vittorio Tognetti**. It's the place to buy stamps and send mail, telegrams, and faxes (the latter to anywhere but the US). There are tables for writing postcards, though chairs are always disappearing because many of Florence's old-timers come here and sit for hours. ♦ M-F (no midday closing); Sa morning. Via Pellicceria 3 (between Via Porta Rossa and Via degli Anselmi). 2382101

51 Caffè La Posta

★$ If the post office across the way is crowded, come to this friendly neighborhood bar for stamps, simple stationery, and tasteful cards. Sandwiches, a limited selection of salads, and pasta are made fresh daily and offered at lunchtime. The house aperitif (ask for the *aperitivo della casa*—it's made with Spumante, Martini rosso, Campari bitter, and gin) is guaranteed to send you special delivery. ♦ M-Sa, 7AM-7:30PM. Via Pellicceria 24r (at Via de' Lamberti). 214773

52 Hotel Pierre

$$$$ Located in a 19th-century building designed in a Gothic style, this refurbished hotel has 44 contemporary rooms with double-paned neo-Gothic windows, ensuring monastic quiet in the center of town. All rooms have parquet flooring and marble bathrooms, air conditioning, minibar, and satellite TV. There is no restaurant, but the hotel offers an "American bar." They will also arrange parking for you. ♦ Via de' Lamberti 5 (between Via dell'Arte della Lana and Via Calimala). 216218; fax 2396573. www.venere.it/firenze/pierre

53 San Carlo dei Lombardi

This simple 14th-century church, its façade cut into golden *pietra forte* like a giant Romanesque cookie, is an oasis of serenity amid the bustle of the pedestrian traffic outside. Inside, its *Deposition* by Niccolò di Pietro Gerini was borrowed from **Orsanmichele** across the street. ♦ Via dei Calzaiuoli and Via dei Cimatori

54 Vini dei Chianti

Another of Florence's typical watering holes—among its nicest claiming to be one of its oldest (since 1875), and definitely its smallest—this extraordinary hole-in-the-wall establishment is run by two brothers whose Chianti is accompanied by a wide selection of sandwiches, such as wild boar salami and *porchetta* (gorgeously generously sliced roast pork). Souvenir Chianti flasks, wrapped in rice straw as in days of old, are also for sale in many sizes. ♦ M-Sa, 8AM-8PM. No credit cards accepted. Via dei Cimatori 38r (between Via dei Cerchi and Via dei Calzaiuoli). 2396096

55 Passamaneria Valmar

This shop is jam-packed with home-decorating trimmings that make lovely gift items. You'll find everything from fat twisted cords and decorative borders to silk tassels in every color combination, all made with exemplary Italian textiles and workmanship. ♦ M-F, Sa morning Mar-Oct; M afternoon, Tu-Sa Nov-Feb. Via Porta Rossa 53r (between Via Pellicceria and Piazza de Davanzati). 284493

56 Borsalino

This marvelous, old-fashioned hatter is not mad, just proper. The shop features Panama hats that roll up into wooden carrying boxes like pencil cases, straw trilbies, flat woven linen caps, and a good selection of classical summer hats for ladies. The shop also carries a small selection of linen shirts. A lovely, dignified little place. ♦ M-Sa 9:30AM-7:30PM. Via Porta Rossa 40

57 Antica Farmacia del Cinghiale

This *erboristeria* (herbalist's shop) claims to be more than 300 years old. It sells herbal teas for the inside, herbal fragrances for the outside, and herbal potpourris for the home. There's also a pharmacy. The herbalists are so justifiably proud of their products that booklets giving the recipes for all their soaps, creams, lotions, and potions are available in several languages for customers. ♦ M-Sa, 9AM-1PM, 4PM-8PM except on holidays. Piazza del Mercato Nuovo 4r (between Via Calimaruzza and Via Porta Rossa). 282128

58 Farmacia Molteni

The neon sign under the green cross of this ancient building says *"Sempre Aperta,"* meaning if one needs a quick fix of pharmaceuticals at any time of the day or night, this is the place to come. And a lovely one it is, with 19th-century ceiling frescoes and gilding intact. The *dottoressa* behind the counter says Dante studied here when the place was part of the university. ♦ Daily, 24 hours. Via dei Calzaiuoli 7r (at Via Porta Rossa). 289490, 215472

59 Caffè Italiano

★★$ This lovely, old-fashioned, almost timeless place has chairs of wrought iron set around tiny marble-topped tables. The glass case on the marble-topped bar holds a selection of delicious-looking pastries (all made on the premises), tiny sandwiches, and filled rolls, and the smell of really, really good coffee is in the air. Caffè Italiano specializes in chocolate—which comes with cream, with cinnamon and cream, with chili pepper . . . almost any way you like. And you will like. There is a full menu of light meals—the composed salads are good, as are the daily-

MICHELANGELO IN FLORENCE

Throughout his 75 years of artistic production, **Michelangelo Buonarroti**'s (1475-1564) lifelong mission was to portray the human soul as it expresses itself within the structure of the human body. Landscapes were of little importance to him, and the art of painting was a distant second to sculpture. When asked to compare the two arts, Michelangelo replied that "the nearer painting approaches sculpture, the better it is, and that sculpture is worse the nearer it approaches painting." Nevertheless, Michelangelo would go down in the annals of global art known as much for his magnificent frescoes that cover the ceiling of Rome's Sistine Chapel as for *David,* the one sculpture with whom he is most often identified. The occasional commission in architecture and painting was usually swiftly completed so that he might return, with the rent paid, to his true loves–stone and sculpture.

Born in the tiny village of Caprese near Florence to an impoverished but proud noble family, Michelangelo was sent to be nursed in Settignano, a village above Florence known for such sculptors as Desiderio da Settignano and the Rossellini family. As a young boy he lived in Florence in the house on the corner of Via dell'Anguillara and Via Bentaccordi (a neighborhood better known now, perhaps, for the famous **Gelateria Vivoli**) and, like most young artists, constantly struggled with his family for its approval to pursue his artistic aspirations. Eventually his parents gave in and allowed him to apprentice in the workshop of Domenico Ghirlandaio, the most popular fresco painter of his day. He must have already excelled at age 13, since he received an annual salary rather than having his father pay the master for his instruction, as was the custom. Even though Michelangelo came to disdain fresco painting, he certainly learned well from the great Renaissance master: He painted the Sistine Chapel some 20 years later with the same clear brilliant forms and colors that were the Tuscan tradition, while such artists as Leonardo da Vinci were moving toward oil painting with darker, more atmospheric tones.

Michelangelo's early steps toward artistic acclaim came with an invitation to work in the free art/sculpture school near the church of **San Marco**, a project sponsored by superpatron Lorenzo de' Medici. Recognizing the young man's potential, Lorenzo invited Michelangelo to live in his own home, obtaining approval from the artist's down-and-out father by arranging for the latter to work at the customs office. Surrounded by the tutelage of the sculptor Bertoldo di Giovanni (an assistant of Donatello) and the members of the Platonic Academy–Lorenzo's philosopher/translator friends–the young artist formed an early style that brought together classical Greek profiles and an unprecedented emphasis on musculature, infused with great emotional depth.

Many of Michelangelo's adolescent works can be seen in **Casa Buonarroti**. The bas-relief *Madonna of the Stairs* (1489-1492), in a style reminiscent of Donatello, has been generally accepted as Michelangelo's first work. Also on display is *The Crucifix* (1492), his only sculpture in wood, reportedly carved for the prior of the church of **Santo Spirito** in exchange for permission to perform dissections on the cadavers of the adjacent hospital.

Having recently completed the statue of the *Pietà,* now in St. Peter's in Rome, Michelangelo was just 26 years old when he finished the 15-foot-tall *David* in 1504 (known then as "The Giant"). This masterpiece established him as one of the leading sculptors of the Renaissance and secured his favor with wealthy art patrons and popes whose commissions kept him busy, solvent, and often frustrated in the years to come. When people realized that the statue was too magnificent to put on one of the buttresses of the **Duomo** where it was intended, a decision was made to place the masterpiece in front of the **Palazzo Vecchio** in **Piazza della Signoria**, playing on the statue's symbolism: David is the young

Bacchus and a Satyr

changing pastas. There is always a good warming soup on offer, and the soufflé of vegetables or cheese is worth trying. The quality of the food is not surprising when you know that the caffè shares its charming proprietor with the renowned **Alle Murate**. ♦ Daily (lunch served noon-4). Via della Condotta 56r (at Via dei Calzaiuoli). 291082

60 LIBRERIA EPT

An amazing little corner store that specializes in you, the traveler. There is a surprisingly good selection of guidebooks and travel writing (especially if you are planning to do some walking or cycling), as well as maps for countries all over the world, dictionaries, and phrase books. There is even a little *cambio*, boy poised to kill the evil tyrant Goliath to save his people, just as the new Florentine Republic was trying to defend her freedom from a Medici return to power. The statue remained outdoors—suffering serious wear and tear from the elements, and the victim of jeers and derision by those who hated it for its colossal nudity—until 1873, when it was laboriously hauled over moving logs to a new wing of the **Accademia** built expressly for this purpose (today a copy stands in Piazza della Signoria). The statue overshadows some of the artist's later works in the Accademia that deserve more attention, including the unfinished *Slaves*.

Other important sculptures, such as *Apollo* and *Bacchus and a Satyr* (1496-1497), are in the **Bargello.** Some art historians believe *Apollo* to be a pre-*David* study, and *Bacchus* Michelangelo's first work of importance. A solitary painting, the *Doni Madonna* (1503), is in the **Uffizi**. The work was commissioned to celebrate the marriage between the powerful Doni and Strozzi families and is the only preserved panel painting in existence entirely done in Michelangelo's hand.

After a long absence from Rome, where he painted the Sistine Chapel, Michelangelo returned to Florence to work on the façade of the church of **San Lorenzo**. In 1520 he also started the **Sagrestia Nuova** (New Sacristy) in the **Cappelle Medicee** (Medici Chapels) that would mirror **Brunelleschi**'s **Sagrestia Vecchia** (Old Sacristy) and provide a final resting place for two Medici dukes, Lorenzo the Magnificent and his brother Giuliano (it also holds the tombs of Lorenzo II and Giuliano, Duke of Nemours). The façade project was abandoned after three years of work on drawings and quarrying marble (there is still no official front to San Lorenzo) and much of the Sagrestia Nuova was left incomplete, to be finished decades later by **Vasari** and **Ammannati**. Still, the sacristry is the only one of Michelangelo's architectural-sculptural fantasies to be realized anywhere near its entirety and is considered to be the central monument of the movement known as the "Mannerist Crisis." Here the supermuscular figures of *Night and Day* and *Dawn and Dusk,* atop the tombs of Lorenzo II and Giuliano, Duke of Nemours, respectively, seem to be slipping off their console. This is perhaps because the statues of the river gods—which were supposed to sit below and complete the circular composition—were never completed.

Michelangelo was also responsible for designing the **Biblioteca Medicea-Laurenziana** at the **Chiostro di San Lorenzo** (Cloisters of San Lorenzo), built to house the great collection of Medicean books. The most dramatic part of the library is the internal stairway leading up to it, for which Michelangelo drew a model; he never saw the completed project. Vasari and Ammannati finished it.

The most dominant creative personality of the High Renaissance, Michelangelo's influence was so widespread throughout the 16th century that no other artist living during this time could ever escape it completely. The force of his turbulent, emotional, and powerful works continues even today.

Dawn and Dusk

so you can get euros at the current exchange rate. There is a small selection of wines for sale (to console you for that terrible exchange-rate thing), some soft drinks, and a few postcards and trinkets. This is a really useful little place. ♦ Daily, 9AM-7PM.

Via della Condotta 42. 294551.
www.maps-store.com

61 GustaVino

This very cool, modern-looking *enoteca* offers a set-price lunch (Tuesday through Friday) and a good selection of snacks and full meals alongside its enormous wine list. You can sit at a table or up at the brushed aluminum bar, where you can watch the chefs prepare your meal of, for example, raviolini with ricotta and lemon . . . or perhaps you would prefer a little foie gras? ♦ Tu-Su. Via della Condotta 37r. 2399806. www.gustavino.it

61 Alessandro Bizzari

The old jars in the shop window (not to mention its name) are an intriguing invitation to Florence's only spice and mineral shop, a musty, family-run business that has been selling a medieval mix of spices, gums, extracts, and essences since 1842. ♦ M-F, Sa morning Mar-Oct; M afternoon, Tu-Sa Nov-Feb. Via della Condotta 32r (between Via dei Magazzini and Via dei Cerchi). 211560

62 Il Cesello

Bronzes are what this showroom sells. Bronze statues—from a tiny, palm-sized reproduction of the famous boar from the Mercato Nuovo to life-sized ladies with very few clothes on. You can buy them all here. ♦ M-Sa, 11AM-7PM. Via Condotta 14/16r

63 Badia Fiorentina (Florentine Abbey)

Badia Fiorentina, or, to give the old girl her full name, Santa Maria Assunta e Santo Stefano Protomartire, is regarded by Florentines as the most important of the ancient monastic complexes. It sits at the southeast corner of the rectangle that is ancient Roman Florentia—"inside the old walls," as Dante described it (Paradiso XV: 97). The Badia was founded in 978 by a German princess named Willa, daughter of the Duke of Spoleto and mother of Marquess Ugo of Tuscany, who moved the seat of imperial government from Lucca to Florence in the year 1000. In the 10th century it was an important seat of ecclesiastical learning, and in 1284–1285 was included in the new Palazzo del Podesta (built behind the apse of the abbey church) and restructured in Gothic style. The Campanile was finished in 13th century, and over the next two centuries in the corridor to the church, in the "all antica" doorway, various sculptures and the frescoes in the Cloister of the Oranges were added. In the 17th century the church assumed its present form—that of a Greek cross, oriented from north to south. From 1624 the architect Matteo di Marco completely refashioned the interior at the behest of Serafino Casolani, the then abbot. Felice Gamberani's gorgeous wooden ceiling and the frescoes in the presbytery by Giandomenico Ferretti were all part of this restructuring. In 1988 the Badia became the home of the Monastic Fraternity of Jerusalem, which was founded in Paris in 1975. ♦ Open Monday afternoons only. Via del Proconsolo (at Piazza di San Firenze). 264402

64 Bargello

This fearsome 14th-century palace (see illustration below) was originally Florence's first town hall; then it became the residence of the city's chief magistrate, or *Podestà,* and later the residence of its police chief, or *Bargello*. It was also the site of public hangings, and to make sure the people learned their lesson, artists frescoed gruesome scenes of the executions on the outside walls. Sometimes artists were even given public commissions, as when Andrea del Sarto was granted the task of depicting the hanging of the Pazzi conspirators here (Botticelli got to decorate the **Palazzo Vecchio** with the same subject). Leonardo da Vinci made a famous drawing (now in Bayonne, France) of one of the conspirators hanging from the window, whose fashion statement was carefully noted: tawny cap; black satin vest; black, lined sleeveless coat; turquoise blue jacket lined with fox; collar appliquéd with black and red velvet; black hose. Today the building is a museum, housing the most important collection of Tuscan Renaissance sculpture in the world. Have a look at the arcaded courtyard before going into the ground-floor gallery. The gallery contains Michelangelo's *Pitti Tondo*, *Brutus*, and *Drunken Bacchus,* as well as Jacopo Sansovino's *Bacchus* made in response. The colorful Mannerist sculptor-goldsmith Benvenuto Cellini (whose *Autobiography* is a delightful definition of the pseudo-Italian word *braggadocio*) is here represented by his model for the *Perseus,* as well as *Perseus and Andromeda* from the actual sculpture's base. He attributed the shape of *Narcissus* to a flaw

Bargello

in the marble rather than to an artistic conceit. The exquisitely grandiose bust of *Cosimo I* by Cellini and *Victory of Florence over Pisa* by Giambologna are also on display.

Upstairs in the loggia are Giambologna's *Mercury* and his bronze menagerie made for the Medici. The **Salone del Consiglio Generale** has two panels from the competition to design the **Baptistry** doors, *The Sacrifice of Isaac* as interpreted by **Filippo Brunelleschi** and **Lorenzo Ghiberti** (the latter won). Among the Donatellos are *St. George* from the church of **Orsanmichele** and two Davids, one in marble and the other in bronze; the latter was the first nude sculpted since ancient times and reflects the classical appreciation of young male beauty. Young female beauty is represented by Desiderio da Settignano's *Pensive Girl*; equally enchanting are the various della Robbias (Luca and Andrea), here and in the rooms on the next floor. Before ascending, take a look at the large collection of decorative art.

The first room on the next floor has Cellini's *Ganymede,* as well as the Roman Baroque sculptor Gian Lorenzo Bernini's bust of *Costanza Bonarelli*. The **Sala di Verrocchio** contains that artist's *David,* a less willowy solution than Donatello's treatment of the same subject. In addition to Antonio Pollaiuolo's *Hercules and Antaeus,* the room contains a number of memorable portrait busts, Mino da Fiesole's *Piero de' Medici* being the first in the genre since Roman times. Finally, as its name implies, the **Sala del Camino o dei Bronzetti** houses Italy's finest collection of small bronzes, displayed before a *pietra serena* chimneypiece by Benedetto da Rovezzano. The Capella di Santa Maria Maddalena on the first floor is also worth a visit. The frescoes were created in Giotto's workshop, and the one on the back wall—entitled *Paradiso*—includes a portrait of Dante. One of the sweetest pieces in the Bargello has made a very recent return to the place. Donatello's *Attis* has undergone a careful and prolonged restoration in the Opificio delle Pietro Dure and, at the time of writing, was specially displayed on the ground floor—in a sort of welcome-home exhibition—but by now should be back on the first floor in the Donatello Room. It was created between 1430 and 1440, and as to who commissioned it from Donatello, no one really knows. In 1568, Vasari mentioned it being the property of Giovan Battista; later that century it was wrongly considered to be a work of great antiquity. In the 18th century it was sold to the Grand Duke and rerecognized as a Donatello. In 1778 it was placed in the Uffizi, thereafter to be moved to the Bargello in 1865. More recent research has revealed that the original owners were probably the Bartolini family, whose family coat of arms bears the heads of poppy seeds, like those on the wide belt worn by the figure. In its day *Attis,* or *Love,* as the sculpture was originally named, has variously been thought to be Mercury, Bacchus, Aeon, Pantheus, and Eros. His upper body is like that of a Cupid, but "down below" (if you will excuse the nontechnical description) he has a faun's tail, little winged feet, snakes entwined around his boots, and open-fronted trousers revealing bared private parts. Such trousers are considered to indicate castration, which is one of the things that suggests he might indeed be Attis, son of Cybele. ♦ Admission. Tu-Sa, 8:30AM-1:50PM; same hours the second and fourth Sunday of each month and the first, third, and fifth Monday of each month. Via del Proconsolo 4 (at Via Ghibellina). 2388606

65 Mercato Nuovo (New Market)

Designed by **Giovanni Battista del Tasso**, this "new market" was a 16th-century annex to the old emporium in what is now **Piazza della Repubblica**. Today it still functions as such, although filled with stalls selling tourist trinkets, leather bags, and embroidered tablecloths (manufacture of the old Italian straw hat for which Florence was once famous, alas, has moved to Asia). The Florentines call the market the *"Porcellino"* (piglet) after their nickname for Pietro Tacca's bronze statue, *Wild Boar,* at its south end.

Tradition dictates that if one rubs the beast's nose or tosses it a coin, it ensures a return to Florence. In the middle of the market is a stone symbol in the shape of a cartwheel. This was the spot where dodgy merchants were punished by being made to drop their trousers "exposing the pudenda" and receive a sound thrashing on the bare buttocks. One can't help feeling that there are some dodgy modern merchants who deserve no less.

In the southwest corner of the marketplace is one of Florence's dying traditions, the tripe vendor. Cow innards are a local delicacy, and the tripe stand is kept much busier than all of the handbag vendors put together. ♦ Daily, Mar-Oct (no midday closing), Tu-Sa Nov-Feb (no midday closing). Piazza del Mercato Nuovo and Via Porta Rossa. No phone

66 Libreria del Porcellino

A welcome respite in a heavily trafficked part of town, this browser-friendly bookshop's selection covers all aspects of Italian culture—art, food, history, travel, etc.—in many languages and warrants a long stay. ♦ M-F, Sa morning Mar-Oct; M afternoon, Tu-Sa Nov-Feb. Piazza del Mercato Nuovo 6-8r (at Via Calimaruzza). 212535

67 Pineider 1774

When Italians present their calling cards, they like to draw a line through their titles to show how modest and well-bred they are, a charming if disingenuous gesture that somehow sums up the Janus-faced Italian culture in one swift stroke. The best-bred (and made) cards in the country come from this stationery store founded in Florence in 1774. There are branches throughout the country, but this is the flagship store. Through the ages, notables from heads of state to Hollywood stars have had their names engraved here. ♦ M afternoon, Tu-Sa (no midday closing) Sept-June; M-F (no midday closing) July-Aug. Piazza della Signoria 13r (at Via Calimaruzza). 284655. Also at Via dei Tornabuoni 76r (between Via degli Strozzi and Via de' Corsi). 211605

68 Il Cavallino

★★$$ On **Piazza della Signoria** near Giambologna's equestrian monument and convenient to surrounding sights, this dining spot serves reliable Tuscan specialties to a clientele of discriminating locals and tourists. Try the ribboned *pappardelle* pasta and the juicy *bistecca alla fiorentina* (a slab of steak grilled, then drizzled with olive oil). They also offer a decent set Tuscan menu, which hits all the traditional spots. ♦ M-Tu, Th-Su, lunch and dinner. Piazza della Signoria 28r (at Via dei Cerchi). 215818

69 Palazzo Uguccioni

Mariotto di Zanobi built this palazzo in 1550, according to tradition, to the designs of **Michelangelo** or **Antonio da Sangallo**. From the balcony, a bust of Cosimo I overlooks the piazza, including his equestrian monument just below. ♦ Piazza della Signoria 7 (between Via dei Magazzini and Via dei Cerchi)

70 Pane & Co

The wine shop you have always dreamed about. Part deli, too! It offers a fantastic selection of Tuscan delicacies and, generally handmade by small local producers, pasta and biscotti, panforte and wonderful breads, herbs and olives and oils and preserves, bottled sauces and pestos, top-notch cheeses, sausages, salamis, and hams, salads and pickles, and even some ready-to-go crostini. To say nothing of the extraordinary selection of wines. If you are a discerning drinker, just fancy trying a Supertuscan, or have already fallen in love with Brunello di Montalcino and Chianti Classico Riserva on your trip, then take your wallet here. There is an unusually good selection of half bottles, a huge range of dessert wines and grappas, and even (can it get any better?) two tables right here in the enoteca so you can try it all without carrying it home. *Then* you can buy more and take *that* home. *Buon appetito!* ♦ M-Sa, 9AM-8PM. Piazza San Firenze 5r. 2654272. www.paneeco.com

70 Palazzo Gondi

Designed by **Giuliano da Sangallo**, this is another fine 15th-century monumental Renaissance palace in private hands. Peek into the courtyard to see the fountain and Roman statue, perhaps the spoils from the Roman amphitheater that formerly stood nearby. ♦ Piazza San Firenze 2 (between Via dei Gondi and Via della Condotta)

Within Palazzo Gondi:

Al Portico

The most wonderful location for a garden shop in the world must be the ancient portico of the Piazza Gondi. For twenty years, around the fountain in the middle and in the shelter of the portico itself, this shop has offered a huge selection of flowers—in bunches and bouquets, in arrangements and growing in pots. There is also a vast stock of seeds in packets for flowers, fruit, vegetables, and herbs. Plus there is everything you could want in your garden that can be made in terra-cotta . . . statues and pot holders, wall plaques and water features. Plus a predictable scattering of variously sized *"pezzi di David"* (pieces of David—plaster noses and ears, etc.). ♦ Daily. 213716. www.semialportico.it; www.italianseed.com

71 San Filippo Neri and San Firenze

San Fiorenzo's ancient oratory stood on the spot now occupied by the 18th-century church of **San Filippo Neri**, a rare and rather restrained example of Baroque architecture in Florence. On its right, and connected to it by a neoclassical palazzo, is **San Firenze**, built as an oratory for the monastic order known as the Filippini, who commissioned the ensemble. Today the palazzo and oratory are occupied by the Law Courts, hence the armed police always outside. ♦ Piazza San Firenze (between Borgo dei Greci and Via dell'Anguillara)

72 Piazza di Parte Guelfa

Two buildings dominate this tiny, atmospheric little piazza. The first is the **Chiesa di Santa Maria Sopra Porta**, built in 1038 and then rebuilt in the 13th century, when it was used for the meetings of the Capitani di Parte Guelfa (the Parte Guelfa being a powerful political party of the day). In the 14th century, the Capitani di Parte Guelfa called in the foremost artists and architects of the day to work on a palazzo next door, the earliest Renaissance palace in Florence. **Filippo Brunelleschi** created the high-ceilinged interior during remodeling in the 15th century, and **Giorgio Vasari** added the coffered ceiling itself and the loggia. Meanwhile the church, now discarded by the politicos, was rededicated to St. Blaise, but it was deconsecrated in the 19th century and used as a fire station. Its beautiful frescoes were all destroyed. It is now the **Biblioteca Palagio de Parte Guelfa**—a library. The palazzo—the **Palagio dei Capitani di Parte Guelfa**—is now the headquarters of the Calcio Storico Fiorentino (the historical soccer society of Florence). All things must change! ♦ Library, M-W, Sa; times vary. Piazza di Parte Guelfa 1 (at Via Pellicceria). No phone

73 Tabasco

Since 1974 the town's chic rendezvous spot for the gay crowd is a stone's throw from the copy of Michelangelo's *David,* whose "camp" aspect has been adopted as the place's logo. Local, twentysomething gay life as witnessed in this deconsecrated church consists of that combo of refined surface and provincial substance that permeates the Florentine *genius loci,* and it doesn't come cheap, with peak Saturday-night admission. ♦ Tu-F, Su, 10PM-3AM; Sa, 10PM-4AM. Piazza Santa Cecilia 3r (off Via Vaccherecciа, between Piazza della Signoria and Via Por Santa Maria). 213000

74 C.O.I.

There's nothing coy about the **Commercio Oreficeria Italiana**, a bustling gold market with the largest imaginable selection of merchandise at some of the best prices in town (and you don't have to bargain for them). Prices are quoted in US dollars at this shop located, oddly, in an apartment and office building. ♦ M-Sa (no midday closing) June-Oct; Tu-Sa Nov-May. Via Por Santa Maria 0 (between Via Lambertesca and Via Vaccherecciа), third floor. 283970

75 Rivoire

★★$$ This was Florence's first chocolatier, founded by a Piedmontese who acquired the sweet vice from French sources. It remains the most elegant such emporium in town as well as a designated landmark bar/caffè. Take the harsh edge off the **Piazza della Signoria** with a cup of hot chocolate topped with a mound of whipped cream, or in warmer weather—at the most coveted tables in the piazza—iced tea or cappuccino dusted with rich cocoa. For those who can't afford to find the tiny boxed Rivoire chocolates on their pillows at the **Hotel Excelsior**, they are available here. You can also pick and choose from an appetizing array of sandwiches and salads that the waiter will bring to your table. ♦ Tu-Su, 8AM-midnight. Piazza della Signoria 5 (at Via Vaccherecciа). 214412

76 Piazza della Signoria

The piazza has been the center of civic life for centuries, and there's nothing like the sight of two elegantly dressed Florentines walking arm-in-arm in deep discussion here to catapult one's spirit back to the Middle Ages. Called an "open-air museum" (though what isn't in outdoor Florence?), the piazza and the **Loggia dei Lanzi** are filled with an impressive collection of monumental sculpture celebrating the schizoid Florentine fascination with tyrants, both in life and in death. From north to south, the assemblage in the piazza begins with Giambologna's equestrian monument to Cosimo I and his attributed bronze figures decorating the base of Bartolommeo Ammannati's **Neptune Fountain**. Much derided by Florentines, it gave rise to the taunt *"Ammannato, Ammannato, che bel marmo hai rovinato!"* ("What beautiful marble you've ruined!") and to this day is known locally as *"Il Biancone"* (The Great White One). Then come copies of Donatello's *Judith and Holofernes* (the original is inside the **Palazzo Vecchio**) and his *Marzocco,* the heraldic lion of Florence (original in the **Bargello**), Michelangelo's *David* (the original is in the **Accademia**), and Bandinelli's *Hercules and Cacus* (the original is here—the town governors don't seem to feel it's worth sheltering from the elements; most art historians seem to agree).

The piazza was the subject of an uproar when it became an open-air quarry years ago. What began as a routine cleaning of its paving stones led to an archeological excavation of Roman and medieval sites beneath. When it came time to repave the piazza in 1993, most of the stones had disappeared, allegedly into the driveways of some wealthy local residents. Furthermore, the remaining stones had been ruined in the cleaning (shades of Ammannati) and no longer fit in place. Florentines wanted to take the opportunity to pave the space in a redbrick and gray *pietra serena*, as it appears in 15th- and 16th-century paintings, but instead the authorities gave them a literal cover-up—too-perfect, brand-new rectangular *pietra serena* paving stones, which hardly live up to their name. This was the hottest scandal since Savonarola was hanged, then burned in the piazza in 1498 (a granite disk marks the spot), just a few years after he incited the Florentines to make the original bonfires of their vanities in the piazza. ♦ At Via dei Gondi and Via Vaccherecciа, and Piazzale degli Uffizi and Via dei Cerchi

On Piazza della Signoria:

Newsstand

Besides selling an ample selection of international newspapers and magazines to the tourist throngs, this understandably mercurial *giornalaio* (newsstand) stocks a terrific selection of postcards and calendars. There are cards of everyone's favorite Florentine scenes and works of art here, from risqué details of David's anatomy to stigmata on the most pious of saints. ♦ M-Sa; Su, 8AM-1PM. North side (at Via dei Calzaiuoli). No phone

77 Erboristeria Palazzo Vecchio

Conveniently located, this shop offers one of the widest selections of medicinal herbs and other natural remedies. The charmingly packaged aromatic soaps, perfumes and perfumed extracts, candles, and Tuscan herbs and spices make lovely gifts. ♦ Daily Dec; M-Sa Mar-Oct; Tu-Sa Jan-Feb, Nov. Via Vaccherecciа 9r (between Piazza della Signoria and Via Por Santa Maria). 2396055

78 Loggia dei Lanzi

Located on the south side of **Piazza della Signoria**, this arcaded space was designed by **Benci di Cione** and **Simone di Francesco Talenti** for public ceremonies in the 14th century and last used as such to receive Queen Elizabeth II. It was originally called the Loggia della Signorina, but became known as the Loggia dei Lanzi because Cosimo I used to station his Swiss mercenaries (known as Lanzi because they were armed with lances) there to remind the populace just who was in charge. **Michelangelo**, with the same eye for symmetry he used to rework Piazza Campidoglio in Rome, once suggested that the loggia be continued around Piazza della Signoria. What a wonderful piazza it would have been! Stand in the piazza and gaze at Giambologna's *Rape of the Sabine Women* and *Hercules Slaying the Centaur,* a classical lion and its 16th-century copy. A lineup of Roman priestesses brings up the rear. Cellini's *Perseus,* the making of which he touchingly writes about in his autobiography, was removed in 1997 to repair the ravages of pollution. It can now be viewed in the **Uffizi** (see page 43); a copy is to be put in the loggia. ♦ Piazza della Signoria (between Piazzale degli Uffizi and Chiasso de' Baroncelli)

Back in the 16th century, Catherine de' Medici married King Henry II of France, and her cousin Maria de' Medici married Henry IV. The women took their cooks, their recipes for creams, sauces, and pastries, provisions of olive oil and ice cream, and the Italian invention of the *forchetta* (the fork) to the French court—along with their trousseaus. As an Elizabethan poet said, "Tuscany provided creams and cakes and lively Florentine women to sweeten the taste and minds of the French."

79 Palazzo Vecchio (Old Palace or Palazzo della Signoria)

This embodiment of the imposing, rustic side of the Florentine character was originally built in 1298 by **Arnolfo di Cambio** to house and protect the ministry of the republican government, the Signoria. In 1540, Cosimo I brazenly set up house here, moving in from the **Medici Palace**. After 10 years, wife Eleanor of Toledo talked him into transferring the official residence to the **Pitti Palace**. Ever since, this building has been known as the **Palazzo Vecchio**. Under Cosimo's reign, it was decorated with sycophantic alacrity by Giorgio Vasari, who virtually became the court painter. He indiscreetly mythologized the entire Medici line with help from some of the finest artists available, primarily late Mannerists. The modern visitor should exercise more discretion in visiting the palazzo, since, unless you're a specialist, it is a waste of energy to try to sample all the often overripe fruits of Vasari's labors.

The courtyard contains a copy of Verrocchio's bronze *Putto* in the fountain (the original is upstairs in the **Cancelleria**), surrounded by frescoes of Austria, which Vasari commissioned to honor Francesco de' Medici's marriage to Joanna of Austria. If you're wondering why the throngs here don't seem to be admiring the works of art but passing through with disgruntled looks on their faces, it's because the palace now serves its original function as City Hall. A more immediate function might be use of the public toilets in this area.

Upstairs are the **Quartieri Monumentali** (Historical Rooms). Visit the **Salone del Cinquecento**, a gigantic room frescoed with Florentine battle scenes—all victorious, of course. Of more interest are the statues: In the center of the longest wall is Michelangelo's *Victory*; on the opposite wall is Giambologna's *Virtue Overcoming Vice*; and scattered throughout are the almost comically labored *Labors of Hercules* by Vincenzo de' Rossi. A door to the right of the entrance leads to the **Studiolo di Francesco I**, which Vasari provided as a hideout for Cosimo I's son Francesco. The walls represent the four elements—earth, air, fire, and water. (It was Pope Boniface who remarked that the world is made up of five elements—the above, plus Florentines.) Bronzino's portraits of Francesco's parents, Cosimo I and Eleanor of Toledo, face each other from either end of the room. They presumably kept an eye on young Francesco as he meditated over his paintings and bronzes on the subject of science.

Of interest on the next floor are the private apartments of Eleanor of Toledo, among which is a chapel frescoed by Bronzino. The *Cappella della Signoria* contains an *Annuncia-*

tion by Ridolfo Ghirlandaio, whose father, Domenico, frescoed the **Sala dei Gigli**. (The *giglio,* which means lily but actually depicts an iris, is a symbol of the city, and City Hall marriages downstairs always end with a bouquet of them for the bride.) The Sala dei Gigli dates from before the Medici occupation of the palace and sticks to mere classical and religious subjects. Outside this room are the sculptures *Judith and Holofernes* by Donatello (in the **Sala dell'Udienza**) and Verrocchio's original *Putto* (in the Cancelleria). Before leaving, take the stairs in the Sala dei Gigli to the tower for a guard's-eye view of the Piazza della Signoria. By paying a little extra, you can take small guided tours through the *percorsi segreti* (secret ways)—lots of little hidden passageways, one of which takes you into the roof of the Salone del Cinquecento. You can also visit the **Museo dei Ragazzi**. This is a great little place—actors dressed as Cosimo and Eleonora encourage your kids to dress up as their kids (Bia and Garcia) and play with the kind of toys they would have played with. Kids can also build and (more enjoyably) take apart models of the Palazzo Vecchio, peer through Michelangelo's binoculars (don't panic about breakages, they are a copy), or see a multimedia show on the Palazzo's history. All information on the "extras" is available just behind the main ticket office. ♦ Courtyard: free. Palazzo: admission. M, F, 9AM-11PM; Tu, W, Sa, 9AM-7PM; Th, Su, holidays, 9AM-2PM mid-June–mid-Sept; M, W, F, 9AM-7PM and Th, Su, holidays, 9AM-2PM the rest of the year. Piazza della Signoria (at Via dei Gondi). 2768224

80 Hotel Bernini Palace

$$$$ Like the others in this upmarket group (seven of them in Italy), the Hotel Bernini Palace has just undergone a major refurbishment. And boy does the old girl look good! The lobby and ground-floor bar and restaurant are jaw-droppingly dramatic in deep olive greens and purples with gossamer floor-to-ceiling ivory drapes, accessorized with huge beaten gold pots and vases. The wow factor is off the charts. Upstairs, one whole floor has been refurbished in this style and called the Tuscan Floor. The entire floor is exclusive to the occupants of these twelve ultra-luxurious rooms done in old wood and velvets, leather upholstery, and terra-cotta tiled floors. Here there is a permanent Champagne Buffet, which guests can nibble on to their hearts' and wallets' content. The rest of the hotel is much more standard, old-style five-star. There are of course all modern conveniences, even though they might be housed in antique cabinets. ♦ Piazza San Firenze 29 (at Borgo dei Greci). 288621; fax 268272. www.bagiolinihotels.com

Within the Hotel Bernini Palace:

Brunello Restaurant and Bar

★★$$$ You will feel like a movie star eating here, amid the glamour of the décor, the lovely staff, the premium spirits, the well-made cocktails, and the good wine list. The small menu runs the gamut from a lightly marinated salmon salad to the old rib-sticking Tuscan favorite of *pasta e fagioli* (pasta and bean soup) for starters. They offer tagliatelle with wild boar in the list of pasta dishes (or try a more ladylike breast of chicken with rolled grilled vegetables). Their take on the classic zabaglione uses Grand Marnier. ♦ M-Sa, 12:30PM-2:30PM, 7PM-10:30PM; bar 11PM-1AM

81 Raffaello Romanelli

This shop has the kind of window you just cannot pass without stopping, huge marble statues, and works in marble and onyx of all sizes, right down to little mosaic-inlaid boxes. But it's the huge statues that grab the attention. They are exactly the sort of thing where size *does* matter. ♦ Tu-Su, 9AM-1PM and 3:30PM-7PM; M, afternoon only. Lungarno Acciaiuoli 72

82 Hotel Torre Guelfa

$$ Not just a hotel, but a great, fat slice of Florentine history. The main building, on the Borgo Santi Apostoli, is a palazzo built by Niccolò Acciaiuoli, a politician and, at one time, prime minister of the Kingdom of Naples. On his return to his home city of Florence, he built himself a home he felt befitted his importance. The tower was built in 1280 by the Buondelmonti family, who had previously owned the site. At the time it was a tradition among noble Florentine families to erect tall towers as part of their residences—the taller your tower, the more important your family. In the 14th century, the Acciaiuoli family made the tower part of their palazzo. It is one of the most ancient towers still standing. On the façade you can still see the wrought-iron torch holders, banner holders, iron rings for tethering horses, and R-shaped hooks that supported poles for hanging laundry. The hotel has been owned and run for the past ten years by three Florentines, one or another of whom is generally to be found at reception. A tiny elevator takes you up to the third floor of the tower and the marble-tiled entrance. There is a sweet little breakfast room (a carbohydrate-and-coffee breakfast is served there each morning) and 15 bedrooms. All are fine, but some are particularly atmospheric, particularly the one reached by an interior stone staircase, with

the bed romantically behind voile drapes and a garretlike view of Florentine rooftops. There is a junior suite (a triple room) and the highly desirable Room 15—a lovely suite with its own private terrace on the roof of the tower. There are six more rooms in the slightly cheaper Residenza on the first floor of the tower. The main difference seems to be that rooms in the Residenza do not have TV, and so are a better bargain. This is a lovely place to live—just a stone's throw from the Ponte Vecchio, the Piazza della Signoria, and the Via Tornabuoni. The hotel is peaceful, but just step outside and you are in the middle of everything. ♦ Borgo Santi Apostoli 8 (between Via Por Santa Maria and Chiasso de' Manetto). 2396338. www.hoteltorreguelfa.com

82 Enoteca Romano Gambi

A delightful place presided over by a quintessentially Tuscan mama. This lady knows a thing or two about the wines and oils she sells. The ground floor stocks packages of pasta, candies and cakes, jars of sauces, honeys and condiments, great single-estate oils, and well-aged balsamic vinegars. Upstairs is an impressive selection of wines. There are some old, dusty (and probably undrinkable) bottles of Chianti Classico, Brunello, and other Tuscans—and when I say old, I mean from 1960 and thereabouts. Who wouldn't be thrilled with a bottle of wine from the year of their birth? There are even a few plaster-covered, distressed-looking bottles that are survivors of the great flood of 1966. This is not just wine (again, probably undrinkable), this is history you are buying. ♦ Tu-Sa, 11AM-7PM. Closed Sunday and Monday afternoon. Borgo Santi Apostoli 22/23r. 292646

83 Mandarina Duck

The Florence branch of this Italian chain is known for trendy, heavy-duty rubber bags and briefcases and smaller accessories. ♦ M-F, Sa morning Mar-Oct; M afternoon, Tu-Sa Nov-Feb. Via Por Santa Maria 18-25r (between Borgo Santi Apostoli and Via delle Terme). 210380

84 Cirri

The delicate Florentine art of hand embroidery is alive and well in this shop. It's well stocked with thousands upon thousands of table linens, collars, kerchiefs, and lingerie in cotton, silk, and linen, as well as exquisite outfits and accessories for infants and toddlers. ♦ M-F, Sa morning Mar-Oct; M afternoon, Tu-Sa Nov-Feb. Via Por Santa Maria 38-40r (between Via Lambertesca and Via Vaccherecia). 2396593

85 Relais Uffizi

$$ Ten lovely, spacious rooms, and large glass windows in the lounge that provide glorious, priceless views of Piazza Signoria, guarantee that this charming hotel in a refurbished 14th-century palazzo is a real winner. There's no restaurant, but there is a bar. ♦ Chiasso del Buco 16 (off Via Lambertesca, between Chiasso de' Baroncelli and Via Por Santa Maria). 2676239; fax 2657909. www.venere.it/firenze/uffizi

86 Casa-Torre degli Amadei

This 14th-century tower, rebuilt after it—like most of the immediate vicinity—was destroyed during World War II, now houses the conservative jeweler **Ugo Piccini**. Once upon a time, it was the residence of one of the most reactionary families of medieval Florence. The Amadei (the name, ironically, means "love of God") arranged for the murder of Buondelmonte dei Buondelmonti, who had jilted their daughter. The Florentines affectionately call this tower *"La Bigonciola,"* meaning the tub—only the Amadei know why. ♦ Via Por Santa Maria 9-11r (between Lungarno Acciaiuoli and Borgo Santi Apostoli)

87 Matassini

Friends who have an eye for Bulgari, Cartier, and the like tip their hats to the Matassini sisters, who have a knack for knocking off the spirit rather than the letter of the big-name jewelry designers. ♦ M-F, Sa morning Mar-Oct; M afternoon, Tu-Sa Nov-Feb. Via Lambertesca 20r (between Chiasso de' Baroncelli and Via Por Santa Maria). 212897

87 Caruso Jazz Internet Cafe

★★$$ It's difficult to know how to describe this place. It is beautifully spacious and calm inside, with vaulted ceilings in honey-colored stone. The tables are topped with rich red cloths and are generously spaced. Food ranges from bar snacks to a full menu that offers 10 spaghettis and 10 tagliatellis (including versions with pesto and fresh tomato, with salmon and porcini, and with truffle cream). There are raviolis and gnocchi too. Main courses include a choice of 10 composed salads, and meats like leg of pork cooked in beer can be accompanied by an impressive choice of fresh vegetables. The wine list is good, and there are several beers on draught as well as a choice in bottles. Jazzwise, a baby grand sits at the back of the hall, and almost every night around 9 there is really good live music. And as if that weren't enough, slip away into the next room and you have top-speed Internet access. ♦ Daily. Via Lambertesca 14/16r. 281940. www.carusointernetcafe.com

88 Ken's Art Gallery

If you are all done with the 15th and 16th centuries and ready to be brought up to date, then come here. The gallery features interesting, intelligent work—an international gathering of paintings and sculptures and generally 21st-century stuff. ♦ Daily, 3:30PM-7:30PM. Via Lambertesca 15/17. 2396587. www.kensartgallery.com

89 Antico Fattore

★★$$ The "old farmer" of the name doesn't really exist, but his spirit lives on in the rustic country cooking (try the classic Tuscan white-bean soup, *ribollita*), with offerings like wild boar sausage and pigeon with olives. The setting is homey and relaxed. It's a favorite of neighborhood merchants and tourists in the know. ♦ M-Sa, lunch and dinner. Closed 15 July–end August. Via Lambertesca 1-3r (between Via dei Georgofili and Via Por Santa Maria). 288975

89 Olive Tree

Memorials can be difficult things to get right, but this one does. It is an olive tree, given to the city by the Comitato Georgofili Lambertesca on 27 May 2004 to commemorate the young people killed by the bomb that wrecked the Accademia Georgofili in 1993. The olive tree was chosen because of the way it overcomes adversity: it survives anything that is flung at it, and it goes on to bear fruit. A plaque on the wall of the adjacent Accademia tells how the whole tower was rebuilt after the attack. And the school goes on. ♦ Via dei Georgofili at Via Lambertesca

90 Galleria degli Uffizi (Uffizi Gallery)

In 1560, Grand Duke Cosimo I commissioned **Giorgio Vasari** to design a building for offices (*uffici* in Italian, corrupted to "uffizi" by the Florentines). Construction was completed by **Bernardo Buontalenti** under Francesco I, who turned the top floor into a museum of art and curiosities and installed artists' and artisans' studios there. Vasari's first architectural commission, the building is a masterful blend of classical elements with the Tuscanisms of *pietra dura* (semiprecious stone) and white stucco walls. The Medici family put together the collection, whose unrivaled strong points are paintings from the Florentine Renaissance as well as works by Flemish and Venetian masters, and an impressive array of antique sculpture. The last of the Medici line, Anna Maria Ludovica, donated it to the people of Florence in 1737.

The most important single museum in Italy, the Uffizi is surprisingly manageable, laid out more or less chronologically in a series of human-scale rooms. It is also the most crowded museum in the country. To avoid the squeeze, try to visit it first thing in the morning, during the lunch hour, or late afternoon. In high season, "standing in line" can mean a wait of up to three hours. If it makes you feel any better, the waiting is in part due to an attempt to limit the number of people inside at any one time to 780. As with most Italian museums, but particularly frustrating at this one, don't expect every room to be open (the principal rooms, however, almost always are).

Stop for a look at Andrea del Castagno's frescoes of *Illustrious Men* (mostly Florentines) next to the ticket office in the remains of the 11th-century church of **San Piero Scheraggio**, which Vasari incorporated into his building. Across from the elevator is a fresco of the *Annunciation* by Botticelli. Vasari's monumental staircase leads to the prints and drawings department, which usually has an exhibition or two mounted from its rich collection. (If climbing the staircase seems too monumental a task, take the elevator to the right of it, pretending not to understand the sign that says it's for staff only.) The painting galleries are on the top floor. Walking from *sala* to *sala* (room to room), don't overlook what may seem to be decorative background elements—lively ceiling frescoes, Flemish tapestries, and antique sculpture. Take a break now and then to gaze out the windows at Florence and the countryside, or into the courtyard when it is filled with a flower show in the spring.

In 1993, a car bomb allegedly set by the Mafia damaged 15 rooms in the west wing of the Uffizi. Thankfully, none of the great masterpieces were affected and exhibits scattered throughout the museum illustrate the bomb damage and completed restoration work. To recuperate from the following tour, go to the museum bar at the end of the corridor, overlooking **Piazza della Signoria** from the roof of the **Loggia dei Lanzi**. Highlights of the Uffizi (*sala* numbers refer to floor plan on page 45): **Sala 2** Three imposing altarpieces depicting the Madonna enthroned (*Maestà* in Italian) open the show with deserving majesty. On the right side of the room is the earliest version, by Cimabue, considered the father of modern painting, though his panel still shows close ties to Byzantine painting in the classical stylization of its angels and drapery. In the center of the room is the more realistic (and, for its day, revolutionary) interpretation by Cimabue's alleged pupil, Giotto. ("Cimabue thought that he held the field in painting, but now Giotto is acclaimed and his fame obscured," writes Dante in *Purgatory*.) To the left is a work by Cimabue's contemporary from nearby Siena, Duccio di Buoninsegna, whose attention to graceful humanity, rich color, and surface pattern was seminal to the Sienese school. **Sala 3** What Duccio sowed may be seen in this room of Sienese pictures. Simone Martini's *Annunciation* is full of grace, whereas Pietro Lorenzetti's *Madonna in Glory* and his brother Ambrogio Lorenzetti's *Presentation in the Temple* and *Story of St. Nicholas* continue the Sienese preoccupation with surface pattern, here combined with an awareness of Giotto's sense of space and solidity. **Sala 4** Here is an assemblage of what used to be referred to as "Primitives." What these panels by followers of Giotto lack in artistic innovation they make up for by capturing the intimate and intense spirituality of the era (the 14th century), their saints performing various impassioned acts before gently glowing gold-leaf backgrounds. **Sale 5-6** These two rooms bring the Gothic period to a close with Lorenzo Monaco's *Coronation of the Virgin* and *Adoration of the Magi*. In Gentile da Fabriano's treatment of the same subject (*Adoration of the Magi*) across the room, the Gothic marches out with charming pageantry. **Sala 7** Masaccio and Masolino, whose work is seen here in the collaborative *Madonna with Child and St. Anne,* are the most sought-out early-15th-century artists in this room. But there are other masterpieces, namely a rare picture by Domenico Veneziano (*Sacra Conversazione*), *Federico da Montefeltro* and *Battista Sforza* by Veneziano's pupil Piero della Francesca, and the epic *Battle of San Romano* by Paolo Uccello. Uccello was obsessed with perspective, a fact that becomes all the more frightening when you consider that this busy picture, bristling with lances and fantastically colored horses, is but one of three panels that once decorated the **Medici Palace**. The other two sections are now in the Louvre and London's National Gallery. **Sala 8** Paintings by Masaccio's pupil Filippo Lippi indicate a return to the tender and decorative style of the Gothic period. **Sala 9** Paintings by the brothers Antonio and Piero Pollaiuolo, particularly *The Feats of Hercules* by Antonio, show a strong interest in the Renaissance study of human anatomy. Botticelli's *Finding of the Body of Holofernes* has some of Antonio's energy, though his *Return of Judith* derives more from his master, Filippo Lippi. **Sale 10-14** Botticelli's—and the museum's—most famous paintings are in these rooms, which have been joined into one large space. They are *The Birth of Venus* and *Primavera* (Spring). The former masterpiece is a fairly straightforward representation of the goddess of the sea, received by a nymph and the personified wind. *Primavera* is a flowery Renaissance interpretation of classical mythology (depicting, from right to left, Zephyr, Chloe, Flora, the Three Graces, and Mercury). In addition to the other Botticellis in the rooms, there are two Flemish masterpieces—Hugo van der Goes's *Portinari Altarpiece* and Roger van der Weyden's *Entombment of Christ*—as well as works by Domenico Ghirlandaio, Filippo Lippi, and Lorenzo di Credi. **Sala 15** This room displays the formative years of Leonardo da Vinci—although for really early Leonardo you should pop back to Room 14. The misty landscape and the sad little angel seen in profile within the *Baptism of Christ* by Verrocchio were painted by Leonardo, who was 18 and an apprentice. In this room you can see—among other works—his *Annunciation* and his sketch of the *Adoration of the Magi*. Leonardo shares his room with Raphael's teacher Perugino and some fascinating works by Piero di Cosimo. **Sala 17** The "Room of the Hermaphrodite," as it is also known, is often closed. Inside (enter from **Sala 18**) is the Hellenistic sculpture that gives the room its name, as well as other bits of classical sculpture. **Sala 18 Buontalenti** designed this octagonal (like the **Baptistry**) room, known as **"La Tribuna"** (The Tribune). It is made of lavish materials that represent the four elements—lapis lazuli for air, mother-of-pearl for water, red walls for fire, and green *pietra dura* floors for earth. It was meant to showcase the gems of the Medici collection, especially the *Medici Venus,* a Roman copy of a Greek original, which caused longing sighs during the Grand Tour era. The room is a veritable temple to Mannerist portraiture, with Medici likenesses by Vasari, Bronzino, and Jacopo Pontormo. Another Mannerist, Rosso Fiorentino, painted the delightful *Musical Angel,* a popular image that graces everything from postcards and calendars to T-shirts. **Sala 19** Notice Luca Signorelli's *Holy Family* (there's a similar composition by Michelangelo in **Sala 25**) and Perugino's *Madonna* and *Portrait of Francesco delle Opere*. **Sala 20** German Renaissance painting in all its intensity is exemplified by Lucas Cranach's *Adam and Eve,* not to mention Dürer's treatment of the same subject, as well as Cranach's *Adoration of the Magi* and *Portrait of the Artist's Father*. **Sala 21** The beginnings of important Venetian painting are seen here in Giovanni Bellini's *Sacred Allegory*. **Sala 22** Works by more northern Europeans are on view in this room, including Hans Holbein the Younger's *Portrait of Sir Richard Southwell* and Albrecht Altdorfer's *Martyrdom of St. Florian* and *Departure of St. Florian*. **Sala 23** Spend some time with Correggio's *Rest on the Flight to Egypt* and religious works by his master, the northern Italian painter Andrea Mantegna. **Sala 24** The *Cabinet of Miniatures* is an example of the kind of curiosities collectors favored in times past. **Sala 25** This houses Michelangelo's only painting in Florence, the *Doni Tondo* (a *tondo,* or round painting, of the Holy Family made for the Doni family), which through its strongly modeled and muscular forms of figures of both sexes shows the artist's clear preference for sculpture. Its garish colors, which were meant to disturb, inspired Florentine painters Fiorentino (his violent *Moses Defending the Daughters of Jethro* is in this room) and

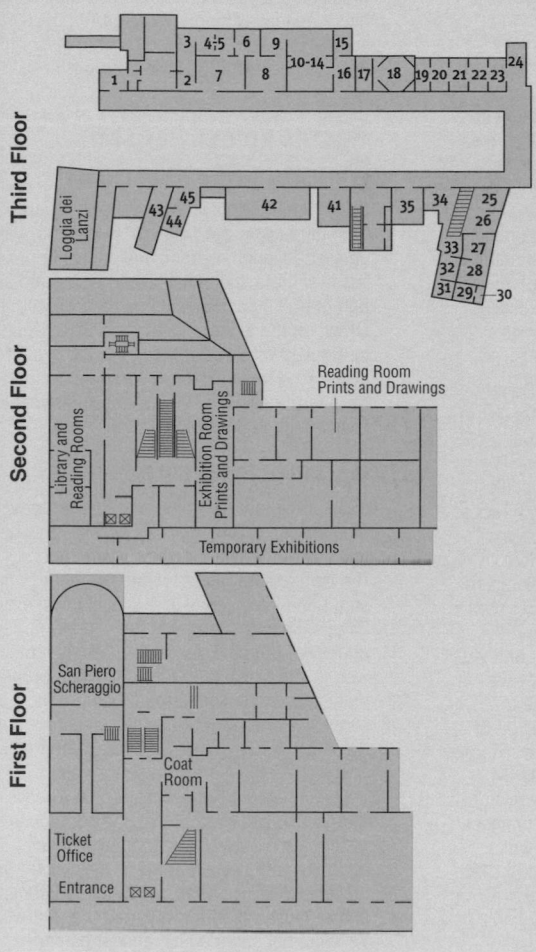

GALLERIA DEGLI UFFIZI

1 Archeology Room
2 12th C and Giotto
3 13th C Sienna School onwards
4 13th C Florentine School onwards
5-6 Gothic – International Collection
7 Early Renaissance
8 Filippo Lippi
9 Piero and Antonio Pollaiolo
10-14 Botticelli
15 Leonardo da Vinci
16 Map Room
17 Room of the Hermaphrodite
18 La Tribuna – Bronzino
19 Perugino and Signorelli
20 Albrecht Dürer
21 Giambellino and Giorgione
22 Fiamminghi and the German Renaissance
23 Mantegna and Correggio
24 Miniatures Room
25 Michelangelo and the Florentine School
26 Raffael and Andrea del Sarto
27 Pontormo and Rosso Fiorentino
28 Titian and Sebastiano del Piombo
29 Dosso and Parmigianino
30 15th C Emilian School
31 Paolo Veronese
32 Bassano and Tintoretto
33 15th C: The Vasari Corridor
34 15th C: Lombard School
35 Baroccio and Tuscan Counter-Reformation School
41 Rubens
42 Niobe
43 16th C Italian and European Schools
44 Rembrandt and 16th C Flemish School
45 17th C Italian and European Schools

Pontormo to begin working in the style known as Mannerism. **Sala 26** Enjoy a moment of serenity here with Raphael's *Madonna of the Goldfinch*, which owes its restful pyramidal composition to Leonardo. The other Virgin, *Madonna of the Harpies*, is by Andrea del Sarto. Raphael is also represented by the *Portrait of Pope Leo X*, a Medici. **Sala 27** A high-pitched frenzy of early Florentine Mannerism is reached in this room with Pontormo's vivid *Supper at Emmaus* and Bronzino's *Holy Family*. The movement's counterpart in Siena is also represented, albeit weakly, by Domenico Beccafumi's *Holy Family*. **Sala 28** This salon of Titians is invitingly presided over by the sensuous *Venus of Urbino*. *Flora* and *Eleanora Gonzaga della Rovere* are part of the lustrous and illustrious company. **Sala 29** Central Italian Mannerism, certainly less spiritual than the Tuscan but equally contorted and distorted, is here typified by Parmigianino's *Madonna of the Long Neck*. **Sala 30** Emilian painting, with works by Battista Dossi and Dosso Dossi, is the focus here. **Sala 31** showcases Paolo Veronese, while next door you will find Bassano and Tintoretto. One of the paintings most severely damaged by the 1993 bomb was del Piombo's *Death of Adonis*. Its restoration is a breathtaking tribute to the skills of the restorers who worked here in the aftermath. What was just tatters is now once again whole. See it. Marvel at the skill it represents on both levels. **Sala 41** Don't overlook this room, home to works by Van Dyck and Rubens, among them the latter's *Portrait of Isabella Brant*. **Sala 42** The **Sala della Niobe** is named after the Roman sculptures of *Niobe and Her*

Children, here ogled incongruously by a collection of 20th-century self-portraits by artists from around the world. **Sala 43** Return to 17th-century Italy to view some of Caravaggio's earthy and realistic responses to the squeamishness of Mannerism–the mad *Medusa,* decadent *Bacchus,* and emotionally charged *Sacrifice of Isaac*. There are also the more bucolic *Summer Diversion* by Guercino and *Seaport with Villa Medici* (this villa is at the top of the Spanish Steps in Rome) by Claude Lorraine. **Sala 44** The Dutch paintings here, including two self-portraits by Rembrandt from his early and later years, are worth the long walk. The collection ends with a rococo flourish of paintings by Tiepolo, Canaletto, Guardi, Chardin, and Goya.

The fabulous sweeping staircase (by Buontalenti) guarantees you can make a great exit in the **Exit Hall**. At the top you will meet one of Florence's lucky charms–the *Wild Boar*, a Roman copy of a third-century Greek sculpture. It was then copied again by Pietro Tacca, who used it as the model for his *Porcellino*, which sits in the Mercato Nuovo. ♦ Main Gallery, Tu-Su, 8:15AM-6:50PM. Bookings in advance by phone carry a $3 surcharge (call 294883) but are worth it. The Uffizi is the busiest single building in the country, and you can't see much of Florence from the ticket line in the Piazzale degli Uffizi. Entry is free to visitors over 65 and under 18. Admission is often increased when there is a special exhibition on. Rooms in the Uffizi are frequently closed without notice, so if you are coming to see something in particular, it's best to check the board at the entrance telling you which rooms are open each day. Piazzale degli Uffizi 6 (between Lungarno Archibusieri and Via della Ninna). 2388651/2

Within the Galleria degli Uffizi:

The Vasari Corridor

Room 33 is described on the plan as "the 15th Century Corridor," but it is better known as the Vasari Corridor. It was commissioned and built within 5 months (which might not sound like much, but wait till you see it!) in 1565. It runs all the way from the Palazzo Vecchio to the Palazzo Pitti, allowing the Medici to get from one to the other without any danger of encountering the hoi polloi. It runs right through the Uffizi, across the Ponte Vecchio, and along the top of the lovely church of Santa Felicità and is lined with a wonderful collection of portraits and self-portraits. There are works by Raphael, Andrea del Sarto, Bronzino, Bernini, Rubens, Rembrandt, Velázquez, Delacroix, and Ingres. Only 30 people at a time are allowed along the corridor and visits have to be arranged separately (and well in advance; this is a hugely popular part of the Uffizi). ♦ The Corridor opens (usually–"*dipende*" is what the gallery says, a marvelously Italian concept which means "it all depends . . .") on Friday and Wednesday mornings as part of the special tour known as the *Percorso del Principe*. Call 2654321 for bookings or call the main ticket office.

Restauro del Perseo (Perseus Restoration)

Benvenuto Cellini's great statue, removed from the **Loggia dei Lanzi** for protection against pollution, is being restored. The process–and the statue itself–can be viewed as part of an interactive multimedia exhibit in the **Uffizi**, on the ground floor of the West Wing, to the right off the entrance hall. The exhibit accommodates only a few people at a time; be sure to reserve. ♦ W-Su, by appointment. Loggiata degli Uffizi 6. 2612758

91 Gallery Hotel Art

$$$$ If modern art is your thing, ever considered staying in a modern art gallery? This new hotel might just be the chicest one around. The immaculately kept minimalist lobby is a smart and intelligently lit art gallery with exhibitions running throughout the year. If modern art leaves you cold (let's face it, there's plenty else to see here), then this is still one of the most impressive hotels you'll find. Not so surprising when you discover it is the work of the latest generation of the Ferragamo family, who know a thing or two about quality, elegance, and design. There are 74 rooms and suites (including 3 amazing penthouse suites with beautifully appointed terraces affording you a view you might never want to leave–luckily, the hotel has excellent room service) just a breath away from the Ponte Vecchio, but set in a tiny, almost hidden courtyard that is amazingly peaceful. Rooms have all the modern conveniences you could shake your credit card at, plus Wi-Fi, video conferencing on request, a garage (very rare in Florence these days), and a chauffeured limousine service. The bedrooms are classily minimalist and the elegant creams and browns of the décor are marvelously calming–a boon, should you have spent your day in line at the Uffizi. The hotel has the most wonderful open lounge and reading room they call The Library, a breakfast area (the excellent buffet breakfast is included), and one of Florence's smartest, hippest bars–**The Fusion Bar**. If you have any aspirations to being a smart sophisticate-around-town, book now. ♦ Vicolo dell' Oro 5. 27263 (booking line 27264000). www.lungarnohotels.com

Within the Gallery Hotel Art:

Fusion Bar

★★$$$ This is a seriously cool place. It looks so 21st-century-fusion-chic that you might think you won't be allowed in if you weigh more than 75 pounds and paid less than 75 hundred dollars for your outfit. But all are truly welcome here. The young lady in charge is an absolute delight, speaks perfect English, and will take great care of you.

The Fusion Bar is not just a bar, but a restaurant too. It opens at noon for very good cocktails and remains open all afternoon, when you might like to try the house special of two pieces of foie gras sushi and a glass of champagne. The Fusion Lunch offers a smart buffet selection of salads and composed salads (broccoli and char-grilled chicken in a tasty dressing or pasta salads), which are impressively lined up along the bar. Or you can order dishes like spicy tuna tartare with salmon roe and gazpacho jelly. The fusion element is showcased in such offerings as their miso soup, which comes (unlikely as it may seem) with clams or Gorgonzola. At 7PM the bar is filled with an incredibly generous selection of free hors d'oeuvres, such as tiny taste-bomb sandwiches, crudités with a selection of tasty dips and sauces, or strips of papadam with a chili dressing. I washed my platter down with a plum sour—the Fusion version of a whiskey sour, and very nice it was, too. Most of the cocktails have been given a twist. If you are a Negroni fan, their version is definitely worth a try. Dinner is à la carte and features dishes like lobster in lemon and garlic sauce. Desserts range from the traditional (tiramisù) to the exotic (white chocolate and coconut risotto). They serve brunch on Sundays, and dining spills out onto the wooden decking in the tiny piazza in summer. ♦ Daily, noon-3PM and 7PM-11PM; bar, noon-midnight

92 Torre dei Donati Consorti

Located near the **Casa-Torre degli Amadei**, this little 12th-century tower was affiliated with the Guelph family, whose daughter Buondelmonte chose to marry and who murdered him for jilting her. Talk about unfriendly neighbors! The atmosphere here is warmer these days, since it houses part of the **Hotel Continental**. ♦ Lungarno Acciaiuoli 2 (at Via Por Santa Maria)

93 Santo Stefano al Ponte

The lower part of the Romanesque green-and-white marble façade of this church dates from 1233, though records claim it was built in 1116 or earlier. The interior was rebuilt in the 17th century by **Ferdinando Tacca** and includes his bronze relief *The Stoning of St. Stephen*. (The church itself was reduced to rubble during the German retreat in World War II, then damaged in the 1966 flood and again in the 1993 bombing of the **Uffizi Gallery**.) Much of the interior was originally made for other churches—the elaborate marble staircase by **Bernardo Buontalenti** stood in **Santa Trinità**, and the altar by Giambologna was in **Santa Maria**. The church is usually open only for noteworthy concerts and occasional exhibitions. A recently opened small museum adjacent to the church houses a collection of ecclesiastical art and sculpture taken from the diocese's small churches in the surrounding Tuscan countryside that are closed or were victims of theft and vandalism. A Virgin Mary that experts think might be an early Giotto is a main feature here. ♦ Museum: Sa, Su, 3PM-7PM. Piazza Santo Stefano al Ponte (off Via Por Santa Maria, between Lungarno Archibusieri and Via Lambertesca)

94 Caffè delle Carrozze

★$ Silvia, the friendly Italian-Canadian co-proprietor of this café, knows her co-continentals' tastes. Lick your cups clean of the berry flavors (all natural, made only with fruit and water) and the sinfully delicious *semifreddo* specialty of *nocciolato* (a cool, creamy chocolate mousselike concoction). There is even a Mousse Al Ferrero Rocher! For those watching calories or fat, there are frozen yogurts. The freshest panini are justifiably best-sellers. ♦ Daily Apr-Oct; closed Monday in winter. Closed in January. No credit cards accepted. Piazza dei Pesce 3-5r (off Vicolo Marzio). 2396810

94 Hotel Hermitage

$$ A restoration incorporated the neighboring **Archibusieri** hotel into this 27-room hostelry. Housed in the top four floors of a medieval tower two steps from the Ponte Vecchio, some of the accommodations have a view of the bridge and the Arno River. The guest rooms are of average size, tastefully done, with new bathrooms (some with Jacuzzi) and air conditioning; units in the back, facing the **Duomo**, are quieter. The vista from the top-floor roof garden at sunset will take your breath away, while the perfume from the honeysuckle that grows in profusion there will replace it in the nicest possible way. There's no restaurant. ♦ Piazza dei Pesce (at Vicolo Marzio). 287216; fax 212208. www.hermitagehotel.com

94 Casa Artigiana dell'Orafo

In this goldsmith's house you can watch more than 30 jewelers go about their timeless craft, producing what's in store for you in the elite shops on the Ponte Vecchio. ♦ M-F, Sa morning Mar-Oct; M afternoon, Tu-Sa Nov-Feb. Vicolo Marzio 2 (at Volta de' Girolami). 292382

95 Cellerini—Forniture per Orafi

If all you do is look in the window, this is a fascinating place. It sells everything you need to work with gold–from digital scales to powerful eyepieces, drill bits and files, little hammers and sets of pliers. I like to watch people going in and out . . . goldsmiths come in some unexpected shapes! ♦ Su-F, 9AM-12:30PM and 3:30PM-7PM. Piazza di S Stefano 2

96 Loggia del Grano

★★$ Originally commissioned in 1619 by Cosimo II and built by **Giulio Parigi**, this was a granary. Over the years it has become many things, including, just a few years ago, a movie theater opened by a famous Italian actor. Well, there are still screens here, but now they are small and are on the computer terminals in one corner which offer you, at the click of a key, all the information you could want on Florence. Of course, you have your Access Guide . . . but should you want to get some in-depth information, these computers have it all. You just can't carry them around.

In addition to the Tourist Information section, this vast pillared space houses a bar, a café, and a restaurant. The bar has premium spirits, a very decent wine list (with a good selection by the glass), and serves orange juice squeezed right before your eyes. They even use delicious Sicilian blood oranges in season. There are always little free nibbles on the bar, and the staff is absolutely lovely. The café serves up freshly made, well-filled panini, crostini, very good pastries (served warm), and light salads. The coffee and wide selection of teas is good, and there are always free newspapers and magazines around for you to browse. The restaurant menu offers tempting things, from a mix of local cheeses served with fresh pear and honey, through a selection of four freshly made pizzas, to hefty main courses like *tagliata di manzo* (sliced grilled fillet steak served on a salad of arugula). Their tiramisù (should you stretch to dessert) is as good as anything in Florence's most expensive restaurants.

Everything is in the one lovely, airy space (which stretches out onto midnight blue-clothed tables under the vaulted ceiling of the Loggia's gorgeous portico when the weather is good), and there is no need to choose between menus. You can sit and have a full meal, or just a glass of chilled Prosecco. Even better, the menus run throughout the day, so you can breakfast at 11:30AM and lunch at 4PM, should you desire. Cosimo should certainly approve of the use that is being made of his granary. It is a real contribution to the welcome Florence gives her guests. ♦ Daily, 7:30AM-midnight. Corner of Via Castellani and Via dei Neri

97 Ponte Vecchio

Florence's 12th-century "Old Bridge" was so named to distinguish it from the Ponte alla Carraia upstream, built in thoroughly modern 1220. The very first mention of a bridge across the Arno at this point is in 972. Destroyed by flood in 1177, it was rebuilt only to be destroyed again in 1333. The Ponte Vecchio crosses the Arno at its narrowest point in the city. It was probably where the Romans built a bridge for the Via Cassia, the ancient road that ran through Florence on its way from Rome to what are now Fiesole and Pisa, much more important cities in those days. A statue of Mars once stood at the northern end of the bridge, the scene of a seminal event in the history of Tuscany. There, on Easter Sunday in 1215, assassins killed Buondelmonte dei Buondelmonti, who had spurned his fiancée of the Amadei family in favor of a more attractive member of the rival Donati clan.

The present bridge and its shops replaced the 12th-century structure swept away in the flood in 1333. Although **Vasari** writes that **Taddeo Gaddi** reconstructed it in 1354, he may have been trying to reinforce his own link with Florentine artistic tradition, since he himself designed the corridor running over it, buying up property on either side of the bridge to do so. (For all his power, Vasari was not able to persuade the Manelli family to let him run it through their residence, however, so it twists briskly around the Manelli tower at the Pitti end of the bridge.) The Ponte Vecchio's medieval character persists, albeit dazzling with the glint of gold in its shops. (Medieval spectacle can be fully appreciated by watching the *Calcio Storico* parade march over the bridge, with participants in full period garb, each 24 June and two other days in June, varying each year.) After Vasari built his corridor, Ferdinand I de' Medici, annoyed at having to pass over the shops of butchers, tanners, and other practitioners of the "vile arts," as he called them, rousted the low-rent tenants and raised the rates. In came the goldsmiths and jewelers whose professional descendants line the bridge today. A tribute to their craft is the bust of the goldsmith/ sculptor Benvenuto Cellini in the middle of the bridge. During the German retreat of World War II, this was the only bridge Hitler's troops did not blow up. Instead, they reduced the buildings on either side of it to rubble (which is why Via Por Santa Maria is so modern-looking), effectively blocking passage across the Arno. In 1966, the Ponte Vecchio's jewelers were among the first to witness the river's flood, and they played a crucial role in alerting the townspeople. Their shops and Vasari's corridor suffered some damage, but the bridge beneath them remained intact.

These days the Ponte Vecchio bustles with upscale shoppers—particularly tourists. At night during the warmer months, however, the last hippies in Italy (who seem to have somehow become embedded in the structure in the 1966 flood) congregate in the two terraces in the middle of the bridge, twanging guitars and performing street theater. Jewelers on the Ponte Vecchio come and go (talking not of Michelangelo, but no doubt of Cellini), but the current crop is likely to stay put for a while. ♦ Between Via de'Guicciardini and Via Por Santa Maria

On the Ponte Vecchio:

Padlocks

In the middle of the bridge, where there is a gap in the shops, you will find on the walls a great dangling cluster of padlocks—all sizes and colors, all padlocked to each other and so, eventually, to the bridge. Each padlock is inscribed with the names of modern-day lovers. It was an inventive way around the Florence Commune's prohibition of writing names on the stone of the bridge itself. Very sweet. And less anatomically drastic than leaving your heart in San Francisco.

T. Ristori

The jewelry here has a contemporary feel, though it is timeless in the cut (and price tag) of its precious stones. The semiprecious stock is equally inventive and, naturally, more reasonably priced, and many of the settings make bold use of both precious and semiprecious sparklers. ♦ M-F, Sa morning Mar-Oct (no midday closing); M afternoon, Tu-Sa Nov-Feb. Nos. 1-3r. 215507

U. Gherardi

Having corralled the coral market in Florence (most of it is produced in Naples), this jeweler sells buckets of the stuff in pale white, blushing pink, and beet red. The bounty of the sea continues in an enviable selection of cultured pearls and cameos. ♦ M-F, Sa morning Mar-Oct (no midday closing); M afternoon, Tu-Sa Nov-Feb. No. 5r. 211809

Tozzi

If you are interested in cameos, then this is where to come. Cream and coral, ivory and white, the cameos come in all sizes and in all forms. There is even a cameo lampshade and an entire conch shell turned into a cameo. ♦ M-Sa, 9:30AM-7:30PM. No. 19

Fratelli Piccini

The Piccini brothers have been crowning heads ever since Queen Elena married Vittorio Emanuele III at the turn of the 19th century. Their current designs are on the street level; upstairs are antique pieces that the descendants of the king and queen could easily have pawned upon their abdication. ♦ M-F, Sa morning Mar-Oct (no midday closing); M afternoon, Tu-Sa Nov-Feb. No. 23r. 294768

Cassetti

Among the most creative of the bridge's jewelers, the Cassetti family is also among its oldest and most respected. They are the exclusive distributors of Bulgari jewelry in Tuscany and are known for their unique selection of antique jewelry. ♦ M-Sa Mar-Nov (no midday closing); M afternoon, Tu-Sa Jan-Feb. No. 52r. 2396028

98 Istituto e Museo di Storia della Scienza

Anyone wondering how to set up a museum could do worse than come here and see how it should be done. The medieval **Palazzo Castellani**—which houses the museum—dates back to before 1180 when it was a fortifying castle, built into the walls of the city. It passed from the Altafronte to the Umberti family. The Castellani were the last private owners. In 1574 the palazzo passed to the Giudici di Ruota (magistrates), and the coat of arms of two of the magistrates can still be seen over the entrance. The palazzo also housed the Accademia della Crusca (The Academy of Letters), an organization set up by a Florentine fraternity to safeguard the purity of the Italian language. But science, it seems, is more important than language, and in 1930 it became the seat of the Science Museum. The museum houses some of the most important collections of scientific instruments and models in the world. Initially gathered together by the Medici family (where would the world be without the Medici?) and then the Dukes of Lorraine, the collections were held in the **Palazzo Vecchio** and then in the **Uffizi**, where they were held along with the art collections. In the mid-18th century art and science went their separate ways, and the collections were moved. The museum, which underwent a stunning refurbishment in 2003/4, currently holds about 5,000 instruments, of which 1,500 are on permanent display in 21 rooms open to the public. ♦ Admission. M, W-F, 9:30AM-5PM and Tu, Sa, 9:30AM-1PM June-Sept; M-Sa, 9AM-5PM, Tu, 9:30AM-1PM, and 2nd Su of month, 10AM-1PM Oct-May. Piazza dei Giudici 1 (at Lungarno dei Medici). 2398876

COLLI

Even before Luca Pitti built his palazzo at the foot of what are now the **Boboli Gardens**, Florentines were heading for the hills—*colli* in Italian—across the **Arno**. According to a medieval legend, one of the first to do so was the martyr St. Minias, who in AD 250 carried his severed head from Florence's Roman amphitheater to the **Mons Florentinus**, now the site of the beloved hilltop church of **San Miniato**.

Many have followed through the ages, including **Michelangelo**, who built fortifications around San Miniato to protect Florence from a siege, and the Medici, who greatly expanded the already grandiose palazzo begun by Pitti. Others have been great Florentine families such as the Guicciardini, Torrigiani, and Serristori, who built palazzi

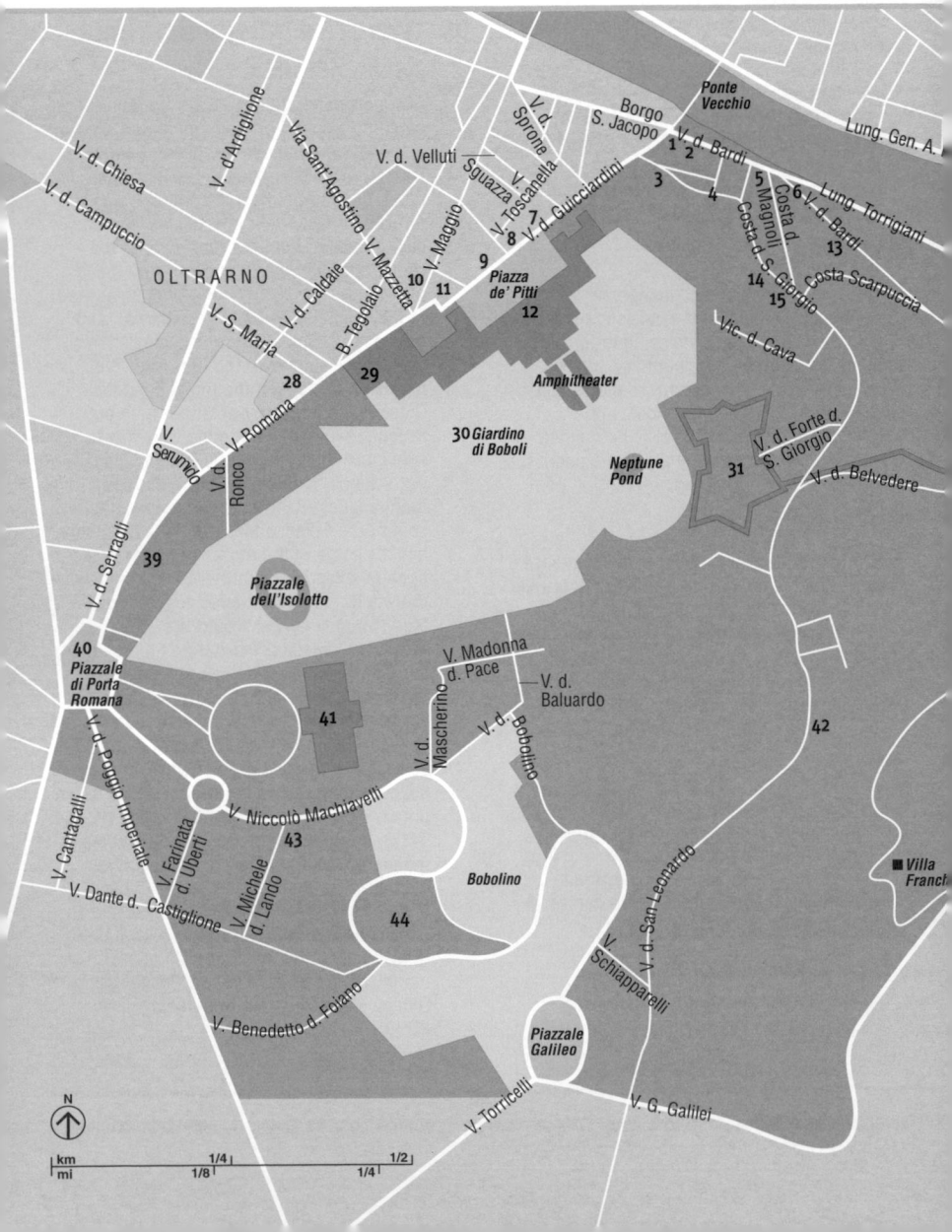

from the Middle Ages onward, and 20th-century plein-air painters, including Ottone Rosai, who immortalized the landscape of **Via di San Leonardo**, the Florentines' favorite country road.

The Colli continue to provide a bit of country in the city, on **Via di San Leonardo** as well as in the panoramic Boboli Gardens, the **Forte di Belvedere**, and **Piazzale Michelangiolo**, all ideal spots for a picnic. Even the most famous museum in the area, **Palazzo Pitti**, is uncrowded (though the arrangement of the art is not) compared with other Florentine institutions.

So as not to lose your head like St. Minias, be forewarned that much of the area is as hilly as its name implies. Before you begin to explore it, put on some sturdy walking shoes.

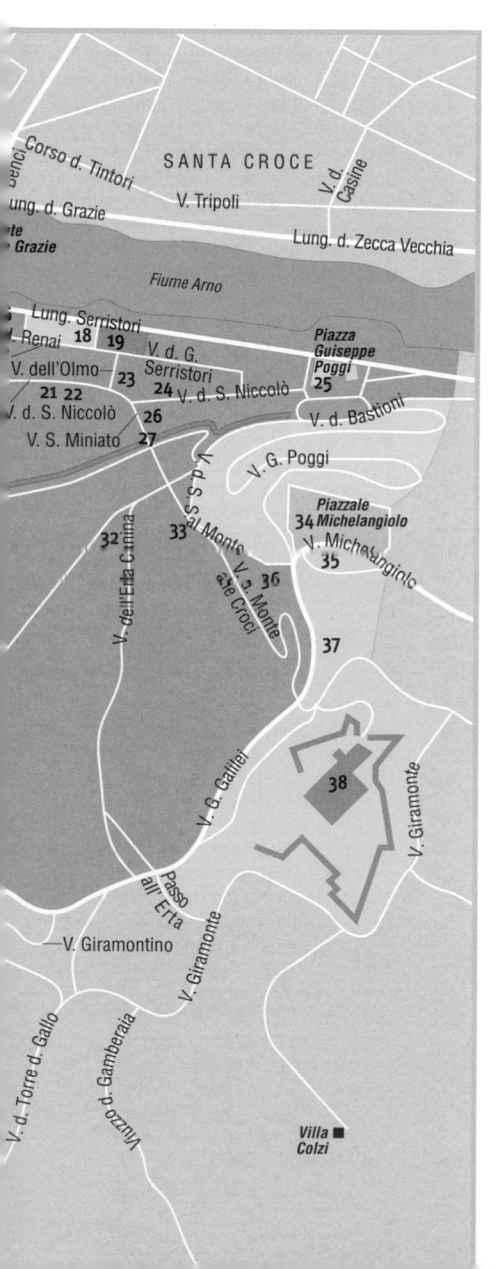

1 Via Giucciardini

This narrow bustling little street leads you up from the **Ponte Vecchio** to where it opens out into the **Piazza Pitti** (which is hard to miss, being the largest palace in Florence). The street is jammed with tiny stores, many selling leather goods, shoes, and porcelain.

On Via Giucciardini:

Madova

This is Florence's prime glove emporium, hands down. The firm makes its own gloves—including custom sizes—of various leathers, linings, and colors and will ship anywhere free of charge. ♦ M-Su, 9:30AM-7:30PM Mar-Oct; M, 3:30PM-7:30PM, Tu-Sa, 9:30AM-7:30PM, Su, 10:30AM-1PM, 2:30PM-7:30PM Nov-Feb. Via de' Guicciardini 1r. 2396526

Guido Longhinotto

Beautiful handmade shoes for men and women, ranging from the coquettish slipper to the businesslike brogue. This is the kind of workmanship you come to Italy for. All the shoes are signed with the maker's name. ♦ Daily. Via Giucciardini 9

Del Secco

This little place sells utterly lovely clothes and accessories for little people. If you know someone age 0–10 (as the sign in the window says), then pop in. The clothes for tiny ones are especially adorable. ♦ Daily, Via Giucciardini 20

Per Modo di Dire

This unique shop is not to be passed by if you know anyone with a decent sense of humor. Fausto Gelormini, the hugely likeable owner, took a degree in Business Economics and spent years in marketing before returning to his first love as a graphic artist and extremely witty cartoonist. His shop sells good-quality T-shirts and sweatshirts, jeans and shorts, dresses and silk scarves, nightshirts, bags, and cute notebooks, all hand printed with his clever pictures and word play. "Stress!" reads the shoestring-strapped top with the drawing of a porcupine, brows furrowed, quills up. *"Mi faccio un giro!"* (I'm going for a little tour) says the legend under a smiley goldfish in a bowl. I bought the T-shirt that shows a sad, weedy, worried-looking little gladiator flanked by two huge lip-licking lions. *"L'importante e partecipare!"* (Important to participate!) it says. Witty, well-made, and very Italian. How much better does it get? ♦ Daily, 11AM-7PM. Via Giucciardini 110r. 2657272. www.permododidire.it

Emporium

The kind of place you go in to buy a gift and end up with half a dozen little bits of gorgeousness for yourself. The window is full of the chicest, smartest tableware and cutlery you can imagine. You will find sweet little espresso cups—white porcelain with a red heart—in sets of six, lovely sets of colored glasses for every imaginable beverage, vases molded like clusters of rosebuds, glass and ceramic candlesticks, and even some smart designer clothes, including chic little jackets in felt with their own corsage worked into the collar. Warning: if you browse, you'll buy! ♦ Daily, 10AM-7PM. Via Giucciardini 122r. 212646

Pasticceria Maioli

★★$ This glitzy modern establishment is the newest makeover for one of Florence's oldest *caffè*/bars. It's a convenient location for a light lunch of pasta, pizza, fresh sandwiches, or salads, either standing at the bar or sitting in the back. ♦ M, W-Su, 6AM-8:30PM. Via de' Guicciardini 43r (between Piazza de' Pitti and Via dei Bardi). 214701. Also at Via dei Bardi 73r (at Ponte Vecchio). 284108

Palazzo Guicciardini

Historian Francesco Guicciardini was born in this 15th-century palazzo and lived here from 1482 to 1540. Rebuilt in 1620–1625 to designs of **Ludovico Cardi da Cigoli** by **Gherardo Silvani,** its elegant courtyard contains a stucco representation of Hercules in the style of Antonio Pollaiuolo. It is one of the few historical buildings that escaped World War II destruction on this street connecting the Ponte Vecchio and the **Palazzo Pitti**. ♦ Via de' Guicciardini 15 (between Piazza de' Pitti and Via dei Bardi)

2 La Porcellana Bianca

White porcelain is the specialty of this housewares shop. Spots of color among the sea of white dishes, cups, and platters include lovely country dish towels and brass-handled stainless-steel cookware. ♦ Daily (no midday closing). Via dei Bardi 53r (between Costa del Pozzo and Via de' Guicciardini). 211893

3 Santa Felicità

This is arguably the oldest church in Florence, although looking at the beautifully restored interior with its wonderful pale gray pillars, you'd never know the old girl wasn't a youngster. It is thought to have been founded in the second century AD and dedicated to the Roman martyr St. Felicity (a bit of a misnomer, given that she was put to death along with her seven sons in the year 165AD). There was certainly a church here in the fifth century, which was replaced in 972 by a proto-Romanesque church, and then in 1060 a Romanesque church was consecrated with a convent of Benedictine nuns. Santa Felicità was again rebuilt between 1340 and 1354 (a few traces of this incarnation remain in the cloister and the nuns' Chapter House). In the 15th century **Brunelleschi** designed the Barbadori-Capponi Chapel (1418) and a new sacristy was built (1470) which now houses Neri di Bicci's altarpiece of Santa Felicità and Luca della Robbia's *Madonna and Child*. The Barbadori-Capponi Chapel was decorated by Jacopo Pontormo between 1525 and 1528, and it is his works that are the church's main claim to fame. Under the cupola are four tondi of the Evangelists, on the right wall is his *Annunciation,* and on the altar, his *Deposition* or *Carrying of Christ to the Sepulchre*. This work is generally held to be one of the true masterpieces of Florentine Mannerism and is regarded, somewhat dramatically, as signaling the end of the Renaissance here. It is an extraordinary piece, very physical, very emotional, and representative of the turmoil and fragility of Italy at the time—Florence had fallen to the Medici, Italy was being invaded, the Lutheran Reformation was red in tooth and claw. The world in this image is disoriented and full of fear; there is no architectural reference or substantive perspective. Everything revolves around an empty center. It is powerful. And in the crowd of mourning figures, Pontormo included a self-portrait. Forty years later, a triple-arched loggia was added to the façade to accommodate the **Vasari Corridor** (which stretches from the **Palazzo Vecchio** to the **Palazzo Pitti**), and in 1587 the **Grand Ducal Balcony** was added so that the ruling family could assist at the liturgy. From 1550, when the Medici moved into the Pitti Palace, until 1776, Santa Felicità was the parish church of the Grand Dukes. The definitive alterations were made between 1736 and 1739, when **Ferdinando Ruggieri** completely reconstructed the church in the late Baroque style. ♦ M-Sa, 9:30AM-12:30PM and 3PM-6:30PM. Piazza Santa Felicità 3 (off Via de' Guicciardini, between Piazza de' Pitti and Ponte Vecchio). 213018

3 Celestino

★★$$ This bright eatery offers a menu of such dishes as *ravioli rose* (in a tomato-and-cream sauce), *scaloppine alla boscaiola* (veal with tomato and mushroom), and *scampi alla pescatore* (shrimp with tomato and garlic). In warm weather, a few tables spill out into the little piazza for dining *all'aperto*—don't ask to eat *alfresco,* which means "in the slammer" in current Italian. ♦ M-Sa, lunch and dinner. Piazza Santa Felicità 4r (off Via de' Guicciardini, between Piazza de' Pitti and Ponte Vecchio). 2396574

4 Le Volpi e L'Uva

★★$ This great, thinking drinker's wine bar is run by Emilio and Riccardo, two young wine enthusiasts who have created a stylish, relaxing niche for a sip and snack. As with so many of these *enoteca*, the guys behind the counter really know and love the wines and grappas they are selling you, so don't just ask for your usual. Ask for their advice and discover something new! Dozens of changing wines-by-the-glass are posted daily, with small sandwiches and a good cheese selection as an aside. Most interesting are the lesser-known Italian wines and those of small and not as well-known producers—and the chance to sample them all at a few outdoor tables, which you can now do no matter what the weather, thanks to the advent of new canopies and big standing heaters . . . there was much alfresco enjoyment even in the snow, apparently, and that was not just northern Italian machismo. And, of course, what you really like, you can buy by the bottle and take home. ♦ M-Sa. Piazza de' Rossi 1r (at Costa di San Giorgio). 2398132

4 Neri

Anyone who thinks pearls are unlucky should come here. Nothing this beautiful could bring bad luck. The whole window of this tucked-away jeweler is dedicated to the labors of oysters everywhere. The pearls here are generally cultured, but none the less lovely for that. There are big pearls and tiny pearls, black pearls and creamy white pearls, Japanese, Chinese, and Australian pearls. They come individually or as necklaces, collars, brooches, rings, and earrings. There are even fascinating framed shells showing the development of the cultivated pearl from one month to three years. ♦ M-F. Via Stracciatella 8r. 282933

5 Osteria Vasari

★★$ This place is the dream of two Florentine men who gave up their businesses to plow the money into this atmospheric trattoria. The building was once used as a charcoal burner but has been brightened with the help of some wonderfully sunny yellow paintwork. It has great vaulted ceilings and delightful nooks and crannies. There is a tiny courtyard with a huge Doric capital, and visitors to the "facilities" will find their activities watched over by a variety of ancient (and naked!) stone Florentines. The *padroni* are charming, helpful, and fabulously enthusiastic about their menu and wine list. The menu is flag-wavingly Tuscan—game stews and roasted meats abound. There is boar and hare and venison and game birds. Homemade pappardelle made with chestnut flour (particularly delicious) comes with wild boar sauce, and their gorgeous ravioli is stuffed with artichoke and served in a meaty pheasant sauce. Should you opt for a roast, there is a good choice of vegetables to accompany it, including wild mushrooms with olive oil and fresh herbs and grilled baby onions. Those looking for something lighter will enjoy the spaghetti with cherry tomatoes and fresh basil. Portions are very Italian in their generosity! If you have room, try their superb selection of seasonally available aged Pecorino cheese. Some are around for only two months of the year, but there is always something delicious—the version aged in the purée of grape left after wine pressing is unforgettable. Their wines (nice list!) and olive oil come from small individual local producers. This place is a find. You should find it too! ♦ Tu-Su, lunch and dinner. Via dei Bardi 25r. 2346435. www.osteriavasari.it

6 Arte & Mestieri

A tiny treasure on the Colli bank of the Arno. This shop has beautifully hand-worked leatherbound diaries and photo albums, the paper as well as the loose-wrap covers handmade by the young Florentine owner. There are lovely reproduction antique photograph postcards, delightful, fragile-looking packs of cards (playing and tarot) faced with sepia-tone photos of long-ago ladies, beautiful antique-style calendars, handmade bookmarks, and, most intriguing of all, a sort of guidebook to Florence. Far be it from me to suggest you navigate using anything other than your Access Guide, but these hand-printed, antique-looking maps come folded and wrapped in leather. Beautiful things. A charming shop. ♦ Daily, 10AM-7PM. Piazza di Santa Maria Soprarno 1

7 Pitti Gola e Cantina

For those looking to buy edible souvenirs for friends back home, this small wine-and-food boutique is a veritable delight. It's known for top-of-the-line labels and small-production wine and food selections, and you're sure to find high-quality pasta, sauce, pâté, extra-virgin olive oil, and a well-priced selection of wines representing all regions of the country. Also available here are English-language cookbooks on Italian regional cuisines. Periodic wine tastings are held in the downstairs *cantina,* sometimes free of charge. They're almost always conducted in Italian, but after a few glasses of wine, you'll catch their drift. ♦ M-Sa. Piazza de' Pitti 16 (between Sdrucciolo de' Pitti and Via dei Velluti). 212704

8 Giulio Giannini & Figlio

Beautifully marbleized Florentine paper goods are the specialty of this fifth-generation shop, which has also been doing custom bookbinding for some of those years. The products are expensive, but there's a good quality-for-your-money ratio. ♦ M-F, Sa morning Mar-Oct; M afternoon, Tu-Sa Nov-Feb. Piazza de' Pitti 37r (between Sdrucciolo de' Pitti and Via dei Velluti). 212621. Also at Via Porta Rossa 99r (between Via Monalda and Via dei Tornabuoni). 215448

9 Pitti Mosaici

It's rare to see the younger generations continuing the Florentine tradition of *artigianato* (craftsmanship), but Ilio de Filippis has taken up the 16th-century Florentine specialty of *pietra dura,* the inlay of precious and semiprecious stones in jewelry, artwork, and furniture. ♦ Daily Apr-Sept; M-Sa Oct-Mar. Piazza de' Pitti 23-24r (between Via de' Marsili and Sdrucciolo de' Pitti). 282127. Also at Via de' Guicciardini 60r (between Via dello Sprone and Borgo San Jacopo). 282127

9 Mr. Jimmy's Dolci

A little piece of America in Florence—by which, of course, one doesn't mean the blight of McDonald's restaurants across the city. No, this is real down-home America—bagels in six varieties, cupcakes and brownies, muffins and hot dogs that come with a choice of mustard, mayo, or ketchup. The talented bakery here turns out birthday cakes and pumpkin pies, apple pie and peanut butter cookies. The little individual cheesecakes have to be eaten sitting down, because you will probably faint with pleasure when you taste them. Mr. Jimmy (well, his mom, actually) does great American-style coffee, and anything in the shop can be delivered "downtown," as the notice says. Their goodies are also available at the Edison Bookstore in Piazza della Repubblica. ♦ Tu-Su; M, noon-3PM. Piazza de' Pitti 6r. 285312. www.mr-jimmy.com

10 Casa Guidi

The poets Robert Browning and Elizabeth Barrett Browning lived and held court on the first floor of this 15th-century palazzo for 15 years. Their son, Pen, was born here, and this was where Elizabeth developed her romanticized support of the unification of Italy. She died here in 1861 and is buried in Florence's **English Cemetery**. All that's left of the Brownings' sojourn in this house is a plaque. The **Casa Guidi Windows**, immortalized in Elizabeth's poem of the same name ("I heard last night a little child go singing . . . O bella libertà, O bella!"), remain intact. Should you wonder what it would be like to live somewhere like this, why not find out? The Casa Guidi is now owned by Eton College (yes, *the* Eton College) and run by the Landmark Trust. It sleeps six and can be rented by the week. ♦ Piazza di San Felice 8 (at Via Maggio). For information on rental, contact Landmark Trust, 00 44 1628 825925. www.landmarktrust.co.uk

10 San Felice

This old church has been here since 1066 and was taken over by the Benedictines in 1153. **Michelozzo di Bartolomeo** is thought to have designed the current façade in the 13th century, built the chapels at the east end of the church, and added the triumphal arch (not quite so triumphal anymore, sadly). San Felice's main claim to fame is a great Crucifixion by the School of Giotto and works by Neri di Bicci, Starnina, and the School of Botticelli. There is also a *Last Supper* by Matteo Roselli in the refectory. In the 16th century the church was taken over by nuns, and in the 18th it became a conservatory for poor girls. ♦ Piazza di San Felice (at Via Maggio)

11 Caffè Pitti

★★$ Considering its position here opposite the **Pitti Palace**, it is a tribute to the charming staff and owners here that the welcome is so genuinely friendly, the staff so helpful, the food and wine so good, and the prices so reasonable. All this and the surroundings are a delight, with dark wood and flattering lighting, comfy chairs, and interesting little nooks and crannies to sit in. You are welcome just for coffee and a (generous) glass of Prosecco, for one of their excellent pastries in the morning, or for a more extensive breakfast. The lunch menu is enticing, with interesting pastas such as *pici al burro cacio e pepe* (little rolled pasta pieces with butter, local cheese, and black pepper). But the real draw here is their Menu al Tartufo, an entire menu dedicated to the joy of truffle eating. It really is wonderful. And the truffles—the *funghi di Aphrodite*—used are from a nature reserve owned by the café's proprietor and boasting over 5,000 of the luscious little lumps. Next door you will find the *bottegha*—a shop where you can buy anything that has stood still long enough to be truffled: pasta and sauces, salsas, honey, and oil. There are also white and black truffles in jars and a limited edition of *salsa del tartufaio* (truffle hunter's sauce), which comes with a *sigillo di garanzia* (a guarantee) and is produced by Savini, who have been truffle experts since 1940. ♦ Tu-Su, 9AM-2AM. Closed Monday afternoon. Piazza de' Pitti 9. 2399863. www.caffepitti.it

11 Firenze of Papier Mâché

You won't believe it, but everything in this amazing workshop/shop is handmade from papier mâché—masks and plaques, reproductions of famous sculptures, and intricately worked murals. A group of artists creates these beautiful lightweight objects. They're the perfect gift idea when you are near your baggage weight limit! Daily, 10AM-7:30PM. Piazza de' Pitti 10. 2302978; fax 365768

12 Palazzo Pitti

Florence's largest if not most beloved palazzo was commissioned circa 1457-1470 for Luca Pitti, a wealthy importer of French cloth who was trying to keep up with the Joneses (in his day named Medici and Strozzi). Legend has it that Pitti's pitiless ambition called for a plan with windows larger than the doors of the **Palazzo Medici** and a courtyard that could contain the entire **Palazzo Strozzi**. (Though the former palazzo was under construction at the time, the latter existed only as a plot of land.) Somewhere between legend and fact is the story that architect **Luca Fancelli** built the palazzo according to a grandiose plan his master **Brunelleschi** had presented to Cosimo Il Vecchio. According to **Giorgio Vasari**, when the Medici rejected it, Brunelleschi "tore the drawing into a thousand pieces in disdain." The original palazzo consisted of only the seven central bays of the present structure, built—as were later additions—out of rough-hewn golden *pietra dura* quarried from the **Boboli Gardens** behind it. Even so, it was most imposing. Machiavelli called the palazzo "grander than any other erected in the city by a private citizen," and Vasari wrote that the view from it was *"bellissima,"* commenting that the surrounding hills in the Boboli made it "almost a theater."

Work on the palazzo had been at a standstill for decades when Cosimo I's wife, Eleanor of Toledo, bought it from Pitti's impoverished heirs in 1549. From then on, the palazzo became the official residence of the rulers of Florence. The Medici brought in **Bartolommeo Ammannati**, who added the wings toward the Boboli and the courtyard in 1558-1577. (He did not ruin any marble here, as the Florentines say of his statue of *Neptune* in **Piazza della Signoria**, but instead enlarged the palace with more stone from the Boboli brought with the help of a mule, whose efforts are commemorated on a plaque in the courtyard.) After Ammannati's interventions, the estate, with its grounds, was the most magnificent in Europe, a rustic and rambling precursor to Versailles. (It was this version of the palace that Eleanor's homesick granddaughter, known as Marie de Médicis when she was married off to Henry IV of France, tried to recall when she commissioned the Palais du Luxembourg in Paris.)

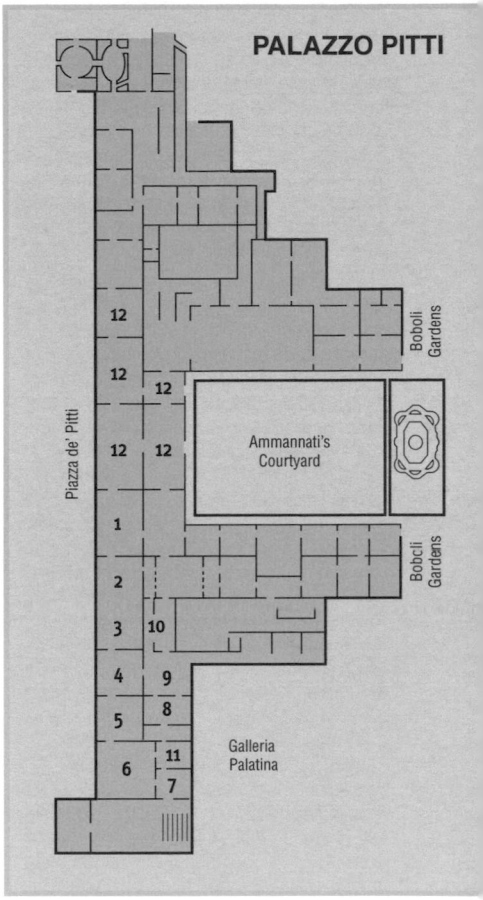

During the 17th century, at the behest of the Medici, **Giulio Parigi** added the three bays on either side of the original seven, and his son **Alfonso** extended the two lower floors to their present dimensions. The two porticos reaching into the **Piazza de' Pitti** were added in the 18th century under the house of Lorraine, giving the palazzo the exterior aspect you see today (see drawing page 56). Meanwhile, as the Florentine *genius loci* that brought about the Renaissance and the Medici began to wane, the royal rulers looked increasingly beyond the city to embellish the palace with suitably magnificent paintings and decoration. The Pitti became the residence of the Italian royal family when Florence was the capital of Italy in the last century. In this century, Victor Emmanuel III gave it to the state. It now houses no fewer than seven museums (many of which have erratic hours or are indefinitely closed from time to time).

Centuries after Luca Pitti commissioned the palazzo, his name lives on in another Florentine institution–the trade shows collectively known as *Pitti Imagine*. These Italian fashion shows, which originally took place in the palazzo's **Sala Blanca**, are now held at the **Fortezza de Basso** and market everything from housewares to international fashion, including the latest versions of those French textiles Luca used to import over half a millennium ago. Ammannati's monumental 140-step staircase leads to the most famous museum in the palazzo, **Galleria Palatina** (see floor plan on page 55 for Palazzo Pitti). The first five rooms are decorated with Pietro da Cortona's allegorical ceiling frescoes, which give the rooms their names. In the **Sala di Venere** [1] (Venus Room; numbers refer to the floor plan) are Titian's *Concert*, *La Bella*, and *Portrait of Pietro Aretino*, as well as Rubens's *Landscape with the Wreck of Ulysses* and Salvator Rosa's *Harbor View*. The **Sala di Apollo** [2] (Apollo Room) has more rich Titians (notably a *Mary Magdalene*) and works by Rosso Fiorentino, Andrea del Sarto, and the maudlin Guido Reni, considered the greatest painter of all time during the Grand Tour days. In the **Sala di Marte** [3] (Mars Room), look for Tintoretto's *Portrait of Luigi Cornaro* and numerous Rubens paintings. The **Sala di Giove** [4] (Jove Room), used as the throne room, contains one of the most famous paintings in the gallery, Raphael's *La Velata*. There are also important works by his master, Perugino, as well as by Fra Bartolommeo and Andrea del Sarto. The **Sala di Saturno** [5] (Saturn Room) houses the painting most singularly identified with the Pitti, Raphael's *Madonna della Seggiola*, as well as other Raphael Madonnas and portraits. Of particular interest in the remaining rooms are Raphael's *La Gravida* in the **Sala dell'Iliade** [6] (Iliad Room); Cristofano Allori's *Judith*, a sensual exception to the cloying 17th-century Florentine school; and Pietro da Cortona's flamboyant Baroque frescoes depicting *The Four Ages of Man* in the **Sala della Stufa** [7] (Stove Room; *stufa* has no mythological significance–it refers to the warmth of the room–but the subjects were taken from Ovid's *Metamorphoses*). Also look for Cigoli's *Ecce Homo* in the **Sala di Ulisse** [8] (Ulysses Room); Filippo Lippi's *Madonna and Child* in the **Sala di Prometeo** [9] (Prometheus Room); and Francesco Furini's *Hylas and the Nymphs*, another exceptional example of the Florentine Baroque, in the **Galleria Poccetti** [10] (Poccetti Gallery). More Florentine Baroque paintings are in the **Sala Volterrano** [11] (Volterrano Room).

On the same floor as the Palatina, the **Appartamenti Monumentali** [12] (State Apartments) are often closed. They contain 17th-century portraits of the Medici by Justus

Palazzo Pitti

Sustermans, 18th-century Gobelin tapestries, and 19th-century decorations commissioned by the house of Lorraine.

Don't be misled by the name **Galleria d'Arte Moderna** (Gallery of Modern Art) one flight up, which contains mostly uninteresting 19th- and 20th-century Tuscan paintings. The quite notable exceptions are the *macchiaoli*. These plein-air painters, whose name means stainers, were long considered to be the Italian counterpart (if not predecessors) of the French Impressionists, but are becoming increasingly appreciated abroad in their own right. **Museo degli Argenti** (Silver Museum), too, is a bit of a misnomer since, rather than silver, the museum (accessible from the courtyard) is primarily a "camp" glorification of the Medici. It is also known for Lorenzo de' Medici's collection of precious-stone vases. They spawned a vogue for *pietra dura*, so associated with Florence during the days of the Grand Tour that it became known in English as Florentine mosaic. There are some examples of it on display here; it reaches its apotheosis in the **Medici Chapel** across the river.

The west wing of the Pitti houses **La Meridiana**, where King Victor Emmanuel chose to stay instead of in the more imposing palace. Its *Collezione Contini-Bonacossi* (Italian and Spanish paintings and decorative art) is dwarfed by that of the main Palazzo Pitti, but works by such artists as Giovanni Bellini, Paolo Veronese, Tintoretto, Gian Lorenzo Bernini, Goya, and El Greco are more than rewarding for those with the stamina. It also houses the *Galleria dei Costume,* a costume collection of largely Italian fashion from the mid-18th to the mid-20th centuries. Despite being housed in the Pitti, La Meridiana is under the auspices of the **Uffizi**. ♦ Admission. Galleria Palatina: Tu-Su, 8:30AM-6:50PM. Galleria d'Arte Moderna: Tu-Sa, 8:15AM-1:50PM and alternating Su/M. Museo degli Argenti, as above. Galleria del Costume, as above. A combined ticket for all the galleries and museums is available. Reduced prices after 4PM. 2388614. La Meridiana: By appointment only. Piazza de' Pitti (between Via Romana and Via de' Guicciardini) 213440; 23885

13 Il Torchio

This *torchio* (printing press) produces some of the loveliest (and more moderately priced than at centrally located stores) marbleized paper in Florence, applied to notebooks, boxes, picture frames, and other gift items. It's well worth the walk. ♦ M-F, Sa morning. No credit cards accepted. Via dei Bardi 17 (between Costa Scarpuccia and Costa de' Magnoli). 2342862

14 Casa di Galileo Galilei

Galileo lived in this palazzo, now covered with faded frescoes and closed to the public. Grand Duke Ferdinando II de' Medici used to stop by on his morning walks from the family residence in the **Palazzetto di Belvedere**. ♦ Costa di San Giorgio 19 (between Vicolo della Cava and Piazza de' Rossi)

15 Spirito Santo

Despite its heavy outward appearance, this Baroque church (erected in the 14th century and remodeled in 1705 by **Gian Battista Foggini**) is one of the lightest in Florence on the inside. It is filled with 17th-century paintings, including Alessandro Gherardini's *The Glory of St. George* (the church is also known as "San Giorgio," after this ceiling fresco). To the right of the altar is *Madonna and Child with Two Angels,* considered an early work by Giotto. ♦ Costa di San Giorgio 31 (between Vicolo della Cava and Piazza de' Rossi)

16 Centro Di

This art bookshop stocks material from many periods in many languages and has a distinguished small press of its own, specializing in museum and exhibition catalogs. ♦ M-F, 5:30PM-7:30PM; Sa, 4PM-7PM. Via dei Renai 202.2342666. www.centrodi.it

17 Silla

★$ This small (36-room) hotel still retains the flavor of the 15th-century palazzo in which it is housed. It's just far enough away from the center of town to be relaxing (the greenery helps too), yet within convenient walking distance to most of the major sights. There's a lovely terrace with a view for breakfast or afternoon tea, but no restaurant. There is now Internet access for guests. ♦ Via dei Renai 5 (between Via dell'Olmo and Piazza dei Mozzi). 2342888; fax 2341437. www.hotelsilla.it

17 Negroni

★$ One of Florence's new wave of chic, almost Milanese bar/restaurants. Everything from the music to the light fixtures is cool here. Except the value-for-money buffet lunch, which is hot (an eclectic mix of noodle dishes, bubbling Eastern-spiced sauces, composed salads, *frittata,* and garnishes. The bar stocks premium spirits and has an impressive cocktail list. The eponymous Negroni comes served on the rocks and in generous quantities. You can sip yours while browsing through the pile of newspapers that are spread fresh each day on the side bar. Happy hour here offers a free buffet of hors d'oeuvres. The restaurant menu is small but practical and includes dishes like risotto with saffron, peas, and prawns. If you are looking for a bit of late-night life here, you could do worse than come down on a Tuesday evening when the Florentine owners organize "The Club." Each "Club" being themed around the cool sounds coming from the deck of Negroni's official DJ, Leo Daddi! ♦ Daily, 8AM-2AM. Via dei Renai 17r. 243647. www.negronibar.com

18 Piazza Nicola Demidoff

This piazza is named after the wealthy Russian ambassador and philanthropist who lived in Florence from 1773 to 1828 and died in the nearby **Palazzo Serristori** (see below). The main feature of the piazza is an elaborate monument to Nicola Demidoff, covered with a glass canopy to protect it from the elements. The monument, by the neoclassical sculptor Lorenzo Bartolini, is composed of allegorical figures of the virtues that Demidoff was said to personify. ♦ Between Via dei Renai and Lungarno Serristori

19 Palazzo Serristori

Rebuilt in 1873 by **Mariano Falcini**, this 16th-century palazzo takes its name from one of Florence's most distinguished noble families. The Serristori gave Italy numerous men of state, from 15th-century soldiers to a 20th-century senator. (It is now best known for its wines, among them Chianti Classico Machiavelli, named for Niccolò Machiavelli, a clever marketing ploy that would undoubtedly have pleased him.) In the 19th century, family members also became landlords, renting to Russian ambassador Nicola Demidoff, King of Westphalia Jerome Bonaparte, and King of Naples and Spain Joseph Bonaparte, who died here in 1844. Gone are the days of the *grandes fêtes* given by Countess Ortensia Serristori. Severely damaged during the 1966 flood, the palazzo is of interest to the passerby today who can peek into its vast garden (also visible from **Piazzale Michelangiolo**). The palace is not open to the public. ♦ Lungarno Serristori 21-23 (between Via Lupo and Piazza Nicola Demidoff)

20 Palazzi dei Mozzi

These adjacent 13th-century medieval palazzi, now private residences, were originally owned by the now extinct Mozzi family, wealthy bankers who belonged to the Guelph party. Pope Gregory X stayed here in 1273 to negotiate a peace, albeit temporary, between the Guelphs and Ghibellines. The palaces are not open to the public. ♦ Piazza dei Mozzi and Via dei Bardi

21 Fallani Best

A recent change of address has resulted in Paola Fallani's change of specialty as well. After being known for years as a purveyor of Art Nouveau and Art Deco, she now offers modern and contemporary art. ♦ M afternoon, Tu-F. Via di San Niccolò 70r (between Via dell'Olmo and Piazza dei Mozzi). 241861

22 Alessandro Dari

Step through this unassuming, easy-to-miss doorway and you will see some of the most beautiful works of art in Florence. They are the work of Alessandro Dari, a young jeweler and goldsmith whose creations—he specializes in rings—are breathtakingly beautiful. His work is actually wearable art. He uses gold, bronze, silver, precious stones, and—occasionally, recently—even marble to create the kinds of pieces that are already treasures and will, without doubt, be heirlooms. Dari's work comes in "collections," including the collection of rings in the form of castles that he calls *"Il Guardino dell'Anima"* ("guardian of the soul"), rings (and some bracelets) in the form of tiny, fabulous crowns, and rings in a series entitled "Metamorphosis" that includes a stunning interpretation—as a pendant—of a female form emerging from a chrysalis. There are rings in human form, rings as musical instruments, and rings as philosophy.

The jewelry is displayed in sympathetically lit cases, some having Alessandro's own poetry set beside them by way of an introduction to the spirit of the collection. You move around the shadowy, atmospheric studio/showroom to the accompaniment of his personally chosen music.

These heartstoppingly lovely pieces of jewelry are alone worth the trip to Florence . They are unique. And you can not only watch the artist at work, but buy his creations as well! I don't believe it is exaggerating to say that the rings created by this intense, darkly handsome young Italian are the real reason human beings developed hands. See them. You will agree. The Maestro has recently taken to working on bigger pieces—still "wearable sculpture," for the most part, but on a larger scale. One of his biggest creations, however, is a huge, figured golden goblet, now occupying pride of place in the museum at Fiesole. While you are coming to Florence to see the work of Michelangelo, your children's children may well be coming here to see the works of Alessandro Dari. See them first! ♦ M-Sa, 9:30AM-1:30PM and 4PM-7:30PM. Via di San Niccolò 115r. Tel/fax 244747. www.alessandrodari.com

23 San Niccolò sopr'Arno

The simple façade of this 12th-century church has a portal and rose window added during the Renaissance. The interior contains numerous 15th- and 16th-century paintings by minor local artists. Also in the interior is one of Florence's little plaques indicating how high the flood waters reached in 1966 (about 4 meters, or 12 feet). ♦ Via dell'Olmo (between Via di San Niccolò and Via del Giardino Serristori)

24 Osteria Antica Mescita San Niccolò

★★★$ I'm almost tempted not to tell you about this place, and keep it for myself and the tables of local workers and clusters of gray-haired, round-hipped Florentine *nonne* who were my fellow diners. The ceiling is hung with bunches of herbs, salami, and cheeses; an old-fashioned fan whirls the delicious scents from the food around the room; the white tiled walls are lined with bottles; the tabletops are old marble, and the floor is immaculate Tuscan terra-cotta. The menu is immaculately Tuscan too. Vast platters of crostini piled with freshly made chicken liver pâté and chunks of local cheese are swept past. Great helpings of juicy, perfectly cooked lamb, beef, and pork are accompanied by world-class roast potatoes. But the real treasure of this warm, wonderful place is its buffet lunch. A simmering pot of just about the best *ribollita* (a delicious thick vegetable and bean soup) to be tasted in Florence, a big dish of pasta twists superbly sauced with tomato and herby pork, a steaming casserole full of local creamy white beans and chunky aromatic local sausage, a platter with slices of the best beef I have tasted in many years, and a warm bowl of a spicy cabbage dish that would turn Dracula into a vegetarian are all offered buffet-style. I ate my own weight in the stuff. And then there is a choice of three desserts—a delicious chocolate cream, a vanilla cream, and a fabulous caramel-topped panna cotta. All of this is accompanied by the house Chianti or mineral water. This is superb Tuscan food in the most convivial of surroundings. The feast is yours for 10 euros, and at the time of writing, there are no plans for it to change. This *osteria* epitomizes almost everything that is good about Italy. Please leave room for me! ♦ M-Sa, lunch and dinner. Via di San Niccolò 60r (at Via del Monte alle Croci). 234286

25 Porta San Niccolò

This imposing three-story medieval tower was built for defense purposes in 1324. ♦ Piazza Giuseppe Poggi (between Lungarno Cellini and Via di San Niccolò)

26 Gelateria Frilli

All the climbing in this part of town will doubtless make you appreciate the mounds of homemade ice cream the Frilli family produces daily in its little grocery store. Flavors change according to the season, but year-round treats include *caffè* (coffee), *mousse al cioccolato* (chocolate mousse), and *crema* (vanilla custard). An outdoor terrace upstairs is open in warm weather. ♦ Summer, 3PM-8PM and 9PM-midnight; winter, 3PM-8PM. Via San Miniato 5r (at Via di San Niccolò). 2345014

27 Porta di San Miniato

This relatively small medieval city gate for centuries provided passage from Florence to the church of **San Miniato**. These days, most people take the long staircase at the end of the street just outside it, rather than the road. At the top of the staircase, turn left and find yourself in **Piazzale Michelangiolo** (see page 61), whose views make the hike up worthwhile. ♦ Via San Miniato and Via del Monte alle Croci

27 Enoteca Bar FuoriPorta

★★$ The name of this wine bar refers to its location just outside the old city gates. The setting is particularly enjoyable when you can have a glass at one of the tables outside and gaze at the ancient ramparts. The bar sells hundreds of wines by the bottle (from as far afield as Chile and South Africa or as close as the Chianti vineyards), but it is most popular for wines sold by the glass and a wide range of *crostini* or *crostoni* (small or large slabs of grilled bread) served with a choice of toppings—mushrooms, cheese, cold cuts, vegetables—and toasted. ♦ M-F, noon-3:30PM, 7PM-12:30AM; Sa, noon-3:30PM, 7PM-1AM. Via del Monte alle Croci 10r (at Via San Miniato). 2342483. www.fuoriporta.it

28 Annalena

$$ This 15th-century palazzo had quite a checkered career before ending up as this quietly comfortable, old-style hotel. The eponymous Annalena fell in love with Baldaccio di Bicci dei Medici, and they were married in 1493. Soon after, they had a son. Unfortunately, Annalena's charm and good looks attracted the attentions of one Bartolomeo Orlandi, who took it—to put it mildly—rather badly when she spurned his advances: He murdered her husband and son before her eyes. Cosimo de' Medici gifted her the house, which she turned into a convent when she herself decided to become a nun. The convent became a refuge for tragic women over the centuries, beginning with Caterina Sforza, widow of Giovanni di Lorenzo de' Medici, and continuing as a home for young widows (under the Dominicans), a school for girls in 1880, and a hiding place for political refugees under Fascism. It first became a *pensione* in 1919. All 20 rooms, ranging in size from singles to quads, are furnished with antiques, many of which have been in the palazzo for generations. All have bathrooms, hair dryers, minibars, and other

amenities. Some have wood-burning stoves, and a few open out onto a lovely gallery overlooking the former Giardino di Annalena, which is now a plant nursery. The lobby is a comfortable place to sit, with big velvet-covered chesterfields and a small bar. A buffet breakfast in the lovely breakfast room is included in the price. ♦ Via Romana 34 (between Via Mori and Via Santa Maria). 222402; fax 222403. www.hotelannalena.it

29 Museo La Specola

Grand Duke Peter Leopold acquired this ancient palazzo from the Torrigiani family in 1771. He subsequently added an observatory (*specola*), giving the palazzo and museum its name. It houses a monument to Galileo, the **Tribuna di Galileo**, built in 1841 on the occasion of a scientific conference. Its main attraction, however, is the morbid part of the **Zoological Museum** (also founded by the Grand Duke) that contains graphic wax models of every imaginable part of the human anatomy by Clemente Susini and Felice Fontana, as well as memento mori wax tableaux by Gaetano Zumbo representing such upbeat subjects as *The Plague*, *The Triumph of Time*, *Decomposition of Bodies*, and *Syphilis*. ♦ Admission. Zoological Museum: Th-Tu, 9AM-1PM. Anatomical Museum: Tu-Sa. Via Romana 17 (just southwest of Piazza de' Pitti). 2288251

30 Giardino di Boboli (Boboli Gardens)

Providing the *bellissima* view Vasari enthused about, the gardens were laid out in 1550 by Niccolò Tribolo on the hilly slopes behind the **Palazzo Pitti**. Probably named after a family that owned property on the site, the park combines a formal, groomed appearance with whimsical Mannerist statuary. It was once the private property of the Medici and other courts, but now its expanses provide fresh air and soothing views for one and all. Matrons, young lovers, au pairs with babies, and travelers welcoming the green expanse all pass their afternoons in the park with its resident legion of feral cats.

The main entrance is on the left side of the Palazzo Pitti facing it from its piazza. Just inside to the left (see map below) is Valerio Cioli's statue of Cosimo I's favorite dwarf, *Pietro Barbino Riding a Turtle,* whose image is almost as popular as that of David. A gravel path leads to the **Grotto**, which was designed by **Vasari** and **Buontalenti** and contains copies of Michelangelo's *Slaves* and the original of Giambologna's *Venus*. As in much of the gardens, the room with *Venus* once contained *giochi d'acqua* (surprise jets of water), which were the Mannerist equivalent of water pistols. The **Amphitheater**, which extends behind **Ammannati**'s courtyard (both were used to stage court frolics), was modeled on an ancient Roman circus and contains such authentic Roman relics as a granite basin from the Baths of Caracalla and part of an Egyptian obelisk brought to the Eternal City. To the left towers the red **Kaffeehaus**, a semicircular structure with a fanciful dome, built by **Zanobi del Rosso** during the reign of the Lorraine. It offers refreshments and a terrace with nice views of Florence and Fiesole. From here a path leads up to the **Neptune Pond**, which surrounds a bronze statue by Stoldo Lorenzi. Above it, completing the perspective down to the Pitti, is a colossal statue of *Abundance* designed by Giambologna and finished by the workshop of

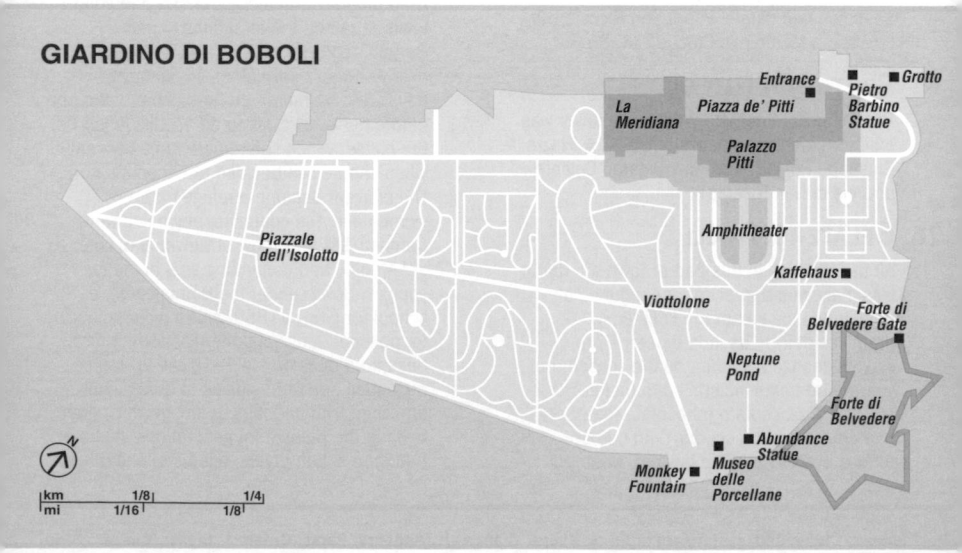

Piero Tassi. Near it is the **Giardino dei Cavaliere**, where the **Museo delle Porcellane**, a museum of European porcelain, has been installed. Its playful *Monkey Fountain* is by Pietro Tacca, and its terrace has lovely views of the surrounding slopes. From here a path leads to the **Viottolone**, a magnificent cypress alley studded with classical and neoclassical statues. The spectacular path leads downhill to the **Piazzale dell'Isolotto**, the centerpiece of which is Giambologna's *Ocean Fountain*, containing a copy of his *Oceanus*. ♦ Admission. Daily, 8:15AM-8PM June-Aug; 8:15AM-7PM Apr-May, Sept; 8:15AM-6PM Mar, Oct; 8:15AM-5PM Nov-Feb. Piazza de' Pitti (at Via de' Guicciardini).

31 Forte di Belvedere

Entered from Costa di San Giorgio and occasionally from the **Boboli Gardens**, the fort—constructed in 1590-1595 by **Bernardo Buontalenti**—affords beautiful panoramic views of Florence and the vicinity from all sides, as its name promises. The rustic fortress was designed to fortify Grand Duke Ferdinand I de' Medici's ego more than anything else—notice the heavy-handed Medici coat of arms. The star-shaped bastions are topped by the **Palazzetto di Belvedere**, designed by Buontalenti in the Mannerist style, with windows set on the sides and decreasing in size on the higher stories; it was the temporary residence of Grand Duke Ferdinando II de' Medici during the plague of 1633. The **Porta San Giorgio** entrance to the fort has a fresco of the *Madonna and Saints* by Bicci di Lorenzo and a relief of St. George. There are often indoor and outdoor exhibitions at the site, which also hosts outdoor film screenings in the summer. ♦ Via del Forte di San Giorgio (off Costa di San Giorgio). At the time of writing, it is closed for renovations.

32 La Beppa

★★$$ This homey trattoria offers home-style cooking—if your home is in the Tuscan countryside. Particularly good are the simple first-course soups (*ribollita, pappa al pomodoro, minestrone*). After dinner you might like to work off the calories at the "Jaragua" Caribbean Disco Bar opposite. ♦ Daily, dinner. Via dell'Erta Canina 6r (between Viale Galileo Galilei and Via del Monte alle Croci). 2347681; fax 2269821

33 Via de San Salvatore al Monte

This is not so much a street, but more a huge stairway. Shorter but steeper than the alternative route to the **Piazzale Michelangiolo**, it climbs the hill in the shade of pine trees and with the stations of the cross marked on its incline with wooden crucifixes, offering a sort of combination worship opportunity and thigh workout.

34 Piazzale Michelangiolo

Piazzale means big piazza, and *Michelangiolo* is a Tuscan spelling of Michelangelo, to whom this panoramic piazza is dedicated. It could just as easily be dedicated to Cupid, given the amorous Florentines who park their cars in the postcard-perfect scenic overlook of the city, famous for its sunsets that silhouette the cypresses and major monuments and render the Arno golden as it passes beneath a succession of bridges. Michelangelo was originally supposed to be commemorated here with a museum of all his works in Florence brought together under one roof in **La Loggia**. As if that idea weren't ill-advised enough, in 1873 architect **Giuseppe Poggi** devised as a monument an odd bronze hybrid of some of Michelangelo's most famous works in Florence—*David* and the sculptures from the Medici tombs—the end result of which some have called a giant paperweight. Under the olive trees to the right of the piazza is an iris garden. The flower, which (originally in a stylized white and later in a red version) became the symbol of Florence, is celebrated in the piazza each May with an international iris show. The incredible view over Florence and what seems like most of Tuscany is definitely worth the climb. ♦ Viale Galileo Galilei and Viale Michelangiolo

35 La Loggia

★★$$$ Instead of architect **Giuseppe Poggi**'s originally planned Michelangelo museum, this space is now occupied by an elegant restaurant popular for those special occasions when you want a touch of theatricality. The unbeatable view overshadows the standard Tuscan fare—ask for an outdoor table, or a window seat in cooler weather. Patio tables are also available for bar service only. Be aware that, should you want a dish of ice cream, it will cost you upward of $12. ♦ M, Tu, Th-Su, lunch and late dinner. Piazzale Michelangiolo 1 (at Viale Michelangiolo). 2342832. www.ristorantelaloggia.com

36 Gelateria Michelangiolo

★$ If it's hot or if you've hiked all the way up to the piazzale and need some refreshment, have one of the numerous homemade ice creams at this hangout for young Florentine roadsters, who also appreciate its pinball parlor. Things are calmer on the open terrace, whose afternoon views make a simple pasta lunch a lifelong memory. Tuesday is—they say—fresh fish day. This place also says it is an "American Bar"—which simply means it mixes drinks (quite well and not too expensively). Consider the view, and they are a giveaway. ♦ M, W-Su, 7AM-1AM. Viale Galileo Galilei 2r (between Via del Monte alle Croci and Piazzale Michelangiolo). 2342705

37 San Salvatore al Monte

Michelangelo called this simple late-15th-century Franciscan church, high on the hills overlooking Florence, "my pretty little country girl." No doubt he appreciated the three windows on the façade, which used alternating triangular and curved pediments (a Roman convention) for the first time in Florence, just as the columns in the simple interior used alternate orders for the first time locally. ♦ Piazza di San Salvatore al Monte (off Viale Galileo Galilei, between Via del Monte alle Croci and Piazzale Michelangiolo)

38 San Miniato al Monte

Florence's most beloved church (and a favorite wedding site) crowns the highest hill in the vicinity and is well worth a detour. It was built circa 1018-1207 on the spot where, according to legend, an early martyr, known in English as Minias, carried his head from the Roman amphitheater across the Arno and up the hill. The geometric green-and-white marble façade (the green is from Prato, the white from Carrara), which ranks with the **Baptistry** among the finest examples of Romanesque architecture in Florence, is embellished with a 13th-century mosaic of Christ and the Virgin and San Miniato above the central window. Inside is a 13th-century mosaic-like marble pavement with signs of the zodiac (considered one of the prettiest of its kind); **Michelozzo**'s 15th-century **Crucifix Chapel**; the 15th-century **Chapel of the Cardinal of Portugal**, with a monument to the cardinal, who died in Florence, by Antonio Rosellino; an *Annunciation* by Alesso Baldovinetti; angels by Antonio Pollaiuolo; a terra-cotta ceiling by Luca della Robbia; and a pulpit alive with Romanesque animals. In the crypt, along with the *Reliquary Altar of Saint Minias,* are ancient columns and frescoes by Taddeo Gaddi. Benedictine monks sing vespers in Gregorian chant followed by a Mass here each day at 4:30PM. The adjoining cemetery offers a remarkable selection of gravestones and tombs, including that of Tuscan-born Carlo Lorenzini, aka Carlo Collodi, author of *Pinocchio*. On the church grounds are **Andrea del Mozzi**'s 1295 **Palazzo Vescovile**, built for the bishop of Florence as a summer residence; a bell tower, built on a preexisting structure in 1523 by architect **Baccio d'Agnolo** and never finished; and fortifications put up by **Michelangelo** barely in time for the 1529 siege of Florence and finished by **Francesco da Sangallo** and others in 1553. ♦ Daily, 8AM-7PM May-Oct; 8AM-12:30PM and 2:30PM-7:30PM Nov-Apr. Via del Monte alle Croci 34 (between Via di San Miniato al Monte and Viale Galileo Galilei)

When the Black Death hit Florence in 1348, the population was swiftly cut in half. In order to increase the local workforce, slavery was legalized in 1363, and Tartars, Russians, Moors, and Ethiopians were purchased in the nearby ports of Venice and Genoa.

39 Ficaibi & Balloni

Trompe l'oeil painting is the specialty of Stefano Ficaibi and Maurizio Balloni, who decorate everything from large murals to tiny boxes in neoclassical style. ♦ M-F, Sa morning Mar-Oct; M afternoon, Tu-Sa Nov-Feb. Via Romana 49r (between Piazza della Calza and Via del Ronco). 2337697

40 Porta Romana

This and a few other gates to the city are remnants of the medieval walls that once surrounded Florence. They lasted from the end of the 12th century until 1865, when, in an effort to modernize the short-lived capital of Italy, they were largely demolished. The *viali* (boulevards) now follow their outline. (The longest sections of remaining walls extend on either side of **Porta Romana**.) The road here led to Rome, hence the gate's name. Its portal and fresco of the *Madonna with Child and Saints* date from the 14th century. The large white statue by Michelangelo Pistoletto on the grass outside the portal is a contemporary (and therefore much contested) addition to the roundabout. ♦ Piazzale di Porta Romana and Piazza della Calza

41 Gipsoteca dell'Istituto d'Arte

To get to this curious little museum, follow the gravel path from the gate next to a tripe stand popular with students from the art school in which the museum is housed. Walk through the run-down park filled with dogs and their walkers to the building at the end of the path, formerly the royal stables. The collection consists of plaster casts of famous sculptures (Michelangelo's *David* and *Prisoners*), quite dusty but supposedly used for didactic purposes by the art academy surrounding it. ♦ M-F, by appointment only. Piazzale di Porta Romana 9 (between Viale Niccolò Machiavelli and Piazza della Calza). 220521

42 San Leonardo

This little 11th-century church gave its name to the street where it stands, Via di San Leonardo.

The Best

Marcella Hazan

Chef/Cookbook Author

The historic open-air fish and produce market at the **Rialto**. Along with the markets in Cagliari and Palermo, it is one of Italy's most thrilling displays of food, replenished daily with produce from the farm islands of the Venetian lagoon and with a dazzling variety of fish pulled in each night from the seemingly inexhaustible Adriatic.

After 11PM, the *No. 1 vaporetto* going up the **Canal Grande** toward **San Marco**. At sunset, the *No. 52 vaporetto* from the **Fondamente Nuove** to the **Giudecca**.

The **Museo Storico Navale** (Naval Museum).

The church of **Santa Maria dei Miracoli**.

The astonishing marble interior of the church **dei Gesuiti**.

Chamber music concerts at the **Vivaldi Church** (**La Pietà**).

Pizza alfresco at **Bar Al Teatro**, while watching everyone in Venice who has not gone to bed walk by. Saturday lunch at **Da Fiore**, the best seafood restaurant in the Western world.

Chocolate ice cream at the bar by the **Albergo Cipriani** pool: the most beautiful people in Venice and the darkest, richest chocolate anywhere.

The embankment on the **Giudecca**: the best place in Venice to look at Venice. Sit on a bench and watch the sun setting or take a long, uncrowded walk.

11PM on the Saturday before the third Sunday in July, sitting in a boat anchored in the **San Marco** basin, watching the fireworks burst out of the blue-black Venetian night.

The road is every Florentine's favorite country passageway—it's lined with olive orchards and stone walls and yet is surprisingly close to town. The Romanesque church, restored in 1899 and 1921, contains a lovely pulpit of the same period moved here from the demolished church of **San Piero Scheraggio** in 1782. ♦ Via di San Leonardo 23 (between Viale Galileo Galilei and Via di Belvedere)

43 Villa Carlotta

$$$ An elegant place with all kinds of plusses for those who like to lodge away from the center, but not too far away. The hotel has lovely gardens, and even in the pouring rain (as there was when I visited) the smell takes you instantly miles away from the city, so you get natural aromatherapy with your room. There are 32 rooms—19 double, 6 triple, and 7 single. All have air conditioners, private bath or shower, hair dryer, minibar, and complimentary courtesy kits. There is 24-hour room service, Wi-Fi and Internet access, and facilities for the disabled. The Carlotta has a fine little American bar for the evenings and a charming breakfast room for the mornings. ♦ Via Michele di Lando 3 (between Via Dante da Castiglione and Viale Niccolò Machiavellì). 2336134; fax 2336147

44 Grand Hotel Villa Cora

$$$$ And old Cora certainly is grand. She is about 100 years old and sits in beautifully kept grounds. The Cora has a huge swimming pool to entice the occupants of its 44 rooms—15 suites, 20 twin, and 9 double. "Sumptuous" is the word that springs to mind when describing the rooms. All have air conditioning, and the beds have hypoallergenic mattresses and covers. There are minibars and separate fridges, fluffy bathrobes, 24-hour room service, and not only Internet access, but computers made available for the use of guests. You get a welcome gift along with a selection of fruit and a complimentary bottle of wine when you arrive (which you can do at any time of the day or night, thanks to the Cora's 24-hour reception and check-in and check-out facilities). The hotel has its own currency exchange and offers laundry and dry cleaning, babysitting, medical facilities, access for disabled guests, and a health center offering massage. Your pets will be made welcome and your children will have their own playground to romp in while you enjoy your excellent breakfast and complimentary newspaper. They really look after you here. The hotel's two restaurants—**The Taverna Machiavelli** and **The Veranda**—offer local cuisine, vegetarian food, and buffets daily for breakfast, lunch, and dinner. ♦ Viale Niccolò Machiavelli 18 (at Via Dante da Castiglione). 2298451; fax 229086

The Austrians ended Venice's sea-only access in 1846 by building a causeway with 222 arches that linked the city to Mestre on the mainland.

SANTA MARIA NOVELLA

Tourism is nothing new to this part of town. As a plaque in **Piazza Santa Maria Novella** states, the area was once called *la Mecca degli stranieri*—the mecca of foreigners. Indeed, as the marker reads, Henry Wadsworth Longfellow stayed in the neighborhood, as did numerous other foreign writers. Henry James wrote *Roderick Hudson* in a house on Via della Scala. John Ruskin took his inspiration for *Florentine Mornings* from Francesca Alexander, who stayed in a hotel on the piazza. And William Dean Howells, Ralph Waldo Emerson, and Percy Bysshe Shelley all sojourned here as well.

For nos. 33-100, see pg. 73

Today the most conspicuous contingent of nonnatives is made up of Third World immigrants who congregate in the piazza on weekends. At all times, however, foreigners pour out of the nearby train station (a masterpiece of Functionalist architecture), named after the church of **Santa Maria Novella**, to see the sights or attend conferences at the **Palazzo dei Congressi**, the **Palazzo degli Affari**, or the nearby **Fortezza da Basso**.

Almost as if deliberately designed to accommodate foreigners, many of the streets are broad avenues. It is no accident that **Via dei Tornabuoni**, Italy's most elegant shopping street, is filled with shops in the best Florentine mercantile tradition. It is the widest and most welcoming (if you can call the somewhat sinister lineup of palazzi welcoming) expanse in the historical part of the city. Almost as wide, if not quite as welcoming because of their barrackslike buildings funneling a barrage of Vespa mopeds and car traffic, are many of the other streets near Santa Maria Novella. But at least they are more easily negotiated than most parts of Florence, having been laid out straight and oddly intersecting, just as the lances intersect in Paolo Uccello's painting *The Battle of San Romano* in the Uffizi.

Another aspect of the area seems almost to have been predestined to attract a certain group of nonnatives. It is the legacy of its former residents, the Vespucci family, who as merchants and Medici civil servants had a great deal of contact with outsiders. A bridge over the Arno, a stretch of street along it, and chapels in the church of the Ognissanti were all named after them. And one of its members, Amerigo, gave his name not only to the New World but to the Americans, who continue to return to this part of Florence to their consulate and their church, and the city's finest deluxe hotels.

---

1 Fortezza da Basso

Alessandro de' Medici commissioned this imposing fortress, built by **Antonio da Sangallo** in 1534-1535. Some 450 years later, its extensive grounds now defend the **Padiglione Espositivo** (built in 1975 by **Pierluigi Spadolini**), a modern space hosting trade shows throughout the year, many of them (such as *Firenze a Tavola*, a culinary show) interesting and open to the public. ♦ Viale Filippo Strozzi 1 (between Viale Spartaco Lavagnini and Viale Fratelli Rosselli). 49721

2 Palazzo dei Congressi

This 19th-century neoclassical villa by **Giuseppe Poggi** was refashioned by **Pierluigi Spadolini** into a 20th-century meeting center. His splendid 1,000-seat underground auditorium is celebrated for its perfect acoustics. ♦ Piazza Adua 1 (at Via Bernardo Cennini)

3 Palazzo degli Affari

Another rare example of modern architecture in Florence, this palazzo—built in 1974 by **Pierluigi Spadolini**, brother of the late prime minister of Italy Giovanni Spadolini—has a prefabricated white cement exterior pierced with upside-down arched windows in dark glass. The modular structure of its interior can be adapted to just about everything from large receptions to small exhibition spaces. ♦ Piazza Adua 1 (at Via Bernardo Cennini)

4 Hotel Mario's

$$ This spotless and tasteful 16-room hotel conveniently located near the station is popular with Americans who are in town to see the sights or to attend the trade shows held in the nearby **Fortezza da Basso**. There is no restaurant. ♦ Via Faenza 89 (at Via Bernardo Cennini). 216801; fax 212039

4 Hotel Porta Faenza

$$ Convenient to trade shows in the **Fortezza da Basso**, this small hotel opened in June 1997. It has 25 rooms with en-suite bathrooms, a bar, and breakfast room, but no restaurant. It is housed in a charming, completely refurbished 18th-century building and is completely soundproofed. ♦ Via Faenza 77 (at Via Bernardo Cennini). 217975, 284119; fax 210101

Healing with Herbs: Florence's *Erboristerie*

The history of today's characterful *erboristerie* (herb shops) dates back to the darkest period of the Middle Ages, when medicinal herbs were already recognized for their curative powers. It was a time when hygienic conditions were particularly bad, a time of plagues and epidemics. A bewildered populace looked to the abbeys and monasteries for tinctures, potions, pomades, and lotions to cure malfunctions of the body often believed to be punishments from God. Each thriving monastic community had an obligatory herbal or botanical garden and a resident alchemist, and secular folk came to regard these earthly vicars of Christ as quasi-divine saviors in times of desperate illness or imminent death.

In the centuries that followed, the vast majority of these natural vegetable- and mineral-based remedies continued to be regarded as highly effective in treating simple maladies, from *mal di luna* (moon sickness)—a condition brought about by a full moon—to swollen gums and flat feet. Today's revival of holistic medicine and organic self-cures has reconfirmed the timeless appeal of these natural medicines. They are widely used for such mundane contemporary ailments as indigestion, insomnia, and dandruff.

Many present-day *erboristerie* still do business in a somewhat hallowed atmosphere, often keeping the centuries-old décor of wooden apothecary cabinets that contain antique pestles, scales, glass decanters of colorful essences, and large porcelain jars of dried herbs. Herbal liqueurs are also displayed. Once distilled and imbibed under the comforting pretense that these spirits had medicinal powers, they kept many a monk warm during damp and arduous winters. The liqueurs are still brewed today—in the same medieval cloisters of monastic communities—following ancient formulas. Honeys from a variety of blossoms abound, too, as do endless mixtures of teas that are said to cure love pangs, sluggishness, and the blues.

Florence has a number of these ancient shops still in existence. To experience the time warp, just step into the 300-year-old **Antica Farmacia del Cinghiale** near **Piazza della Signoria** for some of its special herbal teas, fragrances, and soaps. The small **Erboristeria Palazzo Vecchio** (also near **Piazza della Signoria**) is well stocked with medicinal herbs, shampoos, scents, and tanning creams. The **Officina Profumo-Farmaceutica di Santa Maria Novella** (next to **Santa Maria Novella**) is the oldest and most theatrical, but the least browser-friendly. Active since 1542, it still produces the Dominican monks' recipes for liqueurs, antifainting scents, and antihysteria water.

5 Hotel Albani

$$$$ In an early-20th-century building restored in the stripes and flowers of the *bella epoca* with Florentine furniture and exclusive fabrics and carpeting, this hotel has 90 rooms, all air conditioned; an American bar with complete international menu, and a restaurant-*enoteca* with one of the city's best wine cellars. ♦ Via del Fiume 12 (between Via Nazionale and Via Bernardo Cennini). 26030; fax 211045. www.hotelalbani.it

6 Fountain

This contemporary fountain represents the river Mugnone, which flowed into the Arno near here before it was diverted. Opposite it is a marble relief, *The Arno and Its Valley* by Italo Griselli, set before the linear **Sala d'Onore** (Reception Hall). The depiction is a rare and outstanding example of Roman-style Fascist-era art and architecture in Florence. ♦ Piazza Adua and Via Valfonda

7 Porta al Prato

Built in 1284, this is one of the ancient gates to the city left standing after the walls were knocked down to make way for the *viali* (broad avenues) now running in their stead. ♦ Piazzale di Porta al Prato and Via Il Prato

7 Baldini

★★★$$ This place makes you feel like you have been taken into the warm, motherly heart of Florence. Baldini is about 100 years old, and you just don't last this long if you are not doing something right. Even Garibaldi used to hang out here, and who would want to quarrel with Garibaldi? The rooms are comfortable, and you will feel marvelously at home. The house red is a good basic Chianti and comes to your table in a huge traditional *fiasco*, from which you help yourself and are charged accordingly. This place serves good, sound Tuscan home cooking. There is excellent prosciutto, or *bresaola* in a *salsa limoncello*. The generous choice of pasta dishes includes a delicious *paglia e fieno alla checca* (thin egg and spinach tagliatelle with barely cooked sweet cherry tomatoes and basil) and a tasty *tortelloni verdi alle noci* (pasta parcels in a walnut sauce). Main courses are a butcher's showcase. The Tuscans love their meat, and they don't stint when they serve it. Pork, lamb, and beef come cooked all ways—there are grills and roasts, stews, and an utterly unmissable *bollito misto*, which arrives with the assorted meats (beef, tongue, chicken, pork knuckle, and musetto sausage) in a bowl of the delicious broth in which they have been poached, along with chunks of carrot and unbelievably flavorful zucchini. It is a wonderful basic dish and works only when the meats are really good. It works here. The other thing this place is famous for is its *fritto misto*—feather-light batter-frosted fried vegetables and little meaty tidbits (including *cervelli*, or brains). The vegetable dishes are wonderful, especially the roasted potatoes! If you can leave room for dessert, they do a very good panna cotta with caramel and another with chocolate. The coffee is topnotch. And the walk back into town will do you good. ♦ M-F, Su, lunch and dinner. Via Il Prato 96r (at Piazzale di Porta al Prato). 287663

8 Il Gourmet

★★$$ This basically Tuscan restaurant lives up to its name, offering refined versions of such specialties as crostini (bread rounds spread with a rough chicken-liver pâté or a vegetable puree), ravioli or tortellini stuffed with spinach, and the ubiquitous *bistecca alla fiorentina,* here served as it should be with a side dish of Tuscan cannellini beans drizzled in olive oil. ♦ M-Sa, lunch and dinner. Via Il Prato 68r (between Via Palazzuolo and Piazzale di Porta al Prato). 294766

9 St. James

It is interesting to note that this is the only church in Florence set back from the sidewalk, behind a railing-topped wall, a stretch of lawn, and a gravel drive. One wonders what this says about the relative approaches of Catholicism and Anglicanism to their flocks. Whatever it says, this is a beautiful church. A baby in Florentine terms, the neo-Gothic St. James was commissioned by Pierpont Morgan and built, over three years starting in 1908, by **Riccardo Mazzanti, Marani and Carrère**. The beautiful stained-glass front window, representing Christ's entry into Jerusalem, was designed by Ezio Giovannozzi and added in 1911. English-speaking services are held here, as well as cultural talks, rummage sales, and a famous spring bazaar at which the burgers and hot dogs are as good as anything served at home. ♦ Via Bernardo Rucellai 9 (between Via Palazzuolo and Via della Scala). 294417

10 Otello

★★$$ This large dining spot, hovering somewhere between a rustic trattoria and a more refined restaurant, has a varied menu of all the classic Tuscan dishes. You can enjoy *trippa* (tripe), *cervelle* (brains), or *baccalà* (dried salt cod), or hit the hard protein with a *grigliata mista* (mixed grill—served for two). After that you might just be fit for their *fragile al limone* (strawberries in a light lemon sauce). ♦ Daily, lunch and dinner. Via degli Orti Oricellari 36r (at Via della Scala). 215819

11 Stazione Centrale di Santa Maria Novella

Florence's central train station—built in 1935 by the late **Giovanni Michelucci** and other members of the *gruppo toscano,* **Piero Berardi**, **Nello Baroni**, **Italo Gamberini**, **Baldassare Guarnieri**, and **Leonardo Lusanna**—was the first example of Functionalist architecture in Italy and has been granted the status of a national monument. It is so functional-looking, in fact, that when its plans were first made public one critic wrote, "The papers made a mistake, careful! They published the packing crate. The model is inside." Instead, inside and out the station is filled with intelligent references to the Florentine vernacular, from its *pietra forte* skin to its striped marble pavement and the landscape paintings by Ottone Rosai in the cafeteria. Other functional aspects of the station include its always-open pharmacy (just inside the entrance, to the left) and a mailbox outside the always-open postal dispatch center (behind *Binario* 1, or Track 1) where you can shave a few days off delivery of those important cards and letters.

The *pensilina* (a covered platform in front of the station), built by **Cristiano Toraldo di Francia** and **Andrea Noferi**, has also received its share of criticism. Its detractors say that, unlike the station, the *pensilina* is functionless, since it apparently serves mainly to block the view of the entrance to the station (the structure actually houses newspaper stands and booths selling bus tickets). When Michelucci died in 1990, a few pundits wanted to honor him by blowing up the *pensilina*. But the platform lingers on, an almost deliberately discordant Postmodern appropriation of such Florentine architectural traditions as marble stripes, impassably narrow sidewalks, and a Vasarian propensity to blot out previous architects' work. The final insult to Michelucci's Functionalism is the fact that the platform severely limits station access to a single opening—a convention of military architecture reinforced by a siren that goes off each time pedestrians are given the green light. In its favor, one can say that it sort of looks like—a train?—boat?—Renaissance spaceship? The architects also designed a less assertive small station, the **Terminal di Via Valfonda**, in 1991, adjacent to the main station. Via Valfonda, incidentally, is bridged by an overpass designed by **Gae Aulenti**, also in 1991. The multilevel parking area beneath the station has greatly alleviated much of the nightmare of the parking situation in the Centro Storico, now almost entirely closed to traffic. It makes a convenient, central, and safe spot to leave your car, with hourly and long-term rates available. ♦ Piazza della Stazione

12 Grand Hotel Villa Medici

$$$$ The hotel occupies a beautiful 18th-century villa that sits in a fairly extensive private garden with its own swimming pool. There are 89 rooms and 14 suites, including a new rooftop suite that comes with a Jacuzzi on its private terrace. All rooms have double telephones with personal voice messaging, telefax, satellite TV, minibar, safe, and Internet connection. The décor is impressive—plenty of antiques and fine, rich fabrics. There is a fitness center with gym, sauna, and steam room. The public rooms are fabulous—all gilt and frescoes and imperial colors. The **Jockey Bar** is modern, with pale cream wingback chairs and ash-blond parquet. In the summer, tipplers trip out into the gardens with their glasses. Apparently it is one of the places to tipple! There are two restaurants—the **Lorenzo di Medici** (more formal, with a Tuscan menu) and the newer **Conservatory** (more informal with, as you will guess from the name, a lovely garden view). ♦ Via Il Prato 42 (at Via Palazzuolo). 277171. www.villamedicihotel.com

13 La Carabaccia

★$$ This charming trattoria strikes a successful balance between traditional Tuscan food and creative presentation without ever approaching the padded prices of Florence's more expensive restaurants. Besides the titular dish, a type of sweet-and-sour onion soup, such items as *crespelle florentine* and *sformato di carciofi* (a light mousse prepared with artichokes) or *di pesce* (prepared with fish) make regular appearances, as do a number of vegetarian possibilities, fish dishes, and roasts. There are many dishes on the menu that you do not see very often, such as the roast duck that comes "on salad," or the baked salmon with potatoes. The caramelized pear is the dessert to go for, by the way. In summer, dining spills out onto the quiet little square where the restaurant sits. ♦ M, dinner; Tu-Sa, lunch and dinner. Via Palazzuolo 190r (between Via degli Orti Oricellari and Via Bernardo Rucellai). 214782

14 L'Bambino

★★$$$ Such typical Tuscan dishes as roasted meats are served at this small restaurant that's moved from its old Via del Parione location. A modern take on Renaissance murals covers the walls, and blackened iron candlesticks and heavy wooden tables fuse the historical with the contemporary. The place got its name from the sobriquet of the owner, otherwise known as Raul, and hardly a *bambino*—he was one of Florence's most beloved *Calcio in Costume* football players, a colorful personality in the annual June event when neighborhoods vent centuries-long grudges, and has worked as a bodyguard as well. ♦ M-Tu, Th-Su, lunch and dinner. Corso Italia 35 (at Piazza Vittorio Veneto). 2675612

15 Teatro Comunale

This 19th-century theater by **Telemaco Bonaiuti** was burned in 1863, firebombed in 1944, and flooded in 1966. But the show goes on, the big one being the annual *Maggio Musicale Fiorentino,* an international (and internationally renowned) music and dance festival under the baton of Zubin Mehta held between May and early July (for more information on this event, see "Maggio Musicale" on page 24). The program for the rest of the year is filled with symphonic performances, opera, and ballet. ♦ Corso Italia 12 (at Via Magenta). 211158, 213535; www.maggiofiorentino.com

16 Hotel Kraft

$$$ Slightly off the beaten track and close to the river, the Kraft is one of a tiny number of Florentine hotels to offer a swimming pool—which, even better, is located in its rooftop garden. There is also an American bar up there, so you can indulge in both healthy and unhealthy pursuits within a towel's throw of each other! The hotel has 80 rooms (20 of which are strictly nonsmoking), all of which are air-conditioned, with minibar, TV, pay TV, direct dial telephone, and hair dryer. There are fax and e-mail facilities, international newspapers are available in the lobby, and the hotel will book museum and gallery visits for you on request. ♦ Via Solferino 2 (between Via Palestro and Via Giuseppe Garibaldi). 284273; fax 2398267

17 Baldini

The *bottega* (workshop) of this master *bronzista* (bronze worker) is where upper-crust Florentines have their antique furniture refitted with metal accoutrements, but it also offers such items as doorknobs, handles, pulls, towel racks, sconces and other lighting fixtures, and additional elegant decorations. ♦ M-F. Via Palazzuolo 99-105r (between Via Maso Finiguerra and Via di Santa Lucia). 210933

18 Santa Maria Novella

In 1246, the town fathers erected the present church on the site of a 10th-century oratory for the dogmatic, inflammatory Dominican preaching order. The colored-marble façade was begun in the 14th century by **Fra Jacopo Talenti**. In 1470, **Leon Battista Alberti**, a true Renaissance man (in addition to being an architect and architectural theorist, he was a painter, scientist, musician, and playwright), finished the Romanesque-Gothic façade in Renaissance style, complete with a plug for his patron, Giovanni Rucellai, emblazoned in

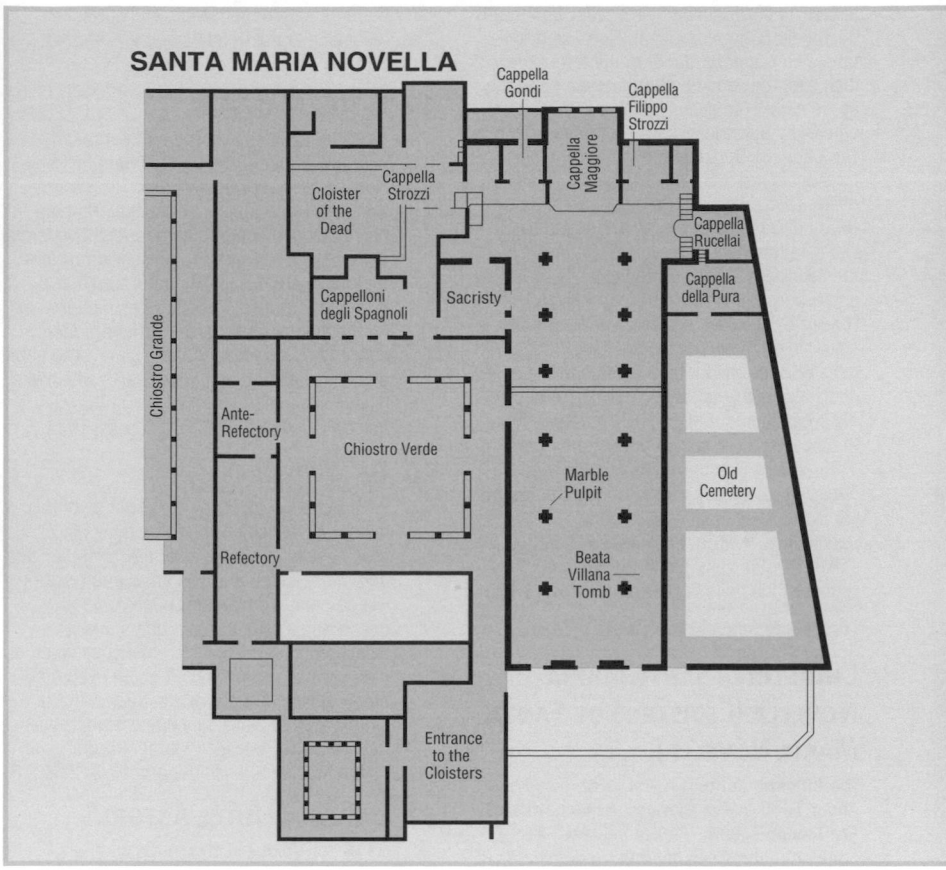

Latin along with the date of completion beneath the pediment. Alberti wrote the first Renaissance treatise on architecture (*De re aedificatoria*), and his design for the façade was the first Renaissance use of his theories of harmonic proportions. The system was remarkably well named; despite the theorizing, the façade remains pleasingly undogmatic, if a bit two-dimensional with what appears to be a false front, like so many Florentine church façades. Alberti was the first to use those scroll-like shapes known as volutes on either side of the upper portion of the façade. In this case they were meant to mask the nave aisles. Not inappropriately, given Alberti's scientific bent, astronomical instruments were added to the façade in 1572 by the Dominican Egnazio Danti, astronomer to Cosimo I de' Medici. The pointed *pietra forte* (strong stone) bell tower to the left of the façade (attributed to **Fra Jacopo Talenti**) is complemented in visual volume and often surpassed in acoustical volume by the starling-filled cypresses above the old cemetery niches to the right, which are called *avelli* and give their name to the short street along the side.

The vast Gothic interior (see floor plan above) was richly decorated in the early Renaissance and later refurbished by **Giorgio Vasari**, who characteristically whitewashed over a number of frescoes. In the second bay on the right aisle is the 15th-century tomb of Beata Villana by Bernardo Rossellino. At the end of the right transept is the **Cappella Rucellai** (Rucellai Chapel), which has a 14th-century statue of the Virgin by Nino Pisano and the 15th-century bronze tomb of Leonardo Dati by **Lorenzo Ghiberti**. To the right of the altar is the **Cappella Filippo Strozzi**, with a 15th-century tomb of Filippo Strozzi by Benedetto da Maiano and frescoes from the same period by Filippino Lippi. Boccaccio chose the chapel (before it was given its present embellishment) as the fictitious meeting place of the young storytellers at the beginning of *The Decameron*. The high altar has a bronze crucifix by Giambologna. Behind it, in the **Cappella Maggiore**, is the dazzling 15th-century fresco cycle by Domenico Ghirlandaio, allegedly depicting the lives of the Virgin and St. John the Baptist, but actually a delightful and historically important document of everyday life in Florence at the time. The **Cappella Gondi** to the left of the high altar, designed by **Giuliano da Sangallo** in the early 16th century, has a 15th-century crucifix by Brunelleschi, his only work in wood. The Cappella Strozzi at the left end of the transept is frescoed with 14th-century scenes of *The Last Judgment*, *Paradise*, and *Hell* by Nardo di Cione, and has an altarpiece by Orcagna from the same period. Behind it in the sacristy is a 13th-century crucifix by Giotto and a delicate, glazed terra-cotta *lavabo* (basin) by Giovanni della Robbia. Down the left aisle off the entrance, the next-to-last pilaster is adorned with a 15th-century pulpit designed by **Brunelleschi** and executed by his adopted son, Buggiano. Just behind it is the most popular work in the church, the 15th-century fresco *Holy Trinity with the Virgin, St. John the Evangelist, and Donors* by Masaccio, a seminal work of early perspective. ♦ M-Th, Sa, 9AM-5PM; F, Su, 1PM-5PM. Piazza Santa Maria Novella (between Via della Scala and Via degli Avelli)

Adjacent to Santa Maria Novella:

Chiostri di Santa Maria Novella (Cloisters of Santa Maria Novella)

The **Chiostro Verde** (Green Cloister) was built about 1350 by **Fra Giovanni Bracchetti** and **Fra Jacopo Talenti**. The chapel takes its name from the green tint that predominates in Paolo Uccello's masterpiece fresco cycle of the *Universal Deluge*, which he painted here almost a century later. This chef d'oeuvre is as concerned with movement and perspective as Uccello's *Battle of San Romano* in the **Uffizi**, but is more charged with emotion. The **Refectory** has a 16th-century *Last Supper* by Alessandro Allori. The **Chiostro Grande** (Great Cloister) is now part of the noncommissioned officers' school of the *carabinieri* (police) and is closed to the public. Still, the guards sometimes honor a visitor's request to see the cloister's **Cappella dei Papi** (Chapel of the Popes), frescoed in the 16th century by Jacopo Pontormo and Ridolfo del Ghirlandaio. The **Cappelloni degli Spagnoli** (Spanish Chapel), so-called because Eleanor of Toledo, wife of Cosimo I de' Medici, gave her fellow Spaniards burial privileges there, is completely covered with 14th-century frescoes by Andrea da Firenze glorifying the Dominican order founded by the Spaniard St. Dominic. Note the symbolic pooches (*domini cane,* Latin for "dogs of God," is a play on the name of the order) and the famous Dominican saints Dominic, Thomas Aquinas, and Peter Martyr (all of whom preached at **Santa Maria Novella**) refuting heretics. In two rooms that used to be the convent's foyer there are vestments, relics, and some art belonging to the Dominicans. ♦ Admission. Sa-Th, 9AM-2PM. 282187

19 Hotel Majestic

$$$$ An absolutely horrid modern façade in a primarily 19th-century piazza fronts this efficient, modern 103-room hotel. The inside won't rock your artistic boat either. Its piano bar-restaurant is a popular late-night watering hole, particularly with the business travelers that make up most of the hotel's regular clientele. It is also a popular destination for the kind of tourist groups that are more concerned with location than charm. The hotel does have an underground garage, which is useful. ♦ Via del Melarancio 1 (at Piazza dell'Unità Italiana). 264021; fax 268428

20 De' Medici

★$$ Don't be put off by the expanse of this restaurant, which seems to do things in a big way, beginning with its specialty, *bistecca alla fiorentina,* a slab that you know immediately will demand a doggie bag. One room is devoted to a wine bar and offers a large selection of inexpensive light lunches, such as pasta or pizza; the other offers an even bigger menu of Florentine favorites. Stick with the simple stuff. ♦ Daily, lunch and dinner. Via del Giglio 49r (between Via dei Panzani and Piazza Madonna degli Aldobrandini). 218878

21 Boscolo Hotel Astoria

$$$$ You don't exactly get the warmest welcome here, but the surroundings are quite glorious, from the vaulted ceilings of the reception hall to the heavy drapes, frescoes, and rich colors of the antique-style bedrooms and suites. There are 98 rooms, including 7 junior suites, some with balconies and wonderful views. All have direct-dial phones, air conditioners, and work desk areas. The hotel offers laundry and dry cleaning services, express check-in and -out, currency exchange, babysitting, and car rental. For the safety conscious, rooms are fitted with smoke detectors and sprinkler systems. The one place in the hotel where you do get a warm welcome is in the **Arrighetti Bar**, where a twinkly-eyed barman shakes a mean cocktail. The **Palazzo Gaddi** restaurant is formal in ambience and Tuscan in menu. ♦ Via del Giglio 9 (between Via dei Panzani and Piazza Madonna degli Aldobrandini). 2398095; fax 214632. www.boscolohotels.com

22 Sabatini

★★★$$$$ The formal Old World charm of this dean of Florentine restaurants makes it the kind of place where men feel that jackets and ties are in order whether required or not (they're not), where the service is polished and professional, and where Japanese tourists feel

The Best

Janice Verrocchia

Owner, Trattoria Antellesi

Taking in the morning hustle and bustle in the **Mercato Centrale** food market.

A cold one at the piano bar of the **Hotel Excelsior**. Make sure not to miss the incredible marble bathrooms.

Palazzo Davanzati, the Gothic-to-Renaissance palace that "puts the pieces together" for me on what life must have been like then, beyond the paintings.

Browsing the **Seeber** bookstore on Via dei Tornabuoni and taking my purchases next door to read while enjoying a truffle sandwich and glass of spumante at **Procacci**.

compelled to eat. The extensive international menu is ambitious and generally successful. Begin with the house specialty, *spaghetti alla Sabatini* (a variation of carbonara). Best choices are such Tuscan classics as *bistecca alla fiorentina* and such generic Italian dishes as osso buco and saltimbocca. After a meal here, you'll understand why this place has staying power. ♦ Tu-Su, lunch and dinner. Via dei Panzani 9A (between Via del Giglio and Piazza dell'Unità Italiana). 211559

23 Hotel Dèco

$$ New and charming, this hotel has only 17 rooms, all of which are doubles (albeit not very big doubles) except one. They are simply furnished, and all have bath or shower, air conditioning, cable TV, double glazing, and a safe. Like very many city center hotels, the Dèco is situated on the upper floors of the building—but it has thoughtfully installed a stairlift for those who need it. The staff are young, multilingual, and very helpful. A generous buffet breakfast is included, and they are proud to offer guests Nutella on their morning croissant. The hotel will also arrange parking facilities. ♦ Via dei Panzani 7. 284469; fax 2302947. www.hoteldeco@dada.it

24 Hotel delle Tele

$$ Given its central location and top-to-toe renovation, this hotel is surprisingly at the very low end of its price category. Double-paned windows ensure quiet, even for the eight rooms in the front (seven others face a side street or courtyard). Terra-cotta floors, air conditioning in each room, trompe l'oeil decoration, and a number of large reproductions of Renaissance works (the hotel's name, "Hotel of the Canvases," refers to these) are handsome touches uncommon at these rates. There is also now Internet access in every room. There is no restaurant, although the hotel's guests do get preferred rates at a local restaurant. And there is a bar and breakfast room in the hotel. ♦ Via dei Panzani 10 (between Via de' Cerretani and Via del Giglio). Phone/fax 2382419, 290797. www.welcomehotels.info

25 Bellettini

$ Set in a handsomely restored Renaissance building, this place is a well-kept secret in Florence, so hope for an available room and then don't tell a soul about it. It offers a central location (quiet nonetheless), air conditioning, tiled private bathrooms, and a frescoed breakfast room (there is no restaurant) where you can indulge in a delightful prodigious buffet. Some of the 27 rooms overlook the **Duomo**, others the church of **San Lorenzo**; most have color TV. There is now an annex with an extra five deluxe rooms. The hotel also now offers full Internet access to guests. The extended family/owners speak fluent English, and are always available and helpful. ♦ Via dei Conti 7 (between Via dell'Alloro and Piazza Madonna degli Aldobrandini). 213561; fax 283551

26 Hotel Principe

$$$$ This small, classic 20-room hotel is a favorite with visiting Americans, who appreciate its river views and garden. It is just far enough off the beaten track to be relatively quiet (and within walking—well, hiking—distance of the major sites) but still remains convenient. There is no restaurant. ♦ Lungarno Amerigo Vespucci 34 (between Via Melegnano and Via Curtatone). 284848; fax 283458

27 Il Profeta

★★$$ This small, discreet restaurant has an Italian menu of such dishes as *pennette Profeta* (macaroni in a creamy tomato sauce with wild mushrooms and ham) and scalloppini in a full-flavored balsamic vinegar sauce. Be sure to save room for the homemade tiramisù. ♦ M-Sa, lunch and dinner. Borgo Ognissanti 93r (between Via Maso Finiguerra and Via Curtatone). 212265

28 Il Contadino

★$ Good, inexpensive home cooking is the order of the day here, as witnessed by the fact that the two spotless, modern dining rooms are always packed with handsome young men who've just left home to do their military service.

Two prix-fixe menus limit the choice, but the selection, at these prices, pleases both palate and pocketbook. ♦ M-Sa, lunch and dinner. Via Palazzuolo 69-71r (between Via dei Porcellana and Via Maso Finiguerra). 2382673

29 Officina Profumo-Farmaceutica di Santa Maria Novella

This centuries-old *erboristeria* (herbalists' shop) was opened to the public in 1612 by Dominican monks from the church of **Santa Maria Novella**, who prepared medicinals for local hospitals and such clients as Catherine de' Medici. Today the tradition continues with all sorts of exotic products, including handmade soaps, skin creams, shampoos, liqueurs (the Medici's own is still sold as *liquore mediceo*), and pungent smelling salts called *aceto dei sette ladri* ("seven thieves' vinegar," from the plague days when corpse robbers, each knowing one of its secret ingredients, used it to protect themselves on their gruesome rounds). The monks are gone, but the knockout neo-Gothic salesroom is presided over with Dominican astringency by the white-coated high priests and priestesses of Florentine *erboristerie*. ♦ M-Sa, 9:30AM-7:30PM; Su, 10:30AM-8:30PM. Via della Scala 16 (between Piazza Santa Maria Novella and Via Santa Caterina da Siena). 216276

30 Aprile

$$ In a 15th-century palazzo once owned by the Medici, complete with faded traces of frescoes, high vaulted ceilings, and a small breakfast courtyard within sight of **Santa Maria Novella**'s campanile, this 30-room hotel has a graceful air of antiquity. Rooms have bathroom and minibar. There is an elevator, a bar, a garden, and garaging for your car. And breakfast is included in the price. Some guest rooms in the back have a limited view of the **Piazza Santa Maria Novella**, while those in the front have double-glazed windows to keep noise out. There is no restaurant. ♦ Via della Scala 6 (between Piazza Santa Maria Novella and Via Santa Caterina da Siena). 216237; fax 280947. www.hotelaprile.it

31 Grand Hotel Minerva

$$$$ The (in Florentine terms) rather bland façade conceals a pleasant hotel, completely renovated in 1995, preserving the design features of architect **Carlo Scarpa**, who created the hotel from an ancient building as a monument to modern architecture in 1958. Many of the 100 rooms (which include 6 suites, 10 junior suites, and 1 presidential suite) have views of **Piazza Santa Maria Novella** or the church cloisters. "Superior" rooms have Jacuzzis. Other amenities include the **Sala Garden** restaurant, serving an international menu and overlooking a quiet private garden, and a small rooftop swimming pool for those who want to cool off amid a sea of terra-cotta roofs and Florentine monuments. The hotel will also rent you a mobile phone for the duration of your stay. ♦ Piazza Santa Maria Novella 16 (between Via della Scala and Via degli Avelli). 27230; fax 268281. www.grandhotelminerva.com

32 Piazza Santa Maria Novella

Once used by the Dominicans of the church of **Santa Maria Novella** for preaching to the multitudes, this piazza was later adapted for public spectacles, including jousts and horse races run around the giant obelisks resting on Giambologna's bronze turtles. Today its pervading calm is enlivened at sunset, when the Hitchcockian starlings swoop down into the cypresses in the church cemetery and chatter endlessly into the night. It is the only piazza in town with grass, and it has a few benches where you can sit, have a picnic lunch, and take it all in. ♦ At Via dei Banchi and Via della Scala, and Via delle Belle Donne and Via degli Avelli

On Piazza Santa Maria Novella:

JK Place

$$$$ This is a smart, sexy place, one of the latest to join Florence's growing list of "designer hotels." The outside is fairly unassuming—well, as unassuming as a tall 18th-century building can be. The idea here is to minimize the "hotel" feeling and make you feel more like a valued house guest. There is a hostess as opposed to a receptionist, you help yourself from the bar, and the tables for breakfast in the glass-roofed dining room are generous communal affairs. There are just 20 rooms, which enhances the homey feel of the place. Having said which, lucky is the home that has bedrooms kitted out by designer Michele Bonan. He is the talent behind the look of the Ferragamo Lungharno hotels, and any man who can design for Ferragamo is obviously doing something right. The place is gorgeous, a beautiful mix of the old and the new—a little like Florence herself. There are Louis XVI fireplaces (this hotel is aglow in winter!), wingback chairs, and four-poster canopied beds . . . but there are also snazzy zebra-print framed mirrors, chic minimalist desks and chairs, and elegant neutral décor set off with big vases of roses or bowls of lemons everywhere. The rooms are delightful and decently sized. There are all the modern conveniences you could want, plus the added luxury of fine linen sheets and a staff-to-room ratio of one-on-one. Many of the rooms have fireplaces, and the Master Room—all cappuccino drapes and king-sized bed—has a balcony. The Penthouse Suite has views from every possible angle and a lovely roof terrace.

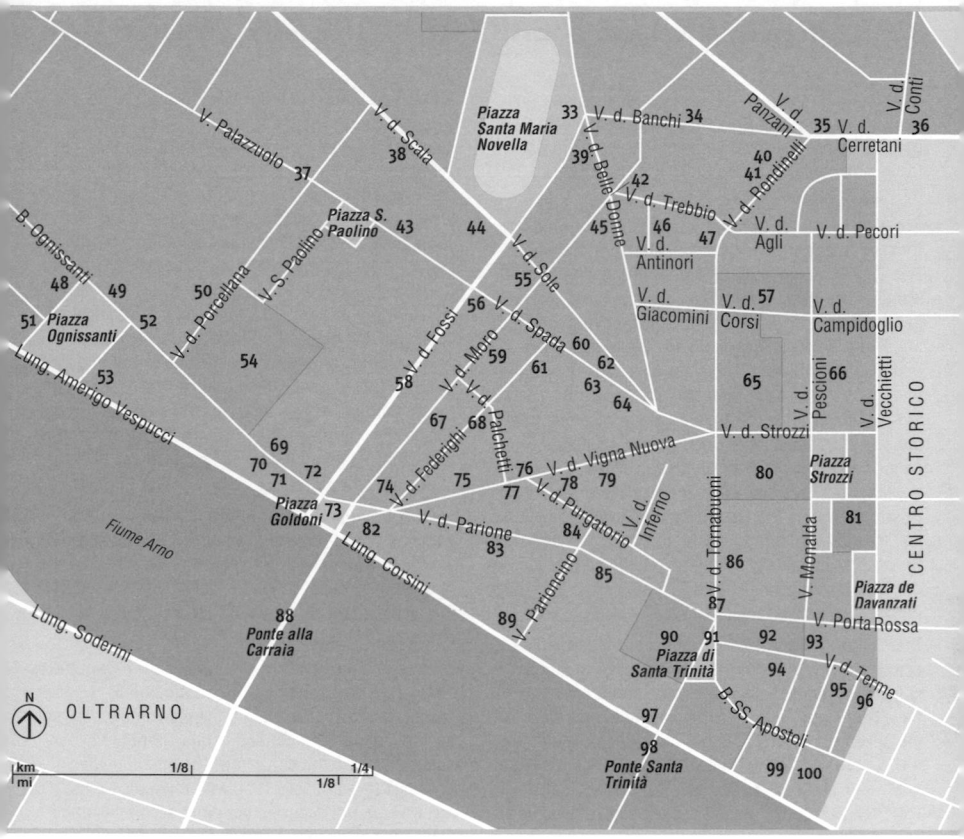

But just in case you can't book The Penthouse, there is another little roof terrace for the other guests. There is also an impressive library for guests to dip into should Florence and the DVD player in the bedroom be insufficient to amuse. The JK Place has been raved about in just about every style and travel magazine in print, and it is not hard to see why. Even the concierge (who can arrange anything from a visit to the Uffizi to a personal shopper) is gorgeous. ♦ Piazza Santa Maria Novella. 2645181. www.jkplace.com

33 Hotel Santa Maria Novella

$$$$ Why can't all hotels be like this one? It is stunningly beautiful and breathtakingly impressive as you enter the lobby. Created from a building that has been here since 1500, the hotel was born, after massive amounts of reconstruction, in 2004. This lovely place is the perfect example of the advantage of the independent hotel ethos over the chain mentality. The public rooms are decorated in rich colors and fabrics much in keeping with the antiquity of the building. The rooms are lovely too, with burnished parquet flooring, well-chosen antique pieces, and wildly romantically draped beds—some of them four posters. Rooms come standard and superior, and there are several Junior Suites and the fabulous sixth-floor Bellavista Suite with 70 square meters of private roof terrace. All rooms have marble bathrooms with polychromatic inlay inspired by the architecture of Leon Battista Alberti. Whoever inspired them, they are just the glamorous place to swank around in your complimentary bathrobe and slippers, smelling sweetly of something from the world-famous Officina Profumo Farmaceutica di Santa Maria Novella, which supplies all the hotel's toiletries. There are, of course, all the usual modern conveniences, and most rooms look out over the lovely Piazza Santa Maria Novella. The hotel has valet parking facilities and a first-class fitness center with sauna and Turkish bath. A buffet breakfast (included in room rate) and, later, light snacks are served in the hotel's restaurant. An elegant American bar and **The Napoleon Room** are where fine cognacs and equally fine cigars are the thing. And, should archeology interest you, the hotel has its own

Eat, Drink, and Be Merry at Florence's Wine Bars

As recently as World War II, wealthy families with vineyards in Tuscany sold their wine from a window in their palazzo. You can still see some of the tiny windows (now cemented over) from which wine was passed, in the façades of palazzos across the city.

But there is still the possibility of buying your wine from the man who made it. At the **Fiaschetteria Zanobini** (Via Sant'Antonino 47r), the utterly charming *padrone* will offer you wines from Le Lame, his family's vineyard in Chianti country. Stand at the tiny marble-topped bar and Signor Zanobini or his son will pour you a glass of their Chianti or Riserva. If I might offer some advice, ask them for a glass of the Coacerbato–a gorgeous, lively red–or Tra I Lusco e I Brusco, a unique rosé that has the seal of approval from Britain's Prince Charles himself. The only other *fiaschetteria* (the name given to a retail outlet for a vineyard–of which there used to be 86 in Florence) is the **Fiaschetteria Nuvoli**, which lurks just a cork's pop from the Duomo (Piazza dell'Olio 15r). Here there is a tiny restaurant as well and a selection of delicious bite-sized rolls filled with marvelous things like porcini scented with truffle.

There are many wonderful, atmospheric little *vinai* all across the city. **Vini dei Chianti** (Via dei Cimatori 38r) is quite literally a "hole in the wall," and it claims to have been here since 1875. You more or less stand on the pavement (there is room for four people under the tiny canopy) and order a glass of Chianti and maybe a hearty panino bursting with *porchetta* (roast pork). You'll feel like a local before you are wiping the crumbs from your coat!

All' Antico Vinaio (Via de' Neri 65r) is a wonderful place to put on your "eat, drink, and enjoy life" itinerary. It's another tiny place–there are just four high stools along a shallow shelf, plus some room for standing and sipping. The walls are lined with bottles of locally produced red, and the marble-topped bar supports a vast, delicious-looking pork roast with perfect crackling and a whole young velvety Gorgonzola, both of which can be on top of crostini and in your hand in the time it takes to refill your glass. You'll like this place! In Oltrarno, you will always be assured of a warm welcome at **Bene Vobis** (Via de' Serragli 78r), a lovely, brick-walled wine bar that does terrific food as well as delicious bar snacks. And the selection of good-quality wines on offer is perfectly matched by the helpful advice you can get from the charming lady owner.

In Colli, **le Volpi e l'Uva** (Piazza de' Rossi 1r) has garnered a well-deserved reputation among fine-wine lovers. There is always an interesting selection by the glass from their collection of over 100 labels, excellent bar nibbles, and top-notch advice from the wine-obsessed owners.

Of course, if you want to go upmarket, the **Cantinetta Antinori** (Palazzo Antinori, Piazza Antinori 3) is your sort of wine bar. Sit at the bar on the high stools and order something from the Antinori catalog from the hyper-smart man with the corkscrew. The little bar snacks are delicious (the tiny rolls filled with truffled pâté are a legend here in Florence), but don't even think about staggering in wearing trainers and jeans.

"archeological corner," where Roman artifacts uncovered during the restoration of the building are on display. They include an ancient stone bathtub and sections of the Matildine Walls. How many hotels have their own museum? ♦ Piazza Santa Maria Novella 1. 271840. www.hotelsantamarianovella.it

34 Hotel Paris

$$ The brochure says "a real Florentine jewel," and it is right. This is a really lovely, atmospheric hotel. Housed in what was originally called "Venturi Mansion," a 16th-century palazzo by the architect **Bernardo Buontalenti**, its 59 rooms (including the gorgeous Presidential Suite) were completely renovated in 2000. All rooms have bath, minibar, satellite TV, hair dryer, and air conditioning. These kinds of surroundings at this kind of price are a gift from Florence to you. ♦ Via dei Banchi 2. 280281; fax 268505. www.parishotel.it

35 Hotel Sofitel

$$$$ Situated in a renovated 17th-century palazzo, the Sofitel could not be much more central without taking over the Duomo itself. There are 84 rooms and a junior suite with a wonderful marble bath. All are soundproofed and have everything you would expect–adjustable air conditioning, satellite TV, "guestlink" radio, two telephones, Internet access, minibar, safe, bathrobe, hair dryer, and 24-hour room service. There is even a cell-phone recharge plug! Guests can also enjoy a vast buffet breakfast in the lovely patio restaurant, where they can sample many regional specialties as well as the more familiar day-starters. ♦ Via de' Cerretani 10 (at Via dei Panzani). 2381301, 800/221.4542, 800/SOFITEL; fax 2381312. www.sofitel.com

36 Libreria Feltrinelli

This is Florence's first mega-bookstore. They'll take special orders for those hard-to-find books and ship anywhere in the world. Foreign visitors will appreciate the architecture, art, and history departments; fully stocked travel section with guidebooks for all destinations; and wide selection of English-language fiction and nonfiction. The store stays open at midday except on Sunday, making this a great place to spend an air-conditioned lunch hour when the shops shut down. ♦ Daily. Via de' Cerretani 30-32r (between Via F. Zannetti and Via dei Conti). 2382652

37 Ostaria dei Centopoveri

★★★$$ For an Italian cuisine that isn't Tuscan, try this small restaurant (just 40 seats) dedicated to the seafood dishes of Apulia, run by authentic Pugliesi Donato Cofano and Donato Mizzi, in a romantic atmosphere of soft lighting, wood fires, arched ceilings, and red brick. Try the *impepata di cozze* (mussels with pepper) or a salad of jumbo shrimp with avocado and valerian leaves to start, then move on to fish of the day in a marinara with black olives and lemon. ♦ W-Su, lunch and dinner; Tu, dinner. Via Palazzuolo 31r (at Via della Porcellana). 218846

38 Hotel Croce di Malta

$$$ Housed in a former convent, this pleasant 98-room hotel conserves a feeling of privacy and simplicity in its understated and serene décor, with a touch of modernity in the small plunge swimming pool located in a shady, tranquil garden. **Il Cocodrillo** restaurant (M-Sa, 7AM-midnight) has a simple Tuscan and international menu, and offers a "light lunch" option at a decent price, and the poinsettia-fringed **PianoBar** is always entertaining and open every night till late. ♦ Via della Scala 7 (between Piazza Santa Maria Novella and Via dei Porcellana). 2183551, 282600; fax 287121; www.crocedimalta.it

39 Palazzo Pitti

Luca Pitti lived in this relatively humble palazzo before his family went bankrupt building their more famous digs across the river. A plaque on the façade recalls Giuseppe Garibaldi's sojourn when it was a hotel in 1867. Here the unifier of Italy stirred the crowds with the words "Rome or die." While not in keeping with the piazza's tradition as a mecca for foreigners, the speech was in line with the great Dominican preachers who once filled the piazza. ♦ Piazza Santa Maria Novella 21 (between Via del Sole and Via delle Belle Donne)

40 Bojola

Walking sticks, umbrellas, bags, briefcases, luggage, and accessories are manufactured with an eye to modern style by this more-than-a-century-old Florentine institution, long known for its leather craftsmanship. ♦ M-F, Sa morning (no midday closing) June-Sept; M afternoon, Tu-Sa (no midday closing) Oct-May. Via de' Rondinelli 25r (at Via dei Banchi). 211155

41 Richard Ginori

The Ginori line of porcelain began in the 18th century, merging in 1896 with the Milanese ceramic firm Richard to create the present partnership—the most famous porcelain manufacturer in Florence, indeed in Italy. Over the years it has become a veritable household name in the US. Most of the current production is based on historical patterns; other internationally known names such as Waterford and Lalique are for sale as well. ♦ M-F, Sa morning Mar-Oct; M afternoon, Tu-Sa Nov-Feb. Via de' Rondinelli 17 (between Piazza Antinori and Via dei Banchi). 210041

42 Croce al Trebbio

In 1308, this cross was erected at the intersection of three narrow streets (now five) where Dominicans, inflamed by the preaching of St. Peter Martyr at nearby **Santa Maria Novella**, battled members of the heretical Paterini sect. ♦ Via del Moro and Via delle Belle Donne

43 Amon

★★$ One of the happier (and less expensive) options for ethnic dining in town, this tiny stand-up sandwich shop serves Egyptian specialties on pita bread, freshly baked twice a day (whole wheat only). One room has a counter where you can order a *shauerma* (like a Greek gyro but served, if you want, with a spicier sauce) or a falafel (owner El Karsh's version is made with a purée of white broad beans). Thursday night is, according to the note on the wall, couscous night. You can then dig into your Egyptian find in the adjoining room, decorated with tongue-in-cheek tomb paintings. ♦ No credit cards accepted. Tu-Su, lunch and dinner. Via Palazzuolo 28r (between Via de' Fossi and Via della Porcellana). 293146

44 Loggia di San Paolo

Fronting the **Hospital of San Paolo**, this late-15th-century loggia was built in the style of **Brunelleschi**'s loggia for the **Hospital of the Innocenti** in **Piazza della Santissima Annunziata**. Its medallions, by Luca and Andrea della Robbia, depict saints and include a lunette by Andrea illustrating *The Meeting of St. Francis and St. Dominic,* which supposedly took place in the hospital. **Il Quadrifoglio**, a floral shop in a former chapel of the loggia (No. 9B, 283010), sells little sachets of long-lasting Florentine lavender, which make lovely gifts or souvenirs. ♦ Piazza Santa Maria Novella (between Via de' Fossi and Via della Scala)

45 Franco Maria Ricci

This small publishing house is the very definition of esoteric, with book titles such as *Lost Florence*, *Erté*, and *Casanova*, as well as limited and original editions and small *objets* that make nice souvenirs for bibliophiles. ♦ M-Sa. Via V. d. Belle Donne 41r (at Via del Moro). 283312

46 Loretta Caponi

Prepare to abandon that old set of stretch cotton sweats you normally sleep in, throw away all your plain old underwear (and I am talking to you guys, too!)—Loretta is here to show you the way to feel fabulous even if no one can see you except your teddy bear, Jay Leno, and anyone with X-ray vision. This shop would have Homer Simpson thinking about wearing satin and lace. There is lingerie in beautiful fabrics and glorious colors, gorgeously frivolous slippers, and bathrobes that could render you housebound just so you don't need to change out of them. In the adjoining shop (I say shop, but just look around at the vaulted, frescoed ceilings and the polished oak floors and you'll know this is a restored palazzo) you will find absolutely the best that Italy can offer a baby. Not just adorable clothes and nightwear for babies and little ones, but cot covers, cushions, sweet mini-bathrobes, a delightful range of hats and even bedclothes and drapes for your little princess's four-poster. This is the kind of place that could change the quality of your life. ♦ M-F, Sa AM Mar-Oct; M AM, Tu-Sa Nov-Feb. Via degli Antinori 5r and Via V. d. Belle Donne 28r (the store is on a corner and there are entrances on both streets). 213668

47 Palazzo Antinori

This rustic 15th-century palazzo by **Giuliano da Malano** anchors the northern end of the boutique-lined Via dei Tornabuoni. For centuries it has been part of the property of the Marchesi Antinori, known internationally for their wines. A small art gallery is operated on the premises. In the quiet courtyard of the palazzo you will find little scale models of the Antinori family's many vineyards from all over Europe, not just Italy. ♦ Gallery: daily. Piazza Antinori 3 (at Via degli Antinori). 223907

Within the Palazzo Antinori:

Cantinetta Antinori

★★$$$ A beautiful old and genuinely classy little place to eat lunch or dinner, or just prop yourself up on one of the high stools at the bar and snack. The Cantinetta has many of Antinori's masterful wines by the bottle or glass, and much of the food served features fruit and vegetables grown—and even game hunted—on the same hillsides that furnish the grapes for the wines. The menu is fine old Tuscan. The little rolls of glazed veal and artichoke cooked in white wine are delicious, and some of the dishes here are virtually a Florentine institution. ♦ M-F, lunch and dinner. 292234

47 Buca Lapi

★$$ This restaurant is located downstairs on the north side of the **Palazzo Antinori**. *Buca* is a typically self-deprecating restaurant name meaning "hole." This one, founded in 1880 and papered with faded travel posters, prides itself on its *bistecca alla fiorentina* and its various preparations of artichokes. Typical of Tuscan cuisine, rabbit and boar feature on the menu, as does a decent osso buco. ♦ M-Sa, dinner. Via del Trebbio 1r (between Piazza Antinori and Via del Moro). 213768

48 Palazzo Lenzi

Built in 1470, this Renaissance palazzo is covered with intricate two-tone stucco designs (called *sgraffiti*) by Andrea Feltrini. It is the home of the **Istituto Francese**, the Florence branch of the **University of Grenoble**, which sponsors a variety of cultural activities, including art exhibitions and film series. ♦ Piazza Ognissanti 2 (at Borgo Ognissanti)

Within the Palazzo Lenzi:

Giotti Bottega Veneta

This prestigious leather chain is known for its distinctive woven treatment of butter-soft hides. ♦ M-Sa Mar-Oct; Tu-Sa Nov-Feb. 294265

49 Ognissanti

This church (dating from 1256 and rebuilt in 1627 by **Bartolomeo Pettirossi**) has one of the earliest Baroque façades in Florence (built in 1637 by **Matteo Nigetti**). Inside, above the second altar on the right, is Domenico Ghirlandaio's fresco *The Madonna of Mercy Protecting the Vespucci Family*. The Vespucci were parishioners, and the boy to the right of the Madonna is probably the young Amerigo Vespucci, whose later voyages (and boastful, perhaps apocryphal, writings about them) gave the New World the name America. In the sacristy is a fresco of the *Crucifixion* by Taddeo Gaddi and a crucifix by Giotto. In the left transept is a monk's robe believed to be the one St. Francis was wearing when he received the stigmata. ♦ Piazza Ognissanti 38 (at Borgo Ognissanti)

49 Refettorio della Chiesa di Ognissanti (Refectory of the Church of Ognissanti)

The refectory houses three important paintings. *The Last Supper*, a fresco by Domenico Ghirlandaio, was painted for the space, as can be seen by the clever use of the room's real window as a light source. The other two paintings, *St. Jerome* by Ghirlandaio and *St. Augustine* by Botticelli, originally hung in the church of **Ognissanti**. ♦ M, Tu, Sa, 9AM-noon. Piazza Ognissanti 42 (at Borgo Ognissanti). 2396802

50 Sostanza

★★★$$ Known to Florentines as *"Il Troia"* (the pigsty, or more colorfully, a loose woman), this restaurant–one of the city's no-nonsense eateries–is hardly bigger than a pigsty, so expect a pretty tight squeeze. Fashion buyers sit at communal tables alongside the workers who still make up a small fraction of the clientele at this former butcher's shop. Better than the people-watching, however, is the food itself, which still includes the best *bistecca* in town. Noncarnivores might want to try the excellent *omelette di carciofi* (artichoke omelette). ♦ M-Sa, lunch and dinner. Reservations required. No credit cards accepted. Via dei Porcellana 25r (between Borgo Ognissanti and Via Palazzuolo). 212691

51 Grand Hotel

$$$$ And very grand it is too, having been originally designed for the Giuntini family by no less a person than **Brunelleschi**. Yup, the guy who designed the great dome of the Duomo. Now, just over 400 years later, and after lavish restoration and refurbishment, it offers 107 bedrooms and 13 suites furnished in 15th- and 16th-century grandeur, with upholstery and drapes handmade in traditional Florentine style. Most bedrooms have impressive frescoes of Florentine life. All the rooms have top-of-the-line TVs and DVD/CD players and all the modern conveniences you could wish for. Some bathrooms have separate bath and shower areas; all are done in pink Portuguese and polychromatic marble, and have double washbasins. The Grand has 24-hour room service, car rental, and babysitting, a 24-hour state-of-the-art fitness center, high-speed Internet connection in every room, and accessible rooms for disabled patrons, and you can book yourself a butler, a tour guide, or a personal shopper at the front desk. The public rooms are quite fabulous–the Grand Ballroom has seen royal marriages and receptions given by the very cream of Florentine aristocracy over the centuries. The Winter Garden is stunning. The stained-glass room and the antique furnishings make you feel like royalty yourself! Best of all, as a guest, you can breakfast on the balcony here in refined splendor. The hotel's restaurant and bar–**The Incanto**–seems quite soulless compared to the rest of the place. But to those who like modern chic, it probably looks wonderful. It's certainly elegant, in a very Italianate way. The restaurant serves a sort of Mediterranean-flavor-with-Tuscan-influences menu from chef Fabrizio Innocenti's open kitchen. If you opt to dine there, it is interesting to take up the sommelier's wine suggestions with each course. The bar is surprisingly hip for an old place like this! It does great cocktails and also offers a quick lunch. Afternoon tea is very civilized here, especially in good weather, when you can move out to the terrace. You might ask to see the much-respected wine cellar in the basement, in what is a natural cave in the rock beneath the hotel. ♦ Piazza Ognissanti 1 (at Lungarno Amerigo Vespucci). 288781, 800/325.3589 in US; fax 217400. www.luxurycollection.com

52 Palazzo Liberty

Nothing patriotic and no English snobbery was intended by the name of this building, designed in the early 20th century by **Giovanni Michelazzi**. It is one of the few examples of florid Art Nouveau (called *liberty* in Italian, as in Liberty of London, the store that helped introduce the style in Italy) in Florence. ♦ Borgo Ognissanti 26 (at Piazza Ognissanti)

52 Kartell

This shop features very smart, very 21st-century furnishings and lamps designed by Ferrucio Laviani. There are chairs and occasional tables, folding beds, and clever accessories. Most of the pieces are in clear or tinted acrylic and are very "Philippe Starck." Tricky to get in the hand luggage, but they won't give you a weight problem. ♦ Tu-Sa. Borgo Ognissanti 50

53 Westin Excelsior

$$$$ A little lacking in the "wow" factor of the Grand Hotel across the piazza, but still oozing quality, the Excelsior has 168 rooms furnished in true old-style luxury. It is part of the Starwood Luxury Collection, so you know what you will get (which some people regard as a plus). The most recent renovation was to the tune of $25 million, so you can expect the best. The 16 suites are even more luxurious than the guest rooms (although they come with a surcharge if you want a view of the Arno). There is a lovely air of calm in the public areas, and the stained-glass ceiling in the lounge is worth gasping at, even if you are not staying here. The **Donatello Bar** is pleasantly laid back for a place like this, and there is even a choice of herbal teas on tap at reception! The restaurant here is **Il Cestello**, now on the ground floor and offering an international menu that changes regularly. The

Don't Leave Florence Without . . .

1. Shopping in the **Mercato Centrale**. Shop with your eyes and your nose and your senses of touch and taste, like Italians do. Decide never to go to a supermarket for anything except toilet tissue and ketchup.

2. Visiting the **Fiaschetteria Zanobini** near the Mercato Centrale and enjoying a glass of excellent local wine from the man whose family makes it. The charming Signor Zanobini will recommend something to suit you for about $1 a delicious glass, and there will always be someone from among his clientele to enthuse with.

3. Discovering the genius of the current generation of Florentine silversmiths and goldsmiths. In a gloomily atmospheric cavern across the Arno, **Alessandro Dari** creates the works of art that future generations might have to line up outside a museum to see. And this art is wearable—rings are his specialty. This is possibly the most beautiful exhibition in the whole of Florence. P.S., you can buy as well as look!

4. Having an ice cream from the outrageously delicious selection at the newly opened **Grom,** in Via delle Oche. If Michelin awarded stars to ice-cream parlors, this place would have a constellation. And should you be at the other side of town, the ricotta and fig ice cream at the **Gelateria dei Neri** will also have your taste buds dancing a tango of delight.

5. Joining the in crowd at **Teatro di Cibreo**. Not only is this club/restaurant/theater/heaven one of the best places to spend a morning/afternoon/evening/-whole day in Florence, but when you fill out the form and join the club you will forever be in touch with Florence, because the wonderful people here will e-mail you about everything that is happening there each week.

6. Eating a little platter of tripe at one of the carts that you will find all over the city. I know I keep twittering on about this. But look on it as a cultural experience.

7. Starving yourself for a day and then ordering *bistecca alla fiorentina* somewhere that really does it well—like **I Latini, Alla Pentola d'Oro**, or **Baldini**. Walk back to your hotel slowly.

8. Wandering around the **Boboli Gardens**—they are just extraordinary, with some little surprise around every corner.

9. Getting on the tour of the **Vasari Corridor**—even if you are not particularly interested in the paintings (to be honest, I am not), just to walk along here, in the steps of the Medici, in this corridor that was closed to anyone but the very highest in the land for so long raises goose pimples in a way that very few actual artworks do.

10. Walking and walking and walking and walking. Clutching your *Access* guide, of course.

emphasis at the moment is very much on health, and their "Wellness Menu" features vegetable, fish, salad, and steamed dishes. Unless there is a good medical reason, I'd eat out, if I were you. ♦ Piazza Ognissanti 3 (at Lungarno Amerigo Vespucci). 27151. www.westin.com, www.starwoodhotels.com

Within the Excelsior:

Il Cestello

★★★$$$ Though the rooftop view is a thing of the past—the restaurant, refurbished as part of the hotel's recent renovation, is now located on the ground floor—the tastefully elegant décor has made a successful transition. The international menu changes with the seasons. ♦ Daily, lunch and dinner. 264201

54 Ospedale di San Giovanni di Dio

Designed and built by **Carlo Andrea Marcellini** in the early 1700s, this hospital, connected with the nearby church of **Ognissanti**, was funded by the Vespucci family. It incorporated the family houses, in one of which Amerigo (the Florentine cartographer after whom America was named) was born in 1454. It contains a fresco by Vincenzo Meucci in the vault. Attached to it is **Marcellini**'s remodeled church, **Santa Maria dell'Umilità**. ♦ Borgo Ognissanti 20 (at Via dei Porcellana)

55 Cellerini

Silvano Cellerini, one of Florence's master leather crafters, prides himself on his original creations. Here you'll find exquisitely handmade handbags, wallets, and suitcases, as well as a limited selection of men's and women's shoes and a collection of Hermès look-alikes. ♦ M afternoon, Tu-Sa. Via del Sole 37r (at Via del Moro). 282533

56 Buca Mario

★★$$ This downstairs restaurant has drawn a steady crowd (largely tourists) since 1890 for reliable versions of Tuscan soups and the place's specialty—*bistecca alla fiorentina* (a slab of steak grilled, then drizzled with olive oil). ♦ M, Tu, F-Su, lunch and dinner; W, Th, dinner. Piazza degli Ottaviani 16r (at Via de' Fossi). 214179

57 San Gaetano

Though originally erected in the 11th century, this church has the truest-to-form of Florence's few Baroque church façades—the 17th-century work of **Matteo Nigetti**, **Gherardo Silvani**, and **Pier Francesco Silvani**—complete with billowy statues and imposing coats of arms (Medici, of course). Among the works of art within are *The Martyrdom of San Lorenzo* by Pietro da Cortona and *Crucifix with Saints Mary Magdalene, Francis, and Jerome* by Filippo Lippi. ♦ Piazza Antinori and Via dei Tornabuoni

58 Via dei Fossi

If antiques are your thing, then get away from the shopaholics on the Via dei Tornabuoni and come here. Almost every shop holds antiques or handwoven carpets, marbles, and artworks.

On Via dei Fossi:

Antonio Frilli

Among the most fun of the shops is this one, here since 1860. From tiny reproductions of the big brass boar you can touch for good luck in the Mercato Nuove to full-size copies of Michelangelo's *David* (now wouldn't *that* give you problems with excess baggage!), the gallery is full of marble and bronze works, mainly reproductions of famous sculptures, all cast or sculpted by hand. ♦ M-Sa, 9AM-12:30PM and 3PM-7:30PM. Via dei Fossi 26

Hotel Unicorno

$$ This imaginative little hotel is a fantastic example of how the old buildings of Florence, with their nooks and crannies and balconies and pillars, can be brought into the 21st century without being standardized. It is housed in a 15th-century building that has been renovated in the most sympathetic way, resulting in rooms that are each unique and full of character yet offer all the modern conveniences you could want. Hotels like this are, indeed, almost as rare as unicorns. ♦ Via dei Fossi 27. 287313. www.hotelunicorno.it

59 L'Osteria di Giovanni

★★$$$ An airy, open place with roomy tables and big old-fashioned cupboards that give it almost the feeling of an old family kitchen. Talking of family, this restaurant is the newest pride and joy of the Latinis—Giovanni, Carole, Chiara, and Caterina—yes, the family whose name is above the door of **I Latini**, virtually a Florentine institution. So you can expect the best in terms of atmosphere, service, generosity of portion, and quality of food. The welcome is certainly as genuinely warm, even on a cold winter's Sunday. Here there is a shorter, more refined menu than there is around the corner. Starters include salmon cured with salt and pink peppercorns served with melon and sour cream, spaghetti *alle Lampade* (with cherry tomatoes), and tortelli filled with Burrata (an ultra-creamy fresh cheese) and asparagus. Steaks come various ways—including with an anchovy-and-caper sauce on a bed of radicchio—and there is an utterly fabulous milk-fed veal chop with roasted cherry tomatoes. There is always a fish of the day (and if you really feel like pushing the boat out, you should order the outrageously opulent *Piatto del Buon Ricordo*—5 lobster tail-stuffed tortelli served with half a lobster), and you will bitterly regret it if you don't leave room for the homemade desserts, which are fabulous. Don't worry about missing the Latini way with tradition—*ribollita* and *bistecca alla fiorentina* are on the menu too. There is champagne and superb wines by the glass, and a regular red and white of the month. This place is a real addition to your options for eating well in *molto simpatico* surroundings during your stay in Florence. ♦ W-M, noon-1AM. Via del Moro 22. 284897. www.osteriadigiovanni.it

60 Rafanelli

The Bronze Age is going strong at the showroom of master *bronzisti* (bronze workers) Enzo and Renato Rafanelli, whose workshop is in the artisans' quarter across the river. Bedsteads, fireguards, doorknobs, knockers, and other handcrafted bronze and copper objects are the dazzling inventory of this unusual shop. ♦ M afternoon, Tu-Sa Sept-June; M-F, Sa morning July-Aug. Via del Sole 7r (at Via della Spada). 283518

61 Museo Marino Marini

A permanent one-man show is housed within the deconsecrated 14th-century church of **San Pancrazio**. The man is Marino Marini (1901-1980), who, though he was born and died in Tuscany (in Pistoia and Viareggio, respectively), became an international figure in 20th-century art. The show features 179 works, many examples of his most famous subject, the horse and rider, which he treated with almost Cycladic simplicity and abstraction in bronze and wood sculptures. ♦ Admission. M, W-Su. Hours are erratic; call to confirm. Piazza San Pancrazio and Via della Spada. 219432

62 Assolibri

Here in this light and lively contemporary bookstore is a nice selection of art, photography, graphics, design, and fashion books from Italian and European publishers (with a number of books in English), as well as posters and postcards. Regular exhibits of an art-and-graphics bent make this spot even more browser friendly. ♦ M-F, Sa morning Mar-Oct; M afternoon, Tu-Sa Nov-Feb. Via del Sole 3r (between Via della Spada and Via del Moro). 284533

63 Cappella Rucellai (Rucellai Chapel)

Within this chapel, once part of the church of **San Pancrazio**, is **Leon Battista Alberti**'s 1467 funerary monument to Giovanni Rucellai. Called *The Aedicule of the Church of the Holy Sepulchre,* it is a scaled-down version of the eponymous church in Jerusalem. ♦ Via della Spada (between Via dei Tornabuoni and Via dei Federighi)

64 Marione

★★$ Basic, low-key but friendly, and run by *il padrone* behind the counter and a young and enthusiastic staff, this restaurant offers a taste of completely genuine Tuscan home cooking at almost unbelievably low prices. Excellent lamb comes with roast potatoes, beef with salad, and pork with beans. Spaghetti comes with butter, *ragu* (meat sauce), or tomato. Try the *ribollita,* Tuscany's most famous regional dish (after their beef)—a thick soup made with vegetables (especially cabbage), beans, and bread. Now that may not sound very good, but it is. *Very* good. The best I've eaten in Florence! For devout carnivores, they do a good *bollito misto* (mixed cuts of meat poached together in a light broth) served with excellent *salsa verde* (a tangy green condiment). Desserts are made *a casa* and are all—like the *torta di mele* (apple cake)—simple but satisfying. The wine list is very fair, the house red very good. If you want a *real* meal in Florence, come here. ♦ Daily, lunch and dinner. V. d. Spada 27r. 214756

65 Palazzo Corsi

This rambling palazzo, built in the 19th century to a design by **Telemaco Bonaiuti**, replaced a 15th-century palazzo by **Michelozzo**, whose courtyard stands invitingly intact within. ♦ Via dei Tornabuoni 76 (between Via degli Strozzi and Via de' Corsi)

Within Palazzo Corsi:

Procacci

★★★This tiny, family-run café/winebar/deli/patisserie is not to be missed. It has been here since 1885, and standing (or sitting at one of the minuscule tables) here is like stepping back in time. The selection of wines is a joy—I don't think there is one bad bottle. Even the tomato juice is fresh pressed. The delicious pastries are all homemade, and the savories (the *frittate* of spinach or of cheese, the imaginative composed salads, or the truffle and asparagus pie) are a perfect light meal. If there is a problem, it is the tiny panini—little finger rolls. They are two-bite-sized and come filled with truffle sauce or with truffled liver pâté. And they are immediately addictive. I had six before I could stop myself. While you are eating, you can peruse the excellent selection of their own label preserves, jellies, honeys, sauces, and jams that are for sale. There is a good selection of all things truffled (of course), cakes and pastries in gift boxes, interesting liqueurs—including one called Dolcefuoco, made from chocolate and chili—and all manner of confectionary. Under a glass counter there is also a fine selection of cheeses (including a local truffled Pecorino) and salami. A civic treasure is here. You really must visit. ♦ M-Sa, 10:30AM-8PM. 211656

Mark Twain, who lived outside of Florence in Settignano while working on *Pudd'nhead Wilson* in the 1890s, said he wrote more there in four months than he could in two years at home.

66 Hotel Helvetia & Bristol

$$$$ One of Florence's—and Italy's—finest hotels, this stately 19th-century hotel (where Gabriele D'Annunzio, Igor Stravinsky, Luigi Pirandello, and Giorgio de Chirico, among others, stayed) is rich in character, offering the ambience of a quiet urban villa and Old World hospitality. Paintings and antiques give the public area and 52 guest rooms individual charm, and the building's principal façade on **Piazza Strozzi** is one of an elite city palazzo. The **Giardino d'Inverno** restaurant is a bright, airy space for breakfast, lunch, or snacks. ♦ Via dei Pescioni 2 (between Via degli Strozzi and Via del Campidoglio). 266651; fax 288353. www.royaldemere.com

67 Garga

★★$$$ Florentine-born owner Giuliano, known as "Garga," gives his name to this lively, friendly restaurant. Lamb is served *al rosmarino,* and spaghetti comes *al carciofi* (with artichokes) or with *bottarga* (pressed roe) as well as in more predictable forms. Garga's Canadian wife Sharon's contribution—*cheesecake della Sharon*—needs no translation, even to the local contingent of the polyglot crowd that has come to appreciate the wonderfully aromatic, herb-based cuisine of this restaurant. Sharon is now running a *scuola di cucina* (cookery classes) for those interested in taking more than a memory of great food away with them; information is available on the web site. ♦ Tu-Sa, lunch and dinner; Su, dinner. Via del Moro 48r (between Piazza Goldoni and Via dei Palchetti). 2398898 www.garga.it (classes). e-mail: garga@fol.it

68 Il Latini

★★★★$$ This place is so great that the hospitality even extends to those standing in line to get in (and many, many people do). Waiters regularly fortify those waiting with little glasses of wine and chunks of local cheese. But once you are inside, prepare to be treated with love and expertise. The avuncular and big-hearted owner and his team of charming waiters adopt you, feed you their wonderful, gutsy Tuscan dishes, and present you with *cantucci* (little almond-studded cookies) and excellent *vin santo* (dessert wine) at the end. The *sopressata* (sausage) is homemade and fabulously rich and even more generously cut than the superb prosciutto (look at the number of hams dangling above your head to get an idea of how popular this stuff is!), the house special *penne* in an intense meat sauce is a joy, the *ribollita* and *zuppa di fagioli col grano faro* are better than those made by any mama I know (including my own), and the meats . . . oh, let us just say that the way they cook the beef, the veal, and the lamb here would turn Gandhi carnivorous. All the meats are priced by weight. Newish on the menu is their *assagi* of starters—a tasting platter with a little bit of everything. A great way to explore the menu. Each table has huge *fiaschi* of very decent red wine, from which you help yourself. Other drinks can be ordered from the impressive wine list. Superbly fruity estate-bottled olive oil also adorns each table. Don't try to enjoy your *ribollita* fully without it. In the basement lies a treasure trove—the Latini wine cellar. Brunellos and Barolos, Chiantis and the best of Italian wines are there alongside bottles of top-vintage Chateau d'Yquem the size of a toddler. There is Krug and Crystal; there are brandies and grappas and a very impressive malt whiskey collection—all good bottles from good years. Wine tastings are planned. Ask about them and give your tastebuds a treat. Such is the popularity of the place that they now have their own merchandising, and you can take home a painted ceramic I Latini ashtray (in various sizes, from social to chain smoker) . . . given that in Italy as in the US, home is just about the only place you can legally use an ashtray now. ♦ Tu-Su, lunch and dinner. Reservations recommended. Via dei Palchetti 6r (between Via della Vigna Nuova and Via dei Federighi). 210916. www.ilatini.com

69 Paolo Romano Antichità

Signor Romano, a third-generation antiques dealer whose Neapolitan grandfather started the *Fondazione Salvatore Romano* of Romanesque sculpture, extends the tradition with his stock of primarily Italian furniture from the 17th to 19th centuries. ♦ M-F, Sa morning Mar-Oct; M afternoon, Tu-Sa Nov-Feb. Borgo Ognissanti 20r (between Piazza Goldoni and V. d. Porcellana). 293294

70 Palazzo alla Rovescia

The story goes that Alessandro de' Medici, when asked if he would approve the plans for a balcony on this palazzo, remarked sarcastically, "Yes, in reverse." To many, that would mean "no," but the literal-minded builder interpreted it as a go-ahead to design it upside-down, as it remains today. ♦ Borgo Ognissanti 12 (between Piazza Goldoni and Piazza Ognissanti)

71 Harry's Bar

★★$$$ The name is the only thing this place shares with the higher-priced Harry's in Venice. This spot is good for the best burger in town, as well as a variety of more classic Italian dishes. It's also the quintessence of what Italians are fond of calling an "American bar"—a place that serves mixed drinks—and its selection of premium spirits is impressive. Charming, urbane bartender Leo Vadorini is justly proud of his martinis (stirred, not shaken), which come served in a chilled shot glass. The house special dessert of an Italianate variation on crêpes Suzette (crêpes Susanna, I guess) is absolutely delicious, to say nothing of dramatic. ♦ M-Sa, lunch and dinner. Lungarno Amerigo Vespucci 22r (between Piazza Goldoni and Piazza Ognissanti). 2396700

72 BM Bookshop

The wide selection of English-language books (many on Florence and Italy, many others Italian fiction in translation) may be more expensive here than at home, but you can't think of everything. Happily, the owners of this place just might well have—there are guidebooks, cookbooks, and children's books in English and Italian. ♦ Daily, 9:30AM-7:30PM. Borgo Ognissanti 4r (between Piazza Goldoni and V. d. Porcellana). 294575

73 Munstermann of Florence

"Cosmetical and homeopathical products," says the little sign in the window. And it is not wrong. Founded in 1897, this shop has kept up with the times. Now, alongside its multitude of herbal remedies and jars of homeopathic help, there are flight socks and anti-cellulite patches. They stock "Drinkwell"—a tiny bottle of drops to put in drinking water you are not entirely sure of—and a huge range of creams and lotions to get rid of everything from oily scalps to wrinkles around the eyes. There are hand therapy gloves and pure-bristle hairbrushes.

And the place smells wonderful. ♦ Daily. Piazza Goldoni 2r. 210660. www.munstermann.it

74 Antico Caffè del Moro

Known locally (and even internationally) as "the Art Bar," this small café has the best mixed drinks in town (unusual in an Italian café), discreetly served in an upscale ambience. Even those who don't drink alcohol can enjoy an expertly made fruit cocktail garnished with enough top-quality fresh fruit to allow you to skip dinner. There is popcorn on the tables and a fascinating collection of old photographs on the walls. This is a great place to spend your cocktail hour. Happy hour is between 7 and 9PM (hours are long here . . .), when all cocktails are 4 euros. Should you prefer something hot, the bar offers a cocktail list of coffees. A New York cappuccino is hot chocolate, milk, Kahlúa, and cream, while a San Francisco cappuccino substitutes brandy for the Kahlúa. ♦ M-Sa, 7PM-1AM. No credit cards accepted. Via del Moro 4r (between Piazza Goldoni and Via dei Palchetti). 287661

75 Beltrami

High-fashion shoes and leather goods for men and women (classical clothing was never its biggest draw) are featured at this elegant store of Florentine origin. It's been known for generations for excellent-quality leather and craftsmanship, as well as some surprisingly imaginative designs. ♦ M-F, Sa morning Mar-Oct; M afternoon, Tu-Sa Nov-Feb. Via della Vigna Nuova 70r (between Via dei Palchetti and Via dei Federighi).

76 Palazzo Rucellai

One of the most handsome of Florence's Renaissance palazzi, this structure was built in 1446-1451 by **Bernardo Rossellino** to designs of **Leon Battista Alberti** for textile merchant Giovanni Rucellai. The family emblem, "Fortune's Sail," can be seen on the building's façade, a classicized and refined version of the rusticated architecture prevalent at the time this palazzo was built. ♦ Via della Vigna Nuova 18 (at Piazza dei Rucellai). At the time of writing, the palazzo was closed for renovation, but call to check for its reopening.

Within the Palazzo Rucellai:

Museo di Storia della Fotografia Alinari (Alinari Museum of the History of Photography)

Temporary photo exhibitions here draw on the extensive collection of the Alinari brothers (whose shop and archives are in the same building). The museum also displays the work of acclaimed international photographers. ♦ Admission M, Tu, Th-Su; special exhibitions, call to confirm. Via della Vigna Nuova 16. 213370

77 Desmo

A front-runner in high-quality, high-fashion leather manufacturing, this boutique carries bags in strong, bright colors and materials ranging from fine calfskin and stamped leather to trendy nylon. Women's purses are the highlight, but it's worth a visit to check out the beautifully made accessories, travel bags, and a small line of leather clothing. ♦ M-F, Sa morning (no midday closing) July-Aug; M afternoon, Tu-Sa (no midday closing) Sept-June. Piazza dei Rucellai 10r (at Via della Vigna Nuova). 292395

77 Ermenegildo Zegna

Known for its luxurious fabrics and stylishly conservative tailoring, this elite menswear manufacturing firm offers what Italians call the "total look"—everything from top to toe. ♦ M-F, Sa morning (no midday closing) July-Aug; M afternoon, Tu-Sa (no midday closing) Sept-June. Piazza dei Rucellai 4-7r (at Via del Purgatorio). 283011

78 Loggia dei Rucellai

Now glassed in, this loggia was built in 1460-1466 on the occasion of the marriage of Giovanni Rucellai's son Bernardo to Cosimo II Vecchio's granddaughter Nannina. Today it is used for art exhibitions. ♦ Via del Purgatorio 12 (at Piazza dei Rucellai)

79 Giorgio Armani

This is the Florence home of the revered Milanese designer, known for his sophisticated interpretations of classic American tailoring, loosely cut in luxury fabrics. ♦ M-F, Sa morning Mar-Oct; M afternoon, Tu-Sa Nov-Feb. Via della Vigna Nuova 51r (between Via dei Tornabuoni and Piazza dei Rucellai). 219041

In the 13th century, one third of Florence's population was engaged in either the wool or the silk trade, which were responsible for a period of extraordinary prosperity.

In the 12th century, interfamily feuds were widespread, and more than 150 square stone towers—built for defense by influential families right next to their homes—dominated Florence's skyline. The building of towers became a real "fashion" with families vying to better and dwarf one another's efforts. Apparently size really did matter to the old Italians!

80 Palazzo Strozzi

Florence's most beautiful Renaissance palazzo was begun in 1489 as the private residence of wealthy merchant Filippo Strozzi, and construction (under architect **Benedetto da Maiano**) continued intermittently as the family was exiled. Though work was completed in 1504 by **Simone Pollaiuolo**, known as **Il Cronaca**, and **Jacopo Rosselli**, the great cornice atop the heavily rusticated building was never finished, as can be seen from the Via degli Strozzi side. The palazzo now houses a number of organizations (such as the **Gabinetto Vieusseux**, a private library and reading room) and is used for exhibitions. The most prestigious of these is the *Mostra-Mercato Internazionale dell'Antiquariato,* an international antiques biennial held in September in odd years. A fire at an antiques fair in Todi occasioned the hideous practicality of the fire stairs in the otherwise harmonious courtyard. As we go to press, the palazzo is host to the fabulous Botticelli exhibition celebrating the masters (www.boticellipalazzostrozzi.com). ♦ Piazza Strozzi and Via degli Strozzi

81 Palazzo dello Strozzino

Filippo Strozzi lived in this palazzo (begun in 1458 by **Michelozzo** and completed by **Giuliano da Maiano** in 1462-1465) while overseeing construction of his big place across the piazza. Its three "layers," or stories, were built in three periods and styles. ♦ Piazza Strozzi 2 (at Via degli Anselmi)

Within the Palazzo dello Strozzino:

Cinema Odeon

Want to know where to find Mel Gibson, Michelle Pfeiffer, Richard Gere, and Arnold Schwarzenegger during your stay in Florence? The Anglo-American community (and with 32 junior-year-abroad university programs, it's large and growing) lives for Monday-night showings of original-version English-language movies—with an occasional French or Spanish flick thrown in—at this gorgeous Art Nouveau theater built in 1922. There's even a bar where the local youths linger in hopes of critiquing a film's virtues with the American *studentesse*, most of whom, however, are more interested in stocking up on ice cream and Milk Duds. The **British Institute of Florence**, the sponsor of this successful program, is also housed in the palazzo. ♦ M-Sa, 3:30PM-10:45PM. 214068

82 Palazzo Ricasoli

This 15th-century palazzo, built for the Ricasoli family, had the strange name of **Hotel de New York** in the 19th century, when this part of town was known as the "mecca of foreigners." Today the palazzo is closed to the public. ♦ Piazza Goldoni 2 (at Lungarno Corsini)

83 Galleria Corsini

Here you'll find the greatest private art collection in Florence, put together by Lorenzo Corsini (nephew of Pope Clement XII—the family has produced a number of religious figures, including a saint), whose idiosyncratic arrangement (à la **Palazzo Pitti**) includes important works by Antonello da Messina, Pontormo, Signorelli, and Raphael. ♦ Admission. By appointment only; call M, W, F, 9AM-noon. Via del Parione 11 (between Via Parioncino and Piazza Goldoni). 218994

83 Il Bisonte

Tanned, undyed leather in casual designs was once the hallmark of this shop, which has since added an array of bright colors as well as sheepskin jackets and coats. ♦ M-F, Sa morning Mar-Oct; M afternoon, Tu-Sa Nov-Feb. Via del Parione 31r (between Via Parioncino and Piazza Goldoni). 215722

84 Coco Lezzone

★★$$ Though the name of this small dining spot is Florentine dialect for "big, smelly cook," the food is good and aromatic in nothing but a positive sense. The sight of well-heeled Florentines and foreigners packed into the simple white-tile surroundings of this much-frequented restaurant is an amusing lesson in radical-chic eating. The dish for which the restaurant is famous is *baccalà alla livornese* (salt cod sautéed and served with tomato sauce); Tuscan specialties (the full range of peasant soups, roast meats accompanied by cannellini beans or cooked or fresh vegetables, Pecorino cheese, and an extensive selection of Chianti wines) predominate. The place has great attitude—a notice tells you "the trilling of cell phones disturbs the cooking of the ribollita," and the menu announces that *bistecca* (the great Florentine beefsteak) will *only* be served rare. They don't serve coffee, and they don't take credit cards. But they do accept *any* foreign currency. ♦ M, W-Su, lunch and dinner. Tu, dinner. Via Parioncino 26r (between Via del Parione and Via del Purgatorio). 287178

85 Chiostro del Convento di Santa Trinità (Cloister of the Convent of the Holy Trinity)

This former cloister, constructed in 1584 by **Alfonso Parigi** to designs by **Bernardo Buontalenti**, is now occupied by the **University of**

Florence Law School. In the refectory are 17th-century frescoes of *The Story of Christ* by Giovanni da San Giovanni and Nicodemo Ferrucci. ♦ Via del Parione 7 (between Piazza di Santa Trinità and Via Parioncino)

Within the Chiostro del Convento di Santa Trinità:

Alimentari Orizi

There's something comfortably down-to-earth about Mariano's invitingly simple downstairs grocery store in a neighborhood of lavish shops, whether it's the barrel seats at the side counter or the lunch itself, which consists of sandwiches made to order out of such cheeses as mozzarella and stracchino and such cold cuts as *prosciutto crudo* (cured) or *cotto* (baked) and *bresaola* (dried salted beef). Coffee is also available. ♦ M, Tu, Th, F; W, Sa morning. No credit cards accepted. Via del Parione 19r. 214067

86 Erboristeria Inglese (at the Officina de' Tornabuoni)

At No. 97 you will see a beautiful old sign for the *Profumeria Inglese*. Luckily for Florence, and for us, the *profumeria* is not gone—it has just been moved to much smaller premises farther down the street. And beautiful premises they are. The 16th-century Palazzo Lardarel was designed and built by the sculptor and architect **Giovanni Antonio Bosio** and makes the perfect setting for the sweet-smelling, health-giving, skin-saving potions and lotions that have been made by this little company since the "English and American Chemist and Druggist" was first opened in 1843 by Henry Roberts. All their own products are completely natural, many from organic sources, and their remedies range from tinctures to improve your immune system to serums to stop your face from wrinkling, and from herbal remedies for your circulation to delicious-smelling creams to make your age spots disappear. Their vitamin E body cream is almost magical. Alongside their own products you will find those of L'Artisan Profumeur, Lalique, Luxe, and Dyptique (whose fabulous candles scent the air here). The staff are incredibly helpful and multilingual. ♦ Daily, except Monday morning. Via de' Tornabuoni 19. 210628. www.officinadetornabuoni.com

Dante described his fellow Florentines in the *Inferno*. XV 61-68, as "that ungrateful, malicious lot . . . miserly, jealous and proud."

Maledetta e sventurata fossa ("cursed and unlucky ditch") is what Dante called the Arno River, which has overflown its banks some 70 times since its first recorded flood in 1177. The worst flood ever was the most recent: On 4 November 1966, the Arno rose 4.92 meters—more than 16 feet. The aftermath of mud mixed with fuel oil flushed out from basement storage tanks engulfed paintings, sculptures, books, manuscripts, and other objects. Thousands of such items were extracted from the morass by teams of local and international volunteers the Florentines dubbed "angels of the mud" in an atypical fit of gratitude, if with a characteristically ambivalent moniker.

87 Via dei Tornabuoni

The gang's all here, and after all, that's why many come to Florence. Some think Michelangelo is the greatest artist, others Salvatore Ferragamo. And this road is lined with big names. There is **Tiffany** at No. 25, **Yves St. Laurent** at No. 27, and **Prada** at No. 51. Keep walking on the same pavement and you'll pass **Dior** at No. 57, **Bulgari** at No. 61, and more **Prada** at No. 67. **Gucci** has more or less taken over a block from Nos. 73-81. The view across the road is not too shabby, with **Trussardi** at No. 34, **Cartier** at No. 39, and **Armani** at No. 48. Taking up the corner where Tornabuoni meets **Via della Spada** is Italy's designer of choice for anyone with a penchant for turning heads, **Roberto Cavalli**. Stopping here is ideal because the Cavalli emporium also houses a gorgeous little café—the **Café Giacosa**, which does teas and coffees, cocktails and snacks in the most elegant way imaginable. Come and sip with the beautiful people (closed Sunday).

Also on Via dei Tornabuoni:

Hotel de la Ville

$$$$ A handsome hotel in a stylish location, this top establishment with 71 totally renovated rooms is quiet and discreet. It's quite desirable for its Via dei Tornabuoni address (and the noiseproof windows in the guest rooms facing that street). There's no restaurant. ♦ Piazza Antinori 1 (at Via dei Tornabuoni). 2381805; fax 2381809. www.hoteldelaville.it

Within Hotel de la Ville:

Bar Belle Donne

The hotel's lobby bar is the size of two baseball fields, furnished with comfy sofas and chairs. Each evening a happy hour serves drinks at half price and offers free plates of hors d'oeuvres. The charming barmaid makes a mean cocktail. ♦ Daily, to 2AM

Gucci

The world's most famous fashion statement started right here in the firm's flagship store, where the full line of loafers, scarves, bags, luggage, and men's and women's clothing are displayed before the admiring eyes of status-conscious shoppers and the famously condescending raised eyebrows of the sales help. ♦ M-F, Sa morning Mar-Oct; M afternoon, Tu-Sa Nov-Feb. Via dei Tornabuoni 73r (between Piazza di Santa Trinità and Via della Vigna Nuova). 264011

Emilio Pucci

The Marchese Emilio Pucci was famous for his vibrant silk patterns, which began adorning the jet set almost as soon as there were jets. Apparently loving a woman in uniform, he then extended his line to brighten the costumes of flight attendants and Florence's meter maids. His silk scarves have become the colorfully uniform uniforms of young-minded old money and the new rich alike. Scarves are but the most classic and accessible items available here; the boutique also sells blouses, dresses, and palazzo pajamas—the designer's contribution to the evening wear of the 1960s. ♦ M-F, Sa morning Mar-Oct; M afternoon, Tu-Sa Nov-Feb. Via dei Tornabuoni 20/22r. 294028

Beacci Tornabuoni

$$ This charming former *pensione* on the top three floors of a 15th-century palazzo is decorated like a house in the Tuscan countryside, and all 29 guest rooms have private baths. A clientele of regulars makes it necessary to reserve well in advance. Many guests welcome the chance to eat dinner here, particularly in the rooftop garden when weather permits. You have only to check the huge library of visitors' books to see how well loved this place is. They even have a thank-you letter from Barbara Bush! ♦ Via dei Tornabuoni 3 (between Piazza di Santa Trinità and Via della Vigna Nuova). 212645; fax 283594. www.bthotel.it

87 Hotel La Residenza

$$ The entrance on Via Tornabuoni is, to say the least, understated. And the first communication from the hotel is a notice telling you that children under 12 are not allowed in the elevator. But this really is a lovely place, where the greeting from the sparky, sparrowlike lady owner and her charming deep-voiced son twinkles like the jewelers' windows on the Ponte Vecchio. They both speak perfect English while both being perfectly Florentine. They make you feel at home here in their city. The hotel has just 24 nicely furnished and decorated rooms (and generally decently sized too). They have air conditioning, minibar, direct dial TV, etc., and a recent refurbishment has given them new bathrooms. All rooms are soundproofed—a boon on this busy street. There is a beautiful wood ceiling in the lounge should you wish to sit and make a shopping list for the day, and your excellent (and generous) breakfast is taken in the simple but comfortable dining room. Unexpectedly for such a small establishment, La Residenza offers restaurant service (excellent stuff), room service, and laundry service. Best of all there is a gorgeous, flower-filled rooftop terrace. This hotel is a real gem. ♦ Via Tornabuoni 8 (between Via Porta Rossa and Via degli Strozzi). 218684. www.laresidenzahotel.com

Palazzo Spini-Ferroni

Built as the residence of a family of wool merchants in 1289, this greatest of the medieval palazzi in Florence today houses the shops and offices of their contemporary counterparts (it's understandably also referred to as "Palazzo Ferragamo"; see below). ♦ Piazza di Santa Trinità 2 (at Borgo Santi Apostoli)

Within Palazzo Spini-Ferroni:

Salvatore Ferragamo

This is the flagship store of the famous family-run shoe firm begun by Naples-born Salvatore Ferragamo, who came to Florence after early years of success in Hollywood, where he became known as "shoemaker to the stars" by attending the feet of the likes of Mary Pickford and Douglas Fairbanks. Ever since, Americans have appreciated his family's designs, which now also include exquisite clothing and such accessories as silk scarves and ties. ♦ M-F, Sa morning (no midday closing) July-Aug; M afternoon, Tu-Sa (no midday closing) Sept-June. Via dei Tornabuoni 16r (between Lungarno Acciaiuoli and Piazza di Santa Trinità). 292123

Museo Salvatore Ferragamo

In response to the worldwide success of a traveling exhibit of the designer's choicest creations, the Ferragamo family opened this museum showcasing the history of shoes and their company. Also featured is a research center, library, and archives. You can also see the wooden "feet" of everyone from Katharine Hepburn to Madonna. These models were used to fashion tailor-made shoes. ♦ Free. M-F, 9AM-1PM and 2PM-6PM. Booking by phone at least 10 days in advance is advised. Via dei Tornabuoni 2 (at Lungarno Acciaiuoli). 3360456; fax 3360444

88 Ponte alla Carraia

Originally called the Ponte Nuovo (New Bridge) to distinguish it from the Ponte

Vecchio, the bridge (built and rebuilt) on this spot was washed away in a flood in 1274, crushed by a crowd watching a spectacle on the Arno in 1304, destroyed in another flood in 1333, reconstructed by **Ammannati** in 1557, and blown up by the Germans in 1945—sort of a bridge over troubled waters in reverse. The current version was put up in the old style after World War II. ♦ Between Piazza Nazario Sauro and Piazza Goldoni

89 Palazzo Corsini

A bit of the Baroque adorns the Renaissance underpinnings of this palazzo, built in the 17th century by **Pier Francesco Silvani** and **Antonio Maria Ferri**, the grandest of the many palazzi associated with the Corsini family in Florence. If the U-shaped courtyard seems a little oddly placed, it is because it was meant to be in the middle . . . but the palazzo was never completed. The most interesting feature inside is the spiral staircase known locally as the *lumache* (the slug). ♦ Lungarno Corsini 10 (between Via Parioncino and Piazza Goldoni)

Within Palazzo Corsini:

Peter Bazzanti & Son

If you've ever harbored a perverse Pygmalion-like desire to appreciate a statue for more than strictly aesthetic reasons, now is your chance. Since 1822 this shop has sold high-quality marble and bronze replicas of the world's most famous masterworks. While the prices are considerably higher than picture postcards, it's still less of an investment than breaking into the **Bargello**. ♦ M-F, Sa morning Mar-Oct; M afternoon, Tu-Sa Nov-Feb. Lungarno Corsini 46r (other entrance on Via del Parione 37-39r, between Via Parioncino and Piazza Goldoni). 215649

90 Santa Trinità

This is a lovely, lofty, atmospheric old church. It was founded in 1092 by Giovanni Gualberto, a local nobleman. The story says that he set off one Good Friday to avenge the murder of his brother, but, having found the murderer, decided to spare his life because it was Good Friday. He then popped into San Miniato for a word with the Almighty and a crucifix there is said to have bowed its head to him in honor of his merciful act. He went on to become a Benedictine monk and founded the Vallombrosan order. His church was rebuilt over about 30 years starting in 1300 (probably by **Neri di Floravante**) and parts have been being added ever since. So what you get is a mainly Gothic interior with a Romanesque interior façade and a Mannerist exterior façade by **Bernardo Buontalenti**. Inside there are Ghirlandaio's famous frescoes from the life of St. Francis, commissioned by Francesco Sassetti. The artist basically took the narrative of the life of the saint and transplanted it into 15th-century Florence. So, for example, we see St. Francis healing a sick girl in Piazza Santa Trinità. In one of the other works—*St. Francis Receives the Rule*—Lorenzo the Magnificent and his sons have roles as "extras" and a little portrait of Sassetti himself pops up in the crowd, along with his son. In the second chapel, the **Capella Scali**, in the left transept you can see the tomb of Bishop Benozzo Frederighi by Luca della Robbia. And, of course, the miraculous crucifix that started it all is here, in the **Capella Doni**. ♦ M-Sa, 10AM-noon and 4PM-5:30PM; Su, 4PM-5:30PM. Piazza di Santa Trinità and Via dei Tornabuoni

91 Colonna della Giustizia

This ancient granite "column of justice," taken from the Baths of Caracalla in Rome, was given to Cosimo I de' Medici by Pope Pius IV after Medici forces had won the battle of Montemurlo (1537) and established the family's absolute power. The statue on top (1581) is by Francesco del Tadda. ♦ Piazza di Santa Trinità and Via dei Tornabuoni

92 Palazzo Bartolini Salimbeni

This 16th-century palazzo by **Baccio d'Agnolo** was the first in Florence to embody the principles of the High Renaissance used by **Raphael** and **Bramante** in Rome. The palazzo was initially criticized for looking more like a church than a residence (note the cross-shaped window sashes). The Salimbeni family motto, *"Per Non Dormire"* ("not to sleep"—they were no slouches, it seems), and its counterpoint, poppies, appear throughout the palazzo. The small courtyard is decorated with ebullient *sgraffiti,* the two-tone designs drawn in stucco on many Renaissance palazzi. ♦ Piazza di Santa Trinità 1 (at Via Porta Rossa)

93 Hotel Porta Rossa

$$ The Old World setting of leaded glass and antique furnishings draws a regular crowd of English and French guests to this hotel that's part of the **Palazzo Bartolini Salimbeni**. Its history as a hostelry dates back to the 14th century. The hotel's 81 rooms are cavernous, perfect for large families. All have private bath or shower, minibar, safe, and satellite TV. The hotel is run today by a direct descendant of the Torigiani family, whose palazzo it was in the 16th century. In its years as a hotel Byron stayed here, as did Stendhal, Balzac, and Emperor Leopold of Austria. And that was before the bathrooms were renovated! A nice touch is that the hotel has "adopted" (as part of a Florentine hoteliers' scheme) the **Museo Stibbert**, which houses a collection of 16th- to 19th-century armor, costume, art, tapestries, and furnishings. ♦ Via Porta Rossa 19

(between Piazza de Davanzati and Piazza di Santa Trinità). 287551; fax 282179

94 Oliviero

★★★$$$ Well-prepared Tuscan specialties and other creative dishes are offered at this comfortably elegant restaurant. Piano music, top-notch service, banquettes, and candlelight create an appropriate backdrop for a special evening. The kitchen is directed by Francesco Altomare, who is largely responsible for the continuing fame of this historical restaurant frequented by a global Who's Who. Even such classic dishes as *minestra di farro* (a barleylike soup) and *risotto di zucca gialla* (risotto with pumpkin) are given special and delicate interpretation; or try the broccoli ravioli with mussels and clams. Accompany your choice with a selection from the impressive wine collection. ♦ M-Sa, lunch and dinner. Reservations recommended. Via delle Terme 51r (between Chiasso Ricasoli and Piazza di Santa Trinità). 287643

95 Al Lume di Candela

★★$$$ This dining spot offers a romantic, candlelit atmosphere for a pricey dinner, with a menu based on seasonal ingredients, including some of the freshest fish in town. ♦ M-F, lunch and dinner; Sa, dinner. Reservations required for lunch, suggested for dinner. Via delle Terme 23r (between Chiasso Ricasoli and Piazza di Santa Trinità). 294566

96 Casa-Torre dei Buondelmonti

This 13th-century medieval tower belonged to the Buondelmonti family, whose scion's fickleness touched off the Guelph-Ghibelline conflicts in Tuscany. ♦ Via delle Terme 13r (at Chiasso Ricasoli)

97 Capocaccia

★$$ This is part of a chain that originated in Monaco and really comes into its own in the later evening, when the DJ is on the decks and it becomes the haunt of the young, the beautiful, and the achingly hip of Florence. It has been voted their favorite nighttime rendezvous several times. Even during the day it is not the kind of place that does one's self-confidence much good if one can name more than three US presidents in one's lifetime but not the designer of one's clothes. Talking of designers, the interior is well designed and roomy; the panini are imaginative, tasty, and freshly made; the salads are ideal for a light lunch; the coffee is excellent, and the cocktails are topnotch. Capocaccia is not overpriced for such a trendy hangout and is very convenient if you have shopped till you are about to drop. ♦ Tu-Sa, noon-4PM and 6PM-1AM. Lungarno Corsini 12-14r (between Via dei Tornabuoni and Via Parioncino). 210751

98 Ponte Santa Trinità

Simple and graceful curves make this the most beautiful bridge in Florence, maybe even the world. Designed by **Bartolommeo Ammannati** in the 16th century using the curves from Michelangelo's tombs in the **Cappelle Medicee**, it was built of stone from the **Boboli Gardens**. The bridge was blown up during the German retreat at the end of World War II, and has been painstakingly reconstructed from as many of the original pieces as could be salvaged and from new stone taken from the original quarry, using the original plans and 16th-century stonecutting tools. The original statues at either end represent the four seasons, the head of *Spring* having been retrieved from the river only in 1961 and replaced with great fanfare. ♦ Between Lungarno Guicciardini and Lungarno Corsini

99 Santi Apostoli

Legend (and legend only) has it that this small 11th-century church (rebuilt in the 15th to 16th centuries) was founded by Charlemagne. Within its Romanesque interior, partially built with material from the nearby Roman baths, is a 16th-century *Immaculate Conception* by Vasari. ♦ Piazza del Limbo (between Lungarno Acciaiuoli and Borgo Santi Apostoli)

99 Hotel Berchielli

$$$$ This hotel's lobby is a monochromed splendor of polished marble. The 76 rooms upstairs are quieter in all senses (all of them are soundproofed), and those in the front have views of the Arno. All rooms are air conditioned and have televisions and minibars. There is no restaurant, but there is an "American bar." ♦ Piazza del Limbo 6r (between Lungarno Acciaiuoli and Borgo Santi Apostoli; another entrance is at Lungarno Acciaiuoli 14). 264061, fax 218636. www.berchielli.it

100 La Bottega dell'Olio

A veritable shrine to olive oil, this gorgeous little shop sells shampoos and soaps, creams and bath gels made from the stuff, plus olive oil servers, T-shirts, and theme-printed towels. Then there are the olives—big and small, black and green, flavored and marinated. And, of course, the oil—over 50 different kinds, which, delightfully, you are encouraged to taste by the owner, Andrea Trambusti. ♦ M-Sa, 10AM-1PM and 2PM-7PM. Piazza del Limbo 2

SAN LORENZO

The area around **San Lorenzo**, the Medici parish church, is something of a Medici theme park. Cosimo Il Vecchio, founder of the dynasty, had **Michelozzo** build the imposing **Palazzo Medici-Riccardi** here, embellished with playful frescoes of the family by Benozzo Gozzoli and sycophantic ones by Luca Giordano (commissioned by later owners). Around the same time, Cosimo commissioned Michelozzo to build the monastery of **San Marco**, keeping aside two cells within it for his personal use. Cosimo also founded the manuscript collections that are kept in the library of San

Marco as well as in the **Biblioteca Medicea-Laurenziana**, a library specially commissioned by Medici Pope Clement VII and housed within the cloisters of San Lorenzo. The church of San Lorenzo itself, greatly expanded by the Medici and housing the family's last remains in its chapels, the **Cappelle Medicee**, epitomizes the beginning and end of the entire dynasty.

The Medici legacy lives on in a number of noble palazzi that were built in the area over the centuries. It also continues in the surrounding streets, from the numerous coats of arms (they have any number of balls on them—usually six—giving rise to predictable jokes about Medici anatomy) above palazzo entrances to names of cafés and restaurants. Sadly, the family's original profession as bankers has its modern counterpart in the increasing commercialization of the area with tacky boutiques and pizza parlors. Still, one can't help thinking that Lorenzo Il Magnifico (who wrote such lines in praise of love and youth as the famous *"quant'è bella giovinezza/che si fugge tuttavía,"* roughly, "how beautiful is youth/which quickly flees") would have enjoyed the large number of university students in the area, and that the livelier members of the Medici family would have appreciated the spirit of the bustling indoor food market and the outdoor vendors' stalls in the shadow of San Lorenzo today.

1 Residenza Johanna Uno

$ The two charming ladies who own and run this 11-room *residenza* (more personal and informal than a hotel) are doing something right, since Johanna now has three sister establishments within the city center. Here at the original establishment and situated in a charmingly understated 19th-century building behind wrought-iron gates in a leafy corner close to San Marco, you will find all the rooms en suite, simply but faultlessly furnished, and there is a sweet little library of books and international magazines for guests to dip into. Credit cards are not accepted. The Residenza's twin sister **Residenza Johanna Due**, is not very far away to the northwest, and offers all the same facilities, pleasant rooms, and attentive, enthusiastic service. Johanna Due is a 1920s town house set in its own private garden. Here there is private parking space (a real boon in this city). Johanna's other sisters are **Johlea I** and **II**. ♦ Via Bonifacio Lupi 14 (between Via Zara and Viale Spartaco Lavagnini). 481806. www.johanna.it

2 Don Chisclotte

★★★$$$ Owner Walter Viliglardi's mother was a cook for descendants of the Corsini princes, and he carries on the princely tradition with such dishes as *risotto dell'ortolano* (with garden vegetables) and *filetto al sale con salsa alle erbe aromatiche* (filet of beef with herb sauce). This superlative dining experience is further enhanced by an excellent Chianti-based wine list and extensive collection of malt whiskies. The airy and elegant dining room features pictures of Don Quixote, whose name, Italianized, is the restaurant's. ♦ M, Su, dinner; Tu-Sa, lunch and dinner. Reservations recommended. Via C. Ridolfi 4r (at Via di Barbano). 475430

3 La Macelleria

★★$ The husband-and-wife team of Danilo and Daniela does marvelously refined justice to this space's past as a 1920s butcher shop with such dishes as *tagliata al pepe verde e rosemarino* (beef with green pepper and rosemary), and they extend their talents to land and sea in *riso verde con pignoli al burro di salmone* (green risotto with pine nuts and salmon butter). ♦ M-Sa, lunch and dinner. Via San Zanobi 97r (between Via F. Bartolomei and Via delle Ruote). 486244

Within La Macelleria:

Virgo Fidelis

God bless the Bank of Tuscany! Here, set into the corner wall of the restaurant **La Macelleria**, is another of the artworks saved by their money: *Spozalizio di Santa Catherina d'Alessandra e San Pietro Martiro* (The Wedding of St. Catherine of Alexandria and St. Peter the Martyr), thought to be by Domenico Puglio, painted about 1526. It was rescued by the bank and preserved here in 1978.

3 VinOlio

★$ Florence is changing—a massive influx of other nationalities and the relentless march of consumerism is taking the *signorile* (noble) atmosphere from much of the city. But occasionally you find a place that, although it is 21st century, feels like old Florence. This is such a place. At the front, it looks like a small, dark bar with some snacks. Look more closely and you will see that those inside are twirling whites and sniffing reds, admiring colors and checking clarity. This is a real wine bar. Step through the tiny front area and you are in a dark-ceilinged, terra-cotta-tiled restaurant with white linen placemats and long-aproned staff. The food is divided into tasting platters of salamis, lardo (cured lard), prosciutti and cheeses, pastas (including *pici,* fat spaghetti served with a rich duck sauce), and soups (including a chickpea soup made with the infrequently seen red chickpea), all of which are freshly made on the premises, as well as carpaccios and salads. There is also a chance to try Tomatin, a soft Tuscan cheese stuffed with truffle pâté and served warm from the oven with porcini mushrooms and a delightful little brown paper bag of warm bread. Wines are intelligent and reasonably priced. Staff are knowledgeable. The whole atmosphere is one that would not disgrace a Michelin-starred establishment. But you are in the back room of a bar on quite a seedy street. Now *that* is Florence! The bar also organizes regionally and seasonally themed dinners and tastings with the emphasis on great wines. ♦ M-Sa. Restaurant, M-Sa dinner only. Via San Zanobi 126r. 489957. www.vinolio.com

4 Taverna del Bronzino

★★★$$$ Set in a 16th-century landmark palazzo, this antiques-filled restaurant offers such imaginative dishes as *tortelloni al cedro* (large tortellini with lime). You will always find a list of specials, which change with the season. There is also a large selection of local and international wines and the potent grappa, the Italian aquavit. ♦ M-Sa, lunch and dinner. Closed August. Via delle Ruote 25-27r (between Via Santa Reparata and Via San Zanobi). 495220

5 Hotel Cimabue

$ The prices here would be considerably higher if this charming, 16-room hotel run by the friendly Rossi family were just a block or two closer to the Centro Storico—it offers attentive service, tasteful décor, private baths, and color TVs. Named after Giotto's master teacher, this place boasts artistic touches that can be found in the preserved ceiling frescoes, hand-painted and -decorated furniture, and the tasteful refurbishment of the 19th-century palazzo, with Liberty-style appointments. There's no restaurant, but plenty of attention is given to a healthy breakfast buffet. All things considered, it's a real find. ♦ Via Bonifacio Lupi 7 (at Via Santa Reparata). 475601; fax 471989

6 Residenze Johlea I and Johlea II

$$ The two newest sisters of the well-known **Residenza Johanna** are twins—two beautifully restored, side-by-side 19th-century palazzi. Each room is individually decorated with antiques and Tuscan leather. They are all en suite, with TV, air conditioning, hair dryer and Internet connection. Some have a mezzanine-level entrance. All of them are relaxing, friendly places to be, and benefit from the friendliness and enthusiasm of the service that Johanna's residents have come to enjoy. There is even a lovely terra-cotta-tiled roof terrace. ♦ Via San Gallo 80 and 76. 4633292 (Johlea I). 461185 (Johlea II). www.johanna.it

7 Palazzo Pandolfini

Based on designs by Raphael, this elegant 16th-century palazzo was built by **Giovanni Francesco** and **Aristotele da Sangallo** for Bishop Giannozzo Pandolfini, as the strange inscription under the cornice indicates. Peek through the iron gate to see the statue-studded garden, in which the bishop presumably contemplated the pressing theological issues of the day. ♦ Via San Gallo 74 (at Via Salvestrina)

8 Hotel Cellai

$$ This is a family-owned hotel set in an 18th-century building with gorgeous dark-paneled ceilings and terra-cotta-tiled floors. There are 60 rooms, all decently sized and all with private bath, air conditioning, minibar, and the rest. There is also a lovely roof terrace with roses, a canopy in case of bad weather, and terrific views. The ground floor has lots of nooks and crannies with comfortable, rich red upholstered armchairs to relax in, and there is a tiny bar for guests only. The truly excellent buffet breakfast (which is included in the price of the room) is served in the delightful atrium-like dining room. On the back of its clever little brochure, the Cellai lists the time it takes to reach many of the things you are bound to want to see in Florence: for the record, it is 3 minutes from Michelangelo's *David* and 7 minutes from the Duomo. ♦ Via XXVII Aprile 14 (between Via Reparata and Via San Zanobi). 489291. www.hotelcellai.it

9 Hotel Genesio

$ Basic and friendly, the Genesio is part of a small, city-wide chain run by a local family. It is two flights up, so not for the disabled, but the rooms are perfectly fine, the staff couldn't be more helpful, and a generous buffet breakfast in the sweet terra-cotta-tiled breakfast room is (amazingly) included in the price. Rooms have telephone, television, and tub or shower. If you are not interested in frills, this hotel is a great bargain. ♦ Via XXVII Aprile 9. 496208. www.hotelgenesio.it

10 Chiostro dello Scalzo

Andrea del Sarto's 16th-century frescoes here include remarkable representations of scenes from the life of St. John the Baptist, such as *The Visitation*, *Charity*, and *Justice*. ♦ Admission. Tu-Su; call to confirm. Via Camillo Cavour 69 (between Piazza San Marco and Via Salvestrina). 2388603

11 Miró

$$ This eatery's stylized design in a large space creates an ambience not usually associated with Tuscan food. In fact, the seasonally changing menu often emphasizes such inventive fish preparations as *pesce spada con capperi e ricotta* (swordfish with fresh capers and ricotta cheese). More conventional Tuscan specialties and meat dishes are also served, along with a stunning list of 200 wines. ♦ M-Sa, lunch and dinner. Via San Gallo 57-59r (between Via XXVII Aprile and Via delle Ruote). 481030

12 Antica Farmacia di San Marco

Like the Dominicans of **Santa Maria Novella**, the Dominicans of **San Marco** founded a pharmacy, and the variety of products at this one would have made Savonarola start a pharmaceutical bonfire of the vanities. Creams, soaps, shampoos, and eau de cologne seem even more appealing amid the antique fixtures. You can also fill prescriptions here. ♦ M-F, Sa morning Mar-Oct; M afternoon, Tu-Sa Nov-Feb. No credit cards accepted. Via Camillo Cavour 146r (between Piazza San Marco and Via della Dogana). 210604

13 Casino di San Marco

Built in 1574 as a laboratory for Francesco I de' Medici by **Bernardo Buontalenti**, today this large palazzo is the headquarters of the Court of Appeals. ♦ Via Camillo Cavour 57 (between Piazza San Marco and Via Salvestrina)

14 Monastero di Sant'Appollonia

This former monastery (begun in the 11th century and remodeled in the 14th century), which now houses various departments of Florence's university, has a lovely portal (attributed to **Michelangelo**) that leads to a cloister and on to Poccetti's fresco of the *Last Supper* in the former refectory. ♦ Via San Gallo 25A (between Via Guelfa and Via XXVII Aprile)

Within Monastero di Sant'Appollonia:

Cenacolo di Sant'Appollonia

Andrea del Castagno's 15th-century *Last Supper* fresco unfolds dramatically beneath three scenes of the Passion. ♦ Free. Tu-Su, 8:15AM-1:50PM. Via XXVII Aprile 1 (between Via San Gallo and Via Santa Reparata). 2388607

15 Cenacolo di Fuligno

One of the finest *Last Suppers* (see "Cenacoli [Last Suppers]" on page 132) is by Raphael's master, Perugino, located in the former Convent of San Onofrio. Similar in composition to the Florentine *Cenacoli* by Andrea del Castagno and Domenico Ghirlandaio, this treatment of the subject contains a background depicting the Sermon in the Garden set in the Umbrian hills. ♦ M, Tu, Su, 9AM-noon. Via Faenza 42 (between Via Nazionale and Piazza del Crocifisso). 286982

16 l'Toscano

★$$ The menu of this reliable place is proudly Tuscan, with first courses featuring local dishes such as *ribollita* (*the* Tuscan first course, a thick vegetable-and-bean soup); *mamme,* stuffed artichokes baked in a rich white sauce; and *faggotini al pomodori picante,* a type of little ravioli served with a punchy, spicy tomato sauce. Main courses feature the traditional *bisteca alla fiorentina* and *filetto al Chianti e pepe rosso* (fillet of beef cooked in Chianti and flavored with pink peppercorns). ♦ M, W-Su, lunch and dinner. Via Guelfa 70r (between Via Santa Reparata and Via San Zanobi). 215475

17 Palazzo Marucelli

Go through the bizarre doorway of this 17th-century palazzo by **Gherardo Silvani** to see 18th-century frescoes by Sebastiano Ricci depicting *Scenes from Roman History*, *The Labors of Hercules*, and *Hercules Ascending Olympus*. The palazzo now serves as the seat of the **University of Florence Law School**. ♦ Via San Gallo 10 (between Via Guelfa and Via XXVII Aprile)

Under Cosimo I (16th century), Jewish men were forced to wear a yellow badge on their hats and the women the same marker on the sleeves of their coats or dresses. Their business privileges were curtailed, and they were forbidden to deal in the wholesale market or in art objects. It was Cosimo who first confined Florentine Jews to the Old Market area, where the Piazza della Repubblica now stands.

18 Museo di San Marco (San Marco Museum) or Museo dell'Angelico (Fra Angelico Museum)

The church and convent of San Marco were built in 1299 on the site of Vallombrosian (later, Sylvestrine) monasteries. Dominicans from the nearby town of Fiesole took them over in the 15th century (Savonarola became Prior of **San Marco** before he was dragged from it to his death in **Piazza della Signoria**). Cosimo Il Vecchio financed its expansion in 1437-1453 by **Michelozzo**, setting apart two cells for his own meditations. The decorations of those cells by Fra Angelico and his assistants, along with other works by the 15th-century Dominican friar/painter, are what still draw visitors inside beyond the almost generic façade designed in 1780 by **Giocchino Pronti**. Michelozzo's **Chiostro di Sant'Antonino** (Cloister of St. Anthony) is reached through the entrance vestibule to the right of the church. The **Ospizio dei Pelligrini** (Pilgrim's Hospice), which once hosted religious pilgrims, now houses 20 paintings by Fra Angelico, among them *The Madonna of the Linen Guild* and the altarpiece, which, in addition to the church's patron saint, Mark, represents the Medici patron saints Cosmas and Damian. The **Sala Capitolare** (Capitolary Room) across the courtyard has Fra Angelico's *Crucifixion* and a *Last Supper* by Domenico Ghirlandaio. Upstairs is Fra Angelico's *Annunciation* and the monks' cells frescoed by the friar and his assistants. Fra Angelico's hand is most evident in the cells on the left side of the corridor, especially (numbers refer to the floor plan) Nos. 1 (*Noli Me Tangere*), 3 (*Annunciation*), 6 (*Transfiguration*), 7 (*The Mocking of Christ*), and 9 (*Coronation of Mary*). Savonarola stayed in No. 11 (his portrait, by Fra Bartolommeo, is on the right side of the vestibule of No. 12), Fra Angelico in cell No. 33, and old Cosimo de' Medici in Nos. 38 and 39. The passage between Nos. 42 and 43 is where the crowd nabbed Savonarola; beyond it is Michelozzo's harmonious library, today displaying the manuscript collection started by Cosimo. ♦ Admission. Tu-F, 8:30AM-1:50PM; Sa, 8:30AM-6:50PM; every 2nd M, 8:30AM-1:50PM; every 2nd Su, 8:30AM-6:50PM. Piazza San Marco 1 (between Via Giorgio La Pira and Via Camillo Cavour). 2388608

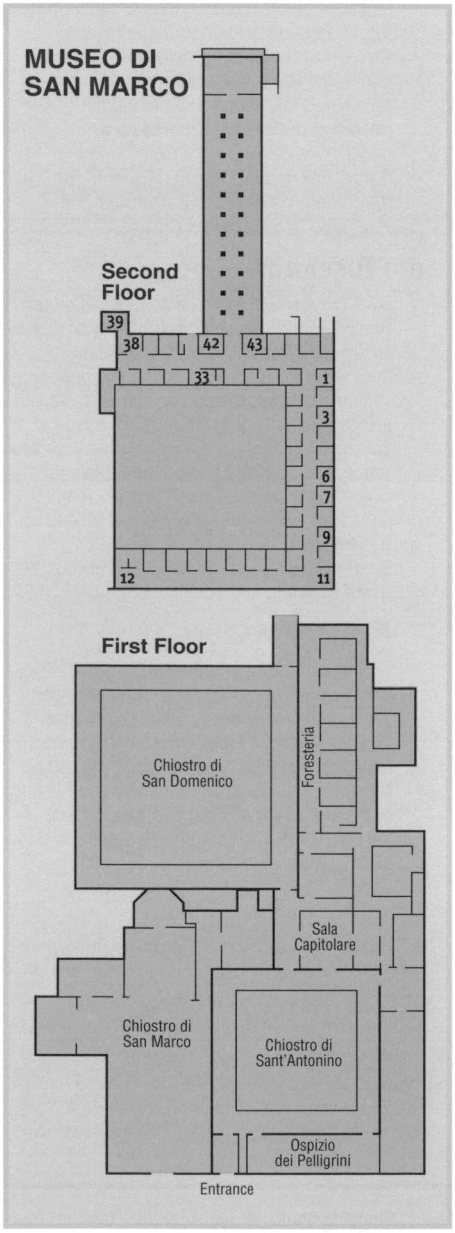

19 Piazza San Marco

This Italian provincial piazza looks like a hundred others of its ilk in Italy. And like the others, it is a pleasant place to rest with the requisite trees, benches, and cumbersome monument to an obscure war hero. The administration building of the **University of Florence** is on the southeast side of the piazza at **No. 4**. ♦ At Via Cesare Battisti and Via XXVII Aprile, and Via Ricasoli and Via Giorgio La Pira

20 La Biscotteria

Abandon hope, all ye dieters who even pass this fabulous little place, let alone enter. You may think you have tasted cantucci (the little almond-studded, sliced cookies you get to dip into your *vin santo* at the end of the meal), but you have not. Not until you have tasted theirs. This shop is devoted to them. Here, delicious, more-ish cantucci come traditional (crunchy with almonds), but also studded with big chunks of rich, dark, high-quality chocolate or nuggets of chewily delicious baby fig, or dark with chestnut flour and mined with pine nuts, or sweet with a generosity of glossy raisins. The most savory-minded will develop an instant sweet tooth. This is a revelation in biscuit eating! On Sundays (only), lines form for the fantastic focaccia they bake and sell by the length. There is a terrific selection of *vin santi* and a smaller selection of olive oils and Chiantis. ♦ M-Sa, 9:30AM-7:30PM; Su, 11AM-7PM. Via Nazionale 121. 283566. www.biscottisanti.com

21 Le Fonticine

★★★$$ This could just be the restaurant you have dreamed of. It was named for the 16th-century fountain by Luca della Robbia just outside. Once inside you will feel cared for, relaxed, and increasingly well fed. The food is *cucina casalinga*—home cooking. No fancy frills. No towering presentation. Just good, straightforward, generally Tuscan cooking. The antipasti include a *porcini trifolati* (porcini mushroom caps sliced, gently cooked, and scented with truffle) that you should not miss, and the fritters of *fior di zucca* (zucchini blossom) are light as air but very much more tasty. Pasta is all homemade and excellent. Tagliatelle comes with fresh asparagus and prosciutto—delicate but delicious—and the house version of ravioli has a fresh ricotta stuffing and a punchy, *piccante* tomatoey sauce that are a great combination. Main dishes include all the classics, and the *bisteca alla fiorentina* is terrific. The osso buco is also excellent, featuring veal that really tastes like something and a terrific, tangy sauce. However, don't even consider not leaving room for dessert, because the true treasure of Florence is not Michelangelo's *David* or Brunelleschi's Duomo, but the Fonticine's *crema di mascarpone*. Unbelievable! Pair its light, creamy sweetness with fresh strawberries, and heaven has nothing left to offer you. The couple at the table next to me had been coming to the Fonticine for 30 years to eat it. Understandably. Another treasure to be found here is Giampiero—son of *il padrone,* maître d', and sommelier combined. He is admirably knowledgeable, passionate about good food and wine, and, if you place yourself in his care, will give you the best night possible in Florence that the Access Guide could write about. Let him guide you through the wine list. And let him pour you a glass of the restaurant's special grappa before you go. If you are interested in finding out what is so wonderful about Italy and Italians, come to Fonticine. You'll come back. ♦ Tu-Su, lunch and dinner. Via Nazionale 79r (between Via Faenza and Via Guelfa). Tel/fax 282106. www.lefonticine.com

22 Il Triangolo delle Bermude

This splashy *gelateria,* named after the Bermuda Triangle, offers such adventurous ice-cream flavors as rose, whiskey, peanut, and coffee crunch. ♦ Tu-Su, 11AM-midnight. Closed 1-20 January. No credit cards accepted. Via Nazionale 61-63r (between Via Faenza and Via Guelfa). 287490

fonte dei dolci

23 Fonte dei Dolci

This is another shop that is exactly what it sounds like. But apart from all manner of candy—sugared almonds and *panforte*, chocolate and *marrons glacés*—and a huge selection of *vin santi*, grappas, and aperitifs, the specialty of this store is those little *bonbonnières* that the Italians are so good at—tiny figured and ornamented boxes holding a couple of slivered almonds, little edible posies, the kind of tiny beautiful wonders that Italians give at weddings or Christmas to each guest as a memento. They're unbelievably lovely, and they aren't made anywhere else. ♦ M-Sa. Via Nazionale 120/122. 294180. www.fontedeidolcifirenze.com

24 Cafaggi

★★$$ Another of Florence's family affairs, this one offers a very reasonable, and genuinely interesting, set lunch alongside a main menu that has excellent seafood (spaghetti comes with a rich seafood sauce or with sardines) and grilled fish, a good choice of meat dishes like *bocconcino di vitello* (little rolls of veal), and some marvelous old traditional offerings such as tripe in a tomatoey sauce and little fritters of brain with artichoke. Just look at the huge joint of beef in the window and judge the quality of the ingredients. ♦ M-Sa, lunch and dinner. Closed August. Via Guelfa 35r (between Via de' Ginori and Via Sant'Orsola). 294989

Florence Nightingale, considered to be the founder of modern nursing, was born in Florence on 12 May 1820 and given the name of her birth city.

25 Biblioteca Marucelliana (Marucelli Library)

This library, founded in 1752 with the collection of Francesco Marucelli, contains over 400,000 works, among them rare books, manuscripts, and prints. ♦ M-F (no midday closing); Sa morning. Via Camillo Cavour 43 (between Via Guelfa and Piazza San Marco). 210602

26 Galleria dell'Accademia

Michelangelo's *David* is the highlight of this gallery. The towering masterpiece is at the far end of the gallery, standing majestically in its own room. The chamber was built for the statue in the 19th century when it was moved indoors from **Piazza della Signoria** (where a full-size replica now stands in its place). Carved from a block of white Carrara marble that had been worked and abandoned by another sculptor, *David* is a mature representation of the biblical subject, which had been portrayed more youthfully (some say effeminately) by Donatello and Verrocchio, and also represented Michelangelo's coming of age as a sculptor (he was barely 26 when he began it). A clear Plexiglas screen was placed around the base of the statue in 1992, after a deranged devotee smashed *David*'s toe (it was restored within weeks).

The **Sala del Colosso**—the first room you enter—is dominated by a plaster model of Giambologna's *Rape of the Sabine,* and has several other interesting paintings including a fresco of the *Pietà* by del Sarto, works by Fra Bartolommeo, and a *Deposizione* begun by Lippi and finished by Perugino. A corridor off this room has the four Michelangelo *Prigioni* (1530) sculpted for the tomb of Pope Julius II, the statue of *St. Matthew* (1506), and an odd and unfinished *Pietà*. All of these pieces are—like many Michelangelo works—unfinished. He is said to have done this deliberately, to allow observers to be a part of the creative process, in that they have to "complete" the work in their mind when they see it. Hmmm. Another theory is that Michelangelo was such a perfectionist that he never felt he had *finished* a work . . . only stopped working on it. The gallery also has a good collection of primitive painting, as well as works by Alesso Baldovinetti and Botticelli. Arrive before 8:30AM to avoid the crowds. ♦ Admission. Tu-F, Su, 8:15AM-6:50PM; Sa, 8:15AM-10PM mid-June-mid-Sept; 8:15AM-6:50PM mid-Sept-mid-June. Via Ricasoli 60 (between Via degli Alfani and Piazza San Marco). 2388609

27 Hotel Nuova Italia

$$ This Italian/Canadian collaboration is a veritable work in progress—every season a new project is launched to improve this family-run and tourist-friendly hotel: triple-paned, soundproof windows installed one year; ultrarare window screens the next. All 20 rooms have been completely refurbished with custom-made furniture and have private newly retiled bathrooms, air conditioning, and new carpeting. The carefully tended, house-proud atmosphere creates a comfortable oasis just two steps from the bustle of the San Lorenzo market. There's no restaurant, but breakfast is served in the bright ground-floor bar. Credit cards are accepted, but you can get yourself a discount by paying by traveler's check or in cash. ♦ Via Faenza 26 (between Via G. B. Zannoni and Via Nazionale). 268430, 287508; fax 210941. www.hotelnuovaitalia.com

27 Lobs

★★$ This is a marvelous bargain of a place, considering the variety and quality of the fish it serves. Huge platters of *frutti di mare* or *crostacei al vapore* (steamed) are served up for two. All manner of fish from sea bass to salmon and John Dory to turbot come grilled and sauced (the bass with balsamic vinegar and a crispy salad on the side is delicious). There is lobster and very good oysters, and there is even a rather appetizing vegetarian selection. Desserts include a delicious and refreshing *sorbetto di limone e basilico con vodka.* The lunch menu is an astoundingly good value and offers a long and enticing list of pasta and gnocchi dishes. The wine list is pleasing, the staff are young, good-looking, and totally charming, and the music is chilled jazz. A very relaxing, enjoyable place to eat. ♦ Via Faenza 75r. 212478.

27 Alice's Masks Art Studio

Professor Agostino Dessi has been creating masks in Florence for more than 30 years. Now his daughter Alice has joined the business. The professor's masks are exhibited and used all over the world from the Venice Carnevale through theatrical productions in Tokyo, international exhibitions in New Orleans, and teaching courses in Helsinki. There are pigs and foxes, harlequins and carnival queens, angels and devils. There is something for everyone to hide behind here along with puppets and miniature theaters. Like a little bit of Venice in Florence . . . which is like finding a little bit of diamond in gold! ♦ Daily, 9AM-1PM and 3:30PM-7:30PM. Via Faenza 72r. 287370. www.alicemasks.com

28 Mercato Centrale (Central Market)

Bei harshofini! is how the greengrocers here sing the praises, in their aspirated Florentine accents, of their beautiful little *carciofi*, or artichokes. The market's hangarlike iron structure was designed in 1874 by **Giuseppe Mengoni**, the architect of Milan's stylish Galleria Vittorio Emanuele II. This being Florence, however, it draws a more rustic assemblage of shops and shoppers than its Milan counterpart. Downstairs are butcher shops selling all types of meat (their proud displays of skinned rabbits, dead pheasants, and decapitated boars' heads are inevitable turnoffs for first-timers), grocers' shops, and an open-air (and what air—both fish and foul!) fish market; many fish vendors still use their booths' original 19th-century marble counters. Upstairs are endless displays of fruits, vegetables, and local color. ♦ M-Sa, 7AM-2PM. Bounded by Piazza del Mercato Centrale and Via dell'Ariento, and Via Sant'Antonino and Via Panicale

Within the Mercato Centrale:

NERBONE

★$ If you can't find this restaurant on the ground floor of the bustling market, just ask: Everyone knows it as the best place around for a quick bite and a glass of local wine. Alessandro, the amiable owner, is the son of well-known local restaurateurs. Try his grilled vegetables, daily soup and pasta specials, or the typically Tuscan *bollito* (beef chunks boiled in broth). Rub elbows with the market merchants and enjoy the high spirits and low prices. ♦ M-Sa, lunch. No credit cards accepted. Ground floor. 219949

29 LOGGIATO DEI SERVITI

$$$ Like **Le Due Fontane** (see page 97), this even smaller and far more charming hotel faces Florence's most architecturally satisfying piazza. Originally a 16th-century convent, this 29-room hotel offers some of the more tastefully decorated lodgings in town, with period wrought-iron beds, decorative trompe l'oeil details, and terra-cotta floors. There are also four suites. All rooms have minibar, safe, hair dryer, and television. It's almost always full, so book well in advance. There's no restaurant. ♦ Piazza della Santissima Annunziata 3 (between Via dei Servi and Via Cesare Battisti). 289592; fax 289595. e-mail: loggiato.serviti@italyhotel.com

30 SANTISSIMA ANNUNZIATA

Long one of the Florentines' favorite churches, this is the first choice for society weddings. The entrance to the 13th-century church, rebuilt in 1444-1481 by **Michelozzo** (see floor plan opposite), called the **Chiostrino dei Voti** (Cloister of the Ex-Votos), once held wax votive offerings (ex-votos) left by pilgrims. It has lovely 16th-century Mannerist frescoes. On the right portico wall are a *Visitation* [1] (numbers refer to floor plan) by Jacopo

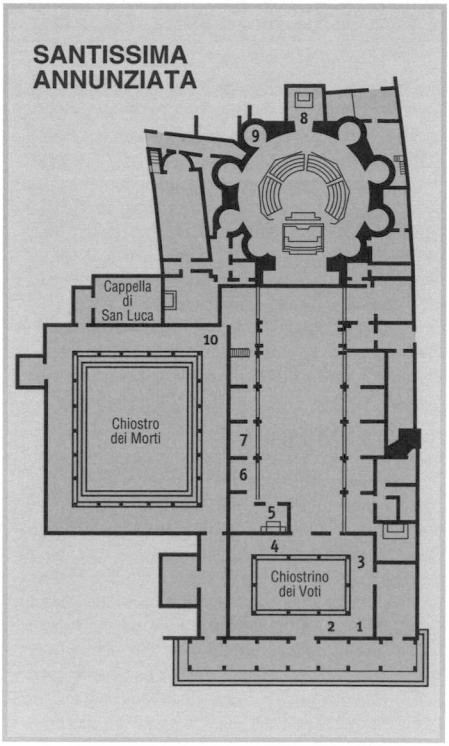

Pontormo (he is buried in the **Cappella di San Luca**, as is Benvenuto Cellini) and an *Assumption* [2] by Rosso Fiorentino. At the end of the right wall is Andrea del Sarto's *Birth of the Virgin* [3]. An earlier work, Alesso Baldovinetti's *Nativity* [4] (containing one of the earliest landscapes in Italian painting), is to the left of the nave entrance. Inside the nave, immediately to the left, is Michelozzo's *tempietto* (little temple), which houses the miraculous image of the *Annunciation* [5]. The nave itself is a Baroque extravaganza relieved by Andrea del Castagno's 15th-century *Vision of St. Julian* [6] above the altar and his *Holy Trinity* [7] in the second chapel on the left. At the far end of the circular presbytery is a chancel [8] decorated in the late 16th century by Giambologna as the tomb for the sculptor and his fellow Flemish artists working in Florence; to its left is a 16th-century *Resurrection* [9] by Bronzino. The **Chiostro dei Morti** (Cloister of the Dead), to the left of the church, contains Andrea del Sarto's masterpiece the *Madonna dei Sacco* [10], which takes its name from the sack on which St. Joseph is leaning in this representation of the Holy Family. ♦ Daily, 7:30AM-12:30PM and 4PM-6:30PM. Piazza della Santissima Annunziata (at Via Gino Capponi)

Fiesole: A Jewel in the Florentine Hills

Five miles out of the congested city (a half hour on bus *No. 7* from **Piazza San Marco** or 20 minutes by cab or car) is the glorious hill town of Fiesole, a municipality that predates Florence by many centuries. On the road to Fiesole are magnificent villas hidden from the streets by imposing walls and gates. These boast spectacular gardens—and views—for those lucky enough to gain admittance. Even if you don't have a personal invitation, the drive still offers enough of a glimpse into the lifestyles of these hillside estates and some timeless vistas to make the pilgrimage worthwhile. And the town itself has a number of sights to keep serious archeology buffs, churchgoers, and aimless wanderers busy for hours.

Fiesole sits on a hill just north of Florence and is believed to have been inhabited since 2000 BC. The Etruscans built **Faesulae** into the most important city of the region, coming down off the hill only to trade at the markets held by the swampy and constantly overflowing **Arno**'s riverbanks. The Romans set up camp by the river in 59 BC and the Etruscans found themselves without a trade route, and soon gave in to the powerful army's squeeze. When the empire fell, being on the hill helped Fiesole defend itself from hostile attacks by barbarian invaders. Fiesole's destiny became forever tied to Florence's in AD 1125, when the rising merchant city in the valley defeated the hilltop village. Fiesole never lost its dignity, though, and the 15,000 people who live in the *comune* of Fiesole still look down from their beautifully tailored hills and quietly majestic terraces to the commercial hubbub and congestion of Florence.

The **Piazza Mino da Fiesole**, named after the 15th-century sculptor, is the town's hub. It features some inviting cafés and pizzerias, a large parking lot, and the tourist information office (No. 36, 055/598720; fax 055/598822). Also here is the **Palazzo Pretorio**, a beautiful example of Renaissance civic architecture that boasts an array of coats-of-arms on its façade, one for each visiting magistrate. The **Duomo di San Romolo** at the other end of the piazza was originally built in 1028 but was heavily altered in a 19th-century restoration effort. Step inside and see works by Mino da Fiesole (note the tomb of the bishop Leonardo Salutati, up the steps on the right) and a 1440 altarpiece of the *Madonna and Saints* by Lorenzo di Bicci. The Duomo's original 13th-century bell tower has long been a landmark for the town, easily visible from any rooftop garden in Florence. Just behind the apse of the Duomo is the **Museo Bandini** (Via Dupré 1, no phone). It has a number of sacred works from the 1300s and 1400s, including della Robbia family terra-cottas and paintings by Lorenzo Monaco, Neri di Bicci, and Taddeo Gaddi. The museum is open Monday, and Wednesday through Sunday; there's an admission charge.

Past the rear of the Duomo is the large **Zona Archeologica** (Via dei Partigiani 1, 055/59477), most famous for its well-preserved, 3,000-seat Roman theater. The arena is still used today for the annual *Estate Fiesolana*, which features music, dance, theater, and film events from June through August. Contact the tourist information office (see left) for program listings. This ancient city center also includes the remains of two Roman temples, ancient baths circa the first century BC, and a long stretch of Etruscan wall. Near the entrance is an early-20th-century temple that houses the **Museo Civico**, with a modest collection of bronze figurines, pottery, funerary urns, and stelae. The archeological zone is open Monday, and Wednesday through Sunday; admission is charged.

On a clear day, the hike up to the **Convento di San Francesco** will be highlighted by a spectacular panoramic view of Florence. Look for the steep

31 Piazza della Santissima Annunziata

Florence's most perfectly proportioned piazza is surrounded by loggias on three sides. Within it is some rather less harmonious sculpture—two strange fountains by Pietro Tacca depicting sea creatures (they were destined for the Medici port of Livorno, but were so well liked they remained in Florence) and a pompous equestrian statue of *Fernando I de' Medici,* begun by Giambologna and finished by Tacca. The piazza has been the center of folkloric activity in the city for many centuries. Its church's namesake image of the *Annunciation,* according to legend begun by a monk and finished by an angel, was a popular pilgrimage destination. Annunciation Day used to mark the beginning of the Florentine calendar and is still commemorated with a celebration by city officials and a little fair in the piazza on 25 March. On 8 September children carry lanterns to the piazza from the **Duomo** down Via dei Servi, which becomes an open-air candyland for the *Festa delle Rificolone* (Lantern Festival). ♦ At Via della Colonna and Via Cesare Battisti, and Via dei Servi and Via Gino Capponi

32 Palazzo della Regione (Palazzo Riccardi-Mannelli)

This imposing 16th-century palazzo by **Bartolommeo Ammannati**, an administrative building shared by the province of Florence and the region of Tuscany, is unusual in Florence for its exposed brick. ♦ Piazza della Santissima Annunziata (at Via dei Servi)

pedestrian-only **Via di San Francesco** just west of the Duomo and set off on the challenging climb to the monastery's church, courtyard, and museum. The inviting Gothic church contains an *Annunciation* by Raffaellino del Garbo and an *Immaculate Conception* by Piero di Cosimo, both Renaissance painters of the early 16th century. Come for Mass and you may hear the friars singing from 14th-century walnut choir stalls. The museum features an interesting collection of documents and materials amassed by the friars during their missionary travels in China and Egypt, as well as local archeological finds. The museum is open daily; entrance is free.

Long, scenic walks are a Fiesolan specialty. A number of walking trails are clearly marked; one good choice is to take **Via Belvedere** to **Via Adriano Mari**, site of the abandoned stone quarries that provided the materials for many Renaissance buildings and streets. The tourist office (see page 96) has information on the walks. East of this area is the **Villa I Tatti** (Via di Vincigliata 26, 055/603251, 055/608909; fax 055/603383), a 75-acre wonderland where the famous American art critic Bernard Berenson lived. Berenson left the villa, his painting collection, and a library of over 50,000 volumes to Harvard University, his alma mater; it is one of many Fiesole villas affiliated with American university programs. Today the villa is an international post-doctorate center for the study of Renaissance topics. It is open for visits by appointment only; call ahead and be sure to ask for directions.

For those who want to enjoy Fiesole and the surrounding area for longer than a day, we recommend two places to stay. Fiesole's stellar hotel is the **Villa San Michele** ($$$$; Via della Doccia 4, at Via del Pelagaccio, 055/59451; fax 055/598734). Once a rather austere 15th-century Franciscan monastery, today it is one of Italy's most elegant and beautifully situated hotels. Formerly spartan monastic quarters are now 36 sumptuous rooms with state-of-the-art bathrooms and canopy beds. Some guest rooms boast the views that inspired **Michelangelo**, who is said to have designed the villa's façade and loggia. Tables on the terrace for drinks or dinner offer nonguests the chance to experience the hotel of choice of the rich and famous. A charming alternative to such budget-breaking accommodations is the 42-room **Pensione Bencistà** ($$; Via Benedetto da Maiano 4, south of Via Giuseppe Mantellini, 055/59163; fax 055/59163), which sits below the Villa San Michele in both location and price. But the gorgeous views are the same and if you don't mind the half-board provision enforced in high season, you'll enjoy the setting just as much.

Le Cave di Maiano (★★$$; Via delle Cave 16, Maiano, 055/59133) is equally delightful whether dining outdoors under the linden trees on a terrace overlooking the **Arno Valley** or indoors in a setting that is warm, cozy, and rustic. The *cucina toscana* menu features excellent prosciutto, local *finocchiona* salami studded with fennel seeds, canapés of mozzarella and mushrooms, homemade ravioli, and *gallina al mattone* (grilled spring chicken flavored with black pepper and olive oil). It is open Monday for dinner; Tuesday-Wednesday, Friday-Saturday, lunch and dinner; and Sunday, lunch. Reservations are required. **La Panacea dei Bartolini** (★★$$; Via Bosconi 58A, Olmo, 055/548972, 055/59485) also has a beautiful terrace view of the countryside, and the locale's high standard of cooking has earned it enthusiastic accolades from the food world. To get in touch with the spirit of Fiesole's Etruscan past, order the prix-fixe four-course Etruscan meal featuring rabbit and veal pâté and grilled beef. It's located eight miles north of Fiesole and is open Tuesday-Saturday, lunch and dinner; Sunday, dinner. Reservations are required.

33 Le Due Fontane

$$$ The two fountains by Pietro Tacca that face this small, modern hotel with 57 rooms give it its name. Rooms and views (they'll try to accommodate your request for a view of the square) are a nice balance of cleanliness and pleasantness, and this is a particularly quiet location for being just five minutes from the **Duomo**. All rooms have a bath or shower, and some have a Jacuzzi. They also have air conditioning, a safe, refrigerator, and TV. The hotel offers bus service from the airport. There's no restaurant. ♦ Piazza della Santissima Annunziata 14 (between Via dei Fibbiai and Via dei Servi). 210185; fax 294461. www.leduefontane.it

34 Ospedale degli Innocenti

Since 1988, part of this facility has been used as a research center by UNICEF. The façade of the foundlings' hospital is by **Brunelleschi**. Decorative medallions by Andrea della Robbia depict a baby in swaddling clothes. Under the portico to the left is the little revolving door where the abandoned children were left to be taken in by what was Europe's first orphanage. Many Florentine family names, including degli Innocenti and Nocentini, originate from this place. Inside is the Galleria degli Innocenti, a gallery that contains works by Piero di Cosimo, Filippo Lippi, and Domenico Ghirlandaio. ♦ Admission. Th-Tu, 8:30AM-2PM. Piazza della Santissima

Annunziata 12 (at Via della Colonna). 2491708

35 Museo Archeologico

Widely regarded as one of Italy's best, this museum is very helpful on the information front—every room has detailed explanatory notes in several languages, copies of which can be taken by visitors. There is an extensive Egyptian collection, an Etruscan section including the marble Sarcofago delle Amazzoni (Amazon's Sarcophagus) from Tarquinia and the Sarcophagus of the Fat Man, and a huge collection of Greek pottery including the François Vase, a fifth-century BC vase signed by Kleitias and Ergotimus. A great deal of the Medici family's treasures are here too. Many of the exhibits were damaged in the flood of 1966, and the restoration work continues today. ♦ Admission. M, 2PM-7PM; Tu, Th, 8:30AM-7PM; W, F-Su, 8:30AM-2PM. Via della Colonna 38 (between Via della Pergola and Via Gino Capponi). 23575

36 Morandi alla Crocetta

$$ This quiet and distinguished 10-room hotel is furnished with antiques, paintings, icons, and medieval manuscripts. The latter accoutrements are quite fitting, considering the place is housed in a former convent dating from the 16th century. (Room 29 still has original frescoes filling one wall.) The genteel Anglo-Italian owners make guests feel they have been welcomed into a private home. There's no restaurant. ♦ Via Laura 50-52 (between Borgo Pinti and Via Gino Capponi). 2344747; fax 2480954

37 La Norcineria

This unbelievable shop would turn Gandhi into a carnivore just for the chance to try its stunning array of sausages and hams, salamis and pressed meats. Huge hams hang from the roof, and sausages of all sizes are in strings and jars, slices and chunks. Huge boars' heads gaze down on the shoppers, and there is an entire tusked beast (stuffed, I hasten to add) sitting in the middle of the store atop a pile of delicious products featuring his friends. Wild boar salami is a Tuscan specialty, and they prepare it wonderfully here. All the products are handmade by small producers. The range of cheeses is just as carefully selected. The store also stocks a gourmet's choice of risotto rices, handmade dried pastas, preserves, honeys, pickles, olives, and even a range of local cold-pressed olive oils, aged balsamic vinegars, and Chiantis. In season they have fresh truffles; out of season they have butters and oils flavored with the regional specialty. And until you make up your mind whether you want a huge chunk of air-cured ham or sopressata, salsicce or salami, you can try them all on one of the store's made-to-order paninis. ♦ Daily, 8AM-8PM. Via Sant'Antonino 19-21r. 294859

The first eyeglasses appeared in Italy in the 14th century, supposedly introduced by Alessandro di Spina of Florence. Spectacles were also seen in China about this time; it is not clear who got the idea first.

38 Palle d'Oro

★★$ Neighborhood office workers pack the stand-up lunch counter in the front of this popular, inexpensive restaurant, so try to come early or late unless you'd like to sit in the back, where table service is available for a slightly higher price. The daily *primi piatti* (first courses) are your best bets for a light but filling lunch, and usually include some sort of pasta, risotto, and minestrone. On Friday the special is *cacciucco,* the tomatoey seafood stew of nearby Livorno. ♦ M-Sa, lunch and dinner. Via Sant'Antonino 43-45r (between Via dell'Ariento and Via Faenza). 288383

39 Sieni

Signor Zanobini (see **Fiaschetteria Zanobini**, page 100) recommends this place, and Signor Zanobini knows his stuff. Sieni has been here since 1909, and the wood-fired ovens are still in the wall of the front of the house café to prove it. The current owners have had it in the family for 30 years. There is a small bar in front and a sunnily painted restaurant in the rear. The restaurant offers 15 salads and a list of homey pasta and polenta dishes. But it is the pastries and cakes that are the thing here. Terrific cantucci are sliced off a ciabatta-size length for you, and fruit tarts and rich chocolate cakes are tempting. *Un infinita di dolce* is how the charming proprietress puts it—"an infinity of sweet things." But when you leave, don't go without a cake of their famous *panforte* to take home—concentrated, densely packed deliciousness. And Sieni does it just about as well as it can be done. ♦ Tu-F, Su. Via Sant'Antonino 54r (at Mercato Centrale). 213830. www.pasticceriasieni.it

40 Trattoria Garibardi

This good, down-to-earth trattoria offers proper Tuscan cuisine (it's in the Cucina Toscana organization), a great wine list featuring Supertuscans, and a whole range of interesting liquid accompaniments to your meal. The menu has the typical Tuscan dishes marked with a little fleur-de-lys. They include, for starters, a terrific simple dish called *salvio fritto*—a mini "sandwich" made with an anchovy fillet between two sage leaves that is then lightly dipped in batter and deep fried. There is also *panzanella* (a sort of cross between a salad and a very thick gazpacho) and *pappa al pomodoro* (a tomato soup thickened with bread). Main courses include the usual list of roasted and grilled meats, but also the epic *fritto misto toscana* (a vast pile of lightly battered and fried rabbit, lamb, and chicken with a good assortment of vegetables, including zucchini blossoms). It comes served on a bed of brown paper and, for the health-conscious, exudes almost no oil. Desserts include the rarely seen *zucotto,* made from fresh ricotta. Service is absolutely charming, the surroundings are lovely, and all in all you could be miles away from the tourist-driven heart of the city. ♦ Daily, 11:30AM-11PM. Piazza del Mercato Centrale 38r. 212267. www.garibardi.it

41 Il Guelfo Bianco

$$$ Florence at the time of the Medici is revived in this efficiently run, 29-room hotel where architectural details of the original 15th-century palazzo, such as leaded glass windows, wooden coffered ceilings, and an occasional fresco, were painstakingly saved and restored. Now a bright and pleasantly decorated hotel, its other pluses include location (midway between the **Duomo** and the **Piazza San Marco**), beautiful bathrooms, a helpful staff, and a peaceful courtyard. There are an additional eight rooms in the adjacent **Cristallo** annex. There's no restaurant. ♦ Via Camillo Cavour 57 (at Via Guelfa). 288330; fax 295203

42 Colomba

$$ Great for the young at heart, this hotel is tranquil and as traditionally Italian as they come. The charming owner and his Australian wife are incredibly friendly and helpful. Some of the 15 large, tiled rooms are spacious enough to sleep four and all are newly repainted, with air conditioning, little refrigerators, safes, satellite TV, and phone. There are also two rooms equipped for the disabled, although the tiny elevator won't accommodate a wheelchair. There's no restaurant. ♦ Via Camillo Cavour 21 (between Via dei Gori and Via Guelfa). 289139; fax 284323

43 Casci

$ The incredibly charming and warmly welcoming Lombardi family has created one of the city's loveliest budget hotels in a former 15th-century convent, where Gioacchino Rossini lived from 1851-1855. Look up at the 17th-century frescoed ceilings in some of the public rooms, and you have visited your first monument without leaving your hotel! It is but a guidebook's throw from the Duomo itself. The 25 rooms all have private baths with showers, as well as such amenities as minibar, color TV, CNN (or BBC World if you prefer), air conditioning, telephones, and hair dryers. Add to that the excellent breakfast buffet, impeccable housekeeping, a laundry service, help with train schedules, parking, good information on almost anything you could want in Florence, and free Internet access, and you know that this place is a real find. There's no restaurant. ♦ Via Camillo Cavour 13 (between Via dei Gori and Via Guelfa). 211686; fax 2396461. www.hotelcasci.com

44 Opificio delle Pietre Dure

Florentine mosaic, the art of inlaying semiprecious stone, was popular during the days of the Medici Grand Dukes, as seen in the **Cappelle Medicee**. Here you can see it in a museum. Though these mosaics seem precious indeed to modern eyes, it is amusing to see them depict views of Florence like grandiose postcards. There are also examples of mosaics used in various types of furniture. The workshop was joined with the Laboratori di Restauro in 1975 and is now famous throughout the world for its work in art restoration. Its real title is now the **Istituto Specializzato per il Restauro**, but most people still know it as the Opificio. Visits last no more than one hour. ♦ Admission. M-W, F-Su, 9AM, 10:45AM, 12:20PM; Th, 2PM, 3:45PM, 7:30PM. Via degli Alfani 78 (between Via dei Servi and Via Ricasoli). 265111

44 Biblioteca del Conservatorio di Musica Luigi Cherubini (Library of the Luigi Cherubini Conservatory of Music)

Among the collection of the library of Florence's prestigious music academy are ancient instruments as well as violins, violas, and cellos by Stradivarius and other famed Italian instrument makers. ♦ By appointment only. Via degli Alfani 80 (between Via dei Servi and Via Ricasoli). 292180, 210502

45 La Mescita

★$ *Mescita* is another Tuscan term for wine shop (like *fiaschetteria*), and this one has quite a mix of wines, Tuscan and otherwise, including fizzy Lambrusco from Emilia-Romagna. Cheese, salami, and three hot dishes *di giorno* (of the day)—such as *pappa al pomodoro* (pasta with a fresh tomato sauce), *salsicce con fagioli* (local spicy sausage with cannelli beans), or *baccalà* (salt cod)—are also served on inviting granite-topped wooden tables. Much to the *padrone*'s delight, the restaurant won a "Little Wonders Award," proudly displayed on the wall. ♦ M-Sa, 8AM-9PM. Via degli Alfani 70r (between Via dei Servi and Via Ricasoli). 2396400

46 Robiglio

Florence's most revered *pasticceria*, this shop has been known for over a half-century for such goodies as *torta campagnola*, a rich cake stuffed with fresh and candied fruit. But the shop also does delicious *salatini*—little savory pastry nibbles—and delicate candied violet petals, rose petals, and fresh mint leaves. ♦ M-Sa, 8AM-8PM. Via dei Servi 112r (between Via degli Alfani and Piazza della Santissima Annunziata). 212784

47 Trattoria Antellesi

★★$$ Janice hails from Arizona; her husband, Enrico, is from a line of respected Florentine restaurateurs. Together they are the spirit of this popular and comfortable trattoria in the shadow of the **Cappelle Medicee**. With the central food *mercato* just around the corner, a meal here is guaranteed to be fresh, delicious, and a memorable, authentically Tuscan dining experience. Janice will guide you to an appropriate selection from the wine list to accompany the seasonally changing menu of good homemade pastas, grilled meats, and desserts made on the premises. ♦ M-Su, lunch and dinner. Reservations recommended. Via Faenza 9r (between Piazza Madonna degli Aldobrandini and Via Sant'Antonino). 216990

47 Oscuro Medioevo Fiorentino

This is a new museum for Florence—and one with a sign outside warning that it is not for anyone of a particularly sensitive nature, or anyone suffering from claustrophobia. The Secrets of Medieval Florence offers just what it promises: exhibits on torture, death, plague, and deprivation. They include a working Florentine home from the 1300s, audiovisual effects, short films, and, shall we say, a degree of interactivity. Looking at the visitors' book at the exit—some of the comments are both cryptic and enticing ("I shall think twice now about taking a pee in the Florentine streets," wrote one visitor, conjuring up a myriad of questions . . . maybe visiting the museum will answer some of them). ♦ Daily, 11AM-11PM. Via Faenza 13r. 282432. www.oscuromedioevo.com

48 Palazzo Riccardi-Mannelli

One of many palazzi in Florence that were covered with frescoes in the 16th century, this small building boasts a bug-eyed bust above the entrance that is a sycophantic tribute to Francesco I de' Medici, who is buried in the colorful mausoleum chapel across the piazza. According to tradition, Giotto, the father of modern painting, was born in one of the simple houses from which the palazzo was built. ♦ Piazza Madonna degli Aldobrandini 4 (at Via Faenza)

48 Palazzo Benci

$$$ The Benci family built this mansion in 1574; in the 1960s it was transformed into a 35-room hotel, which underwent extensive refurbishment in 1989. Try to get one of the extra-quiet back rooms, with views overlooking the Cappelle Medicee. All rooms are air conditioned, with double-glazed windows, and have their own safes, satellite TV, and Internet access. Breakfast is available, and the gorgeous leather seating in the lobby and bar area makes it a really comfortable place to sit. There is no restaurant. ♦ Piazza Madonna degli Aldobrandini 3 (at Via Faenza). 2382821; fax 288308

48 Fiaschetteria Zanobini

This is one of only two wine shops in Florence that sell wine from their own vineyards by the bottle or the glass. Its label, Le Lame, appears on Chianti Classico and *vin santo*, a sweet dessert wine. In exceptional years (most recently, 1990), the Zanobini family produces a Chianti Classico Riserva called Vigna di Sorripa, named after one small tract of its tiny vineyard. There are some old photographs of the Zanobini house and vineyard on the walls—an idyllic scene—and to stand drinking Chianti while the old gentleman whose grapes gave up their juice for it shows you on the photograph the room where he was born, and the rows of vines the wine you are drinking came from, is a memorable experience indeed. No less a person than Prince Charles of Great Britain himself, on a trip to Florence to see restored artworks, enjoyed a glass of the Zanobini rosé. This year Signor Zanobini recommends his newest creation—Coacerbato, a fruity young red. And so, most heartily, do I. Other than the many, many wines, Signor Zanobini sells a huge selection of grappa and other premium spirits. If you are, for example, a malt whiskey fan, you will find his range and his prices hard to beat anywhere—even if you are planning a trip to Scotland! ♦ M-Sa. Via Sant'Antonino 47r (between Via dell'Ariento and Via Faenza). 2396850; fax, 296708. e-mail: zanovini@tin.it

49 Palazzo Inghiarini

More interesting than its more rusticated neighbor, **Palazzo Bonaluti**, this 16th-century palazzo boasts a bust of Cosimo I by Baccio Bandinelli, whose monument to Giovanni delle Bande Nere stands in the piazza below and whose descendants once lived here. ♦ Piazza San Lorenzo 2 (at Borgo La Noce)

Within the Palazzo Inghiarini:

Sergio

★$ This is another typical neighborhood trattoria in one of the most typical of Florentine neighborhoods. Open for lunch only, it features daily pasta specialties and grilled meats and caters to market vendors with serious appetites. Don't expect to linger (they make their money on fast turnover), but do try the house wine from the Gozzi family's Chianti vineyard. ♦ M-Sa, lunch. No credit cards accepted. Piazza San Lorenzo 8r. 281941

50 Palazzo della Stufa

The Stufa family (the name means stove) made enough money running medieval steam baths to build this 14th-century palazzo, where a 16th-century loggia and the modern stovepipe openings in the windows one floor below apparently still help let off steam. ♦ Piazza San Lorenzo 4 (between Via de' Ginori and Via della Stufa)

Within the Palazzo della Stufa:

Passamaneria Toscana

The best and most extensive selection of home-décor trimmings and accessories in Florence can be found here, including fabrics, borders, and cord tassels (one of the city's most versatile gifts). ♦ Daily (no midday closing) Mar-Oct; Tu-Sa (no midday closing) Nov-Feb. Piazza San Lorenzo 12r. 214670. Also at Via della Vigna Nuova and Via dei Federighi. 2398047

51 Palazzo Medici-Riccardi

This palazzo by **Michelozzo** was commissioned in 1444 by Cosimo de' Medici for the Medici family, who received such visitors as Emperor Charles VIII and Charles V of France. The corner arches were originally an open loggia, filled in with the first examples of the bracketed kneeling windows (designed by **Michelangelo**) that became all the rage on Florentine palazzi and to this day enrage tourists who bump into them. In the 18th century, the Riccardi family had the façade lengthened by seven windows on the Via Camillo Cavour side. The Riccardi also had the first-floor galleria designed. You will notice that they were not exactly into minimalism. The whole room glistens with gold leaf and the ceiling fresco by Luca Giordano is sumptuous, with curvaceous figures looming out at you. Entitled *The Apotheosis of the Medici,* it was commissioned to commemorate the original owners of the palazzo. All that remains of the extensive Medici art collection once installed in the palazzo is in the **Capella di Benozzo Gozzoli**, also referred to as the *"Cappella dei Magi."* The tiny chapel contains important frescoes by 15th-century artist Benozzo Gozzoli depicting the *Journey of the Magi,* in which various members of the Medici family take part in a delightful procession through the Tuscan countryside. Because the chapel really is very small, staff here restrict entry to 15 people every 15 minutes. ♦ Admission. M, Tu, Th-Su, 9AM-7PM. Via Camillo Cavour 3. 2760340

52 Mercato di San Lorenzo (San Lorenzo Market)

Don't be fooled by the low-rent, almost souklike air of this outdoor clothing and souvenir market, which snakes through a number of streets. The simple canvas-covered vendors' stalls, called *bancarelle,* are equipped with electricity, cellular phones, and charge card machines. (Many of the free-spirited vendors also have near-perfect American accents, one product of their nocturnal trysts with junior-year-abroad coeds who, along with Italian and foreign tourists, make up the market's clientele.) Best buys are woolens, scarves of all sizes and designs, gloves of all leathers and linings, and other leather goods. Also be on the lookout for (besides pickpockets) the latest in T-shirts and sweaters. Bartering is a thing of the past, but customers buying more than one item and paying with cash should give it a try. ♦ M-Sa Mar-Oct (no midday closing); Tu-Sa (no midday closing) Nov-Feb. Piazza San Lorenzo, Via dell'Ariento, and surrounding streets

53 San Giovanni Evangelista

Begun in 1579 by **Bartolommeo Ammannati** and finished in 1661 by **Alfonso Parigi the Younger**, this small neighborhood church was restored after World War II along with Ammannati's Santa Trinità Bridge. ♦ Via Martelli and Via dei Gori

54 Frette

This Milan-based firm has been supplying the world with luxury bed, bath, and table linens and lingerie for more than 125 years. Traditional, classic, and contemporary prints appear on beautiful quality cottons, silks, and linens. ♦ M afternoon; Tu-Sa. Via Camillo Cavour 2 (at Via dei Pucci). 211369

55 Viceversa

There is a sleek, often humorous touch of Milanese design evident here in the tabletop objects that look like they belong in a modern art museum. A back room is dedicated to designs by Alessi for the kitchen and beyond, one of the better-known home-design labels in this signature-obsessed consumer culture. ♦ M-F, Sa morning Mar-Oct; M afternoon, Tu-Sa Nov-Feb. Via Ricasoli 53r (between Via dei Pucci and Via degli Alfani). 2398281

56 Palazzo Niccolini

This 16th-century palazzo by **Baccio d'Agnolo** is decorated with 19th-century *sgraffiti,* the two-tone stucco designs popular during the Renaissance. Go inside to see the two courtyards, and if the *portier* will let you in, you can also admire the 17th- and 18th-century frescoes. ♦ Via dei Servi 15 (between Via dei Pucci and Via degli Alfani)

57 Museo di Leonardo

Somehow Florence just seems to do museums better than anywhere else in the world. This is one of the newest and most fun. Yes, that's right: fun. Bring your children here, whatever age they are, and they will have more fun than you could ever imagine possible in a museum. And they'll learn. This is an interactive museum. Well laid out, with generous space, it holds dozens of beautifully made, fully functional reproductions of Leonardo da Vinci's famous (and not so famous) inventions. There's his rolling mill for metal sheets, his printing machine, and his hydraulic saw. And his cannon! There are his flying machines—one is a prototype helicopter (sadly, you can't fly in them here)—and a sort of bird he made for the theater that flies across the room balanced on a rope. There is the famous Archimedean screw, an olive oil press, and a system for walking on water! If anyone could walk on water (close relatives of God aside), it would be Leonardo. This is the man who, in 1495, invented the first humanoid robot. There are huge blowups of his manuscripts, some drawings, and, of course, the Vitruvian Man, now set forever in the public imagination as a clue in a fictional murder mystery. Come here and marvel at the sheer genius of the man. For me, this is so much more impressive than the *Mona Lisa.* ♦ Daily, 10:30AM-6:30PM. Via dei Servi 66. 282966. www.mostredileonardo.com

The Medici always had parties in a grand style and made sure no guest went away hungry. For Lorenzo de' Medici's wedding to Clarice Orsini, five banquets were held in the space of three days, featuring 150 cuts of veal, 4,000 capons, and many barrels of wine, both Italian and foreign.

58 Brunellesco

This tiny bar spills its (generally young) customers out under the trees and canopies of the square in good weather. It is unusual—and welcome—in that it is one of very few places to offer freshly made (to order) vegetable and fruit juices. A pile of top-quality carrots and apples, celery and fennel, and ginger and lemons sit beside their juicing machine, and you simply ask for the mix you want. They also offer soy and rice milk, herbal teas, and excellent Italian coffee, and their panini come filled not just with prosciutto and cheese, but with (should you wish) tofu as well. They do bagels and pastries, and there are newspapers to sit and read. Needless to say, there is a full bar on offer too! ♦ M-W, F-Su, noon till 10:30PM. Via degli Alfani 69r

58 Rotonda di Brunelleschi

This rather academic-looking octagonal church was begun by **Brunelleschi** sometime after 1433. It was to have been the Rotonda di Santa Maria degli Angioli and lined with chapels—and would have been one of his most original works if the money hadn't run out. Rendered usable in 1936, the building now houses the **University of Florence**'s **Centro Linguistico**. ♦ Via degli Alfani (at Via del Castellaccio)

59 Palazzo Giugni

Bartolommeo Ammannati's palazzo, built about 1577, has a lovely fresco, *Allegory of Art,* in its courtyard. ♦ Via degli Alfani 48 (between Via della Pergola and Via dei Fibbiai)

60 Centrale

$ The young French owner of this homey 18-room hotel is responsible for the attention to detail and palpable charm here. A regal Renaissance palazzo houses this quiet oasis, with classical music wafting through the lobby and soothing pastel-painted guest rooms. Many have views of **San Lorenzo**'s cupola, and 15 have private baths. An abundant buffet breakfast will sustain you through hours of shopping at the city's largest—and noisiest—outdoor market just steps away. ♦ Via dei Conti 3 (between Via dell'Alloro and Piazza Madonna degli Aldobrandini), second floor. 215761; fax 215216. www.pensionecentral.it

61 San Lorenzo

Built on the site of a church consecrated in 393 by St. Ambrose and enlarged in the Romanesque era, the present exterior (which was developed 1418-1421 by **Filippo Brunelleschi**, initiated soon thereafter, and completed 1447-1460 by **Antonio Manetti**, though lacking a finished façade, is one of the handsomest piles of brick and stone in Italy. When viewed by day from a few paces behind the shoulders of the overlooked 16th-century monument to Giovanni delle Bande Nere (by Baccio Bandinelli) in **Piazza San Lorenzo**, its jumble of curves and angles seems almost Byzantine, a Florentine Hagia Sophia looming over a veritable souk, a rich visual backdrop for the heartbreaking bells that ring from **Ferdinando Ruggieri**'s Baroque campanile. When the piazza is deserted on Monday morning and at night, it is easy to imagine the cloaked Medici and their minions hurrying off to attend to affairs of state, or even affairs of the heart.

Financed by the Medici, the great cake of **San Lorenzo** was never iced (they rejected **Michelangelo**'s model for the façade, now on display at **Casa Buonarroti**) but filled instead with the fruits of the best artists of the era, which became almost too candied for the contemporary palate in the *pietra dura* extravaganza of the **Cappella dei Principi** (see below). Brunelleschi's interior magnificently lives up to the name of the *pietra serena* (literally "serene stone," a warm-colored stone) used throughout. The inside wall of the façade is by Michelangelo. In the second chapel on the right is the 16th-century *Marriage of the Virgin* [1] (numbers refer to floor plan) by Rosso Fiorentino. Just before the transept are two 15th-century bronze pulpits [2, 3] designed by Donatello; behind the right one is a 15th-century marble tabernacle [4] by Desiderio da Settignano, and behind the left one is the 16th-century fresco *The Martyrdom of St. Lawrence* [5] by Bronzino. In a chapel in the left transept is Filippo Lippi's 15th-century *Annunciation* [6]; Brunelleschi's harmonious **Sagrestia Vecchia** (Old Sacristy), based on the architectural convention of a circle within a square, is just ahead. It was decorated by Donatello in the 15th century with medallions depicting the life of St. John the Evangelist, roundels of the Evangelists, and doors of the Apostles and Martyrs. To the left of the **Old Sacristy** entrance is Andrea Verrocchio's 15th-century monument to Piero and Giovanni de' Medici [7]. ♦ Piazza San Lorenzo (between Borgo San Lorenzo and Via del Canto de' Nelli)

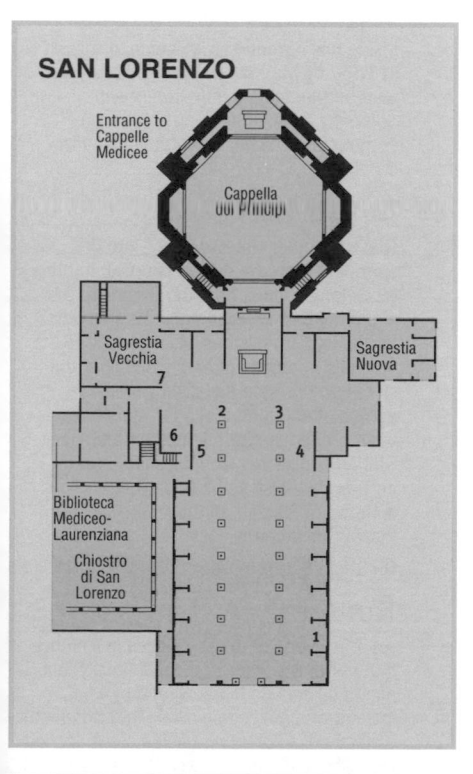

Within San Lorenzo:

Cappelle Medicee (Medici Chapels)

The entrance to these chapels leads to the **Cappella dei Principi** (Chapel of the Princes), built in 1604 for Giovanni de' Medici by **Matteo Nigetti** and home of the Medici mausoleum, which once ranked among the must-see monuments in Florence—the Graceland of its day. Despite the proto-psychedelic brightness of the mother-of-pearl, lapis lazuli, coral, and other *pietra dura* (semi-precious stone) materials, the chapel leaves the modern eye cold, a frozen object lesson in grandiosity. Note the octagonal plan (see floor plan left), similar in style to the **Baptistry**, the **Tribune room** in the **Uffizi**, and the cupola of the **Duomo**. By contrast, the **Sagrestia Nuova** (New Sacristy) begun by **Michelangelo** in 1521 and completed by **Vasari** and **Ammannati** in 1555, seems almost restful, though Michelangelo designed it as an uneasy response in part to **Brunelleschi**'s **Sagrestia Vecchia** (see above). It contains the tombs of four more members of the Medici family—two Lorenzos and two Giulianos. Lorenzo Il Magnifico (the Magnificent) and his brother Giuliano (killed in the **Duomo** during the Pazzi Conspiracy) lie in the simple tomb opposite the altar. On top of it is Michelangelo's *Madonna and Child*. The remains of the more grandiose, but less important, 16th-century Lorenzo and Giuliano de' Medici are in the more elaborate tombs to the left and right, from which Ammannati took the unusual curve for his Ponte Santa Trinità. The tomb of Lorenzo, Duke of Urbino, on the left of the altar is crowned with Michelangelo's reclining allegorical statues *Dawn* and *Dusk*; opposite, the tomb of Giuliano, Duke of Nemours, has *Night* and *Day*. Michelangelo is said to have been brooding about the decline of the Florentine Republic when he made these sculptures; it's unclear what he was thinking when he painted the remarkably spontaneous frescoes in a room beneath the sacristy. Discovered in 1976, the room is now open to the public. ♦ Admission. Tu-Su, 8:15AM-5PM; 8:30AM-1:50PM on holidays. Piazza Madonna degli Aldobrandini (between Via dei Conti and Via del Canto de' Nelli). 2388602

Chiostro di San Lorenzo (Cloister of San Lorenzo)

A remarkably tranquil break from the bustling market outside, the cloisters (note the views of the **Duomo** and the dome of the **Cappella dei Principi**) lead to the **Biblioteca Medicea-Laurenziana** (Laurentian Library), which was begun in 1524 by **Michelangelo** and completed in 1578 by **Vasari** and **Ammannati**.

The *pietra serena* is less serene here in the Mannerist vestibule, which gives a dramatic slant on the classical elements rediscovered during the Renaissance in anticipation of the Baroque. Things settle down once again inside the library, where the Medici motifs on the wooden ceiling are echoed on Tribolo's marble floor. Michelangelo designed the reading benches. Works on display from the rare book collection (begun by Cosimo Il Vecchio) include the *Medici Virgil* and autographs of Petrarch, Poliziano, Machiavelli, and Napoleon. ♦ Free. M-Sa morning.

62 Palazzi Pucci

Historians have attributed the design of these connected palazzi to **Bartolommeo Ammannati** and **Paolo Falconieri**. Note the coats of arms of Cardinal Pucci and Leo X (a Medici pope), the latter badly deteriorated. The Emilio Pucci boutique—once located within—was relocated around the corner on Via Ricasoli, following the death of the Marchese Emilio Pucci in 1992. The palazzo is still used for administration offices and as residential quarters for the Pucci family. ♦ Via dei Pucci 2-6 (between Via dei Servi and Via Ricasoli)

63 Hong Kong

★$$ None of the Chinese restaurants in Florence are on a par with those in the rest of the West—or with this one, formerly known as **Fior di Loto**. The names of some of the dishes have been Italianized (the spring rolls appear on the menu as *cannelloni primavera*), but the Beijing specialties remain the same. Dim sum become *ravioli al vapore,* and desserts include not only *frutta fritta* (assorted fried fruit), but also *gelato fritta*—fried ice cream! There is also a grappa-like *digestivo* called *mautai* on offer. Fortissimo! The Italian word for chopsticks is *bastoncini*. If you really want to enter into the spirit of things, there is a shop right next door selling Chinese clothes, shoes, and accessories. ♦ M-W, Th-Su, lunch and dinner. Via dei Servi 35r (between Via dei Pucci and Via degli Alfani). 2398235

64 Dino Bartolini

This shop stocks a vast array of Italian housewares and unabashedly displays high-tack cookie jars alongside genuinely high-tech contemporary designs by Alessi and others. ♦ M afternoon, Tu-F, Sa morning July-Aug; Tu-Sa Sept-June. Via dei Servi 30r (at Via Maurizio Bufalini). 211895

65 San Michelino

Inside this Baroque-style church, designed in 1660 by **Michele Pacini**, at the second altar on the right, is *Holy Family with Saints* by Florentine Mannerist Jacopo Pontormo. ♦ Via dei Servi (at Via Maurizio Bufalini)

66 Borgo San Lorenzo

There are other streets feeding into the sprawling **Mercato di San Lorenzo**, but this block-long conduit from the **Duomo** to the church of **San Lorenzo** prepares shoppers for the retail maelstrom. As a prelude to the market's hundreds of awninged stalls, the stores on this strip are slightly more upmarket and formal and for years have been predominantly oriented toward shoes, with an occasional clothing shop thrown in. There are also some bookstores. ♦ Between Piazza San Giovanni and Piazza San Lorenzo

On Borgo San Lorenzo:

Nuti

★$ This is one of the few places in Florence that not only serves food continuously, but allows customers to eat what they want, instead of a full-course meal. They bone their *bistecca alla fiorentina* (grilled steak drizzled with olive oil), offer *ravioli alla Nuti* (with cream and walnuts), and serve spaghetti with clams, shrimp, and mussels in a spicy tomato

The Best

Mary Westerman Bulgarella

Textile and Costume Conservator

My favorite places and activities vary from season to season and year to year. I never tire of Florence, and I can always discover something new and exciting. Lots of my "haunts" and treasures are found off the beaten path, so I suggest to anyone to explore.

One of my favorite summer nighttime activities is stopping at the local watermelon stand for a fresh slice (**Giacomo** is our closest one on the corner of Via dello Statuto and Via XX Settembre—very close to the **Fortezza da Basso**). In the autumn he sells porcini mushrooms, in the early winter the *best* roasted chestnuts, and at Christmas he sells the *best* trees!

Culturally speaking, I like to go to exhibitions way after the opening date to avoid the crowds and enjoy the show. I also go to some smaller, less touristy museums from time to time, such as the **Museo Stibbert**, **Museo Salvatore Ferragamo**, and the **Cappella Brancacci** (Masaccio frescoes in the **Santa Maria del Carmine**). On Monday when the state-run museums are closed, it's fun to roam around and see the outdoor monuments and take the time to visit churches.

Shopping is one of my favorite pastimes, and I could probably write my own book on the art of shopping in Florence. My theory here is go into any store, no matter what it looks like from the outside or what you see in the window. You never know what goodies lie within! Lots of foreigners do not know that Tuesday is market day in Florence at the **Cascine** park. If you like to market shop, it's a must!

sauce. They also have another Nuti right across the street. Things just keep getting "Nuti-er" around here! There is a vast choice of other dishes, but most locals come for the pizza. ♦ Tu-Su, lunch and dinner. No. 39r. 210410

67 Teatro Niccolini

This 17th-century theater, modern on the inside, is one of the most active in Florence. ♦ Via Ricasoli 5 (between Piazza del Duomo and Via dei Biffi). 213282

68 Ospedale di Santa Maria Nuova

Florence's oldest hospital was founded in 1287 by Folco Portinari (coincidentally the father of Beatrice, Dante's beloved). Its portico, perhaps designed by **Bernardo Buontalenti**, contains busts of the Medici; inside the portico are frescoes by the 16th-century artist Taddeo Zuccari and the 17th-century artist Pomarancio. Within the hospital complex itself are the 15th-century church of **Sant'Egidio** and the former monastery of **Santa Maria degli Angeli**, as well as a 15th-century fresco of the *Crucifixion* by Andrea del Castagno. ♦ Piazza di Santa Maria Nuova 1 (between Via Sant'Egidio and Via Maurizio Bufalini)

69 Teatro della Pergola

Court spectacles took place in a wooden theater built on this spot by **Ferdinando Tacca** in 1656. Subsequently rebuilt more than once, the present 18th-century structure by **Giulio Mannaioni** was heavily altered in the 19th century. It is still one of the city's busiest theaters. ♦ Via della Pergola 12-32 (between Via Sant'Egidio and Via Nuova de' Caccini). 2479651

70 Museo di Firenze Com'Era

This museum recounts the history of the city's growth from the Renaissance on, displaying topographical maps, prints, and paintings. Its grounds, the **Giardino delle Oblate**, are peaceful proof that even today Florence hasn't grown by too many leaps and bounds. ♦ Admission. F-Tu, 9AM-2PM. Via dell'Oriuolo 4 (between Via Sant'Egidio and Via Folco Portinari). 2616545

71 Teatro dell'Oriuolo

Another of Florence's theaters, this house presents plays primarily in Italian. The theater and its street take their name from an old Florentine word for clock. ♦ Via dell'Oriuolo 31 (between Piazza G. Salvemini and Via del Proconsolo). 2340507

SANTA CROCE

The church of **Santa Croce** is where Lucy Honeychurch becomes flustered in E. M. Forster's novel *A Room with a View,* not having brought along her *Baedeker.* These days, most of the frustration in Santa Croce comes from tourists not having brought along their credit cards to the area's numerous leather and souvenir stores.

Since Lucy Honeychurch's time (not to mention that of Michelangelo, who lived in the neighborhood as a boy), Santa Croce has changed from a place of lowlife to a place of hard sell. Shady ladies used to operate in the area between the churches of Santa Croce and **Sant'Ambrogio**, and the debtors' prison once occupied the site of the **Teatro Verdi.** While much has remained the same (prisons still occupy its eastern end, and minor drug dealing in Florence currently occurs around the area of **Borgo Allegri** near **Piazza dei Ciompi**), the area continues to be gentrified. **Via Ghibellina** has become something of a restaurant row for all budgets; other entrepreneurs are opening shops and restaurants in the surrounding streets. Once one is off the well-trodden tourist track between the parking lots on the *viali* and the leather shops surrounding **Piazza Santa Croce**, the area can still be a rather pleasant place for a stroll.

---

1 Cimitero degli Inglesi (English Cemetery)

This Protestant burial ground contains the mortal remains of such immortals as Elizabeth Barrett Browning, Frances Trollope, and the American preacher and abolitionist Theodore Parker. ♦ Piazzale Donatello (between Viale Antonio Gramsci and Viale Giacomo Matteotti)

2 Palazzo Panclatichi Ximenes

Enlarged in 1620 by **Gherardo Silvani**, this palazzo was the residence of the architects **Giuliano** and **Antonio da Sangallo**, who built it circa 1499. Napoleon slept here in 1796. ♦ Borgo Pinti 68 (at Via Giuseppe Giusti)

3 Hotel Liana

$ Housed in a 19th-century palazzo once occupied by the British embassy and now decorated in Art Nouveau style, this hotel has 26 peaceful rooms (all but three with private baths), many of them facing a garden planted with lonesome pines. There's a breakfast room, but no restaurant. A nearby garage offers discount parking. ♦ Via Vittorio Alfieri 18 (between Piazza Massimo d'Azeglio and Viale Antonio Gramsci). 245303; fax 2344596

4 Hotel Regency

$$$$ There's something refreshingly un-Florentine about the air of respectability suffusing this elegant hotel in a 19th-century palazzo: It could be that the colors of the décor have taken William Morris to an enthusiastic extreme, or that the tranquil green expanse of the shady **Piazza Massimo d'Azeglio** outdoors is disturbingly rare for this city of stone. There are flowers all over the place, inside and out. If you need to relax, there can hardly be a better place to do so without leaving the city. ♦ Piazza Massimo d'Azeglio 3 (between Via Silvio Pellico and Via Vittorio Alfieri). 245247; fax 2346735

Within the Hotel Regency:

Relais Le Jardin

★★★$$$ In two dazzlingly decorated dining rooms (one overlooking a garden that offers warm-weather seating, the other with a zodiac painted on the ceiling), chef Paolo Bisogno offers refined regional cooking from all over Italy and quality well above what you'd expect from a hotel restaurant. Some recurrent examples are *risotto alla milanese* (a creamy rice and saffron dish from Milan) and *orecchiette con broccoli* (ear-shaped pasta and broccoli, a specialty of Apulia). ♦ M-Sa, lunch and dinner. Reservations required. Piazza Massimo d'Azeglio 5. 245247

5 Santa Maria Maddalena de' Pazzi

The highlight of this church—rebuilt 1480-1492 by **Giuliano da Sangallo** for the Pazzi family and dedicated to St. Mary Magdalene—is Perugino's fresco of the *Crucifixion* in the chapter house. In the church itself are paintings by 17th-century Neapolitan artist Luca Giordano (on either

side of the high altar) and a modern stained-glass window by Isabella Rouault (in the fourth chapel on the right), which is a hint that the church is now in the hands of French Franciscans. ♦ Donation. Tu-Su. Borgo Pinti 58 (between Via dei Pilastri and Via della Colonna). 2478420

6 Acquacotta

★★$$ The signature dish of this warm Tuscan trattoria is *acquacotta*—not cooked water, as its name translates, but thick slices of toasted Tuscan bread smothered in vegetable soup and topped with a poached egg. The rest of the menu features traditional Tuscan fare. ♦ M-Sa, lunch and dinner. Via dei Pilastri 51r (between Via de' Pepi and Via Fiesolana). 242907

7 Hotel Monna Lisa

$$$$ Look up the road and you won't notice this place. And that would be a mistake. This old palazzo was built, in part, before 1300 and is thought to have been a convent. By 1439 it was the home of the Ferranti family, and Joseph, Patriarch of Constantinople, 23 Greek metropolitan bishops, many theologians, and several scholars were the palazzo's first guests—although I don't expect they paid. In the early 1500s the palazzo passed to the Neri family, and Filippo Neri was born here in 1515 (thought to be in room 19 or 21, in case you are a particular fan!). Neri's portrait, along with those of four other past owners, is still in the hotel lobby. The palazzo is currently owned by the Ciardi Dupre family, who turned it into a hotel in 1956, and the Monna Lisa houses many of their personal collection of antiques and original oil portraits. The floors are still original *cotto fiorentino* from the 1500s, as are the wooden ceilings in the sitting rooms and some of the bedrooms. A huge painting in the sitting room near the staircase is *Golden Rain* (the sifting of wheat through sieves in the old Sardinian method) by Gaetano Spinelli in 1929. Opposite this is a rough marble of Giambologna's famous *Rape of the Sabine Women*. It was this work that won the competition for the award to make the sculpture, now in the Piazza della Signoria. The ceiling of the loggia here was painted by Bernadino Poccetti Barbatelli (1542–1612) and is yet to be restored. His other works can be seen in Santa Maria Novella, San Marco, and the entrance vault to Santi Annunziata Cloisters, The sculptures around the hotel are by a distant relative of the owners, neoclassicist Giovanni Dupre. All the public rooms are simply lovely. The courtyard and garden are a a joy to sit in during warm weather. The 25 rooms (classic, superior, junior suites, and suites) are less gloriously lavish, but still very pleasant, many with whirlpool bath and all with direct dial, Internet, minibar, hair dryer, and TV. There is also a small gym and solarium. The American bar is a place that will have you rushing back from a day in town to relax with a cocktail before dinner. ♦ Borgo Pinti 27 (between Via Sant'Egidio and Via Nuova de' Caccini). 2479751. www.monnalisa.it

8 Da Noi

★$ A smart little hybrid place for foodies, Da Noi is part deli and part café. Anything on the menu can be bought to take away, so you could taste test a few dishes and then take out your favorite to eat tomorrow. It is all good, homemade fare and the menu is surprisingly wide-ranging, from *crostini* (little crisp bits of bread with an assortment of toppings) through homemade sauces, mixed antipasti platters, soups (like cream of yellow pumpkin), salads, and interesting, traditional main courses such as osso buco and smoked turkey with walnut sauce. The inside is full of natural woods and great smells. Service is helpful and smiling, and while new, the place seems to have a regular clientele already (always a good sign). Of course, you could just have a great cup of coffee and a slice of their crumbly orange and almond tart. It's a great place to pop in for a short break. ♦ M, Th, F, lunch and dinner; W, Sa, lunch only. Via Fiesolana 46

9 Mago Merlin Tea House

★★$ If you are all coffeed out, then come and relax at this temple to tea. The atmosphere is definitely east of Italy, with one room strewn with huge cushions and laid with thick carpet. You must remove your shoes before entering this room. If you prefer to remain shod, you can drink tea and eat delicious pastries and cakes at one of Merlin's sweet little tables. Teas have been brewed here since 1977 and come as "classic" teas (China, Assam, Darjeeling, etc.), special "mixtures" of the house (spiced chai, for example), tea "cocktails" (with rum, whiskey, or other spirits), and herbal and medicinal teas. There is also a list of *pozioi*—teas that can be "prescribed" for you, according to your personal and emotional state. Hookah pipes (contents legal and herbal only) are available for those who would like to smoke. Poetry readings, belly dancing, theatrical events, and music are on offer on winter evenings, and—almost best of all—you can have your tea leaves read once you have drunk your fill! ♦ Daily, 5PM-2AM. Via de Pilastri 31r. 242970

10 Ruth's

★$$ Right next door to the **Jewish Temple** is this, Florence's best-known kosher restaurant. The food has a generally Middle Eastern bias; there is a vegetarian couscous on offer alongside a *caponata alla giudea* (sweet-and-sour vegetable stew), and of course there is smoked salmon. Puddings are predictably serious, and blintzes, strudel, and halvah are featured. ♦ Daily, except Friday PM and Saturday. Lunch, 12:30PM-2:30PM; dinner, 8PM-10:30PM. Reservations recommended. Via Luigi Carlo Farini 2A. 2480888

11 Tempio Israelitico (Jewish Temple)

The first stone laid for Florence's synagogue came from Jerusalem; the rest is a fanciful neo-Moorish pile of intricately carved, particolored stone topped with a copper dome. It was constructed 1874-1882 to the designs of **Mariano Falcini**, **Marco Treves**, and **Vincenzo Micheli**. ♦ Call for appointment. M-Th, Su, 10AM-1PM, 2PM-4PM; F, 10AM-1PM. Via Luigi Carlo Farini 4 (between Via dei Pilastri and Piazza Massimo d'Azeglio). 245252

12 Sbigoli Terrecotte

Terra-cotta—plain, glazed, and painted—is the specialty of this well-known shop, which stocks earthenware from all over Tuscany. Reliable shipping can be arranged, though it can double the price. If you're interested in learning this craft yourself, ask about the ceramic classes that are held at the shop's *bottega* (Via di Camaldoli 10r, between Piazza Torquato Tasso and Via dell'Orto, Oltrarno). ♦ M-F, Sa morning Mar-Oct; M afternoon, Tu-Sa Nov-Feb. Via Sant'Egidio 4r (between Borgo Pinti and Via della Pergola). 2479713; fax 2479713

13 Pentola dell'Oro

★★★$ Another of Florence's treasures, this place looks like a tiny run-of-the-mill local trattoria. But finding it is like finding a perfect pearl in an oyster. The chef/patron is Giuseppe Alessi, a man who started as an artist and musician, began the study of the history of Italian cooking, and in 1985 published one of the seminal works of culinary history—*The Etruscans: The Legend at the Table*. He has written regularly in the Italian press on Italian cuisine and its history and even took on the Florentine local government for funding to host scholarly dinners to explore and discuss the history of cuisine. In 1988, Alessi opened the Pentola dell'Ora. Here you can taste masterful cooking, cooking that ranges through the traditional, the innovative, and the genuinely historical. Yes, the proof of the Renaissance pudding recipe is in the eating. And you can eat it here. The ground floor is nicknamed *"l' Bettolino"* (the little tavern). Here, at friendly, communal tables under a wonderful old dark wood ceiling, you can enjoy a fresh handmade cheese in a sweet-sour marinade on arugula salad, or a *risottino delicato sui porri* (a small, surprisingly light risotto with leeks). There is still the marvelous tripe and *lampredotto* (cow intestine) that Giuseppe and his chefs de cuisine Margherita Alessi and Anna Berti (who describe themselves as his "right and left arms") do so well, along with other traditional main courses such as *strachetti di manzo* (strips of tender beef served with roast vegetables). Save some room for the *torta alla crema sciantilli con le fragole* (chantilly cream tart with strawberries)—it's luscious!

Downstairs, Alessi and his team let their inner Renaissance chefs out to play in *lo Studiolo*, with a menu that draws on Giuseppe's vast knowledge of historical cuisine. First courses include *carabazada alla fiorentina*—fabulously velvety yellow pumpkin soup delicately flavored with a mix of spices and aromatics dating back to the Renaissance—and pappardelle that come with what is described as *"sugo alchemico di cinghiale,"* an "alchemist's sauce of boar." The star main course is, in season, the legendary *peposo di Brunelleschi* (a peppery beef stew much beloved by the great architect, and which he used to have sent up to him in pots as he worked on the Duomo). Even vegetarians can dine fabulously here. The *tegamaccio* is a delicious vegetarian stew with fresh basil, from Maremma. Even ubiquitous dishes are different here. *"Il mito della cucina Toscana"*—"the legendary Tuscan dish"—*bistecca alla fiorentina* is cooked "bloody, in accordance with the ancient ritual pagan sacrifice." The desserts are mouthwatering; some, like the *semifreddo Mediceo,* are cooked according to those 17th-century recipes. This is a very, very special restaurant. Oh, one more thing: if you are in Florence on New Year's Eve, the candlelit *Cenone dell Ultimo dell Anno* (New Year's Eve Dinner) here is absolutely the only way to celebrate. ♦ M-Sa, dinner. No credit cards accepted. Via di Mezzo 26r (between Piazza Sant'Ambrogio and Via de' Pepi). 241821. www.lapentoladelloro.it

14 Hotel J & J

$$$$ Housed in a 16th-century monastery, this hotel still provides an air of peace and tranquillity in a just-off-the-beaten-track part of town. In the public areas as well as in the 20 guest rooms, soft modern furnishings, including plenty of pillows, play off the solid wooden ceilings and stonework. There's no restaurant. ♦ Via di Mezzo 20 (between Piazza Sant'Ambrogio and Via de' Pepi). 263121; fax 240282

15 Palazzo Altoviti

The portrait busts of famous Florentines (Dante, Petrarch, Boccaccio, Amerigo Vespucci, etc.) adorning the façade of this 16th-century palazzo attributed to **Baccio Valori** earned it the nickname *"Palazzo dei Visacci"* ("of the ugly faces"). ♦ Borgo degli Albizi 18 (between Piazza San Pier Maggiore and Via del Proconsolo)

16 Palazzo degli Albizi

This is considered the most imposing of the palazzi of the Albizi family, one of many Medici rivals. Built in the 16th century, it is attributed to **Gherardo Silvani**. ♦ Borgo degli

The Best

Faith Willinger

Food Writer/Longtime Florence Resident

Best *caffè*—**Caffè Italiano**. I stop by daily if I can for the best coffee and—in the summer months—the best fruit juices mixed with the café's subtly fizzy *acqua antica*.

Best restaurant—**Il Cibrèo**. If it's on the menu, don't pass up the *passatelli in brodo,* homemade pastalike strips in a mixed meat broth—Italian comfort food.

Best wine bar—**FuoriPorta**. I prefer sitting outdoors, and order from their excellent selection of Chianti Classico wines.

Best bookstore—**Pitti Gola e Cantina**. Its discerning selection of wines and gourmet foods is worth the visit, and I find that the selection of food and cookbooks, as well as guidebooks on Tuscany and Italy, is the best in town. Many are available in English.

Best markets—**Mercato di Santo Spirito** may not have many farmers, but those who show, show up with the best; it's one of Florence's most authentic markets. Saturday morning is the best time to go. The **Mercato di Sant'Ambrogio** is much bigger and busier, the perfect prelude to lunch at nearby Il Cibrèo.

Best accessories shopping—I have an ever-growing collection of Moschino scarves, almost all of which I've chosen from the varied and colorful selection of accessories at **Aramis**. This is easy and fun souvenir shopping.

Best housewares store—**Viceversa** offers the greatest variety of of-the-moment contemporary home design items and makes souvenir shopping for difficult or fussy friends a breeze. **La Ménagère** has an equally good selection, but of more classic, traditional wares in an appropriately Old World setting.

Best olive oil—While you're at Pitti Gola e Cantina for books or FuoriPorta for a Chianti break, check out the stock dedicated to the region's best olive oils. The bottle should always state that it is bottled and produced at a particular estate, and give the year of harvest; never buy anything older than one year.

Best cheese—When visiting Tuscany's small towns, stop in any local *latteria* (dairy goods store) or food shop for a thick hunk of Pecorino cheese. If it is aged longer than 30 days—and usually most of it is—you'll have no problem getting it past US Customs.

Best informal lunch—I love the **Trattoria Casalinga** in my neighborhood (**Santo Spirito** in the **Oltrarno**). Unpretentious and reliable, its traditional Tuscan dishes are all great: Begin with the *ribollita* (white beans, bread, black cabbage, and onions) or *pappardelle alla lepre* (homemade noodle strips with a tomato-and-rabbit sauce.)

Albizi 12 (between Piazza San Pier Maggiore and Via del Proconsolo)

17 Palazzo degli Alessandri

Built in the 14th century, this is one of the oldest and most distinguished of the palazzi in this palazzo-populated area. ♦ Borgo degli Albizi 15 (between Piazza San Pier Maggiore and Via delle Seggiole)

18 I Ghibellini

★★$ Eat outdoors in the small and lovely piazza in the warm weather or inside at this clean and modern place known for its large selection of inexpensive and decent pizzas and pastas. ♦ M, Tu, Th-Su, lunch and dinner. Piazza San Pier Maggiore 8r (at Borgo degli Albizi). 214424

19 Loggia di San Pier Maggiore

This piece of real estate (it can hardly be called a building) is all that remains of the **Matteo Nigetti**-designed 17th-century church of **San Pier Maggiore**. (It's also called "San Piero"; Piero is a Tuscan diminutive for Pietro, or Peter.) The church was demolished in 1784, and its former loggia was subsequently altered with uncharacteristic architectural nonchalance. Two of its arches were filled in (the one on the left now houses a butcher shop), and a string of flats was built on top of it, the overall effect being rather more like devil-may-care Baroque Rome than rigid Renaissance Florence. The *piazzetta* is still one of the more colorful corners of the city, with a daily produce stand and outdoor tables at **I Ghibellini**. ♦ Piazza San Pier Maggiore and Via San Pier Maggiore

20 Vestri

Abandon calorie counting, all ye who enter here! *"Cioccolata d'Autore"* says the sign. And, oh, what chocolate!!! Handmade on the very premises, it comes in beautifully wrapped bars, in truffles and chunks, in ice creams and in *Bacione di Firenze* (rich chocolate bombs they call "big Florentine kisses"), even in a reproduction of Michelangelo's *David* (and don't think you'd be able to resist a nibble . . .). Absolutely best of all, it comes thick and intense and hot in little plastic cups. Florentines drink it with a little *peperoncino* (chili pepper) sprinkled on and mixed in. Try it. It is liquid heaven. Vestri now has a little ice-cream stall in its doorway, offering chocolate ice cream in several degrees of richness plus *affogato*—ice cream with topping of strawberries in syrup, mint syrup, or, best of all, hot chocolate. ♦ M-Sa, 10AM-8PM. Borgo degli Albizi 11r. www.cioccolateriavestri.com

21 Stand

OK, it's not very historical, but it *is* incredibly useful. Stand is a supermarket with good ready-to-eat fruit (all peeled and cored and nicely sliced, if that is how you like it), plus fresh whole fruit, prepared salads, fresh-baked bread, fish, meat, and a terrific deli counter. Plus everything else in packets and cans that you might expect. And a decent beverage section! ♦ M-Sa, 8AM-9PM; Su, 9AM-9PM. Via Pietrapiana 96

22 Piazza dei Ciompi

Woolworkers in medieval Florence, called *ciompi,* were a frustrated and rebellious lot who finally revolted in 1378, winning themselves the right to organize into guilds like the other professions. Their modern counterparts, in a sense, surly flea market vendors, occupy this piazza today, and on the last Sunday of the month they hold an outdoor market. At one end of the piazza is **Vasari**'s **Loggia del Pesce** (1567). It once housed a fish market in the center of Florence, but it was salvaged from the ill-advised urban renewal that created **Piazza della Repubblica** in the last century, and was reconstructed here in 1955. ♦ Tu-Sa (no midday closing); last Sunday of the month. At Via Pietrapiana, Via Martiri del Popolo, and Borgo Allegri

23 Il Pizziuolo

★★$ The simplicity in the name "The Pizza Maker" is the same simplicity you'll find in the perfect pizzas that come out bubbling and crusty from the full-throttle wood-burning ovens. Pizza is a Neapolitan institution, so when Carmine Calascione arrived from Naples with 30 years of experience and his own supply of oregano and garlic, Florence eagerly awaited his pizzeria's opening. They are now waiting for the next free table (and these are folks with reservations). Almost everyone seems to be digging into the lengthy menu's most uncomplicated selection, the *pizza margherita* made with fresh tomatoes, mozzarella, and oregano. ♦ M-Sa, lunch and dinner until midnight. Reservations required for dinner. No credit cards accepted. Via dei Macci 113r (between Via dell'Agnolo and Piazza Sant'Ambrogio). 241171

24 Sant'Ambrogio

This site has had churches on it since well before the 13th century, from which the present structure dates. The plain façade was applied in 1888. The interior, redone in 1716, contains a tabernacle by Mino da Fiesole housing some miraculous blood, a 15th-century fresco by Cosimo Rosselli depicting a procession in front of the original church façade, and a 15th-century panel by Alesso Baldovinetti, *Angels and Saints*. ♦ Piazza Sant'Ambrogio (at Borgo la Croce)

24 Cibrèo: Teatro del Sale

★★★★$$ Some things just defy description. The latest in the constellation of star-quality Cibrèo outlets is such a thing. What can be said is that coming here makes going to heaven a gamble—because heaven is probably going to be a disappointment after this place. The Teatro del Sale has been created out of what remains of an ancient convent. It is a deli and a restaurant, a theater and a place to relax and talk. It is also a kind of club—a "good-living society." Before entering, you sign a form agreeing to abide by the rules, including "to show respect to other members . . . ask before assuming," and to exchange news and information of interest from around the world—a great restaurant in your hometown, a new play that opened in New York, or a book that must be read. "Any member discovered in the act of non-communication," say the rules, "will not have membership renewed." Once inside, you first pass the shop where all manner of edible goodies are sold, most bearing the Cibrèo label. The interior is all polished wood floors and comfy chesterfields and armchairs, very clubby. And then it opens out into a full theater with stage, where every evening there is some kind of event—theater, music, a workshop, a "tasting," or a reading. You may wander at will and help yourself to wine, water, and coffee. Meals are everything you would expect from the Cibrèo kitchens and are served at a big table where guests help themselves. Have as much as you like. And you will like. There is always a big selection of hot and cold antipasti (all with absolutely top-quality fresh ingredients), followed by a succession of pasta and risotto dishes. There is always excellent salad, and *secondi* (main dishes) tend to be top-quality grills—lamb or chicken, beef or pork. Desserts are on little trays dotted around the place and usually feature fresh fruit. You can take as long as you like to linger . . . and can in fact stay all day relaxing, chatting, and enjoying life. There is nowhere like this in the world. And one does not often get the chance to write that. ♦ Daily, breakfast 9AM-11AM; lunch noon-2PM; dinner 7PM-9PM. Via dei Macci 111r. 2001492. www.teatrodelsale.com

25 Cibrèo

★★★★$$$ This restaurant offers not just a meal, but almost a relationship and certainly a delicious education in the art and craft of Tuscan cuisine. Fabbio Picchi's kitchen is a national treasure. Ask anyone who knows about food in Tuscany and he will rhapsodize about this place. You will find a tiny cluster of Cibrèo on this corner. The main restaurant is simply decorated, but exudes an air of quiet quality. Damask tablecloths, serious cutlery, elegant dried rose posies, candles on every table—even at lunch—and absolutely perfect service from a charming and knowledgeable staff give a hint of how good the food will be. And then you meet Christina. She comes to each and every table and talks her guests through the menu of the day, explaining and suggesting. There is no written menu. Every restaurant should throw away its menu and get a Christina. The antipasti are works of art—buttery polenta with a *ragù* of tuna . . . a *passata di peperoni gialli* (cream of yellow pepper) that seems to have captured the very soul of the pepper . . . an incredibly delicious salad of veal tripe. Main courses run the gamut from brilliantly executed peasant fare like *inzimino* (a spicy stew of calamari) through reconstructed peasant food like *collo di pollo* (neat medallions of chicken neck, boned and stuffed with a fabulously light mousse) to the most 21st-century cuisine—the sashimi-like marinated tuna being an example. These are tastes you will remember all your life. They even do a Tuscan kebab, the meats marinated for 24 hours in lemon juice and herbs and spit roasted to juicy perfection. Sweets—including a simple *panna cotta*—are to die for. The wine list is extensive and worth exploring, especially when you have the help of someone like Cibrèo's drop-dead gorgeous Alfonso to guide you. As you enter and leave, there is a little section where you can buy the wines and the sauces, olive oil, preserves, cookies, and even Fabbio's recipes in a small Cibrèo cookbook. ♦ Tu-Sa, lunch and dinner. Closed August. Via Andrea del Verrocchio 8r. Reservations necessary. 2341100.

26 Mercato di Sant'Ambrogio

Intended for neighborhood use, this market is more functional than its flamboyant counterpart, **Mercato di San Lorenzo**. It houses a few inexpensive stand-up lunch counters, along with kiosks where staples cost less than in other shops. Just outside are a number of stalls selling fresh farm produce and a ragtag assemblage of housewares and clothing. ♦ M-Sa, 8AM-1PM. Piazza L. Ghiberti (at Via Ferdinando Paolieri and Via Andrea del Verrocchio, and Via S. Verdiana and Via della Mattonaia)

> This is the fairest picture on our planet, the most enchanting to look upon, the most satisfying to the eye and spirit. To see the sun sink down, drowned in his pink and purple and golden floods, and overwhelm Florence with tides of color that make all fine lines dim and faint and turn the solid city to a city of dreams, is a sight to stir the coldest nature, and make a sympathetic one drunk with ecstasy.
>
> —Mark Twain

27 Cose Così

A full line of classic porcelain Tuscan ovenware made by Linea Tuscia is offered at this housewares shop, as well as such well-known names as Alessi and Villeroy & Boch. It features such items as a *fagioliera* for cooking beans, a boar's head-shaped dish for stews, and numerous baking dishes and casseroles. ♦ Tu-Su, 9AM-1PM and 4PM-8PM. Borgo la Croce 53r (between Piazza Cesare Beccaria and Via della Mattonaia). 2343474

28 Borghese Palace Art Hotel

$$ Get here while you can: given the quality of this place, prices are surely bound to go up. For starters, it is not just *called* the Borghese Palace, it is located *within* the Borghese Palace. At the time of writing, it had been open one day and Fabrizio Romeo, the gently worried-looking owner, was on his own in the place. But I still got the tour. The foyer is breathtaking—high vaulted ceilings, square brown leather seats the size of a New York block, Regency-style gilt and silk upholstered chairs, and a series of stunning sculptures arranged along each side of the hall to the tiny, ultra-chic bar. Your room (on the second or third floor) is reached via a central glass elevator, or by the open-plan stairway that curls around it like a ringlet. The marriage of ancient building and modern design works to incredible effect here. The 25 rooms are beautiful, and all have a bas-relief above the bed individually sculpted by the same artist responsible for the lobby artworks. You get a lot of space for your money here, which is another plus. The hotel has a lovely roof terrace with awe-inspiring views. At the other end of the building in the basement there is a small gym, a sauna, and a Turkish bath. Some of the stonework you run your hands over is actually Roman. The rest is relatively modern—medieval, in fact. Your generous buffet breakfast is served in the lovely marble-floored breakfast room and is included in the price. This is where I'll be staying next time I'm in Florence. ♦ Via Ghibellina 174r. 284363. www.borghesepalace.it

29 Danny Rock

★$$ This "pub," besides gathering a crowd of Florence's gilded youth, is one of the few places in the neighborhood for late-night crêpes, pizza, and hamburgers. ♦ Tu-Su, lunch and dinner until 1:30AM. Via dei Pandolfini 13r (at Via Matteo Palmieri). 2340307

30 Salimbeni

One of the best art and antiquarian bookshops in the country (with many titles in English), **Salimbeni** also operates a small press that produces Italian-interest books. ♦ M afternoon; Tu-Sa. Via Matteo Palmieri 14-16r (between Via Ghibellina and Via dei Pandolfini). 2340904

31 Palazzo Quaratesi

Look up at the lovely loggia with Doric columns in this 14th-century medieval palazzo. ♦ Via Matteo Palmieri and Via Ghibellina

32 Acqua al Due

★★★$ This unique, forever-crowded restaurant has found long-lasting success with its *assaggi* (tastings), as well as a full menu. The first-course *assaggio* may be different types of pasta paired with anything from tomato to mushrooms, eggplant, salmon, or zucchini (the choice is up to the kitchen); risotto may appear with Gorgonzola cheese, artichokes, or *sugo verde* made with green vegetables. Both salads and desserts are given the same *assaggio* treatment. The restaurant's other branch, interestingly enough, is in San Diego! ♦ Daily, dinner until 1AM. Reservations required. Via della Vigna Vecchia 40r (between Via Isola delle Stinche and Via dell'Acqua). 284170

33 Sam's Market

A little bit of America in the heart of Florence, Sam's Market stocks over 250 imported products to make Americans feel a little more at home in their city. So if you are having withdrawal symptoms from Reese's Pieces, Saltines, Cheez-it, Nutter Butter cookies, Mountain Dew, or root beer, then come down to Sam's. Betty Crocker, Heinz's 57 Varieties, Hellmann's Mayo, and Quaker Instant Oats are all there. And on Sundays it is rumored they do hot dogs that are the equal of anything you'll taste in the USA. ♦ M-F, 11AM-7PM; Sa, 11AM-3PM. Via Ghibellina 117r. 7189020. www.sams-market.com

34 Osteria del Caffè Italiano

★★★$$ The latest star of the gastronomic empire of the indefatigable Umberto Montano is this handsomely furnished rustic trattoria. Its simple name emphasizes the importance of the wine cellar's selection of Tuscan labels, but the location in a landmark 14th-century palazzo confirms that it is as much about historical ambience and simple dishes as about spirits. Try any of the homemade pastas or thick, grilled meats while indulging in a Chianti Classico Riserva or a Brunello di Montepulciano. The less formal (and less expensive) front room is warmed by rich 18th-century wooden panels and an open 17th-century hearth, where roast meats are prepared. It's a relaxing place to sip a glass of wine and nibble on slabs of homemade sausage and aged cheese during "off hours." ♦ Tu-Su, noon-1AM. Via Isola delle Stinche 11-13r (at Via della Vigna Vecchia). 289368

35 Il Pallottino

★★$$ The eponymous first course of this restaurant, *penne Pallottino,* is made with seven p's—penne, *porri,* pancetta, *pomodoro, peperoncino, panna,* and Parmigiano (tubular pasta, leeks, Italian bacon, tomato, hot pepper, cream, and Parmesan cheese). Expect good renditions of all the Florentine classics, from the typical soups (*ribollita*, with white cannellini beans, bread, and black cabbage; *pappa al pomodoro*, with tomatoes, bread, olive oil, and onions; and *zuppa di farro*, with barley) to the *bistecca alla fiorentina* (a slab of steak grilled, then drizzled with olive oil). The inexpensive lunchtime *menù turístico* is the latest draw. ♦ Tu-Su, lunch and dinner. Via Isola delle Stinche 1r (between Via delle Burella and Via della Vigna Vecchia). 28952573. www.trattoria.pallottino.com

35 Vivoli

One of Florence's best, and certainly its best-known, this *gelateria* can be found by following the discarded paper cups to their well-lit and jam-packed point of origin, a third-generation family business that prides itself on its ability to make lip-smacking ice cream out of the freshest ingredients. ♦ Tu-Su, 8AM-1AM. Closed January. No credit cards accepted. Via Isola delle Stinche 7r (between Via delle Burella and Via della Vigna Vecchia). 292334

36 San Simone

This 14th-century Gothic church was redone Baroque-style by **Gherardo Silvani** in 1630, but it retains some medieval frescoes as well as a terra-cotta garland in the style of the della Robbia family. ♦ Piazza San Simone and Via dei Lavatoi

37 Teatro Verdi

The neighborhood's ancient theatrical tradition is alive and well here. (The outlines of the Roman amphitheater may be traced by following the curves of Via Torta—"crooked street"—and Via Bentaccordi a block away.) The modern entrance to Florence's most popular theater leads to a 19th-century interior with a capacity of 3,000. ♦ Via Ghibellina 99 (at Via Giuseppe Verdi). 2396242

Taste of Tuscany

There is no such thing as Italian cookery—only a wonderful mix of Italian regional cuisines. And every Italian region thinks it has the finest cuisine. The Tuscans certainly have one of the most widely known and influential. It is powerful, rich, passionate stuff.

Antipasti

Typical Tuscan antipasti will include *crostini*, those little rounds of crisped bread lightly smeared with oil and scraped with garlic, then spread with a traditional soft liver pâté or perhaps a plate of local salami—*finocchiona* (a fat local salami flavored with fennel seeds), prosciutto *di cinta senese* (from Siena), or prosciutto *di cinghiale* (made with wild boar meat). Local salami and prosciutto tend to be darker and stronger in flavor than those from surrounding regions.

Primi

Famous Tuscan first courses include chunky thick soups that are, as the saying goes, "a meal in themselves." There is *ribollita* ("reboiled"), a delicious dish made from fresh vegetables (especially *cavolo nero*), beans, and bread. Then *pappa al pomodoro*, a similar, but lighter, summery soup made from bread and tomatoes and served either hot or cold. *Aquacotta* is made with thick slices of Tuscan bread covered in fresh vegetable soup and served with a lightly poached egg on top. *Carabaccia* is a wonderful sort of sweet-and-sour onion soup. In summer you should try *panzanella*, which has very much the same ingredients as *pappa al pomodoro*, but serves as a salad of summer tomatoes over bread with onion, vinegar, and oil. All of these soups and salads are traditionally served with a "*C'd'olio*, a curving splash of local oil.

There are some marvelous rich pasta dishes on the traditional Tuscan table, many with game sauces—like *pappardelle sulla lepre*, thick pasta ribbons in a sauce made from chunks of hare stewed with celery, tomato, onion, and bacon.

Secondi

Although meat is the first thing you think of as being Tuscan, there is a good tradition of fish cookery here. In *anguilla alla fiorentina*, regional cooks prepare eel with white wine and sage. *Anguilla marinata* is eel floured, then fried and left to marinate in a spicy vinegar. *Cieche* are newborn eels, fished from the rivers in springtime, fried in oil, and baked. *Cacciucco* is Tuscan fish soup made with a huge variety of local fish, cooked with chili, garlic, wine, and herbs and served over garlic *crostini*. The lovely legend behind the dish is that after a fisherman was killed at sea, his poor widow and children were starving. When the hunger became too much, she sent her children out to beg for food among their dead father's workmates. The fishermen were all poor, but each gave what he could—a little scrap of one thing or another . . . a few shrimp or a few shellfish . . . The woman collected the fish, adding everything she could find growing in her garden and a few spices from her larder. The wonderful smell from the pot brought all the neighbors around to find out what it was, and *cacciucco* was born!

Secondi Carne

Meat is the red heart of Tuscany. *Bistecca alla fiorentina* is a massive slab of prime Tuscan beef on the bone, gently massaged with local olive oil, expertly grilled over red-hot coals (and served *al sangue*, according to ancient tradition, although you can ask for it *ben cotto*, or well done. Or ruined, in other words.). *Arista alla fiorentina* is a hunk of pork loin, pierced with holes that are filled with fresh rosemary, pepper, and salt and spit roasted (the dish got its name when it was served to the Ecumenical Council in Florence in 1430 and the Greek bishops pronounced it *arista*, which is

38 L'Enoteca Pinchiorri

★★$$$$ I admit I have never eaten here—just watched and listened and sniffed. It is Florence's only Michelin-starred restaurant. And it has everything that normally comes with that coveted star status—a sumptuous setting in a Renaissance palazzo; tables set with Gambellara linen, Ricci di Alessandra silver, Reidel Crystal, and perfect floral centerpieces; and quasi-militarily immaculate service. Cuisine is in the talented hands of a Frenchwoman (I am sure this didn't harm the restaurant's Michelin prospects), Annie Feolde, and her French influence is apparent. Risotto is served with onions and frog's legs! Dishes are evolved and luxurious (but not overwhelmingly so)—you can start with sautéed sea scallops served with an eggplant puree, garlic, oregano and a stew of whelks; try red mullet with black olives, a potato and lemon cream, chickpeas, and pork crackling; or opt for turbot—which comes spit roasted or deep fried. One eye-catching suggestion is the Taleggio fondue with pear and licorice marmalade. There is a gloriously luxurious eight-course menu (with suggestions as to accompanying wines for each course) and—sweet-toothed travelers take note—four separate dessert menus. Giorgio Pinchiorri's wine list is encyclopedic and, with the help of L'Enoteca's sommelier, an education. If you want out-and-out luxury, and a revel in conspicuous consumption, then this is the

Greek for excellent!). In season you will find *lepre* (hare), *cinghiale* (boar), *coniglio* (rabbit), *capriuolo* (roebuck), and *cervo* (venison). In fact, most of them are used together in another traditional dish, *scottiglia*, a rich mixed stew of all sorts of game meat and birds cooked with tomato, herbs, wine, garlic, and onion.

Now, you cannot come to Tuscany (and most especially Florence) without confronting the question. Just try it. You might well not like it, but you might just be missing out on a wonderful eating experience. Good grief—hundreds of generations of Florentines can't *all* be wrong! *Trippa* and *lampredotto* are two different kinds of tripe. They are cooked *alla fiorentina* (in a rich tomatoey sauce) or simply *lesso* (poached in broth). The latter you eat with a slick of hot oil and a dollop of tangy fresh *salsa verde*. Now, when you have tried and enjoyed *trippa*, there is a whole new delicious world out there. Take a trip through the Mercato Centrale and discover *cervelli, mammella* and *polmone* (brains, udder, and lung).

Contorni

Vegetables here are good—*cavolo nero* (a kind of kale), *cardo* (cardoon), and, of course, porcini are beloved. As are the fat white beans (*fagioli*) that come cooked any number of ways. *Fagioli al fiasco* are cooked slowly in a sealed bottle, then poured out and dressed with oil, salt, and pepper, and *fagioli all'uccelletto* are cooked with tomato, garlic, and sage. Such is the mutual love affair of Tuscany and beans that the Tuscans are known as *mangiafagioli* (the bean eaters).

Tartufi—truffles, black and white—are a real Tuscan treasure. White truffles are gathered between 10 September and 31 December only, and black between 15 November and 15 March, with much partying and celebrating. You will find their musky, sexy scent in everything—in pastas and oils, honeys and pâtés, sauces and purees and cheeses.

Formaggi

Take a look at any decent cheese stall and you will realize there are enough different types of Pecorino here to eat a different one every day of your vacation and still have dozens left to try. It comes fresh or aged. And the aging can be done under wine lees, in caves, under ashes, in walnut leaves, in oak barrels . . . every way you can imagine and many you can't. There is a particularly lovely one, *delle colline Senese* (from the hills around Siena), made only from evening milking. It is sweet and mild when young, and tangy and crumbly when aged. And there is a fabulous young Pecorino studded with truffle. No one will object if you ask to taste before you buy, and it is great fun finding your favorite.

Dolci

There are some fabulous *pasticcerie* and *biscotterie* here in Florence. As everywhere else in Italy, the cakes and pastries you find are largely dependent on what time of the year you go. *Schiacciata* is a pastry that comes covered in almost anything from icing sugar to grapes. *Biscotti di prato* are almond-studded biscuits that are eaten dunked into *vin santo*. *Bomboloni* are terrifyingly more-ish baby doughnuts—crispy on the outside and dredged with sugar, then filled with cream, custard, or even chocolate. Get to your baker early and eat them still warm. Be prepared to experience sheer bliss. *Fritelle di riso* are delicious rice fritters you will find in March, when the feast of San Giuseppe is celebrated. *Cenci* are another celebratory sweet, prepared for the last day of Carnival—little raggedy scraps of pastry, deep fried and dredged with sugar. *Panforte* is a great creation, a dense, almost nougaty cake, heavy with candied fruits, nuts, and spices, that is served in tiny slices. There are various types, some spicier than others, but all of them last forever (until you eat them).

place to go. ♦ M, W, dinner; Tu, Th-Sa, lunch and dinner. Via Ghibellina 87 (between Via dei Pepi and Via da Verrazzano). 242777

39 Casa Buonarroti (Michelangelo Museum)

Michelangelo did not live here (but rather in a house on the corner of Via dell'Anguillara and Via Bentaccordi west of **Piazza Santa Croce**), but he did buy the land for his nephew Leonardo, whose son Michelangelo Il Giovane (the Younger) had it decorated. On the death of Cosimo Buonarroti, the last of the line, in 1858, it was left to the state, which waited until 1964 to restore it. The space is sometimes used for interesting temporary exhibitions. Of special note in the permanent collection are Michelangelo's relief sculptures, *Madonna della Scala* (1490-1492) and *Battle of the Centaurs*, believed to be two of his earliest works. Other pieces by the master on display are a wooden crucifix (attributed) and his wooden model for the never-completed façade of **San Lorenzo**. ♦ Admission. M, W-Su, 9:30AM-1:30PM. Via Ghibellina 70 (at Via M. Buonarroti). 241752

40 Alle Murate

★★★$$$ A lesser man than Umberto Montana might have settled for having designed the menu for the restaurant at the Metropolitan Opera House in New York City, owning and running one of the most important hubs of Florentine life—the elegant *Caffè Italiano* strand (the cafés are too nice to be called a chain) now expanding across the city—and being *il padrone* of one of Florence's most treasured culinary institutions, Alle Murate. But now Montana has taken this shining jewel in his culinary crown and given it a unique setting. Jaws always dropped for the cuisine at Alle Murate. Well, now your jaw will drop before you even get to your table. Signor Montana joined forces with the Sovrindenza delle Belle Arte and architect Elio di Franco to renovate the Palazzo dell' Arte dei Giudici e Notai. As you eat, archeological excavation is going on in the basement, which is thought to contain remains of a building dating back to the first century. The first floor contains many beautiful 14th-century frescoes. But it is the ground floor, under the beautiful, curving, frescoed ceilings of the *Volta di Jacopo di Cione*, that you can now enjoy the famed cooking of Alle Murate and Giovanna Ioro, Umberto Montana's not-so-secret weapon in the kitchen. As you dine, you are looked down on by scenes of medieval Florentine life, and by extraordinary portraits of Petrarch, Boccacio, and—most interesting of all—of Dante. But don't let him put you off your food! For Giovanna is still at the top of her form in the kitchen. The menu changes almost every day, according to what is good in season and in the local markets. Everything here is fresh. Dishes are still based on regional Italian culinary tradition, given a little personal spin. Carnivores are going to be very happy here. Duck comes roasted and also as a deliciously slow-cooked *sugo* for *garganelli* (pasta parcels), and one of the constants on the menu (by popular request) is the deep-flavored and delicious beef stewed in Brunello di Montalcino. The wine list is marvelously Italian and one of the best you will ever pick from. You might be hard-pressed to find a more Florentine dining experience. ♦ Tu-Su, dinner. Lunch by reservation only. Via del Proconsolo 16/r (between Borgo Allegri and Via M. Buonarroti). 240618. www.caffeitaliano.com

41 La Baraonda

★★★$$$ The hearty and varied dishes here are prepared by Elena and served by husband Duccio in a refined dining room. There are always six first courses, including homemade tagliatelle, often served with *ragù alla fiorentina* (made with chicken liver). Of the six main courses, you're always sure to find a vegetarian dish. Desserts include a *torta di mela* (apple pie), topped with cream, or you can finish with a selection of local cheeses served with *mostarda di frutta* (fruit preserved in a syrup infused with mustard). Unusual, and delightful, is *nicino,* the walnut liqueur from Emilia-Romagna. ♦ M, Su, dinner; Tu-Sa, lunch and dinner. Via Ghibellina 67r (at Borgo Allegri). 2341171

41 Dino

★★★$$ A modernized Renaissance palazzo sets the tone for such historical dishes as the house specialty, *stracotto dei granduca* (beef with garlic, rosemary, almonds, pine nuts, mint, and cinnamon), and *garetto ghibellino* (roasted pork shank in a leek, celery, and sage sauce); each dish is paired with the owner's selection of fine Italian wines from one of the city's most distinguished cellars. Chef Renza Casall oversees the daily homemade pastas and personally gathers the herbs used to season the popular *risotto alla Renza*. ♦ Tu-Sa, lunch and dinner; Su, lunch. Via Ghibellina 51r (between Via dei Macci and Borgo Allegri). 241452

42 Leo in Santa Croce

★★$$ Constructed on the site of a former Roman amphitheater, this restaurant retains original columns and capitals from that era and the early Renaissance. Even the atmosphere is somewhat theatrical, with an enormous international menu catering to tourists. House specialties include *tagliarini della casa* (pasta with mushrooms in a creamy tomato sauce) and *costola di vitella alla Leo* (veal chop prepared in a white wine-based sauce flavored with lemon and parsley). ♦ Tu-Su, lunch and dinner. Via Torta 7r (between Piazza Santa Croce and Via dell'Anguillara). 210829

43 La Maremma

★★$$ Tuscany's Maremma area prides itself on its rough and independent spirit, as the rustic decoration of this restaurant, complete with Maremma wagon wheels, bears out. The antipasto table is popular with the locals. Game in season is the specialty here (sausage and prosciutto made from *cinghiale,* or wild boar, rabbit, etc.), as are the many dishes based on the more generic *tartufo,* or truffle, when in season. This restaurant is understatedly chic, and the rustic nature of the Maremma is reflected only in the food . . . and in the cartwheels the restaurant wryly takes and uses as pseudo-chandeliers. ♦ M, Tu, Th-Su, lunch and dinner. Via Giuseppe Verdi 16r (between Piazza Santa Croce and Via Ghibellina). 244615

44 Palazzo Serristori

The studied classical elements of this Renaissance palazzo built between 1469 and 1474, more Roman than Florentine, have given rise to various attributions as to its architect, among them **Baccio d'Agnolo** and **Giuliano da Sangallo**. ♦ Piazza Santa Croce 1 (at Via Torta)

The Best

Umberto Montana

Restaurateur

Galleria degli Uffizi: Botticelli's masterpieces—*Spring, Birth of Venus*; Michelangelo's *Doni Tondo*; Piero della Francesca's portraits of *Federigo da Montefeltro* and *Battista Sforza*; the great Mannerists—Pontormo, Rosso Fiorentino.

Palazzo Pitti—Galleria Palatina: Raffaello's *Madonna dei Granduca, Madonna della Seggiola, La Dama Velata*; Tiziano's *Flora, Venus of Urbino*; Caravaggio's *Bacco Adolescente*.

Bargello: Sculpture collection from the 14th through 17th centuries—Donatello's *San Giovanni Battista*; Michelangelo's *Madonna col Bambino e San Giovannino*.

Museo di San Marco: Fra Angelico's frescoes.

Santa Maria del Carmine—Cappella Brancacci: Frescoes by Masolino and Masaccio.

L'Enoteca Pinchiorri always manages to amaze.

Cibrèo offers the best *cucina toscana*.

Hike up **Via di San Niccolò** or **dell'Erta Canina** to **Piazzale Michelangiolo** and to the splendid romantic church of **San Miniato al Monte** to enjoy the view of the city. On the way down, stop for a glass of good Tuscan wine at **FuoriPorta**, a popular spot with young Florentines.

Visit the **Mercato Centrale** in the heart of the city's tourist center: You'll be fascinated with the voices, colors, and the gaiety that permeates the place.

45 Peruzzi

The mercantile tradition of the medieval Peruzzi family continues in this spacious ever-expanding store, laid out to accommodate bewildered tour groups paraded in like cattle to peruse an array of leather goods, including bags, clothing, and wallets. Quality increases significantly upstairs, with such designer labels as Armani, Valentino, and Moschino. ♦ Daily. Borgo dei Greci 8-14r (between Piazza Santa Croce and Via Bentaccordi); another entrance is at Via dell'Anguillara 7-15r (between Piazza Santa Croce and Via Bentaccordi). 289039

46 Piazza Santa Croce

This large, open piazza is lined with stately corbelled palazzi on one side and their gawky poor relations on the other. Both sides are more interesting than the green-and-white marble church façade, which was added just in the last century, as was the campanile. As the Dominicans preached in the piazza in front of **Santa Maria Novella**, so the Franciscans preached in the piazza before **Santa Croce**. This piazza was also used for public spectacles, including jousts in honor of such noble families as the Visconti, Sforza, and Medici, and of course that most popular of public spectacles, the executions of heretics. As in centuries past, it is still used as a soccer field by the local urchins (the marble disk dated 1565 in front of **Palazzo dell'Antella** marks the center line), who daily reenact the ancient rite as if hired by the city to do so. In June a more deliberately historical spectacle, *Calcio Storico Fiorentino,* takes place in the piazza. A soccerlike game that used to be played throughout Florence in the Middle Ages and Renaissance, it fell into disuse in the early 18th century but was revived in 1930. Played in costume and by medieval rules, replicating the famous match of February 1530, it ends up resembling less its modern equivalent than a Renaissance drawing by Antonio Pollaiuolo, as it degenerates into a giant wrestling match with balletic overtones. ♦ At Largo Bargellini and Via Torta, and Via Antonio Magliabechi and Via dei Pepi

47 Palazzo dell'Antella

The colorful frescoes on the façade of this 17th-century palazzo by **Giulio Parigi** were assiduously applied by a team of artists in an astounding 20 days. The current restoration of the delicate façade took much longer. ♦ Piazza Santa Croce 21 (between Via Antonio Magliabechi and Via dei Benci)

48 Arte del Mosaico

This workshop continues the art of *pietra dura,* the inlay of semiprecious stone, so popular during the days of the Medici grand dukes. Elaborate tables and wall-hangings are available, at prices only a grand duke could afford; more portable (and affordable) items are the attractive jewelry boxes and cigarette cases. ♦ M-F, Sa morning Mar-Oct; M afternoon, Tu-Sa Nov-Feb. Largo Bargellini 2-4 (between Via delle Pinzochere and Via dei Pepi). 241647

49 Santa Croce

Begun in 1294 by **Arnolfo di Cambio**, with additions made in 1560 by **Giorgio Vasari** and a façade finished in 1863 by **Niccolò Matas**, this vast church is not quite in

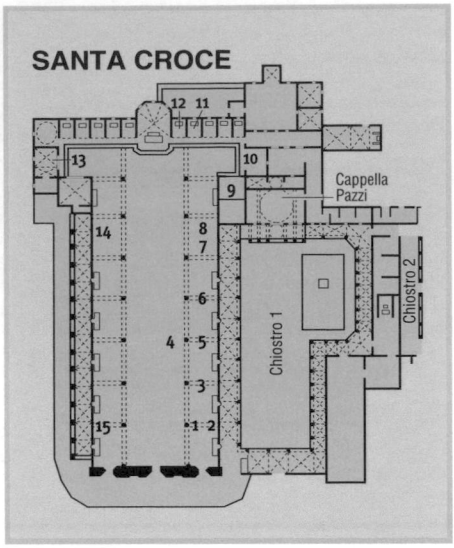

keeping with the humble practices of St. Francis. The town fathers erected it (on the site of an earlier church) as a showplace for the glory of Florence as much as for the gentle preaching order of the Franciscans. In the former function, the church contains the tombs and cenotaphs of many of the city's illustrious citizens, a sort of Gothic (then neo-Gothic) Pantheon. The Franciscans' principles come through in its fresco decoration by Giotto and his pupils, which is at once vivid and faded.

Within the vast, simple space are an equally vast number of tombs, cenotaphs, and works of art (see floor plan above). At the first pilaster in the right aisle is Antonio Rossellino's 15th-century tomb of Francesco Nori [1] (numbers refer to floor plan), topped by his *Madonna and Child*. In front of it is Vasari's 16th-century monument to Michelangelo [2] (buried here). Just ahead is Stefano Ricci's belated 19th-century cenotaph to Dante Alighieri [3] (buried in Ravenna; he is also commemorated by a statue outside). Farther on is Benedetto da Maiano's 15th-century pulpit with marble reliefs of *Scenes of the Life of St. Francis* [4]; on the wall behind it is Antonio Canova's 19th-century monument to poet Vittorio Alfieri [5]. Farther along is Innocente Spinazzi's 18th-century monument to Niccolò Machiavelli [6] (buried here), followed by Donatello's 15th-century *Annunciation* [7], in the unusual medium of gilded *pietra serena* (warm-colored stone), and Bernardo Rossellino's elaborate 15th-century tomb of Leonardo Bruni [8], a Florentine statesman. The church is designed as a main chapel (**Cappella Maggiore**) with five minor chapels on either side of it. The right transept has the **Cappella Castellani** [9], frescoed with scenes from the lives of saints in the 14th century by Agnolo Gaddi and his pupils; and the **Cappella Baroncelli** [10], with wonderfully human 14th-century frescoes of scenes from the life of the Virgin, the masterpiece of Taddeo Gaddi, who also created the fresco of the **Crocifissione** in the **Sagrestia** (sacristy), an enchanting 14th-century room itself. Two chapels to the right of the chancel, the **Cappella Peruzzi** [11] and the **Cappella Bardi** [12], have 14th-century frescoes by Giotto, damaged in the course of having been whitewashed, uncovered, and restored. Another Cappella Bardi [13], in the left transept, contains a 15th-century crucifix by Donatello. The left aisle has Desiderio da Settignano's 15th-century lavish tomb of Carlo Marsuppini [14], a Florentine statesman, and Giulio Battista Foggini's monument to Galileo [15] (buried here). The final chapel's wonderful frescoes by Maso di Banco include one that is worth seeing for the title alone—*Miracolo del Santo che Chiude le Fauci del Drago e Risuscita due Maghi Uccisi Dall'Alito del Mostro* (The Miracle of the Saint Who Shuts the Dragon's Jaws and Brings Back to Life the Magi Killed by the Monster's Breath). It is worth noting that many of the frescoes in these chapels are not illuminated until you switch on the lights by inserting money into a machine.

Within Santa Croce:

Scuola del Cuoio

A side entrance leads you around the back of the church, through some tranquil gardens and up a stairway to the School of Leather. Here you can see all the machines and tools, traditional and modern, used in the making of the leather goods for which Florence is so famous. You can watch the apprentices at work . . . and buy their best efforts on the way out. ♦ Daily, 9:30AM-6PM. Piazza Santa Croce (at Largo Bargellini). 244534

50 Baldovino

★$$ This friendly eatery rambles over three big rooms on a corner of the Piazza Santa Croce. The open kitchen means that if you sit in the center space, you are never short of entertainment. It has an interesting menu, dotted with vegetables like cardoon served as side dishes (and absolutely delicious the cardoons are too, in their rich tomatoey sauce) and ingredients that are not too frequently seen. My *fagottini* (plump pasta parcels) came *ripieni di burrata e pomodoro, pesto di rucola* (stuffed with burrata—a fabulous cream-filled cheese—and tomatoes, with a pesto of arugula). They do lots of robust dishes, like the *rigatoni alla Norcina*, a pasta with a sauce of spicy sausage, but also do more refined dishes like a chicken breast with fennel and saffron. Their pizzas look and smell terrific, as they are pulled out of the restaurant's roaring wood-fired oven, all crisp and fresh and mounded high with a generosity of topping. The wine list is fine, and there is a small selection by the glass. ♦ Daily, lunch and dinner. Via San Giuseppe 22/r (at Piazza Santa Croce). 241773. www.baldovino.com

51 Ruggini

This *pasticceria* is known for its *crostate* (pies) and *millefoglie* (the rough Italian version of the French pastry millefeuilles). ♦ Tu-Sa, 7:30AM-8PM. No credit cards accepted. Via dei Neri 76r (between Via della Mosca and Via dei Leoni). 214521

52 All Antico Vinaio

★★$ The "old wine shop" has been here for 100 years and, for the sake of visitors to come, it is hoped it will be here for another 100. You don't need a guide book to tell you this place is worth a visit. Just sniff the air as you pass, then turn and look in the window. The shop is—be warned—tiny. There is standing room only in front of the glass-topped counter. And the place doesn't even do that many things. But what it does do, it does superbly. Well enough to bring me right across the city on three consecutive days to enjoy their *crostini* with truffle topping and their crispy, olive-oily bread nibbles, but most of all to worship at the twin altars of the enormous pork roast (complete with the ultimate crackling and served with the perfect mustard), which lies resplendent across the white marble worktop, and the single finest Gorgonzola I have ever encountered. A whole round of it, young and creamy and unctuous and utterly delicious. The friendly chap behind the bar scoops out generous spoonfuls of it and dollops them on little bread rounds. And they make little *brutti ma buoni* (odd-shaped fritters) of it as well. There are also good hams and salamis, some squeaky-fresh mozzarella di bufala, and enormous pillows of focaccia to be filled at your request. And, of course, there is wine served in tiny round goblets at even tinier prices. Be prepared to stand in line at peak times; you won't regret it. ♦ Closed Sunday afternoon and Monday. Via dei Neri 65r. 2382723

53 Elto

★$$ One of Florence's two Japanese restaurants, this place maintains strict standards, not because the city is so gastronomically cosmopolitan (Florentines, in fact, are notoriously unadventurous in their eating habits), but because of the large groups of Japanese tourists who eat here. Specialties are sushi and *yakizakan* (grilled fish). ♦ Tu-Sa, lunch and dinner. Su, lunch only. Via dei Neri 72r (between Via della Mosca and Via dei Leoni). 210940

54 Piazza dei Peruzzi

This evocative little piazza retains the original residences and the name of the medieval banking family Peruzzi, whose descendants run some of the better leather shops in the vicinity. The young Michelangelo lived around the bend when he apprenticed at local *botteghe* (workshops). ♦ At Via delle Brache and Via Bentaccordi

55 Migliori

This shop stocks a colorful array of terra-cotta and ceramic housewares and decorative objects from Tuscany and other parts of Italy. ♦ M-Sa, 10AM-1PM, 3:30-7:30PM; Su, 10AM-1PM. Via dei Benci 39 (between Piazza dei Peruzzi and Borgo dei Greci). 283681

56 San Remigio

Founded on the site of an 11th-century inn for French pilgrims, this Gothic church dating from the 13th and 14th centuries has a *Madonna and Child* by a follower of Cimabue, who was known as the "Master of San Remigio." ♦ Piazza San Remigio and Via Vinegia

57 Da Benvenuto

★$ Yet another typically Florentine neighborhood trattoria, the fare here includes wonderful first-course soups and good *bollito misto* (or boiled meats) served with *salsa verde,* a sauce made with parsley and olive oil. Artists frequent the place; some of them left paintings in lieu of cash that now decorate the walls. ♦ M-Tu, Th-Sa, lunch and dinner. Via della Mosca 16r (at Via dei Neri). 214833

58 McRae Books

Should you find yourself in need of a good dictionary or phrasebook, some really good writing on Florence, Tuscany, or elsewhere in Italy, or—perish the thought—be thinking of buying another guide book, then this is the place to come. Even if you have simply found yourself dreading the journey back without a little stack of reading material to see you through it, McRae's is a boon. They have everything from a superb range of cookery and foodie books to terrific children's books, novels (including a good range of crime writers), art books, and a delightful section devoted to Italian authors translated into English. This has to be the best and most imaginative selection of English-language writing in Florence, probably in all of Tuscany. ♦ Daily, 9AM-7:30PM. Via dei Neri 30r

59 Fiaschetteria Vecchio Casentino

★$ This inviting neighborhood watering hole, with its old marble tables and wood bar, offers a large selection of freshly prepared foods and sandwiches against a background of soothing classical music. ♦ Tu-Su, noon-3PM, 6PM-midnight. No credit cards accepted. Via dei Neri 17r (between Via dei Benci and Via della Mosca). 217411

59 Gelateria dei Neri

There are many who will swear on Michelangelo's *David* that this is the best gelateria in Florence. They might well be right. A terrific choice of flavors takes you from all the standards through *cassata Siciliana* (with chunks of candied fruit), cookies (with chunks of cookie), *croccantino* (with crunchy chunks of honeycomb brittle), *pinoli* (with pine nuts), and a pretty impressive pistachio. All are homemade on the premises, as is the range of mousses (or *semifreddi*), which offers chocolate, tiramisù, and *panna montana* (like whipped sweetened cream). Best of all, though, and worth crossing Tuscany for, is their Gorgonzola ice cream. There are Michelin-starred establishments that would love to have something like this on the menu. It's delicate, delicious, and something to put on your "must try" list. As with all good things in this marvelous country, this is a seasonal treat. Should you arrive when there is no *gelato di Gorgonzola* on offer, console yourself with the stunning, fresh, and utterly unforgettable ricotta and fresh fig ice cream. ♦ Daily, 9AM-midnight. Via dei Neri 20/22r. 210034

60 Piccolo Slam

If you're wondering where fashion-conscious *bambini* get their threads, look no further. This high-toned boutique outfits children from 6 to 16 years old in Italian-made fashions by Armani, Simonetta, and C. P. All the design sensibility, workmanship, and quality fabrics that have set Italian adult fashion apart from the rest are available here for the younger set. Party outfits for special occasions (*da cerimonia*) will make you sigh, while across the street at **No. 9-11r**, newborn to six-year-old customers can be outfitted in mostly French labels. ♦ M afternoon; Tu-Sa. Via dei Neri 9-11r (between Via dei Benci and Via della Mosca). 210070

61 Palazzo Spinelli-Rasponi

The façade and interior courtyard of this Renaissance palazzo are decorated with the two-tone stucco work known as *sgraffiti*. ♦ Borgo Santa Croce 10 (between Via Antonio Magliabechi and Via dei Benci)

62 Cappella Pazzi and Museo dell'Opera di Santa Croce (Pazzi Chapel and Santa Croce Museum)

Here in the freestanding 15th-century chapel, **Filippo Brunelleschi** used the same harmonious circle-in-a-square idea that he had used in the **Sagrestia Vecchia** in the church of **San Lorenzo**. Despite the chapel's name (it means "crazies" and actually derives from the family name of its patrons, also known for their role in the notorious Pazzi Conspiracy), it is one of the most peaceful spots in Florence, as are the surrounding cloisters. Decoration of the chapel is by Luca della Robbia, who was responsible for the 15th-century tondos of St. Andrew over the door and the Apostles in the chapel. Brunelleschi may have made the tondos of the Evangelists. In the museum, Cimabue's *Crucifixion* has become somewhat of a symbol of the 1966 flood, which totally submerged it and lifted huge patches of paint from its surface. It has since been restored. Also on display are Donatello's 15th-century *St. Louis of Toulouse* and a 14th-century *Last Supper* by Taddeo Gaddi. ♦ Admission. M-Tu, Th-Su. Piazza Santa Croce 16 (between Via Antonio Magliabechi and Largo Bargellini). 244619

63 Hotel Balestri

$$$ This old-fashioned riverside hotel has been run by the Balestri family since 1888. Twenty of the rooms face the Arno, and another 30 face a quiet courtyard or the adjoining square. Even the view-deprived will find the hotel's location within easy walking distance of all major sites. Buffet breakfast is included, and there is now Internet access for guests at a small fee. There's no restaurant. ♦ Piazza Mentana 7 (at Lungarno Generale Armando Diaz). 214743; fax 2398042

64 Museo Horne

The late-15th-century Renaissance Palazzo Corsi, which was designed by **Cronaca**, was home in the early 1900s to Herbert Percy Horne, a rich Brit abroad. He renovated the whole house in an effort to re-create the original Renaissance feel. One interesting feature is the original kitchen, which is—as was the custom—on the top floor. The art collection includes a number of paintings by the so-called Primitives (Agnolo Gaddi, Bernardo Daddi, Pietro Lorenzetti, Filippo Lippi), as well as some interesting Mannerist art (by Domenico Beccafumi and Dosso Dossi). There are also some appealing pieces of decorative art scattered throughout the museum. It was all bequeathed to the city in 1916.

♦ Admission. M-Sa, 9AM-1PM. Via dei Benci 6 (between Lungarno delle Grazie and Corso dei Tintori). 244661

65 Biblioteca Nazionale (National Library)

The core of the national library's collection includes one of the greatest assemblages of incunabula and illuminated manuscripts in the world. On public view in this imposing early-20th-century building by **Cesare Bazzani** are early editions of Dante's *Divine Comedy*, as well as sculpture by Giovanni della Robbia and Antonio Canova. ♦ M-F; Sa morning. Piazza dei Cavalleggeri 1 (at Corso dei Tintori). 244443

66 Plaza Hotel Lucchesi

$$$$ This comfortable, stylish hotel is just far enough away from the hustle and bustle of the center of town to be quiet (with the help of soundproof windows), yet still an easy walk to most tourist attractions. Of the 97 rooms, those 12 with room-length terraces and views of the Arno best justify the high rates charged. Guest rooms in the rear have the slightly less desirable, yet still pleasurable, view of **Santa Croce**. The hotel restaurant, **La Serra**, is a spacious and serene spot for breakfast, lunch, or dinner, but it's open only to hotel guests. The hotel has joined the 21st century, and guests have free Internet access. ♦ Lungarno della Zecca Vecchia 38 (between Via delle Casine and Piazza dei Cavalleggeri). 26236; fax 2480921

Cappella Pazzi and Museo dell'Opera di Santa Croce

OLTRARNO

For centuries Florentines have made a distinction between the *Arno di quà* (this side of the Arno River, spreading from its more developed north bank) and the *Arno di là* (that side of the Arno, along the south bank), also known as the Oltrarno, or the other side of the Arno. Perhaps because of that enduring distinction, based more on attitude than on actual distance, the Oltrarno has largely been spared the myriad shops and high-volume pizzerias that have sprung up across the river.

The Oltrarno embodies Florence in both its most palatial and most popular aspects. **Via Maggio** (the name is said to be derived from *maggiore,* or major), historically its most important street, is lined with noble palazzi housing elegant antiques shops. The **San Frediano** area, quite different in character, is a tight-knit neighborhood appreciated by outsiders who have strolled its colorful streets or read about it in the late

Vasco Pratolini's book *Le ragazze di Sanfrediano* (The Girls of Sanfrediano), which beautifully captured the everyday drama of its working-class residents. In between is the **Santo Spirito** neighborhood, where the high- and low-rent aspects of the Oltrarno come together in perfect harmony.

It is easy to see why Florentines have a soft spot for the Oltrarno. Here you can still hear the hammering of craftspeople in their workshops (take a stroll down **Via Toscanella**) and the peal of bells from the campanile of **Santo Spirito**. Workshops and palazzi somehow take on a friendlier air, and even the pace seems slower and quieter in the Oltrarno.

1 Arte di Gioire

An extraordinary place full of statues and sculptures. It looks as if many of the objects have simply been frozen, so flowing are the fabrics in the dresses the figures wear, their hair, the droop of a hat, the plumage on a bird. This is because all the sculptures here are made in cloth or leather or plastic treated with a new substance called Powertex. I am assured Powertex is entirely naturally based, but it has the effect of hardening any fabric it coats like metal. So fabrics keep their fluidity, but that fluidity is frozen, as it were. Interesting stuff! ♦ Closed Tuesday and Friday afternoon. Via Lorenzo Bartolini 14. 333 7432060. www.artedigioire.it

2 Antico Setificio Fiorentino

This 500-year-old silk manufacturing mill was revived years ago by the late Marchese Emilio Pucci, who was anxious to keep alive this important element of local history. It is currently run by Sabine Pretsch, an architect and Pucci's former right hand. Exquisite fabrics woven on wooden looms predating the industrial revolution are available in limited quantities, while others may be commissioned on a special-order basis; inquire at the small retail outlet within. ♦ M-F. Via L. Bartolini 4 (at Via Sant'Onofrio). 213861; fax 218174

3 Granaio di Cosimo III

Built as a granary under the Medici, this wheat bin (constructed in 1695 by **Ciro Ferri** and **Gian Battista Foggini**) is now used as a military building. ♦ Piazza di Cestello 10 (at Lungarno Soderini)

4 Porta San Frediano

This towering ancient city gate (part of the old wall is still attached) was built in 1332-1334 by **Andrea Pisano** and still sports its original wood and ironwork, to which visitors once hitched their horses. ♦ Piazza di Verzaia (between Viale Ludovico Ariosto and Via Lungo le Mura di Santa Rosa)

5 Tripperie

Look, I know you think you won't like it, but you should at least try Florence's most famous contribution to feeding the people of Italy: *trippa* (tripe) It is delicious. And it is especially delicious served at this little outlet that looks like a hot-dog van. Your *trippa* comes *alla fiorentina*, in a rich tomato sauce. Then there's *lampredotto* (cow intestine) also delicious, although it looks like something from a horror sci-fi movie. But just think–it is one of the lowest-fat foods in town! It is all cooked fresh and comes to your little plastic tray (or panino) steaming from the pot, expertly chopped up by the young man in the van and spiced with *piccante* (chili oil) or *salsa verde* (a tangy herby, garlicy green sauce). Have it with beer or red wine (yes, he sells that too) and feel like a real Florentine. ♦ Closed Sunday. Piazza dei Nerli

6 Antico Ristoro di Cambi

★★$$ The Cambi family has been running this rustic restaurant in an old *fiaschetteria* (wine shop) for decades. All the Tuscan soups are well prepared here. If you're feeling adventurous, try the *trippa* (tripe) or *lampredotto* (cow intestine); otherwise, an excellent *spezzatino* (beef stewed with tomatoes, potatoes, and herbs) should hit the spot. There's outdoor seating in warm weather. Check out the wine list. For such an unassuming place it is very "Florentinely" impressive, with 11 Brunello de Montalcinos and 23 Supertuscans from which to choose. You can quaff them outside at the Cambi's tables on the Piazza del Tiratoio in summer months. ♦ M-Sa. Via Sant'Onofrio 1r (on the corner of Piazza Tiratoio). 217134. www.anticoristorodicambi.it ♦ M-Sa, lunch and dinner. Via Sant'Onofrio 1r (between Borgo San Frediano and Piazza del Tiratoio). 217134

7 San Frediano in Cestello

This rare Florentine-Baroque church, constructed 1680-1689 by **Antonio Maria**

Ferri with the interior renovated in the late 18th century by **Giulio Cerrutti**, is best admired from a distance, where its cupola adds a nice shape to the city's profile. *Cestello* in Italian means crate, though in Florence it was a corruption of Cistercense or Cistercians, the monks who once inhabited the site. The church's interior decorations, primarily by 18th-century Florentine painters, are inoffensive if uninspiring, though the third chapel on the left has a blissed-out 13th-century smiling *Madonna*. ♦ Piazza di Cestello and Via di Cestello

7 Borgo di San Frediano

This is one of the very oldest parts of the city, claimed by its inhabitants to have been the first settled street from which the rest of Florence then grew. It is still well known as a street of artisans and artists—the *"mani d'oro di firenze"* (the golden hands of Florence). Among the best examples today is the bottega of **Maestro Antonio Abussi** at No. 72. Maestro Abussi creates beautiful ceramics, restores old ceramics, and offers courses in both. At **No. 77r** you will pass the glowing windows of **Il Paralume** (Su-F, 8:30AM-1PM, 3:30PM-7PM, 2396760, www.ilparalume.it), a lovely shop/workshop where the friendly (and surprisingly modest, considering he has won several international craft awards) gentleman behind the counter makes and sells all manner of lampshades. There is a window devoted to the delightful stained-glass animals he crafts—glass snails and owls, ducks, and a gorgeous tortoise—all of which light up beautifully at the touch of your switch. There are Tiffany-style glass shades, old-style card shades, and carved wood bases . . . everything the well-dressed lightbulb might be wearing tomorrow. And talking of well-dressed lights, on the other side of the road at **No. 44r** you will find **Enneti** (M-F, 9:30AM-1PM, 2PM-6:30PM, 284257, www.pepsrl.com). You will want to go into this lovely, wood-paneled, calm and spacious showroom just for the thrill of standing under the gorgeous chandeliers they make and sell here. Suddenly you won't be able to think of a reason not to have one in your room.

8 Ugolini

Romano Ugolini carries on a long family tradition as a *bronzista* (bronze worker). His specialty is lamps of all types, with a minimum order of four. ♦ M-F, Sa morning Mar-Oct; M afternoon, Tu-Sa Nov-Feb. No credit cards accepted. Via del Drago d'Oro 25r (between Via dell'Orto and Borgo San Frediano). 215343

The period we now know as the Renaissance was first called a *rinascita* (rebirth) by Vasari in 1550. People living at that time certainly were aware that something new was happening, but the word had no wide currency until used by Swiss historian Jacob Burckhardt in his classic *The Civilization of the Renaissance in Italy* (1860).

9 Del Carmine

★★$$ One of the most popular trattorias among Florentines and visitors alike (especially during the warmer months, when its tables move outside), this warm and friendly restaurant serves a substantial *tagliatelle a funghi porcini* (ribbons of pasta with porcini mushrooms) and fillet of beef given the same tasty treatment. ♦ M-Sa, lunch and dinner. Piazza del Carmine 18r (between Piazza Piattellina and Borgo San Frediano). 218601

10 Marino

There are two shifts of fresh-baked bliss at this *pasticceria* (pastry shop). Croissants, plain or filled with jams and custards, emerge from the oven each morning until noon and then again after 4PM right into the eager hands of waiting Florentines. ♦ Tu-Su, 6:30AM-8:30PM. Piazza Nazario Sauro 19r (between Borgo San Frediano and Lungarno Soderini). 212657

11 Momoyama

★★$$ The current place of choice in Florence for sushi and sashimi is this elegantly designed interior, with sushi bar, upstairs dining room, and downstairs art gallery. Tempura is available (Tuesdays only), along with what the owners call *cucina inventiva* ("inventive cooking") of Japanese-French fusion: fried gyoza (called *tortelli* on the menu) with poppy seeds and foie gras mousse with Port. ♦ Tu-Sa, dinner; Su, lunch. Borgo San Frediano 10r (at Via dei Serragli). 291840

12 Francesco

This shop specializes in beautiful, simple handmade shoes, from sandals to brogues and loafers to moccasins, exemplifying wonderful old-fashioned craftsmanship. It also sells wallets and purses. ♦ Tu-Su, 9AM-1PM and 3:30PM-7PM. Via di Santo Spirito 62

13 Beccofino

★$$$ The night I went, thanks to the howling wind and driving rain in March, in accordance with tradition coming "in like a lion" to Florence, I had the entire restaurant and bar to myself. I had expected dining here to be more welcoming—partly because the owner is Scottish (and the man who also has the much more relaxed **Baldovino** restaurant just off Piazza Spirito Santo). But the food had also come highly recommended. The menu is certainly smart and sophisticated, as is the space, with its open kitchen at the back and semicircular bar at the front. The interesting antipasti include *flan di ortiche con capperi* *e asciughe* (a nettle flan with capers and anchovy) and *tortelli di zucca gialla e amaretti al burro, salvia e mandorle tostata* (pasta parcels stuffed with pumpkin and amaretti, sauced with butter sage and toasted almonds). The vegetables here are notable—served on an oblong platter and lightly slicked with oil and basil (there were Jerusalem artichokes, broccoli, smoky roasted peppers, silky eggplant, braised fennel, baby asparagus, and new potatoes). The main courses run from light fish dishes to a *guanciale di vitello brasato* (braised veal cheek), which is incredibly rich. Desserts are interesting—the *semifreddo* of ricotta is nice (but not as good as the ricotta ice cream at the little Gelateria dei Neri in Santa Croce). The wine list is excellent, and the house Prosecco the perfect aperitivo. ♦ Closed Monday. Piazza degli Scarlatti 1r. 290076. www.beccofino.com

14 Dolce Vita

Named after the Fellini film about the good life in Rome in the 1960s, this modern-looking nocturnal hangout for Florentine and foreign youth brings a sweet smile, especially when its clientele's earnest and urgent interactions take over the parking lot in true Roman fashion. ♦ Daily, 11AM-1:30AM Apr-Oct; Tu-Sa, 5:30PM-1:30AM Nov-Mar. No credit cards accepted. Piazza del Carmine and Borgo Stella. 284595. www.dolcevitaflorence.com

15 Banchi Lamberto

Master bronze worker Lamberto Banchi makes intricate tiny objects (frames, paperweights, candlesticks) and larger items (lamps, tabletops) in bronze and copper. He also repairs antiques made of those metals. ♦ M-F, Sa morning Mar-Oct, M afternoon, Tu-Sa Nov-Feb. No credit cards accepted. Via dei Serragli 10r (between Via Santa Monaca and Borgo Stella). 294694

16 Arredamenti Castorina

Florence's antiques dealers and restorers come here for the little bits of sculpted wood they use to mend and embellish their frames and furniture. Many of the pieces—ranging from *putti* (cupids) to abstract geometrical shapes—are lovely objects in and of themselves and make unusual souvenirs, gifts, and even Christmas tree ornaments. A vast selection of elaborately carved frames also makes a stop here worthwhile. ♦ M-F, Sa morning Mar-Oct; M afternoon, Tu-Sa Nov-Feb. Via di Santo Spirito 13-15r (between Via de' Coverelli and Via Maffia). 212885

17 Mariotti

If you are by any chance looking for a chandelier to complete your home, then this would be the place to come. Even if you are not looking for a chandelier, this place is so gorgeous you might just buy one anyway! There is Bohemian crystal and burnt bronze . . . drops and strings and globes and clusters. All sizes and styles of chandelier are here. Even if you are just looking, it is a lovely place to spend awhile. Any purchases can be shipped home! ♦ M-Sa, 9AM-12:30PM and 3PM-7:30PM. Via di Santo Spirito 9. 283300; fax 2728787. www.mariottilampadari.it

18 Il Cantinone

★$$ This is an outrageously atmospheric place, in a huge vaulted cellar with exposed brick walls and chunky Tuscan tables. As the name suggests, the wine list is enormous and impressively sourced. The menu is pretty enticing too. There are Tuscan standards like *ribollita*, and the Italian classic *tagliata di manzo con rucola* (sliced grilled fillet steak on a bed of arugula that comes in five subtle variations). Charcoal-grilled garlic bread comes eight ways, including with tomato and Pecorino and with white beans and black cabbage, and there are specials like their delicious-sounding veal stew with tomato and black pepper. ♦ Tu-Su, lunch and dinner. Via di Santo Spirito 6r. 218898. www.ilcantinonedifirenze.it

18 Olio & Convivium

★★$$ If you have a foodie bone in your body, you will love this place. Set in the Palazzo Capponi, it is a world-class deli, a very impressive wine shop, and a delightful restaurant all rolled into one. And let's face it, anywhere that lines up four chunky legs of prime prosciutto *crudo*—Parma, Gaiole, Cinta, and Pata Negra—to be sliced off for your delectation gets the foodie vote anywhere! This is the retail outlet of a society set up in 1980 to promote the enjoyment and understanding of good food and wine. And this place really helps you understand. There are shelves of crusty artisanal breads, gleaming rows of balsamic vinegars of various ages, and a range of cold stone-pressed olive oils, including some pressed from stoned olives from all over Italy that would bring tears to the eyes of any Mediterranean-friendly gourmet. One marvelous thing you can enjoy here is the tutored olive-oil tastings and fascinating hints on the pairing of different oils and foods. There is a range of organic honeys from Tuscany; there are fabulous handmade jellies, jams, pickles, and preserves, and, of course, yards of glorious-smelling cheeses and salami. On opposite shelves you will find biscuits and candies, top-of-the line chocolate, and wonderful patisserie. Then there is the fantastic selection of wines—more than 250 labels from 45 producers (including many small vineyards you will love to discover), alongside a hugely impressive selection of grappas. The dining area is walled with dark wood shelves of wine bottles, and a big blackboard tells you the menu of the day. The food is all freshly prepared and, of course, features daily selections from the best the store has to offer. The owners describe the space as an *atelier gastronomico*—a studio or workshop where you come to learn, to expand your experience of good foods and wines and, most especially olive oils. It is a wonderful place to find foodie presents and to treat yourself. ♦ M, 10AM-3PM; Tu-Sa, 10AM-3PM and 5:30PM-10:30PM. Via di Santo Spirito 4. 2658198. www.conviviumfirenze.it

19 Palazzo dei Frescobaldi

Dating back to the 13th century, this is the oldest of the palazzi associated with the Frescobaldis. The family gave birth to a number of distinguished members, including ambassadors, composers, writers, and—currently—vintners. ♦ Piazza Frescobaldi 2r (at Borgo San Jacopo)

20 Angela Caputi

If you've just damaged your credit card buying designer delights, come here for accessories to the crime. The eponymous owner's imaginative costume jewelry coordinates conspiratorially with the strongest of fashion statements. It is the quintessence of Italian chic—everyone will want to know where you bought it. ♦ M-F, Sa morning Mar-Oct; M afternoon, Tu-Sa Nov-Feb. Borgo San Jacopo 82r (between Piazza Angiolieri and Piazza Frescobaldi). 212972. There is also a larger branch at Borgo Santi Apostoli 44.

21 Parenti

A corner shop full of gorgeous things from this well-known Florentine firm. From faux Fabergé eggs to gold-edged porcelain dinner services and from vast ornate mirrors to Belle Epoque occasional furniture, this shop is a wonderful place to look . . . and maybe to buy. ♦ Via Maggio 1 (at Via dello Sprone). 214438. Also at Via Tornabuoni

21 Waterline

On the wall at the junction of the Via dello Sprone and the Via Maggio is one of those marks that you will find all over the city showing the height that the flood waters reached on 4 November 1966. The line here is so far above my head I could barely reach it. Makes you think!

Stendhal, the 19th-century French writer, was—so the story goes—so overwhelmed by the magnificence of the Basilica that he was unable to walk because he was so near to fainting. Florentine doctors are said to treat a dozen cases of *"Stendhalismo"* (or Stendhal's Syndrome) per year. You have been warned!

22 Caffè Santa Trinità

★$ A pleasant, modern, and unhurried place for a coffee or sandwich break, this café features an of-the-moment rock music selection. It also has what must be the highest stool anywhere in the café world, so stand at the bar if you suffer from vertigo! At noontime there's a variety of interesting salad combinations and a daily-special pasta that sells out quickly. ♦ M-Sa, 7:30AM-8PM. Via Maggio 2r (at Piazza Frescobaldi). 214558

23 Guido Bartolozzi

One of Florence's leading and most exclusive antiques dealers, Signor Bartolozzi presides over a rambling space filled with furniture, paintings, and objets d'art ranging from the times of the Medici to those of Mussolini. ♦ M-F, Sa morning Mar-Oct; M afternoon, Tu-Sa Nov-Feb. Via Maggio 18r (between Via de Michelozzi and Piazza Frescobaldi). 215602

24 Bartolozzi e Maioli

Fiorenzo Bartolozzi, Italy's finest wood-carver, is best known for his restoration of the famed choir stalls in the Benedictine abbey of Monte Cassino outside of Naples after it was destroyed during World War II. These days he and his workshop of master crafters continue to carve and gild practically everything imaginable for churches, palaces, and other distinguished clients. His two-floor showroom is filled with his creations great and small, from smiling cupids to fanciful life-size pythons and ostriches. ♦ M-F, Sa morning Mar-Oct; M afternoon, Tu-Sa Nov-Feb. No credit cards accepted. Via Maggio 13r (between Via dei Vellutini and Piazza Frescobaldi). 298633

25 Cammillo

★★$$ The owners of this family-run restaurant pride themselves on their homemade pasta and dishes based on porcini mushrooms and truffles (when in season). When they are not in season, pasta is still worth the trip over the Arno with dishes like *malfatta di ricotta e spinachi al burro e salvia* (dumplings stuffed with ricotta and spinach and sauced with butter and sage). ♦ M-Tu, F-Su, lunch and dinner. Borgo San Jacopo 57-58r (between Via de' Sapiti and Via dello Sprone). 212427

26 Hotel Lungarno

$$$$ The local Ferragamo family now owns this old-time, riverside favorite, and has outfitted it in the same classic, distinguished style and elegance with which the clan built its fashion empire. The hotel's tailored image incorporates an important collection of 20th-

century art that is generously displayed in the guest rooms, as well as throughout the public areas. Each of the 69 refurbished rooms—18 of them in the renovated medieval tower next door—boasts a new beige marble bathroom. Six large guest rooms (most of which are on the sixth floor) open onto grand terraces with exceptional views of the **Arno** and the **Ponte Vecchio**. The restaurant specializes in seafood. ♦ Borgo San Jacopo 14 (at Piazza Angiolieri). 27621; fax 268437. www.lungarnohotels.com

27 Mamma Gina

★$$$ Set in a vaulted 15th-century palazzo, this elegant trattoria specializes in all the Tuscan classics. Particularly good to start with are the *minestrone di riso* (vegetable soup with rice) or *ribollita* (traditional Tuscan soup made with beans). The traditional entrée is the succulent *bistecca alla fiorentina* (a slab of steak grilled, then drizzled with olive oil), but you'll also find a host of other roasted and grilled meat dishes vying for your palate's attention. Mama Gina's *ribollita* is so good she has a certificate of excellence for it from the Accademia Italiana della Cucina; it hangs just inside the door. There is also an extensive wine list. ♦ M-Sa, lunch and dinner. Borgo San Jacopo 37r (between Piazza Angiolieri and Via Toscanella). 2396009

28 Le Barrique

★$$ The sophistication of the place belies its location. It's more fun in good weather, when the trellis-covered romantic little garden is a tranquil place for a meal, but the small interior is charming too. The menu changes according to season and market, but there is always a choice of good fresh fish like *branzino con mandorle* (sea bass with almonds) and a good *tagliata* of beef (fillet served in strips on a bed of arugula salad). The wine list is impressive, and the new owner, Alessandro, will make sure you enjoy yourself. ♦ Tu-Su, dinner 6PM-1AM. Via del Leone 40r (between Piazza Torquato Tasso and Via dell'Orto). 224192

29 Santa Maria del Carmine

The "Carmine," as it is known locally, was built in 1268 for the Carmelite nuns and suffered a devastating fire in 1771. Though the fire destroyed most of the church (it was rebuilt in 1782 by **Giuseppe Ruggieri** and **Giulio Mannaioni**), the **Cappella Brancacci** (Brancacci Chapel) was untouched. The chapel contains restored early-15th-century frescoes begun by Masolino, continued by Masaccio, and completed by Filippino Lippi. Masaccio's contribution was a watershed in the history of art, combining perspective, chiaroscuro, and the vivid rendering of emotions with unprecedented boldness, seminal to the painters of the later Renaissance. Two of Masaccio's sections dominate the cycle—the agonizing *Expulsion from Paradise* on the extreme upper-left wall, and the serene and noble *The Tribute Money* just to its right. Below it, *St. Peter Enthroned* contains a portrait of Masaccio, the figure gazing out at the viewer in the group of four men at the right of the composition. If you feel like looking at anything else ever again, the left transept of the church contains the 17th-century **Cappella di Sant'Andrea Corsini**, with three relief sculptures by Giovanni Battista Foggini, and the dome has Luca Giordano's 17th-century fresco *The Apotheosis of St. Andrew Corsini*. ♦ Brancacci Chapel: admission. Church: daily. Chapel: M, W-Sa; Su, 1-5PM. Piazza del Carmine (between Via Santa Monaca and Piazza Piattellina). 2382195

30 Albrici e Paderni

You're not going to find much here you can get away with packing in the average carry-on bag. But you will find wonderful big chunks of old Florence—huge stone urns, marble fountains, and even a vast stone fireplace (the kind that makes you want to change into doublet and hose just to lean against it!). History in stone, in effect. Yes, they ship. ♦ Closed Monday morning and Sunday. Via dei Serragli 20. 211095

31 Bene Vobis

This new *enoteca* for Oltrarno is open till the wee small hours of the Florentine morning. You can enjoy its lovely, relaxed atmosphere perched at the bar or sitting at one of the tables farther in. Bottles line the walls, and exposed brickwork sets them off to advantage. The food is great too! The good variety of bruschette are perfect to nibble while you make your way down the wine list—they are freshly made to order. *Pimzimonio* (Tuscan crudités) are a healthy option for nibblers. Fusilli pasta is served with red radicchio, and ricotta and chicken is cooked in a secret blend of aromatics including fennel. The charming lady with the corkscrew wouldn't give me the recipe. There is a generous choice of single-variety grappas and some excellent coffee available. ♦ Tu-Su, 10:30AM-3AM; M, 6PM-3AM. Via dei Serragli 78r. 218952

32 Luciano Ugolini

Signor Ugolini makes exquisite copper tubs and jugs in patterns inspired by the collection of the **Museo degli Argenti** (Silver Museum) in the **Palazzo Pitti**. The pieces are ideal as planters, since their timeless quality works well with practically any kind of décor. ♦ M-F, Sa morning Mar-Oct; M afternoon, Tu-Sa Nov-Feb. No credit cards accepted. Via del Presto di San Martino 23 (between Via dei Michelozzi and Via di Santo Spirito). 287230

33 Nava & Nencini

These silversmiths specialize in small birds and animals, but they also do custom work and will faithfully etch each feature of Felix or Fido should you wish a tony tribute to the family pet. ♦ M-F, Sa morning Mar-Oct; M afternoon, Tu-Sa Nov-Feb. Via dello Sprone 4-4r (at Via Toscanella). 283224

34 Pitti Palace

$$ This refurbished former *pensione,* while offering an excellent location and modern facilities, has, alas, very little character. The views from many of the 72 smallish rooms—you can almost reach out and touch the **Ponte Vecchio**—and the lovely roof terrace come close to making up for it. There's no restaurant. ♦ Via Barbadori 2 (at Via de' Guicciardini). 23987011; fax 2398867. www.vivahotels.com

35 Alla Vecchia Bettola

★★$$ A *bettola* was a sort of prototypical lunch counter in old Florence, a place where peasants ate and ran. Perhaps you'll want to linger, though, in this ceramic-tiled trattoria. The atmosphere is warm; communal tables are understandably for lovers of fun, and the specialties of tripe and the like are for lovers of the heartiest of Florentine food. The less adventurous will be happy with the classic standbys that change daily. ♦ Tu-Sa, lunch and dinner. No credit cards accepted. Viale Ludovico Ariosto 32r (between Via Villani and Via San Francesco di Paola). 224158

36 Vino Olio

A full line of Italian wines and olive oils by such famous names as Antinori, Frescobaldi, and Ruffino are stocked at this shop. Other delicacies include grappa, various liqueurs, truffled olive oil, aged balsamic vinegars, and vinegars made with Champagne and fermented apples. ♦ M, Tu, Th-Sa; W morning. Via dei Serragli 29r (between Via della Chiesa and Via Sant'Agostino). 2398708

37 Fondazione Salvatore Romano

The only part of the Gothic monastery of **Santo Spirito** spared by the fire of 1471 is this foundation, established by a Neapolitan antiques dealer who worked in Florence. Housed in the former refectory just west of the church, it is also known as "*Cenacolo Santo Spirito*." Among the works on display are a *Last Supper* and a *Crucifixion* attributed to Andrea Orcagna. Also here is a Romanesque sculpture and other pieces believed to have been done by Jacopo della Quercia, Donatello, and Bartolommeo Ammannati. ♦ Admission. Tu-Sa, 9AM-2PM; Su, 8AM-1PM. Piazza Santo Spirito 29 (between Via dei Michelozzi and Via Sant'Agostino). 287043

38 Santo Spirito

This has been called "the most beautiful church in the world" by no less a person than Bernini, who knew rather a lot about beautiful churches. Built in 1434, it was more or less the swan song of the great **Brunelleschi**. The façade was not completed until much later and is today just a simple white plaster wall. Inside, the church is breathtaking. Brunelleschi designed 38 chapels around the outside of his floor plan, with 35 columns lining the nave, transept, and chancel. The artworks here are an unusual collection, in that the majority of them were commissioned at the same time in the aftermath of the terrible fire that destroyed most of Santo Spirito's medieval works and frescoes. One of the most famous works here is Filippino Lippi's *Nerli Altarpiece*, a Madonna and child. Through a door in the north aisle you will find the vestibule and **Sacristy** designed (and built 1489-93) by **Giuliano da Sangallo**, in imitation of Brunelleschi's own Cappella dei Pazzi. The wooden crucifix that hangs here is thought to be by Michelangelo. The *Chiostro dei Morti* you can glimpse through the glass door here in the vestibule (unfortunately usually locked) is the only cloister that was part of the Augustinian monastery—almost all the rest having been destroyed in the fire of 1471. The only other original part of the monastery is the adjacent Refectory, but the only supper you'll get here these days is the *Cenacolo di Santo Spirito*. There is also a massive fresco of *The Crucifixion* by Orcagna and his workshop. ♦ M, Tu, Th-Sa, 8:30AM-noon and 4PM-6PM; Su, 4PM-6PM. *Cenacolo di Santo Spirito*, Tu-Su, 9AM-2PM. Piazza Santo Spirito (between Via dei Michelozzi and Via Sant'Agostino)

39 Casa di Bianca Cappello

This ancient palazzo, covered with delicate and restored *sgraffiti* decoration by Poccetti, was altered by **Bernardo Buontalenti** between 1570 and 1574 for the mistress (and later wife) of Francesco I de' Medici, the Venetian Bianca Cappello, whose family's coat of arms (featuring a *cappello,* or hat) appears above the entrance. ♦ Via Maggio 26 (between Via dei Michelozzi and Piazza Frescobaldi)

40 Borgo Antico

★$$ A young crowd always fills this simple dining spot, particularly on Sunday evenings, when most of Florence is closed. But the good pizza keeps regulars coming back any day of the week. And when warm weather arrives and the tables are brought outdoors, this becomes the best place in the neighborhood to dine while taking in the goings-on of Florence's most characteristic piazza. *Grigliata di verdure e formaggio* (grilled vegetables and Camembert) will elate vegetarians, as will many of the pizzas, "super salads," or pasta selections. ♦ Tu-Su, lunch and dinner. Piazza Santo Spirito 6r (between Via Mazzetta and Via dei Michelozzi). 210437

41 La Casalinga

★★★$ This basic, friendly place gives you just what it says it does—*casalinga* (home cooking). The bread is good, the house wine fine, the napkins are linen, and the service is warm-hearted. The menu is as Florentine as the River Arno, but if you don't feel like getting really meaty about your meal, the pesto ravioli with butter and sage is lovely, the carpaccio is well nigh a perfect example, the salads are as fresh as a seventeen-year-old on a first date, and there is a selection of vegetable side dishes that is quite astounding in this city. It has to be said that the *bollito misto*, a platefull of deliciously poached tongue, beef, pork knuckle, *sopressata* (sausage), and chicken, served with a tangy salsa verde, is one of the most delicious bargains to be had with a few euros. It was terrific. And the portions of mixed steamed vegetables (French beans, potatoes, and beets) was a simple joy. The ladies at the table next to me ordered the roast potatoes with their pasta dishes, which looked terrifyingly more-ish! The cheeses are top quality, the homemade tarts and cheesecake on offer for dessert are heavy on flavor while light in texture, and the coffee is just what you need to get you on your feet again after such generous feeding. A genuine taste of Tuscany. ♦ M-Sa, lunch and dinner. Via dei Michelozzi 9r (between Via Maggio and Borgo Tegolaio). 218624

42 Piazza Santo Spirito

This piazza, which extends before the Augustinian church bearing the same name, is as down-to-earth as **Piazza Santa Maria Novella** and **Piazza Santa Croce** are grand. A peaceful oasis, it is shaded by trees, cooled by a fountain, and enlivened by vendors who sell produce on weekday and Saturday mornings. On the second Sunday of the month, there is a small open-air flea market here. This is also a favorite nighttime hangout for young people during the warm months. ♦ At Via dei Michelozzi, Via Mazzetta, and Via Sant'Agostino

43 Pensione Sorelle Bandini

$$ One of the last old-fashioned *pensioni* in Florence, this quirky place is installed on the third floor of the Renaissance **Palazzo Guadagni** (attributed to **Cronaca** or **Baccio d'Agnolo**). Five of its 12 large, simply furnished rooms have private baths, and all have views, either of Piazza Santo Spirito or of the historic neighborhood and nearby hills. It's wonderfully atmospheric, dripping with history, and the huge wraparound loggia terrace promises the most memorable sunset in town. Credit cards are not accepted. ♦ Piazza Santo Spirito 9 (at Via Mazzetta). 215308; fax 282761

44 Franceschi

Frames from stately Renaissance style to Minimalist modern are the specialty of this shop. Though meant for paintings, they can also be used to make mirrors pretty as a picture. Even those weary of shopping should seek out this narrow street full of artisans whose *botteghe* (workshops) and skills are often centuries old. ♦ M-F, Sa morning Mar-Oct; M afternoon, Tu-Sa Nov-Feb. No credit cards accepted. Via Toscanella 34-38r (between Sdrucciolo de' Pitti and Via Sguazza). 284704

45 Diladdarno

★★$$ This is the local option for local cuisine in a typical trattoria. Tuscan first-course soups (minestrone; *ribollita*; and *pappa al pomodoro*—tomatoes, bread, olive oil, and basil) are favorites. Also on offer are Italian classics *mozzarella in carozza* (basically a sort of delicious deep-fried mozzarella sandwich) and *vitello tonnato* (veal in a tuna fish sauce. Don't for a second think you wouldn't like it.). ♦ M-Sa, dinner only; Su, lunch and dinner. Via dei Serragli 108r (between Via del Campuccio and Via della Chiesa). 225001

46 Prezzemolo

Some of the young and the restless (and rich) Florentines come to this nightspot to play board games (and bored games) in an unusual setting of catacomb-like rooms divided up Italian-style into little seating areas for the local lounge lizards. ♦ Tu-Su, 9PM-2AM Sept-June. Closed July and August. No credit cards accepted. Via delle Caldaie 5r (at Via della Chiesa). 211530

47 La Baruciola

★$$ This comfortable restaurant, popular with the neighborhood's well-heeled antiques dealers, prides itself on its home-style Tuscan menu. Homemade potato gnocchi with spinach and ricotta and *gran pezzo* (standing rib roast) are reliable choices here. ♦ M-Sa, lunch and dinner. Via Maggio 61r (between Piazza di San Felice and Sdrucciolo de' Pitti). 218906

ADDITIONAL FLORENCE HIGHLIGHTS

As if the many character-filled neighborhoods of Florence weren't packed with enough must-see, -eat, and -do possibilities, it is even more daunting to know that just a cab ride away is a sprinkling of temptations, and more often than not, the crowds are virtually nonexistent. What follows are some recommended destinations outside the main flow of traffic.

1 Museo Stibbert

The **Villa Stibbert** houses the eclectic collection of Frederick Stibbert, a Scotch-Italian who was active in the unification of Italy during the 19th century. That aspect of his life is easily inferred from room after room of displays of arms and armor from East and West, enough to glut any *Camelot* or *Shōgun* fantasies. The exhibit is considered to be one of the most important private collections in the world.

Besides arms, the man also collected furniture, paintings, porcelain, clocks, and objects of every sort—most of which are now collecting dust in this oddball, slightly out-of-the-way museum, sure to appeal to obsessive-compulsives of all ages. ♦ Admission; M-W, 10AM-2PM; F-Su, 10AM-6PM. Closed Thursday. Via Federico Stibbert 26 (between Via Vittorio Emanuele II and Via di Montughi). 475520. e-mail: museostibbert@tin.it

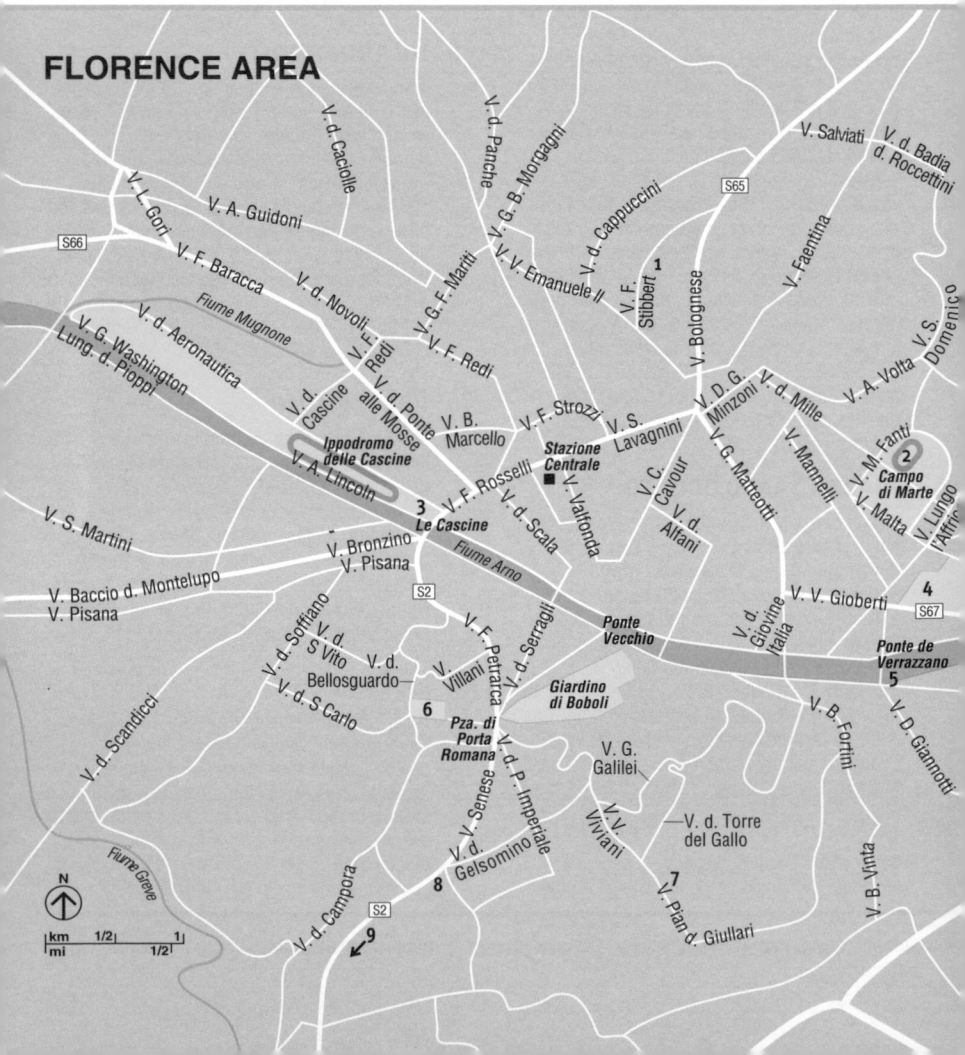

2 Stadio Comunale

Florence's soccer stadium (seating capacity 40,000) is a 1932 Modernist masterpiece of reinforced concrete by **Pier Luigi Nervi**, master of the medium, who designed for it an expansive cantilever roof and widely flying spiral staircase. Beside the stadium rises his **Torre di Maratona** (Marathon Tower). ♦ Open during soccer matches. Viale Manfredo Fanti and Viale Pasquale Paoli. 572625

3 Le Cascine

Florentines of all ranks have long loved their public park, named after the Medici dairy farms, or *cascine*, that once occupied the area, extending almost two miles along the Arno west of the city center. Though the park saw its heyday as center of the carriage trade in the last century, the well-heeled still make use of its private tennis courts and swimming pool (as can foreigners). At the other end of the social scale are the ladies of the night (and the men who dress like them), plying their trade along its alleys. Children can ride merry-go-rounds year-round, or take part in the *Festa del Grillo*—a festival of crickets, which chirp away in tiny cages—on Assumption Day (15 August). On Tuesday morning a large open-air market offering everything from live chickens to antique embroidered linens extends west of **Piazza Vittorio Veneto**. Though few visitors seem to take advantage of the breezy expanses of the former farm, one who did was Shelley, who was inspired to write "Ode to the West Wind" here. At the west end of the park is the **Piazzaletto dell'Indiano**, a little piazza named after the Indian maharaja Raiaram Cuttaputti, who died in Florence in 1870 and was cremated in accordance with the Brahmanic rite and laid to rest nearby, where the Mugnone River joins the Arno. ♦ North bank of the Arno (between Piazza Vittorio Veneto and Piazzaletto dell'Indiano)

4 Cenacolo di San Salvi

This *Cenacolo* (muraled refectory) in the former monastery of San Salvi, now an asylum, houses a magnificent *Last Supper* by Andrea del Sarto. The fresco, painted between 1519 and 1525, represents the apogee of the High Renaissance in Florence, as do Leonardo da Vinci's *The Last Supper* (painted between 1495 and 1498) in Milan and Raphael's *School of Athens* and *Disputa* (painted between 1509 and 1511) in Rome. Though del Sarto is less well-known than the other two painters, Michelangelo is said to have warned Raphael, "There is a little fellow in Florence who would make you sweat if ever he got a great commission to do." *The Last Supper* was del Sarto's greatest commission and is his masterpiece, embodying the Renaissance principles of solid composition and movement in its figures and drapery. It was painted at the moment in art history shortly before his Florentine contemporaries Jacopo Pontormo and Rosso Fiorentino were to take movement and color to a disconcerting extreme in the style that became known as Mannerism. ♦ Daily, 8:30AM-1:50PM. Closed 1st and 3rd Sunday and 2nd and 4th Monday of each month. Via di San Salvi 16 (between Via Lucrezia Mazzanti and Piazza di San Salvi). 2388603

5 La Capannina da Sante

★★$$ An old-fashioned country-style restaurant, Signor Sante's modestly named "little shack" is prettily located along the Arno, with furnishings that have reminded some of Florence's old ATAF buses of the 1950s. There are tables outdoors during the warmer months. He specializes in *acquacotta*, tripe, *spezzatini*, and *inzimino* (Tuscan stewed squid). Wines are good, and the kitchen stays open past midnight, when the dining rooms are packed to the gills. ♦ M, dinner; Tu-Sa, lunch and dinner. Piazza Ravenna (just south of Ponte Giovanni da Verrazzano). 688345

TORRE DI BELLOSGUARDO

FIRENZE ITALIA

6 Torre di Bellosguardo

$$$ Escape the seasonal crush while staying at the remarkable home of the charming Barone Amerigo Franchetti, one of the nicest of Florence's historical villas-turned-hotels. Guests bask in any of 16 handsomely renovated rooms, common areas, and a park with botanical gardens, all steeped in history and decorated with impeccable taste. One of the many attractions of this Renaissance time capsule is the landscaped pool with views of Florence seemingly light-years away. Just in case you feel the need to work off the fabulous food you are enjoying in Florence's restaurants, this hotel has just added a sports center to its facilities: Indoor pool, Jacuzzi, sauna, and gym are all there to keep you in tip-top physical form. There is no restaurant, but breakfast is served on a big sunny veranda. ♦ Via Roti Michelozzi 2 (follow signs heading southwest from Piazza Torquato Tasso to Piazza di Bellosguardo). 2298145; fax 229008

7 Omero

★★$$ This lovely rustic-looking restaurant has recently had a facelift, and it looks

Cenacoli (Last Suppers)

Although Leonardo da Vinci's *Last Supper* in the church of Santa Maria delle Grazie in Milan is the best-known interpretation of this famous event, seven *Cenacoli* (the word derives from *cena*, meaning supper or dinner) await the curious traveler in the cloisters of seven monasteries in Florence. The monks felt that there was no more appropriate image for them to ponder while eating in silence (although holy scriptures were often read during meals) than a larger-than-life portrayal of Christ and the disciples gathered for his last repast. While they satisfied their earthly appetites, their souls turned to spiritual nourishment.

The *Last Supper* portrays a Passover seder attended by Christ and his twelve disciples. It was at this repast that Christ gave them bread and wine, saying, "This is my body" and "This is my blood." The moment is commemorated by Christians in the sacrament of Holy Communion, also known as the "Lord's Supper." During the course of the meal Christ also proclaimed, "One of you shall betray me." He continued, "He that dippeth his hand with me in the same dish shall betray me." The apostles were so taken aback that each asked, "Lord, is it I?" St. John, the closest to Christ, is often pictured as putting his head on Christ's chest in the desperate hope that it would not be him. Judas (the betrayer) is often depicted sitting alone on the viewers' side of the table, with Christ and the other apostles together facing the observers.

Florence's oldest *Cenacolo,* and one of its largest, is in the treasure-filled **Museo dell'Opera di Santa Croce** (formerly a cloister) in **Piazza Santa Croce**. Taddeo Gaddi, a follower of Giotto, painted this rendition in about 1340. Unlike other versions, this *Cenacolo* shows a group of disciples relatively emotionless: The reaction to Christ's pronouncement seems to have alarmed no one. The black background also sets this one apart from others; later *Cenacoli* are more elaborate in their display of both backdrops and the psychological tension of this important moment.

There remains only a fragment of the *Cenacolo di Santo Spirito* in the **Fondazione Salvatore Romano** in **Piazza Santo Spirito**, and a healthy imagination is needed to visualize its long-lost splendor. The painting's artist is unknown. Below it is the scene of the Crucifixion by Andrea Orcagna (ca. 1370).

The *Cenacolo of Sant'Appollonia* in the **Monastero di Sant'Appollonia** by Andrea del Castagno—one of the great early-15th-century Renaissance artists—is just around the corner from the piazza and convent of **San Marco**. The most stylized of Florence's *Last Suppers,* this highly three-dimensional work was painted for the nuns of the Benedictine convent and dramatically focuses on the configuration of Peter, Judas, Christ, and John. Judas dips his bread into wine blessed by Christ, reminding all that those who receive the sacrament of the Holy Eucharist and are unworthy of it can be compared to Judas the betrayer. The devil has clearly entered into Judas, giving him a diabolical aspect—dark robe, hooked nose, jutting beard, and pointed ears. Peter looks on, terribly upset, and John throws his head down before Christ. The drama of the moment is further reflected in the six white-framed marble panels above these central characters' heads—it is tensely veined like lightning bolts and may remind the modern observer more of a 20th-century abstract painting than a Renaissance fresco. This is one of Castagno's few existing works. The *Cenacolo* found in the **Refettorio della Chiesa di Ognissanti** (Refectory of the Church of Ognissanti) at **Piazza Ognissanti** was sponsored by the *umiliati* ("humbled") monks and signed by Domenico di Ghirlandaio (ca. 1480). One of the most sought-after painters of his day, Ghirlandaio was renowned for his penchant for focusing on the everyday details of the lifestyles around him, including those of his patrons—the wealthy merchants of Florence. Ghirlandaio's *sinopia* (preparatory underdrawing of the fresco) is in the same room.

The **Museo di San Marco** in **Piazza San Marco**, dedicated to the works of Fra Angelico, houses Ghirlandaio's

terrific. Now there are two large light, airy rooms, a gorgeous terrace for diners, and a terrific little deli, where the hams hang so thick you can't actually see the ceiling. In case you don't have time to dine you can still enjoy the excellent local salami, cheeses, and other products the Omero offers. Food here is Tuscan through and through, as are most of the 200 wines in the cellar. The *fettunta* (bread toasted, drizzled with olive oil, and scraped with garlic) is toasted at the restaurant's fireplace; you know the *ribollita* and pasta with *ceci* (chickpeas) has been simmering away in the kitchen for hours; and the *fritto misto* (a pile of tiny fritters of chicken, rabbit, and brain) is deliciously fresh and surprisingly light. ♦ M, W-Su, lunch and dinner. Via del Pian de' Giullari 11r (south of Via della Torre del Gallo), Arcetri. 220053. www.ristoranteomero.it

8 Ruggero

★★$$ This rustic eatery—owned by a former cook at **Coco Lezzone**—is somehow more authentic in its location just outside the city gate. Tuscan soups take first place here—*pappa al pomodoro* (tomatoes, bread, olive oil, and basil); *ribollita* (white beans, bread, black cabbage, and onions); and *zuppa di farro* (barley other Florentine *Cenacolo* (a third rendition is at the monastery of Badia a Passignano in Tavarnelie Val di Pesa in Tuscany). This reduced version for the small refectory was completed about 1482. It is one of the most elegant *Last Suppers,* done as Ghirlandaio was approaching the apogee of refined Renaissance painting. The apostles, well-groomed and courtly-looking—unlike the farmers and fishermen they were—seem listless and uninvolved compared to the tension and drama found in Castagno's masterpiece (see page 132). The background is a typical Tuscan garden. Raphael's master teacher, Perugino, painted the *Cenacolo di Foligno,* dated about 1495. Located in the ex-convent of the Franciscan order of **San Onofrio** (see "Cenacolo di Fuligno" on page 91) near **Santa Maria Novella**, its bright Umbrian background features a garden and a forest of pillars that recede into the distance, perhaps representing that which awaits Christ after this powerful moment. It is one of the elements that makes this masterpiece stand out from other *Cenacoli,* though some art historians believe the figures were painted by the artist's assistants. This is the only *Last Supper* where more than a crust of bread and the presence of wine appears on the table. Perugino even included silverware.

Franciabigio's (1514) *Cenacolo della Calza*—the name *Calza* comes from the special hood once worn by the monks—at the **Convento della Calza** (Piazza della Calza 6, between Piazzale di Porta Romana and Via dei Serragli) in the Oltrarno covers the entire back wall of the large refectory of the convent formerly known as **San Giovanni alla Porta di San Pier Gattolino**. It is the most poorly restored of all the *Last Suppers* discussed here. It is open daily 11AM-noon, 3:30PM-5:30PM; an offering is requested.

The *Cenacolo of San Salvi,* one of the best and most famous of the Florentine *Last Suppers,* was painted by Andrea del Sarto (begun 1519) in the old refectory of **San Salvi** in what once was the outskirts of Florence (see page 131). The brilliant colors and lifelike figures make it his most beautiful masterpiece, with the attention and body language of each participant at the dinner drawn toward the central figure of Christ. This background is unique in that it features two servants who are eavesdropping from a balcony above the table. In fact, the Renaissance art historian Vasari apologized in one of his many works about not being able to say enough about its "infinite grace, grandeur and majesty." During the devastating siege of Florence in 1529 by the combined troops of the pope and Emperor Charles V of Spain, as Vasari relates, soldiers came to demolish all the buildings of the suburbs. After having destroyed the church and bell tower of San Salvi, they started to tear down the convent when the leader of the wrecking crew came upon the *Last Supper.* He was so awed by the painting that he ordered it saved and abandoned all further destruction.

Hours for all of the above *Cenacoli,* with the exception of Franciabigio's at the **Convento della Calza**, are listed in the entries in their respective chapters. Note: Schedules for viewing these paintings can be somewhat erratic; be sure to check with the tourist office (see "Visitors' Information Office" in the Orientation chapter, page 16).

soup). ♦ M, Th-Su, lunch and dinner. No credit cards accepted. Via Senese 89r (just south of Via del Gelsomino). 220542

9 Stefano

★★★$$ Generally regarded as just about the best seafood restaurant in Florence. Well-known chef Stefano Corsini opened the place in the 1990s and still helps you choose a delicious dinner (the restaurant doesn't open for lunch—Stefano's motto is "*solo pesce, solo fresco, solo la sera*"—"only fish, only fresh, and only in the evening"). There are vast seafood platters, an excellent spaghetti with lobster, and the legendary *gran tegame*, a huge pot of mixed seafood in a gorgeous stew. The wine list is extensive. Take Stefano's advice and you won't go wrong. And sit on the terrace in summer and gaze out over the cypresses on the hillside. You'll feel like you're an extra in *Under the Tuscan Sun.* ♦ M-Sa, dinner. Closed August. Via Senese 271, Galluzzo. 2049105

Seravezza
Forte dei Marmi
Pietrasanta
Viareggio
Lago Massaciuccoli
Torre del Lago Puccini
Migliarino
Fiume Serchio
Bagni di Lucca
Lucca
Collodi
Pescia
Segromigno in Monte
Montecatini Terme
Montecarlo
Pistoia
Prato
Poggio a Caiano
Sesto Fiorentino
Vinci
Montelupo Fiorentino
Scandicci
Empoli
San Giuliano Terme
Pisa
Santa Croce sull'Arno
Fucecchio
Fiume Arno
Autostrada Firenze-Mare
Cascina
Pontedera
San Miniato
San Casciano
Ponsacco
Castelfiorentino
Capannoli
Fiume Elsa
Certaldo
Leghorn (Livorno)
Poggibonsi
San Gimignano
Colle d Val d'E
Volterra
Casole d'Elsa
Pomarance
Fiume Cecina
Pievescola
Cecina
Castagneto Carducci
Mare Ligure
Campiglia Marittima
Massa Marittima
Piombino
Follonica
Portoferraio
Elba
Porto Azzurro
Castiglione della Pescaia
Grosseto
A12
A11
S12
S435
S436
S64
S325
S66
S67
S555
S439
S429
S2
S206
S1
S68
S541
S329
S398
S441
S73
S322
S223

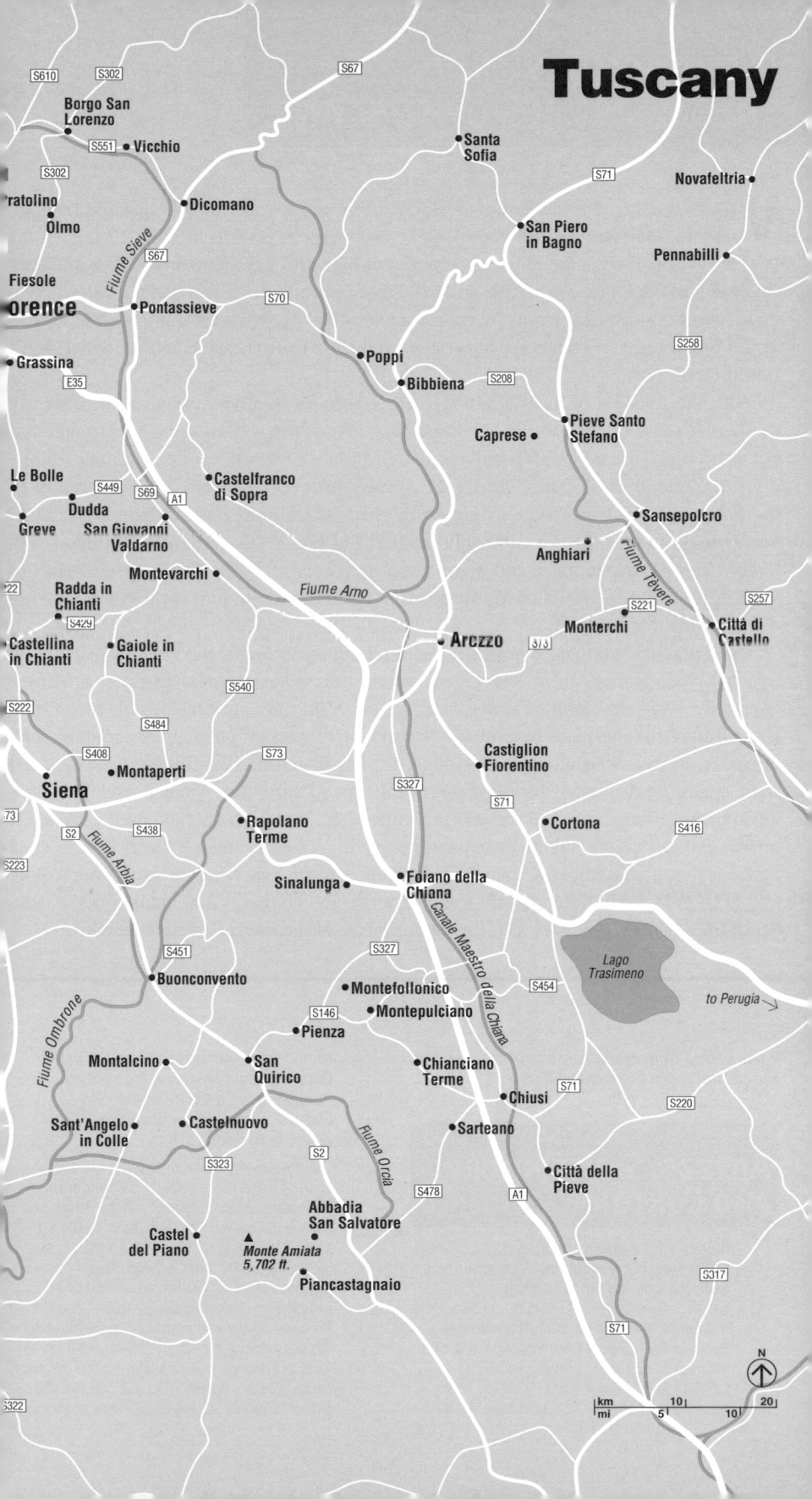
Tuscany
S610
S302
S67
Borgo San Lorenzo
S551
Vicchio
Santa Sofia
S71
Novafeltria
S302
ratolino
Dicomano
Olmo
San Piero in Bagno
Pennabilli
Fiume Sieve
S67
Fiesole
orence
Pontassieve
S70
S258
Grassina
Poppi
E35
Bibbiena
S208
Pieve Santo Stefano
Caprese
Le Bolle
S449
S69
A1
Castelfranco di Sopra
Dudda
Greve
San Giovanni Valdarno
Sansepolcro
Anghiari
Fiume Tevere
Montevarchi
Fiume Arno
Radda in Chianti
S429
S221
S257
Monterchi
Città di Castello
Castellina in Chianti
Gaiole in Chianti
Arezzo
S540
S222
S484
S408
S73
Castiglion Fiorentino
Montaperti
Siena
S327
S71
Rapolano Terme
Cortona
S416
S2
S438
Fiume Arbia
Sinalunga
Foiano della Chiana
Canale Maestro della Chiana
S451
S327
Lago Trasimeno
Buonconvento
Montefollonico
S454
to Perugia
S146
Montepulciano
Pienza
Fiume Ombrone
Montalcino
San Quirico
Chianciano Terme
S71
Chiusi
S220
Sant'Angelo in Colle
Castelnuovo
Sarteano
Fiume Orcia
S2
S323
Città della Pieve
S478
A1
Abbadia San Salvatore
Castel del Piano
Monte Amiata 5,702 ft.
Piancastagnaio
S317
S71
N
km
mi
10
20
5
10

FLORENCE DAY TRIPS: THE TREASURES OF TUSCANY

Visitors can spend a few hours or many lifetimes meandering through the treasure trove that is Florence. Yet venturing beyond the city's walls into the Tuscan countryside that inspired some of Italy's greatest minds and palettes brings other delights: small, uncrowded museums with artworks rivaling many of the **Uffizi**'s masterpieces; quasi-deserted medieval towns; *cucina toscana*; drinking wine on centuries-old estates in **Chianti** where the grapes are harvested; and the unsurpassed beauty of the region's fabled landscape.

With the freedom of a car and a few unfettered days, adventurers can confidently throw maps and caution to the wind and take off for the less-traveled back roads that wind through Tuscany's olive-grove-covered hills. Those who prefer organized planning over the glories of spontaneity or chance discovery can mix and match any of the following day trips—some as easy and close as an hour outside Florence (**Lucca**; **San Gimignano**), others considerably farther, but less known (**Pienza**, **Volterra**). The larger cities of **Arezzo**, **Pisa**, and **Siena** are a perfect contrast to the beachside resort of **Viareggio** or the spa town of **Montecatini**. And architecture buffs will enjoy viewing the historical Medici villas.

Some practical matters: If possible, avoid taking a trip on the weekend—especially on Sunday, when traffic can be heavy, restaurants full, stores closed, and many museums open only a half-day. Rent a car before leaving the US; rates are considerably lower than last-minute bookings made in Florence. If you'll be relying on public transportation, look into train and bus schedules before setting off to avoid getting stranded (we have included some recommended hotels for those desiring to spend more than a day outside the city). For train information, contact **Stazione Centrale di Santa Maria Novella** (Piazza della Stazione, 055/147888088). Bus companies servicing Tuscany include **Lazzi** (Piazza della Stazione 4-6, across from the train station, 166856010) for the western part of the region, and **SITA** (Via Santa Caterina da Siena 17r, between Via Luigi Alamanni and Via della Scala, 055/214721, 055/4782231) for the southeast and eastern part of the region.

When calling from inside Italy or within a city, dial the city code and the local number.

AREZZO, SANSEPOLCRO, AND CORTONA

Arezzo is 80 kilometers (50 miles) southeast of Florence via autostrada **A1** or state road **S69**. To continue from Arezzo to Sansepolcro, travel 38 kilometers (24 miles) northeast of Arezzo on **S73**. If heading to Sansepolcro directly from Florence, it's 118 kilometers (73 miles) on A1 and S73. Cortona is 31 kilometers (19 miles) south of Arezzo on **S71**; from Florence, take A1 97 kilometers (60 miles) southeast to **Val di Chiana**. From here follow the signs to **Perugia**, turning left (north) on S71 to Cortona. There's frequent train service to Arezzo from Florence.

The metropolis of Arezzo is set at the confluence of three green valleys—the **Valdarno**, the **Casentino** (the upper valley of the Arno), and the Val di Chiana. The **Old City** is built on a terraced hill and is topped by a fortress, an indication of the strategic importance this site has held since its earliest days. Arezzo was a prosperous city under the Etruscans and the Romans, and a free commune with Ghibelline leanings during the Middle Ages until it fell to Guelph Florence in 1289. Early in the following century, however, the short but decisive reign of Guido Tarlati (1312-1327)—one of a series of warrior bishops—lifted Arezzo to prominence. It is the city's 14th-century character that remains in evidence today.

After the Black Plague killed half the city's population in 1348, the French troops of Louis d'Anjou sacked Arezzo and refused to move on until they were given 40,000 florins. Florence paid the ransom, effectively purchasing Arezzo's independence. Although Arezzo then became an economic backwater, some important Italians have been born here: Guido d'Arezzo, the 11th-century Benedictine monk who invented the first versions of modern musical notation and the "do-re-mi" names of the notes; Petrarch (1304-1374), the great pre-Renaissance poet; and **Giorgio Vasari**, the Renaissance painter, architect, and historian. Piero della Francesca may have been born in nearby Sansepolcro, but Arezzo holds him as one of its dearest sons. The **Basilica di San Francesco** (see below) is filled with his works. Modern Arezzo is one of the wealthiest cities in Tuscany, boasting one of the largest jewelry industries in Europe; it is also a center for furniture-making and antiques.

At the top of the series of terraces on which the town is built is the **Passeggio del Prato**, a spacious public park that overlooks the surrounding countryside. Arezzo's Gothic **Duomo** stands to one side of it. Begun in the late 13th century and not finished until the beginning of the 16th century, the cathedral contains the stained-glass windows of Guillaume de Marcillat, a famed 15th-century French artist; a fresco of Mary Magdalene by Piero della Francesca; and a memorial to Guido Tarlati (although he is not buried here), completed in 1330 by Agostino di Giovanni and Agnolo di Ventura. At the high altar is the 14th-century tomb of St. Donatus.

A few blocks north of the Duomo is the 13th-century church of **San Domenico** (Piazza San Domenico, at Via Sasso Verde and Via San Domenico), with a beautiful wooden crucifix that is an early work of Cimabue. Not far away is the house of Giorgio Vasari (Via XX Settembre 55, west of Via San Domenico, no phone), who supervised its construction and furnishing and decorated it himself with frescoes between 1540 and 1548. Call the tourist office (see page 138) for hours, which are erratic; there's an admission charge.

Arezzo's main attraction is Piero della Francesca's fresco cycle illustrating *La Storia della Croce* (The Legend of the True Cross). Recently restored, the frescoes are behind the main altar in the **Basilica di San Francesco** (Piazza San Francesco, at Via Madonna del Prato), a barnlike 14th-century church that is the spiritual nucleus and geographical center of the Old City. Della Francesca is considered one of the most important Renaissance painters; his fresco cycle is a marvelous chronicle of the social history, especially fashion and jewelry, of the 15th century.

Nearby is **Piazza Grande**, a sloping trapezoid-shaped square that has been the center of urban life for centuries. The piazza is surrounded by palazzi reflecting the architectural styles of several centuries. Giorgio Vasari's 16th-century **Palazzo delle Logge**, with its open portico of shops, is on the north side and is flanked by several handsome Renaissance palazzi and medieval homes; the façade of the **Palazzo della Fraternità dei Laici** (Palace of the Lay Fraternity) is part Gothic and part Renaissance; and the magnificent **Pieve di Santa Maria**, a 12th- to 14th-century church, features a 13th-century Pisan-Lucchese Romanesque façade. The church's campanile, completed in 1330, is known as "of the hundred holes" because of its 40 mullioned windows.

On the first Sunday of every month and the Saturday preceding it, Piazza Grande and the surrounding streets become the site of the largest (700 vendors) antiques fair in Italy. The last Sunday in August and the first Sunday in September, the market moves to the **Passeggio del Prato** behind the Duomo to make room for the annual *Giostra dei Saracino,* a colorful re-creation of a medieval jousting tournament in which eight knights representing the city's four quarters attack an effigy of a Saracen, the infidel enemy. A historical procession of lance-carrying knights—decked in full armor—on brilliantly adorned horses takes place at the same time. This dazzling spectacle fits in quite easily with the Old City's cobblestone streets and picturesque piazza. Tickets are sold at the tourist office (see page 138). To order tickets in advance, call the tourist office to reserve them, and then send an international money order.

Also of interest in Arezzo are the remains of a Roman amphitheater near the **Museo Archeologico Mecenate** (Via Margaritone 10, between Via Niccolò Aretino and Via F. Crispi, 0575/20882), which contains a collection of the corallini vases made by Aretine (residents of Arezzo) artists from the first century BC to the first century AD. The museum is open Monday-Saturday, 9AM-2PM, and Sunday, 9AM-1PM; there's an admission charge.

On the first weekend of each month, Italy's top antiques market takes place in Arezzo. Over 600 dealers and thousands of buyers crowd the Piazza Grande and the surrounding streets.

And if all that buying makes you hungry, be assured that eating in Arezzo is good! The **Caffè dei Constanti** is all Old World charm, as you can see in the film *Life Is Beautiful,* in which it is featured. Three generations of the

Olive Oil: Liquid Gold

You are in Tuscany now—oil country. Not black gold, but green gold. Olive oil. The ancient Greeks and Romans considered the olive holy. Olive branches are used to symbolize peace, and wreaths of olive leaves were used to crown heroes.

You can see acres of the little gnarled gray-green trees across the hills of the region. And never make the mistake of thinking that olive oil is olive oil is olive oil. Every little estate and farm will produce a slightly different-tasting oil, which will change from year to year. The difference comes from the soil, the weather conditions, the time of pressing, and the mix of olives. Every grove contains a different mix of trees and olive types. Leccino and Scarlinese, Arancino and Madonna della Impruneta, Razzaio and Leccio del Como, Seggianese and Pesciatino . . . these are the names of just some of the most popular olives in Tuscany alone. There are dozens more. And the mix is individual to each estate. Harvesting (the *raccolta*) is usually carried out in November after enough of the olives are ripe but before the first frosts can damage them. Traditionally, the harvesting is done by hand, or with tiny stubby plastic rakes that the workers use to comb down the branches. Usually a tarpaulin or parachute silk is laid all around the base of the tree, the olives plucked or combed down onto it, the tarpaulin gently gathered up, and the contents decanted into buckets and boxes. Experts (and almost everyone in Tuscany with an olive grove is an expert) say you should not harvest in the rain because the water rots the olives if they are left to dry in boxes or dilutes the oil if they are pressed when still wet, but the fact is once a harvest starts, you have to finish it, and having worn out my hair dryer and given up two of my blankets to dry olives on, I know that there is more than one way to dry an olive!

The harvest should be pressed as soon as possible after picking. The traditional method takes the olives to the local *frantoia* (mill), where they are weighed, sorted, washed, and slowly crushed to a khaki paste by stone wheels rolling round and round. The paste is spread out onto a series of circular rope mats piled one on top of another and pressed by another great stone weight till the oil drips, single drop by single drop, out of the paste and down into the collecting vat. Anyone who has watched those single drops form and remembers the single olives they collected to make the drops will never quibble about the price of good olive oil again.

It takes time for the paste to be pressed dry, and then, after a quick whirl in the centrifuge to remove the impurities (you can watch the brown sludge swoosh out of the back of the tank), you can see the extraordinary, electric green liquid foam and pour out of the pipe and into the holding tank. From there it is released into containers for transport and storage. Taste the oil now and it is peppery, zingy, unbelievably grassy, and lively. Within even a month it will have deepened in color and mellowed in flavor.

The new olive oil is celebrated at its birth—toasts are drunk not only to it, but in it. I know the idea of a shot glass of pure new olive oil might sound appalling, but it is delicious. It is spread on crostini served with *pinzimonio* or vegetable crudités to dip in it.

Go and find a real oil merchant. He will encourage you to taste. Do taste! Look for cold-pressed and stone-pressed oil. Look for estate name and dates of pressing. Know your oils—extra virgin has less than one percent acidity, virgin has under four percent. Other olive oils are higher in acidity, which means they go rancid sooner. Never use the commercially produced gloop.

Once you have your oil, look after it. Don't let it get too hot or too cold. Don't expose it to too much light. It is precious stuff. Take it from one who has given up her blankets for it!

Good places to buy olive oil: **Olio & Convivium** (see Oltrarno), **Cibreo** (see Santa Croce), **La Bottega dell' Olio** (Santa Maria Novella).

same family have served gelati here (Piazza San Francesco 19, 0575/21660). It's open Tuesday through Sunday, 7AM-10PM. **Le Tastevin** is regarded as offering some of the best cooking in the city, plus occasional jazz played by the owner (Via de Cenci 9, 0575/28304). **Antica Osteria l'Agania** is a fun trattoria where you drink from huge flagons and pay only for as much as you down. Food is robust, including *grifi e polenta* (veal tripe with polenta) (Via Mazzini 10, 0575/295381). The most famous eatery is **La Buca di San Francesco** (Via San Francesco 1, 0575/23271), located in the former cantina of a 14th-century palazzo. It's pretty historic itself, having been run here by the de Fillipi family for 70 years. The food is terrifically Tuscan, and the *saporita del buonconte,* a big stew of assorted meats, and the white bean soup are top-notch comfort food. It's open daily except Tuesday.

Arezzo's tourist office (Piazza della Repubblica 28, between Viale Michelangelo and Viale Piero della Francesca, 575/377678; fax 575/20839) is open Monday-Saturday, and the first Sunday of each month from April through August, closed Sundays in September; Sunday hours from October through March vary.

Before heading to Sansepolcro—a "must see" for any pilgrim seeking treasures by Piero della Francesca—detour off S73 on **S221**, stopping in **Monterchi** to see the artist's extraordinary *Madonna del Parto*. This recently

The Outlets

Okay, ladies, we all know what this trip to Florence is about. And Renaissance art it isn't. Florence may be Michelangelo and Brunelleschi and Donatello and Dante, but Florence is also Ferragamo and Cavalli and Prada and Gucci.

And you go to buy at the outlets. Anything from 30 minutes to 2 hours outside Florence, you can experience retail therapy that will cure you of anything. Many companies will organize tours to one or more of these marvelous malls, but some are accessible by train or bus, and all of them if you have a car.

The biggest is also the newest. Simply called **The Mall** (Via Europa 8, Leccio Reggello. 055 865 7775), there are over 90 shops in this massive shopper's paradise, as well as, you will be glad to know, a very nice café. You'll find Alexander McQueen, Armani, Balenciaga, Burberry, Ungaro, Fendi, Gucci, Pucci, Ferragamo, Stella McCartney, Valentino, and YSL, among many others. Buses leave Santa Maria Novella Station in Florence at 9AM and noon Monday through Friday, and at 9AM only on Saturday. They return at noon and 5PM.

The **Barberino Outlet** will offer you Prada, Gucci, and Versace, as well as private parking and a children's playground to engage those too young to be excited by Prada. Take A1 in the direction of Milan, exit at Barberino di Mugello, and the outlet is 200 meters down the road. Open Tuesday through Sunday 10AM-9PM.

Dolce&Gabbana have their outlet in Rignano Sull'Arno at Santa Maddalena 49 833 1300. Trains run frequently from Santa Maria Novella Station in Florence.

Roberto Cavalli's (www.robertocavallioutlet.it) extroverted creations can be found at knockdown prices at Via Volturno 3/3 in Osmannoro (take the A1 heading north for a half hour and look for the sign to Osmannoro). It is open weekdays in winter and Monday through Saturday in summer.

www.enjoyvenice.com can organize tours to **The Outlet Store** (Max Mara, Moschino, and Versace) and **The Prada Outlet** (Helmut Laing, Miu Miu, and Jil Sander). You can book online or call them at 055 295 206.

www.caftours.com will take you to The Mall, Prada, and Dolce&Gabbana in luxury coaches (as well as offering many other good day trips in Tuscany). Again, you can book online or at CAF Tours, Via San Antonino 6r. (210612). Open daily, 8AM-7PM.

restored fresco on the wall of a small chapel in a country cemetery is a rare depiction of the Virgin Mary late in her pregnancy. It is an intimate work, revealing a very personal moment for Mary—she seems weary and melancholy, with one hand on her hip and the other on her stomach. Check with Arezzo's tourist office (see page 138) for information and hours.

Sansepolcro is famous for its lace, pasta, and most of all Piero della Francesca, who was born and lived most of his life (1416-1492) here. His father, a shoemaker, died before his birth, and he was given his mother's family name. Although he worked in the region of the Marches to the east, Arezzo, and Rome, Sansepolcro is where the artist spent most of his life, painting and writing on geometry and perspective until he became blind at age 60.

The **Piazza Torre di Berta** in the town's center is where the *Palio della Balestra* takes place on the second Sunday in September. This ancient contest between the crossbow archers from Gubbio (in Umbria) and Sansepolcro is enacted in medieval costume. Walk down **Via Matteotti** to catch a glimpse of many of the city's 14th- to 16th-century palaces. Most notable are the **Palazzo delle Laudi** and the 14th-century building housing the **Museo Civico**. This museum in the old **Town Hall** features one of the most important art collections in Tuscany outside of Florence.

The museum's pride is the *Resurrection*, Piero della Francesca's masterpiece of the risen Jesus stepping out of his tomb while holding a standard with a cross and surrounded by the sleeping soldiers who were guarding the tomb. The second soldier from the left is said to be the artist's self-portrait, and the Sansepolcro countryside is the background. Also on display is *Madonna della Misericordia* (The Virgin of Pity), another of the artist's masterpieces. This gold-background multipaneled altarpiece represents a giant Madonna using her cloak to shelter the members of the confraternity who commissioned the picture (confraternities were groups of guild heads who did anonymous good works, often wearing hooded cloaks). Other works include fragments of frescoes by Piero della Francesca; a *Crucifixion* by the artist's pupil Luca Signorelli; Pontormo's *Martyrdom of San Quintino*; works of 16th-century painters Santi di Tito and Giovanni de' Vecchi; a 17th-century Mannerist *Last Supper*; Renaissance terra-cottas; a collection of sinopias (sketches drawn directly on the walls); church vestments and reliquaries; and prehistoric artifacts found

The Best

Laura Kramer

Historian/Journalist/Tour Designer, Custom Tours in Tuscany

Rummaging around looking for treasures at the antiques fair in **Piazza dei Ciompi** the last Sunday of the month.

Walking through **Piazza Santo Spirito** on a summer's night to see the locals "in action." There are usually throngs of hip people hanging out, chatting with one another and on the ubiquitous cell phones, deciding where to go dancing after midnight.

Listening to the monks chant at 4:30PM at **San Miniato al Monte** church.

Basking in the glory of the Medici family in a visit to the Benozzo Gozzoli frescoes in **Palazzo Medici Riccardi**.

Getting up early and joining the Italian *mamme* in battle for the best produce at the **Mercato Centrale** or at the farmers' market at **Sant'Ambrogio**.

Strolling through the iris garden at **Piazzale Michelangiolo** in May and marveling at the seemingly infinite number of different color combinations.

Hunting down that perfect pair of new shoes after looking in absolutely every store window between the station and **Ponte Vecchio**.

Stepping back in time with a visit to the **Museo Horne**, a restored Renaissance house filled with period art and home furnishings.

in the upper Tiber Valley. There's also a lovely little courtyard with plants and benches. The museum is open Monday-Saturday, 10AM-4PM; admission is charged.

Other notable artworks appear in three of Sansepolcro's churches: The 11th-century **Duomo** on Via Matteotti (at Piazza dei Duomo) houses a fresco by Bartolomeo della Gatta and a polyptych by Matteo di Giovanni; the Gothic **San Francesco** (Piazza San Francesco) features a beautiful rose window and portal; and **San Lorenzo** (Piazza San Lorenzo) boasts a *Deposizione* by Rosso Fiorentino.

Cortona is another treasure trove of artists. The Renaissance painter Luca Signorelli, the Baroque master of the rooms in Florence's **Pitti Palace**; Pietro Berrettini (known as Pietro da Cortona); and the Futurist artist Gino Severini (1883-1966) were all born here.

Set high above the Val di Chiana plain, this small hill town of steep narrow streets (only **Via Nazionale** is level) is pre-Etruscan. Legend says that the city was founded by Dardanus, who, when fighting against a neighboring tribe, lost his helmet (*corythos*) on top of a hill. Dardanus went on to found the city of Troy (the Dardanelles are named after him). Many historians believe that the Etruscans came from western Anatolia in approximately 900 BC, because inscriptions on the Greek island of Lemnos (near Troy) are very similar to Etruscan, and there are cultural similarities in the Iron Age artifacts found in Anatolia and Tuscany. During the medieval period, which the town still reflects, Cortona remained independent but suffered internal struggles between the Ghibellines—supporters of the Holy Roman Emperor—and the Guelphs, who were defenders of the pope. The Ghibellines ultimately won out, but the Casali—the ruling family of the 14th century—created havoc in the city and turned against itself in an orgy of self-destruction. This ended in 1409, when the city was captured by King Ladislas of Naples and then sold to Florence. Begin a stroll through town in the asymmetrical **Piazza della Repubblica**, whose architectural highlight is the 13th-century **Palazzo Comunale** (Town Hall), with its tower built in 1503. The adjoining **Piazza Signorelli** features the 13th-century **Palazzo Pretorio** (also called the "Palazzo Casali"), which houses the **Museo Accademia Etrusca** (0575/630415). In its great central hall hangs the prize of the museum's collection: an amazing Etruscan chandelier of the fifth century BC that features a gorgon's head for the base, surrounded by stylized waves and dolphins, and 16 squatting figures supporting as many oil burners. The chandelier is the largest and most richly decorated of its kind anywhere. Also in the museum's eclectic collection are Etruscan bronzes, Greek vases, Egyptian mummies, and a fine group of paintings dating back to a Roman portrait of the muse *Polyhymnia*. The museum is open Tuesday-Sunday; there's an admission charge.

At **Piazza del Duomo** is an 11th-century **Duomo** (rebuilt in 1560) that houses a mosaic by Gino Severini. From the ramparts is a wonderful view of the whole valley. Across the piazza in a former church with a fine wooden coffered ceiling (1536) is the **Museo Diocesano** (Piazza del Duomo 1, 0575/62830). Stop in to see, among other works, Luca Signorelli's *Descent from the Cross* and Fra Angelico's ethereal *Annunciation*. Ambling down the town's picturesque lanes—**Via Jannelli**, **Via Ghibellina**, **Via Guelfa**, and **Via Giuseppe Maffei**—it's easy to imagine life here during the Middle Ages.

Notice the small side doors—*porte del morto* (doors of the dead)—visible in the façade of some palazzi. More common in medieval Umbria than in Tuscany, the doors were used during the Black Plague to carry the deceased out of the house, as it was considered bad luck for the living to use the same exit.

If you want to shop rather than look, then the **Antica Drogheria** is a great place for gift ideas, stocking local wines and grappas, but more interestingly all the potions and health products created by the Camaldolesi monks (daily, 9AM-1PM and 3PM-8PM). (Via Nazionale 3)

Eating is good in Crotona too. **Preludio** (Via Guelfa 11, 0575/630104) offers modern Tuscan cuisine—light twists on traditional dishes—in the ancient setting of a Renaissance palazzo.

Beautifully situated in a tiny, privately owned 17th-century hamlet just 5 kilometers (3 miles) north of town is the rustic yet very elegant **Il Falconiere** (Località San Martino, 0575/612679; fax 0575/612927) restaurant/inn. Silvia and Riccardo Baracchi run what is regarded as one of the best restaurants in the region. It's expensive, but a real, all-around treat. Eat outside on a flagstone terrace overlooking Cortona in summer; in cooler weather, meals are served in a former *limonaia* (an enclosed lemon garden) that features stucco walls and a vaulted brick ceiling. There are nine delightful guest rooms in an old villa for those who wish to spend the night. All are air conditioned and tastefully furnished with antiques and white linen curtains. The restaurant (reservations are recommended) is open Monday-Tuesday; Thursday-Sunday, lunch and dinner. The hotel is open year-round.

Cortona's tourist office (Via Nazionale 42, between Vicolo Vagnucci and Piazza della Repubblica, 0575/630352) is open daily; it is closed October through May.

Chianti Classico Country

The Chianti Classico region may be explored on a number of roads. If time is limited, take autostrada **A1** southeast, getting off at any of the exits before or at **Montevarchi**, and drive west. The **Via Cassia** (also called **S2**) from Florence to Siena follows the route of the ancient Roman road. Just before reaching **San Casciano** (12 kilometers—7 miles), turn left (east), following signs for **Greve** (18 kilometers—11 miles). A more picturesque route to Siena is via the **Chiantigiana** (**S222**), which winds up and down the hill towns of central Chianti. Pick up the road outside Florence at **Grassina** (9 kilometers—6 miles) and head south to Greve for 19 kilometers (12 miles). Continue south 20 kilometers (12 miles) to **Castellina in Chianti**, then head east 10 kilometers (6 miles) on **S429** to **Radda in Chianti**. Travel east 10 kilometers (6 miles) on S429 to **Badia a Coltibuono**, then head south 5 kilometers (3 miles) on **S408** to **Gaiole in Chianti**. **SITA** buses go from Florence to Greve.

The word *Chianti* can signify two things: an often complex and ever-changing red wine, and a 170,000-acre geographical region that is one of Italy's most beautiful and, to the gastronomically inclined, most alluring. Yet the two are inseparable; this region of rolling hills covered with forests, olive groves, cypress trees, and orchards reaches its maximum form of expression in a glassful of its historic beverage. The Chianti area is divided into seven subzones; the most famous is the Chianti Classico region, which extends roughly from Florence to Siena.

Its history goes back to the 13th century, when the three cities of **Radda**, **Castellina**, and **Gaiole** joined the Florentine-backed league known as the *Lega dei Chianti* (Chianti League). The confederation was set up to halt the expansionist acts of neighboring Siena and took the *gallo nero* (black rooster) as its symbol. Today the wine consortium that produces Chianti Classico uses the same emblem.

In the last 30 years the Chianti Classico area has been called home by an ever-increasing community of Americans, Dutch, English, and Germans, many of whom bought dilapidated *case coloniche* (farmhouses)—and sometimes castles and mills—and restored them into enviable residences with breathtaking views and often histories to match. It is not always with a smile that Tuscans will talk about how their region has come to be known as "Chiantishire."

Castles, sleepy hill towns, wineries, countryside churches, and weekly markets make up a storehouse of different options for exploring the area's treasures. The region's beauty unfolds when you go where the back roads take you. Up and over the next cypress-studded hill may lie a time-locked town, your favorite meal, the most sophisticated unsung wine producer, a field of sunflowers, or an ancient olive grove. Unless you're following a prearranged agenda, a carefree, adventurous style should play a large role in your wanderings around the region; it rarely disappoints. The following are just some of the area's highlights. One caveat: Try to avoid driving on Sundays and holidays, when Italians flood the roads in search of an escape from the city.

Along S222 near **Le Bolle** (about 24 kilometers—15 miles—from Florence) is **Castello di**

The Best

Donatella Cinelli Colombini

Owner/Director, Fattoria dei Barbi

Castello Banfi, Montalcino. The castle was built before AD 1000 and includes a museum of wineglasses and a restaurant. Surrounding the castle are more than 700 hectares of vineyards. The large, modern cellar with big barrels looks like a cathedral dedicated to wine.

Badia Coltibuono, Gaiole in Chianti. A monastery founded by Benedictines in AD 1076. The cellars under the cloister date back to the 16th century. In the monastery is the cooking school of Lorenza de' Medici. The students attending the courses sleep in the friars' cells. The restaurant, serving typical dishes, is joined to the monastery.

Vicchiomaggio (055/854079). The winery here is owned and run by Englishman John Matta, and visitors can stop in and sample (and buy, of course) the vineyard's products. Leonardo da Vinci mentions the medieval castle in his writings and may even have been a guest. A couple of kilometers farther south on S222 just before **Greve** is the cutoff for **Castello di Uzzano**. Take the signposted, winding road up to this beautiful spot, where you can taste and buy the winery's excellent Chianti Classico. The estate has beautiful, extensive gardens. The 13th-century castle was sacked endlessly by enemy Ghibellines and repeatedly rebuilt until it took its present form in the 1400s.

Greve is considered the center and unofficial capital of the Chianti Classico region. Its most famous son is Giovanni da Verrazzano, who is credited with the discovery of the Bay of New York. He is remembered by a large bronze statue in the center of **Piazza Matteotti**, a picturesque triangular "square" lined with loggias. A walk around the piazza provides an introduction to some of Chianti's main products: salami, cheeses, pottery, terra-cotta pots, straw baskets, wine, and olive oil. Every Saturday from 8AM-1PM the piazza is the site of an open-air market featuring food, clothes, toys, and household wares. Greve's annual wine festival, which includes tastings, presentations, and concerts, takes place on the piazza at the beginning of September. Check the local tourist office (open Monday-Saturday) in the **Municipio** (Town Hall) building (Piazza Matteotti, 055/8545245) for exact dates. In good weather, the hotel/restaurant **Giovanni da Verrazzano** (Piazza Matteotti 28, 055/853189) has outdoor dining on its upstairs terrace overlooking the piazza. The restaurant is open Tuesday-Sunday, breakfast, lunch, and dinner.

For a delightful meal in the hills above town, head to the **Borgo Antico** restaurant (055/851024) in **Lucolena**. To get there, go east 10 kilometers (6 miles) to **Dudda**, then head south for 4 kilometers (2 miles) to Lucolena. This dining spot (a few rooms are also rented out here) tucked away in a medieval hamlet serves every Tuscan grandmother's favorite recipes, either inside or outdoors on the wide patio. It is open Monday, Wednesday-Sunday, lunch and dinner March through November (daily, June-September); Friday-Sunday, lunch and dinner December through February. Reservations are recommended. Another rustic, charming restaurant near Greve is **Le Cernacchie** in La Panca (055/8547968). Local dishes and some unexpected New Wave inventions, including pasta with cocoa, are served here. It is open Monday, Wednesday-Sunday, lunch and dinner; reservations are recommended.

The hill town of Castellina in Chianti dominates three valleys—**Arbia**, **Pesa**, and **Elsa**. As a result, it was a critical stronghold in history's endless battles between Florence and Siena. When Florence won final control in 1554, Castellina lost its strategic importance but retained its distinction as one of the region's most picturesque towns. Houses were built over the old fortress ramparts, creating a tunneled or "vaulted" street known as **Via delle Volte**. At the top of today's village of about 2,700 inhabitants is the looming **Rocca** (Fortress), now the home of the mayor's office. The tourist information office (Via della Rocca 12, 0577/740620; fax 0577/740620) is open Monday-Saturday.

Wine-tasting visits may be made at **Fonterutoli** (S222, 5 km/3 miles south of Castellina, 0577/740309), a traditional Chianti producer; and at the **Fattoria Querce Sola** (0577/743016), whose 1988 Rufone won a gold medal in 1996 at the prestigious International Challenge du Vin at Blaye-Bourg sur Gironde in France. The restaurant **Albergaccio** (Via Fiorentina 35, just northwest of the S222/S429 intersection, 0577/741042) offers regional cooking at its best in a converted farmhouse (and, despite its name, it is not an *albergo,* or hotel). It's open Monday, Friday, and Saturday, lunch and dinner; Tuesday-Thursday, dinner. Reservations are recommended.

High up (1,700 feet) in a more rugged landscape than other spots in Chianti sits Radda in Chianti, a mostly agricultural outpost of fewer than 2,000 residents. The town center is beautifully preserved within heavy walls; walk up the main road to see the **Palazzo del Podestà** (Via Roma), covered with the coats of arms of visiting magistrates, and then lose yourself in the winding, picturesque back streets. Just outside the wall at the end of the park is **La Ghiacciaia** (Viale Matteotti 10, 0577/738739); it's open Monday, Tuesday, Thursday-Sunday. This former multileveled ice cellar was built into the hill by the Medici grand dukes for preserving their meats and perishables. Today it is a charming store that features antiques and local handicrafts. Radda's tourist information office, open Monday-Saturday, is located in the **Palazzo del Podestà** (577/738494).

A special place to spend the night is the stylish 18th-century villa-turned-hotel **Fattoria Vignale** (Via Pianigiani 9, 0577/738300). The 22 rooms in this sophisticated hostelry are both comfortable and charming, and many boast lovely views of the countryside and pool area. An elegant dining experience awaits at the hotel's nearby restaurant, **Relais Vignale** (Via XX Settembre 23, 0577/738094). One of the area's best caterics, this place offers many homemade Tuscan delicacies, including pasta and grilled meat. The hotel is closed mid January to mid March; the restaurant is open Monday-Wednesday and Friday-Sunday for lunch and dinner; closed mid-January to mid-March. Reservations are recommended.

Close to Radda, off the road back to Florence, you will find the **Villa Rosa**, a beautiful, old, warm pink-walled villa set in gorgeous gardens with its own swimming pool. There are 11 rooms with wrought-iron beds draped with fine Italian fabrics and handmade and hand-painted furniture. All are en suite, with minibar and all modern conveniences. Two have their own terraces. Breakfast is served on the rear terrace when the weather is good (and the view glorious) and in the old wine cellar when it is not. Four-course home-cooked Tuscan dinners are available on request. As if that were not enough, the Villa can furnish you with a chauffeur-driven car for trips into town (Florence is 20 miles away, Siena slightly nearer), pick you up from the airport or train station, organize wine tours, and host wine and olive oil tastings in the Villa itself. The Villa Rosa even welcomes your pets! And all at a price that would not get you anything remotely in the same class in the city. (Via S Leone 59 Panzano in Chianti, 852577, www.resortvillarosa.it)

From Radda, head east 14 kilometers (9 miles) to Gaiole in Chianti. Gaiole is peaceful and quaint, although it lacks the charm of Radda. It has been a market town since early medieval times, because of its strategic position as a low crossroad between the area's hilltop towns, monasteries, and castles. Immediately above Gaiole lies the early-medieval religious center of **Castello di Spaltenna**. Beautifully preserved from the outside with a characteristic tower, the hamlet dates back at least to AD 1003 and is now a luxury hotel (0577/749483) with 15 rooms, a restaurant, and a panoramically situated pool.

On the way to Gaiole is **Badia a Coltibuono**, an ancient abbey set amid a forest of pine and fir overlooking the Arno Valley. Today it's a noted winery and restaurant (0577/749948), in a lovely setting. It is open Tuesday-Sunday, lunch and dinner. And if you really take to it, why not enroll in **Lorenza de' Medici**'s cookery school? She teaches well—her son runs the restaurant. Don't let the name panic you; the Medicis no longer poison people. (At least, that we know about.)

Montecatini Terme, Collodi, Montecarlo, and Lucca

Montecatini Terme is 47 kilometers (29 miles) west of Florence on autostrada **A11**. Collodi is 13 kilometers (8 miles) west of Montecatini Terme via **S435**. To get to Montecarlo from Montecatini, take S435, detouring south at **Pescia**. From both Collodi and Montecarlo, pick up S435 to continue west to Lucca—it is 17 kilometers (11 miles) from Collodi, or 15 kilometers (9 miles) from Montecarlo. Lucca is 73 kilometers (45 miles) from Florence on A11. Trains run about every hour during the day from Florence's **Stazione Centrale di Santa Maria Novella** to Lucca and Montecatini; buses frequently leave from the **Lazzi** station.

What Vichy is to France and Baden-Baden is to Germany, Montecatini Terme is to Italy. The resort's heralded mineral waters have had a salutary effect on many people, including Giuseppe Verdi (who wrote the last act of *Otello* here), Arturo Toscanini, and Sophia Loren. To "take the waters" in Montecatini means to settle into a hotel, undergo an obligatory clinical consultation with a hydro expert, and then make tracks each day—almost always in the morning on an empty stomach—to one of the town's *stabilimenti termali* (thermal establishments) to drink the prescribed measure from any of the five springs: **Tamerici**, **Torretta**, **Regina**, **Tettuccio**, and **Rinfresco**. The waters from two other springs, **Leopoldine** and **Giulia**, are for mineral baths only, and an eighth spring, **Grocco**, is expressly for mud baths.

Montecatini was first frequented by the soldiers and leaders of the ancient Roman legions, who soothed their war-weary bodies by soaking in and imbibing its curative waters. The *termi* were once the private property of the Medici, but it wasn't until the late 19th century that the waters' curative powers became well known. Early in the 20th century the various springs were taken over by the government, a massive building program was undertaken, and fashionable hotels were constructed. Today Montecatini's hostelries number over 400, with most operating from Easter through November. A select few are open year-round, though the town pretty much shuts down in the empty winter months.

A serious treatment should last 12 days, so if you're here just a day or two, don't expect miracles. But even for those who don't take the cure, a peek at one of the *stabilimenti,* all laid out in a vast green park—**Parco degli Stabilimenti**—is enlightening. The most beautiful is the **Stabilimento Tettuccio** (just south of Viale Fedeli), built in 1927 in the classical style. From early morning until noon here, an orchestra plays under a frescoed dome; attendants replenish cups at fountains spouting from counters of inlaid marble set before scenes of youth and beauty that are painted on walls of ceramic tile; and patrons stroll through the colonnades, peruse newspapers, or chat. The entrance fee is stiff because it includes water for those who are taking the cure as well as the otherworldly atmosphere, and there is a lovely, conventional coffee bar inside. Off-season only the less theatrical **Stabilimento Excelsior** (Viale Verdi), built in 1915 with an ultramodern wing, is open.

Other attractions here include expensive boutiques; sports facilities—there's horse racing from April through October, and the **Montecatini Golf Club**, a challenging 18-hole golf course 10 kilometers (6 miles) from Montecatini near **Monsummano Terme** (Via dei Bragi, 0572/62218; fax 0572/617435); and seemingly endless, beautifully groomed flower gardens and forests of century-old oaks, pines, palms, cedars, magnolias, and oleanders. Pick up booklets on different walks at the tourist information office (Viale Verdi 66, between Viale Manzoni and Via Grocco, 0572/772244; fax 0572/70109). It is open Monday-Saturday and Sunday morning. For information on the spas, contact **Direzione delle Terme** (Viale Verdi 41, 0572/7781); it's open daily in the morning.

Open since 1870, the **Grand Hotel e La Pace** (Via della Torretta 1, between Piazza del Popolo and Viale Amendola, 0572/9240; fax 0572/78451) features an Old World setting of grandiose décor and a pampering staff. There are 150 air-conditioned rooms, three restaurants, a heated pool in an extensive park, tennis courts, and a health center. The hotel is open April-October. The more intimate and far more affordable **Cappelli-Croce di Savoia** (Viale Bicchierai 139, between Viale Manzoni and Via Grocco, 0572/71151; fax 0572/71154) has 72 rooms—50 with air conditioning—and has been run by the amiable Cappelli family since the 1930s. The spacious lobby, with marble floors, Persian carpets, and pots and vases of flowers, is a bit grander than the more modest rooms, but there is a beautiful flowering back patio with a pool and a good restaurant, all only about 100 yards from the spa. It's open April—mid-November. The town's most highly recommended restaurant is **Gourmet** (Viale Amendola 6, 771012), known for its lobster *crespelle* and sea bass in Champagne. It's open Monday, Wednesday-Sunday, lunch and dinner; reservations are required for dinner.

Midway between Montecatini and Lucca is the tiny, isolated hill town of Montecarlo, known in the culinary world for its well-respected white wine and delightful restaurants such as **La Nina** (Via San Martino 54, 0583/22178), which features alfresco dining in a lovely garden. It's open Monday, lunch; Wednesday-Sunday, lunch and dinner; reservations are recommended.

A perfect place for children is the **Parco di Pinocchio** (0572/429342) in Collodi, the mythical setting for Carlo Lorenzini's wooden puppet's adventures (Lorenzini took the name of his hometown as his nom de plume) written in 1881. This indoor/outdoor museum and sculpture garden boasts larger-than-life representations of Pinocchio and other characters from the famous book, a maze, and mosaics of scenes from Collodi's work. The park is open daily, 8:30AM to sundown; admission is charged.

Although Lucca is a fair-sized city (100,000 residents), it has the air of a charming, elegant town. A favorite with locals and visitors alike, most of Lucca's treasures—food, art, architecture, shopping, and gardens—are found within the painstakingly maintained historic district. Lucca's third and final set of city walls was built in the 16th and 17th centuries—a swath of magnificent ramparts that are still perfectly intact. They are both broad and low enough to be topped with a tree-lined promenade, a public traffic-free thoroughfare that's an intrinsic part of city life Within the walls, Lucca's architecture is a mingling of Roman, Gothic, and Baroque, with neoclassical and Art Nouveau (called "Liberty style in Italy) featured as well.

Giacomo Puccini was born here; the old-fashioned bar, **Fanciulla del West** (Via Mordini 19, between Piazza del Carmine and Via Fillungo, 0583/47343), is one of the more lighthearted memorials to him. But the composer preferred the cozy, wood-paneled **Antico Caffè Di Simo** (Via Fillungo 58, between Via Sant'Andrea and Via San Giorgio 0583/496234), where excellent ice cream is still served.

At the center of town is **Piazza Napoleone**, named for the French ruler who conquered the city and made his sister Elisa duchess. Take **Via del Duomo** out of the square to the **Duomo di San Martino** (Piazza San Martino and Piazza Antelminelli). A church has occupied the site since the 6th century; this incarnation dates back to the 11th century. The cathedral is noted for its asymmetrical Romanesque façade of carved-column loggias—this imbalance is said to be caused by architect **Guidetto da Como** accommodating the preexisting campanile on its right. Also striking is the church's soaring 14th-century Gothic interior.

In the middle of the nave is the town's beloved *Volto Santo* (Holy Visage), a dark wooden statue of Christ on the cross that's probably of 12th-century Eastern origin. According to legend, however, it was carved by Nicodemus immediately following the Crucifixion and procured by a Lucchese bishop during a pilgrimage to the Holy Land. The statue was extremely famous throughout Europe and became a popular veneration stop-off for pilgrims on their way to Rome. A special ceremony takes place here every 13 September to honor the statue; it is dressed in fine silks and paraded through town in a candlelight procession after sunset. Another masterpiece is the exquisite marble tomb of Ilaria del Carretto (1379-1405), beloved wife of nobleman Paolo Guinigi, the powerful ruler of independent Lucca. Their politically arranged marriage turned into a union of love; Paolo's world was shattered when Ilaria died just after the birth of their daughter. His immense love and grief shows through in this expensive sepulcher commissioned to the Sienese sculptor Jacopo della Quercia, who delicately portrays the beauty in premature death, with Ilaria's faithful dog at her feet. The 19th-century critic John Ruskin called the sarcophagus the "loveliest Christian tomb in Italy." Townspeople still come here today to revere this icon of a good—and dearly beloved—Italian wife. While a recent restoration caused an upheaval in the city—some felt that stripping the natural wear of the centuries had left a brand-new-looking Ilaria in its stead—most now feel that there was no choice but to restore the statue. There's daily access to the statue, currently in the sacristy; buy tickets for the tomb at the **San Giovanni** church across from the **Duomo**.

An antiques fair of about 200 exhibitors takes place in the streets around the Duomo on the third Sunday of the month and the Saturday preceding it. For more information, call 0583/978282.

The bustling **Piazza San Michele** northwest of the Duomo was the site of the old Roman

Chiesa di San Michele in Foro, Lucca

The Best

Lorenza Sebasti

Owner and Chief Executive Officer, Castello di Ama S.P.A.

I would like to suggest to everyone who is traveling in Tuscany to take a deep breath in the **Chianti Classico** area. Four or five days will be enough to fall in love with a marvelous region. Here you can find a perfect combination of art and nature that lives from century to century.

Radda, **Gaiole**, and **Castellina in Chianti** are in the old triangle of what was already known as Chianti in the 12th century.

Relais Vignale in Radda and **Castello di Spaltenna** in Gaiole.

My favorite restaurant is in Castellina in Chianti: **Albergaccio**, where Francesco and his wife will offer you a perfect Tuscan meal with the best raw materials (wine, cheese, vegetables, and meat . . .) of the area.

The market in **Greve** on Saturday mornings.

Sunday is the day to go to **Montalcino** and stop at the **Abbazia di Sant'Antimo** to hear the priests singing the Gregorian chants during the Mass. It is a unique atmosphere, and you will never forget it!

Forum, and the unusual church that is the centerpiece of the piazza is officially called **San Michele in Foro** (St. Michael in the Forum). Built in the 12th and 13th centuries, the church has a Romanesque façade constructed in the Pisan-Luccan style. Four levels of columned arcades, of which no two are alike, are topped by a colossal statue of the warrior St. Michael nonchalantly killing the dragon. Inside the cavernous church are a *Madonna and Child* by Andrea della Robbia and a panel of four saints by Filippino Lippi. Some beautiful 14th-century brick houses and two fine statues are also on the piazza: A marble figure of Luccan Executive Council head Francesco Burlamacchi (1498-1548) stands in the square's middle, and a pensive, seated bronze of Renaissance sculptor Matteo Civitali (1435-1501) sits under the loggia of the **Palazzo Pretorio**. A large outdoor market is held here daily the last two weeks of September.

A block east of San Michele in Foro is **Via Fillungo**, one of Lucca's busiest shopping streets. It is lined with medieval houses and towers and chic modern stores displaying clothes, jewelry, and food. West of the thoroughfare is the **San Frediano** church in **Piazza San Frediano**. Note the Romanesque bell tower of this 12th-century church and the reliefs by Jacopo della Quercia inside in the **Capella Trenta**. Cross back over Via Fillungo to the second-century **Anfiteatro Romano**, another remnant of Lucca's Roman past. All that remains of the amphitheater is the oval outline, traced by soft-yellow stuccoed medieval-style houses. Exit from the opposite side and proceed to **Via Guinigi**, a medieval street featuring several palazzi owned by the noble 14th-century family. The tall Guinigi family tower is easily recognizable by the holm oak trees crowning its top. It is one of Lucca's most photographed images.

Music and opera lovers will want to visit the birthplace of Puccini (1858-1924), Lucca's most famous son. The 15th-century palazzo just one block from **Piazza San Michele** (Corte San Lorenzo 9, at Via di Poggio, 0583/584028) houses some of the maestro's original manuscripts and documents, as well as the piano on which he composed *Turandot*, his final opera. Check with the tourist office (see page 147) for days open; there's an admission charge.

Piccolo Hotel Puccini

Nearby is the charming and reasonably priced hotel **Piccolo Puccini** (Via di Poggio 9, 0583/55421; fax 0583/53487); it boasts 14 rooms, but no restaurant. This is also the neighborhood for **Buca di Sant'Antonio** (Via della Cervia 1-3, 0583/55881), Lucca's most upscale dining spot. Rustic, yet elegant, it serves the best local fare. The restaurant is open Tuesday-Saturday, lunch and dinner; Sunday, lunch; reservations are recommended.

The more informal **Da Giulio** (Via delle Conce 45, just north of Piazza San Donato, 0583/55948) is a large, simple trattoria that is known for its *cucina lucchese* served in a relaxed atmosphere. As is **La Mora a Moriano** (Via Sesto di Moriano 1784, 0583/406402), where the specialty is *cacciucco* (fish stew).

If you fancy a tiny excursion outside the town, visit the really rustic trattoria **Solferino** (Via delle Gavine 50, 0583/89118), a great place that is very popular for Sunday lunch. The kitchen prides itself on using local small game and ingredients gathered in the woods around the restaurant itself, in such dishes as cakes made with sweet chestnut flour and delicious porcini mushrooms.

The main office of the tourist bureau is at Vecchia Porta San Donato, Piazzale Giuseppe Verdi (0583/419689). It offers a complete listing of local museums and concerts and is open daily April-October; Monday-Saturday, 9:30AM-3:30PM November-March. Bike rentals are available March-October at the **Servizio Noleggio Biciclette** (Piazzale Giuseppe Verdi, 0583/491243), a good idea in this traffic-free city where two-wheelers are the basic means of transportation. It's also the best way to experience the tree-lined path around the top of the ramparts.

The countryside around Lucca, known by locals as the **Lucchesia**, is an area of rolling hills dotted with olive groves (Lucca is famous for its olive oil), thick woods, and a number of stately villas worth visiting. The **Villa Torrigiani** (0583/928008; fax 0583/928041), 12 kilometers (7 miles) northeast of Lucca off S435 in **Camigliano**, has an exquisite 16th-17th-century garden with grottoes, nymphs, and fountains. The villa is open for guided visits (in English) Monday, Wednesday-Sunday March through December; admission is charged. In nearby **Segromigno in Monte** is the equally spectacular park and mansion of **Villa Mansi** (0583/920234, 920096; fax 0583/928114), a 1630s restructuring of an older villa with extensive grounds. The park and villa are open Tuesday-Sunday; there's an admission charge.

Although the **Villa Reale di Marlia** (0583/30108; fax 583/30009)—take **S12** north 6 kilometers (4 miles) and turn off to the right after about 10 minutes, following signs for Marlia—is not open to the public, its grounds are worth visiting. Take a stroll through the formal lemon garden, the romantic ruins of the 15th-century bishop's palace, and the theater made out of cleverly staged hedges and statues. The beautiful gardens were the pride and joy of its most famed owner, Elisa Baciocchi Bonaparte, duchess of Lucca from 1805-1814 (open Tuesday-Sunday March through November). Guided visits of the garden (in Italian only) are at 10AM, 11AM, 3PM, 4PM, 5PM, and 6PM; admission is charged.

For an unforgettable meal, return to S12 and continue north for about 2 kilometers (1 mile) to the refined and intimate **La Mora** (Via Sesto di Moriano 1748, Ponte a Moriano, 0583/406402), where exquisite *Lucchese* specialties of soup, pasta, fish, and game reach their maximum expression and earned the owners a Michelin star. Specialties include *gamberi di fiume con fagioli* (river shrimp with Tuscan beans), *bavettine* pasta with eels, and pigeon in casserole. Wine lovers will want to visit the restaurant's *enoteca* located across the street. The eatery is open Monday, Tuesday, Thursday-Sunday, lunch and dinner; it is closed in October. Reservations are recommended. The *enoteca* is open Monday-Friday, and Saturday morning.

Travelers with deep pockets can enjoy a semblance of the lifestyle of the land-owning aristocracy (expect hotel rates to match) by checking into the **Locanda l'Elisa** (0583/379737; fax 0583/379019), a deluxe country inn 3 kilometers (2 miles) south of Lucca on Via Nuova per Pisa. This early-18th-century villa was once owned by a French army official in the employ of Elisa Baciocchi Bonaparte. The common areas and 10 suites were re-created to cater to a princess's every caprice, with furniture, fabrics, and carpets designed from period prints. Luxuriant gardens and landscaping include a brook, walking paths, and a large pool. The restaurant, located in the Victorian style conservatory, looks out onto the pretty grounds. It is open year-round except in January and the last week of November. Nearby is the **Villa la Principessa** (Via Nuova per Pisa, 0583/370037; fax 0583/379136), a less-expensive hostelry under the same ownership as the **Principessa Elisa**. This elegant 19th-century villa turned 44-room hotel boasts spacious gardens, a pool, a large staff, and complete serenity. It is open year-round.

Medici Villas

During the years of fighting between the Guelphs and the Ghibellines, Florence's nobility felt safer staying within the protective custody of the city's walls than going into the Tuscan countryside. But with the onset of the Black Plague in 1348, when city living meant unhygienic and crowded circumstances that permitted the disease to run rampant, and a subsequent end to the conflicts—more than half of the city's population died—the idea of fleeing to the countryside became popular.

For the Medici family, building country villas and the requisite formal gardens that surrounded them became an extravagant hobby that would be passed down from generation to generation. By the end of the 1500s, the family possessed some 15 villas in the Florentine countryside. Although today most of them are privately owned, a number are open (some only partially) to the public.

About 7 kilometers (4 miles) northwest of Florence on the road to Sesto Fiorentino is the 16th-century **Villa della Petraia** (Via della Petraia 40, off Via Reginaldo Giuliani,

The Best

Amerigo Franchetti

Hotelier/Owner, Torre de Bellosguardo

When it is raining, sleep as long as possible.

At twilight sit on the **Ponte Santa Trinità** and dream while the lights go on along the **Arno** and on the **Ponte Vecchio**.

Eat a memorable sandwich of boiled beef with green sauce at **Nerbone** in the central **San Lorenzo** food market. Then go upstairs and wallow in the fruit and vegetable stands.

Admire the 18th-century looms still clattering away, weaving wonderfully patterned cloths at the **Antico Setificio Fiorentino**.

Bribe the guardian of the **Chiostro dello Scalzo** to open the little door and let you see the wonderful chiaroscuro frescoes of Andrea del Sarto on all four sides of the cloister.

Restore your energy at my favorite tratoria, **Alla Vecchia Bettola**—wonderful *penne alla Bettola* and the best steaks.

Castello, 055/451208). For those without a car, **ATAF** bus *No. 28* from Florence will get you here. Set on a steeply sloping hill, the villa was originally built by the Brunelleschi family as a castle. It then passed on to the powerful Strozzi family until the Medici family took it over about 1532. Under the direction of Medici Cardinal Ferdinando, the turreted castle was rebuilt from 1575-1590 by **Buontalenti** into an elegant, square villa for the cardinal's rest and leisure activities. The prominent tower rising from the center of the roof is the only remaining evidence of the medieval building. When Florence became the capital of Italy in 1801, the villa became the royal palace of the Savoy family. King Vittorio Emanuele II proceeded to make heavy-handed alterations, adding an iron-and-glass skylight over the courtyard and giant billiard tables for his game room. Don't miss Giambologna's statue of *Venus Wringing Water from Her Hair,* located in a small room. After the villa, proceed on to the shady cypress groves of the back garden. The villa is open Tuesday-Sunday (until 4PM in winter); there's an admission charge.

Villa di Castello is just down the road; walk down the hill to **Via di Castello**, turn right, and go about 500 yards. By the 1630s the properties were already linked by this broad avenue. The villa is not open to visitors, but it's worth a stop here to see the beautiful gardens. Castello was originally bought in 1477 by cousins of Lorenzo ("Il Magnifico") de' Medici. Cosimo I de' Medici was brought up here and remained attached to the villa throughout his life. In 1537 he commissioned **Il Tribolo** to design the villa's gardens, including fountains and statues that represented the cycle of nature and a highly complicated hydraulic system to supply the fountains. After Tribolo's death in 1550, **Vasari** and, later, Buontalenti worked on the plan of the first Medicean garden, which became known throughout Europe for its geometrically patterned terraces, labyrinths, avenues, and arching plants. Cosimo I moved to the villa permanently when he retired from public life and lived here with his second wife, Camilla Martelli, until his death in 1575. The gardens are open daily except the second and third Monday of every month; admission is charged.

The magnificent **Villa di Poggio a Caiano** (Piazza dei Medici 12, Poggio a Caiano, 055/877012) is 17 kilometers (11 miles) west of Florence near Prato on **S66**. It differs from the other villas in that it was expressly built as a farm estate; the cultivation of hundreds of different varieties of fruits and vegetables covered vast expanses of land in the area. After Lorenzo de' Medici purchased the villa from Giovanni Rucellai in 1485, he began to rebuild it with the help of **Giuliano da Sangallo**. Sangallo's temple colonnade and sculptured frieze on the façade (the original is on view inside) is one of the first examples of a classical front on a secular building. This launched a long tradition that spread to the Veneto region and the seminal architect **Palladio**, then to England, and finally to the United States in the form of plantation homes. After the death of Lorenzo de' Medici, the construction of the villa was finished by his son, Giovanni, soon to be Pope Leo X, who commissioned a monumental fresco cycle in the second-floor ballroom (**Salone di Leone X**). The paintings by Andrea del Sarto, Franciabigio, Pontormo, and Allori date from 1512-1580 and celebrate classical allegories of the Medici family. Much of the villa's heavy-handed décor shows signs of King Vittorio Emanuele II and Queen Margherita of Savoy—especially the theater, billiard room, and bedrooms. The villa is open Tuesday-Sunday February through October; Tuesday-Sunday, 9AM-1PM November through January. There's an admission charge.

Florentines and visitors alike love to stroll the lawns and parkland of **Villa Demidoff**, 11 kilometers (7 miles) north of Florence on **S65**, Pratolino (055/409427). Once the

Siena: The Palio

The Palio—dating back to the Middle Ages—is a fast and furious horse race run each year at the beginning of July and the middle of August. Imagine the Kentucky Derby ridden bareback around Times Square and you're getting close.

The backbone of Il Palio are Siena's 17 *contrade,* which you can liken to city wards or administrative districts. These well-defined neighborhoods were designated in the Middle Ages, basically to aid the many military companies hired to defend Siena's fiercely earned independence from Florence and other nearby city-states. Each *contrada* runs its own horse under its own colors in the race, the "official" motivation of which, since the 11th century, has been to give thanks to the Madonna. The horses that tear around the Piazza del Campo at breakneck speed, with or without jockeys on board, wear the colors and designs of the *contrade:* Tortoise, Wave, She-Wolf, Goose, Shell, Porcupine, Dragon, Owl, Snail, Panther, Eagle, Caterpillar, Unicorn, Ram, Giraffe, Forest, and Tower. The actual horse race, is, incredibly, just 90 seconds long.

The night before the race, the streets are filled as dinner is served for an average of 25,000 Sienese and their visitors. Each *contrada* lays out rows and rows of 50-foot-long tables in its largest square, and local restaurateurs serve up huge bowls of pasta, gigantic platters of meat, and legendary sides of vegetables.

Il Palio really starts months before the race, when each neighborhood carefully selects its race officials for the coming year. The captain is responsible for managing the *contrada*'s money, and is in overall control in the days leading up to the race. The *barbaresco* takes care of the horse once it's chosen. The *comparsa,* the pages and costumed characters, represent the neighborhood during the pre-race pageant. The two most important *comparsa* members are *il paggio maggiore,* who carries the *contrada*'s official banner, and *il duce,* who parades in full body armor as he impersonates the military commanders of ancient days.

Six trial races are held so that the jockeys (racetrack professionals who receive astronomical sums from the *contrade*) can get to know their mounts. Locals say the fifth trial is the most dangerous day of all, because spectators can no longer control their emotions. Then there is a "dress rehearsal" dinner, albeit the idea of Italians having to rehearse celebration is mindboggling.

Tickets tend to sell out months in advance, and for those aiming to occupy a freestanding place in the center of the circuit, waiting on line for days is the only way to do it. The center of Siena is absolutely jam-packed.

There is a great deal of pageantry and flag tossing before the horses line up behind the length of ancient rope, which is the starting line.

Historically, the race was carnage—horses and jockeys suffered terrible injuries. But thanks to a a layer of sand strewn over the cobbles and safety shoes on the horses, injuries are few and far between nowadays.

Medici **Villa Pratolino**, the estate was masterminded by the Medici garden-lover Francesco I, who entrusted Buontalenti to devise one of the most sensational and extravagant gardens Europe had ever seen. In 1580, Montaigne visited the gardens and wrote about the wondrous grottoes, statue-filled "rooms," and complex system of waterworks that propelled moving figures through the park. Unfortunately, little remains of this monumental 16th-century Disneyland. The park already seemed dated by the 17th century, and later Medicis abandoned it entirely. In 1819 the park was transformed into an English garden, and the villa was destroyed in 1822. Some treasures still remain and are worth the visit: Giambologna's enormous *Appenine* sculpture, the **Cupid Grotto**, and the **Fountain of the Masks**. The old **Paggeria** (courtesans' quarters) were transformed into a villa in the late 19th century and inhabited by the noble Demidoff family of Russian descent until the early 20th century. Today the villa belongs to the city and is open Thursday-Sunday, 10AM-8PM April-September; there's an admission charge.

Montalcino, Pienza, and Montepulciano

Montalcino is 109 kilometers (68 miles) south of Florence and 41 kilometers (25 miles) south of Siena. To get to Siena, take the **Superstrada del Palio** or the picturesque **Chiantigiana** (**S222**). From Siena, take **S2** to Buonconvento, make a right turn at the Montalcino sign, and follow that road for 11 kilometers (7 miles). To get to Pienza, head northeast on the road to **Torrenieri** for 9 kilometers (6 miles), then go southeast 6 kilometers (4 miles) on S2 to San Quirico, and finally 10 kilometers (6 miles) east on **S146**. Continue east 13 kilometers (8 miles) to Montepulciano. There is no train service from Florence. Take a **SITA** bus to Siena and connect with **TRA-IN** service in Piazza San Domenico (0577/204111) for Montalcino, Pienza, and Montepulciano.

The three small towns of Montalcino, Pienza, and Montepulciano line up from west to east in the southern reaches of Tuscany near the Lazio and Umbria borders. Although they can be visited as a long day trip from Florence, another option is to stay overnight in Siena or in the lovely countryside surrounding the city. This is Tuscany's lesser-known and -visited corner, and together with the Chianti Classico region, a particularly interesting niche for those curious about the local wine production.

Montalcino is situated on a hill that has been inhabited since Etruscan times. The site subsequently belonged to the extant **Abbazia di Sant'Antimo**, a nearby abbey. Montalcino later became a free commune that the Sienese and Florentines fought over until Siena defeated Florence in 1260. When Siena itself fell to Florence in 1555, Sienese patriots fled here to form a short-lived "Republic of Siena at Montalcino," until the town was forced into submission by Cosimo I de' Medici in 1559. In recognition of this hospitality, to this day a delegation from Montalcino occupies a place of honor in the historical procession that precedes Siena's twice-yearly *Palio* race.

Most of Montalcino's stately architecture shows medieval Sienese influence, particularly the imposing 14th-century **Rocca** (0577/849211), a fortress that stands as a symbol of Montalcino's strength and bravery. Climb the ramparts for an excellent view of the surrounding countryside. An informal *enoteca* (wine bar) downstairs serves sandwiches, cheese, and glasses of the local Brunello di Montalcino—one of the most celebrated and costly wines in Italy. The fortress is open daily; admission is charged. The other spot where townsfolk converge is the handsome 19th-century **Caffè Fiaschetteria Italiana** (Piazza del Popolo 6, 0577/849043). The *Sagra del Tordo*—part archery contest, part thrush-eating festival—is held here on the last Sunday in October. The tourist office (Via Mazzini 66, 0577/849471) organizes visits to wineries and farms in the area. It's open Monday through Saturday.

La Cucina di Edgardo (Via Soccorso Saloni 21, 0577/848232) serves very good local cuisine with a limited—but discerning—selection of the area's best labels. It's open daily, lunch and dinner; reservations are required. Two family-run trattorie that have wine cellars stocked with the best Chianti and Brunello vintages are **Giardino** (Piazza Cavour 2, 0557/848257), open Monday, Tuesday, and Thursday-Sunday, lunch and dinner; and **Giglio** (Via Soccorso Saloni 5, 0577/848167), open Tuesday-Sunday, lunch and dinner. The latter also rents 12 rooms.

Abbazia di Sant'Antimo is a 10-kilometer (6-mile) drive south of Montalcino—follow the signs for Castelnuovo dell'Abate and Sant'Antimo. When seen from afar, this abbey stands out as a golden jewel isolated in an open expanse of olive trees. An excellent example of Romanesque architecture, the present building was begun in 1118; according to legend the abbey dates back to the time of Charlemagne (742-814). After being abandoned for more than 500 years, the monastery was restored in 1870. Today it is run by the Norbertini, a group of seven French clerics who continue the painstaking work of repairing the structures. The best-preserved building is the church. Its rounded apse boasts a French-style ambulatory, and the elegant tower is made of travertine (alabaster from Volterra was used for the trim). Try to time your visit to hear the monks sing Gregorian chants (Monday-Saturday, 9AM, 5PM; Sunday and holidays, 11AM, 6:30PM). Sexts are celebrated daily at 12:45PM and Nones at 2:45PM. To confirm times, call 0577/835659.

Poggio Antico (0577/849200) is a working farm/restaurant 4 kilometers (2 miles) south of town on the road to Grossetto that has deservedly earned much acclaim. The setting is informal and rustic, but the approach to dining is serious and rewarding. Most of the produce used is grown on the enormous property that surrounds this refurbished farmhouse. The menu offers a host of delicious reliable Tuscan standbys, as well as such innovative creations as melt-in-

Many writers have waxed poetic about the Apuan Alps (Tuscan Apennines). From one of the most renowned: "I like to imagine that amidst those mountains dwell the spirits of great sculptors and that it is their invisible hands that shape the clouds in splendid, majestic forms. . . . There is a hint of Michelangelo in that white cloud set off by that dark shadow."

—Aldous Huxley

Medieval city dwellers were wary of spending too much time in the countryside. "The farm makes good animals but bad men" was a common phrase of the 14th century, as farmers spent all day with animals and not enough time in the company of other presumably intelligent people.

your-mouth goose liver cooked in *vin santo*. The restaurant is open Tuesday-Saturday, lunch and dinner; Sunday, lunch; reservations are recommended. **Villa Banfi** (0577/840111; fax 577/840205) is a vast estate of more than 2,000 acres of vines, producing Brunello and Rosso di Montalcino, Moscadello, a California-style Chardonnay, olive oil, and balsamic vinegar. Take the road for Sant'Angelo in Colle 10 kilometers (6 miles) south of Montalcino. It's open by appointment. Founded in the late 16th century by the ancestors of the Colombini, its present owners, the **Fattoria dei Barbi** (0577/849357; fax 577/849356) has been winning medals and accolades for its wines for centuries. The panoramic vineyards and working farm supply its rustic restaurant, **Taverna dei Barbi**, with many of its excellent wines, meats, cheeses, and oils. It serves authentic Tuscan cuisine at its best, Monday, Tuesday, Thursday-Sunday, lunch and dinner (closed Tuesday dinner November through April). Take the road to Abbazia di Sant'Antimo 3.5 kilometers (2 miles); at the fork, bear left and follow signs for **Fattoria Barbi**. Wine tastings are available daily; call 0577/849357 for specific hours.

Once called **Corsignano**, Pienza is a perfectly preserved town that once belonged to the powerful Piccolomini family. Aeneas Sylvius Piccolomini was born here and grew to be an exceptionally clever Renaissance man, and in 1458 became Pope Pius II. As an acclaimed humanist, he dreamed of creating the perfect Renaissance city, executed to a precise urban plan, and so he commissioned the famous architect **Bernardo Rossellino** to create this small jewel out of his birthplace. It became a papal annex and summer home for Pius II, who officially changed its name to Pienza (after himself) in 1462.

Rossellino's plan is centered on **Piazza Pio II** (Pius II Square), a beautiful Renaissance square surrounded by the **Duomo**, the **Palazzo Piccolomini**, the **Palazzo Comunale** with a loggia, and the **Palazzo Vescovile**. The cathedral has a simple Renaissance façade with only the Piccolomini coat of arms and the papal keys carved on the pediment for decoration. The interior shows a Gothic influence and has several important 15th-century Sienese paintings. It appears exactly as it did when it was completed in 1462; Pius's papal bull issued that year forbade any changes. The piazza's columned well and the Palazzo Piccolomini were also designed by Rossellino. Be sure to walk behind the church for a sweeping view of the **Val d'Orcia** (Orcia Valley) and **Monte Amiata**, a dormant volcano, and a glimpse of the charming **Via della Fortuna** (Street of Luck), **Via del Bacio** (Street of the Kiss), and **Via dell'Amore** (Street of Love). Franco Zefferelli chose to film *Romeo and Juliet* in Pienza because of its historically authentic setting. The tourist information office (Piazza Pio II, 0578/749071) is open daily.

Dal Falco (Piazza Dante Alighieri 3, 0578/748551) is a rustic and unassuming trattoria where patrons dally at outdoor tables in the shady square just outside the town gate. Try *pici*, the tasty homemade pasta found only in this area of southern Tuscany, and on Wednesday enjoy the fish of the day, an uncommon sight in this landlocked, game-loving part of Tuscany. The restaurant is open daily, lunch and dinner; reservations are recommended. It also includes a six-room *albergo* (hotel). The **Relais Il Chiostro di Pienza** (Corso Rossellino 26, 0578/748400; fax 578/748440) hotel, featuring 27 comfortable rooms, great views, and a reputable restaurant, is located in a 15th-century convent in the heart of town. It is closed January-15 March.

Hotel Relais
Il Chiostro di Pienza

Located in the country 7.5 kilometers (5 miles) northeast of Pienza is the lovely **La Saracina** (0578/748022; fax 0578/748018), a 19th-century Tuscan farmhouse-inn owned and operated by the McCobbs, an amiable American couple. Each of the five elegantly cozy guest rooms and the one apartment have a fireplace. There's no restaurant, but plenty of amenities; the beautifully landscaped pool and tennis court command magnificent views of the surrounding hills dotted by the occasional medieval hill towns. It's closed January and February.

Montepulciano, famous for its wine—Vino Nobile di Montepulciano—was founded in the sixth century by people from Chiusi who were fleeing the Barbarian invasion. The refugees named the place **Mons Politianus**, and even today the inhabitants are called *poliziani*.

The town is perched 2,000 feet above sea level, with the spacious **Piazza Grande** at its highest point. Montepulciano is most noted for its 16th-century monuments, the many handsome palazzi lining the square, and its two main streets—**Via Roma**, which begins at **Porta al Prato** and continues to the other side of town under several names, and **Via Ricci**. The Gothic **Palazzo Comunale** and slender bell tower on the west side of the square offer sweeping panoramic vistas of the environs. The late Renaissance **Palazzo Avignonese** (Via Roma 37) is attributed to **Giacomo Vignola**, and the early-16th-century

The Best

Piero Antinori

President, Wine Company Antinori

Mercato Centrale of **San Lorenzo**—food market.

Lunch at **Nerbone**—exceptional local food, in the **Mercato Centrale**.

Officina Profumo-Farmaceutica di Santa Maria Novella—beautiful location where they sell perfumes and aromas.

Procacci—Stop for a truffled sandwich.

Giacosa café on Via dei Tornabuoni.

Cappella Brancacci in the **Santa Maria del Carmine** church.

Antico Setificio Fiorentino—silk produced in the old ways.

Palazzo Cocconi (Via Roma 72) is believed to have been designed by **Antonio da Sangallo the Elder**. On the right as you continue down the street is the church of **Sant'Agostino** with its elegant Renaissance façade designed by **Michelozzo**, and the much beloved, aged clock tower just across the street with a masked Pulcinella striking the hours. The town is a joy to discover, with its winding *vicoli* (alleys), majestic door knockers, and decorative window ironwork. West of town (a mile-long walk down the **Strada di San Biagio**), sitting in an open field overlooking the valley, is the **Tempio di San Biagio**, a 16th-century church in pale gold travertine by Antonio da Sangallo the Elder.

Montepulciano is a great place for little shops and *enotece*. **Pulcino** (Via Gracciano nel Corso 80) is a foodie paradise offering samples of salamis, wines, and grappas from the owner's family's farm. It's open daily, 9AM to 8PM. Nearby is **Avignonesi/Classica** (Via Gracciano nel Corso 91), which is basically the tasting room of the wine producer. Take a credit card; these wines are good. Open daily, 10AM-1PM and 3PM-7PM. **Maledetti Toscana** (Via Voltaia nel Corso 40) features all manner of Tuscan handicrafts—leatherwork, copperware, wrought ironwork, and the rest. Open daily, 10AM-8PM. There is more copperware at the **Bottega del Rame** (Via dell'Opio nel Corso 64), open daily 9:30AM-7:30PM. And, if you are feeling flush, **Aliseda** (Via Gracciano del Corso 68) showcases beautiful gold jewelry, the designs of which are based on ancient museum pieces. Open daily, 9:30AM-8PM.

Right in town and for lean budgets is **La Terrazza** (Via Piè al Sasso 16, 0578/757440; fax 0578/757440), a renovated 16th-century residence-turned-hotel that's a short walk from **Piazza Grande**. Each of the 14 rooms is furnished differently, and there are also three mini-apartments with kitchenettes. No credit cards are accepted. Restaurants include **Diva e Maceo** (Via di Gracciano nel Corso 92, 0578/716951), a longtime favorite that never disappoints. Although its décor is nondescript, this noisy and friendly trattoria right in town features typical Tuscan home cooking that makes dining here a memorable experience. Specialties include an ever-changing homemade pasta and delicious roast meats.

It's open Monday, Wednesday-Sunday, lunch and dinner; no credit cards are accepted. **Evoè** (Via dell'Opio nel Corso 30, 0578/758411) is new on the restaurant scene; the modern décor somehow fits in perfectly with the 15th-century wooden beam ceilings. This is the place to go for a free cooking lesson, since the kitchen is behind a low counter right in the center of the restaurant. Offerings include traditional fare plus pizza. It's open daily,

lunch and dinner. For a more serious meal, **Caffè Poliziano** (Via di Voltaia nel Corso 27, 0578/758615) oozes Old World charm and offers fine regional specialties such as ravioli in chervil sauce, tortelli with local Pecorino, *agrodolce* of wild boar, and pigeon with black truffles. Founded in 1868 and recently restored to its original splendor, it's also a great place for a quick bite or an espresso on the run, or sitting and watching the world go by. It's open Monday, Tuesday, and Thursday-Sunday, 7AM-2AM; closed February.

Montepulciano's tourist office (Via Ricci, 0578/758687) is open Tuesday through Saturday.

The **Fattoria Pulcino** (Strada per Chianciano 37, 0578/758711), just out of town in the direction of Chianciano Terme, is a medieval monastery-turned-farm-turned-restaurant. Walk past the open wooden ovens and through a tempting maze of olive oil, wines, Pecorino cheese, and beans before entering the large dining room, where delicious meals are served at communal tables. The restaurant is open daily, lunch and dinner.

The well-known **La Chiusa** restaurant (Via della Madonnina 88, Montefollonico, 0577/669668) can be reached by backtracking a few miles west of Montepulciano on S146 and then turning north, following signs to the town of Montefollonico. There are also 12 delightfully decorated guest rooms. Imaginative cuisine is blended here with Tuscan dishes both traditional and rarely found, such as *farro* and *piccione al vin santo* (wild pigeon in sweet wine). The restaurant is open Monday, Wednesday-Sunday, lunch and dinner; closed 8 January-25 March, 6-23 November, 10-26 December; reservations are required.

PISA

Pisa is 94 kilometers (58 miles) from Florence via the **A11** autostrada; or via **Autostrada Firenze-Mare**, the southern route, which goes past Empoli, San Miniato, and Vinci. Train service from **Santa Maria Novella** is approximately every hour and takes one hour.

Visitors invariably rush to **Piazza dei Miracoli** (Field of Miracles), also known as the **Piazza del Duomo**, to see the famous leaning **Torre**. Most are not prepared, though, for the other stunning structures that appear on the spacious green lawn—the **Duomo**, the **Battistero**, and the white wall of the **Camposanto**. The Duomo set the style in Italy known as Pisan Romanesque, or simply Pisan, with its stripes and blind arcades; it was one of the most influential buildings of the time, with its roots in the great Moorish architecture of Andalusia.

This city on the **Arno** was a naval base for the Romans, and during the darkest days of the Middle Ages it kept the Tyrrhenian coast free from marauding Saracens. Pisa established early trading connections with Spain and Africa; much of the great medieval Arab cultural centers sent their scholars in science, philosophy, and architecture to Europe through the port of Pisa. A fleet of Pisan ships sailed off to the First Crusade, which proved to be an economic bonanza. By the 11th century, Pisa had developed into a maritime republic rivaling Genoa and Venice. By the 12th century it had reached the height of its artistic splendor and military supremacy when it defeated the maritime republic of Amalfi in 1135.

But the forces that eventually caused Pisa's decline—internal rivalries and external strife with nearby Lucca, Genoa, and Florence—were already taking form during this period. Pisa's greatest rival became Genoa, with its thriving port. The two cities engaged in years of constant warfare, and the Pisan navy was overwhelmingly defeated at the Battle of Meloria in 1284; Pisa never recovered from this upset. The Arno also crushed Pisa. The silt of the river closed the port and debilitated the economy of the city (today the mouth of the Arno is 11 kilometers—7 miles—from Pisa). In 1396 the city was seized by the Visconti of Milan, and in 1406 it was overtaken by Florence. The Medici rule of Pisa provided a period of well-being for the city and support for the university.

The Duomo was begun in 1064 and finished by the end of the 13th century. Its façade of four graceful galleries of columns was widely imitated. The bronze doors facing the Battistero are from the 16th century, replacing originals lost in a fire, but the highly stylized bronze doors facing the Torre, by **Bonanno Pisano**, date from 1064. As you go through the cavernous interior, close to 400 feet long with 68 columns, find your way to Giovanni Pisano's ivory *Madonna with Child*. This carving, leaning backward along the curve of the elephant's tusk from which it was created, and Pisano's intricate pulpit—nine years in the creation (1302-1311)—are the cathedral's greatest treasures. Be sure to note Cimabue's wonderful mosaic of *Christ Pantocrator* in the apse, and the portraits of the saints by Andrea del Sarto in the choir. The 16th-century bronze Galileo Lamp that hangs opposite the pulpit is also of special interest. Legend holds that Pisa-born Galileo arrived at his theory of pendulum motion by studying the swinging lamp set in motion by a sympathetic sacristan. However, historians date the manufacture of the lamp six years after Galileo wrote his theory.

The Battistero, the largest baptistry in Italy, was begun in 1152 but not finished until the end of the 14th century. The lower portion of the building is typical Pisan-style stripes and arcades. A second colonnade was planned, but as Pisa lost its trade routes to Genoa, money was short. In the 1260s, **Giovanni** and **Nicola Pisano** redesigned and completed the upper half in Gothic style. The most famous interior feature is the pulpit, carved by Nicola Pisano in 1260. Notice the relief panels depicting New Testament events, similar in concept to the reliefs on old Roman triumphal arches.

The baptistry is noted for its remarkable acoustics—for a small contribution the guards might provide a demonstration, or try a few notes from the center of the floor yourself. There's an admission charge. Construction on the cylindrical Torre was begun by Bonanno Pisano soon after the Battistero was started. The work progressed quickly, but as the third floor was completed the building began to tilt, and work was suspended for a century. Construction resumed in 1275, and the finishing touches were made 1350-1372. A few romantic historians say that the architect purposely planned the leaning in order to demonstrate his inordinate skill; however, most experts attribute it to shifting soil. The 187-foot tower leans 16 feet off of the perpendicular; the tilt has continued to increase by an average of .07 inches a year, although recent experiments seem to have stabilized the structure for the first time. After the 1997 earthquakes in nearby Umbria, steel girders were fastened to the tower and connected to nearby buildings. If you can walk up the tower's 294 steps (it reopened to visitors in 2001), you could enjoy the view from the top terrace where Galileo held his experiments that established the laws of gravity.

The Camposanto, a long low building, gleams in its absolute simplicity with a blind arcade along the façade and a Gothic tabernacle of the enthroned Virgin over the entrance. The legend is that the cemetery was begun in 1277 when the Archbishop Lanfranchi (who led the Pisan fleet to the Crusades) returned from the Holy Land with boatloads of earth for extra-holy burials. Many of the frescoes that once decorated the interior of the Camposanto walls were destroyed or heavily damaged in World War II, but some by Benozzo Gozzoli escaped undamaged, and enough remains of the enormous and famous *Triumph of Death, Last Judgment,* and *Inferno* by Florentine artist Bonamico Buffalmarco to suggest the uneasy turn of the 14th-century mind. Sinopias of the frescoes, uncovered during postwar restoration, are now in the **Museo delle Sinopie** across the street from the Duomo. The museum is open daily; there's an admission charge. The frescoes can be seen in the nearby **Museo Camposanto Monumentale** (Piazza dei Miracoli), which is open daily; admission is charged. On the other side of the cathedral is the little-known, fascinating **Museo dell'Opera del Duomo** (Duomo Museum) (Piazza Arcivescovado 6, between Via Corta and Piazza dei Miracoli), which is located in a former Capuchin monastery. On display in the museum's 19 rooms are fine examples of Islamic art, remnants of Pisa's tradition as a trading power; sculptures by father and son Nicola and Giovanni Pisano; and a magnificent frescoed dining room. It is open daily; there's an admission charge. All three museums can be reached by calling 050/560547.

Torre di Pisa

Beyond the Campo, Pisa holds many other joys for the sightseer. **Santa Maria della Spina** is a fantastic Gothic creation, built 1230-1323 by Giovanni and **Nino Pisano** as a place in which to enshrine a thorn, said to be from Jesus' crown, brought to Pisa by a local crusader. **San Paulo a Ripa d'Arno** is truly ancient, having been started in 805. And if you've had enough of churches, the **Tenuta di San Rossore** is a lovely coastal wildlife reserve with deer, wild boar, and waterfowl. It was at this spot that Shelley's body was washed ashore after he drowned when his boat capsized.

The tourist information office (Via Carlo Cammeo 2, at Piazza dei Miracoli, 050/560464; fax 050/40903) is open Monday and Thursday; Tuesday, Wednesday, and Friday, 9AM-1PM. There's another branch at the railroad station (050/42291).

Pisans are avid fish eaters, and the top-notch **Emilio** (Via Carlo Cammeo 44, between Piazza Daniele Manin and Via Contessa Matilde, 050/562131) keeps them happy with a fine selection of the day's freshest. The homemade pasta is also superb. It's open Monday-Thursday, Saturday-Sunday, lunch and dinner; reservations are recommended. The less expensive **Antica Trattoria "da**

The Best

Puccio Pucci di Barsento

Marchese

Gipsoteca dell'Istituto d'Arte—The most extraordinary selection of masterpieces of plaster busts and monuments.

Museo Stibbert—Impressive collection of armor from the Middle Ages.

Officina Profumo-Farmaceutica di Santa Maria Novella—One of the oldest Italian pharmacies, set in a 600-year-old monastery. Fabulous flower potpourri and the *agua isterica* for fainting women.

Loretta Caponi—The finest outfits for table, bed, and bathroom, and infants' and children's wear in the best fabrics, mostly hand-embroidered. A shop with beautiful layout and atmosphere.

Bruno" (Via Luigi Bianchi 12, between S12 and Via Giuseppe Abba, 050/560818) is a traditional spot that specializes in such typical Pisan cuisine as *pasta e ceci* (a tomato-based soup with chickpeas), *polenta con funghi* (with mushrooms), and *baccalà con porri* (dried salt cod with leeks). The restaurant is open Monday, lunch; Wednesday-Sunday, lunch and dinner. The **Trattoria Sant'Omobono** is situated in the square of the outdoor market around a medieval column. *Baccalà* (salt cod) and *brachetti alla renaiola* (an ancient recipe of pasta squares in a sauce of smoked fish and turnip greens) are the kind of local specialty on offer.

The **Grand Hotel Duomo** (Via Santa Maria 94, between Piazza Cavallotti and Piazza dei Miracoli, 050/561894; fax 050/560418) is a busy, modern hotel with 94 rooms and a restaurant. But the **Villa Kinzica** (Piazza Arcivescovado 2, 050/560419, 050/561736; fax 050/551204) is less expensive and just as hard to beat in terms of location. This former private residence has 30 guest rooms and a small restaurant just a few steps from the major monuments. The tower can be seen from some of the rooms.

San Gimignano

San Gimignano is 54 kilometers (33 miles) south of Florence. Take the **Superstrada del Palio** autostrada south, exit Poggibonsi, and head west 13 kilometers (8 miles), following the signs for San Gimignano. There are frequent **SITA** buses from Florence that connect in Poggibonsi.

Ringed by three sets of walls, San Gimignano bristles with 14 (or 13 or 15, depending on what you count) of its original 72 medieval towers. Its unique hilltop skyline has secured its fame as *"San Gimignano delle Belle Torre"* (San Gimignano of the Beautiful Towers) or, more comically, as "Medieval Manhattan." Each tower was attached to the private palazzo of a patrician family and was used partly for defense against attack from without and to some extent for protection against feuding families inside the city walls. Height was an indication of prestige; some of the remaining towers are over 150 feet. The city has recently been declared part of the World's Architectural Heritage by UNESCO.

The town was called **Castel della Selva** until, in the mid-sixth century, an obscure saint—Gimignano, the martyred bishop of Modena—was called upon to save the city from a sacking by the Gothic army of Totila. He appeared at the city gates and commanded a heavy mist to fall on the attackers; it staved off the attack and the city was saved, and then renamed for Gimignano.

The town became a free commune in the 12th century, and life would have been tranquil except for the destructive conflict between two warring factions—the Guelph, led in San Gimignano by the Ardinghelli family; and the Ghibelline, headed locally by the Salvucci family (the city was predominantly Ghibelline). In 1300, Guelph Florence sent Dante to San Gimignano as an ambassador to make peace between the warring factions, but he was unsuccessful. Internal strife grew so volatile that 53 years later, an exasperated San Gimignano willingly surrendered to the Florentines, whom they had resisted for so many centuries.

The two main shop-lined streets of this beautifully preserved medieval town, **Via San Giovanni** and **Via San Matteo**, feed into two splendid squares, **Piazza della Cisterna** and the adjoining **Piazza del Duomo**. At the center of Piazza della Cisterna is the 13th-century well from which it takes its name. The piazza is paved with bricks inlaid in a herringbone pattern and surrounded by an assortment of medieval palazzi and towers.

In the adjoining Piazza del Duomo, the 12th-century cathedral, known as **La Collegiata**, is flanked by more stately palazzi and seven towers. The **Cappella di Santa Fina** in the **Duomo** is a Renaissance addition to the cathedral that is decorated with Domenico Ghirlandaio's frescoes of the life of a native saint who died here at the age of 15.

FROM THE GRAPEVINE

Tuscany is the picture-perfect home of some of Italy's best wines. A driving tour through the undulating hills of this preeminent wine region will expose oenophiles to everything from easy-drinking *vino della casa* (house wine) to the assertive and costly *riserva*. The following explanations of some government-controlled standards will guide you on your wine-tasting tour.

Denominazione semplice is the lowest of the three designations, implying a good table wine, but generally not a wine of note. *Denominazione di origine controllata* means the wine has met certain quality requirements and comes from an officially recognized wine-producing area. The most prestigious ranking goes to *Denominazione di origine controllata e garantita (D.O.C.G.)*; these wines meet the highest quality standards and must pass the demands of a special government-established tasting committee.

When a particularly good vintage is produced, a wine maker will set aside a *riserva* to be aged longer than other wines. *Riserve* are usually aged in French oak barrels and are released for sale in the market by the winery after about three years.

Tuscany's hilly topography affords a perfect environment for producing some of the country's finest wines: its reliably sunny exposure; altitudes between 820 and 1,970 feet, which create a natural drainage; a soil suited for viticulture; and a number of different microclimates throughout the area that imbue each wine with a certain individuality.

Ancient castles, stone farmhouses, and *fattorie* (vast wine estates) line the back roads of Tuscany's countryside. Some of the more renowned vintners require appointments (and offer such services as guided tours, guest rooms, and trattorie), but most *fattorie,* large and small, post *"Vendità Diretta"* (Direct Sales) signs. At these locales, visitors can spontaneously stop in to sample the goods and hopefully drive away with a bottle or case—or at the very least, with vivid memories and a valuable experience. A language difference is rarely a problem; it's not difficult to interpret the pride on the face of the wine maker or the rapt appreciation of visitors from abroad. (For those unable to get out into the hills, an excellent place to get an overview of Tuscan—and other Italian—wines is at the **Enoteca Italiana** in Siena. The attractive, brick-vaulted wine cellar boasts 774 labels from all over Italy.)

Tuscany is a land of ancient viticulture traditions—it was settled by the wine-making Etruscans as far back as the eighth century BC. The ancient Romans, enthusiastic followers of the wine god Bacchus, made large quantities of wine for personal consumption as well as for export throughout the empire. The almost mystical transformation of grapes into wine lent itself well to the adoption of wine in sacred rituals of Romans, Jews, and Christians.

In medieval times, the Tuscan countryside was the battleground for the fierce conflicts between the Guelphs (defenders of the pope) and Ghibellines (supporters of the Holy Roman Emperor). Many fortified villages, castles, and monasteries built in this period became peaceful communities or residences when the wars subsided. By the mid-1400s, many vast forests were cleared to open up space for the cultivation of vines, setting an early stage for an economic development that is still growing today.

At the beginning of the 18th century, the grand dukes of Tuscany officially established the production zones of **Chianti** and **Carmignano**. During this time, the sharecropper system was set up and the layout of the properties and farmhouses assumed their present forms—major estates, rural villas, and the houses of farmers and peasants clustered in small villages.

In the mid-1800s, Baron Bettino Ricasoli introduced a mixture of grapes for Chianti wine at his farm, **Fattoria di Brolio**, thus inventing "modern" Chianti. His blend included predominantly Sangiovese and Canaiolo (red grapes), with small amounts of Malvasia and Trebbiano (white grapes). This recipe was adopted even beyond the confines of the Chianti territory and has remained largely unmodified until fairly recently. In the 1960s, the replanting of vineyards after the disastrous phylloxera plague and the transition from the sharecropping system to individual farms encouraged farmers to expand their vineyards. As a result, there was overproduction and a drop in quality that put the entire wine community into a deep economic crisis. Thanks to a few courageous wine makers who sought to make quality wine without regard to cost or other factors, and to the introduction of stricter wine-growing and -making guidelines, Tuscan wines have made an enormous comeback since the 1980s.

The **Palazzo del Popolo** (when facing the cathedral, to its left) is the home of San Gimignano's small **Museo Civico** (0577/940340). In addition to paintings from the 14th and 15th centuries, the museum houses the room from which Dante delivered his harangue in favor of the Guelphs. It also provides access to one of San Gimignano's towers—**Torre Grossa**, which affords a 360-degree view of the town and surrounding hills. The museum and tower are open Tuesday-Sunday; there's an admission charge.

San Gimignano's second-most-visited church is the 13th-century **Sant'Agostino**

Chianti is by far the most famous wine in Tuscany, and has the correspondingly largest zone of production. All Chianti wines carry the *D.O.C.G.* specification. The region is divided into seven districts, reaching from **Pisa** to **Arezzo** and from **Florence** to **Siena**. The **Chianti Classico** zone, covering the area just south of Florence to Siena, is the best-known district and thought by most experts to produce the finest Chianti wines.

Although most Chianti wines today are made almost entirely from Sangiovese grapes, they may vary greatly in style and taste from one another because of different grape blends, microclimates, and lengths of aging. Chianti is the perfect accompaniment to Tuscan food, enhancing it with its delightful tartness. The best recent vintages for Chiantis at press time include 1983, 1985, 1995, and 1997. There are more good producers than there is space to note them, but among the best are **Castell'in Villa**, **Castello di Ama**, **Castello di Fonterutoli**, **Castello di Rampolla**, **Castello di Volpaia**, **Fattoria di Felsina**, **Fontodi**, **Isole e Olena**, **Monte Vertine**, **San Felice**, **Selvapiana**, **Villa Antinori**, and **Vecchie Terre di Montefili**.

Brunello di Montalcino gets its name from the brownish hue of the grapes, and the credit goes to Ferruccio Biondi-Santi of the **Biondi-Santi** cellars around **Montalcino** for its conception. The 20-year-old vintner broke from tradition in the 1850s by moving away from the Chianti recipe and vinifying just one clone of Sangiovese. He abandoned the common practice of *governo* (making the wine ferment a second time by introducing some slightly dried grapes) and began to age the wine, which gives the spirits their intensely concentrated and tannic flavors. Brunello ages in the barrel at least 3.5 years (another 1.5 for *riserva*), and stays in the winery another 1.5 years before being released for sale. The wine is best when aged for 5 to 15 years; just be sure to let it breathe a few hours after it is opened before having a glass. The production zone of Brunello is limited to Montalcino and today boasts 130 growers.

Rosso di Montalcino is a less expensive version of Brunello, made from the same grapes (and by the same producers), but with a shorter amount of aging in the barrel. It is ready to drink much sooner than its superstar sibling, costs less, and gives an idea of the power of the bigger wine. Some of the best vintages of these two wines are 1975, 1985, 1988, 1990, and 1997. Look for such producers as **Altesino**, **Argiano**, **Biondi-Santi**, **Caparzo**, **Col D'Orcia**, **Costanti**, **Fattoria dei Barbi**, **Poggio Antico**, **Soldera**, and **Villa Banfi**.

Vino Nobile di Montepulciano is produced southeast of the Chianti zone around **Montepulciano** from the Prugnolo Gentile grape (another clone of Sangiovese) and is aged in wooden barrels for about two years, three for *riserva*. The origins of this wine have been traced back to the 14th century. In the 17th century the poet Francesco Redi called Vino Nobile *"il re di tutti vini"* (king among all wines). Thanks to its promotion to *D.O.C.G.* in the 1980s, today's Vino Nobile from a good wine maker stands up very well to the better Chiantis. Three producers to watch for are **Avignonese**, **Poderi Boscarelli**, and **Poliziano**. Vino Nobile producers also make a lighter wine called Rosso di Montepulciano.

The Carmignano wine region, located in the western end of the province of Florence, was established as a wine region by the grand dukes of Tuscany in 1716. Cosimo III de' Medici imported vines of Cabernet Franc and Cabernet Sauvignon at this time and added their grapes to the traditional Sangiovese to make this characteristically soft and elegant wine. The most notable winery of the area is **Tenuta di Capezzana**, which traces its grape-stomping roots back to the ninth century under the rule of Charlemagne.

Vernaccia di San Gimignano, the only white Tuscan *D.O.C.G.*, is named for the famous hill town of medieval towers located west of the Chianti Classico zone. It was the very first wine to be given *D.O.C.G.* status in Italy and dates back at least as far as Dante. Vernaccia usually has a fresh, almondy flavor, a slightly oily texture, and a hint of bitterness in the aftertaste. It is meant to be enjoyed young and is an inexpensive summer favorite for locals. Producers to look for are **Falchini** (who also makes a great Spumante) and **Montenidoli**.

An excellent time to visit the wine-growing regions of Tuscany is in September and early October, when wine festivals abound. For more information on dates, contact **Movimento del Turismo del Vino**, c/o Donatella Cinelli Colombini, 53024 Montalcino, 0577/697430; fax 0577/849356.

(Piazza Sant'Agostino) at the north end of town, important for its frescoes by Benozzo Gozzoli. The recently opened **Museo della Tortura** (Via del Castello 1, at Piazza della Cisterna, 0577/942243) features items that are well labeled in English (in case you're not familiar with cranium crushers and chastity belts). Most of the works are original; others authentic-looking reproductions. The museum is generally

San Gimignano

ELIZABETH McCLEARY

open daily, but hours may vary; admission is charged.

For a view of the incomparable landscape that surrounds this ancient hilltop outpost, head to the **Rocca**. West of Piazza del Duomo, this former fortress is now a public park that's picnic perfect. To take advantage of the lovely countryside, inquire at the tourist office (see page 159) about guided walks offered Wednesday, Saturday, and Sunday March through October. Be sure to call a day or two ahead to reserve a place.

A favorite pastime for both locals and visitors is to while away an hour or an afternoon at a sidewalk café with a glass of San Gimignano's famous Vernaccia, considered one of Italy's finest white wines. The best time is late afternoon, after the hordes of tour buses have left, leaving the town tranquil.

The **Hotel and Restaurant Bel Soggiorno** (Via San Giovanni 91, between Porta San Giovanni and Via Piandornella, 0577/940375; fax 0577/943149) is located in the former 13th-century **Covento di San Francesco**. The 20 inexpensive guest rooms are simple but some of the nicest in town. Ask for one in the back in order to enjoy the view of the morning mist swirling over the open fields. The same wonderful vista (without the mist) is also prominent in the hotel's acclaimed restaurant, which offers a delicious representation of Tuscan specialties with an emphasis on homemade pastas, grilled meats, and an impressive selection of local wines. It's open Monday, Tuesday, Thursday-Sunday, lunch and dinner; closed 10 January-6 February.

La Cisterna (Piazza alla Cisterna 24, between Via del Castello and Via San Giovanni, 0577/940328; fax 0577/942080) is another moderately priced hostelry housed in a 13th-century palazzo. Conveniently located in the center of town, the 50 guest rooms are more nicely decorated, some with windows and large wooden balconies overlooking the surrounding valley. This panorama is shared with the hotel's **Le Terrazze** restaurant, domain of some very fine Tuscan dining. Film buffs may recognize the setting as the backdrop for the movie *Where Angels Fear to Tread,* adapted from the E. M. Forster novel. The hotel is open March through October; the restaurant is open Monday, Thursday-Sunday, lunch and dinner; Wednesday, lunch March-October.

The elegant **Dorando** restaurant (Vicolo dell' Oro 2, off Piazza del Duomo, 0577/941862), located in a wine cellar, features both innovative and traditional Tuscan cuisine. Try the *pasta con la bottarga* (with fish roe), *cibrèo* (chicken necks stuffed with meat and herbs), and soufflélike *sformati*. As expected in this town, it offers a good selection of local and Tuscan wines. It's open daily, lunch and dinner from Easter through October; Tuesday-Sunday, lunch and dinner the rest of the year.

Relais Santa Chiara (Via Matteotti 15, 0577/940701; fax 0577/942096), one of the loveliest country hotels in the immediate area, is just a minute's drive south of the town walls. The 41 rooms in this sprawling turn-of-the-century villa are contemporary. All have terraces—half overlook San Gimignano, and the rest face the rolling Tuscan hills and the good-sized swimming pool. There is also a Jacuzzi.

The owners of the Bel Soggiorno (see left) in town offer a country alternative—the delightful

The Best

Suzanne B. Cohen

President, Suzanne B. Cohen & Associates, Inc., Travel Destination Specialist

Abbazia di Sant'Antimo—Gregorian chants, Sunday vespers. The best 30 minutes in Tuscany—absolutely magical.

Villa Banfi—Lunch is the perfect meal here, made even better with the vineyard's award-winning wines. The tour of the winery is well designed and executed.

Hotel Pescille (5 kilometers—3 miles—south of town on the road to Volterra, 0577/940186; fax 0577/946165; www.pescille.it). Now an idyllic 39-room country inn, this former farmhouse sits on a hilltop overlooking the towers of San Gimignano. All the guest rooms are decorated with terra-cotta tiles, straw chairs, and country furniture. The Pescille now has a swimming pool and a tennis court.

San Gimignano's tourist office (Piazza del Duomo 1, 0577/940008; fax 0577/940903) is open daily.

Siena

Siena is 68 kilometers (42 miles) from Florence on the **Superstrada del Palio**. More scenic (and longer) routes are the **Chiantigiana** (**S222**) and **Via Cassia** (**S2**). Trains run from Florence's **Stazione Centrale di Santa Maria Novella** to Siena's station (Piazza Fratelli Rosselli and Via Giuseppe Mazzini, 0577/280115), which is located below the city. A bus or cab will be necessary to reach the center. **SITA** buses run almost hourly from Florence to Siena's **Piazza San Domenico**, easy walking distance from the centrally located **Piazza del Campo**.

The late Italian writer Curzio Malaparte wrote that if you ask a Florentine saint for news about heaven, you will get an answer, but in a tone of voice that casts doubt on your worthiness to go there. Ask San Bernardino of Siena, however, and you will be told not only what heaven is, where it is, and the shortest road to take, but also how many rooms it has, how many kitchens, and what's cooking in the pot. Something of the same air of affectionate intimacy pervades this city. Sienese speech is peppered with diminutives (it is said the Sienese speak the country's purest Italian), and Sienese Renaissance painting continued to delight in pretty Madonnas while the Florentines forged on to wrestle with problems of perspective.

Florence was a menacing presence through much of Siena's history; it was largely Florence that arrested Siena's development and caused it to remain the medieval gem it is today. Legend has it that Siena was founded by Senio and Aschilo, sons of Remus, one of the founding brothers of Rome; hence the Roman she-wolf on the Sienese coat-of-arms. More likely, the founders were members of a Gaulish tribe, the Senes. What is certain is that Siena was an important Etruscan city and then a military stronghold under the Romans. Overtaken by the northern Lombards in the early Middle Ages, it did not flourish as a center of commerce, finance, and culture until the late Middle Ages. And prosper it did. Siena's wealth became the envy of its Tuscan neighbors, prompting continual warfare, particularly with the Florentine city-state. By 1235 the mightier military strength of Florence forced Siena to accept harsh peace terms.

But that was merely round one. In 1260, the Sienese dealt the Florentines a resounding defeat at **Montaperti**, a hill east of the city. Under a nine-member government of merchant families (the *Governo dei Nove*) peace was made, and Siena embarked on one of its most enlightened and prosperous periods. The university (founded in 1240), some of the city's most noteworthy buildings, such as the **Palazzo Comunale**, the **Palazzo Chigi-Saracini**, and the **Palazzo Sansedoni**, as well as ambitious plans to enlarge the cathedral date from this time. It was a golden age for painting, too; Duccio di Buoninsegna and Simone Martini were making names for themselves beautifying palaces and churches. The good times lasted until 1355, when, following a severe drought and outbreak of plague in 1348, civil discontent brought about a rebellion of leading noble families and a series of short-lived governments. The decades following the Black Plague saw an increase in religious fervor; the city's two beloved saints, Catherine and Bernardino, emerged during that period. Would-be conquerors came from farther afield until, in 1554, a 24,000-man army of Spanish, German, and Italian troops under the command of the Florentine Medici family laid siege to the city. A year later Siena fell. Cosimo I de' Medici became its ruler, and Siena became part of the Grand Duchy of Tuscany, first under the Medici and then under the French house of Lorraine, until it passed, with Tuscany, to the Kingdom of Italy in 1860.

The Best

Donald and Jessie McCobb

Owners, La Saracina

Pienza (recently named by UNESCO as a patrimony of the world's humanity) is a gem of a small town, rebuilt in the 15th century, reflecting medieval architecture. Presently it is going through a face-lift to bring the buildings back to how they looked several hundred years ago.

Abbazia di Sant'Antimo, an abbey south of **Montalcino**, was originally built by Charlemagne in the AD 780s in the valley where he was camped after his troops recovered from the plague. The current spectacular church, which is beside the original one, dates from the 12th century.

Absorption by Florence kept Siena as small and medieval-looking as it is. Loss of independence also led the Sienese to invest a vibrant civic passion in their annual *Palio*. Over the centuries little of the city's fierce pride has been lost, apparent in the reckless bareback horse race still run today around the Piazza del Campo yearly on 2 July and 16 August. The latter, the more important of the two, dates back to the beginning of the 13th century; the former was instituted in 1656 (for more on this event, see "Siena: The Palio," on page 149).

Today's Siena is still divided into *contrade* (districts). The 17 *contrade*, once 59, have such allegorical names as **Bruco** (Caterpillar), **Tartuca** (Tortoise), **Chiocciola** (Snail), **Drago** (Dragon), and **Leocorno** (Unicorn). Keep an eye on the corners of buildings as you walk around town and you'll see the *contrade* marked off with their symbols, just as streets are with their names. Each *contrada* has its own patron saint, a church where the saint is worshipped, and a feast day in the saint's honor.

Duomo, Siena

Siena seems to gravitate toward the seashell-shaped Piazza del Campo, and almost all of its sights are within walking distance of this magnificent square. (Be aware, however, that the town's narrow streets wind up and down and sometimes turn into steps.) The piazza was built on a difficult curving slant that, resembling a theater, puts the Palazzo Comunale at center stage. The brick paving is divided into nine sections, a number that harks back to the 13th and 14th centuries, when the city was ruled by the *Governo dei Nove*. The sections converge on the piazza's lowest side, in front of the Palazzo Comunale and the adjacent **Torre del Mangia**. Facing them on the higher side is the **Fonte Gaia**, a fountain decorated with reliefs by Jacopo della Quercia (reproductions take the place of the 15th-century originals, which are in the **Museo Civico** in the Palazzo Comunale). Lining the semicircular edge of the piazza are medieval and Renaissance buildings. The *Governo dei Nove* had decreed during the building of Palazzo Comunale that all the other buildings should mimic the triple-mullioned windows on its majestic façade. The only façade nowadays still to have this kind of window is the **Palazzo Sansedoni**, which also curves around the piazza.

The elegant Gothic façade of the Palazzo Comunale is slightly curved, in keeping with the unusual outline of the Piazza del Campo. Siena's town hall since it was built between 1297 and 1310, the Palazzo Comunale also houses the Museo Civico (0577/292263). The **Sala del Mappamondo,** a room named for a world map that's no longer there, now houses the splendidly restored *Maestà* of Simone Martini, the great Sienese painter's first masterpiece, completed in 1315. On the opposite wall is the fresco of *Guidoriccio da Fogliano* (1328), long attributed to Martini (the attribution is now considered doubtful). Below that is a *Madonna and Child* by the earlier Sienese painter Guido da Siena, dated 1221; it may have been repainted a half-century later by Duccio da Buoninsegna. The adjacent **Sala della Pace**, the meeting room of the *Governo dei Nove,* is decorated with a series of allegorical frescoes on the subject of good and bad government. Painted between 1338 and 1340 by Ambrogio Lorenzetti, they are among the first monumental fresco cycles of a secular subject. The museum is open daily, 9:30AM-7:45PM 15 March-15 November; daily, 9:30AM-1:45PM 16 November-14 March; admission is charged.

Adjacent to the Palazzo Comunale is the 332-foot bell tower, the Torre del Mangia. It takes its name from a one-time bell-ringer, Giovanni di Duccio, who was evidently known to the Sienese as a man of prodigal habits and better known as Mangiaguadagni (profit eater). Dedicated stair climbers may still find the hike to the top a challenge, but the view is breathtaking. The pillared and covered structure at the base of the tower is the **Capella di Piazza** (Chapel of the Square), built 1352-1376. The chapel is not open to the public but can be viewed partially through an iron gate. The tower is open daily, 15 March-15 November; daily, 10AM-1:30PM 16 November-14 March. There's an admission charge.

Dedicated to Santa Maria dell'Assunta, the **Duomo** (Piazza del Duomo, between Via del Capitano and Via dei Fusari) is one of the most beautiful medieval churches in Italy. It was begun in 1196, and most of what is standing today was completed by the 13th century. A new addition was planned in 1339 that would have transformed the cathedral into a transept of a much larger basilica, but plague, money problems, and technical difficulties put an end to the dream. The only remnant of the addition is the façade, still visible to the right of the Duomo—the Sienese call it *"Facciatone"* (big façade). The inlaid marble floor, divided into 56 squares of biblical scenes, is the cumulative work of more than 40 artists and spans from the mid-14th to the mid-16th centuries (see floor plan on page 162). Only some parts of the floor are viewable year-round; many sections are covered in the interest of preservation. Another highlight is the marble-and-porphyry pulpit by **Nicola** and **Giovanni Pisano**. An imposing ring of 172 busts of different popes runs along the second-level perimeter of the interior. The **Libreria Piccolomini**, on the left side of the nave, was built in honor of the Sienese Pope Pius II (Aeneas Silvius Piccolomini). Painted with frescoes by Pinturicchio, the scenes describe the pursuits of this quintessential Renaissance man who was a geographer, poet, urban planner, diplomat, and patron of the arts. The library is open daily; there is an admission charge.

The **Battistero di San Giovanni** is down a flight of outside stairs to the right of the cathedral, behind the apse. Amid the frescoed, vaulted 14th-century space inside is a baptismal font designed by Jacopo della Quercia, with panels by Lorenzo Ghiberti and Donatello, among others. The baptistry is open daily (no midday closing), 16 March-31 October; daily, 1 November-15 March; admission is charged.

The **Museo dell'Opera del Duomo** (0577/283048), also known as the Museo dell'Opera Metropolitana, contains mainly works that have been taken from the cathedral. It is housed in the "new" part of the cathedral that was never finished, where visitors can imagine the potential magnificence of the architecture while pondering statues of Old Testament figures carved by Giovanni Pisano for the façade (now replaced

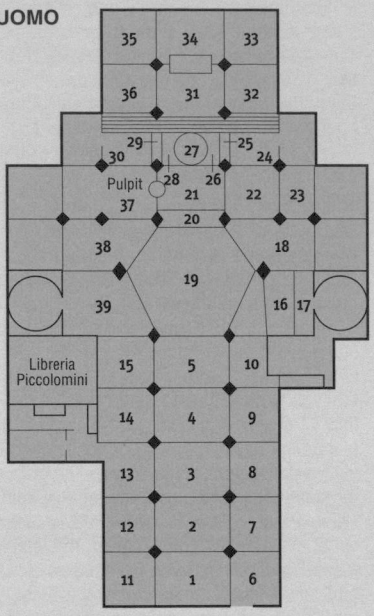

1 *Hermes Trismegistus* (1481-1498)
2 Coat of Arms of Siena and 12 other towns (mosaic)
3 Imperial altar
4 *Allegory of Fortune* (Pinturicchio)
5 *Wheel of Fortune* (Marchese di Adamo, 1406)
6-15 Sibyls (1481 and 1498)
16 *The Seven Ages of Man* (c. 1450)
17 The theological virtues—Faith, Hope, and Charity—and Religion
18 *Story of Jephthah* (1481-1498)
19 *Story of Eli and Ahab* (Beccafumi, 1518-1547)
20 *Moses Smiting the Rock to Bring Forth Water* (Beccafumi, 1518-1547)
21 *Moses on Mount Sinai* (Beccafumi, 1518-1547)
22 *Emperor Sigismond* (1434)
23 *Death of Absalom* (1443)
24 *Battle of Samson against the Philistines* (c. 1425)
25 *Moses and the Tablets of the Law* (c. 1425)
26 *Goliath the Giant* (c. 1425)
27 *David Singing Psalms* (c. 1425)
28 *Young David Armed with His Sling* (c. 1425)
29 *Joshua* (c. 1425)
30 *Hanging of the Five Amorite Kings* (c. 1425)
31 *Abraham's Sacrifice* (Beccafumi, 1518-1547)
32 *Prudence* (Marchese di Adamo, early 15th C)
33 *Temperance* (Marchese di Adamo, early 15th C)
34 *Mercy* (Marchese di Adamo, early 15th C)
35 *Justice* (Marchese di Adamo, early 15th C)
36 *Fortitude* (Marchese di Adamo, early 15th C)
37 *Judith Liberating Bethulia* (1473)
38 *Massacre of the Holy Innocents* (Matteo di Giovanni, 1481-1495)
39 *Herod Losing His Throne* (1481-1498)

by reproductions) and the masterpiece *Maestà* (1308-1311), which made Duccio di Buoninsegna's career. When first finished, the enormous, double-sided painted panel was carried to the high altar of the cathedral in a solemn procession. Originally it showed the Madonna and Child on the front and 26 scenes of the Passion on the back (it was sawed in two in the 18th century), with smaller scenes of the life of Christ and the Virgin above and below. (Nineteen of these smaller panels remain; others are in museums in the US and Great Britain.) Hardy visitors can climb up to the top of the **Facciatone** from the museum for a bird's-eye view of the city. The museum is open daily, 14 March-October; daily, 9AM-1:30PM November-13 March; there's an admission charge.

Directly across from the Duomo is the ancient hospital of **Santa Maria della Scala** (0577/586200, 0577/586410), a hospital since the early 11th century until it closed in 1995 to become a museum and exhibition hall. Of particular note is the **Sala del Pellegrinaio**, where pilgrims, foundling children, the poor, and the sick were all attended to by a fleet of monks, doctors, and wet nurses. Recently restored 15th-century paintings on the walls of this large hall reflecting these activities were carried out by Domenico di Bartolo and others. The museum is open daily; admission is charged.

An easy stroll south of both the Piazza del Campo and the Duomo is the **Pinacoteca Nazionale** (National Picture Gallery, Via San Pietro 29, between Casato di Sopra and Via di Città, 0577/281161), housed in the elegant Gothic **Palazzo Buonsignori**. A good place to get a clear understanding of Sienese art from the 12th through 17th centuries, the museum features 40 rooms filled with Sienese masterpieces by Guido da Siena, Duccio di Buoninsegna, Simone Martini, Pietro and Ambrogio Lorenzetti, Beccafumi, and others. The museum is open Monday, 8:30AM-1:30PM; Tuesday-Saturday, 9AM-7PM; Sunday, 8AM-1PM April-October; and Monday-Saturday, 8:30AM-1:30PM; Sunday, 8AM-1PM November-March. There's an admission charge.

The **Basilica di San Domenico** (Piazza San Domenico) is a massive, severe-looking monastic church begun in 1226 and completed in the 15th century, while the graceful bell tower next to it was built in 1340. Inside, the spacious, simple majesty of the unusual Egyptian cross plan, unencumbered by side aisles, is diffused with shafts of light from modern stained-glass windows. St. Catherine often prayed here, and a chapel in her honor is located on the right side of the nave. Here, Sodoma's early-16th-century frescoes show the miracles of the Sienese saint who is, along with St. Francis of Assisi, Italy's patron saint. The altarpiece contains the head of St. Catherine.

The Best

Kristen Aachengreen Pincenti

Director, Museo Stibbert

San Miniato al Monte church—an architectural gem with a wonderful view of Florence.

The **Oltrarno**—the left bank, with its palaces and artisans' workshops and garden-museum complex.

Palazzo Pitti—with its museums (11 Raphaels!), the old royal residence, and the most wonderful architecture in all Florence.

Via dei Tornabuoni—the elegant shopping street with its two unique churches: **Santa Trinità** and **San Gaetano** (try to look at Christmastime, when the church is "dressed" in fabulous silks of the early 18th century).

Another chapel, the **Capella delle Volte**, contains a fresco portrait of the saint by one of her contemporaries, Andrea Vanni. It is said to be the only authentic portrait of her in existence. St. Catherine lived here from 1347 to 1380 and became a saint under Pope Pius II in 1464. Her home, **Santuario Cateriniano** (St. Catherine's Sanctuary; Costa Sant' Antonio, at Via di Santa Caterina), was then transformed into a series of chapels and a church. Over her humble father's dye shop and the Benincasa family kitchen is an elaborately decorated chapel (Costa di Sant' Antonio) with scenes from her life painted in the 15th and 16th centuries. It is open daily.

A less crowded alternative to the Torre dei Mangia and the Facciatone for a panoramic view is the **Fortezza Medicea**, also known as the "Forte di Santa Barbara," a defensive fortress built in 1560 by Cosimo I de' Medici shortly after his arrival in Siena as the city's conqueror. But the vista is not the only reason to visit this well-preserved fort and city park at the end of a long day of sightseeing. Part of the space has been given over to the **Enoteca Italiana** (Piazza Matteotti 30, between Via del Paradiso and Viale Federico Tozzi, 0577/288497), a wine-tasting center, cellar, and outlet for quality Italian wines from all over the peninsula. Piano music is occasionally played in the evening. The *enoteca* is open Monday, noon-8PM; Tuesday-Sunday, noon-1AM.

Siena has no opera company, but the **Fondazione Accademia Musicale Chigiana** more than makes up for this deficit in July and August, when its music school puts on a series of concerts. The events take place in the **Palazzo Chigi-Saracini**'s music room—Siena's main concert hall—as well as in other palaces and churches. For information, contact the Fondazione Accademia Musicale Chigiana (Via di Città 89, 0577/46152; fax 0577/288124).

If you plan to stay overnight in Siena, be sure to reserve ahead May through October. Because of the small size and the popularity of the town, Siena's 30 or so hotels may be booked solid for most of the prime tourism season. You can make reservations through **Siena Hotels Promotion Office** (Piazza San Domenico, 0577/288084; fax 0577/280290), Monday-Saturday (no midday closing).

The **Palazzo Ravizza** (Pian dei Mantellini 34, 0577/280462; fax 0577/221597) is a charming, 30-room inn built in the 17th century and full of antiques, with a pretty terrace. The restaurant is only for guests in high season. Conveniently located just one block from the intercity bus station is the **Chiusarelli** (Viale Curtatone 15, between Piazza San Domenico and Viale F. Lozzi, 0577/280562; fax 0577/271177), a villa-turned-*pensione* with 50 rooms and a restaurant. The family-owned and run **Piccolo Hotel Etruria** (Via Donzelle 3, between Via Banchi di Sotto and Via Cecco Angioleri, 0577/288088; fax 0577/288461; www.hoteletruria.com underwent some renovation and is rather smart now. The 13 rooms vary among single, double, and triple. They are all en suite and have air conditioning, TV, and phone. There is free parking nearby and an atmospheric restaurant in the vaulted, stone-walled basement, serving traditional dishes.

The 14-room **Certosa di Maggiano** (Strada di Certosa 82, east of Porta Romana, 0577/288180; fax 0577/288189) is nestled among cypress trees and vineyards. An atmosphere of seclusion and meditation pervades the property, which had its beginnings in the 14th century as a Carthusian monastery. A member of the Relais & Chateaux group, the property has several spacious sitting rooms, gardens, a swimming pool, and a very elegant restaurant of the same name.

Four lovely apartments on the top floor of the **Palazzo Antellesi** (Via Sallustio Bandini 31) warrant a splurge. The storied Piccolomini family is one of Siena's oldest and most respected, and this august Renaissance palazzo is one of their ancestral homes. For reservations call 055/244456 in Florence, 212/932.3480 in New York; fax 055/244456 in Florence; 212/932.9039 in New York. Farther away is the **Relais La Suvera** (30 kilometers–19 miles–west of Siena, off S541, Pievescola, 0577/960300; fax 0577/960220), an enchanting luxury hotel and restaurant. Built in the 16th century by the great architect **Baldassare Peruzzi** for Pope Julius II as his summer villa, the hostelry has 25 rooms and 10 suites and is still packed with priceless antiques. Much closer to Siena, the 69-room **Park Palace Hotel** (Via di Marciano 18, between Via Piero Strozzi and Strada Gaetano Milanesi, 0577/44803; fax 0577/49020) was originally a castle-*cum*-villa, built in 1530 for the noble Gori family. The panoramic countryside views, as well as the swimming pool and courts, make it worth the five-minute taxi ride from town. There's also a restaurant.

Siena is a great place to sample delicious meat specialties, as well as game–venison, wild boar, hare, pheasant, quail, and pigeon–in season. Meals may begin with salami and rustic pâté served on toast, followed by hearty vegetable-and-bean soups or pastas with mushrooms and truffles. Cheeses are made from sheep's and cow's milk (Pecorino and caciotta) and can be mild and soft or seasoned and hard. Red wines range from local Chianti to Brunello di Montalcino and Vino Nobile di Montepulciano. Tuscan whites include Vernaccia from San Gimignano and Bianco Vergine della Valdichiana. Siena specializes in sweets, and no trip is complete without a sampling of *panforte,* a heavy cake of candied fruit, nuts, and spices; and *ricciarelli*, light cookies made from almond paste.

It is truly a pleasure to hear the Tuscans speak. Their expressions, full of imagination and elegance, give an idea of the pleasure one must have felt in ancient Athens when people spoke that melodious Greek that resembled a constant stream of music.

—Madame de Staël

Lucca represents the Tuscany that still lives and enjoys, hopes and works. The city is a fascinating and picturesque mixture of ancient and modern; and not only the city but also the countryside–the flourishing, romantic countryside one views from the celebrated walk along the walls.

—Henry James

The moderately priced **Botteganova** (Via Chiantigiana 29, just east of Via Simone Martini, 0577/284230) offers a creative approach to traditional Tuscan fare that has earned it a Michelin star, in an elegant atmosphere. The seasonal menu abounds with such delicacies as porcini mushrooms and truffles, as in a truffle-scented Pecorino tortelli, and other local produce like the Sienese tarragon that flavors the duck in red wine; homemade desserts such as a chocolate *tortino* with white-chocolate sauce and an ample wine list are always offered. The restaurant is open Tuesday-Sunday, lunch and dinner. Just a few steps from the Facciatone is **Al Marsili** (Via del Castoro 3, just west of Via di Città, 0577/47154). Located in a vaulted, 15th-century palace, this dining spot serves Tuscan dishes and some of its own creations as well. It's open Tuesday-Sunday, lunch and dinner. A friendly trattoria near **Piazza del Campo**, **Antica Trattoria Papei** (Piazza del Mercato 6, 0577/280894) is the perfect place to indulge in pasta, beans, and steak without straining the budget. Alfresco dining in the summer in the piazza, directly behind **Piazza del Campo**, is another plus. It's open Tuesday-Sunday, lunch and dinner.

Siena's tourist information office (Piazza del Campo 56, 0577/280551; fax 0577/270676), open Monday-Saturday, offers up-to-the-minute information on museum hours and local events. Cab stands are located at the train station and at **Piazza Matteotti**, or call 49222. Almost the entire city is blessedly closed to traffic. There are well-marked parking areas just outside the city walls.

Viareggio, Forte dei Marmi, and Torre del Lago Puccini

Viareggio, 97 kilometers (60 miles) west of Florence, is most directly reached on autostrada **A11**. If you are heading to Torre del Lago Puccini, drive 5 kilometers (3 miles) south of Viareggio along **Via dei Tigli**, following signs. From Viareggio, Forte dei

The Best

Enrico Giannini

Fifth-generation bookbinder/maker of leather and marbled paper products, Giulio Giannini & Figlio

Walking over to the **Mercato Nuovo** and buying a *lampredotto* (the fattiest part of a cow's intestines) sandwich from the fourth-generation tripe vendor, and devouring it standing up.

Sampling another "lost" Florentine traditional food called *cecina,* a flat yellow crepe made from chickpea flour—sometimes I find it at **Cantinetta da Verrazzano.**

Walking up the long, winding, and steep road to **Via di Belvedere** and **Via di San Leonardo**, where there is a large variety of etchings on the walls, some dating back over a hundred years.

Gazing endlessly at the perfect harmony of the façade of the **San Miniato al Monte** church.

Marmi is 14 kilometers (9 miles) north via autostrada **A12**. There is train service to Viareggio and Forte dei Marmi from Florence.

Named after the medieval road **Via Regia**, which connected Migliarino and Pietrasanta, Viareggio is now Tuscany's largest and most popular seaside resort. It boasts wide, sandy beaches and relatively easy access from Florence. Viareggio's coastal location made it strategically important as far back as the 14th century, when it became Lucca's only access to the sea. This marshy outpost was transformed in the 19th century by Lucca's Duchess Maria Luisa, who drained the swamps, developed the shipping and fishing industries, and laid out the town. By the 1860s cabanas and umbrellas were popping up on the beach. In 1917 a massive fire destroyed almost all of the wooden Art Nouveau buildings that had lined the popular seaside boardwalk, the **Passeggiata Viale Regina Margherita**, but in the 1920s it was almost entirely rebuilt as it appears today, with many of the most significant buildings designed by **Galileo Chini** and **Alfredo Belluomini**. Chini was one of the founders of Italian Art Nouveau. He also designed sets for the earliest New York City Metropolitan Opera productions of *Manon Lescaut*, *Gianni Scicchi*, and *Turandot*, composed by his Lucca-born friend Giacomo Puccini.

Principally a beach destination, Viareggio's wintertime festivities of *Carnevale* now rival those of Venice, though here the atmosphere is of pure frivolity, featuring parades of large, elaborately constructed and designed satirical papier-mâché floats. The ambience here is decidedly more contemporary and commercial than Venice's theatrical and sophisticated rendition. If you can't be here on Mardi Gras or the three preceding Saturdays when the parades take place, you can see where the floats are made in the huge float hangars along **Via Marco Polo**.

The 78-room **Palace Hotel** (Via Flavio Gioia 2, at Viale Giosué Carducci, 0584/46134; fax 0584/47351) is a throwback to the resort's heyday in the 1920s, with the ambience and service somewhat formal and the restaurant (0584/31320) appropriately elegant. Ask for one of the guest rooms with a terrace that faces the sea. It's open year-round.

Ristorante da Romano (Via Giuseppe Mazzini 122, between Via Antonio Fratti and Via Cesare Battisti, 0584/31382) is one of the best fresh fish and seafood dining spots on the Tuscan coast, with a Michelin star to prove it. Order the special of the day and experience a meal to remember (with a price tag to match). It's open Tuesday-Sunday, lunch and dinner February through December.

Viareggio's tourist office (Viale Giosué Carducci 10, between Via Leonardo da Vinci and Via Amerigo Vespucci, 0584/962233; fax 0584/47336) is open Monday-Saturday, Sunday morning June through September; Monday-Saturday October through May.

The **Casa di Giacomo Puccini** (1858-1924), on the shore of **Lago Massaciuccoli** (0584/350567) in Torre del Lago Puccini, is a pilgrimage spot for opera lovers. The Tuscan composer's villa still has its original furnishings, vintage photographs, and the piano on which Puccini wrote *La Bohème*, *Tosca*, and *Madama Butterfly*. On the villa grounds is a small chapel and the tombs of Puccini, his wife, and son. Torre del Lago holds an outdoor *Festival Pucciniano* yearly from the end of July to mid-August, featuring the works of Puccini. Unfortunately, lack of funds are forever threatening the festival's existence, and it is often difficult to get information more than a month or so in advance. The tourist office in Viareggio (see above) has information on the program and tickets, as does the provincial tourist office in Torre del Lago (Viale Marconi 225, 0584/359893; fax 0584/359893). It is open Monday through Saturday.

Forte dei Marmi is one of the largest and most fashionable resort towns on the Tuscan coast; the well-heeled summer residents here make Viareggio seem tacky by comparison. There is relatively little car traffic in Forte dei Marmi, and bicycles and barefoot twenty-somethings add to its atmosphere of innate chic and prestige. Originally founded in 1788 by Grand Duke Pietro Leopoldo as a seaport and fortress to store marble quarried in nearby Seravezza, the old loading pier is now used as a promenade. The white sandy beaches attracted the first summer residents in the 1860s, and even today it retains an understated residential atmosphere drawing the idle rich from Milan and Turin (sandy beaches are scarce on the coastline north of Tuscany toward Liguria and the Riviera), who settle in for the summer.

The town is set back from the beach amid an expansive pine forest that provides a green shady area to escape the summer sun. As with Viareggio, there are no hotels directly on the water; beaches are lined with scores of private *bagni* (bathing establishments) with individual cabanas and other necessities for a luxurious day in the sun. If the sun gets too hot, you can always escape into the many high-fashion boutiques and chic cafés, or stop for homemade gelato. Among the too-tanned and casually gorgeous, you may spot Giorgio Armani if he has opened his villa for the season. A lovely 55-room hotel that blends in effortlessly with its surrounding aristocratic neighbors, the stately **Villa Franceschi** (Via XX Settembre 19, 0584/787114; fax 0584/787471) sits in a small shady parkland, with bikes for its guests; it's a five-minute peddle to the beach. The restaurant is for hotel guests only.

Forte dei Marmi's tourist office (Viale Achille Franceschi 8, 0584/80091; fax 0584/83214) is open Monday-Saturday June-September; erratic hours October-May.

Two small towns of interest are **Seravezza**, 7 kilometers (4 miles) inland from Forte dei Marmi (follow the signs), the marble town where Michelangelo lived in 1517 during one of his great quests to find perfect stone to sculpt, and **Pietrasanta**, 6 kilometers (4 miles) east of Forte dei Marmi (follow the signs). Small and unassuming, this 13th-century village is a home to artists and sculptors who have been coming from points near and far for years. Nearby are the centuries-old quarries of **Massa** and **Carrara**, and the creative spirit lives on here in small workshops and foundries. A creative crowd (or the merely curious) browse the attractive shops, antiques stores, and always-busy restaurants. Housed in a historical palazzo of exposed brick archways and a back room dating to the 1200s, the family-run **Trattoria San Martino** (Via Garibaldi 17, 0584/790190) promises an inexpensive meal of homemade pastas and congenial service. It's open Monday, Wednesday-Sunday, lunch and dinner.

Be sure to visit some of the *museo della contrada*. There are 17 of these "museums" in Siena, each crammed with mementos, drawings, paintings, photographs, sacred art objects, locks of horse mane, military uniforms, tiny sets of jockey silks, and, most important, every single banner (or *palio*) won by the *contrada* since they started handing them out. The oldest extant one, dated 1719, is on view at the museum of L'Aquila (The Eagle). Il Bruco has few of these, but it boasts a lovely fresco depicting the historic noble uprising.

VOLTERRA

Volterra is 81 kilometers (50 miles) southwest of Florence. Take the **Superstrada del Palio** 39 kilometers (24 miles) to Colle di Val d'Elsa, and follow **S68** 30 kilometers (19 miles) to Volterra. There's no direct bus service to Volterra from Florence; take a **SITA** bus to Siena and make a **TRA-IN** connection for Volterra.

It is a dramatic sight to see Volterra from a distance: The city rises up isolated, stark, and aloof from the abandoned countryside. Less known than some of Tuscany's other destinations, Volterra has been the site of 3,000 years of continuous civilization and is of particular interest for those interested in history. As ancient **Velathri**, it was the northernmost and strongest of the 12 city-states of the Etrurian federation, three times larger than Volterra is today. Its medieval city, dating mostly from the 12th and 13th centuries, is protected within the perimeter of another, larger set of walls.

The beautiful central **Piazza dei Priori** is bounded by sober medieval palaces, of which the **Palazzo dei Priori** (Piazza dei Priori, at Via Turazza) is the most prominent. The view from the top of this oldest functioning town hall (built 1208-1254) in Tuscany commands an unrivaled panorama that can reach as far as the Tuscan coast. Behind the Palazzo dei Priori is the **Duomo** (Piazza San Giovanni, at Via Turazza), a Romanesque edifice consecrated in 1120, with Pisan touches added in the 13th century. The **Battistero** (Piazza San Giovanni, west of the Duomo), begun in 1283, remains with its marble façade completed only on one side. Close by (take Via Roma from **Piazza San Giovanni**) is the **Porta all'Arco**, an original Etruscan gate to the city, which affords more extensive and breathtaking views.

A handsome 15th-century palazzo by **Antonio da Sangallo** houses the **Pinacoteca** (Via dei Sarti 1, between Piazza San Michele and Via Buonparenti, 0588/87580). This museum has a small but impressive collection of predominantly 14th-17th-century Tuscan artists, highlighted by Luca Signorelli's *Annunciation* and Rosso Fiorentino's *Descent from the Cross* (1521). The latter has long attracted the attention of art historians as one of the important works that links Renaissance and Mannerist styles. The **Museo Etrusco Guarnacci** (Guarnacci Etruscan Museum; Via Don Minzoni 15, between Porta Selci and Piazza XX Settembre, 0588/86347) has one of the best and largest collections of Etruscan objects in Italy. Its most important item is the famous elongated bronze figure *Ombra della Sera* (Evening Shadow). Other pieces include some 600 funerary urns of tufa, terra-cotta, and alabaster. The latter demonstrates the Etruscans' early skill in working with the local alabaster. Volterra is still famous around the world for its high-quality alabaster crafting. Stop in at one of the myriad souvenir shops that sell inexpensive pillboxes or at gallery-like stores that are full of museum-quality works. Both museums are open daily, 15 March-1 November; daily, 9AM-1PM 2 November-14 March; there's an admission charge for each museum. In the nearby **Museo d'Arte Sacra** (Museum of Sacred Art; Via Roma 13, between Via Ricciarelli and Piazza San Giovanni) are sculpture and architectural fragments and a della Robbia terra-cotta of *San Lino,* Volterra's patron saint, who was the successor pope to St. Peter. The museum is open daily; admission is charged. A single ticket good for all three museums can be purchased at the museums and the tourist office, as well as at hotels around town.

The climb to Volterra's 14th-15th-century **Fortezza** begins not far from the Museo Etrusco Guarnacci. This massive installation serves as a reminder that independent Volterra, like many other Tuscan towns, eventually fell to the superior force of Florence. Lorenzo de' Medici modified an existing 14th-century fortress (**Rocca Vecchia**—Old Tower, which has a tower known as the **Torre Femmina**—Women's Tower) and added a **Rocca Nuova** (New Fortress) of five towers, one of which is known as the **Torre Maschio** (Men's Tower). Only the Fortezza's park is open to the public (the rest is used as a prison), but the whole is an impressive feature of Volterra's silhouette. Typical Tuscan fare is served at **L'Etruria** (Piazza dei Priori 6/8, 0588/86064), a highly acclaimed restaurant housed in a medieval palazzo with vaulted ceilings and turn-of-the-20th-century frescoes. Such local specialties as *farro* soup, *agnello al forno* (roast lamb), and game are especially delightful when dining moves outdoors on the main piazza in warm weather. It is open Monday-Wednesday, Friday-Sunday, lunch and dinner; reservations are recommended.

The 44-room **Hotel San Lino** (Via San Lino 26, between Via Ricciarelli and Porta San Francesco, 0588/85250; fax 0588/80620) is set in a 12th-century cloistered convent that has been thoroughly modernized, with a restaurant and pool (for hotel guests only), and is Volterra's loveliest hostelry. Just beyond the walls, the 17th-century **Villa Nencini** (Borgo Santo Stefano 55, just northwest of Porta San Francesco, 0588/86571; fax 0588/80601) offers a country-hotel setting with a pool as well, and a restaurant that's relatively inexpensive. Some of the 34 guest rooms have a view of the **Val di Cecina** (Cecina Valley).

The tourist office (Via Turazza 2, between Piazza dei Priori and Piazza San Giovanni, 0588/86150; fax 0588/86150) is open Monday-Saturday.

No medieval battle was ever complete without the escort of *carroccil* (war chariots) on each opposing side. Pulled by six white oxen, these carts were like giant floats, carrying tall masts holding the city's emblems, banners, and good luck charms. Often there was space on the cart for a priest to hold a Mass and a large bell that would signal distress or victory to the soldiers and townspeople. A replica of such a chariot can still be seen in Siena when it is taken out for each of the two *Palio* horse races and is led in procession around the Piazza del Campo before the contest.

VENICE ORIENTATION

A dazzling, fabled link between East and West, Venice remains one of the world's most exciting cities to discover, albeit one that thrives on tourism. Seen on foot in the sparkling sunlight of a summer's day or through the brooding mist of a winter's morning, from a gondola in the moonlight or a *vaporetto* drifting down the gently curving **Canal Grande** (Grand Canal), Venice has the power to enchant. The greatest tour in town is aboard the *No. 1 vaporetto,* cruising past weathered palazzi and ancient piazze. While the effects of age, pollution from nearby **Mestre**, and ever-increasing *acqua alta* (high water from the **Adriatic Sea**) take their toll, the theatricality of these Gothic palaces and the absence of automobiles give the city an ageless quality reminiscent of its former epithet, *La Serenissima* (Most Serene).

This unique city, built on 117 islands separated by 177 small canals, started life as a swampy refuge from the violent barbarian invasions of the fifth century. By the time of the Crusades, Venice had become a major power on the Adriatic and its merchants gradually tightened their control of the major trade routes to the Levant. The most famous of all the merchants of Venice was Marco Polo, who grew wealthy selling, to the rest of Europe, silks and spices collected on his Asian adventures. In the heyday of *La Serenissima*, the riches brought from the East made the Venetian court one of the most luxurious and influential in Europe. Among other things the Venetians take credit for is the introduction of coffee and the use of the fork. Of more interest to visitors, though, this vast wealth made it possible to commission great works of art from the likes of Titian, Tintoretto, and Veronese, and of architecture from **Palladio** and **Longhena**—a priceless legacy.

The artistic heritage of Venice draws tourists by the millions, resulting in negatives for visitors and residents alike. Myriad masks and kitsch glass are displayed in every shop window, and prices only occasionally correspond to quality. But today there are still some ties to Venice's mercantile past. Visitors can find—and buy—gilded mosaics made in the Byzantine manner, hand-painted and pleated fabrics sculpted for modern wear, cut velvet and stenciled silk lamps evoking the ever-present glamour of the Far East, beaded and gold-leafed slippers appropriate to wear to a palazzo salon, and the famous **Murano** glass with its airy delicacy. The magic of Venice endures, and through it all, the Venetians somehow remain hospitable and enthusiastic, and eager to direct visitors who get lost in the maze of their city's streets. But getting lost is one of the best parts of a Venetian experience. After all, how else can one find the special tranquillity of a tiny *campo* (square) filled with the sounds of children's laughter and golden sunlight, a picturesque but forgotten canal, and the legendary romance of Venice?

City code is 041 unless otherwise noted. To call Venice from the US, dial 011-39-041, followed by the local number. When calling from inside Italy or within Venice, dial 041 and the local number.

Getting to Venice

Airport

Aeroporto Marco Polo

The closest international airport to Venice is in **Tessera**, 13 kilometers (8 miles) from the city.

Airport Services

Airport Emergencies	2606890
Currency Exchange	5415471
Customs	5415390
Ground Transportation	2609260
Information	2609260, 2606111
Lost and Found	2606436
Police	2606825
Traveler's Aid	2606111

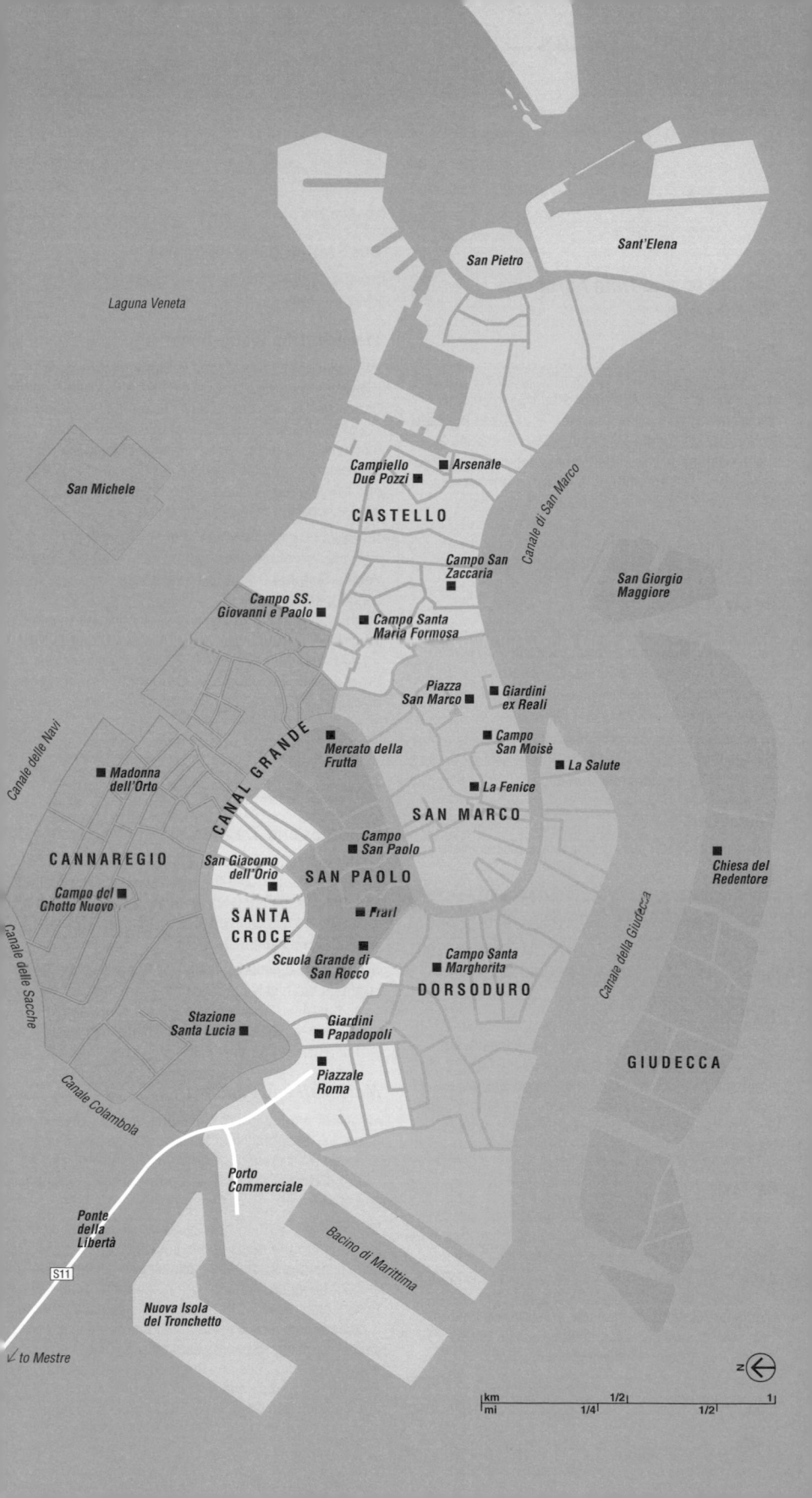
Sant'Elena
San Pietro
Laguna Veneta
San Michele
Campiello Due Pozzi
Arsenale
CASTELLO
Canale di San Marco
Campo San Zaccaria
San Giorgio Maggiore
Campo SS. Giovanni e Paolo
Campo Santa Maria Formosa
Piazza San Marco
Giardini ex Reali
Canale delle Navi
CANAL GRANDE
Mercato della Frutta
Campo San Moisè
La Salute
Madonna dell'Orto
La Fenice
SAN MARCO
Campo San Paolo
CANNAREGIO
San Giacomo dell'Orio
SAN PAOLO
Chiesa del Redentore
Campo del Chotto Nuovo
SANTA CROCE
Frari
Canale della Giudecca
Canale delle Sacche
Scuola Grande di San Rocco
Campo Santa Margherita
DORSODURO
Stazione Santa Lucia
Giardini Papadopoli
GIUDECCA
Piazzale Roma
Canale Colambola
Porto Commerciale
Ponte della Libertà
Bacino di Marittima
S11
Nuova Isola del Tronchetto
to Mestre
N
km
mi
1/2
1
1/4
1/2

Airlines

Air France 167800160, 800/237.2747

Alitalia.....147865641/2/3, 800/223.5730

British Airways.....167287287, 800/247.9297

KLM.....02/216969, 800/374.7747

Getting to and from Aeroporto Marco Polo

By Bus

The least expensive way to travel between the city and the airport is on the **ACTV *No. 5*** bus, which travels across the mainland between the airport and **Piazzale Roma**. Tickets for the 20-minute ride are available at the newsstand in the airport lobby. Schedules for the service are available from the tourist information offices (see "Visitors' Information Offices," page 175) and in *Un Ospite a Venezia* (A Guest in Venice). Local water transportation to destinations throughout the city is available outside the bus terminal in Piazzale Roma.

By Car

While it is possible to rent a car at the airport, automobiles are not allowed in Venice. There are only three places to park: **Piazzale Roma**, **Tronchetto**, and on the **Lido**. Therefore, unless Venice is just one stop on a trip, it's not advisable to bring a car here.

To get from the airport to Venice, follow the signs out of the airport to state road **S14**. In Mestre, go east on **S11** over the bridge to **Piazzale Roma**.

Rental Cars

The following rental car agencies have offices at the airport:

Avis 5415030, 800/331.1084

Europcar (National) 5415654, 800/227.3876

Hertz 5416151, 800/654.3001

Thrifty 5415299, 800/367.2277

By Boat

The service (5415084) is loosely coordinated with arriving and departing flights (leave yourself plenty of time) and connects the airport to **Piazza San Marco** and the Lido. The trip to Piazza San Marco takes about 80 minutes. Service to the Lido runs hourly, and the trip takes about 40 minutes.

By Taxi

Taxi acquei (water taxis) from the airport take passengers as close as possible to their hotels. Many hostelries have their own landings, and those that don't will send a porter to the dock to collect luggage. The taxi landing is outside the arrivals building; the trip to Piazza San Marco takes about 20 minutes, and at press time the cost was about $75. If you need to book a taxi by phone, try one of the following stands:

Ferrovia 716286

Lido 5260059

Marco Polo (airport).....5415084

Radio Taxi 723112

Rialto 5230575/723112

San Marco 5229750

Venezia Taxi 723009

Bus Station (Long-Distance)

The main bus station for Venice (5287886) is at **Piazzale Roma**.

Train Station (Long-Distance)

Venice's central train station is **Santa Lucia** (Fondamenta Santa Lucia, 147888088), located on the Canal Grande. Be sure to buy a ticket to that station and not to the Mestre station across the lagoon on the mainland. (There are, however, shuttle trains that run between the two stations every 15 minutes.) *Vaporetto* and *taxi acqueo* service to other points in the city is available on the pier outside the station.

Those looking to tour in the grand manner of the romantic era of rail travel can hop a ride on the fabled **Venice-Simplon Orient Express**. It starts (or ends) in London, and stops in Paris, Venice, Florence, Rome, Salzburg, Vienna, Budapest, and Istanbul. For more information, contact the Venice-Simplon Orient Express (c/o Abercrombie & Kent, 1520 Kensington Rd, Oak Brook, IL 60521, 630/954.2944, 800/524.2420; fax 630/954.3324).

Getting Around Venice

Gondolas and *Traghetti*

Gondoliers gather at strategic places in the city (in front of the train station and the **Hotel Danieli**, for example) and offer 50-minute tours for about $80 at press time (a supplement is charged after sundown). A gondola comfortably accommodates six.

Traghetti (also called gondolas by Venetians) are less luxurious but highly functional; they are the best way to cross the Canal Grande if you are not near one of the three bridges. Follow signs for *traghetto* or gondola, pay, and hop aboard for the short ride across the canal.

Motoscafi and *Vaporetti*

Motoscafi are enclosed, black-and-white express water buses that stop only at a few places along the canals and cost a bit more than *vaporetti*. Tickets are sold at ACTV booths at all stops. An up-to-date ACTV book is available there, or visit www.hellovenezia.com.

Vaporetti are partially open-air water buses. The stops, indicated on the maps in this book with a "T," are usually named for a nearby church or landmark. *Nos. 1* and *82* travel the entire length of the Canal Grande. Tickets are sold at ACTV booths at the stops. If a booth is closed, purchase a ticket on board; passengers caught traveling without tickets are subject to hefty fines. *Vaporetto* lines and stops change occasionally, so check the schedule and be sure the boat is heading in the direction you want to go. The service is 24 hours,

VENICE VAPORETTO

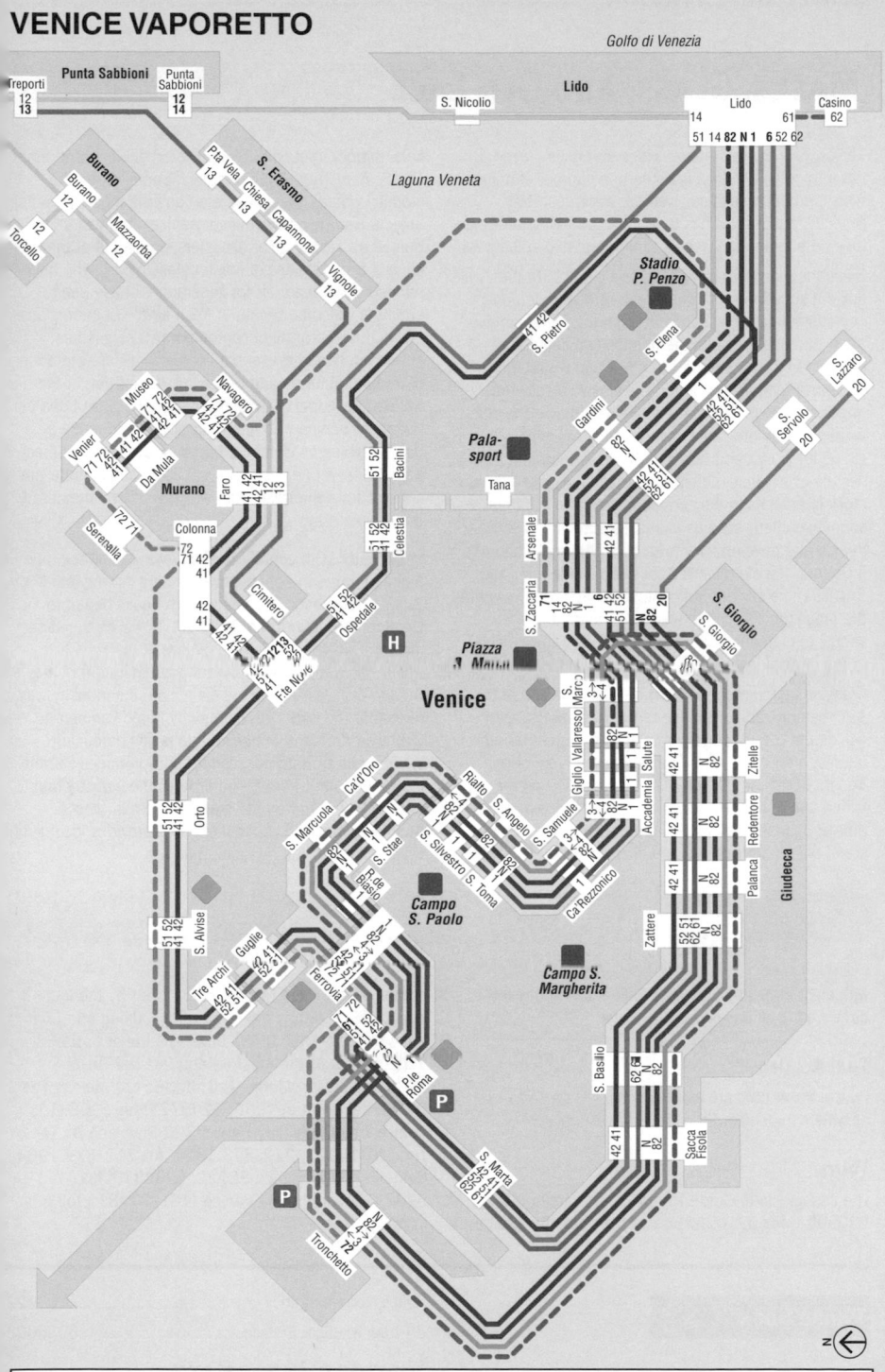

1	12	41	61	82
3	13	42	62	N
4	14	51	71	Garden / P Parking
6	20	52	72	Interest / H Hospital

Routes subject to change

Bold route numbers: Start/End of line

Dashed line: Summer only

Masks, Glass, and Old Lace

Venice, like all major Italian cities that have played a powerful role in history, is home to a number of indigenous crafts that have survived the centuries. Their products make souvenirs that are as authentic today as they were for foreign visitors to the Republic in the past.

Since the reinstatement of *Carnevale* in 1980, the ancient Venetian art of mask making has undergone something of a renaissance. Though the forms are now many and often include the plumes and sequins of cosmic fantasy, there are still a few that would make Casanova feel right at home. The classic mask—the angular white beaklike form that extends over the chin, as depicted in the genre scenes of Pietro Longhi—is called the *bauta* and was once worn by men and women everywhere. Other masks take their cue from the stock characters in the commedia dell'arte (an improvisational comedy style using masks that originated near Venice and traveled from town to town): Pantalone and Il Dottore, the old misers; Arlecchino (Harlequin) and Brighella, the servant buffoons; and Capitano Spaventa, the braggadocio. All the masks are made out of a variety of materials, from the ubiquitous papier-mâché to the original leather and, more recently, ceramic.

Glass has been made in **Murano** since the end of the 13th century, and a furnace or two has always been active, but a 19th-century revival and another rebirth of interest after World War II have kept the fires roaring into modern times. Much of what is hawked on the island and in the city—mass-produced beads and tiny animal figurines—is of little interest, but a few items stand out as authentic or genuinely creative. Chandeliers, mirrors, meticulously replicated goblets, and other classic items from 16th-century Murano—when the industry was at its peak—are among the most appealing objects. Today, a few younger people—many of them trained as architects or designers, and some of them coming from families of master glassmakers who have handed down the craft for generations—have been adding a welcome breath of fresh air to Venetian glassmaking. A vast array of contemporary designs has appeared, based on simple lines or witty interpretations of traditional forms and deserving of inclusion in the world's museums of modern art. Serious glass buffs or visitors to Venice who intend to buy should make a point of going to Murano's **Museum of Glass Art** (see page 284). A brief visit here will help you separate the sublime from the trash, with which you'll be inundated during your stay.

In the early 16th century **Burano** lace was all the rage among European nobility, even finding its way into Mary Tudor's trousseau. Once its pattern books began to circulate throughout the Continent, however, Venetian lacework was soon eclipsed by that of the French, which was nothing more than a good imitation of the Burano art. On the verge of extinction, the industry was revived in the mid-19th century by Paolo Fambri and Contessa Andriano Marcello, and is still producing. While much of what passes for hand-produced Burano lace is imported from Spain or Asia, the industry that put the tiny island on the map survives. Burano's **Scuola di Merletti** (*School of Lace*) provides local girls with subsidized lessons (see Burano)

with night routes being a little different from day routes but covering all bases just the same.

Taxi Acqueo

Private water taxis are expensive but will take you anywhere in Venice. There are stands all over.

Tours

The Associazione Guide Touristiche (Castello 5328, 5209038; fax 5210762) has a list of multilingual tour guides whose fixed rates are approved by the local tourist board. Many agencies offer walking and boat tours and day trips to the outer islands or to the Veneto. Four of the most reliable are Ital Travel (Ascensione San Marco 71G, 5236511), Kele & Teo (Ponte dei Bareteri 4930, 5208722; fax 5208913), Venice Travel Advisory Service (22 Riverside Dr, New York, NY 10023, 212/873.1964; fax 212/873.1964; Castello 4718; Venice 30122, 5232379; fax 5232379), and Enjoy Venice (167/274819 toll free in Italy).

Phone Book

Emergencies

Ambulance 118
Fire 115
Police 112
Police Nonemergency 703222
24-hour Medical Service 5230000

Visitors' Information

Bus 5287886
Customs 5415390
Postal Information 5299111
Train 147888088

Walking

The best way to truly enjoy Venice is to begin walking. It is nearly impossible not to get lost in the city's labyrinth of *campi* (squares), *calli* (streets), and *fondamente* (canalside piers). In fact, getting lost is highly recommended. Some of the most pleasant discoveries can be made this way, and obliging Venetians are always willing to help wayward tourists find their way back to a familiar landmark.

FYI

Accommodations

In high season, making reservations ahead is essential. Hotels follow a high-season calendar of their own. Maximum rates are in effect at *Carnevale* (the two weeks preceding Ash Wednesday); from 15 April to 1 July; in September and October; and for the Christmas/New Year's season. Reserve directly or through Venetian travel agencies, such as CIT Viaggi (Via Mestrina 65, Mestre, 5341388; fax 5341025) or Kele & Teo (see "Tours," page 172). If you arrive without reservations, visit one of the Azienda di Promozione Turistica (APT) offices (See "Visitors' Information Offices," page 175). During summer, many houses owned by religious orders open their doors to paying visitors.

Climate

Good times to visit are May, when temperatures stay in the agreeable 60 degrees Fahrenheit range, and September and October, when they don't drop below a mild 50 degrees Fahrenheit. Summers bring high heat and humidity; winter months are chillingly damp, and the piazze sometimes flood. It rains often November through December and March through April. That said, don't stay away on account of the weather—Venice enchants no matter what the season.

Months	Average Temperature (°F)
January	43
February	48
March	53
April	60
May	67
June	72
July	77
August	74
September	68
October	60
November	54
December	44

Embassies and Consulates

British Consulate: Palazzo Querini, Campiello della Carità 1051, just west of Ponte dell'Accademia, Dorsoduro.....5227207

The nearest Australian, Canadian, and US consulates are in Milan.

Holidays

In addition to the national holidays (see "Northern Italy Orientation"), Venice celebrates the feast day of San Marco, its patron saint, on 25 April.

Hours

A midday break is a fact of life in Venice, as in the rest of Italy. Most businesses are open Monday through Saturday, 9AM-1PM and 3:30-7:30PM March through October; from November through February they are sometimes closed on Monday morning. Food shops are open Monday, Tuesday, and Thursday through Saturday, 9AM-1PM and 3:30PM-7:30PM; Wednesday, 9AM-1PM; and closed Wednesday afternoon and Sunday. Churches are generally open daily, 8AM-12:30PM and 3:30PM-7:30PM, with many exceptions. Most museums close on Tuesday, although that too varies. Opening and closing times are listed by day(s) only if normal hours apply (including a midday break); in all other cases, specific hours are given (e.g., 8AM-3:30PM, noon-5PM, no midday closing).

Medical and Legal Emergencies

In a medical emergency, call Assistenza (118); for legal emergencies, contact Ufficio Stranieri (2715511).

Money

The unit of currency in Italy is now the euro. Luckily for visitors from the US, the value of the euro usually hovers around the same as that of the US dollar. And like the dollar, one euro is divided into 100 cents. Notes come in 5-, 10-, 20-, 50-, 100-, and 500-euro denominations. There are also 1- and 2-euro coins. Any old lira notes can be exchanged at any bank in Italy, but can no longer be spent.

Banks are open Monday through Friday from about 8:30AM to 1:30PM, and reopen for an hour or so (usually 3:30 to 4:30) in the afternoon. A good place to change money is at **American Express** (Campo San Moisè 1471, at Salizzada San Moisè and Rio di San Moisè, San Marco, 5200844). Another choice would be **Guetta Viaggi** (Frezzeria 1289, between Calle Due and Calle Selvadego, San Marco, 5208711), or any of the principal banks displaying the *"Cambio"* sign. Change money at the airport, train station, and private *cambios* around town only as a last resort; these agencies charge high commissions.

Better than any of those is, of course, simply to use one of the many available ATMs in the city.

Personal Safety

It is remarkably safe to wander the streets of Venice at night—to visit Piazza San Marco or the church of Santa Maria della Salute, to window-shop along the Mercerie, to walk back to your hotel after the opera, or have a

The Best

Enrica Abbate

Executive Director, Teatro Fondamenta Nuove

A Day in Venice

Morning

Get up early and take a walk on the **Riva degli Schiavoni**. Reach **Piazza San Marco** and go up to the campanile (it's worthwhile). Keep on walking to the **Pescheria** (on the other side of the **Rialto Bridge**) and enjoy the fish-and-vegetables market (it closes at 1PM).

Lunch

From the Pescheria, get a *traghetto* (gondola) and cross the **Canal Grande**. You are in **Strada Nuova**. Nearby you'll find the **Trattoria Ca' d'Oro**, called "della Vedova" by Venetians, and have some *cicchetti* (finger food) there.

Afternoon

While you are in **Cannaregio**, go to the **Gesuiti** church and admire Titian's painting *La Notte* on your left at the entrance. Then get on the *No. 52 vaporetto*, two minutes away from the **Campo dei Gesuiti**, and take a ride through the **Arsenale** (only the *vaporetti* can go through it), getting off at **San Zaccaria**. You are back in Piazza San Marco. Have a Bellini at **Harry's Bar**, then walk to the **Ponte dell'Accademia** for the best view of Venice at sunset.

Dinner

Get on the *No. 1 vaporetto* and get off at **Ca' d'Oro**, turn left on Strada Nuova until you hit the **Fondamenta San Felice** (a few steps away), and have dinner at **Vini Da Gigio**. Choose seafood and *coquillage*.

Nightlife

End your day with a drink at **Il Paradiso Perduto** on the **Fondamenta della Misericordia**.

The Next Day

Wake up late, and if it's sunny, go to **Le Zattere**, sit at one of the outdoor cafés, and enjoy the view, the sun, and a good restful day.

romantic stroll along a moonlit canal. But take elementary precautions; using common sense will outwit most bag, camera, and wallet snatchers. Never carry more than you can afford to lose—i.e., keep your passport and larger amounts of cash in the hotel safe or well concealed in a money purse—and don't leave any valuables visible in a rented car.

Pharmacies

Pharmacies in Venice take turns operating on a 24-hour schedule. Your hotel concierge can tell you who has the responsibility during your stay; the information is also published weekly in *Un Ospite a Venezia*.

Postal Service

The main post office, Poste e Telecommunicazioni (PTT), is near the Ponte di Rialto (Fondaco dei Tedeschi, Salizzada Fondaco dei Tedeschi 5554, between Calle Fondaco dei Tedeschi and Rio dei Fontego dei Tedeschi, San Marco, 5299111); it's open Monday through Saturday from 8:15AM to 6:45PM. There's a more centrally located branch at Calle Larga dell'Ascensione (between Bocca di Piazza and Calle Selvadego), just west of Piazza San Marco; it's open Monday through Friday, 8:10AM-1:40PM and Saturday, 8:10AM-noon.

Publications

The tourist information office carries copies of the monthly *L'Agenda*, an exhaustive list of nightlife possibilities. (There are also posters plastered about town advertising concerts and the like.) English-language cultural-events listings can be found in *Un Ospite a Venezia*; it is available at most hotels and tourist information offices. *Venezia News*, a monthly publication, is a terrific guide to everything that is going on in the arts in the city. It also has lists of restaurants, pizzerias, bars, and late-night clubs. Most of it is printed in both English and Italian.

Restaurants

Lunch is served 12:30PM-3PM; dinner hours are usually 7:30PM-9:30PM. Most bars and cafés open in the early morning and follow their own particular midday-break schedule; closing time varies from 8PM to midnight. Many eateries close in January, in February, before Carnevale, or in August, as well as between Christmas and New Year's. Reservations, while not required, are suggested and may be essential at the most expensive or most popular restaurants. Most restaurants accept major credit cards, but not all.

Shopping

The main shopping districts are the area surrounding Piazza San Marco and the zigzag maze of streets known as the Mercerie, which lead from San Marco to the Ponte di Rialto. The area west of the piazza is home to most of the high-priced boutiques selling designer clothing and leather goods. Prices drop considerably off the main tourist drags at the shops hidden in Venice's backwater alleyways.

Venetian glass is everywhere, but much of it is of poor quality and design. To get an idea of what to look for, visit the museum and factories on Murano. Papier-mâché *Carnevale* masks are also abundant and range from the traditional to the phantasmagorical. Handmade lace can be fabulously expensive, but simple, affordable pieces can be found (here, again, it's best to be educated—visit the lace school on the island of **Burano**).

Street Plan

Venice is divided into six *sestieri* (literally "sixths"), or districts: San Marco, Dorsoduro, San Paolo, Santa Croce,

Cannaregio, and Castello. The island of Giudecca is considered a seventh area. At the base of a Byzantine system that gets even the locals confused is the duality of all addresses: Each location has a specific street address and a different mailing address. The street address may be, for example, Campo Santo Stefano 240, while its mailing address is San Marco 240. The latter refers to the *sestiere* in which the place is located, and not to its actual *calle* (street).

When giving directions, Venetians will usually use a church, a *campo*, or a number of bridges as a reference. For example: "When you cross the next *campo*, keep going straight ahead and after crossing two bridges . . ." Seeing the bewilderment in the visitors' eyes, and realizing the language difficulties, some kindhearted Venetians have been known to simply show the way.

Telephones

The **SIP-Telecom** office near the central post office and the Ponte di Rialto (Fondaco dei Tedeschi, Salizzada Fondaco dei Tedeschi 5551, San Marco, 5333111) is open daily, 8AM-7:45PM. Telephone calls can be made here using American calling cards or credit cards, or by paying afterward in cash.

Visitors' Information Offices

There are five locations of **Azienda di Promozione Turistica (APT)**: at **Palazzetto Selva** (5208964; fax 6298730) between the **Giardini ex Reali** and **Harry's Bar** in San Marco; at Piazza San Marco (5208964; no fax); in the **Santa Lucia** train station (5298727; fax 719078) in Cannaregio; at Calle del Remedio 4421 (5298711; fax 5230399) in Castello; and at the airport (415887). All offices are open Monday through Saturday from 8:30AM; the one at Palazzetto Selva closes at 3:30PM, the Piazza San Marco at 5:30PM, Santa Lucia at 7PM, and Calle del Remedio at 2PM.

The **Institute of Architecture of the University of Venice** publishes *Veneziapertutti,* a free map and guide to Venice designed specifically for travelers with disabilities. Write to **Assessorato Sicurezza Sociale, Ufficio Inserimenti Sociali** (Ca' Farsetti, Commune di Venezia, 30100 Venezia, Italy) for a copy.

The Best

Eric Denker

Senior Lecturer, National Gallery of Art, Washington

The Seven Best Paintings *In Situ* in Venice

Venice is replete with remarkable museums whose collections reflect the history of art and taste from the beginnings of the Republic to the dawn of the new millennium. The Accademia is *the* world-class collection of Renaissance and Baroque Venetian art; the museum of the Ca' Rezzonico details the late florescence of painting in the 18th century. Yet there is always something slightly wistful about seeing works in museum collections orphaned from their original position and ambience. Conversely, the opportunity to view a work *in situ*, in its original location, can provide the most exhilarating and compelling aesthetic experiences in Venice. Below, listed in chronological order, are seven of the most enthralling works still to be discovered in their original locations. Each continues to yield up its charms through multiple visits of quiet contemplation.

Cima da Conegliano, *The Baptism of Christ*, 1494, Church of San Giovanni in Bragora, Castello. Cima was Bellini's most faithful follower, and the image of the Baptism on the high altar is testament to his abiding interest in the beauty of light in the Veneto landscape.

Vittore Carpaccio, *The Vision of St. Augustine*, Scuola di San Giorgio degli Schiavoni, Castello. The most charming of Carpaccio's entertaining cycle of paintings, executed 1502–1508, represents the saint at his desk accompanied by his faithful dog and surrounded by the typical decorations of a Venetian scholar's study. (The Carpaccios were originally on the upper level of the Scuola, but were moved in 1551.)

Giovanni Bellini, *San Zaccaria Altarpiece*, 1505, Church of San Zaccaria, Castello. Bellini's monumental image of the Madonna and child with saints, with its vivid rendition of limpid Venetian light playing over the landscape background, may be the single greatest altarpiece *in situ* in the city.

Domenico Tintoretto, *The Crucifixion*, 1564–1567, Scuola Grande di San Rocco, San Paolo. Tintoretto labored decorating the Scuola for close to 25 years, but his most clarified vision and crowning achievement is *The Crucifixion* in the Sala dell'Albergo of the Scuola.

Titian, *The Annunciation*, 1566, Church of San Salvatore, San Marco. Others might have chosen the early *Assunta* or the *Pesaro Madonna* in the Church of the Frari, but Titian's late work is molten with the energy of devotion and experience.

Paolo Veronese, *The Triumph of Venice*, 1588, Sala del Maggior Consiglio, Palazzo Ducale, San Marco. Veronese was the preeminent muralist in Venice in the 16th century, and this allegorical homage to his adopted city is his last great painting.

Giovanni Battista Tiepolo, *The Banquet of Antony and Cleopatra*, 1746–1747, Palazzo Labia, Cannaregio. Tiepolo was the heir to the Venetian tradition of large-scale fresco decoration, and the last in the line of Italian muralists that began in the 14th century with Giotto. Tiepolo was assisted by the architectural specialist Mengozzi Colonna in rendering the two sumptuous Antony and Cleopatra frescoes that are a tour de force of trompe l'oeil painting. Open by appointment only.

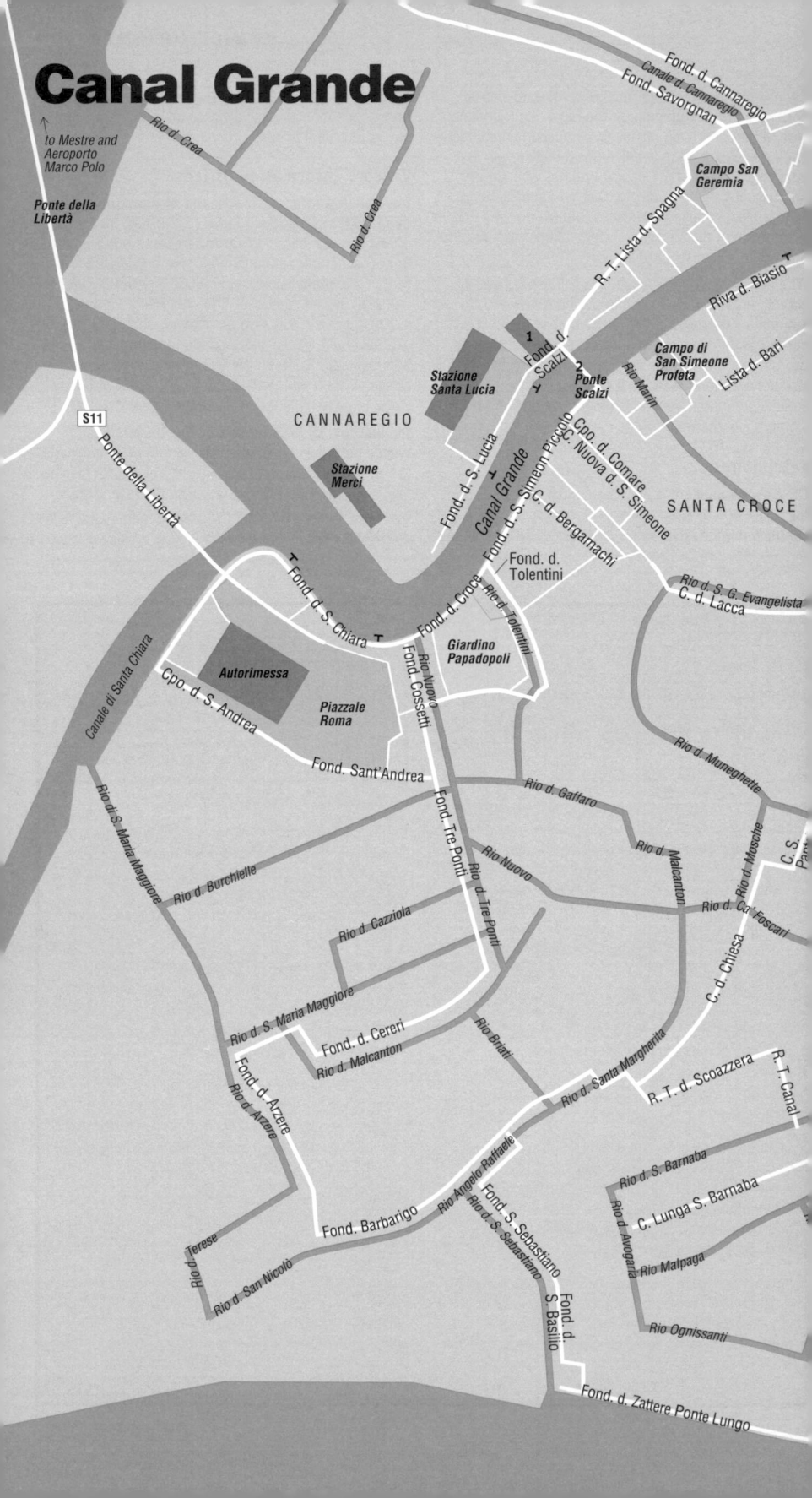
Canal Grande
to Mestre and Aeroporto Marco Polo
Ponte della Libertà
Rio d. Crea
Rio d. Crea
Fond. d. Cannaregio
Canale d. Cannaregio
Fond. Savorgnan
Campo San Geremia
R. T. Lista d. Spagna
Riva d. Biasio
Fond. d. Scalzi
Ponte Scalzi
Campo di San Simeone Profeta
Lista d. Bari
Rio Marin
Stazione Santa Lucia
CANNAREGIO
S11
Stazione Merci
Ponte della Libertà
Fond. d. S. Lucia
Canal Grande
Fond. d. S. Simeon Piccolo
Cpo. d. Comare
C. S. Nuova d. S. Simeone
C. d. Bergamachi
SANTA CROCE
Fond. d. Tolentini
Rio d. S. G. Evangelista
C. d. Lacca
Fond. d. S. Chiara
Fond. d. Croce
Rio d. Tolentini
Giardino Papadopoli
Canale di Santa Chiara
Autorimessa
Piazzale Roma
Cpo. d. S. Andrea
Rio Nuovo
Fond. Cossetti
Fond. Sant'Andrea
Rio d. Muneghette
Rio d. Gallaro
Rio di S. Maria Maggiore
Rio d. Burchielle
Fond. Tre Ponti
Rio d. Tre Ponti
Rio Nuovo
Rio d. Malcanton
Rio d. Moschè
C. S. Pant
Rio d. Ca' Foscari
Rio d. Cazziola
C. d. Chiesa
Rio d. S. Maria Maggiore
Fond. d. Cereri
Rio d. Malcanton
Rio Bratti
Rio d. Santa Margherita
R. T. d. Scoazzera
R. T. Canal
Fond. d. Arzere
Rio d. Arzere
Rio Angelo Raffaele
Fond. S. Sebastiano
Rio d. S. Sebastiano
Rio d. S. Barnaba
C. Lunga S. Barnaba
Rio d. Avogaria
Rio Malpaga
Fond. Barbarigo
Rio d. Terese
Rio d. San Nicolò
Fond. d. S. Basilio
Rio Ognissanti
Fond. d. Zattere Ponte Lungo

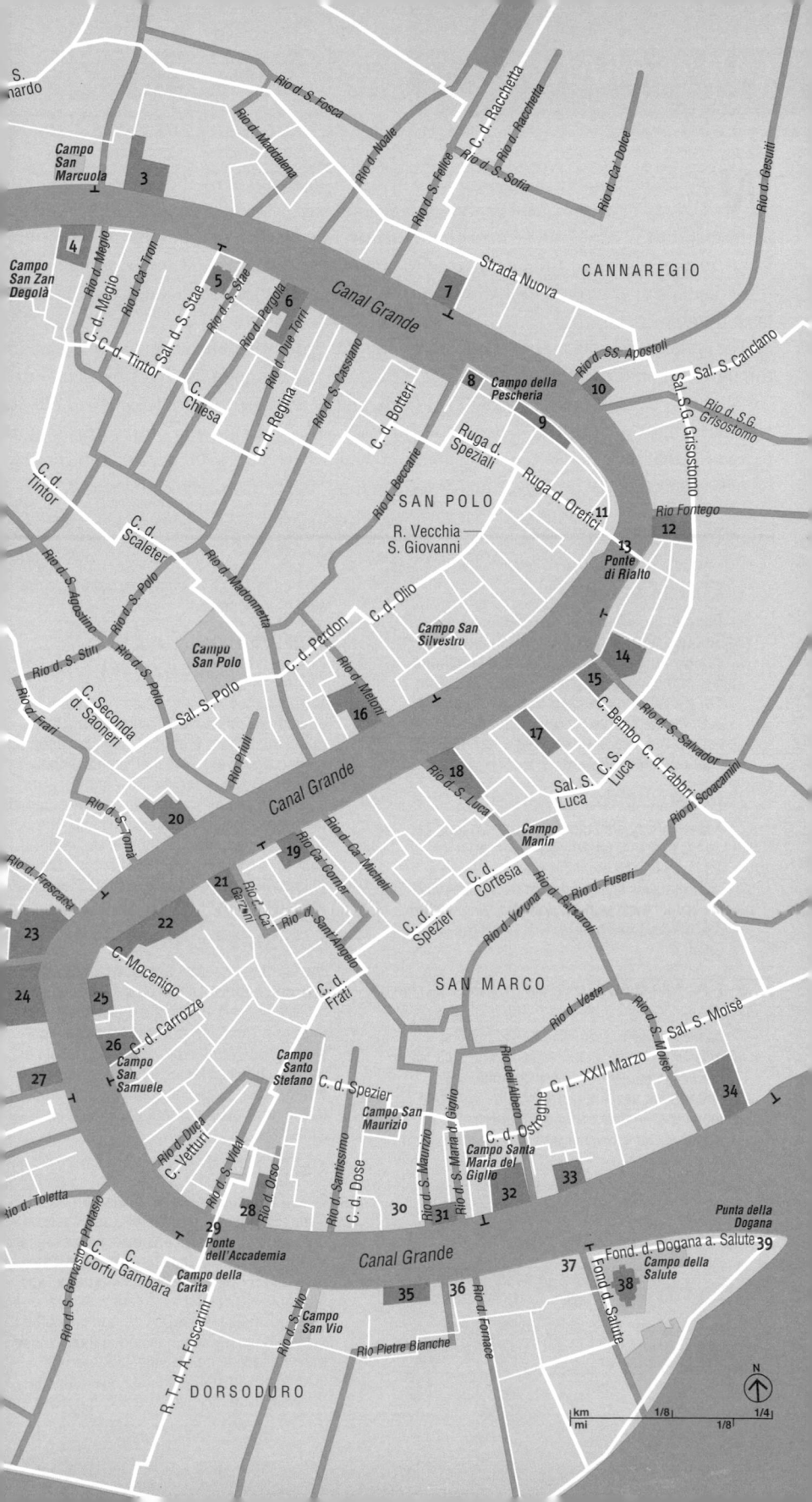
S. nardo
Rio d. S. Fosca
Rio d. Maddalena
Rio d. Noale
Rio d. S. Felice
C. d. Racchetta
Rio d. S. Rio d. Racchetta
Rio d. S. Sofia
Rio d. Ca' Dolce
Rio d. Gesuiti
Campo San Marcuola
3
4
Campo San Zan Degolà
Rio d. Megio
C. d. Megio
Rio d. Ca' Tron
Sal. d. S. Stae
Rio d. S. Stae
Rio d. Pergola
5
6
Canal Grande
7
Strada Nuova
CANNAREGIO
C. d. Tintor
C. Chiesa
C. d. Regina
Rio d. Due Torri
Rio d. S. Cassiano
C. d. Botteri
8
Campo della Pescheria
9
10
Rio d. SS. Apostoli
Sal. S. Canciano
Sal. S. G. Grisostomo
Rio d. S. G. Grisostomo
Ruga d. Speziali
Ruga d. Orefici
11
Rio Fontego
12
13
Ponte di Rialto
C. d. Tintor
C. d. Scaleter
Rio d. Baccarie
SAN POLO
R. Vecchia — S. Giovanni
Rio d. S. Agostino
Rio d. S. Polo
Rio d. Madonnetta
C. d. Olio
Campo San Silvestro
C. d. Perdon
Campo San Polo
Rio d. S. Stin
Rio d. S. Polo
Rio d. Meloni
14
15
16
Rio d. Frari
C. Seconda d. Saoneri
Sal. S. Polo
Rio Pistoi
C. Bembo
Rio d. S. Salvador
C. d. Fabbri
Rio d. Scoacamini
17
18
Rio d. S. Luca
Sal. S. Luca
C. S. Luca
Canal Grande
Rio d. S. Tomà
20
19
Rio d. Ca' Michiel
Campo Manin
Rio d. Frescada
21
Rio d. Ca' Gazzeri
Rio d. Ca' Corner
C. d. Cortesia
Rio d. Fuseri
Rio d. Ferreroli
Rio d. Verona
23
22
Rio d. Sant'Angelo
C. d. Spezier
C. Mocenigo
SAN MARCO
24
25
C. d. Frati
Rio d. Veste
Rio d. S. Moisè
Sal. S. Moisè
26
C. d. Carrozze
Campo San Samuele
27
Campo Santo Stefano
C. d. Spezier
Campo San Maurizio
Rio dell'Albero
C. L. XXII Marzo
34
Rio d. Duca C. Vettori
Rio d. S. Vidal
Rio d. Orso
Rio d. Santissimo
C. d. Dose
Rio d. S. Maurizio
Rio d. S. Maria d. Giglio
C. d. Ostreghe
Campo Santa Maria del Giglio
33
32
28
30
31
Rio d. Toletta
29
Ponte dell'Accademia
Punta della Dogana
Fond. d. Dogana a. Salute
39
Canal Grande
37
Fond. d. Salute
38
Campo della Salute
C. Corfu
C. Gambara
Rio d. S. Gervasio e Protasio
Campo della Carità
35
36
Rio d. Fornace
Rio d. S. Vio
Campo San Vio
Rio Pietre Bianche
R. T. d. A. Foscarini
DORSODURO
N
km
mi
1/8
1/4
1/8

CANAL GRANDE

Whether in high style in a gondola (which will cost you) or on the cheap in *vaporetto No. 1*, a ride on the Canal Grande (Grand Canal) is the perfect, dreamlike introduction to the magic of Venice. Don't worry about identifying the individual sights on your initial visit—once you've seen the Canal Grande you're sure to return. (Many of the places in this chapter are described in further detail elsewhere in this book; check the index for page numbers.)

The canal is actually an extension of the River Brenta, which had been weaving a path through the mudflats and little islands of the lagoon toward open sea. It forms an inverted "S" shape, is 3.5 kilometers (10,500 ft.) long, and is anywhere from 40 meters (120 ft.) wide at its narrowest to 100 meters (300 ft.) at its widest. In case you drop something in, be assured that the canal is generally no more than 6 meters deep. In the fifteenth century French writer Phillipe de Commines described it as "the finest street in the world."

1 Chiesa dei Scalzi

This church, a fine example of Roman Baroque architecture, was built in the 17th century from plans by **Baldassare Longhena**, one of the most celebrated architects of the day (he also designed **La Salute**, the church in Dorsoduro at the eastern entrance to the canal). The façade was added a few decades later by **Giuseppe Sardi**.

2 Ponte Scalzi

A team of city architects built the present bridge in 1934, replacing the one built in 1841 by French architect **A.E. Neville**, in a style that was later judged to be at odds with the rest of the Canal Grande. Amazingly, it is one of only three bridges that cross the Grand Canal.

3 Palazzo Vendramin Calergi

This imposing palazzo, just after the **San Marcuola** *vaporetto* stop, was one of the first Renaissance buildings in Venice. It was built in the 15th century by **Mauro Codussi**, who abandoned the Gothic tradition to introduce the new style derived from Florence and Rome. Richard Wagner was a guest here when he died in 1883. In winter the palazzo is the seat of the **Casino**.

Fondaco dei Turchi

4 Fondaco dei Turchi (Turks' Warehouse)

The elongated supports of this splendid, oriental-looking building's arches and the round medallions in carved stone between them (*patere*) are typical elements of the Byzantine style in Venice. Built in the 12th and 13th centuries and originally the home of the Pesaro family, it was then used by the Turkish community. The façade was rather clumsily restored in the 19th century. The palazzo now houses the **Museo di Storia Naturale** (Museum of Natural History).

5 San Stae

The fine 18th-century Baroque façade, by **Domenico Rossi**, of this church is remarkable for its balanced architectural and sculptural harmony. The three statues at the top represent *Christ*, *Faith*, and *Charity*. This is one of the few churches facing the Canal Grande, with a small, simple piazza opening in front of it. The odd name is in fact Venetian dialect for St. Eustace.

6 Ca' Pesaro

One of the most imposing *palazzi* on the Canal Grande, this building is exquisitely Baroque and conveys an obvious message of wealth and power. The stark-white structure, begun 1657 by **Baldassare Longhena**, was also built out of the characteristically Venetian love for ample loggias. On the top floors the façade is mostly columns and arches. Notice the long façade on the side canal—a real luxury, and an infrequent one, even among the wealthy patricians of Venice. It houses the

Museo d'Arte Moderna and the **Museo d'Arte Orientale**.

7 Ca' d'Oro

This 15th-century palazzo by **Matteo Raverti** is the most admired example of Venetian Gothic in the city. In Venice, Gothic means pointed arches and elaborate–at times flamboyant–stone decorations, as opposed to the austere Gothic cathedrals in Northern Europe. The top two floors here offer an irresistible impression of lightness and grace, in perfect harmony with the water environment. The façade was accurately restored in the 1980s; only the original blue, red, and gold trimmings could not be replaced. Another extensive restoration of the façade was completed in the early 1990s, and the effect is spectacular. The palazzo now houses the **Giorgio Franchetti Gallery**.

8 Pescheria (Fish Market)

Notice the open loggia, built in the Venetian Gothic style in 1907. A gondola service ferries people across the Canal Grande to shop at this important fish market and the adjacent *erberia,* the local fresh produce market.

9 Fabbriche Nuove di Rialto

This long, narrow palazzo was erected 1552-1555 as part of a general plan to reorganize the Rialto area around the new stone bridge over the Canal Grande. Designed by **Jacopo Sansovino**, the palazzo now houses government offices.

9 Santi Geremia and Lucia Church

This newly cleaned façade is that of a church built originally in the 11th century and reconstructed in the early 19th century by **Carlo Corbellini**.

9 Fabbriche Vecchie di Rialto

Right alongside its newer brother building, this was built in the 16th century, designed by **Antonio Scarpagnino**.

10 Ca' da Mosto

One of the oldest palazzi on the Canal Grande, the façade dates from the 13th century (the top floors were added later). The second-floor balcony is one of the finest examples of Byzantine architecture in Venice (narrow arches supported by thin columns, round medallions with stone bas-reliefs).

11 Palazzo dei Camerlenghi

Right at the foot of the Ponte di Rialto, this elegant 16th-century Renaissance palazzo by **Guglielmo Bergamasco** houses government offices.

12 Fondaco dei Tedeschi (Germans' Warehouse)

In its heyday, the Republic of Venice had close commercial ties with Northern Europe. German merchants would buy goods imported from the East by Venetian merchants and would then store them here before shipping them to their homeland. The palazzo was rebuilt in the Renaissance style after a fire in 1508; the façade was originally covered with frescoes by Titian and Giorgione. Today the palazzo houses the Venice post office.

13 Ponte di Rialto (Rialto Bridge)

In the 16th century, the Republic decided to replace the old drawbridge (the only one over the Canal Grande) with a permanent stone structure designed by **Antonio da Ponte**. The arcades on top were necessary in order to strengthen the structure. Heavy buildings were added on both sides of the bridge to keep the foundations in place.

14 Palazzo Dolfin Manin

The ground-floor portico of this imposing 16th-century Renaissance palazzo by **Jacopo Sansovino** is a pedestrian walkway. Today the palazzo houses offices of the Banca d'Italia.

15 Palazzo Bembo

A delightful Gothic façade was added late in the 15th century, changing the original Byzantine look of this old palazzo. As is the case with many similar buildings, the top floor of the structure was added much later.

16 Palazzo Papadopoli

This 16th-century palazzo by **Gian Giacomo dei Grigi** used to belong to the Tiepolo family and contained four paintings by Veronese that are now in a museum in Dresden. It was acquired by the Counts Papadopoli, but now belongs to the Italian Department of Education.

17 Palazzo Loredan

To many a lover of Venice, this 13th-century palazzo and the one next door (the 12th-century **Ca' Farsetti**) epitomize the beauty of the Canal Grande as it appeared before the Renaissance moved in with heavier, more imposing façades. The rows of narrow arches supported by thin columns (a Byzantine feature) created a rare impression of lightness and grace, now partly impaired because of the top floors, which were added later. Today the two buildings house municipal offices.

18 Palazzo Grimani

Begun in 1556 and designed by **Michele Sanmicheli**, this imposing Renaissance structure was built for one of the leading Venetian families. It is now occupied by the offices of the *Corte d'Appello* (Court of Appeals).

19 Palazzo Corner-Spinelli

A masterwork of the Venetian Renaissance, this palazzo was built in 1490 by **Mauro Codussi**, who also designed the **Palazzo Vendramin Calergi** (see page 178).

20 Palazzo Pisani-Moretta

A fine example of Venetian Gothic, this privately owned 15th-century palazzo is currently used for meetings, conferences, and *Carnevale* balls.

21 Palazzo Garzoni

This 15th-century palazzo now belongs to the **University of Venice** and is used by its department of foreign languages.

22 Palazzi Mocenigo

The powerful Mocenigo family had these twin palazzi built in the 16th century. The controversial monk Giordano Bruno lived here in 1592, and Lord Byron in 1818. Two more palazzi, one on each side, completed the properties of the Mocenigo in this stretch of the Canal Grande. All four palazzi are privately owned residences.

23 Palazzo Balbi

Dating from the late Renaissance, this 16th-century palazzo belongs to the state and is currently used as the office of the president of the Veneto Regional Authority.

24 Ca' Foscari

This palace, one of the most sumptuous 15th-century Gothic buildings on the Canal Grande, has a great view because of its location at the canal's curve. It belongs to the **University of Venice**.

25 Palazzo Moro-Lin

Built by **Sebastiano Mazzoni**, this 17th-century structure is also known as the "palazzo with 13 windows." The top floor is a later addition.

26 Palazzo Grassi

This building, designed by **Giorgio Massari**, one of the foremost artists of early 18th-century Venice, was completed only after the architect's death. In the 1980s it was acquired and restored by the Fiat Corporation to be used as a cultural center. It houses expensively mounted art and historical exhibitions and is visited by thousands each day—the highest number of visitors to any building in Venice except for the **Palazzo Ducale**.

27 Ca' Rezzonico

The wealth of the Rezzonico family is evident in this sumptuous 17th-century building, designed by **Baldassare Longhena** and completed by **Giorgio Massari** (top floor). It now houses the **Museo del Settecento Veneziano** (Museum of the Venetian 17th Century).

28 Palazzo Franchetti

This originally Gothic building was heavily, and not very accurately, restored in the 19th century. The palazzo now houses the **Venetian Institute of Science, Letters and Arts**.

29 Ponte dell'Accademia (Accademia Bridge)

As it is now, this wooden bridge is a "temporary" structure, built about 1930 to replace a previous iron bridge too reminiscent of the industrial architecture of the 19th century for the tastes of the time. The temporary structure was restored in the 1980s, and most Venetians are convinced that it will remain here for at least a few generations.

30 Palazzo Corner della Ca' Grande

The tallest building on the Canal Grande, erected in 1537, this palazzo was also one of the first buildings in Venice to express the grandiose ideas of **Jacopo Sansovino**, who soon became the official architect of the Venetian Republic.

31 Palazzo Barbarigo

The structure dates from the early Renaissance; the striking mosaics on the façade were added in the 19th century.

32 Palazzo Gritti

The somber 15th-century Gothic façade was slightly modified in the 19th century. It is one of the great luxury hotels of Venice, offering terrace dining right on the canal.

33 Palazzo Contarini-Fasan

Also known as "Desdemona's palazzo," as in Shakespeare's *Othello*, this small, beautiful building is noted for its carved stone balcony. Built in the 15th century in Gothic style, it was restored in the late 1980s and is now a private residence.

34 Ca' Giustinian

The Giustinian family, one of the oldest and wealthiest in Venice, lived in this 15th-century

Gothic mansion (*ca'* in old Venetian dialect), the first to appear on the Canal Grande outside of the San Marco area (the next, now **Hotel Monaco**, was built in the 19th century). The palazzo belongs to the city of Venice and houses the offices of the *Biennale*, including the headquarters of the Venice Film Festival.

35 Palazzo Venier dei Leoni

The Venier family intended to compete with the **Palazzo Corner della Ca'Grande** across the canal but was never able to go beyond the ground floor. Peggy Guggenheim found the unfinished 18th-century building fascinating and bought it as a residence for herself. At her death it became a museum of modern art, home to the *Collezione Peggy Guggenheim*.

36 Palazzo Dario

A delightful example of early Venetian Renaissance architecture by **Pietro Lombardo**, this dangerously slanted palazzo built in 1487 was acquired in the 1980s by the late Raoul Gardini, an Italian industrialist, as his Venice residence. Gardini was popular in Venice because of his sailboat, *The Moor of Venice*, which competed in the America's Cup in 1992. In 1994, Gardini was implicated in an unprecedented nationwide scandal involving bribes and kickbacks, and he committed suicide while in jail.

Palazzo Dario

ELIZABETH McCLEARY

37 Abbazia di San Gregorio

This former abbey, of which only a Gothic portal has survived, is now a luxury condominium.

38 Santa Maria della Salute (La Salute)

This church is the 17th-century masterwork of **Baldassare Longhena**, the great Baroque architect who redesigned the whole complex at the entrance of the Canal Grande. The statue at the very top represents the *Virgin Mary* dressed as a Venetian admiral. Merchant ships used to stop here for customs upon arrival from all over the Mediterranean and the North Atlantic.

39 Punta della Dogana (Customs Point)

In the 15th century, this was the customs center for all Venetian ships. The long, low building was rebuilt in the 17th century and finished in the 19th. At the very tip of the tower is a large sphere representing the world, supported by two bronze giants; the statue over the sphere represents *Fortune*.

By the mid-13th century nearly 3,000 Jews lived and/or worked in Venice. Since many resided on the island of Spinalunga, its name was subsequently changed to Giudecca.

For 1,000 years, the people of the Venetian Republic spoke *Venessian*—the local form of Latin, which, over the years, collected a bit of Greek and a smattering of German. Venetians don't like their language to be called a dialect; they say it is a proper language. Many words are completely different: *Pistor* (baker) is *fornaio* in Italian; *carega* (a seat) is *sedia* in Italian. Venessian is still spoken to some extent by many people across the Veneto.

SAN MARCO

The most-visited *sestiere* (district) of Venice is San Marco. It centers around **Piazza San Marco**, the only square the Venetians deign to call a piazza (the others are called *campi*). Napoleon supposedly called the piazza "the best drawing room in Europe." Just as in the heyday of the *Serenissima Repubblica* (the Most Serene Republic, as Venice was called), Piazza San Marco today is a drawing room for people of every nationality. Some stroll, others sit, but all gaze spellbound at the sights surrounding the basilica of **San Marco**, about which Henry James wrote, "If Venice, as I say, has become a great bazaar, this exquisite edifice is now the biggest booth." Farther into the district, San Marco becomes a bustling, mazelike marketplace. Here you will find tacky tourist fodder cheek

by jowl with beautiful handcrafted traditional items. The tangle of tiny crisscrossing streets is lined with houses mainly dating from the 14th and 15th centuries. The streets between San Marco and the Rialto have names like **Merceria dell'Orologio** (Clock Market), **Merceria San Zulian**, and **Merceria San Salvador**; and on the other side, toward the **Accademia**, is the shopaholic's paradise that is the long alleyway called **Frezzeria**. Look out for lots of good clothes shops, dozens of shops dealing in figured and handmade paper, mask workshops, lacework, and antiques, alongside the many many boutiques selling tiny glass gondolas in unlikely colors. But there's more to see in San Marco than that exquisite edifice: the campanile, the **Palazzo Ducale**, the **Museo Correr**; and the **Florian** and **Quadri** *caffès*. You may be tempted never to leave the piazza itself, caught up in the comings and goings of the bedazzled crowds that flock here as if they were mimicking the legion of pigeons.

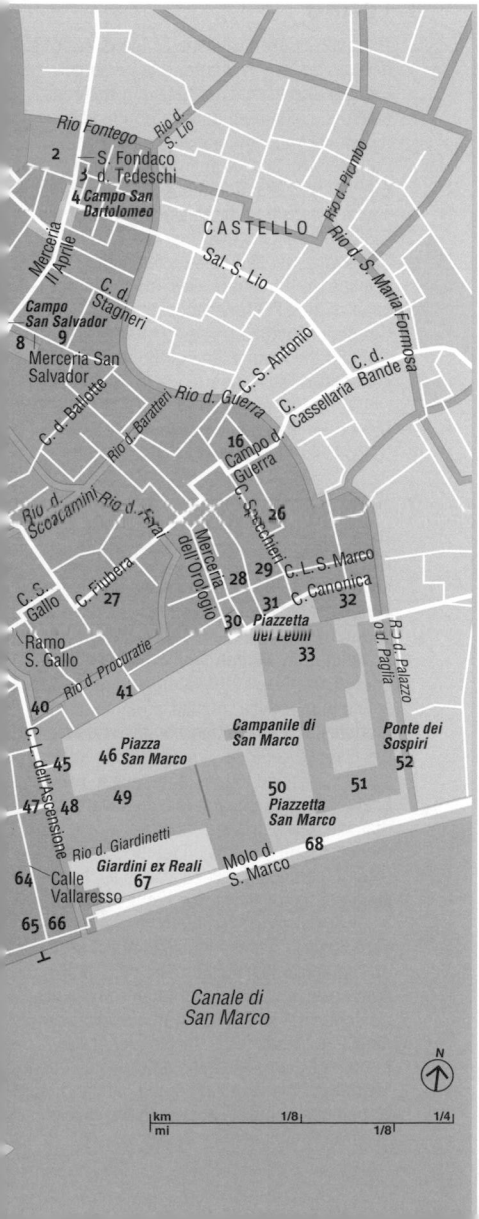

1 Hotel Rialto

$$$ Half of this aptly named hotel's rooms look out on the world-famous bridge (the view is particularly good from the two rooms with small wrought-iron balconies). The location is ultraconvenient, and double-paned windows and air conditioning keep the street noise to a minimum. The décor is a mixture of modern and 18th-century Venice; beamed ceilings give some of the rooms a cozy feel. The restaurant next door is affiliated with the hotel. ♦ Riva del Ferro 5149 (between Calle Larga Mazzini and Salizzada Pio X). 5209166; fax 5238958. *Vaporetto* stop: Rialto

2 Fondaco dei Tedeschi (Germans' Warehouse)

Venice's central post office is headquartered in this Renaissance building designed by **Scarpagnino** in 1505. In the heyday of the Republic it housed the offices and storerooms of German merchants, hence its name. The façade on the Canal Grande was originally frescoed by Renaissance artists, including Titian and Giorgione (some very faded remnants of the frescoes are visible at the **Franchetti Gallery** in the **Ca' d'Oro**). ♦ Daily. Salizzada Fondaco dei Tedeschi 5554 (between Calle Fondaco dei Tedeschi and Rio Fontego). *Vaporetto* stop: Rialto

3 Bácaro Jazz

★★$$ A good mix of a Venetian bar and restaurant with a glass-topped counter offering all the usual *cicchetti* and little plates of fishy deliciousness. The restaurant serves a solid menu of standard Italian fare with jazz and a cocktail bar. The décor (all black-and-white graphics and New Yorkish vibe) is as cool as the (unfortunately taped) jazz that plays until three in the morning. Somewhere "real" just an olive stone's throw from the Rialto Bridge. And if that thought doesn't cheer you, the Bácaro has a happy hour from 4PM till 7PM. Cocktails are good, the wine is fine, and they have a decent selection of beers. ♦ Closed Wednesday, 4PM-3AM. Salizzada Fondaco dei Tedeschi 5546. 5285249. www.bacarojazz.com *Vaporetto* stop: Rialto

4 Campo San Bartolomeo

One of the busiest centers of Venetian life, this *campo* is enlivened by a graceful 19th-century statue of playwright Carlo Goldoni. ♦ At Merceria Il Aprile, Salizzada Pio X, and Salizzada Fondaco dei Tedeschi. *Vaporetto* stop: Rialto

On Campo San Bartolomeo:

Rosticceria San Bartolomeo

★★$ This is the best place in Venice for prepared foods, either to be taken out or eaten at the counter (more formal dining is upstairs). Composed salads, pasta, risotto, roast chicken, *baccalà* (salt cod), and grilled fish keep coming from the kitchen and are quickly consumed by the many customers. The range of small, delicious deep-fried things like crabmeat, cheesy rice, and (believe it or not) creamy custard is not to be missed. The quality is good, much higher even than in some more expensive restaurants. ♦ Tu-Su, 9:30AM-9:30PM; M, 3:30PM-9:30PM. Calle Bissa 5424 (off Campo San Bartolomeo through the Sottoportico de la Bissa). 5223569. *Vaporetto* stop: Rialto

5 Pelliceria Caberlotto

Conspicuous consumption at its most classy, this opulent little shop sells only top-quality furs, leathers, and genuine Kashmiri cashmere. They have been creating and selling classic fashions in leather and fur for 50 years and have become rather good at it. As a tourist, you can buy your beautifully handmade jacket or cashmere throw tax free and have it sent home. *La dolce vita* lives on! ♦ M-Sa, 10AM-noon and 3:30PM-7:30PM. Calle Larga Mazzini 5114. 5229242; fax 2770595. *Vaporetto* stop: Rialto

6 Riva del Carbon

This is one of the few stretches of the Canal Grande flanked by a street and allowing pedestrian passage. The name comes from its use as a pier for unloading coal. The presence of **City Hall**, the Bank of Italy, and other offices guarantees that the street will be crowded with Venetians, particularly in the morning (most state and city employees work 8AM-2PM). Some of the oldest and most charming palazzi in Venice are located here and can be closely inspected from the pier. At **No. 4792** is **Palazzo Bembo**, a Gothic building with remnants of an original Byzantine structure (the frieze on the lower floor); at **No. 4172** is **Palazzo Dandolo**, an early-Gothic building with a stone inscription in memory of Doge Enrico Dandolo, who headed the Fourth Crusade in 1204; and at **Nos. 4137** and **4136** are the two palazzi **Loredan** and **Farsetti** (**City Hall** offices), which have the original Byzantine ground and first floors (the top floors are later additions). ♦ Between Rio di San Salvador and Calle Cavalli. *Vaporetto* stop: Rialto

7 Scuola di San Teodoro (School of St. Theodore)

A Baroque façade by **Giuseppe Sardi** decorates this early-17th-century building, now used for temporary exhibitions. ♦ Campo San Salvador and Calle dell'Ovo. *Vaporetto* stop: Rialto

8 Longo

The quiet-spoken Giuliana Longo is Venice's hat and accessory wizard. She personally designs and makes her hats in a workroom upstairs, using both antique and modern materials. You can choose feathers, pearls, ribbons, and lace or go for straw, fabric, or felt. Everything is made to measure and unique. If you are visiting at the beginning of the year, Giuliana concocts the most fabulous hats for *Carnevale*. Her shop also offers Venice's finest selection of Panamas. Giuliana is the vice chair of the El Felze Association (see Gondola, Gondola, Gondola, page 221) and is responsible for the resurrection of the traditional gondolier's winter hat, made in woolly fabric with a wobbly pompom. ♦ 9:30AM-7:30PM. Closed Sunday. Calle dell'Ovo 4813. 5226454. *Vaporetto* stop: Rialto

9 San Salvador

The façade of this church, designed by **Giuseppe Sardi** in 1663 and cleaned and restored in 1991, is a fine example of Venetian-Baroque architecture. The interior, begun by **Giorgio Spavento** in 1506 and completed by **Jacopo Sansovino**, is of great interest because of the attempt to divide the space into perfectly regular 15-foot-square modules. The space between the entrance and the first two columns is made of four such squares, aligned to form a rectangle. Two identical rectangles, separated by a square, form the side naves. In the central nave, four modules form squares under the domes. Multiples of the square's sides also regulate the length of the columns. The result is a perfectly geometrical space—a bit too abstract when compared with the emotional impact of Gothic or Romanesque churches. The third altar in the right nave contains one of Titian's last works, an *Annunciation* painted with a revolutionary, almost impressionistic, technique. At the bottom of the painting the artist wrote *"Titianus fecit fecit,"* the repetition of the phrase "he did it" perhaps being his answer to the criticism he expected. ♦ Campo San Salvador (between Calle dell'Ovo and Merceria San Salvador). *Vaporetto* stop: Rialto

10 Teatro Goldoni

Named after the great Venetian playwright of the 18th century, this is the same theater where Carlo Goldoni enjoyed some of his successes before moving on to Paris. It was entirely rebuilt in the 1970s, and little of the original structure remains. It remains the best place in town for classic Italian and Venetian-dialect comedy and drama and avant-garde performances. ♦ Calle del Teatro 4650B (between Calle Bembo and Calle del Forno). 5205422; tickets 5207583. *Vaporetto* stop: Rialto

11 Museo Fortuny

If you have a vast amount of cash to put to good use, you could do no worse than rescuing this lovely old palazzo museum. Mariano Fortuny was an outrageously talented artist from Catalonia in Spain who settled in Venice in the early 1900s. This was his palazzo. He was a painter, etcher, sculptor, photographer, designer, and inventor (Fortuny invented the world's first dimmer switch!). In Venice he entered the world of fashion—creating the still famous Delphos Gown, thought to be one of the most flattering designs ever, and beloved by stars of the day such as Isadora Duncan. Following this he entered the world of textile manufacturing, creating his world-famous fabrics. Mariano believed that any artist should maintain total control of the realization of his art—down to the very last detail. And so he designed and made his own brushes, paints, and dyes. He developed (pardon the pun!) his own photographic paper, bound his own books, and designed his own lamps and furniture. When he opened his factory on the Giudecca (which is still creating those fabulous fabrics today), he designed both the factory and the machines that printed the fabrics. The name Fortuny now immediately conjures up an image of rich, jewel-like colors (many unique to Fortuny, the exact mix of the dyes known only to a chosen few), figured silks and velvets, and those fabulous Fortuny pleated silks. They are all here in this beautiful old palazzo, along with an absolutely amazing collection of paintings and photographs by this egregiously gifted man, who died here in 1949. The palazzo itself is set back in a beautiful little gem of a courtyard, and stepping into it is like stepping through a time portal. It even smells historical—if that doesn't sound too fanciful. And now for the bad news. Although the factory on the Giudecca is still functioning and its showroom and gardens are open to the public, the museum is closed, except for the occasional special exhibition. The gently sad curator explained that the palazzo is in need of restoration and they cannot afford to heat it sufficiently to keep it open to the public. The head office of Fortuny is now in New York (979 3rd Ave, Suite 1632, NY, NY 10022. 212/753.7153). *Vaporetto* stop: Sant'Angelo. www.fortuny.com

12 Enoteca al Volto

★★★$ The low, dark ceiling of this marvelous hole-in-the-wall *enoteca* is covered with the labels of bottles long since drunk. Luckily for you, there are plenty more where they came from. This place does everything from a simple local table wine to wash down a homemade *polpette* (meat ball) to top-of-the-line bottles for spending time (and, admittedly, money) on. The bar snacks are excellent, from red cherry chiles stuffed with tuna and capers to slices of steaming hot musetta sausage with a dab of mustard. The *sarde in saor* (sardines in a tangy onion marinade) are as good as you'll find in Venice. And this is a great place to take a little walk on the culinary wild side with *nervetti* (calves' cartilage stewed with onion and served with oil and vinegar) or tiny slivers of *milza* (spleen). Pasta and risotto dishes are good, and everything is always fresh. Your genial host is ever helpful should you need a guide through wine-list or snack selection. The place is never short of a fascinating local character or two propped up at the bar. ♦ M-Sa. Calle Cavalli 4081. 5228945. *Vaporetto* stop: Rialto

13 Fantoni Libri Arte

Originally an outlet of the Electa publishing company (a major Italian art book publisher), this is the best bookstore in Venice for art publications in all languages. ♦ M-Sa Mar-Oct; M afternoon, Tu-Sa Nov-Feb. Salizzada San Luca 4119 (at Calle Loredan). 5220700. *Vaporetto* stop: Rialto

14 Campo San Luca

Strategically located between the Ponte di Rialto and **Piazza San Marco**, this is one of the busiest squares in Venice. During the day it is a traditional meeting place for those who crowd the **Bar Torino** (known for the quality and variety of its *tramezzini*—small sandwiches eaten while standing at the counter) and the **Caffè Rosa Salva**, one of the best pastry shops in town. Before and after dinner, the *campo* is crowded with young men and women—mostly college students—who meet here to gossip and plan their evenings. Tragically, the *campo* has been horribly scarred by the advent of Burger King. Even if you stand with your back to the sight, it seems you are still assailed by the smell. Please don't let Venice sink any further—don't go there! ♦ At Calle San Luca and Salizzada San Luca, and Calle dei Fuseri and Calle del Forno. *Vaporetto* stop: Rialto

15 Bistrot de Venise

★★★$$$ Ignore the French name, this place is all Venetian! From the moment you step through the door you are made to feel not just welcome, but an important guest. The maître d' is arguably the most charming man in the Veneto. At the tiny bar, if you are lucky, you will meet Paolo, the newest generation of the family who own the place. Paolo is charming, tall, dark, and handsome, and he really knows his wines. Ask for the Spritz al Bitters. Paolo makes a spritz with more care and expertise than anyone in the city. It is his personal favorite, and you will taste why. The menu here is unique in Venice. It offers, alongside more modern dishes, recipes from the 14th and 15th centuries. How many restaurants do you know with a "historic and culinary consultant"? So, alongside their imaginative modern dishes—such as venison loin with juniper, apple salad, and crispy cinnamon waffle—you will find the 15th-century ravioli of pumpkin with mixed wild meat in a sweet-and-sour spiced sauce, or sturgeon in a black grape sauce with yellow garlic and almond pudding. Lunches here are a great bargain, and the menus are tempting. A marinated salmon salad with *puntarelle* (young chicory) is fresh and light, the pastas are always imaginative, and the desserts are fabulous. The wine list has been named one of Italy's Top 30 Wine Lists, and many of its interesting offerings are available by the glass. The Bistrot also hosts art exhibitions (just look around you), wine tastings, poetry readings, and musical evenings. Pick up their brochure on your way out. I think you'll like this place. ♦ M, W-Sa, 9AM-1AM. Calle dei Fabbri 4685 (between Rio dei Scoacamini and Calle dell'Ovo). 5236651. www.bistrotdevenise.com. *Vaporetto* stop: Rialto or San Marco

15 Antico Locanda Al Gambero

$$ Sitting right above the Bistrot de Venise and alongside a little canal, this hotel couldn't be more central. It has 31 recently renovated rooms in traditional Venetian style, all with private bath, air conditioning, minibar, safe, direct-line telephones, and hair dryer. A breakfast room on the first floor offers a continental breakfast, which is included. ♦ Calle dei Fabbri 4687. 5200431. www.locandaalgambero.com

Doges, the "presidents" of the Venetian Republic, were elected for life. From AD 697, when Paolo Lucio Annafesto was the first elected Doge, to 1797, when Ludovico Manin handed the Republic over to Napoleon, 120 men (with only 67 different names) held this potent position in unbroken succession.

15 Palace Bonvecchiati

$$$ This impressive hotel, right in the very heart of San Marco, has a huge lobby with amazing sand-colored marble floors, comfortable deep-red leather upholstered chairs, and an original Botero reclining nude to greet you en route to check-in! And should you feel in need of a cocktail, a chic little bar is available. There are 80 modern, generously sized and beautifully appointed rooms (including suites) that have LCD color TV and Internet access along with everything else you might expect. Bathrooms are seriously elegant in black and white, equipped with a set of scales so you can monitor all the weight you lose walking around Venice. The hotel has a gymnasium, solarium, sauna, and steam room. Your excellent buffet breakfast is included. ♦ Calle dei Fabbri 4680. 2963111. www.palacebonvecchiati.it

16 Albergo San Zulian

$$ This newly renovated little hotel, just a moment from San Marco, is a real find. It's been nicely made over with decent-sized rooms done in Venetian style. All have private shower, minibar, air conditioning, direct-dial telephone, and TV. A continental breakfast is included. The décor downstairs is modern and the staff is charming. San Zulian has to be one of Venice's few great bargains! ♦ Campo della Guerra 534/535. 5225872. www.hotelsanzulian.it

Within the Hotel San Zulian:

Cavatappi

★★$$ Hotel San Zulian's wine bar and restaurant, Cavatappi, has swiftly become a destination location. It is tiny, but the minimalist décor makes the most of the space with a well-lit bar on one side and dark wood chairs and comfortable banquettes along the other. The food is terrific. There is a wonderful selection of seasonal cheeses and salamis. Yes, in the land of Monterey Jack no cheese is seasonal, but this is Italy, and everything edible has its day. Frequently behind the bar you will find a huge roast of pork (*porchetta*) offered on a little roll or as a *piatino*—a small plate with mustard and some bread. Delicious! You could opt for one of their delightful selections of *tramezzini* (little sandwiches, filled to bursting). Main meals are imaginative and enticing, with ten freshly made-to-order composed salads to choose from. Or perhaps risotto with artichoke and mascarpone tempts you? Or *spaghettini con pomodoro fresco e calamaretti* (thin spaghetti with fresh tomatoes and baby squid)? Main courses such as swordfish on a bed of roasted potato, eggplant, and tomato come with a suggested glass of wine. Cavatappi's wine list is one of the most admired in the city, with at least twenty wines to choose from by the glass. The service is warm and friendly. Small wonder this new kid on the block has fast become a favorite with Venetians and visitors. ♦ Campo della Guerra 525. M-Sa, 9AM-midnight; Su, AM. 2960252

17 Palazzo Grassi

The Palazzo was built between 1748 and 1772 for the wealthy Bolognese Grassi family and designed by **Giorgio Massari**, who also designed **Ca' Rezzonico**, located just over the canal. It was one of the last palaces built in Venice before the fall of the Republic in 1797. Designed in the classical style, it is built around a large colonnaded courtyard (now glassed in to make a huge atrium) with one of those staircases that make you feel like Scarlett O'Hara, decorated with frescoes by Michelangelo Morlaitor and Francesco Zanchi.

The Grassi family sold the Palazzo in 1840, after which it was owned by an opera singer, a painter, and several industrialists, including Giovanni Stucky and Vittorio Cini. From 1949 onward it housed a center for costume arts. In 1978, a group of businessmen took over the Palazzo and turned it into an art exhibition space. It was purchased by FIAT in 1983 and remodeled by Milanese architect **Gae Aulenti**, in collaboration with Venetian architect **Antonio Foscari**. They introduced some essential modernizations and put their own unmistakable stamp on the interior. In 2005 the Palazzo, now a hugely impressive art gallery which at one time was second only to the Palazzo Ducale in terms of the number of visitors it attracted, changed its look again. This time **Tadao Ando** was the architect. Ando had three tenets: serving the effective presentation of an exhibition by creating a neutral ambience, respect for the Palazzo's architecture, and, in a great display of lack of ego, keeping his alterations reversible. In the rooms specifically intended to house the exhibitions, freestanding white partitions mask the walls without touching them and leaving the passageways and their marble surrounds open to view. The lighting, specially created for Palazzo Grassi, is also self-contained. Hollow metal beams house the safety equipment and lighting appliances.

To mark the reopening of Palazzo Grassi, several works were commissioned for the opening exhibition. "Where Are We Going?" includes a playful installation by the young Swiss artist Urs Fischer in the Palazzo's grand staircase and a new commission for the Canal Grande façade by Danish artist Olafur Eliasson. Known for spectacular installations evoking natural phenomena, Eliasson has designed a luminous "skin" to be stretched over the neoclassical façade. Made from an experimental self-illuminating material, the textile of interwoven cords will be suspended from the Palazzo's roof to the edge of the waters below, radiating a turquoise glow beginning each day at dusk. The Palazzo has a very well-stocked bookshop, open museum hours, and a marvelous café run by Irina Freguia from **Il Vecio Fritolin** (a wonderful restaurant included in your Access Guide). Even if you don't like art, the lunches are worth the trip! ♦ Daily, 10AM-7PM (tickets on sale until 6PM). Café: 10AM-7PM. Campo San Samuele 3231. 523 16 80. www.palazzograssi.it. Advance ticket booking: M-F, 8AM-8PM. 899.666.805. *Vaporetto* stops: San Samuele, San Angelo

18 Piscina San Samuele

A little corner too often missed. Here you will find a collection of shops and galleries selling an interesting cross-section of really beautiful things. At No. 3135 there is **L'Angelo Narciso** (5203963, closed Su and M AM) selling angels—from little cherubs through candle-holding, carved, and stucco angels to big, fat golden angels. A little farther along at No. 3146 is **Venice Design**, a modern gallery where something genuinely eye-catching is always on display. If you suddenly smell something lovely wafting on the breeze, it comes from No. 3149, where a branch of Florence's famous **Officina Profumo Farmaceutica di Santa Maria Novella** has opened. Fabulous perfumes and colognes, creams for every body part, scent for the home, and even ancient remedies for a sore stomach are here. Down at No. 3157(a) is the gallery and shop of the internationally renowned **Livio De Marchi** (M-F, 5285694), whose wonderful wooden carvings are exhibited all over the world. He originated the idea of carving hanging coats and jackets or socks on a washing line in wood. He has even carved a car, which he "drives" up and down the Grand Canal. Surreally beautiful work. At the end of the street at No. 3216 is the gallery of **Marina Barovier** (5226216, M-Sa). This is modern Venetian glass as serious art. The pieces are frequently huge and always stunning. On the other side of the Piscina, **Forme D'Arte** (Tu-Su) is a newish gallery showcasing sculpture, ceramics, and painting. The choice of these modern artworks is intelligent, and you can always have an enjoyable time looking and wishing!

Almost next door, at No. 3337, is **Buengo Fine Arts**, a glass specialist with its own glass furnace. These pieces are gloriously extravagant. Even the tables where the glass is displayed are works of art.

19 Calle delle Botteghe

If you want lovely things, this is one of the best places to take your credit card. Unlike the touristy shops so common in this area, it's full of things you are going to want. The street's name means "alleyway of workshops," and in a way it still is. Some have no name outside . . . but all seem to have something beautiful and fascinating inside. ♦ *Vaporetto* stop: San Samuele

On Calle delle Botteghe:

Gallery Holly Snapp

Venice has many galleries, but the ever-growing collection owned and run by the blondely chic and gamine artistic powerhouse that is Holly Snapp are among the most intelligent and user-friendly. From the original space, Ms. Snapp has now expanded into two others, all along this marvelous little alleyway. Here you might find the powerfully colored portraits of Venice that have become the forte of Geoffrey Humphries, an English painter who has become in the decades he has lived here as much a Venetian treasure as San Marco itself. He is also renowned for his nude studies, and Holly is his shop window to the world. The gallery has many other artists behind its beautifully lit glass and has recently shown some wonderful contemporary sculpture. Whatever is on display, you can rely on Holly Snapp's quality control. She herself says she likes to offer people the kind of works they would find "only in Venice." And Mario Testino buys here . . . so she must be doing something right. Holly and her staff of charming young ladies are helpful, gorgeous, and generally bilingual. You will come out of her gallery feeling not so much like a client as a friend. Check her out at the Biennale, where she is renowned for showcasing the hottest young British artists and organizes performance pieces that are always the talk of the festival. ♦ Tu-Sa, 11AM-1PM and 3:30PM-7:30PM. Calle delle Botteghe 2970/3128/3133. 4592526, 4864015, 4592627. www.gallery-hollysnapp.com. *Vaporetto* stop: San Samuele

Atelier Nube

There's no need to worry about not finding this place; the stunning burst of vibrant colors in the window will stop you—as it does everybody—in your tracks. Pigments are what this man sells: artists' colors as powdered pigment, in pots and in tubes. He sells the brushes too. There is a beautiful selection of modern quill pens and brilliantly colored inks, along with sealing waxes and stamps. Your letter writing will never be the same again. All this beauty shares a space with a section selling household goods and minor ironmongery . . . the artistic alongside the practical. Very Venetian! ♦ M-Sa. Calle delle Botteghe 3457. 5236818. *Vaporetto* stop: San Samuele

Kleine Galleria

This lovely, tiny shop displays and sells antique items from Venice, such as porcelain sets, oil paintings, and books. ♦ Closed Sunday and Monday morning. Calle delle Botteghe 2972. 335388370. *Vaporetto* stops: San Samuele, Sant'Angelo

Artigianato Veneziano

This little workshop has a beautiful collection of snuffboxes in the window and an old gentleman restoring picture frames and objets d'art inside. There are chandeliers and little collections of silverware . . . beautiful things being brought back to life. ♦ M-Sa, 9AM-12:30PM and 3PM-7:30PM. Calle delle Botteghe 2974. *Vaporetto* stop: San Samuele, Sant'Angelo

Antiquus

This shop is one to warm your credit card if antique jewels and silverware are your thing. Nothing here could be described as minimalist, but if the idea of, say, a necklace of old black pearls set in gold to look like acorns, or five strands of seed pearls linked with gold into a bracelet, or indeed drop earrings of the Venetian emblem of the winged lion takes your fancy, this is the shop for you. There is another branch farther along the alley at No. 3131. ♦ Tu-Su, 10:30AM-1PM and 4PM-7PM; M, 4PM-7PM. Calle delle Botteghe 2973. 5206395(3131), 5210106(2973). *Vaporetto* stop: San Samuele, Sant'Angelo

Galleria Marina Barovier

Another window you can't just pass by. Glass is the thing here—huge, beautiful sculptures and artworks in glass. The Muranese skills are safe in the 21st century in the hands of people like the artists here. The main part of this gallery is around the corner and is absolutely worth a visit. ♦ M-F (Saturday by appointment only). Calle delle Botteghe 3126 (and at Salizzada San Samuele 3216). 5236748/5226102. www.barovier.it. *Vaporetto* stop: San Samuele, Sant'Angelo

Al Bacareto

★★★$$ This marvelous restaurant manages the terrifying juggling trick of being both genuine and tourist-friendly at the same time. Most important, the food is excellent, including arguably the best *bigoli in salsa* (traditional fat spaghetti with a delicious anchovy sauce) in Venice. There are excellent local dishes, good grills and fish dishes, and *amoretto*—the house dessert that is one of the most more-ish things you will eat in Italy. Pray that the wonderful Elsa is still in charge of service—she is an Italian treasure. The house wines are excellent, and you will leave feeling like a friend. How much better does it get? ♦ M-F, lunch and dinner; Sa, lunch. Calle delle Botteghe 3447 (at Piscina San Samuele). 5289336. *Vaporetto* stops: San Samuele, Sant'Angelo

G (Gaggio)

Venice's millennium of trade with faraway Cathay introduced luxurious silks and fabrics to Europe, eventually spawning a fabric industry here that took its influence from the Far East. Precious textiles can still be found in limited quantities today; this store is one of the best places to find rich printed velvets. The workmanship is impeccable, so you'll pay handsomely for these high-quality silk and silk/cotton velvets, all hand-stamped and beautifully hand-finished. Home-décor articles for sale here include decorative pillows and bolsters of all sizes and colors, whose designs complement sumptuous throws and romantic bedding in gemlike tones. The store also carries a collection of women's clothing and accessories including shawls, scarves, vests, and jackets appropriate for both day and evening wear. ♦ M-Sa. Calle delle Botteghe 3451-41 (between Campo Santo Stefano and Calle Crosera). 5228574. *Vaporetto* stops: San Samuele, Sant'Angelo

Fiore

★★★$$ This is a truly wonderful little place to eat, drink, and feel a little Venetian for a moment. The window of this tiny bar opens onto the alleyway all day, and you can sit with a glass of local red wine or a *spritz* (Venice's traditional refreshing, but ultimately intoxicating, aperitif) and one of the delicious *cicchetti* (Italian tapas) that are on offer. The specialty here is fish, and the kitchen turns out absolutely the best *sarde in saor* (fresh sardines in a sweet-and-sour dressing with onion) in Venice. Ask for *gamberetti* in season and get a heap of deep-fried, light-as-a-feather baby shrimp. The company is generally fun and everyone hugely helpful to those who speak no Italian. Next door—and sharing the same kitchen—is the **Trattoria da Fiore**. There they offer the same delicious antipasti, but then you can go on to perhaps a pasta with *scampi e castaure* (prawns with artichoke hearts) or a *frittura mista de molecche* (soft-shell crabs). ♦ M, W-Su. Bar, 9AM-11PM; trattoria, noon-3PM and 7PM-10PM. Calle delle Botteghe 3461 (at Campo Santo Stefano). 5235310. *Vaporetto* stop: San Samuele

20 Rigattieri

You don't need a guidebook to tell you this family-run shop is worth a visit. The place is a trove of modern treasures—beautiful glass, ceramics, and pewter, but most of all silver. Each piece is handmade by Italian artists and silversmiths. It is the most gorgeous and extravagant gift shop you can imagine. If you don't have much to spend, you can still find something to delight a friend (or yourself!). If your credit card is healthy, then buy your family an heirloom of the future! Sadly, the huge silver squid that held a crystal hors d'oeuvre dish in its figured tentacles has gone to Australia, but there is always something else. Your purchases can be sent anywhere in the world. ♦ M-Sa, 9:30AM-1PM and 3PM-7:30PM (Dec-Mar, also closed M AM). Calle dei Frati 3532. 5231081.

21 Libreria Linea d'Aqua

This great little bookshop, recently taken over and modernized, stocks lots of books on Italy and Venice, guides, phrasebooks, and lots of English-language novels, including those of Donna Leon—perfect for getting you into the mood for walking around Venice. ♦ Daily, except Monday morning. Calle dei Frati 3717d. 5224030. www.librerialineadaqua.it. *Vaporetto* stops: Maria del Giglio, Sant'Angelo

22 Campo Sant'Angelo (or Sant'Anzolo)

This wide square is characterized, like few others in Venice, by an elevated floor in the center that was built in order to enlarge an underground cistern that collected rainwater for domestic use. The wells at the center (with original wellheads from the 15th century) once reached the cistern's bottom, where the water gathered after being filtered by layers of sand and pebbles; they are no longer used. Composer Domenico Cimarosa died at the Gothic **Palazzo Duodo** at **No. 3585**. ♦ *Vaporetto* stops: Santa Maria del Giglio, San Samuele, Sant'Angelo

23 Ottica, Danilo Carraro

Eyeglass designer/optometrist Dr. Danilo Carraro is one of Venice's more unconventional artisans. The two dozen classic-to-hip models in his limited-edition collection come in a wide range of serious-to-fun colors, from 14 variations of faux tortoise to 35 bold shades of celluloid. They are all guaranteed for life and are offered at surprisingly reasonable prices. The latest ranges include the Rubber Collection—less kinky and more practical and tactile than it sounds!

Carraro can fill any prescription or have any model made up as nonprescription sunglasses, and claims to do it in one hour. Spectacles are sold tax free to tourists and include designs by Gucci, Armani, Calvin Klein, and Swarovski. This place makes you ache for myopia. ♦ M-Sa. Calle della Mandola 3706 (between Calle della Verona and Rio Terrà degli Assassini). 5204258. www.otticacarraro.it. *Vaporetto* stops: Santa Maria del Giglio, Sant'Angelo

23 Trattoria da Arturo

★★★★$$$ Not just a meal, but an experience. And the wonderful Ernesto, *il padrone* of this tiniest of restaurants, nicknamed "the railway carriage," has 33 years' experience. This must be on your list of places to eat in Venice, especially if you love meat. Ernesto's *melanzane in saor* (eggplant in a tangy onion marinade) is famous, and his delicious little composed salads are a legend in many people's lunchtimes. Your bread comes warm and delicious. Pasta chef Alessio prepares his artichoke and radicchio perfectly and properly *al dente*. His roasted potatoes with rosemary are arguably the finest in modern cuisine, but the main reason for coming here is the meat. Scallopine of veal comes with a delicate, silky mustard sauce or simply served with lemon. Fillet of beef is prepared *al pepe verde* (with green peppercorn sauce) or *al stroganoff*. I like the *braciola alla Veneziana*, a seldom-seen ancient Venetian specialty: a pork steak roughly the size of New Jersey is briefly dipped into vinegar, breaded, then fried. If your taste buds love tang, this is the dish for you. And try the *tiramisù*. You'll never taste it like this again. Portions are generous. Ernesto has no patience with the kind of food that merely decorates plates. "If I buy a pair of shoes," he said, pouring me a large grappa, "I would be very unhappy if I only got one!" The wine list befits such a temple to good taste. By the way, Ernesto doesn't take credit cards. ♦ M-Sa, lunch and dinner. Calle degli Assassini 3656. 5286974

24 Pensieri

Dolls. This is what the tiny shop Pensieri sells. Lovely soft dolls. Not rag dolls exactly, but the heads and hands of these chubby, friendly dollies are stitched in fabric. The shop also sells the softest teddy bears a child ever cuddled. Very sweet. ♦ M-Sa, 9:30AM-7PM; Su, 11AM-7PM. Calle della Mandola 3716(a)

25 Scala del Bovolo

This staircase is often seen in paintings and photographs of Venice because of its unusual and elegant snail shape. Its 121 stairs were added to the courtyard of **Palazzo Contarini** at the end of the 15th century in order to permit access to the top floors of the palazzo without the necessity of going through the interior stairs. ♦ Open Sa and Su only. Calle delle Locande 4299 (between Calle dei Fuser and Rio di San Luca). *Vaporetto* stop: Sant'Angelo

26 Hotel Montecarlo

$$$ Small enough to offer guests personalized service, this family-run hotel has 48 contemporary rooms done up in flowered prints with tiled bathrooms, and a restaurant, **Antico Pignolo**. While most hostelries claim to be a stone's throw from the **Piazza San Marco**, this one actually is conveniently close by, on a popular store-lined street. ♦ Calle Specchieri 463 (between Calle Larga San Marco and Campo Guerra). 5207144; fax 5207789. www.venicehotelmontecarlo.com. *Vaporetto* stops: Rialto, San Marco, San Zaccaria

27 Valese

For generations, the Valese family of *bronzisti* (bronze craftspeople) have provided gondolas with their *ferri* (seahorse fittings) and virtually every patrician palazzo in Venice with their massive door knockers. Visitors are more than welcome at the Cannaregio foundry of Gianni and Mario Valese (720234), but shoppers should come directly to this shop presided over by their English-speaking sister Loredana. Many of the store's offerings—drawer pulls, knobs, handles, doorstops, bookends, sconces, and ceiling fixtures sold here in bronze, copper, brass, pewter, and wrought iron—are perfect historical replicas. The Valese family is accustomed to shipping worldwide—they've even sent goods to the White House. ♦ M-Sa. Calle Fiubera 793 (between Rio delle Procuratie and Calle dei Fabbri). 5227282. *Vaporetto* stops: Rialto, San Marco, San Zaccaria

28 Albergo ai Do Mori

$$ This 11-room hotel (1 guest room shares bath) takes its name from the two bronze Moors who strike the massive bell in the nearby clock tower in Piazza San Marco. A recent renovation added air conditioning, double-paned windows, and brand-new bathrooms. The lack of an elevator (guest rooms start on the second floor) might be a problem for some, but if the climb doesn't bother you, be sure to ask for a room on the top (fourth floor) with a postcard view of the campanile or the romantic *mansarda* with a private terrace. You won't find luxury here, but location and price make this place a sure bet. There's no restaurant. ♦ Calle Larga San Marco 758 (at Calle Spadaria). 5204817, 5289293; fax 5205328. e-mail: reception@hotelaidomori.com. www.hotelaidomori.com. *Vaporetto* stops: San Marco, San Zaccaria

29 Elite

Business attire and sportswear are both offered here at one of the most exclusive men's clothing stores in town. ♦ Daily, 10AM-7:30PM. Calle Larga San Marco 284 (between Calle Specchieri and Calle Spadaria). 5230145. *Vaporetto* stops: Rialto, San Marco, San Zaccaria

30 Torre dell'Orologio

The Clock Tower was designed by **Mauro Condussi**—one of the fathers of the Venetian Renaissance—and built between 1496 and 1499. Its gilded and blue enamel dial shows not just the time, but the moon phases, the rotation of the sun through the astrological signs, information on tides, and other navigational information. It was regarded as the greatest scientific achievement of all time. And so, fairly typically of the Venetians at that time, the clockmaker Paulo Ranieri, whose genius had created the workings, and his son Carlo, who assisted him, were rewarded by the Grand Council of Venice by having their eyes burnt out so they couldn't ever replicate the masterpiece. As the clock chimed the hour, statues of three kings and an angel would appear and bow before the Virgin and Child while on the superior terrace, alongside statues of the San Marco Lion, two bronze *Mori* (moors) were animated by a mechanism that strikes a bell with a hammer. Over the centuries, changes and improvements were made to the mechanism. In 1858 the pendulum was replaced and two large paneled wheels were added that rotated and displayed the hours and minutes, a little like the display on a digital watch. In 1952 the mechanism was overhauled and the pendulum again corrected. In 1996 the current refurbishment began, funded by Piaget. Blacksmith Alberto Gorla and orological historian Giuseppe Brusa were entrusted with the work. The renovation has been fraught with controversy. Should clocks be your thing, there is a fascinating insight into it all on www.orologeria.com. In February 1999 the clock was reassembled in the Palazzo Ducale and shown to the press. There it remains, awaiting the completion of structural work being done on the walls of the tower itself. For the time being, as you enter Piazza San Marco, what you see is a vast trompe l'oeil canvas of London's Big Ben covering the tower. Predictably, there is nothing remotely like a completion date being bandied around! ♦ Merceria dell'Orologio 147 (at Piazza San Marco). *Vaporetto* stops: San Marco, San Zaccaria

Torre dell'Orologio

31 Venini

When it was founded in 1921, the Venini glass factory immediately distinguished itself with its innovations in the ancient Venetian glassmaking tradition. The firm introduced new types of glass, and contemporary artists produced new shapes. In the 1980s, Venini vases made in the 1950s fetched as much as a half million dollars at auction. ♦ M-Sa, 10AM-7:30PM. Piazzetta dei Leoni 314 (at Calle San Basso). 5224045. *Vaporetto* stops: San Marco, San Zaccaria

32 Libreria Studium

This is a good place to buy maps, postcards, and English-language paperback novels and books on Venice. Works by local expatriate authors and artists not usually found in other shops are in abundance here. ♦ M-Sa, 9AM-7:30PM (no midday closing). Calle Canonica 337 (between Rio di Palazzo o della Paglia and Piazzetta dei Leoni). 5222382. *Vaporetto* stops: San Marco, San Zaccaria

33 San Marco

Originally begun in the ninth century as the doges' private chapel, this basilica—Mark Twain's "vast warty bug taking a meditative walk"—is a complex conglomeration of medieval, classical, Byzantine, and Romanesque architectural styles (see drawing on page 192). It was built to house the bones of St. Mark, stolen from their Egyptian tomb in Alexandria and smuggled to Venice in a barrel of pickled pork so that Muslim officials would not search its contents. This event, known as the *tranlatio,* is depicted in a 13th-century mosaic on the exterior of the church over the far left arch.

Basilica di San Marco

Also noteworthy on the exterior are Romanesque relief carvings on the three receding arches of the main entrance, as well as the copies of the four 2,000-year-old gilded bronze horses (the originals are in the church museum) carted off by Napoleon and returned to the city in 1815, and the Gothic carvings of religious figures on the roof.

The basilica's interior is a beautifully murky and mysterious space, paved with an intricately patterned undulating mosaic floor and walls and ceilings covered with mosaics dating from the 12th to the 18th centuries. The most important are the 13th-century Old Testament scenes in the vaults, the 13th-century *Ascension* in the central cupola, and the *Christ*, *Madonna*, and *Prophets* on the walls of the nave aisles. Also here is the *Pala d'Oro* (golden altarpiece), made, between the 10th and 12th centuries, of enamels and precious stones; the **Tesoro** (Treasury), containing loot from Constantinople (the 10th-century icon of St. Michael was a real prize); the 15th-century *iconostasis* (choir screen) by the Masegne brothers, located in front of the altar; and the **Cappella dei Mascoli**, to the left of the main altar, where there is a bejeweled 10th-century icon known as the *Madonna Nicopeia*. The highlights of the second-floor **Museo della Basilica** (the entrance is in the portico) are the original four bronze horses, believed to be about 2,000 years old, and the cover for the *Pala d'Oro,* which was painted by Paolo Veneziano in 1345. You may have to wait to enter, as only a certain number of visitors are allowed in the basilica per minute. ♦ Admission: Pala d'Oro, Tesoro, and museum. Daily. Piazza San Marco (between Piazzetta San Marco and Piazzetta dei Leoni). 5225205. *Vaporetto* stops: San Marco, San Zaccaria

In the 12th century, Venice was the only European city that was mandatorily lit at night.

While the rest of medieval and Renaissance Italy and Europe were competing in jousts and tourneys for social recreation, Venice—with no piazzas to accommodate these early sports—held regattas in the Canal Grande and the lagoon. Today, more than 100 of them take place every year, the most important being the Voga Lunga in May and the Regata Storica, held the first Sunday of every September.

34 Santo Stefano

The façade of this 15th-century church is adorned with two rose windows and a handsome Gothic portal. Don't let the peaceful air fool you. This church has been reconsecrated six times to take away the stain of blood left by murderers within its walls! Inside, the carved wooden ceiling has the uniquely Venetian shape of an inverted ship's hull (local master carpenters most likely learned their craft in the shipyards). The church contains many monuments to illustrious Venetians, the most remarkable being *Domenico Contarini* (1650) over the portal, *Antonio Zorzi* (1588) on the left side, and *Giacomo Surian* (1493) on the right side. In the **Sacristy** (enter from the right nave), three large canvases by Jacopo Tintoretto hang on the right wall: *The Last Supper*, *The Agony in the Garden*, and *Christ Washing the Disciples' Feet*. On the same wall is a *Crucifixion* by Paolo Veneziano (1348). ♦ Campiello Santo Stefano (between Campo Santo Stefano and Calle dei Frati). *Vaporetto* stops: Santa Maria del Giglio, San Samuele

35 Daniela Ghezzo

Once the workshop of renowned Venetian master shoemaker Rolando Segalin, this is now home to the work of the young Daniela Ghezzo, who carries on handcrafting beautiful made-to-measure shoes for her well-heeled clientele. Even if you can't buy, the shoes and little boots in soft leather are beautiful to look at. ♦ M-Sa, 9:30AM-12:30PM and 3:30PM-7:30PM. Calle dei Fuseri 4365. 5222115

36 Hotel La Fenice et des Artistes

$$$ Long a favorite with theatergoers and performers, this well-known hotel is located across a *campiello* from the legendary **Teatro La Fenice**. Visitors return year after year—it's one of the few hostelries in this bustling and popular neighborhood—drawn no doubt by the beamed ceilings, Murano chandeliers, red-damask wallpapered guest rooms, and lovely garden. Two separate buildings are connected at the lobby, and the 69 rooms vary widely in size, décor, and ambience; only a few have been renovated. There's no restaurant, but excellent dining is right next door. ♦ Campiello de la Fenice 1936 (between Calle della Fenice and Ramo Feretti) 5232333; fax 5203721. *Vaporetto* stop: Santa Maria del Giglio. www.fenicehotels.it

37 Teatro La Fenice

On 29 January 1996 one of the great disasters of all time hit Venice, when, for the second time in its existence, the beautiful La Fenice Theater was destroyed by fire. Two young electricians were arrested for setting fire to the theater with a blowtorch to avoid paying a fine of 10 million lire for delays in restoration work they were carrying out. Their boss—generally accepted to have planned the whole thing—was imprisoned but escaped and has not been seen since July 2003.

La Fenice originally opened in April 1792, having taken two years to build. It was Venice's greatest theater. In 1836 it burned down, but, true to its name, it rose again. Then, it took Venice 12 months to rebuild the theater. This time it has taken seven years. For the first four, work on the Fenice went nowhere in a tangle of utter incompetence and alleged corruption. In 2000 Paulo Costa, the new mayor of Venice, fired the firm in charge. After that, five builders' yards worked every day from dawn till 10PM with craftsmen working in overlapping shifts.

Almost unbelievably, the main resource for the template for the reconstruction was Visconti's film *Senso*—the only real record of what the Fenice had looked like inside. For this reason, a key member of the reconstruction team was in fact Mauro Carosi, Visconti's scenographer. The architect was **Elisabetta Fabbri**, a Venetian who went on to work on the rebirth of La Scala in Milan. Both agree that the previous mayor's promise to rebuild the Fenice *"com'era, dov'era"* ("as it was, where it was," echoing the promise made to build the campanile in San Marco when it fell) was impossible. The new Fenice is just that—new. The gold glitters; the colors explode. There are no wrinkles or cracks. Nothing is faded or dusty. Think any beautiful Hollywood icon after a really good face-lift! The chief artist was the master mask maker (and another Venetian) Guerrino Lovato. He opened the first mask shop in Venice in 1978, since which time he has been responsible for the sculptures of the Kremlin's cupolas in Moscow, an ancient Venetian ceiling for Givenchy in Paris, a 6-meter Christ for John Paul II in Brescia, and the Venetian hotel in Las Vegas. His was the marathon task of creating in its entirety the extravagant interior of the theater with satyrs and nymphs, cherubs and cupids. Amazingly, much of the sculptural part of the theater had been made of 70% papier-mâché and 30% wood—even the boxes. The result is close to a modern miracle. Purists decry the "newness," but the place is heart-stopping. Opera seasons recommenced in fall 2004 with a sumptuous production of *La Traviata* directed by Lorin Maazel. Guided tours of the opera house take about 50 minutes. Tickets to see any of the shows are difficult to get, so a guided tour is the simplest way to see the inside. Tours can be booked at the ticket office at the Fenice or by phoning Hello Venezia, 0412424. Tours are in English, German, Spanish, and Italian (separately), and times vary according to demand. ♦ Campo San Fantin 1365 (at Calle della Fenice). Reservations, 786580. Information line, 32658010. Free phone from within Italy, 14788211. www.teatrolafenice.it. *Vaporetto* stop: Santa Maria del Giglio

37 Ristorante al Teatro

★★$$ Most of the cozy **Campo San Fantin** is filled in the summer with tables from this old, established restaurant that stays open late. The hours, and the collection of international newspapers with which one can while them away, are more to be recommended than the food. ♦ Tu-Su, lunch and dinner. Campo San Fantin 1916 (at Calle della Fenice). 5221052. *Vaporetto* stop: Santa Maria del Giglio

38 Centrale

★★$$$ If you are looking to go where the beautiful young Venetians go, this is the place. Centrale is a bar and a restaurant with cool music. You will never hear "Volare" at Centrale. This place is so cool you'd better bring a wrap. Offering an upmarket club ambience, terrific cocktails, and maximally chic staff, its house specials are lobster and fresh fish from the lagoon served up as simply or as saucily as you like. Centrale also does a pretty good risotto. Many of the holidays of the Venetian calendar are celebrated here with menus and evening events themed around, for example, *Carnevale*, New Year's, and Valentine's Day. Service is exemplary. Even if you only order a bottle of house white, you'll get the whole cork-sniffing, ice-bucket-rattling, glass-twirling performance. If you want to "chill" as opposed to simply "relax" on a Venice evening, then this is a place for you. ♦ Daily, 6:30PM-2AM. 1659b Piscina Frezzeria. 2960664. www.centrale-lounge.com

39 Frezzeria

The warren of streets around San Marco are the old marketplaces. They are narrow, frequently crowded, a maze of retail opportunities with innumerable identical stores selling glass, masks, and figured paper. Just keep wandering till you find one you like more than the others! I liked the wonderful silver jewelry at **No. 1850**, up where the Frezzeria crosses the Rio dei Barcaroli and becomes the Calle del Frutariol. Opposite at **No 1860**, you'll see gorgeous amber in the window of **Claudia**, who has been selling beautifully crafted jewelry and silks since 1968. Coming back down toward San Marco at **No. 1735** is a mask shop specializing in leather masks. Quite spooky but fascinating. **The Galleria Antiquaria San Marco** at **No. 1725** has breathtakingly monumental pieces in stone, marble, and glass, as well as antique Murano chandeliers. Its other branch, at **No. 1722**, has more modern works, although still on a grand scale. You can't pass **Leon D'Oro** (at **No. 1770**) without gasping. The window is crammed with glittering and golden masks, fabulous puppets, and miniature puppet theaters. It is really a whole *Carnevale* in one shop. And should all this leave you in need of refreshment, you could do a lot worse than the new and very chic **Osteria Enoteca San Marco** at **No. 1610** (5285242, M-Sa). Its impressive wine list is complemented with a good selection of salamis and cheeses at the bar. The main menu is "Venetian with a twist"—tuna comes with sesame, sole with truffle, and scallops with pineapple and balsamic vinegar!

The Venetians invented the income tax, statistical science, censorship, the gambling casino, the ghetto, and easel painting.

Venice is like eating an entire box of chocolate liqueurs at one go.

—Truman Capote

40 Bacino Orseolo

Behind the **Procuratie Vecchie** a canal opens onto this small basin, the main gondola landing for **Piazza San Marco**. Whether you take a ride or not, it is fun just to watch the gondoliers and their customers It's everything you imagined it would be. ♦ At Rio delle Procuratie. *Vaporetto* stop: San Marco

At Bacino Orseolo:

Libreria del Sansovino

Art books, including rare and out-of-print copies, and a wide selection of books on Venice in English are the specialties at this bookstore. It also carries some current English-language best-sellers—the owner refers to them as "jet lag" books—to amuse and bemuse. ♦ Daily, 9AM-7PM. Fondamente Orseolo 84 (just east of Calle Larga dell'Ascensione). 5222623

41 Procuratie Vecchie

With your back to the basilica, the building on the right is the Procuratie Vecchie. This structure, along with the **Procuratie Nuove** directly across the piazza to the left (see page 198), served an important function during the Venetian Republic. The procurators (after whom the edifices were named) were high government officials, and their headquarters next to the **Palazzo Ducale** made **Piazza San Marco** the center of civic life in Venice. The building, attributed to **Mauro Codussi** and erected at the beginning of the 16th century, replaced an earlier Byzantine structure and retains some Byzantine influence in the first-floor arcade. **Jacopo Sansovino**, the official architect of the Republic, created the building's final shape by adding the second floor in 1532. Piazza San Marco (between Merceria dell'Orologio and Ala Napoleonica). *Vaporetto* stops: San Marco, San Zaccaria

At Procuratie Vecchie:

Caffè Lavena

★★$$$ This historical café is forever in the shadow of the world-famous **Caffè Florian** (see page 198) across the piazza. But Richard Wagner preferred this 18th-century *pasticceria* (pastry shop)/bar and used to drink tea or cognac at a regular table (now preserved) on the little upstairs balcony. The Lavena's *barrista* Roberto has been awarded the title *Maestro dell'Espresso*, and his coffee is definitely worth tasting—

The Best

Ennio Montagnaro

Gondolier

Usually considered a tourist attraction, the gondola is still very important for Venetian people on their wedding day, when it carries the bride to the church. The gondola, beautifully decorated and furnished for this occasion, together with the elegant dress of the bride, takes Venice back to the 18th century—and the old Venice is, for me, the real one.

The sophisticated **Caffè Florian**, with its frescoes and old furniture, offers elegant meals to the Venetian upper class and to wealthier tourists. One can spend hours there, delighted by live music.

Ristorante de Romano on the island of **Burano** (famous all over the world thanks to the lace made there) is a typical restaurant where Venetians have parties with family and friends and where everybody can taste excellent dishes of fresh fish.

To eat characteristic Venetian dishes, go to **La Corte Sconta** or **Trattoria da Remigio** (both in the *sestiere* of **Castello**). Try *risi e bisi* (rice and peas), *sarde in saor* (marinated sardines), and *fegato alla Veneziana* (liver with onions and white wine)—you'll never forget them.

If you can afford it, go to the **Hotel Danieli**, the former residence of the Doge Dandolo. Personally, I'd love to spend the night in this hotel.

Venice is romantic, fascinating, and elegant . . . but sometimes it is also fun. Kids and grown-ups love the phenomenon of the *acqua alta* (high water), which is actually a serious problem for the city. In spite of this, nobody can stop laughing when others slip and take a salty bath.

If you're looking for adventure, rent a small motorboat, go visit the islands (**Murano**, Burano, **Torcello**), and have a little swim in the middle of the journey.

especially as part of a delicious *affogato* (ice cream with an espresso coffee tipped over it). There is also one of the most outrageous chandeliers in San Marco (and you have to go some to be that). A dozen or so jet black Moors' heads are impaled around the huge glass confection, with the lights sprouting out of them—gloriously politically incorrect. ♦ Daily, 9AM-midnight. Closed Tuesday in winter. Piazza San Marco 133. 5224070

Missiaglia

Since 1864 the Missiaglia family has been supplying wealthy Venetians and visitors with the best in jewels and gold. Definitely one of the most reliable goldsmiths in town (most items are crafted in their own workshop), this jeweler excels in sober, classic objects, but keeps an accurate eye on the newest trends in design. ♦Tu-Sa, 9:30AM-12:30PM and 3:30PM-7:30PM. Piazza San Marco 125. 5224464

Caffè Quadri

★★$$$ This establishment boasts a rather historic "first": It was this very café that allegedly introduced Venetians (and therefore Europeans and North and South Americans) to Turkish coffee in 1725. Stendhal, Dumas, Byron, and Proust all got their caffeine fixes here in their time. The upstairs restaurant, with a setting befitting a doge (and prices to match), is the only restaurant with windows directly on the square. The food is excellent, but the formal ambience is most appealing to serious diners or expense-account *Biennale* celebs. ♦ Daily, 9AM-midnight. Closed Mondays, Dec-Feb. Piazza San Marco 120. 5222105

42 Antico Martini

★★$$$$ Among the great historical experiences in Venice is a trip down here to the Antico Martini. It will take you back to the 1960s. This basement is all old-fashioned nightclub. And the clientele are a fascinating mix—mainly Venetian, *signori* generally older, *signorine* generally younger. The food is textbook, traditional luxury at luxury prices. The wine list is heavyweight, the cocktails are classic, and the prices are high. But the place has a lovely, gentle air about it. It stays open late—the kitchen until midnight, with live music and dancing till the small hours for those of us who have "graduated" from the aching cool of places like Centrale. ♦ M, Th-Su, lunch and dinner; W, dinner. Campo San Fantin 1983 (at Calle delle Veste). 5237027, 5224121. *Vaporetto* stop: Santa Maria del Giglio

42 Vino Vino

★★$$ Originally a wine bar with snacks, this place quickly became a preferred restaurant for light, informal meals (one or two pastas daily and a changing choice of vegetables and simple entrées) in a casual atmosphere. Choose from a selection of wines by the glass or bottle. ♦ M, W-Su, lunch, dinner, and late-night meals. Calle delle Veste 2007A (between Rio de Fenice and Campo San Fantin). 5224121. *Vaporetto* stop: Santa Maria del Giglio

43 Antiquità M

This antiques store has its own workshop for the production of precious velvets hand-printed in the style of the world-renowned Mariano Fortuny, the Venice-based artist who was all the rage during the 1920s and 1930s. Both the antiques and the velvets are of the highest quality. ♦ Daily, 9:30AM-1PM, 3:30PM-7:30PM. Closed M AM. Frezzeria 1691 (at Calle Bognolo). 5235666. *Vaporetto* stop: San Marco

44 Bacaro

★★$$$ Very new, very chic, and very much one of the places to be, this bar and restaurant is wholly glass fronted, and the bar shares the ground floor of the building with the excellent travel section of the Mondadori bookshop. The bar has an impressive selection of premium spirits, including an intelligent collection of bourbons. There is a good cocktail list along with a list of beers, and they do a hot trade in cold Prosecco. The equally chic upstairs restaurant features a "new" Italian menu. There is *zimino di cozze e vongole verace* (mussels and clams in a broth) and *carpaccio de tonno fresco e valeriana con olio profumato al timo* (a carpaccio of fresh tuna served with a salad of valerian leaves dressed with thyme-scented oil). Pastas come with shellfish or with cuttlefish cooked in its own ink (very Venetian), and main courses include a *gran fritto di pesce* (mixed fried seafood) and sole cooked in Prosecco. This is one of the very few places in Venice where you can eat late. ♦ Daily. 9AM-2AM (restaurant till 1:30AM). Salizzada di San Moisè 1345. *Vaporetto* stop: Vallaresso

45 10 Ala Napoleonica

In 1797, young Napoleon Bonaparte brought about the end of the Republic of Venice after its millennium of glory with a simple letter in which he asked Doge Ludovico Manin to resign and open the way for a new, democratic constitution. Pressed by Napoleon's armies at the Republic's borders, the doge and his men decided to oblige. It was an inglorious end, the only justification for which was that a war would most certainly have ended in defeat for Venice. During their occupation, the French undertook important public works, among them the restructuring on the side of the piazza opposite the basilica.

This west flank of **Piazza San Marco**, designed by Italian architect **Giuseppe Maria Soli** in 1814, includes a grand staircase and the so-called royal apartments, with a ballroom that is today part of the **Museo Correr**. ♦ Piazza San Marco (between Procuratie Nuove and Procuratie Vecchie). *Vaporetto* stops: San Marco, San Zaccaria

Within Ala Napoleonica:

Museo Correr

This museum comprises three sections: the **Collezioni Storiche** (Historical Collections), consisting of 22 rooms on the second floor at the top of the grand staircase, with material related to the history of Venice; the **Museo del Risorgimento e dell'Ottocento Veneziano** (Museum of 18th-Century Venice) on the third floor; and the **Quadreria** (Collection of Paintings), also on the third floor. The Collezioni Storiche include works by neoclassical sculptor Antonio Canova in the **Galleria** (**Room 1**); neoclassical frescoes (**Rooms 4-5**); documents and images related to the doges (**Rooms 6-7**), with some fascinating bound *commissioni* (instructions sent by the doges to Venetian ambassadors and other high officers); a library (**Room 8**); clothes and portraits of patricians (**Rooms 9-10**); Venetian coins from the 12th century (**Room 11**); models of galleys, paintings, and material related to the history of the **Arsenale** and to Venetian navigation techniques (**Rooms 12-13**); maps of Venice, including the original wood dies of Jacopo de' Barbari's famous *Map of Venice in 1500,* an extremely detailed drawing and a valuable resource for reconstructing the shapes of buildings at that time (**Room 14**); weapons (**Room 15**); the *Morosini Armory* (**Room 16**); and small Renaissance bronze sculptures (**Rooms 19-21**). The Museo del Risorgimento e dell'Ottocento Veneziano covers the history of Venice from 1797 to 1866, focusing on the unsuccessful attempt to gain independence from Austria in 1848-1849. At press time, it was closed for restoration. In the **Quadreria**, a large collection of minor paintings documents the evolution of Venetian art from the 13th to the 16th centuries. Included are works by great masters, such as Antonello da Messina's *La Pietà,* painted in Venice; four paintings by Giovanni Bellini (exhibited next to works by Jacopo, his father, and Gentile, his brother); and two portraits by Vittore Carpaccio, *The Courtesans* (though the women portrayed were most likely members of the Venetian upper class) and the striking

The Venetians use the affectionate nickname *ninzioleto* ("little sheet") when referring to the rectangular white street signs that mark bridges and *calli* (streets).

The Venetians are convinced they invented marzipan, explaining that its Latin root, *pan marci* or *pane di Marco* (Mark's bread), refers to a sweet made in honor of the city and the Republic's ubiquitous patron saint.

Young Man in a Red Beret. ♦ Admission. Daily. Piazza San Marco 52 (entrance at Porta del Frumento). 5224951. www.museicivicveneziani.it

Entered through Museo Correr:

Biblioteca Nazionale Marciana (St. Mark's Library)

Jacopo Sansovino started constructing this Renaissance masterpiece in 1537, but left it to be completed by his pupil **Vincenzo Scamozzi** in 1588. The façade was designed to be a continuation of the **Procuratie Nuove**, thus emphasizing the architectural unity of the whole compound. The Roman-inspired solemnity of the exterior was intended to visually represent the power and wealth of the Venetian Republic. Don't miss the two large caryatids that support the vault flanking the library's monumental door.

The library houses a collection of precious manuscripts and incunabula (early printed books). Some 1,000 codices were left to the Republic by Cardinal Bessarione in 1486 and found a home in the upstairs *Sala della Libreria*. The ceiling of the *Vestibolo* (Vestibule) has a centerpiece—*Sapienza* (Wisdom)—by Titian worth seeing, and the wonderful sweeping entrance stairway is a twin to the **Scala d'Oro** in the Palazzo Ducale across the square. A small room on the ground floor is reserved for scholars to consult ancient books or manuscripts (permission must be granted by the library).
♦ M-Sa. Piazza San Marco 13; entrance for general public at Piazza San Marco 7 (at Piazzetta San Marco). Free guided tours of the library in English are available at two-hour intervals M-F, 10AM-4PM. Entrance to the upper rooms is included in the Museum Pass (see **Palazzo Ducale**, page 199.) 5208788.

Museo Archeologico Nazionale

From the 16th to the 18th centuries, many of Venice's patrician families assembled archeological pieces from Rome, Greece, and the Roman-settled territories bordering on the lagoon (Aquileia, Eraclea, and Altinum). The Grimani family bequeathed its collection to the Republic in the 16th century; other donations followed. The assortment of coins, epigraphs, bas-reliefs, and statues here include many exquisite originals from Greece, particularly from the fifth century BC, and from Rome. Among the most interesting pieces are a statue of *Demeter* and one of *Athena* (**Room 4**); the *Ara Grimani* (Grimani Altar), with magnificent sculptures from the first century BC (**Room 6**); and three statues of Gallic warriors, sculpted in Pergamon around the year 200 BC. On a smaller scale, if you like cameos, then this museum has a great collection. ♦ Admission. Daily. This museum is also covered by the Museum Pass (see **Palazzo Ducale**, page 199). Free guided tours in English M-F, 3PM; Sa, Su, 3PM and 5PM. 5225978

46 Piazza San Marco

This square is surely one of the most beautiful and harmonious architectural spaces in the world. Those qualities can be appreciated even while standing amid the bustling hordes of midsummer tourists, though there are special times when the sight is even more breathtaking—in the mist of the early morning, the silence late at night, the light fog that often sets in during the winter, or even during the *acqua alta* (high water), when wooden planks are needed in order to cross the piazza without getting one's feet wet. But at all times, the square symbolizes and traces the history of Venice, from the ninth century (when the basilica was begun and the original campanile was erected) through the Renaissance (when **Jacopo Sansovino** devised the plan for the piazza) to the neoclassical era (when the addition called the **Ala Napoleonica** was built under Bonaparte). Through it all, the pigeons continue to swoop (and pollute the monuments), merchants continue to ply their wares, Venetians pause for refreshments at **Caffè Florian**, and bedazzled visitors gaze in awe at the wonder that is Venice. ♦ At Piazzetta dei Leoni, Piazzetta San Marco, and Merceria dell'Orologio. *Vaporetto* stops: San Marco, San Zaccaria

In Piazza San Marco:

Campanile di San Marco (St. Mark's Bell Tower)

Since the ninth century there has been a campanile here. The design of the current one, the highest monument in Venice (325 feet), dates back to the early 16th century, when **Bartolomeo Bon** gave it its final shape. Nearly three centuries later, on the morning of 14 July 1902, the structure collapsed into the piazza. Miraculously, no one was injured and none of the other buildings in the piazza were damaged. Many shops around Venice sell what purports to be a photographic record of the event. Unfortunately, no film at the time was fast enough to have captured it, so the image is a picturesque fake. It took 10 years to raise the tower again, in the words of the Venetians, *"com'era, dov'era"* ("as it was, where it was"). The original bricks were used, and the one bell in the tower (the *marangona*) is one that had survived the fall. Today, after continuing restoration work, it is looking fabulous, complete with a shining gold figure of the Archangel Gabriel at the top. The view of Venice from the balcony is absolutely unbeatable. Although, interestingly, the one thing you cannot see in Venice from the top of the campanile is the canals! ♦ Admission. Daily. At Piazzetta San Marco. 5224064

At the base of Campanile di San Marco:

Loggetta di San Marco

Jacopo Sansovino designed this structure, which was built between 1539 and 1549. The terrace and balustrade in front were added later. The four bronze statues in the niches, executed by Sansovino, represent *Minerva*, *Apollo*, *Mercury*, and *Peace* as symbols of good government. Over them is *Venice Clad as Justice*, accompanied by bas-reliefs representing Cyprus and Crete, then part of Venice's empire. Together with the **Procuratie** and the **Biblioteca Marciana**, this structure symbolizes the majesty of the Venetian Republic.

Cenedese

The pieces on display in this small shop are elegant samples of this firm, one of the oldest and most prestigious producers of Murano glass. The offerings range from exquisite objets d'art to affordable objets d'everyday. ♦ Daily, 15 Mar-5 Nov; M-Sa, 6 Nov-14 Mar. Piazza San Marco 40. 5225487

47 Vogini

Just barely outside of **Piazza San Marco** is one of Venice's oldest and most respected leather goods stores. Three elegant shops under the Vogini name carry men's and women's accessories from wallets and bags to attaché cases, luggage, belts, and stylish outerwear. The shops feature other designer collections (including the hard-to-find local house of Roberta di Camerino), but the private, classic Vogini label matches them in quality of craftsmanship and materials. ♦ M-Sa. Calle Secondi dell'Ascensione 1257A-1301 (between Rio dei Giardinetti and Bocca di Piazza). 5222573. *Vaporetto* stop: San Marco

48 Nardi

You may not be able to afford anything here, but take a peek at the displays of one of Venice's oldest premier jewelry stores. The more elaborate pieces studded with precious stones are worth a doge's ransom, particularly the museum-quality antique pieces. ♦ M-Sa. Piazza San Marco 69. 5225733. *Vaporetto* stop: San Marco

48 Pauly & C.

Located right under the open porticoes of the **Museo Correr**, this cluster of shops offers a wide selection of exquisite glass objects, mostly produced in its own Murano furnace. Vases, chandeliers, drinking glasses, and statues come in an incredible variety of shapes. While some pieces would be right at home in a museum, others are less elaborate and relatively more affordable. Glass masters since 1866, this firm has an excellent reputation for reliability when shipping abroad. A salesperson at any of the three small shops in the piazza will direct you to their principal location at the end of Calle Larga San Marco, which is open by appointment only. ♦ Daily. Piazza San Marco 72-77. 5209899

49 Procuratie Nuove

Notice that this façade is heavier and more imposing than its older counterpart on the other side of the square (the **Procuratie Vecchie**—see page 194). Construction of these administrative headquarters was started by **Vincenzo Scamozzi** in the late 16th and early 17th centuries. It was completed 100 years later by the Venetian-Baroque architect **Baldassare Longhena**. Napoleon designated this building his Royal Palace and had it connected to the Procuratie Vecchie with the **Ala Napoleonica**. ♦ Piazza San Marco (between Piazzetta San Marco and Ala Napoleonica). *Vaporetto* stops: San Marco, San Zaccaria

At Procuratie Nuove:

Caffè Florian

★★$$$ This most famous of the Venetian cafés was one of the first places in Europe to serve that new and exotic drink—coffee. Today it is still patronized by upper-class Venetians, particularly for afternoon tea inside in the winter, where the original 18th-century décor has been preserved. In the summer, a small orchestra plays popular tunes for guests sitting at the outdoor tables, sipping expensive coffee and cappuccino. Those concerned with budgets can take refuge at the counter inside, where they can sip a Bellini cocktail or glass of Prosecco wine, away from the strains of *"O sole mio"* and *"Volare."* ♦ M-Tu, Th-Sa 9AM-midnight. Piazza San Marco 56-59. 5285338

Biblioteca Correr (Correr Library)

Next to **Caffè Florian**, a doorway leads to one of the inner courtyards of the Procuratie Nuove, where an elevator takes scholars and students to the pleasant reading rooms of this library. A friendly staff of librarians helps them find their way through the ancient catalogs, many of which are handwritten. The rich collection of documents and manuscripts was bequeathed in 1830 by the patrician Teodoro Correr. A collection specializing in Venetian art history was more recently acquired by the library. ♦ M-Sa, 8:30AM-1:30PM. Piazza San Marco 52. 5225625

50 Piazzetta San Marco

This "little piazza," an extension of the **Piazza San Marco** between the south side of the basilica and the lagoon border, is separated from its larger neighbor by the campanile. The white marble pavement was used by the patricians to pace back and forth while Parliament was deliberating inside the **Palazzo Ducale**. When a young patrician came of age, he was officially admitted into the community of rulers here. ♦ Between Molo di San Marco and Piazza San Marco. *Vaporetto* stops: San Marco, San Zaccaria

On Piazzetta San Marco:

Caffè Chioggia

★$$ If you're looking for a splendid way to end an evening in Venice, relax at one of this café's outdoor tables and enjoy the romantic music in the company of the **Palazzo Ducale** in front and the lagoon at the side. This café is the only one in the piazza with a view of the water. The music is consistently good here (from quartets to a solo pianist) and the waiters have less attitude, even encouraging you to linger. ♦ M-Sa, 8AM-2AM Apr-Nov. Piazzetta San Marco 11 (between Molo di San Marco and Piazza San Marco). 5285011. *Vaporetto* stops: San Marco, San Zaccaria

51 Palazzo Ducale (Doges' Palace)

More than just the residence of the doge, this opulent palace was both a symbol and a seat of power. Behind its pink-and-white confectionery façade were the meeting halls of government and the offices of the dreaded secret police and inquisitors. Construction of the building began in the ninth century, and it was enlarged and modified many times, reaching its present state in the 15th century, when the façade facing the **Piazzetta San Marco** and the monumental door on the basilica side were built. The façade on the lagoon side is the oldest: A column at the southwest corner bears the date 1344 (marking the completion of the ground-floor loggias).

Renovations have been made in recent years to improve traffic flow. You now enter the palazzo through the **Porta del Frumento** [1] on the Canal Grande (numbers refer to floor plan below), and leave by the old entrance at **Porta della Carta** [6]. The first works you'll see are in the **Museo dell'Opera** [2], housing 32 of the original late-Gothic columns and capitals that were taken from the south- and west-side loggia and ground-level portico.

In the courtyard, the façades on the south (lagoon side) and west have 14th-century loggias on the second floor; the ground floors were originally just brick walls. In 1602, city architect **Bartolomeo Monopola** performed the amazing feat of replacing those walls with arches and columns by temporarily supporting the structure during construction.

The two bronze wellheads [3,4] at the center of the courtyard were cast during the 16th century. Patricians entered the building by ascending the monumental **Scala del Giganti**

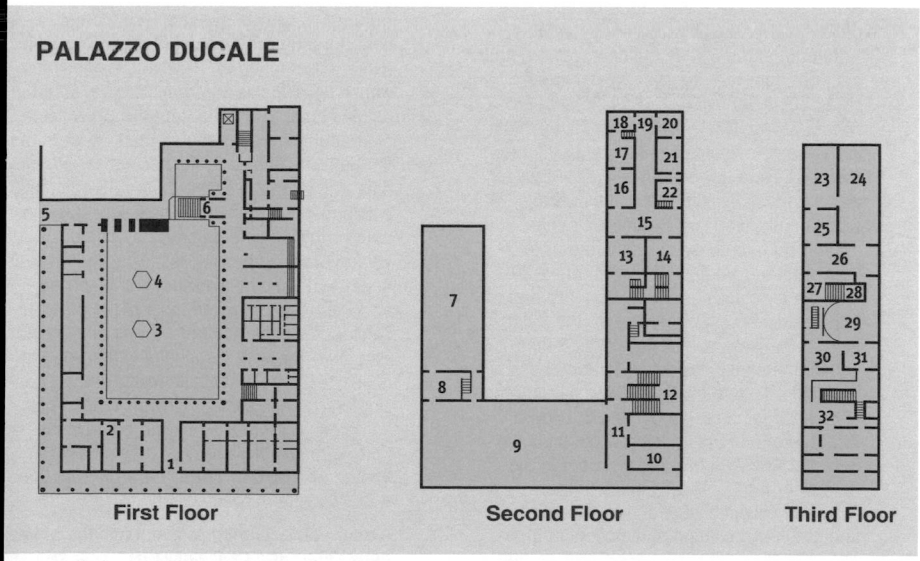

[6] (Giants' Staircase), flanked at the top by statues of *Mars* and *Neptune,* symbols of Venetian power over land and sea.

The interior of the palazzo dates from the 16th century. A fire in 1574 destroyed the original woodwork, ceilings, and walls, as well as important paintings by Carpaccio, Giorgione, and Titian. The imposing staircase, **Scala d'Oro** [12], leads to the **Primo Piano Nobile** (actually the second floor), where the recently reopened doges' apartments [13-22] are located. These rooms are decorated with sculptured fireplaces and paintings by the major artists of the Venetian school. The **Sala Grimani** [16] contains three Venice insignias, among them a famous *St. Mark's Lion* by Vittore Carpaccio. At the **Sala dei Filosofi** [19] is a staircase that leads to the doges' chapel. Notice the fresco of *St. Christopher* by Titian over the door at the stairs.

From the Scala d'Oro [28], continue to the **Secondo Piano Nobile** (third floor). Through the **Atrio Quadrato** (Square Atrium) [27] and the **Sala delle Quattro Porte** (Room of Four Doors) [26] is the small **Sala dell'Anticollegio** [25]. In this room (rebuilt in the 16th century to plans by **Palladio** and **Alessandro Vittoria**), ambassadors and delegations from subject territories would wait to be received by the doges' cabinet. Here, beside the doors, are four paintings by Jacopo Tintoretto. On the wall opposite the window is *Rape of Europa* by Paolo Veronese. The next room is the **Sala del Collegio** [23], where the doges' cabinet would meet to deliberate and to receive its visitors. The ceiling was painted by Paolo Veronese with allegories of virtues and with the famous *Venice Enthroned with Justice and Peace* (center of ceiling, at the far end). The paintings over the entrance are by Jacopo Tintoretto, and those on the right wall are from his workshop. The one over the cabinet's seats, *Doge Sebastiano Venier Offering Thanks for the Victory of Lepanto,* is by Paolo Veronese. The Venice Senate met in the next room, the **Sala del Senato** [24]. The Senate was a body of elected patricians in charge of foreign policy and some domestic affairs. With about 150 members, it was a more agile body than the *Maggior Consiglio,* the 1,200-member legislative assembly that included all male patricians who were of age. The paintings on the walls and ceiling of the Senate's chamber are minor works by Tintoretto and his workshop, Jacopo Palma il Giovane, and other Mannerist painters. Through the Sala delle Quattro Porte [26] and a small atrium is the **Sala del Consiglio dei Dieci** (Room of the Council of Ten) [29]. This much-feared assembly was in charge of the secret police and of the prosecution of members of the patrician class. Like most secret police, those of Venice acquired enormous power, particularly in the last days of the Republic's life.

Three paintings by Paolo Veronese adorn the ceiling in correspondence with the curved woodwork at the back. The central oval is a copy of *Jupiter Striking Vices with Lightning,* also by Veronese (the original is in the Louvre). Past the **Sala della Bussola** [31] is the **Armory** [32]. Up a few steps from the council's assembly room, this salon contains a large collection of weapons, mostly from the 16th and 17th centuries.

The **Sala degli Inquisitori** (Three Inquisitors' Office) [30], off the Sala del Consiglio dei Dieci, can be seen only as part of a guided tour. The Three Inquisitors, selected from among the 10 council members, were the real terror of Venice, particularly in the 18th century. Their trials of real and supposed political criminals were held in secret without the chance of appeal. A small staircase led directly from this room to the torture chamber, while a secret corridor led to the Ponte dei Sospiri (Bridge of Sighs) and the prisons. Inquire at the ticket window for guided tours of these rooms. These tours, called *Itinereri Segreti* (Secret Itineraries), and offered in Italian only, must be booked at least one day in advance.

Return to the **Primo Piano Nobile** and the **Liagò** [11], a veranda with statues of *Adam* and *Eve* by Antonio Rizzo, considered to be among the best works of the early Renaissance in Venice. A door on the left wall goes to the **Sala dell'Armamento** [10], with the large, much-damaged fresco that is all that is left of *Paradise,* painted by Guariento in 1367. After the 1574 fire, a new *Paradise* was commissioned from Tintoretto; it is now in the Sala del Maggior Consiglio. The remnants of Guariento's work were discovered when Tintoretto's canvas was removed for restoration. It was in the Sala del Maggior Consiglio (Great Assembly Hall) [9] that the patricians, whose numbers varied from 1,200 to 2,000, regularly met to run the Republic. They sat in nine double rows parallel to the long walls of the hall. The doge and his cabinet sat on the dais at the entrance wall. Of the 35 paintings encased in gilt frames on the ceiling, the most noteworthy is Paolo Veronese's *Apotheosis of Venice Crowned by Victory* (at the central oval near the dais). The workshops of Veronese and Tintoretto produced most of the other canvases. Behind the dais is Tintoretto's great *Paradise*—the largest painting in the world. It is one of the painter's last works, and his son Domenico and Palma il Giovane helped him complete it. A frieze at the top portrays the first 76 doges of Venice, up to Francesco Venier, who died in 1556. The view from the windows here is spectacular.

A door at the far right goes through the **Sala della Quarantia Civil Nuova** [8]—now the bookstore. The **Sala dello Scrutinio** (Ballot Counting Room) [7], the last great hall of the palace, is richly decorated with paintings by Palma il Giovane, Andrea Vicentino, Aliense, and other Mannerist artists. The room is often used for temporary exhibitions. The *Last Judgment* above the dais is by Palma il Giovane.

Exit at the **Porta della Carta** [5], the palace's original entrance. This is a Venetian-Gothic masterwork by **Giovanni** and Bartolomeo Bon. The figure over the door, on his knees in front of *St. Mark's Lion,* is Doge Francesco Foscari, who led the Republic in the acquisition of new territories on the Italian mainland from 1423 to 1457. Outside, remarkable sculptures adorn the palazzo's corners: Near the bridge on the southeast corner is *Drunkenness of Noah,* and on the southwest corner is *Adam and Eve,* both by unknown artists; on the northwest corner is *The Judgment of Solomon,* attributed to Jacopo della Quercia. Over the columns, the capitals are decorated with animals, warriors, men, women, and representations of vices and virtues and human activities. A high-tech audio guided tour, called Lightman, is available in English and other languages for visitors to the palazzo. The portable infrared system offers detailed information about the artwork in the palace and the history of the Republic. Lightman can be rented at the palazzo entrance and is well worth the additional charge. ♦ Admission. Daily. Molo di San Marco (between Rio di Palazzo o della Paglia and Piazzetta San Marco)

There is now a Museum Pass, which, for very little, will give you entry to Palazzo Ducale, Museo Civico Correr, Museo Archeologico Nazionale and the Sale Monumentali, and the Biblioteca Nazionale Marciana. It is valid for 3 months, so there is no need to feel you have to rush it all at once. 5224951. www.museicivicveneziani.it. *Vaporetto* stops: San Marco, San Zaccaria

52 Ponte dei Sospiri (Bridge of Sighs)

This elegant bridge owes its melancholy name (probably invented by 19th-century travelers) to the fact that it connected the **Palazzo Ducale** with the prisons across the canal. It was built in 1602, and has since figured prominently in countless tales, paintings, and movies. ♦ Rio di Palazzo o della Paglia. *Vaporetto* stop: San Zaccaria

53 Campo Santo Stefano

Though not one of the most elegant *campos* in Venice, this is one of the largest. It marks the crossroads of streets to the **Accademia**, **San Marco**, and the **Rialto** and is ringed with cafés and famous palazzi. On the east side at Nos. 2802/3 is the **Palazzo Morosini**, built in the 17th century for a wealthy local family (you will see the name elsewhere), opposite which at No. 2945 is the Palazzo Loredan, thought to be the last Gothic palazzo built in Venice. ♦ *Vaporetto* stops: Santa Maria del Giglio, Accademia, San Samuele

On Campo Santo Stefano:

Hotel San Stefano

$$ A great location on a popular and sunny square two minutes from the Accademia makes this hotel worth a mention. The 11 rooms are newly and nicely decorated, with whirlpool baths or really decent showers (more worth mentioning than you might imagine). Breakfast is included. ♦ Campo Santo Stefano 2957. 5200166; fax 5224460

Fiorella Gallery

There is nowhere like this in the world. Designer Fiorella Mancini—who claims her inspiration is from Fortuny and *Playboy* in equal measure—fills this corner of Santo Stefano with her outrageous and opulent designs. Her signature velvet smoking jackets hang in rails of rich, deep colors as well as adorning the provocative shop-window dummies. But what makes them unique are the hand-printed patterns—huge rats, crowns, and, now, euro and lire signs. Fiorella's clothes are a statement—and not just a fashion statement. There are amazing three-dimensional corsets and showstopping dresses. This is fashion with intelligence and biting wit. ♦ Daily. Campo Santo Stefano 2806; tel/fax 5209228. www.fiorellagallery.com

Paulin

This landmark café sprinkles its end of the *campo* with tables and chairs. It offers excellent old-fashioned ice cream, teas and tisanes, coffee in every guise imaginable (including the almost sinful *bicerin,* which combines espresso with hot chocolate and tops it with whipped cream), wines, aperitifs, spirits, and a short list of cocktails. There is also a selection of panini, sandwiches, and "toast" (toasted sandwiches). ♦ Daily. Campo Santo Stefano 2962. 5225576. *Vaporetto* stop: San Samuele

Bar All'Angolo

Cheek by jowl with Paulin, this place lacks the ice creams and the heritage but offers better service. The usual *tramezzini* (sandwiches) and bruschetti, panini, and other nibbles—although they are of a generally better and more imaginative standard—are available at the quite modern, brushed steel-topped bar. There is a nice young staff and a more fun atmosphere than at Paulin. This is the place to come for an early-morning pick-me-up. ♦

The Best

P.L. Beggiato

Owner, Metropole Hotel

Trattoria Alla Madonna—If you survive the noise, the lights, and the impossible paintings, you will experience what is probably the best fish in Venice (relative to the low prices).

Fiaschetteria Toscana—Nothing to do with Tuscany, but a lot to do with high quality, seriously inventive cuisine, and attentive waiters (I've been there dozens of times and was disappointed only once).

Harry's Bar (what a bore!)—Go there at 7:30PM just for a drink (the best in town), experience the miraculous transformation of a bar into a restaurant that takes place every day, and, if you have the money and a lack of imagination, stay on for dinner (the standards are monotonously high) and the best pastry in Italy.

Daily, 6:30AM-10PM. 3464/a Campiello Santo Stefano (at Calle della Botteghe). *Vaporetto* stop: San Samuele

Cavalier

Also known as the Bottega de L'Indorador. Alberto Cavalier has mostly taken over from his father in this gilding, lacquering, and restoration business. He works squares of real gold leaf over plain wood and makes it altogether something else. As well as restoring, he makes original objects and he will take commissions. In good weather, there are always a couple of his *moretto* doorstops outside, so you can't miss the tiny shop—wooden figures, in lacquer and gold, representing young Moorish boys of the kind who were popular as servants in the Republic. Should you find the door closed, try the bar next door! ♦ M-Sa, 10AM-7PM. Campo Santo Stefano 2863(a). 5238621. *Vaporetto* stops: Santa Maria del Giglio, San Samuele, Accademia

54 Contini Galleria d'Arte

If you are moved at all by 20th-century art, then this is a terrific gallery to visit—light, white, and intelligently laid out. Some of the pieces inhabit a little open garden area, and the huge torso by Polish artist Igor Mitoraj certainly looks impressive there. The gallery was begun by Stefano Contini, Tuscan by origin, and there are now three Contini galleries in the Veneto. There are permanent exhibits—works by major-league artists such as Chagall, Magritte, Picasso, and Graham Sutherland—as well as temporary exhibitions by some of the world's top "artists of the moment," such as the brilliant Mitoraj, Paulo Borghi, Sandro Chia, and Botero Funando. ♦ Daily, 10AM-1PM and 3:30PM-7:30PM. Calle del Spezier 2765 (at Ponte San Maurizio). 5204942. www.continiarte.com. *Vaporetto* stop: Santa Maria del Giglio

55 San Maurizio

The neoclassical façade of this church was one of the last construction projects undertaken by the Venetian Republic before its fall in 1797. It was designed by **Pietro Zaguri**, a patrician and intellectual who lived in the **Palazzo Zaguri** (see below) on the same *campo*. The interior is a fine example of neoclassical architecture, designed by **Giannantonio Selva**, who was also responsible for the **Teatro La Fenice**. ♦ Campo San Maurizio (at Calle del Spezier). *Vaporetto* stop: Santa Maria del Giglio

55 Alfredo Laggia

A treasure trove of glamorous, sparkling jewels, this shop sells cuffs and collars, earrings and necklets, rings and bracelets. Each piece—be it a jeweled mask or a hugely ornate collar—is unique. All are exuberantly dramatic designs, many in rich colors, and are not to be worn by the shy wallflower. But if you would like to make a glittering impact, these designs are for you! ♦ M-Sa, 10AM-1PM and 3:30PM-7:30PM. Closed January. Calle Zaguri 2627. 5286092. *Vaporetto* stop: Santa Maria del Giglio

56 Antichità V. Trois

In business since 1911, this tiny store specializes in home-furnishing fabrics and objects from 18th-century Venice, including lamps, ceramics, and paintings. Most important, it is also the exclusive agent for the precious textiles produced by the Mariano Fortuny workshop, still operating on Giudecca with the original machinery invented by Fortuny. ♦ M-Sa Mar-Oct; M afternoon, Tu-Sa Nov-Feb. Campo San Maurizio 2666 (at Calle Zaguri). 5222905. *Vaporetto* stop: Santa Maria del Giglio

57 Palazzo Zaguri

While most Venetian palazzi have only one façade, the supremely elegant 15th-century palazzo of the Zaguri family has two, one on **Campo San Maurizio** and another along the canal in back. Pietro Zaguri, the last of his clan to live here, was an intellectual, a freethinker, and a close friend of Giacomo Casanova, who was often a guest here, as was Mozart's librettist Lorenzo da Ponte, who for a time worked as Zaguri's private secretary. When Zaguri was on his deathbed, his brother, a stern Catholic bishop, had to

Child's Play

Have the kids seen one too many Michelangelos? Though the art and architecture of the Renaissance can be aesthetically pleasing and culturally enriching, some of the following activities—with a focus on fun—might well be your children's (and perhaps your) most vivid recollection of travel in Italy.

In Florence

Enjoy a picnic in the farthermost reaches of the **Boboli Gardens**, behind the **Palazzo Pitti**, then stroll the gardens, stopping along the way to pose like the statues. (Keep an eye out for the more grotesque ones!) From the eastern confines of the gardens, you can reach **Forte di Belvedere** by foot, another perfect grassy venue-with-a-view.

Pick up everyone's spirits at any of the city's well-known *gelaterie* (ice-cream parlors), perhaps the world-famous **Vivoli**. There are dozens of flavors to pick from (coconut! melon! black cherry!), and a large cup can accommodate a half-dozen creamy wonders.

Rub the nose of the *Porcellino* in **Mercato Nuovo**.

Roam the **Mercato di San Lorenzo**, an open-air market just north of the **Duomo**, in search of everything from souvenir "Firenze" T-shirts and Italian soccer banners to leather jackets and silk scarves.

In Tuscany

Visit the **Parco di Pinocchio** in **Collodi**, just outside of **Lucca**, hometown of the Tuscan-born author of the world's most beloved wooden puppet.

In Venice

Cruise the small back canals of Venice on a meandering gondola. Or try a far less expensive *vaporetto* ride down the **Canal Grande**: The *No. 1* will transport you past hundreds of proud palazzi and under the Rialto Bridge. As a compromise, take a short *traghetto* ride across the canal—gondola experience but not gondola prices.

Take a trip to **Murano**'s glass-blowing *fornaci* (furnaces), where you'll learn about Venice's thousand-year history as an unrivaled leader in the glass industry, and see firsthand the local masters perfecting this delicate art.

Climb the steep steps inside the **San Marco** basilica up to the **Museo**, where you'll get a close-up view of the famous *quadriga* (four horses) kept here, protected from the elements. Elsewhere in the square, watch the Mori striking the hour in the Torro l'Orologio.

Build sand castles on the **Lido**.

Both the **Parco Savorgnan** (part of the Palazzo Savorgnan: Fondamenta Venier in Cannaregio. *Vaporetto* Guglie) and the **Giardini Pubblici** (*Vaporetto* Giardini) have swing parks.

In the Veneto

Pretend you're a knight on the human-size chessboard at **Marostica**, slaying opponent bishops and pawns as you advance to scale the castle and steal the queen.

make a deal with the family creditors in order to keep the palazzo until his death. Today it is occupied by a public grade school. ♦ Campo San Maurizio 2668 (at Calle Zaguri). *Vaporetto* stop: Santa Maria del Giglio

58 Antica Legatoria Piazzesi

Originally a bookbinding business, this store branched out decades ago into marbled paper and other fancy paper objects. There are now many such shops in Venice, but this one remains among the most professional and elegant. Notebooks, address and appointment books, desktop items, and a large selection of wrapping paper with old Venetian prints make great gifts and souvenirs. A sign in the window tells you this is the oldest paper shop in Italy and has the largest selection of hand-stamped paper. So it's official! ♦ M-Sa Mar-Oct; M afternoon, Tu-Sa Nov-Feb. Campiello della Feltrina 2511C (between Rio di Santa Maria del Giglio and Rio di San Maurizio). 5221202. *Vaporetto* stop: Santa Maria del Giglio

58 Margerie

Margherita Pasotto is a charming young Venetian designer who wanted to open a "non-Venetian" boutique for her designs. And she has done just that. She designs wonderful, contemporary jewelry—necklaces and earrings, bracelets and pendants—and also sells gorgeous, fun handbags in bright fabrics with lighthearted appliqué, truly unforgettable shoes, and great hats. Each of the items is handmade by a local craftsman to Margherita's design. She has recently started working with a glass artist, so who knows what might happen next! Another of the new generation of artists and other creative types who are keeping the real Venice alive. ♦ Daily, 9:30PM-5:30PM. Campiello della Feltrina 2511/B. 5236393. *Vaporetto* stop: Santa Maria del Giglio

59 Santa Maria del Giglio

This fine example of a Venetian-Baroque church, completed in 1683 by **Giuseppe**

Sardi, carries to an extreme the Venetian habit of immortalizing on the façade the patrician families who financed the construction. Here the Barbaros are represented by four statues in the deep niches, while Antonio Barbaro, the dynasty's patriarch, looms over the portal between the statues of *Honor* and *Virtue*. The bas-reliefs on the lower façade represent the maps of cities under Venetian domination. Inside, the organ's doors were painted by Jacopo Tintoretto with figures of the four evangelists. ♦ Campo Santa Maria del Giglio and Calle del Piovan). *Vaporetto* stop: Santa Maria del Giglio

60 Il Prato

This shop sells hand-printed paper, notebooks, albums, and frames in 14th- and 15th-century patterns as well as some more contemporary. The rich colors used in the patterns are mixed by Il Prato themselves. The window is filled with gorgeous papier-mâché figurines, and behind the counter are dozens of intricate little mini-theaters and puppet shows. There are lovely Murano glass pens and a whole section of albums, diaries, and organizers bound in hand-tooled and stamped leather. There is also a branch at Calle de la Mandola 3633 and one on Las Vegas Blvd South (no. 3355). ♦ M-Sa, 9:30AM-7:30PM; Su, 11:30AM-6PM. Calle delle Ostreghe 2436. Tel/fax 5224847. *Vaporetto* stop: Santa Maria del Giglio

61 Calle Larga XXII Marzo

Sort of the Fifth Avenue of Venice, this street continues where the Calle delle Ostreghe ends. Here you will find all the big names—if that is what you are looking for in Venice. **Laura Biagiotti** offers her ladies' fashions at No. 2401, and **Bruno Magli** does it for the smart-suited boys directly opposite. **Bulgari** is at No. 2282 with a huge store of their trademark watches and jewelry. **Gucci** takes up a block from Nos. 2100-2105. (What is particularly fun is that while some shoppers pop inside for their fix of high-end fashion and accessories, others stay outside and buy a really rather impressive fake from one of the throng of counterfeit handbag and wallet salesmen who ply their trade here. And I do mean right outside the store! **Ferragamo** is at Nos. 2097-2099 (with fakes outside) and **Frette** opposite at No. 2070. The Calle Larga XXII Marzo crosses a bridge beside a gondola station and becomes the **Campo San Moisè**, where you'll find **Versace** at No. 1462 and **Prada** (for ladies at No. 1466 and for gentlemen at No. 1470). Exiting the *campo*, the same street is now called the **Salizzada di San Moisè** and is lined with the fake sellers on the right-hand side and stores like **Fendi** (at No. 1474) on the left. Here luxury brand names carry on with **Valentino**'s elegant store at No. 1473. The renowned Italian shoemake **Calzature Fratelli Rossetti** offers to make ladies' and gents' feet fabulous at No. 1477. ♦ *Vaporetto* stop: Santa Maria del Giglio

Also on Calle Larga XXII Marzo:

Ristorante La Caravella

★★$$$$ This is one of the fanciest dining spots in Venice. The kitchen really goes to town on the luxury items like caviar (popular, if less than traditional) and spider crabs (in season). One dessert worth leaving room for is the *semifreddo di torrone in salsa d'aurum* (a nougat frozen confection with orange liqueur sauce). Accompany your meal with a selection from the restaurant's refined wine list. In summer there's outdoor seating in the lovely courtyard, but you'll have to reserve it. ♦ M-Tu, Th-Su, lunch and dinner. Calle Larga XXII Marzo 2397 (between Calle delle Veste and Calle delle Ostreghe). 5208901. *Vaporetto* stop: Santa Maria del Giglio

Frette

This renowned Milan-based company produces high-quality linens for tables, beds, and clothing. The Venice shop is one of a dozen throughout the world, including outlets in London, New York, Paris, and Beverly Hills. ♦ M-Sa Mar-Oct; M afternoon, Tu-Sa Nov-Feb Calle Larga XXII Marzo 2070A (between Rio di San Moisè and Calle del Cristo). 5224914. *Vaporetto* stop: San Marco

Venetia Stadium

This exquisite store specializes in items created with hand-printed fabric and accordion-pleated silks in the style of Mariano Fortuny. The lamps, scarves, and handkerchiefs are delightful. In addition, this shop carries the famous Delphos clothes, also created after designs by Fortuny in gem-colored silk. ♦ M-Sa Mar-Oct; M afternoon, Tu-Sa Nov-Feb. Calle Larga XXII Marzo 2403 (at Calle delle Ostreghe). 5229281. *Vaporetto* stop: Santa Maria del Giglio

Hotel Flora

$$$ One of "the" places to stay in Venice, according to discerning Venetophiles. And they are right. The hotel is on a site, just off the Calle Larga XXII Marzo, once occupied by the ancient School of Venetian Painting, directed by a pupil of Titian. It is a gem. It manages that wonderful double act of having all the efficiency and charming service you could require from a top hotel, while creating an atmosphere that makes you feel you are not in a hotel at all. The Romanelli family, who began it, still run it—the masterfully charming Ruggero and Gioele are the current managers—and the rooms, both the 44 private and 2 public, are furnished and decorated with individually chosen antiques that give the place a very

genuine feel you never quite get in a chain, no matter how many stars. The star of the Flora is its beautiful internal garden—an absolute joy in good weather. Inside, the hotel bar is charming, and frequently the location for a winter game of canasta or backgammon among well-bred ladies. This is a very Venetian place to stay. And compliments don't really come much higher than that. ♦ Calle Larga XXII Marzo 2283A (between Calle del Traghetto and Calle del Pestrin). 5205844; fax 5228217. e-mail: info@hotelflora.it. www.hotelflora.it. *Vaporetto* stop: Santa Maria del Giglio

La Coupole

One of the classiest chains around, this store offers all the buzz-name designers: Blumarine, Calvin Klein, Donna Karan, Anna Molinari, Stella McCartney, Versace, and, of course, Dolce&Gabbana. The service is incredibly charming considering how ultra-chic the stores look. They have an alteration service too. ♦ Daily. Men's: Calle Larga XXII Marzo 2366. 5224243. Ladies': Calle Larga XXII Marzo 2414. 5232754; and at 2031. 2960555. Babies': Calle Larga XXII Marzo 2254. *Vaporetto* stop: Santa Maria del Giglio

Salviati

Some traditional crafts are immutable. The Salviati brand is fabulous proof that Venetian glass is capable of keeping the best of the past and making with it the most strikingly modern works. The brand collects *maestri* of the art of glass offering bottles and vases, plates and lampshades, glasses and candle holders—beautiful, elegant works of art made timeless. This is their exclusive distributor in Venice. These treasures make wonderful gifts. And surely generosity, like charity, should begin at home! ♦ Calle Largo XII Marzo. Daily, 9AM-11PM. 5231191; fax 5285745. www.mareglass.com. *Vaporetto* stop: Santa Maria del Giglio

62 Hotel Bauer

$$$$ This eminent five-star hotel has been welcoming visitors to Venice since 1880. It is a pair of hotels—hotel Siamese twins—one of which is modern, the other old-style classic. The **Bauer Il Palazzo** occupies the 18th-century wing of the building and underwent a $50 million renovation under the new owner, Francesca Borlotto Possati (third generation of the Bennati family who bought the Bauer in 1930). This part of the Bauer has 35 double rooms that start at "Palatial" and 40 suites that range from "Junior" to "Royal." All are individually decorated in high Venetian style. The more modern part of the Bauer got its $25 million face-lift a couple of years ago and now has 115 totally refurnished guest rooms, including 20 suites and junior suites. Again, here, each room has been individually decorated under the eagle eye of Signora Possati. Many have double bathrooms, sitting rooms, and terrific views over the lagoon. The welcome is warm and friendly. The hotel has its own excellent spa and a very efficient concierge service. ♦ Campo San Moisè 1459. 5207022; fax 5207557. www.bauervenezia.com. *Vaporetto* stop: San Marco

Within the Hotel Bauer:

De Pisis Restaurant

★★★$$$$ Quite a destination restaurant now, it serves well-known "modern Italian" cuisine and traditional dishes with international twists. The wine list is eye-watering. In summer, dining is on the lovely terrace overlooking the Grand Canal.

B Bar

Full of character and relaxed for the bar of a five-star hotel, B Bar offers excellent cocktails from a well-considered list, decent beers, premium spirits, and access to that eye-watering wine list. The bar has live jazz every night. It is a "Bond Spot," with amusing little booklets of "Bonds Drinks" and a full cabinet of memorabilia. Order any drink ever consumed in a Bond film, and the barman will produce it! Delicious and unexpected little snacks appear at your table, which is nice. And the men behind the bar are absolutely delightful. ♦ Campo San Moisè 1459. 5207022; fax 5207557. www.bauervenezia.com. *Vaporetto* stop: San Marco

63 San Moisè (St. Moses)

Venice is probably the only city in the world with Catholic churches consecrated to prophets of the Old Testament (technically included among the saints): There are churches for Daniel, Zacharias, and Job, as well as the Archangel Raphael. **St. Moses** was built in 1668 in full Baroque style by **Alessandro Tremignon** with funds from the Fini family. As in many other Venetian churches, statues of the donors were installed over the portals. Here the family's coat of arms is also sculpted on the pediment. The lavish decorations on the façade have often been compared with stage sets for Baroque operas. Equally controversial is the surprising and sumptuous high altar, with a dark and complex sculpture—*Moses Receiving the Tablets on Mount Sinai*. ♦ Campo San Moisè and Salizzada San Moisè. *Vaporetto* stop: San Marco

64 Missoni

The latest colorful designs created for men and women by the Milanese team of Ottavio and Tai Missoni are available here. Particular items to look for include cardigans, coats, skirts, and dresses. Venetians watch for the sales at the end of each season. ♦ M-Sa Mar-Oct; M afternoon, Tu-Sa Nov-Feb. Calle Vallaresso 1312B (between Fondamenta delle Farine and Calle Due). 5205733. *Vaporetto* stop: San Marco

64 Luna Hotel Baglioni

$$$$ Close enough to have Harry's Bar as your "local," this hotel is one of Venice's elegant elder statesmen. It is easy to see why it is listed as one of the "Leading Hotels of the World." Over the years it has checked in famous names from Jean-Paul Sartre to Neil Armstrong and Nelson Mandela to Rod Steiger. There are 115 rooms decorated in period style, with silk wall coverings and hand-blown Venetian chandeliers, as well as the usual TV, minibar, air conditioning, and other amenities. The 18 suites have Jacuzzi, VHS, open bar, and private fax. Many have views of the canal; some have terraces. The **Canova Restaurant** serves excellent cuisine both Venetian and international, the generous buffet breakfast is served in the stunning **Marco Polo** lounge (frescoed by Tiepolo scholars in the 18th century), and the hotel also offers the **Caffè Baglioni**, overlooking the Royal Gardens. ♦ Calle Vallaresso 1312. 5289840; fax 5287160. e-mail: luna.venezia@baglionihotels.com. www.baglionihotels.com. *Vaporetto* stop: San Marco

64 La Bottega Veneta

This famous high-fashion leather accessories firm started in New York City before making its mark in Italy. Their trademark woven-leather skins come in the season's favorite colors. ♦ M-Sa Mar-Oct; M afternoon, Tu-Sa Nov-Feb. Calle Vallaresso 1337 (between Fondamenta delle Farine and Salizzada San Moisè). 5229489. *Vaporetto* stop: San Marco

64 Camiceria San Marco

A large selection of fabrics and years of experience draw customers here for the city's best custom-made shirts, blouses, and pajamas for men and women. Prices are comparable to those of the most expensive department stores. ♦ M-Sa Mar-Oct; M afternoon, Tu-Sa Nov-Feb. Calle Vallaresso 1340 (between Fondamenta delle Farine and Salizzada San Moisè). 5221432. *Vaporetto* stop: San Marco

65 Hotel Monaco and Grand Canal

$$$$ This is the only hotel in Venice to make its way into Condé Nast's top hotels of the world list. As the name suggests, it is really two hotels. One is characterized by the achingly chic reception hall. The Benneton Group took the place over in 1992 and has hugely renovated what began as the palazzo of the well-known Dandalo family, became Venice's first public casino in 1638, and was turned into a theater in 1774. Their chosen Milanese architects' influence is seen in the atrium-like reception hall and the elegant upstairs bar. However, it is not all chic restraint and 21st-century minimalism. The "other half" of the hotel is still old Venice. A grand old staircase connects the reception hall with the Sala di Ridotto . . . and suddenly you take a leap centuries back to the stuccos, marbles, and frescoes of Grand Venice. This is now the hotel's salon, a stunning place for tea or a drink that can be booked as a fabulous location for receptions. It is surrounded by eight rooms with names like Sospiri (Sighs) and Vallaresso. They are available individually for anything from a conference to a private dinner. The hotel has 99 rooms with 7 suites and 6 junior suites. The décor is elegant, rooms have every modern convenience you can imagine, including Internet access, and the hotel is even protected from flooding during periods of "acqua alta." There is a bar and the Grand Canal Restaurant, which offers an international cuisine as well as some Venetian specialties. Dining is possible on the hotel's large canal-front terrace in good weather. ♦ Calle Vallaresso 1332 (at Fondamenta delle Farine). 5200211; fax 5200501. e-mail: mailbox@hotelmonaco.it. *Vaporetto* stop: San Marco.

66 Harry's Bar

★★★$$$$ Nearly 65 years ago a kindhearted barman loaned some money to a guy called Harry. Three months later, Harry gave the barman back his money . . . and tripled it. The barman took his profit, opened his own bar, and called it . . . **Harry's Bar**. The rest, as they say, is history and Hemingway. Distinguished owner Arrigo Cipriani, son of the original owner, claims that many Venetian specialties were created here—the Bellini (a peach nectar and Prosecco wine cocktail, originally available only in summer as the nectar must be fresh, but now available all the time because the "nectar" comes in tins), and carpaccio, for instance. Both were named after Venetian painters. The food is good. And among the luxurious offerings are some very decent pasta dishes. Their *spaghetti al sarde in saor* is a delicious take on the traditional antipasto fish dish and they make, according to friends, the best hamburgers on the planet. The *risotto primavera* (with spring vegetables) is legendary. And so are the prices. ♦ Daily, lunch and dinner. Calle Vallaresso 1323 (at Fondamenta delle Farine). 5285777. www.cipriani.com. *Vaporetto* stop: San Marco

67 Giardini ex Reali

Napoleon's architects razed a building and put a small park in its place to permit a view of the lagoon from the Royal Apartments they had created in the **Procuratie Nuove**. Although far from living up to its name (Royal Gardens), the park offers welcome respite—a rare spot of green in a city of stone and water. ♦ Bounded by Molo di San Marco and Rio dei Giardinetti. *Vaporetto* stop: San Marco

68 Molo di San Marco

Once the main entrance to the city, this quay on the south side of the **Piazzetta San Marco** opens toward the lagoon. Patricians, merchants, and others having business in the city landed here. The two huge columns marking its sides like an imaginary portal were transported on boats from Byzantium in the 12th century. They support the statues of *St. Theodor* (the original protector of Venice, later replaced by St. Mark) and a puzzling winged animal, accepted as *St. Mark's Lion,* although it is probably a chimera made in China or Persia (the wings were added in Venice). The most charming aspect of the pier today is the row of gondolas parked along it, furiously rocking all day long from the waves created by the heavy motorboat traffic. In fact, only a few courageous gondoliers (and their unsuspecting passengers) still brave the rough waters of St. Mark's basin. ♦ Between Rio di Palazzo o della Paglia and Rio dei Giardinetti. *Vaporetto* stops: San Marco, San Zaccaria

69 Conservatorio di Musica Benedetto Marcello

This imposing structure was built between the 17th and 18th centuries for the Pisani family. Today it is occupied by the well-known **Venice Conservatory of Music**. The interior contains two courtyards and a handsome ballroom, now used for concerts by the conservatory's teachers and students. Inquire at the administrative offices about visiting the palazzo. ♦ Campo Pisani (off Campo Santo Stefano). *Vaporetto* stops: Santa Maria del Giglio, San Samuele, Accademia

70 Novecento

$$$ The Romanelli family (who own the lovely Hotel Flora) have created something very different here. This nine-room hotel is almost a little work of art in itself. Each room is decorated in a different style, and the entire place has a multi-ethnic theme, with Turkish carpets and Moorish wall hangings, African carvings and native art. It has a very restful, laid-back feel. All rooms have nonethnic, state-of-the-art bathrooms and all the other facilities you would expect from hoteliers this good at what they do. ♦ Calle del Doce da Ponte 2683. 2413765; fax 5212145. www.locandanovecento.it. *Vaporetto* stop: Santa Maria del Giglio, Accademia

71 Hotel Ala

$$ Furnished with all the modern necessities, this comfortable hotel in a renovated building is conveniently located near the city's major sights. The 85 rooms are individually decorated in various Venetian styles, and the hotel is undergoing continuing renovation to add Internet service, an American bar, a wine cellar, and a cigar divan. There's no restaurant. ♦ Campo Santa Maria del Giglio 2494 (at Calle Gritti). 5208333; fax 5206390. *Vaporetto* stop: Santa Maria del Giglio

72 Gritti Palace

$$$$ The most understated front since the stable at Bethlehem hides the 16th-century palazzo of Doge Andrea Gritti, now and for years Venice's ultimately, historically opulent hotel. It has welcomed kings and queens, presidents and prime ministers, and it has a suite named after Ernest Hemingway. The 80 double rooms, 2 singles, and 9 suites are furnished in such a way that you might expect a guided tour to come around to see them at any minute. The **Club del Doge** restaurant has a Grand Canal terrace and a wonderful international *carte,* while the **Bar Longhi** is a marvelously relaxing place for a cocktail or even just a coffee. For residents and nonresidents alike, the hotel now has a piano bar with live music nightly. It also has its own private beach and sports facilities on the Lido. The whole atmosphere is of quiet quality. And wealth. ♦ Campo Santa Maria del Giglio 2467 (at Canal Grande). 749611, 2961222; fax 5200942. www.luxurycollection.com/grittipalace. *Vaporetto* stop: Santa Maria del Giglio

73 The Westin Europa & Regina

$$$$ This hotel—right on the **Grand Canal** itself—has had a recent magnificent $21 million renovation including a total refurbishment of the 192 rooms, which now boast mosaic floors, spacious closets, Murano chandeliers, heated Cararra marble floors in the bathrooms, and gold-leafed mirrors. The service is impeccable and the view from the canalside windows even more stupendous. Claude Monet painted many of his famous works in this hotel. The hotel has three terraces for dining along one of the most panoramic points on the Canal Grande, one for the very fine **Cusina** restaurant. ♦ Corte Barozzi 2159 (at Rio di San Moisè). 5200477, 800/3253589; fax 5231533. *Vaporetto* stop: San Marco

DORSODURO

While the throngs of visitors pouring across the **Ponte dell'Accademia** are usually drawn to Dorsoduro for its art museums, the **Galleria dell'Accademia** and the **Collezione Peggy Guggenheim** (Peggy Guggenheim Collection), others have long preferred this largely residential area as a place for their own Venetian homes. Poet Ezra Pound lived here, just a few steps from the palazzo where Peggy Guggenheim spent the last decades of her life hosting a parade of international literati and glitterati. But simple folk will enjoy just strolling around, especially along the three small canals with walkable banks, to take in such unassuming sights as the **Campiello Barbaro**, a tiny square that has inspired artists for years.

1 Roberto Tolin

Peek in the window of this little workshop-with-a-window and you will be entranced by the shoes and boots of another of Venice's leather wizards. Roberto has a particular way with little ankle boots . . . they come with interesting cuffs, in multicolored suede, in green crocodile skin, and even as beautifully old-fashioned button boots. All can be made to measure. Signor Tolin is also renowned as a savior of old shoes and boots, with skills to bring almost anything made of leather back to life. ♦ M-Sa, 8:30AM-1PM and 3PM-7:30PM. Calle Vinanti 3773 (at Ponte dei Vinanti). 5242090

2 Ponte della Donna Onesta

The alleyway, bridge, and the bank of the canal are all named for the *donna onesta*—the "honest woman." There are many versions of the reason for this: One says that the tiny sculpted woman's face on the façade of the house over the bridge was once alleged to be the only honest woman in Venice . . . another that here, a Venetian prostitute plied her trade with an honesty unique among those of her profession . . . and the saddest of all tells of the good wife of a local sword maker who was raped by one of her husband's clients and stabbed herself with one of his daggers because she could not live with the shame. ♦ *Vaporetto* stop: San Tomà

2 Trattoria della Donna Onesta

★$$ This charming restaurant is on the corner of the alley and the canal bank. White linen and the sound of the canal outside the window provide the setting. The classic menu offers all manner of fishy starters, as well as a house special of tagliatelle Donna Onesta (in a fresh vegetable sauce) and a fresh *zuppe di verdure* (vegetable soup). Main courses cover almost everything that once swam, grilled, including a simple *grigliata mista* (mixed grilled fish and seafood), along with beef and veal in a variety of guises and—unusual for Venice—*salmone alle erbe* (salmon fillet with fresh herbs). For dessert, the more usual tiramisù and panna cotta are listed alongside petits fours. This is a place with a growing reputation. ♦ M-Sa, lunch and dinner. Calle della Donna Onesta (at Fondamenta della Donna Onesta). 710586. *Vaporetto* stop: San Tomà

3 Campo Santa Margherita

Lined with food shops, cafés, and open spaces where mothers take their children to play, this is one of the most charming and lively of Venice's many squares. On the east side is **Al Capon**, a restaurant and *pensione*. An abandoned church at the northern end is marked by the truncated bell tower. Some of the houses on the *campo* are among the oldest and most attractive buildings in Venice: The one at **No. 2931** (west side) is 13th-century Gothic with original Byzantine elements (such as the 12th-century arch over the main door); a few doors away (**Nos. 2945-62**) are two 14th-century Gothic houses. Fruit-and-vegetable stalls are always a colorful addition to the *campo,* to say nothing of offering a cheap and delicious alternative to pizza for lunch. You'll even get cabaret—watching the stall-holders deftly trim a prickly globe artichoke down to its tender heart! On some days there is also a fish market. ♦ At Calle del Magazen and Calle del Forno, and Rio Terrà della Scoazzera and Calle della Chiesa. *Vaporetto* stop: Ca' Rezzonico

On Campo Santa Margherita:

Planet Earth

This delightful shop is full of handmade treasures such as pleated silk scarves and bags, classily gorgeous iron and glass sconces and candleholders, plates and serving dishes with pressed leaves and flowers suspended in glass resin . . . an intelligent assortment of really nice things. ♦ M-Sa, 10AM-1PM and 3PM-8PM. Campo Santo Margherita 3002. 5286700. planetearth@inwind.it

Caffè Rossa

This café offers big atmosphere in a tiny place with excellent *tramezzini* (sandwiches) and panini, good coffee, and friendly service from young staff. Sit inside and soak up some rock music or outside and soak up the sun. ♦ M-Sa 7AM-1AM. Campo Santo Margherita 2963

Loris Marazzi

A wonderful artist who works in wood, Marazzi's amazing carvings are now all over the world, and the man himself will show you the snapshots to prove it. He gives wood a marvelous liquidity in some works, like his abstract Daliesque *Reality* . . . and then creates everyday items of clothing, draped raincoats and jackets that look terrific on a wall or door and bowties you can really wear. He will carve you something to order, such as the bed he carved for an American couple as a vast, cupped human hand. Go and marvel at the artistry, be charmed by the man, enjoy the smell of wood, and buy your family an heirloom of the future. ♦ Daily (he is always working). Campo Santa Margherita 2903. 5239001. www.lorismarazzi.it

Emporio Pettenello

This wonderful, old-fashioned toy shop is stuffed with great things for kids . . . and a few fun pieces for their moms and dads. The window is full of tiny animal figures, but not just your run-of-the-mill horses and cows. This place has zebras and rhinos, dromedaries and polar bears! Of interest to eco-friendly parents is the fact that Pettenello is one of very few places to stock Popolino diapers. They are made from 100% soft organic cotton and have removable pads inside, meaning you don't throw away the whole thing each time you change the small person in your family. ♦ Daily. Campo Santa Margherita 2978. 5231167. *Vaporetto* stop: Ca' Rezzonico

4 Ca' Foscari

One of the most stately on the Canal Grande, this sumptuous 15th-century Gothic palazzo was built for Doge Francesco Foscari, one of the most remarkable of the Venetian doges. After he had presided over a tumultuous period in Venetian history, the doge was deposed and his son was exiled. Foscari died in disgrace in his home, which is now the main building of the **University of Venice**. In 1999 repair work began on the palazzo, hidden from view by a massive trompe l'oeil façade, which will remain until work is finished. ♦ Canal Grande and Rio di Ca' Foscari. *Vaporetto* stop: Ca' Rezzonico

5 Osteria da Codroma

★★$ This great little place is low and cozy with huge, heavy dark wood tables to share, a

Magic's in the Air

In Venetian, *Carnevale* means magic. Since the festival was brought back in 1980 (Napoleon had declared it illegal almost 200 years earlier), hordes of visitors have arrived here from around the world—as they did in pre-Napoleonic days from all over the European continent—to partake in the fun and frolic of Venice's no-holds-barred annual amusement. Today's *Carnevale* is a tribute to 18th-century Venice and people from all social classes mingle, hidden from each other by masks and sometimes even by the inevitable fog. Traditionally, *Carnevale* lasts two weeks. Last year it lasted six weeks, and the garbage collectors went on strike!

After *La Serenissima* (Most Serene Republic) was in her decline and folly replaced power, *Carnevale* sometimes lasted for six months. People came from all over Europe to the Queen of the Adriatic to partake in the festivities. Among these were organized contests featuring tumbling, boxing, wrestling, goose catching, and bull hunting. Gondolas plied among the frenzy, past parades and puppet plays, by bear baitings, burlesque shows, and bullfights, dodging balloon ascents and fireworks. All of Venice was a stage, filled with theatrical and operatic events, costume parties, and children getting into the act by throwing eggs filled with perfumed water at passersby. There were even "oracles" with long pipes who whispered secrets to the curious.

In today's *Carnevale,* bear baiting has been replaced with live rock concerts and an expensive sound system, and bridge boxing and wrestling with local police officers guiding traffic on the bustling streets. Some things remain constant, though: opera and theater performances, glittering masked balls, wildly colored groups of living dominos parading the streets, and masculine ballerinas twirling with energy. The party still goes on all night, as in Browning's era: "Balls and masks begun at midnight, burning ever to mid-day,/When they made up fresh adventures for the morrow." It all ends with fireworks over the **Canal Grande** on the night of Shrove Tuesday.

For more information about the festivities and getting an invitation to one of the masked balls, contact the tourist office (Palazzetto Selva, 5226356).

glass-topped bar bursting with delicious things to eat, and a few "surprise delights" on offer, such as hot chocolate with grappa. The food is all homemade and includes panini and rolls stuffed with a generosity of *porchetta* (roasted pork), prosciutto, or milky mozzarella and tomato. It comes served on a round wooden platter. There are wonderful fried packages of salt cod mousse, cheese and anchovy and mozzarella-stuffed sandwiches, tiny, high-rise *pizzette* full of rich tomato sauce and a variety of toppings, and *involtini* of eggplant slices marinated and wrapped around an explosion of pepperoncini and capers. This would be a great place to kiss that diet good-bye! The clientele is young, the background music is rock, and the atmosphere is warm and friendly. ♦ M-Sa. Fondamenta Briati 2540. 5246789. *Vaporetto* stop: San Basilio

6 Bazzani Camilla

This lovely shop-*cum*-workshop is filled with the ceramic artistry of Camilla, the equally lovely brunette who sits at the workbench crafting the beautiful tiles and ceramic jewelry she sells. The tiles are frequently detail-perfect miniatures of some of the famous façades of the city. The front of the Ca' Rezzonico becomes a deep green 6-inch-by-6-inch tile. Some are made even smaller, but the sweeping Gothic window arches and intricate stonework is all reproduced. There are lovely necklaces and pendants too. You may never have considered tiles to be worth a second look, but a visit to Camilla will change your mind. ♦ M-F, 10AM-6PM. Campo dei Carmini 30123. 5235277. *Vaporetto* stop: San Basilio

7 Scuola Grande dei Carmini (Great School of the Carmelites)

The name *scuola* is not really correctly translated as "school." In a time when there was no welfare state, the *scuola* was both a religious and community association dealing with, among other things, financial assistance to families of members. The lay members of the *scuola* formed brotherhoods (*confraternità*) dedicated to a patron saint. There were six main *scuole* (*Scuole Grandi*) and about 400 smaller ones. During the 17th century, the charitable organization of Santa Maria del Carmelo (one of many denominations of the Virgin Mary) had some 75,000 people under its wing. The importance of the building today is tied to the extraordinary number and quality of paintings by Giambattista Tiepolo. Nine of his works adorn the ceiling of the main hall on the second floor. The central one, *The Virgin Mary with the Blessed Simon Stock,* is considered one of the high points in Tiepolo's career. A masterwork by Giovanni Battista Piazzetta, *Judith and Holofernes*, is in the passageway between the **Sala dell'Archivio** and the **Sala dell'Albergo**. Alongside the works of art, the interior offers original wooden furniture, beautiful carved ceilings, and stucco work by Stanzio. ♦ Admission. M-Sa, 9AM-6PM; Su, 9AM-4PM. Campo dei Carmini (between Campo Santa Margherita and Fondamenta del Soccorso). 5289420. *Vaporetto* stop: Ca' Rezzonico

8 San Nicolò dei Mendicoli

Some extensive restoration work in the 1970s (funded by the Venice In Peril Fund) uncovered architectural remnants from as far back as the seventh century, making this one of the oldest churches in Venice. The existing structure was built between the 13th and 15th centuries; the magnificent Veneto-Byzantine bell tower dates from the 11th century; and the façade was redone in the 18th century. The interior, unusually welcoming and intimate, is adorned with exquisite 15th-century woodwork. The restoration raised the entire floor of the church, which had been one foot below the level of the canals and so badly damaged in the floods of 1966. It is now out of harm's way. ♦ Campo San Nicolò and Rio di San Nicolò. *Vaporetto* stop: San Basilio

9 Fondamenta del Soccorso and Fondamenta San Sebastiano

These two charming streets, running along two canals, lead to the tall, Gothic **San Sebastiano** church. Across the canals is **Palazzo Ariani Pasqualigo**, with its remarkable Gothic windows and an outdoor staircase, now a *scuola elementare* (grade school). ♦ Between Campo dei Carmini and Calle Avogaria. *Vaporetto* stops: Ca' Rezzonico, San Basilio

10 I Carmini (Santa Maria del Carmelo)

This Gothic church, begun in the 14th century, was modified in the 16th century by raising the central nave (the rose window on the façade was then partly filled). The campanile, by **Giuseppe Sardi**, was added in the 17th century. The rich wood decoration of the church interior also dates from the 17th century. Within the church are two masterworks: In the second chapel on the right is *Adoration of the Shepherds*, one of the last works by Cima da Conegliano; and in the second chapel on the left is *Saint Nicolas, Saint Lucy, Saint John the Baptist, and Saint George Killing the Dragon*, one of the few paintings by Lorenzo Lotto in Venice and much admired for the coastal landscape at the bottom. Behind the church is the convent of the Padri Carmelitani, now used by the **Istituto d'Arte**, which is the main high school for young Venetian artisans specializing in glass, ceramics, and textiles. ♦ M-Sa, 7:30AM-noon and 2:30PM-7:10PM; Su, 7:30AM-noon and 2:30PM-4:30PM. Campo dei Carmini (between Campo Santa Margherita and Fondamenta del Soccorso). *Vaporetto* stop: Ca' Rezzonico

11 Mondonovo Maschere

Since *Carnevale* was reintroduced in 1980, hundreds of mask shops have popped up all over Venice. This store is one of the originals, as well as one of the few where masks are still made with artistic care and respect for tradition. Owners Giorgio Spiller and Giano Lovato, who are well known nationally and internationally, create their traditional and contemporary masks as well as other papier-mâché objects in a workshop behind the counter. ♦ M-Sa (no midday closing). Rio Terrà Canal 3063 (between Fondamenta dello Squero and Rio Terrà della Scoazzera). 5287344. *Vaporetto* stop: Ca' Rezzonico

11 Gualti

Gualti is one of the new wave of Venetian artists and craftsmen. And what a wave! What this man does is somewhere between art and craft and represents the best of both. He works in resin, glass, and nylon to create what can only be described as wearable sculpture. His works have the lightness and delicacy of glass, yet are pliable. Gualti says he sees them as extensions of the wearer's body. I only wish I thought my body were beautiful enough to extend into anything like these earrings and necklaces, headpieces and shoe ornaments. They are like exotic sea anemones, or sometimes flowers or leaves, extending tendrils from a tiny central point—sometimes an eye or a "pool of water"—that frequently is made of glass crystal. The tendrils of his brooches, especially, cascade over the wearer's shoulder like a fabulous corsage. The colors are rich, and each piece is crafted by hand with the point of a hot needle used to bore and solder. Gualti not only creates exuberant shoe ornaments, but hand dyes the handmade silk shoes to match them. The latest addition to the art of Gualti is an array of fabulous wraps and some breathtakingly gorgeous jackets. All come in his wonderful colors—and most are reversible. The wraps and jacket collars are malleable into undulations and peaks as suits the wearer's fancy. Truly this is unique, wearable art. ♦ M-Sa, 10AM-1PM and 3PM-7:30PM.

Rio Terrà Canal 3111. 5201731. www.gualti.it. *Vaporetto* stop: Ca' Rezzonico

12 Ponte dei Pugni

The name, which means Bridge of the Fistfights, dates back to an old tradition that once pitted the residents of San Nicolò (a Dorsoduro neighborhood inhabited mostly by fishermen) against those of Castello (which was comprised mostly of **Arsenale** shipbuilders). The champions of both areas used to hold mock fights on the bridge, trying to push their opponents into the water. Four white footprints still mark the starting places of the opposing fighters. One of the most impressive displays of fresh vegetables and fruit in Venice is here—moored on a barge beside the bridge. ♦ Between Fondamenta Gherardini and Fondamenta dello Squero. *Vaporetto* stop: Ca' Rezzonico

13 Ristoteca Oniga

★★$$ One of the newish additions to the Venice dining scene, this restaurant is prettily situated on the tiny Campo San Barnaba. Tables outside are a lovely place to sit in good weather, especially in the evening, and the interior is chicly modern. As are the staff! The wine list is extensive and covers the whole of Italy. The food is excellent and offers as antipasti various *degustazione,* or tasting plates: one of the vegetable dishes, one of fish (with delicious prawns in a sweet-and-sour sauce, carpaccio of octopus, marinated anchovies, and crayfish with pears), and one of *"antipasti tipici venenziani"* (with cuttlefish in its own ink, thinly sliced flash-sautéed calves' liver, a creamy mousse of salt cod, and the classic sardines in a tangy marinade, *sarde in saor*). Main courses include fish and meat, and everything is top quality—tuna is blue fin and beef is Aberdeen Angus. ♦ T-Su, noon-2:30PM and 7PM-10:30PM. Campo San Barnaba 2852. Tel/fax 5224410. e-mail: oniga@libero.it. *Vaporetto* stop: Ca' Rezzonico

13 San Barnaba

A lovely little church in a lovely little square. The area around San Barnaba was once where the "fallen" aristocracy lived. They were called the *barnabotti* and were looked after on what we would call state benefits. San Barnaba himself was born in Cyprus in the first century AD. He was one of the evangelists who took Christianity to Asia Minor, but ended his days stoned and then burned. The church is thought to have been built in AD 809, destroyed in a fire in 1106, and then rebuilt in 1167. The bell tower is one of the oldest in Venice. The architect of the final rebuilding (in the 16th century) was thought to be **Lorenzo Boschetti.** Inside, the main altar is in seven parts, and artworks include *The Birth of the Virgin* by Antonio Foler. ♦ Daily, hours vary. Calle del Traghetto. *Vaporetto* stop: Ca' Rezzonico

14 Ca' Rezzonico—Museo del Settecento Veneziano (Museum of the Venetian 17th Century)

This famously imposing palazzo was begun by **Baldessare Longhena** in 1667, at the behest of Filippo Bon. Filippo, unfortunately, went bankrupt, and the palazzo was left a half-finished shell until bought by the Rezzonico family (snootily dismissed as "nouveau riche" by the Venetian aristocracy) in 1751 and completed by **Giorgio Massari**. It passed through various owners, including the son of Robert Browning (Browning himself died there in 1889). It opened as a museum in 1936, preserving perfectly a Venetian palazzo of the 18th century for 21st-century viewing—the textiles, the décor and furnishings, and the objets d'art.

On the first of the two "noble floors" (*piani nobili*, the part of the house reached by the grand staircase and used for great occasions of public display), the large ballroom contains furniture by the famous woodcarver Andrea Brustolon. The ceiling of **Room No. 2** has a fresco by Giambattista Tiepolo called *The Marriage of Ludovico Rezzonico and Cristina Savorgnan*. More works by Tiepolo are in **Room No. 6** (*Allegory of Nobility and Virtue,* a ceiling painting) and in **Room No. 8** (*Fortitude and Wisdom,* a canvas). **Room No. 12** is dedicated to Brustolon; the astonishing, extremely elegant furniture was originally conceived for the **Palazzo Venier dei Leoni** (the unfinished building now occupied by the **Guggenheim Collection**). In **Room No. 13**, on the second *piano nobile* is the large, dramatically attractive *Death of Darius* by Giovanni Battista Piazzetta. **Room No. 14**, adorned by a Tiepolo ceiling (*The Triumph of Zephir and Flora*), is called **Sala dei Longhi** because it contains some 30 canvases by Pietro Longhi, a Venetian of the late 18th century who delighted in painting scenes from everyday life (*The Morning Chocolate*, *The Family Concert*). Nothing illustrates the dramatic changes in Venetian life after the loss of independence better than a comparison between the triumphant Tiepolo ceilings and these intimate, bourgeois interiors. In a totally different vein, hints of decadence are also present in the frescoes by Gian Domenico Tiepolo, son of Giambattista and himself a first-rate painter. They can be seen in **Rooms No. 22** and **23**, where they were placed after being removed from the painter's home on the Venice mainland (Gian Domenico had painted them for his own enjoyment). **Room No. 29** contains a famous small canvas by Francesco Guardi, also a painter of the second half of the century—*Il Ridotto*, which portrays one of the many Venetian gambling casinos. On the third floor is an exhibit of a complete 18th-century pharmacy, restored and moved here after it went out of business in 1909. ♦ Admission. W-M, 10AM-6PM. Fondamenta Rezzonico 3136 (east of Calle delle Botteghe). 2410100. *Vaporetto* stop: Ca' Rezzonico

15 Antica Trattoria La Furatola

★★★$$$ Wonderful old photographs of Venice, occasionally featuring earlier generations of the owner's family, line the walls. They are fascinating, but concentrate on the menu. Whatever fish is in top condition, in season, and in the market can be on your plate here. The *antipasti misti* (mixed hors d'oeuvres) is a fishy feast: first a plate of steamed or boiled seafood, then a tiny serving of polenta topped with gorgeously creamy *baccalà mantecato* (salt cod poached and whipped almost to a creamy mousse) with some *schie* (tiny shrimp), and then a plate of different marinated fish, sardines *in saor* (in a tangy sweet-and-sour dressing), fresh anchovies, and absolutely stunning marinated salmon. Pastas are all cooked to order and *spaghetti della casa* comes in a richly fishy *ragù*. All fish can be ordered cooked on the restaurant's special old grill, and they are fabulous so prepared. Don't leave without trying the licorice-and-coffee *scroppino* that maître d' Luigi makes himself. He calls it "the eighth wonder of the world." He's not wrong. ♦ M-W, F-Su, lunch and dinner. Calle Lunga San Barnaba 2869a. 5208594. e-mail: furatola@gpnet.it. *Vaporetto* stop: Ca' Rezzonico

15 Fujiyama

$ A real find! This tiny bed-and-breakfast has just four bedrooms on two floors and a delightful tearoom on the ground floor. The rooms are named for the owner's favorite capitals: Shanghai, Tokyo, Paris, and Harbin (which is the capital of Manchuria!), and are simply but beautifully decorated with Chinese and Japanese antiques and artifacts. The word "unique" can be overused, but it is apt for this place. The charming owner lived and worked for many years in the East and remains in the grip of his love affair with the region. The tearoom is open to the public daily after the residing guests have enjoyed their breakfasts. Chinese and Japanese teas are on offer, along with Italian coffee. The Fujiyama has a delightful and very restful garden and a sweet terrace. In the very heart of Venice, this is a tiny oasis of calm. Impressively, the staff can speak English, French, Japanese, Chinese, German, and Spanish! ♦ Calle Lunga 2727/a. 7241042; fax 2771969. www.bedandbreakfast-fujiyama.it. *Vaporetto* stop: Ca' Rezzonico

16 Ostaria ai 4 Feri

★★★$$ A tiny gem, offering oak tables (which you may be encouraged to share), paper placemats, and a warm welcome. You can be pretty sure that whatever is good in Venice's famous fish market that day will end up on your plate, simply but perfectly cooked. Pastas come with scampi or clams in a fresh tomato sauce, *gnocchi di zucca* (pumpkin gnocchi) perhaps with bay scallops and porcini. For the keen learner at the Venetian table, whatever dish is traditionally on the Venetian family menu in every season and for every festival is served here. The *bancone* (counter) toward the door is also overflowing with staples of the local antipasti—octopus and squid salads, *baccalà mantecato* (creamed salt cod), grilled baby octopus, and *sarde in saor* (sardines in a tangy onion marinade). The wines are both good and a good value. Service is friendly, and if you are lucky and they are generous, you might just get to share a table with some locals—the little place gets very crowded. Once you've eaten here you will understand why. ♦ M-Sa, lunch and dinner. Closed Sunday. Calle Lunga San Barnaba 2754(a). 5206978

17 Chiesa dell' Angelo Raffaele

I probably shouldn't be telling you about this beautiful little church in its own secluded campo, because one of the most beautiful things about the place is its peace and tranquillity. For all that, the Angelo Raffaele is very much a working parish church. It was originally built in the seventh century but, as with many of Venice's churches, it has been rebuilt many times. The current building was started in 1618 by Frances Contin, dedicated in 1639, and consecrated on 15 May 1740. The post-renovation exterior is startling white marble with carved marble figures from the Lombard School of Raphael. Tobias and his dog are at the top of the façade. The interior is quite simple by Venetian standards, but it does boast a very famous series of 16th-century paintings by GianAntonio Guardi. They depict the story of Tobias and the Angel (the angel in question being Raphael) and form a frieze around the organ loft, above the main door of the church. The ceiling fresco is an early work by Nicolo Baldissini, and there are some marvelously dramatic works here, such as *The Punishment of the Snakes* by Antonio Vassillacchi. The Grand Altar of the Archangel Raphael is inlaid with red African marble, the main altar is in polychromatic marble, and the six pillars of the tabernacle are in ancient green marble. Whenever you visit, it seems there are priests and parishioners around. It gives the place a lovely, friendly feel. The parish priest even offers this welcome: "The faith which moved our ancestor to build this church to God, today incites our parish community to welcome all those people who want to visit it as pilgrims and tourists." ♦ Daily. Campo dell'Angelo Raffaele.

17 Pane Vino e San Daniele

★★★$$ There is a little more to this place than (very good) bread and wine. You can make your wine selection not from a list, but from the restaurant's little *cantina*, where shelves are lined with an impressive selection of Friuli's finest gently priced wines. The excellent San Daniele ham is much in evidence on the menu. This was, until a couple of years ago, one of Venice's oldest and best-loved *osterie*, with chunky communal tables for its local clientele. Luckily it has passed into the hands of a couple who care about food and about the joy of eating. Patricia has a welcome as warm as a Venetian summer, although her passport claims she is Canadian. She will talk you through the small but enticing menu. Antipasti tend toward the "platter" variety, with San Daniele figuring, of course. The vegetable platter is delicious and unusual with an imaginative mix of fresh, grilled, and preserved vegetables. The pasta spirals with raddichio and San Daniele are delicious, as are the unusual *gnocchi di pane e San Daniele* (little breadcrumb dumplings with ham). The portions are generous, so don't fill up too soon, because it is in the main courses that the kitchen shows its true colors. And dishes such as *porcheddu* (suckling pig), *cognilio con mirto* (rabbit with myrtle), and *capriolo con ginepro* (kid with juniper) tell you that those colors are Sardinian. Patricia's equally charming husband, Luigi, is in the kitchen, and his cooking is excellent. Try to leave room for one of the ever-changing selections of homemade cakes and tortes to end your meal. ♦ Th-Tu, 10AM-midnight. Campo dell'Angelo Raffaele. 1722. 5237456

18 San Sebastiano

This 15th-century church contains a wealth of 16th-century works by Paolo Veronese, one of the major painters of the Venetian Renaissance. On the ceiling of the main nave are his *Esther in Front of Ahasuerus*, *Esther Crowned by Ahasuerus*, and *The Triumph of Mordecai*. The last painting could be taken as a manifesto of Veronese's ideas about his art: His aim seems to be a kind of high, refined spectacularity, regardless of the nature of the subject (whether religious or, as in the patrician villas, totally secular). The perspectives on the two horses in the foreground, the twisted column, and the top balcony with overlooking ladies are particularly striking. With these paintings, Veronese established himself as the man who could best represent the theatrical, grandiose fantasies of the Venetian nobility in a moment of relentless commercial and political expansion. He also painted the doors to the organ (left wall); the canvas on the main altar (*The Virgin in Glory with Saint Sebastian, Peter, Catherine, and Francis*); the two large canvases in the chancel (*Saint Mark and Saint Marcellino* and his famous *Martyrdom of Saint Sebastian*); the ceiling of the **Sacristy** (this was his first work here); and, visible from a walk over a stair (ask the custodian to accompany you), two frescoes: *Saint Sebastian in Front of Diocletian* and another *Martyrdom of Saint Sebastian*. The church was originally built (in 1455) to face the other way, but architect **Antonio Scarpagnino** was given the task in 1506 of reversing the whole thing—which he did, putting the door where it now is, opening right onto the bridge. To get the best effect, walk in and a little way down the aisle. Then prepare yourself for a thrill and just look up. ♦ M-Sa, 10AM-5PM. Campo San Sebastian (at Rio di San Sebastiano). *Vaporetto* stop: San Basilio

19 Libreria Toletta

This is actually three bookshops all clustered around the corner of the Sacca della Toletta. The **Libreria** is a bookshop par excellence with novels, poetry, dictionaries, history, and the whole literary enchilada to choose from. The **Cube** has CDs and videos, guidebooks, cards, games, and T-shirts. The **Studio** is an academic bookshop specializing in architecture; it also offers Internet access. A classy cluster. ♦ Daily except Sunday morning. Libreria: Sacca della Toletta 1214. 5232034. Cube: Sacca della Toletta 1175/a. 2415371. Studio: Calle della Toletta 1183/d. 5229481. (Between Calle della Toletta and Rio della Toletta). 5232034. *Vaporetto* stops: Accademia, Ca' Rezzonico

20 Pensione Accademia—Villa Meravege

$$ It's unusual in Venice to find a *real* free-standing villa, surrounded by a garden and detached from other buildings. This 27-room hotel is just such a rarity. The halls and common areas are reminiscent of a private home, and guests can enjoy breakfast in the canalside garden. Loyal guests keep this hotel booked,

so try to make reservations well in advance. A recent freshening-up of the place makes it even more attractive. There is no restaurant. ♦ Fondamenta Bollani 1058 (just north of Calle della Toletta). 5237846, 5210188; fax 5239152. www.pensioneaccademia.it. *Vaporetto* stop: Accademia

21 Ponte dell'Accademia

This "temporary" bridge was built of wood in the 1930s to replace a suspended bridge designed and built in the 1840s by **A.E. Neville**. The permanent structure that was supposed to replace it in turn was never built, and now it is a beloved old bridge in its own right, restored in the 1980s. ♦ Between Campo della Carità and Campiello San Vidal. *Vaporetto* stop: Accademia

22 Trattoria da Montín

★$$ When third-generation owner Giuliano Montín was a child, his father ran this trattoria and made it famous, and guidebooks and movies have kept the restaurant popular and the prices high. The food is all right, the pasta homemade (*tortelloni fatto a mano alla rucola con salsa di gamberi*—tortelloni with a ricotta-and-arugula stuffing sauced with prawns—is light and pleasant), and the *fegato alla Veneziana* (grilled calves' liver) as famous as some of the guests. The atmosphere is friendly and informal. Dine in the huge, wonderful garden in good weather. ♦ M, Th-Su, lunch and dinner; Tu, lunch. Fondamenta di Borgo 1147 (at Calle Forno). 5227151. *Vaporetto* stops: Accademia, Ca' Rezzonico

Upstairs from Trattoria Montín:

Antica Locanda Montín

$ The restaurant also rents out 12 rooms upstairs. Six have bathrooms; the others share. Four of the rooms have a marvelous view over the canal, with small terraces and beautiful geranium pots. ♦ 5227151. www.locandamontin.it

23 Avventurino

This is a glorious little shop, unique in Venice, its soft-spoken owner says—although I suspect the owners of a few other unique shops would quibble! Antique Venetian beads and pearls are what it sells. And the real thing, not imported, on their own and looking like sparkling candies or made up into earrings and necklaces. There are truly beautiful glass beads, too, in the rich colors that you will come to know and love. The name of the shop echoes the name for the vitreous paste that is used to make the beads, invented by a Muranese glass artist in the early 17th century. It was so difficult a process that he called it a *ventura* (an adventure)! ♦ Daily. Calle della Toletta 1195. 5223159. *Vaporetto* stop: Accademia

24 Liceo Marco Polo

The building that houses this high school, restored in 1980, has an 18th-century façade by **Andrea Tirali**. Since time immemorial it has been one of two high schools for classical studies in Venice, attended by children of the upper classes. ♦ Fondamenta Sangiantoffetti 1073 (between Campo San Trovaso and Calle della Toletta). *Vaporetto* stop: Accademia

25 Lo Squero

Every so often "the" people in Venice start talking a place up. And at the time of writing, all of "the" people in Venice were talking about Lo Squero. Basically, it's a hole-in-the-wall on a corner beside a tiny canal leading away from the Zattere toward the Accademia. There are no tables, just a counter with a display of ice creams and a tall, thin youth with a scoop. But oh my oh my are these ice creams good! Simone Sambo and his brother-in-law hand make them in the old way, using only whole milk and the finest of natural ingredients, and they taste like they have come down direct from ice cream heaven. The *cioccolato* is the deepest, richest, and creamiest you have ever tasted. The *limone* has the heart of Sicily trapped in ice. They will make you an ice cream from mascarpone to order. Few places do that. Not many places do *gelato di pistachio* either, and none does it as well as this. Made from the finest Sicilian pistachios, and costing 20 cents more than the other varieties, it offers an experience that is not just like eating pistachio ice cream. At the risk of sounding extravagant, it can only be described as like being a pistachio and being made passionate love to by another pistachio. Get there early. The experience tends to be bought up fast! If you cannot be tempted by the ice creams in the winter (although you should be!), Lo Squero also offers dense, dark hot chocolate and a delicious range of filled chocolates and bars incorporating figs, dates, and chili pepper. ♦ Daily. Fondamenta Priuli 989. 2413601. *Vaporetto* stop: Accademia

26 Galleria dell'Accademia

Venice has Napoleon to thank for this unrivaled catalog of Venetian art housed in the former 15th-century school, church, and convent of **Santa Maria della Carità**. As the little emperor began suppressing Venetian churches and monasteries in the 1800s, he gathered up their works of art and shipped them off to this warehouse of a museum. Return trips to savor the wealth of its 24-room collection, arranged more or less chronologically, will cut fatigue and enhance appreciation of the gallery's attempt to illustrate the development of Venetian art from the 14th through the 18th centuries. In

Bridges of Venice

The name *Venice* conjures up such romantic images as moonlight glinting off the four horses standing guard over the basilica of **San Marco** while gondolas row by on the **Canal Grande** rhythmically slapping their oars, the magnificent **La Salute** church standing in silhouette, and masked Venetians cavorting during *Carnevale*. Recounting its charms, one also recalls Venice's 408 *ponti* (bridges), very important structures in this city of 117 islands and 176 *rii* (rivers).

The bridges come in all shapes, sizes, and materials. Only 87 are flat, while 321 are arched—the **Ponte dei Tre Archi** boasts three. An impressive 300 are made of stone, 59 of iron, and 49 of wood. **Tre Ponti** (Three Bridges) is constructed of three stone and two wood bridges (the latter were added later, but the name remained the same). The singular **Ponte dei Bareteri** fans out into five different streets. Private bridges—those that lead directly into an entrance of a building—number 72.

Surprisingly, only three bridges cross the **Canal Grande**. The precursor to the **Ponte di Rialto**, the **Ponte del Quartarolo**, was built in 1180, and connected the political **Palazzo Ducale** side of Venice (**Riva del Ferro**) with the economic **Rialto** bank (**Fondamenta del Vin**). Originally a platform supported by boats that were tied together, the Rialto was rebuilt several times. The final stone bridge still in use today was finished in 1591. Designed by **Antonio da Ponte** (a fitting name), the Rialto was the only overpass spanning the canal until 1854, when the **Ponte della Carità**, later known as the **Ponte dell'Accademia**, was built. An English engineer, **A. E. Neville**, designed the bridge using the then-new method of forged iron. A short three years later an almost identical bridge, the **Ponte Scaizi**, was erected in front of the train station. These two began to show wear after a few decades, and Venetians wanted something more elegant and made of a material that could be arched so that boats could pass easily under them. Although the decision was made to build both new bridges out of stone, today's **Accademia** overpass is still the "temporary" structure that was constructed of wood in a record 37 days in 1930. The airy marble Ponte Scaizi in front of the train station was inaugurated in 1934.

Bridges are named after any number of people and things: saints, powerful Venetian families, doges, religious orders, and miscellaneous trades; even composers and travelers have a handful dedicated to them. The single most popular name is **Ponte Storto**; there are officially seven, while many others are simply referred to that way. *Storto* means crooked, and it would be appropriate to call close to 200 bridges in Venice by this name. Bridges were put up and across canals as the need arose, and they often connected two streets that were not parallel and were of different heights.

The religious theme abounds. Four **Ponti del Christo** (Christ) are spread throughout the city, and there's also a **Ponte della Croce** (Cross). Numerous others are dedicated to the Madonna, Madonneta, or Maddalena. One is consecrated **Ponte della Ca' Dio** (House of God); another **Ponte dell'Angelo** (Angel); and another more precise, **Ponte dell'Anzolo Raffaele** (Angel Raphael). The **Ponte del Diavolo** (Devil) serves as a good balance for the **Ponte dei Miracoli** (Miracles) and the **Ponte del Paradiso** (Paradise). There is a **Ponte dei Fratti** (Friars) and a **Ponte dei Preti** (Priests). Virtues also have their bridges, among which are *pazienza* (patience) and *pietà* (piety).

There are more down-to-earth names to Venetian bridges as well: **Ponte Piccolo** (Small), **Ponte Longo** (Long), **Ponte de Mezzo** (Middle), and **Ponte Nuove** (New). Three scaffolds across different canals are labeled **Ponte Rosso**, since some were painted the preferred color of the Venetians. Some are dedicated to animals: **Ponte dei Cavalli** (Horses), **Ponte delle Oche** (Ducks), and **Ponte delle Ostreghe** (Ostriches). The food groups claim **Ponte de l'Olio**, **Ponte del Pignolo**, **Ponte della Fava**, and **Ponte delle Erbe**, showing the importance of oil, pine nuts, fava beans, and herbs. Naturally, wine was essential to the islanders, and accordingly one bridge takes the name **Ponte del Vin**; while four others are known as **Ponte della Malvasie**, after a dry wine produced in the Peloponnese city of Malvasie.

Finally, bridges with warlike names come from 1292, when the city was divided between the *Castellani*—those who lived in **Castello**, **San Marco**, and the eastern side of the **Dorsoduro**—and the *Nicolotti*, residents of the western half of the Dorsoduro, **Cannaregio**, **San Paolo**, and **Santa Croce**. They battled for control of the bridges, and these structures later became known as *ponti della guerra* (war).

Ponte di Rialto

high season, when the lines can be a nightmare, it is best to arrive at opening time or late in the afternoon.

The earliest paintings in the museum, displayed in **Room I**, are notable mainly for their Byzantine influence, which is especially evident in Paolo Veneziano's glittering *Coronation of the Virgin with Scenes from the Lives of Christ and St. Francis*. The mastery of the 15th century's Giovanni Bellini, whose favorite subject was the Madonna, is amply represented in **Rooms II**, **IV**, and **V**. A particular favorite among his paintings here is the restful *Madonna of the Trees* (**Room V**). Hanging nearby is one of the museum's must-sees, Giorgione's brooding secular masterpiece *La Tempesta*. Among the works by early-16th-century artists in **Rooms VI** through **IX**, the most interesting is *Portrait of a Young Man in His Study,* by Lorenzo Lotto (**Room VII**). The heavyweights of the High Renaissance—Tintoretto, Titian, and Veronese—dominate **Rooms X** and **XI**. The latter's *Feast at the House of Levi* (**Room X**) was originally intended to be a treatment of the Last Supper. When the Inquisition objected to the inclusion of dwarfs and Germans in the painting, the artist, in a stroke of genius, avoided redoing the work by simply changing its title. In the same room, Tintoretto's cycle of paintings on the subject of St. Mark (*St. Mark Freeing the Slave*, *Transport of the Body of St. Mark*, and *St. Mark Rescuing a Saracen*) is another of the museum's major attractions. Nearby is Titian's final work, a *Pietà* that he intended to be mounted above his tomb as an epitaph. Three more masterworks by Veronese (*Madonna Enthroned with the Baptist and Saints Joseph, Francis, and Jerome*, *The Mystic Marriage of St. Catherine*, and *Ceres Paying Homage to Venice*) are in **Room XI**. Among the highlights of the 18th-century works displayed in **Rooms XII** through **XX** are Giovanni Battista Piazzetta's *Fortune Teller* (**Room XVIA**) and Gentile Bellini's *Corpus Domini Procession* (**Room XX**). As you wander among the paintings in **Room XVII**—scenes of 18th-century Venice by Francesco Guardi, Canaletto, and Pietro Longhi—you may begin to think the city outside has been untouched by time. As fascinating for its detailed depiction of 15th-century Venetian fashion as for its poignant story, Carpaccio's *St. Ursula Cycle* (**Room XXI**) is the most popular of the **Accademia**'s paintings. The story unfolds left to right around the room: Young Ursula is betrothed to the king of England, accepts the condition that the marriage remain unconsummated while she undertakes a pilgrimage in the company of 11,000 virgins, and is eventually martyred outside Cologne. The Accademia's other fresco cycle is by a variety of artists of the Scuola de San Giovanni Evangelista and is entitled *The Miracles of the True Cross*—each painting describing a miracle worked by a relic of the True Cross (owned by the Scuola, incidentally). **Room XXIII** is what remains of the original church of **Santa Maria della Carità**, designed by **Bartolomeo Bon** and built between 1441 and 1452. Titian's *Presentation of the Virgin* (**Room XXIV**) should be your last stop before leaving the museum—probably in Madonna overload. The **Quadreria** (Picture Room) features 88 paintings, including works by Tintoretto and Titian. Access to the room is limited; reservations are required (713498; fax 713487). ♦ Admission. Daily. Campo della Carità (between Rio Terrà Antonio Foscarini and Rio Terrà della Carità). 5222247. *Vaporetto* stop: Accademia

27 Hotel Galleria

$ This charming canalside hotel in a 17th-century palazzo was recently transformed into one of Venice's most welcome finds by offering the quintessential room with a view at about one-fifth the price of the grandes dames boasting similar locations. Eight of the ten guest rooms have a private bath. The spectacular vistas of the Ponte dell'Accademia, chandeliers of Murano glass, wood beams, antique furniture, and incredibly pleasant service make this a great deal. Breakfast is included and is served in your room. ♦ Rio Terrà Antonio Foscarini 878/A (between Calle Nuova Sant'Agnese and Ponte dell'Accademia). 5232489; fax 5204172. *Vaporetto* stop: Accademia

28 869

It is not by chance that Paula Carraro's shop sits snugly between the **Accademia** and **Peggy Guggenheim** museums: This young artist gives a new spin to the ancient craft of knitting by marrying it with modern art. Her exquisite (and expensive) oversized sweaters in cotton, mohair, and silk depict some of the contemporary world's greatest masterpieces by artists such as Klee, Warhol, Magritte, and Picasso. You can't miss the window display of colorful sweaters—you'll think you've arrived at the Guggenheim! ♦ Daily. Closed Tuesday morning. Calle Nuova Sant'Agnese 869 (between Piscina Venier and Rio Terrà Antonio Foscarini). 5206070. *Vaporetto* stop: Accademia

29 Galleria di Palazzo Cini

This 17th-century palazzo belongs to the Cini Foundation and houses the **Raccolta d'Arte della Collezione Vittorio Cini** (the Vittorio Cini Art Collection). The 30-plus Tuscan Renaissance paintings here include works by Taddeo Gaddi, Bernardo Daddi, and Sandro Botticelli, a Guariento, and a *Madonna* by Piero della Francesca. While they may not belong in the pantheon of the greatest Tuscan art, the paintings bequeathed to the foundation by the Conte Vittorio Cini (who died in 1977) illustrate the collector's eye for minor gems. Every year the collection displays a different masterwork on loan from a major art gallery. ♦ Admission. Tu-Su. Rio di San Vio 864 (at Piscina Forner). 5210755. *Vaporetto* stop: Accademia

30 Hotel American

$$ This charming and newly refurbished hotel on a quiet canal has 30 rooms, all with brand new bathrooms and charming décor. Some even have a small terrace with a sidelong view of the Canal Grande! All rooms have bar refrigerator, air conditioning, TV, hair dryer, and Internet access. There is a sweet terrace, where your breakfast can be taken. Staff are absolutely lovely and will make you feel most at home. ♦ San Vio 628. 5204733; fax 5204048. www.hotelamerican.com. *Vaporetto* stops: Zattere, Accademia

30 St. Georges

This is the Anglican Church in Venice. Small and cozy compared to many of the churches that surround it, it is a friendly place, and the current chaplain, John-Henry Bowden, is one of the most interesting and delightful native English speakers you could hope to meet in Venice. He preaches not a bad sermon, either! Sunday morning services are something of a social event for the English-speaking community here. And I am sure John-Henry would be delighted to welcome any visitors who feel like attending. ♦ Campo San Vio. www.stgeorgesvenice.org

31 Collezione Peggy Guggenheim (Peggy Guggenheim Collection)

Peggy Guggenheim opened her first gallery in London in 1938, having been encouraged by playwright Samuel Beckett to become a great patron of modern art because it was "a living thing." Throughout 1939 and 1940 she traveled around Europe fulfilling her stated ambition to "buy a picture a day." Not even Hitler stopped her! In 1942 she opened her museum-gallery "Art of This Century" in New York and wrote of the opening night, "I wore one of my Tanguy earrings and one made by Calder in order to show my impartiality between Surrealist and Abstract art." In 1947 she returned to Europe and showed her collection at the 1948 *Biennale*. And—like so many Americans—when she came, she stayed. She bought the Palazzo Venier dei Leoni on the bank of the Grand Canal. It was begun in 1748, designed by **Lorenzo Boschetti** (who also designed the church at San Barnaba). The frontage is in Istrian stone decorated with yawning lions' heads (hence "dei Leoni" perhaps?). Peggy lived here and in 1949 opened her first collection (sculptures arranged around the garden) to the Venetian public. In 1969 she donated her palace and her entire collection to the Solomon R. Guggenheim Foundation.

Peggy Guggenheim lived in Venice for 30 years, famous for her parties, living life to the fullest and enjoying the last privately owned gondola in Venice. She died in 1979, and her ashes are buried in a corner of the palazzo garden, next to the graves of her beloved dogs. The collection is regarded as one of the finest small museums of modern art in the world. The Peggy Guggenheim Collection has, on permanent display, works from the important movements in modern art: Cubism and Dadaism, Futurism (both painting and sculpture), Surrealism, Expressionism, Abstraction-Creation, and Non-Objective Painting. All the modern greats are here—Picasso and Dalí, Matisse and Braque, Paul Klee and Marcel Duchamp, Chagall and Mondrian, Max Ernst and Francis Bacon. And of course, two of Peggy's most famous (some might think infamous) protégés, Mark Rothko and Jackson Pollock. Even if you hate the art, you have to marvel at the passion of the woman. ♦ Admission. Daily, except closed Tuesday. Vaporetto stops: Salute, Accademia. Fondamenta Venier dei Leoni 708. 2405411. www.guggenheim-venice.it

32 *Traghetto* to Santa Maria del Giglio

Taking this gondola service to the other side of the Canal Grande will save you a long detour on foot over the Ponte dell'Accademia, or from having to wait for the *vaporetto*. ♦ Calle del Traghetto and Canal Grande. *Vaporetto* stop: Salute

33 Campo San Gregorio

The church in front of this *campo*, originally built in the ninth century, was renovated in the 15th century and is now used as a laboratory for the restoration of stone monuments. The beautiful apses are visible from the bridge at the back. At the left side, a wall encloses the garden of **Palazzo Genovese**, a neo-Gothic building dating from 1892 with a façade on the Canal Grande. A few steps farther (**No. 172**) are still-visible remnants of the old **Abbey of St. Gregory** (now privately owned), with its 14th-century cloister. ♦ At Calle Abazia, Calle Bastion, and Calle dei Morti. *Vaporetto* stop: Salute

34 Campiello Barbaro

This cozy, quiet little square on the bank of a small canal is one of the most charming in all of Venice. The back of **Palazzo Dario** is visible from the bridge, beyond the wall and the small garden. ♦ At Calle Bastion, Calle San Cristoforo, and Calle Molin. *Vaporetto* stop: Salute

On Campiello Barbaro:

Marangon da Soaze

Near the gentle fountain, you may hear the tapping of cabinetmaker Andrea Da Tos laboring in his workshop, whose name comes straight from ancient Venetian dialect and means, roughly, "wood carpenter specializing in frames." In fact, he restores old furniture and produces gilded wood objects. ♦ M-Sa Mar-Oct; M afternoon, Tu-Sa Nov-Feb. No. 364. 5237738

35 Galleria d'Arte l'Occhio

If you are looking for something modern, this is a good, intelligent gallery showcasing new, young artists. The works are nicely hung and well lit, and the staff of the gallery are well informed and helpful. I've seen some genuinely interesting art here. ♦ Daily. Calle del Bastion 181–85. 5226550

36 Santa Maria della Salute (La Salute)

In the 1630s, to fulfill a vow made during a plague that wiped out more than one third of the population, the city fathers held a competition to design a church in honor of the Virgin of Good Health. The site they had selected for this solemn tribute was of vital importance to Venice, both commercially and aesthetically: It sat at the entrance to the Canal Grande and was visible from almost any point in Venice. **Baldassare Longhena** was then only 26, but his daring project was chosen over those of 11 other competitors. The structure he designed is one of the best examples in Europe of the Baroque concern for large-scale planning (the idea being that a building should not only express its own individual beauty but also should work with the surrounding landscape as a whole).

Longhena's unusual octagonal plan was designed to create the church as a crown for the Mother of God. He set the whole structure aboveground on a huge embankment, to be flooded with light coming through the windows in the walls and dome. In order to support the massive structure, the ground had to be reinforced with more than a million wood piles. The dome of the church was supported by buttresses, or volutes, disguised as stone spirals, affectionately referred to by the Venetians as *"orecchioni"* (big ears), and topped by a statue of the *Virgin Mary* dressed as a Venetian admiral. The front of the church with its imposing staircase and wealth of over 125 statues and other stone decorations, faces the Canal Grande. Behind the dome, Longhena built a second, smaller dome flanked by two bell towers, creating an elongated shape from the door to the main altar, as in the basilica of **San Marco**. It took more than 50 years to build this wonder of European architecture and engineering (Longhena died in 1682, five years before completion but one year after the solemn inauguration).

In contrast with the festive, exuberant exterior, the interior is sober and reverential. On sunny days, a good deal of light enters the main hall of the church, while the high altar, under the smaller dome, remains shaded and intimate. The six open chapels on the sides of the church correspond to the six secondary façades on the outside. In the first chapel at the right, look for Luca Giordano's *Presentation of the Virgin,* part of a larger cycle of paintings celebrating the

Santa Maria della Salut

Gondola, Gondola, Gondola

n *The Aspern Papers* (Oxford University Press, 1983), Henry James describes the thrill of Miss Tina's romantic gondola ride to **Piazza San Marco**: "She had forgotten the splendour of the great water-way on a clear summer evening, and how the sense of floating between marble palaces and reflected lights disposed the mind to freedom and ease . . . the whole thing was an immense liberation. The gondola moved with slow strokes, to give her time to enjoy it, and she listened to the splash of the oars, which grew louder and more musically liquid as we passed into the narrow canals, as if it were a revelation of Venice."

One thing you know is that whoever you see in a gondola, it isn't a Venetian. Of course, you don't get many native New Yorkers at the top of the Empire State Building either–it doesn't mean it isn't a real experience and you shouldn't do it at least once.

A gondola ride can be a great way to see smaller canals and waterways winding away from the broad expanse of the Grand Canal. At nighttime one would have to have a heart of steel not to appreciate the magic there is when the moonlight bathes the buildings in silver, the lights twinkle, the waterways are wrapped in blue velvet, and you glide almost noiselessly through the city. You might even be treated to a songfest by a *gondoliere,* although the city recently enacted laws to limit the hours *"O Sole Mio"* singers and accordion players can croon.

The gondola is as much a symbol of Venice as the lion of San Marco. From the 14th through the 18th centuries they were the normal means of transportation in the city. Originally the *gondolieri* painted their craft all the colors of the rainbow. In the 16th century there was a sort of "gondola census" done, and there were found to be 10,000 in use. The Senate decided in 1630 to encourage modesty and reduce ostentatiousness, and ordained that (in a spooky intimation of the Ford Motor Company) gondolas could be any color their owners liked . . . as long as it was black. In the 19th century, the less expensive *vaporetti* replaced their sleek forerunners as the major means of transport for Venetians. Today fewer than 400 gondolas cruise the canals of Venice.

These canoelike boats–5 feet wide and 36 feet long–sport a *ferro*. This steel apparatus, which resembles a battle-ax resting on a comb with six bristles forward and one extending backward, helps balance the *gondoliere*'s weight when rowing. Seven different kinds of wood are used to make 280 pieces for just the hull of the boat, which has to be asymmetrical, with more of a curve to the left side to compensate for the action of the oar on the right side. A basic model with no gilding, carving, or other decoration (just in case you were thinking of buying your own private transport) costs about $18,000 and takes about a month to build.

There are just over 400 gondoliers working in Venice. New applicants have to go through a *selezione* (selection), which takes place once a year. At present all gondoliers are men.

Gondolas are hired for an initial period of 50 minutes and cost a little more in the evening. They will take up to six people–obviously less of an option if romance is the general intention.

It is worth noting that a gondola ride when the water is low can be a less enthralling experience–the smell can be a little off-putting.

Recently, an association calling itself *El Felze* (after the removable cabin placed at the center of a gondola) has started up. It is the coming together of all the professions that conjoin to make the gondola, promoting, teaching, and raising awareness of their skills and crafts. They have a small guide to the places where anyone interested can see these craftsmen at work. The professions are the *squeranioli* (the carpenters who make the basic boat: Squero San Trovaso–see page 222), the *remeri* (who carve the oars), the *ottonai* and *fonditori* (who make the brass ornamentation), the *fravi* (the blacksmiths who forge the iron *forcola* that rises above the prow), the *intagiadori* (who carve and engrave the intricate decorations), the *indoradori* (who gild the gondola), the *tapessieri* (who upholster the interior), the *sartori* (the tailors who specialize in gondoliers' clothing), the *calegheri* (who make the specialist shoes worn by gondoliers), and the *bareteri* (who make their characteristic hats for summer and caps for winter). El Felze can be contacted by telephone (5200331) or on their web site (www.elfelze.com).

Some of the gondola stands are:

Bacino Orseolo 5289316

Calle Vallaresso 5206120

Danieli Riva degli Schiavoni. 5222254

Ferrovia San Simeon Piccolo. 718543

Isola Tronchetto 5238919

Piazzale Roma 5221151

Rialto Riva del Carbon. 5224904

San Marco Molo di San Marco. 5200685

Santa Maria del Giglio 5222073

Santa Sofia 5222844

San Tomà 5205275

Trinità Campo San Moisè. 5231837, 5223103

Virgin Mary originally planned for the church's interior. The high altar, designed by Longhena, surrounds a Greek-Byzantine icon of the Virgin Mary that is very dear to Venetians (it was taken from Crete in 1672 as war booty). At the third altar on the left is a lackluster Titian, *The Descent of the Holy Spirit,* which the artist repainted (unenthusiastically, it appears) after the original was damaged. A small door at the left of the main altar leads to the **Sacristy**.

The admission price to this section of the church is well worth it if you like Titian. His three very emotional ceiling paintings are on the theme of the struggle: *Caino e Abele* (Cain and Abel), *David e Golia* (David and Goliath), and *Il Sacrificio de Isaaco* (The Sacrifice of Isaac). There are also his eight really sweet medallions depicting saints and his *St. Mark Enthroned* (at the altar). On the right wall is *The Marriage at Cana,* usually considered one of Tintoretto's best works.

Every year on 21 November, a procession takes place from St. Mark's Square to the church to give thanks for the city's good health. ♦ Daily. Sacristy: admission; 9AM-noon and 3PM-5:30PM. Campo della Salute (between Fondamenta della Dogana alla Salute and Fondamenta della Salute). 5225558. *Vaporetto* stop: Salute

37 Seminario Patriarcale

The building between **La Salute** church and the **Punta della Dogana**, designed by **Baldassare Longhena**, was built in 1670 as a school for children of noble families. In 1617, it became the **Venice Seminary** (previously on the island of Murano). Inside is a 17th-century cloister and the **Pinacoteca Manfrediniana**, a collection of minor works of art mostly from the 16th century. ♦ By appointment only. Campo della Salute 1C (east of Santa Maria della Salute). 5225558. *Vaporetto* stop: Salute

38 Punta della Dogana (Customs Point)

Upon arrival in Venice, ships laden with precious cargoes from the Far East stopped here first to be examined for customs duties; they would then continue along the Canal Grande and anchor in front of the patrician palazzi, where they would be unloaded. Beginning in the 1670s, this easternmost point of Dorsoduro was entirely reconstructed as part of a vast plan to design an impressive entrance to the Canal Grande, culminating in the church of **Santa Maria della Salute**. Today the area is rarely crowded, not even with tourists, though in the evening it is a favorite stroll for couples looking for an isolated romantic spot.

The **Customs House**, between the extreme tip of the island and **La Salute**, was built in 1677 (northeast wing) and in the 1830s (southwest wing). The 17th-century tower at the tip supports two bronze giants carrying a gold sphere (designed by Bernardo Falcone) representing the world, surmounted by a huge statue of *Fortune* that acts as a wind gauge. Thus the city welcomed its ships with the symbols of its naval power. ♦ Fondamenta della Dogana alla Salute and Fondamenta delle Zattere ai Saloni. *Vaporetto* stop: Salute

39 Ristorante Riviera

★★$$ This restaurant may not have a wood terrace over the canal, but the tables set on the banks of the Giudecca Canal are inviting and pleasant. The new young owner has taken over and is working hard to maintain standards. The wife of the director of the Cipriani eats here regularly, so he must be doing something right. The menu changes seasonally, but you will always find local specialties like the *granseola* (crab), which comes fresher than fresh as a starter in a classy timbale. Traditional fare like *bigoli in salsa* (thick spaghetti in an anchovy sauce) is done well, as are lesser-known dishes like their *costice di agnello ai mirtilli*—a Sardinian influenced dish of lamb cutlets flavored with myrtle. Their homemade breads are terrific, their olive oil is organic, and the wine list generous. This is a friendly but classy little place to dine. You can also simply enjoy a drink at the bar and watch the sun go down. ♦ Restaurant, Tu-Su, lunch and dinner; bar, Tu-Su, 9AM-2:30PM and 7:30PM-10PM. Fondamenta delle Zattere Ponte Lungo 1473 (between Calle Trevisan and Calle dei Cartellotti). Tel 5227621; fax 2447724. *Vaporetto* stops: San Basilio, Zattere

40 Squero di San Trovaso

Probably the most photographed and painted sight in Venice, this small compound—most visible from Fondamenta Nani across the narrow canal—is now a national landmark. It is one of three places in Venice that still builds and maintains gondolas using traditional methods. The 17th-century wooden buildings (homes of the owners and hangars for boats) are unusual for Venice but were typical of boat builders. They resemble Dolomite mountain homes, and in fact both the wood for the gondolas and the master carpenters often came from that region. ♦ Campo San Trovaso 1092 (between Rio Ognissanti and Fondamenta Sangiantoffetti). *Vaporetto* stop: Zattere

41 Rio Terrà Antonio Foscarini

Flanked by a few trees, this unusually wide and straight alley is as close as Venice comes to a boulevard. It was built in 1863 by filling in a canal (hence the *rio terrà*) to facilitate pedestrian traffic to the Accademia Bridge. The building at **Nos. 898-902** houses the **Istituto Cavanis**, a private grammar and high school founded in the 18th century to provide poor children with free education. It's still free, and the quality of education at the school is so high that Venice's upper crust tries to send their children here.

Across from the school, the Cavanis Fathers (a small, local monastic order) run an inexpensive hotel during the summer months, usually reserved by Catholic groups but theoretically open to anyone. ♦ Between Campo di Sant'Agnese and Canal Grande. *Vaporetto* stops: Accademia, Zattere

On Rio Terrà Antonio Foscarini:

Hotel Belle Arti

$$ This is a hotel to consider if you are here in good weather. Its main selling point is its lovely walled garden, with a loggia scattered with smart cane furniture and a rather romantic-looking swinging sofa with a canopy. The 67 en-suite rooms (which come in single, twin, and triple sizes) are nice, but fairly Venetian standard. A sweet foyer bar and a little dining room for breakfast is included. Rio Terrà Antonio Foscarini 912/A. 5226230. www.hotelbellearti.com

Ca' Pisani Hotel

$$$$ This beautiful hotel is quite un-Venetian in its Art Deco-meets-futuristic chic. It is the dream-come-true of Gianni Serandrei and his sister Marianna, the latest generation of the Venetian family who have owned the well-known Hotel Saturnia since 1908. From the moment you enter the lobby, you know you are in the hands of intelligent, creative people. There are 20 guest rooms, all with private phone and fax, satellite TV, and a minibar. They have bathrooms that will make you want to bathe on the hour, every hour. Your buffet breakfast is included, served downstairs in the bar/restaurant. The hotel's décor is a unique work of fusion art. The beds are original 1930s and 1940s, and sit on beautiful inlaid parquet flooring against smart but sympathetic geometric minimalist walls and upholsteries. You will find your TV, writing desk, personal safe, and minibar in a hand-crafted, silver leaf-covered, modernist cupboard of almost Japanese austerity. The Ca' Pisani boasts a tiny, charming roof terrace, a solarium, and a private steam room, should the delights of the hotel not open your pores enough! The top-floor hallway and rooms are under the eaves of the former palazzo, and the beautiful exposed beams are all original. Each room door has its own uniquely designed wooden inlay. Aptly chosen and very eye-catching artworks are everywhere. The attention to detail is an object lesson to hoteliers everywhere. On what was the *piano nobile* of the palazzo, a vast and impressive hallway is left open and sweeps from one side of the building to the other. This is a special hotel. ♦ Rio Terrà Antonio Foscarini 979/a. 2401411; fax 2771061. www.capisanihotel.it

Within Ca' Pisani Hotel:

La Rivista

★★★$$$ The hotel's bar and little dining room are already a draw for the beautiful and the chic of Venice. Originally offering simply selections of hams and traditional cold cuts, or of cheese from their mouth-wateringly impressive list (including such selections as bagoss, morlacco, and murianengo—an education in Italian cheeses as well as a delicious lunch!), the restaurant also offers a menu of new takes on old favorites. So it is Italian with a twist. Salmon and turbot carpaccio, served with fennel and *bigoli* (fat spaghetti), comes in a fish sauce made with Prosecco, and fillet of veal is honey-glazed and served with foie gras. The cocktails are created with both care and imagination, as is the restaurant's wine list—which offers about twenty of its excellent selection by the glass. ♦ Daily.

42 Calle delle Mende

A walk through the area between this street and Le Zattere (the bank of Canale della Giudecca to the south) is the best way to see why this neighborhood is so dear to foreign lovers of Venice. This is residential Venice at its best. The houses are rarely more than two stories high; frequent, small gardens are visible; and flowerpots line most windows. Quite a few locals still live here, but they are gradually being driven out by soaring real estate prices—apartments here now start at about $3,000 a square yard. Notice the fading fresco of Venice's skyline, by local painter Bobo Ferruzzi, on the **Campiello Incurabili**. The small streets on both sides of the Rio Terrà San Vio allow access to the buildings between the two canals. At the far end of the *Rio Terrà* (**No. 460**), a door opens into the former **Convento dello Spirito Santo** (Convent of the Holy Spirit), used today as a high school; visitors are welcome to look at the courtyard and the 16th-century cloister. ♦ *Vaporetto* stops: Accademia, Salute

43 Ca' Maria Adele

$$$ A gorgeous hotel in a gorgeous location right on its own little canal facing the Chiesa delle Salute, tucked away and reached by its own little wooden bridge. And it is worth

reaching. Just 14 rooms are spread over four floors of an old palazzo. Each has a king-sized bed, LCD TV, air conditioning, minibar, safe, and Jacuzzi or a fabulous "waterfall" shower. In their deluxe rooms, the décor is opulent. There is the Sala dei Mori, done out in rich dark Moorish style; the Sala del Camino, all white drapes and ivory marble; the Sala del Doge, a dramatic riot of Venetian crimson and gold; and the Sala Orientale, in the golds and blues that symbolize Venice's dominance over the sea. Finally there is the Sala Noire, where I plan to live forever. Decorated in tones of pepper, clove, and cocoa, it is a real Casanova of a room! The reception areas are chic and modern—minimalist even, with exposed brickwork and old columns, although the wooden rafters above you date back to the 16th century. A very individual and very sexy hotel. ♦ Rio di Salute 111. 5203078. www.camariaadele.it

44 Le Zattere

From the tip of Punta della Dogana all the way to the cruise-ship terminal at the southwest end of Venice, the Canale della Giudecca is flanked by an uninterrupted walkway called **Fondamenta delle Zattere**, or simply "Le Zattere." *Zattere* means rafts; it was to this extended pier that huge barges once brought their cargoes of supplies from the mainland. The sunny southern exposure of the canal bank makes this a favorite walk for Venetians on mild winter afternoons and on Sunday mornings year-round. Many cafés open onto the street, and some have wooden terraces suspended on piles over the water. A cross-section of the population can be seen here soaking up the sun, sitting at the cafés, or walking along eating ice cream. The Canale della Giudecca, now congested with boat traffic, still offers some memorable sights, including the boats of the Bucintoro rowing club going out for practice and the large cruise ships and cargo ships, taller than any buildings in the area, slowly passing by on their way to the **Stazione Marittima**. Until the 1960s, a small section of the canal was enclosed by a white-and-blue fence, creating a swimming pool right in the canal's water, where most Venetians learned how to swim. Today the canal is polluted (though it has improved in recent years) and few brave its waters. The Fondamenta has recently been widened considerably almost all the way from the Stazione Marittima to the boat stop at Zattere. For me, the most beautiful part of the Zattere is up toward the Punta della Dogana, where it narrows again and travels alongside high-walled gardens and the Accademia di Belle Arte. At certain times of the year, such as February, you can, around five o'clock in the evening, have the unforgettable experience of walking up here in marvelous peace and quiet with the canal on one side, San Giorgio in front of you, with the sun on your back and the moon in your face. It is a real Venice moment. ♦ Between Punta della Dogana and Stazione Marittima. *Vaporetto* stops: Zattere, San Basilio, Salute

45 Gesuati

This church (officially named **Santa Maria del Rosario**) and its adjacent monastery were originally built by the Poveri Gesuati, a local monastic order not to be confused with the *Gesuiti* (Jesuits). In the 17th century the order merged with the Dominicans, who proceeded to rebuild the church entirely, trusting the project to **Giorgio Massari**. The façade is clearly reminiscent of **Palladio** (whose **Redentore** church is visible across the canal). Both churches are flanked by two bell towers, but this one is somewhat more imposing. The canal bank and gondola landing were redesigned to harmonize with the new church, although the effect has been somewhat spoiled by the *vaporetto* stop in front.

The interior is one of the masterworks of 18th-century Venice, consisting of a single nave, as in the church of **La Pietà**, with a large chancel behind the altar. Most of the statues are by the ubiquitous and rather uninspiring Giovanni Maria Morleiter, but the paintings are among the best by Tiepolo and Piazzetta. Tiepolo painted the ceiling (1737-1739) with his *Institution of the Rosary* (center of ceiling) and with stories from the life of St. Dominic in his *St. Dominic Praying to the Virgin Mary* (near the chancel). Also by Tiepolo is the altarpiece dedicated to the Virgin Mary on the first chapel to the right, while Piazzetta painted *St. Dominic* in the next chapel and a splendid *St. Vincent Ferreri* in the following one (third at the right). More frescoes by Tiepolo are on the inside of the apse. A remarkable Tintoretto adorns the first chapel on the left side: It is a *Crucifixion* dated 1526 said to have been restored by Piazzetta himself. ♦ Fondamenta delle Zattere ai Gesuati and Rio Terrà dei Gesuati. *Vaporetto* stop: Zattere

46 Ristorante Alle Zattere

★★$$ This dining spot is best known for its location; it is one of only a few restaurants with a terrace overlooking the Canale della Giudecca. The food is all right, though the prices reflect its monopoly over the canal view. ♦ M, W-Su, lunch and dinner. Fondamenta delle Zattere ai Gesuati 795 (at Sottoportico Trevisan). 5204224. *Vaporetto* stop: Zattere

47 Pensione Seguso

$$ This old-fashioned *pensione,* still run by the Seguso family, is one of very few places in town where half-board—breakfast (sunny canalside breakfasting is on offer) plus one

meal per day—is still required of its guests during high season. All but 15 of the 38 rooms have private baths. ♦ Closed January, February, December. Fondamenta delle Zattere ai Gesuati 779 (between Calle Pistor and Sottoportico Trevisan). 5286858; fax 5222340. *Vaporetto* stop: Zattere

48 La Calcina

$$ Home to 19th-century British author John Ruskin while he wrote *The Stones of Venice* in 1876, this 29-room hotel has been extensively but sympathetically refurbished, and keeps much of the furniture and many of the paintings, books, etc. from the time of Ruskin. It is on the Guidecca Canal, so views can be wonderful, most especially from the hotel restaurant and bar's terrace, which is right on the water. (Talking of terraces, the hotel has a roof terrace, small but absolutely stunning. Breakfast can be taken here and, if you are at all able to manage the many stairs, you will never want to leave it.) The hotel also has three suites and two apartments situated close by, the apartments with their own kitchen. All benefit from the excellent standards of housekeeping in the hotel. ♦ Fondamenta delle Zattere ai Gesuati 780 (between Calle Pistor and Sottoportico Trevisan). 5206466; fax 5227045. e-mail: la.calcina@libero.it. www.lacalcina.com. *Vaporetto* stop: Zattere

Within La Calcina:

La Piscina

★★$$ Starting as the hotel's tiny café/bar, La Piscina is now a better-than-average restaurant. Should you choose to sit outside on the Zattere, you'll have one of the finest views in Venetian catering. They have a large wooden terrace over the Giudecca Canal and several linen-decked tables alongside the hotel. It's worth coming and ordering something just to sit here! The café serves good fresh sandwiches and panini with very good coffee or hot chocolate. The pastries in the morning are terrific too. The restaurant has plenty of choices to offer those who are light eaters or vegetarian. Usually, there are several homemade soups on offer—fresh carrot, broccoli, or pea. Fusilli comes with fresh vegetables and is a wonderful light summer dish. There are seven *insalatone* (composed salads) to choose from, and should you be in the mood for something meaty, the rabbit with sweet herbs and artichoke is highly recommended. The wine list is good, the service lovely (and efficient!). La Piscina has grown up rather well! ♦ Tu-Su, 11AM-10PM. 2413889

49 Ospedale degli Incurabili

The history of this 16th-century building is a chronicle of sadness: It was built for people with incurable diseases (mostly syphilis), then used to house abandoned children, and in the 20th century it became a prison for juvenile delinquents. It now stands semi-abandoned, like many other buildings in Venice, although at press time it was expected to be turned over to the **Accademia**. ♦ Fondamenta delle Zattere allo Spirito Santo 423-26 (between Calle dello Zucchero and Ramo dietro gli Incurabili). *Vaporetto* stops: Accademia, Salute

50 Saloni or Magazzini dei Sale (Salt Warehouses)

An early source of Venetian wealth was the salt trade. The huge building at **Nos. 258-266** was constructed in the 14th century to store the salt supplies the city imported from the East. The façades were redesigned in the 1830s, but the enormous storage rooms are still capable of holding 45,000 tons of salt as originally planned. Today they house the boats of a rowing club, as well as temporary art exhibitions, often held in conjunction with the Venice *Biennale d'Arte*. ♦ Fondamenta delle Zattere ai Saloni 258-66 (between Rio Terrà dei Saloni and Fondamenta Ca' Bala). *Vaporetto* stop: Salute

51 Rio Terrà dei Saloni

This wide street was created in the 19th century by filling in a canal (*rio terrà* means "land-filled canal"). The building at the corner of Rio Terrà dei Catecumeni (**Nos. 107-108**) was rebuilt by **Massari** in 1727. For many centuries it was a center for the education of non-Catholics who intended to convert, among them Lorenzo da Ponte, Mozart's librettist. The handsome **Palazzetto Costantini** (**Nos. 70-71**) dates back to the 14th century and still has the original wood beams over the portico. ♦ Between Fondamenta delle Zattere ai Saloni and Rio Terrà dei Catecumeni. *Vaporetto* stop: Salute

SAN PAOLO

San Paolo has no shortage of distinguished art and architecture. The **Frari** church, for example, ranks among the highest achievements of Venetian Gothic style, and the **Scuola di San Rocco** houses a breathtaking array of canvases by Tintoretto. **Campo San Paolo** itself–vast, luminous, and elegant–is one of the most beautiful squares in all of Venice. For Venetians, San Paolo is the part of town where *real* people live and go about their daily business. The fruit-and-vegetable market and the nearby fish market still serve shoppers from throughout Venice, who arrive by *vaporetto* to buy their weekly food supplies at prices much lower than in their neighborhood shops. The liveliest street is **Ruga degli Orefici** (commonly called **Ruga Rialto**). The narrow streets between Ruga Rialto and the Canal Grande are where market merchants used to have their homes and warehouses. In the labyrinth of tiny streets on the other side of Ruga Rialto hide some of the best wine shops in town. These are real institutions still packed with Venetians who stop for an *ombra* (glass of wine) and a *cicchetto* (the Venetian version of tapas, or finger foods) before lunch or dinner. Among the patrons are pensioners, students, teachers, doctors, lawyers, and architects–the last abound in Venice because of the university's acclaimed school of architecture. Even though the food booths at the **Mercato della Frutta** (Produce Market) are gradually giving way to stalls selling tourist trinkets, San Paolo remains one of the last places where class and money distinctions don't seem to matter and where the locals simply enjoy their city, perhaps more than any outsider ever could.

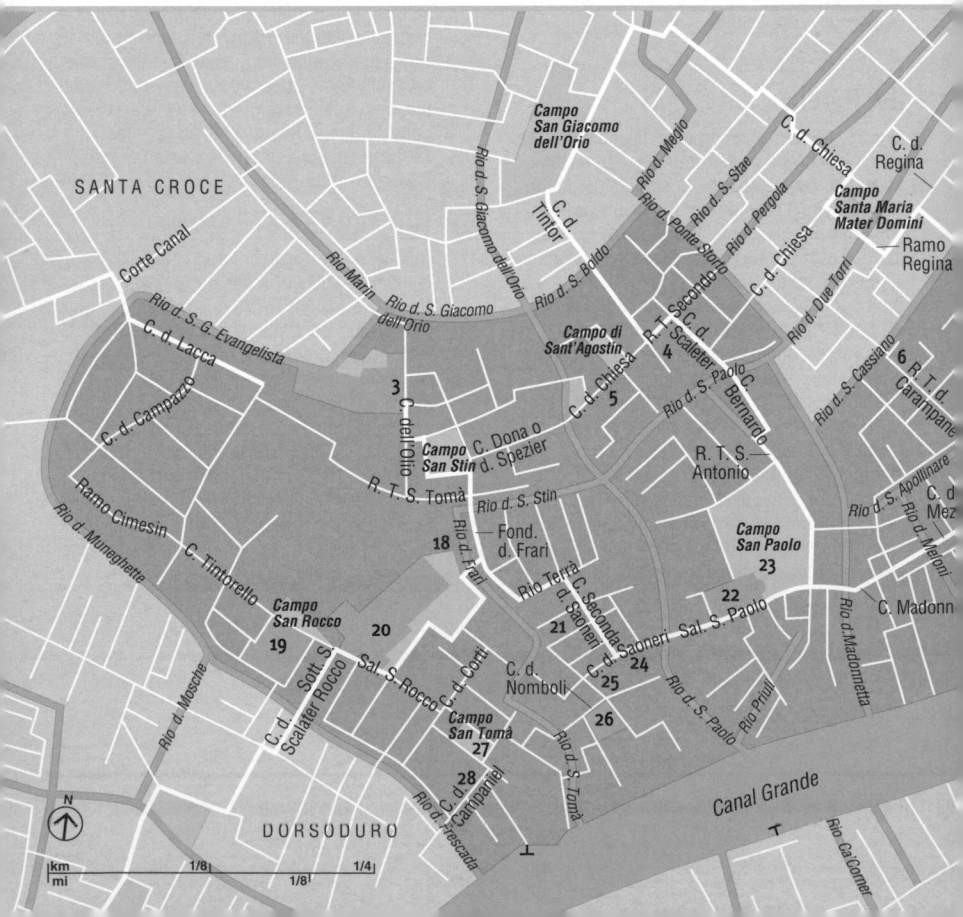

1 Pescheria (Fish Market)

This building—with its neo-Gothic ground floor and Renaissance-style second floor—was erected in the 19th century to provide cover for the colorful and lively fish stands here. Industrial pollution in the waters around Venice has diminished in recent years, and some of the seafood is from local waters: the sardines, which Venetians cook in a variety of succulent ways; some small shrimp; and most of the shellfish and the farmed trout. Live lobsters are the most expensive item for sale, followed by such fish as *branzini* (sea bass) and *orate*. The salmon comes from Norwegian sea farms; the sole is mostly imported from Holland; some of the shrimp come from Sicily or from Adriatic waters, but most are from Norway and Ireland. Most squid and octopus are imported frozen from Thailand and the Canary Islands. ♦ Campo della Pescheria and Canal Grande. *Vaporetto* stop: Rialto

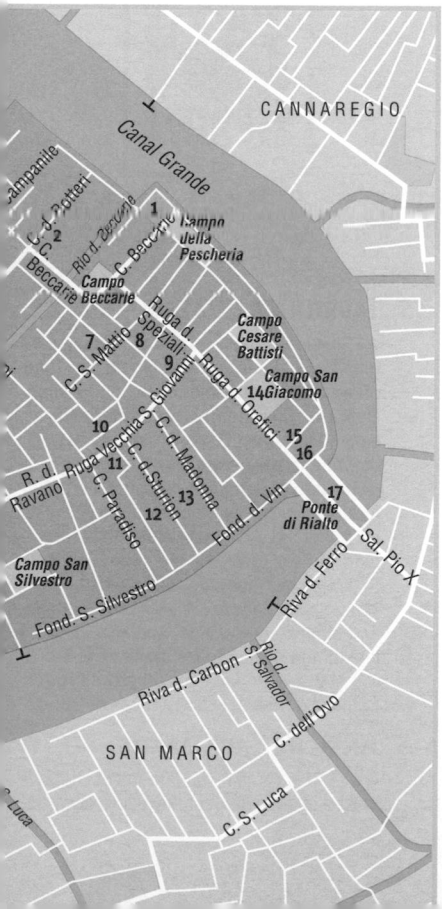

1 Campo Beccarie

The fish market extends into the **Campo Beccarie**. This is the highest point in the city. The area around it was originally called *Rivoalto* ("high bank") and then contracted to become *Rialto*. It was the very first area of settlement on the lagoon islands and became the center of trade and banking for the Republic. Now it is a fish market. ♦ *Vaporetto* stop: Rialto

On Campo Beccarie:

Rialto Biocenter

This new shop is a godsend for those living the organic life—a tiny supermarket offering just about everything organic from fresh fruit and vegetables through packets and tins of pastas, sauces, and soups to wine and beer. A small selection of herbal remedies and cosmetic products is also on offer. ♦ M-Th, 8:30AM-1PM and 4:30PM-8PM; F, Su, 8AM-8PM. Campo Beccarie 366. 5239515. *Vaporetto* stop: Rialto

2 Antica Trattoria Poste Vecie

★★★$$$ Walk across a small wooden bridge to reach this charming restaurant, where you can dine outdoors in the garden or indoors among the 16th-century frescoes. Tradition and perfection are the highest priorities here, and it shows in the food. The pasta is all homemade and comes with artichokes and prawns, or flavored and colored with *nero di seppie* (squid ink) and sauced *al granchio* (with crab). Much of the menu is dictated by the two markets (fish and vegetable) that are but a spaghetti's length from the restaurant. In season you can eat the delicious *moleche* (soft-shell crab) that is a Venetian specialty. The mainly Italian wine list is worth talking through with your maître d'. ♦ Daily, lunch and dinner. San Paolo 1608 (between Rio delle Beccarie and Rio di San Cassiano). 721822. *Vaporetto* stops: Rialto, San Silvestro

At Antica Trattoria Poste Vecie:

Locanda Poste Vecie

$ No, you are not seeing double. This incredibly atmospheric trattoria now offers rooms! There are 10 in all, 7 with private bath and 3 without, but all with air conditioning, TV, phone, etc. Views of the **Ca' d'Oro** from your bedroom window do, however, rather put to shame anything you are likely to see on TV. ♦ Fax 721037. www.postevecie.com

3 Scuola Grande di San Giovanni Evangelista (Great School of St. John the Evangelist)

The rich and powerful brotherhood named after St. John acquired this property early in the 14th century. In 1478, master **Pietro Lombardo**, one of the first architects and sculptors to introduce the Renaissance in Venice, redesigned the little square on the side of the building and in front of the church. He added the elegant marble portal, decorated with an eagle (the symbol of St. John) and two angels, thus creating one of the first Renaissance environments in town.

The brotherhood was housed in the building at the right of the square's entrance (notice the medieval bas-relief *The Virgin and St. John Being Adored by the Brotherhood's Members*). **Giorgio Massari** redesigned most of the interior in the 18th century, but its most interesting feature is the splendid staircase designed and built by **Mauro Codussi** in 1498. The building is not usually open to the general public, except for pre-booked guided tours, although musical performances are held here quite often. ♦ 718243. Campiello della Scuola 2454 (at Calle dell'Olio). *Vaporetto* stops: San Tomà, Riva di Biasio

4 Osteria da Fiore

★★★★$$$$ When you enter the bar of a restaurant to find the owner proffering a basket of delicious hand-cut potato chips still warm from being made in the kitchen, you just know everything is going to be all right. This is Venice's only Michelin-starred restaurant and yet bears none of the overblown formality of Michelin's choices in, say, Britain. The menu changes every day according to what is good in the market, but there is regularly a platter of top-quality seafood carpaccio on offer, together with some genuine Venetian basics such as *bigoli in salsa* (fat spaghetti in a savory anchov sauce). *Filetto di branzino* (sea bass) comes with a balsamic glaze and, in season—as with everything here—the delicious local *moleche* (soft-shell crabs) are deep-fried and served with polenta. The wine list is fabulous. Owner Maurizio Martin, an urbanely charming gentleman, runs the front of the house while his (and Michelin's) "star"—wife Mara—creates the gourmet-pleasing cuisine. For dinner you need to book about a month in advance; lunch is easier. And Maurizio says please note the address . . . there is another da Fiore near San Stefano, where numbers of confused diners clutching Michelin guides have been known to turn up. In case your meal here inspires you to improve your skills, da Fiore now has a cookery school attached! ♦ Tu-Sa, lunch and dinner. (Closed 3 weeks in August and 3 weeks at Christmas/ New Year.) Calle del Scaleter 2202 (between Rio di San Paolo and Rio Terrà Secondo). 721308. www.dafiore.com (restaurant); www.dafiorecooking.com (school). e-mail: reservation@dafiore.com. *Vaporetto* stops: San Silvestro, San Stae

The Archangel Gabriel is sculpted into the left of the downstream side of the Ponte di Rialto; the Virgin Mary receives the celestial message on the right; and there's a dove between the two. This recalls the legend of the founding of Venice on 25 March 421, the same day as the Feast of the Annunciation.

Birre e Vini

5 Taverna da Baffo

★$ This is not really a taverna, but a great wine bar that serves cold platters and sandwiches, bruschetta and panini, and a good choice of wines and beers. **Baffo** (actually an early Venetian erotic poet!) also serves an amazing range of teas, from Darjeeling and jasmine to ginseng and herbal-fruit teas. Atmospheric inside, this place really hits its mark in good weather, when it has a monopoly on tables on the sweet Campiello Sant'Agostin. There are Tuesday-night concerts, Wednesday-night poetry readings, and other literary events. And all tucked away just off the beaten tourist track. ♦ M-Sa, 7:30AM-2AM. Calle della Chiesa 2346 (on Campiello Sant'Agostin). Tel/fax 5208862

6 Antiche Carampane

★★$$ This small restaurant full of charm is tucked in a labyrinth of tiny alleys away from the busiest streets of San Paolo. The fish is good and the prices are reasonable; hence its largely local clientele. ♦ Tu-Sa, lunch and dinner; Su, lunch. Rio Terrà delle Carampane 1911 (between Rio delle Beccarie and Rio di San Cassiano). 5240165. *Vaporetto* stop: San Silvestro

7 Cantina Do Spade

★★$$ This is a well-known *bacaro*—Casanova was a regular when this tavern was already 300 years old—where *cicchetti* (finger foods) and bonhomie abound. Sample the *prosciutto d'oca* (goose ham); try local specialties like *bigoli in salsa* (thick spaghetti in a savory, anchovy-based sauce) or pasta with *baccalà* (salt cod). The wine list is good. The ultra-friendly *padrone,* lorghe, has just opened "Casanova's Room," candlelit and romantic—with the little back door Casanova used as a quick escape route still there. ♦ M-W, F-Sa, lunch and dinner. Calle Do Spade 860 (between Calle San Mattio and Calle Angelo). 5210574. www.dospadevenezia.it *Vaporetto* stops: Rialto, San Silvestro

8 Cantina Do Mori

★★★$$ It's no wonder this *bacaro* (wine bar) is filled with Venetians before lunch and dinner—a good selection of high-quality wines and a long menu of *cicchetti* (finger foods) and *francobolli* (literally, "postage stamps," sandwiches scarcely bigger than a stamp) make it a real crowd-pleaser. This is one of the oldest Venetian *bacari,* and there's no seating, but you won't want any . . . it's much more fun to stand and soak up the unbeatable atmosphere. ♦ M-Sa, 8:30AM-8:30PM. Calle dei Do Mori 429. 5225401. *Vaporetto* stops: Rialto, San Silvestro

9 Ruga Vecchia San Giovanni

This narrow, busy *ruga* (old Venetian for the French word *rue,* or street) is the main connection between the Rialto and **Campo San Paolo**. Until the 1960s it was also the main shopping street for Venetians, as opposed to the Mercerie across the canal in San Marco, where goods and prices were geared toward tourists. ♦ Between Ruga degli Orefici and Calle Donzella. *Vaporetto* stops: Rialto, San Silvestro

10 Ostaria Antico Dolo

★★$$ At this old-fashioned wine shop the owner lines the counter with a pot of hot *musetto* (boiled sausage), an enticing selection of fishy antipasti including a terrific *sardine in saor* (fresh sardines in a tangy dressing), and little pots of olives, pickles, and crunchy nibbles. It is a great, characterful place to eat and drink. If you want to do things properly, table service and more ambitious dishes such as *seppiolina alla griglia* (grilled baby octopus) and a terrific *risotto di pesce* (seafood risotto) are available. The Antico Dolo have recently instigated "Bacco Time" (two glasses of wine for the price of one) at the bar from 3:30PM-6:30PM. You may never want to leave, but bar service finishes at 7:30, although the kitchen stays open till midnight. ♦ M-Su. Closed July. Ruga Vecchia San Giovanni 778 (between Calle Occhialera and Calle Donzella). 5226546. *Vaporetto* stops: Rialto, San Silvestro

11 Ruga Rialto

★★$ This is a genuinely friendly place with a bar serving *cicchetti* (little tapas-type snacks) ranging from *baccalà mantecato* (a sort of soft pâté made from salt cod) and *fritto misto* (fried seafood) to the most delicious little meatballs you can imagine. Enjoy any or all of these and more, either at the counter or sitting down. Through the back are dining tables and a menu that covers more substantial pastas and main dishes. The food is down-home-good cooking. Don't leave without their most recent house specialty—*nocciolo* (a chocolatey liqueur) served in tiny frozen chocolate thimbles. Mmmm. Come on a Friday night to enjoy live music till late. ♦ Daily. Ruga Vecchia San Giovanni 692 (between Calle del Sturion and Calle Paradiso). 5211243. *Vaporetto* stops: Rialto, San Silvestro

12 Locanda Sturion

$$$ This place has Grand Canal views without grand rates. Amenities such as heated towel racks, coffee-making facilities (instant coffee . . . don't get too excited), and air conditioning make a stay at this smart, 11-room establishment even more enjoyable. There is a small library (multilingual), a selection of videos available, and now Internet access for guests within the hotel. There's no elevator, so steady yourself for the three-flight walk up. If you're not lucky enough to procure one of the two rooms on the canal, take solace with breakfast in the pretty canalside dining room. ♦ Calle del Sturion 679 (between Fondamenta del Vin and Ruga Vecchia San Giovanni). 5236243; fax 5228378. e-mail: sturion@tin.it. *Vaporetto* stops: Rialto, San Silvestro

The Best

John-Henry Bowden

Anglican Chaplain in Venice at St. George's Church

My bests vary as I discover more, but at present they are:

The great **St. George's Dragon Hunt** (also featured on our web site). You will have seen around the city, though you may not have noticed, several bas-relief panels depicting St. George slaying the dragon, generally attached to random buildings at first-floor height and about two or three feet square. The object of the Dragon Hunt is to locate as many of these as you can, and in the process to discover some other corners of the city that you mightn't have thought of visiting. If the visitor contacts the Chaplain's house by phone, 041 520 0571, we will supply, for the modest outlay of 10 euros payable to the St. George's Appeal Fund, a treasure hunt that is a set of instructions and a map for finding most (but not all) of them, and on return here with the locating questions duly answered, a magnificent Souvenir Certificate to record their achievement. The full route takes five to six hours, or one can see just the central ones in about two to three hours. A sense of curiosity and adventure are recommended for success.

For a spiritual experience, I would choose to see the mosaic **Madonna and Child** in the apse of the cathedral at Torcello and the **Veronese Crucifixion** in room 10 of the Accademia. Both will repay long periods of silent meditation. For the Veronese, you need to take your Bible and read one of the Gospel accounts of Jesus' passion as you look at it and see how many details of the story are to be found in the picture.

Explore the lagoon—preferably, if you are lucky (or rich) enough to get the use of one, in your own boat.

Even if you have your own boat, the ACTV trip by *vaporetto* to the Lido—bus no. 11, ferry, bus again, boat—and down to Chioggia is fun, and gives you a whole different insight on life here. It's also a good way to get the maximum value of your lagoon boat ticket, which covers the Lido buses as well.

I'd recommend the former cathedral of **San Pietro in Castello**. It's quiet there and retains a spiritual quality; and then there's also the sense of wonder that such a leaning campanile can possibly still stay up!

Hope this is helpful. I would have given **San Giorgio Maggiore** a mention of its own, being in my opinion Palladio's best, but it comes into the Dragon Hunt anyway!

12 Locanda Ovidius

$$ On the floor (soon to be two floors) immediately beneath the Locanda Sturion, the **Ovidius** has nine traditionally furnished rooms at present but will be expanding very soon. Two of the rooms have canal views, and all have air conditioning, Jacuzzi, bath or shower, hair dryer, minibar, and television. The breakfast room (with canal-front terrace) is sweet, and the charming gentleman in charge bears an almost spooky resemblance to a younger version of Dirk Bogarde in *Death in Venice*. ♦ Calle del Sturion 677a. 5237970; fax 5294101. e-mail: info@hotelovidius.com. www.hotelovidius.com. *Vaporetto* stops: Rialto, San Silvestro

13 Trattoria Alla Madonna

★★$$ One of the few restaurants in Venice that serves really fresh fish at decent prices, this place is a local favorite. It dates back more than 50 years, and the eclectic clientele keeps it lively. Dine here and you rub elbows with everyone from upper-crust Venetians and tourists to gondoliers who park their craft on the nearby stretch of the Grand Canal. Try the risottos and the *granseola* appetizer (a type of delicious crabmeat). In season you can try *tartufi de mare* (sea truffles—delicious!) by the half dozen. ♦ M, Tu, Th-Su, lunch and dinner. Calle della Madonna 594 (between Fondamenta del Vin and Ruga Vecchia San Giovanni). 5223824. *Vaporetto* stops: Rialto, San Silvestro

13 Ostaria al Diavo'lo e l'Aquasanta

★★$ This little hole-in-the-wall *osteria* is quintessential Venice: the people, the wine and the food. The *cicchetti* (little snacks) on offer behind glass on the bar are a truly delicious Italian adventure for your taste buds. Just point and say *uno di questi* (one of those). They are also the greatest bargain since the Native Americans sold Manhattan. Many of them are offered in different-size portions—a snack size or a meal size. Alongside these there is always a good choice of lasagne or pasta with meatballs—all homemade, all excellent. Eat at a table or just stand at the bar. There is a good choice of wines and beers. ♦ M, 10AM-3PM; W-Su, 10AM-3PM and 6PM-midnight. Calle della Madonna 561b. 2770307; fax 2775757. *Vaporetto* stops: Rialto, San Silvestro

14 Campo San Giacomo

During the daytime it's hard to see the beauty of this little square, crammed as it is with vegetable stands and shabby canopies. But at night the little church, fondly called **San Giacometto** by the locals, evokes a time when human size was more important than imperial magnificence. Its 12th-century portico, once common in front of churches, is one of very few left in Venice. The handsome clock on the bell tower dates back to the 15th century, and the original Greek marble columns inside feature 11th-century capitals.

From the early times of the Republic until the 18th century, this square was the Wall Street of Venice. Here, the modern banking system was first invented: Bankers had their tables on the square or under the nearby colonnade, and they would record transactions in their books, avoiding the transfer of real gold and silver. ♦ At Ruga degli Orefici. *Vaporetto* stop: Rialto

15 Mercato della Frutta (Produce Market)

Despite the rapid transformation of the rest of the market into a tourist trap, the fresh produce market (also called *Erberia*) is still very much alive at the foot of the Rialto Bridge near the **Pescheria** (Fish Market). ♦ M-Sa. Ruga degli Orefici (between Ponte di Rialto and Campo San Giacomo). *Vaporetto* stop: Rialto

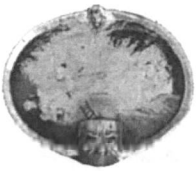

La Bottega dei Mascareri

16 La Bottega dei Mascareri

Woody Allen is a signed-up fan of this guy, so he must be all right. Amid the produce stands and tourist shops on the San Paolo side of the bridge, this mask shop is a standout. Sergio Boldrin's small *botteghe* (workshop) has been praised for its high-quality collection of masks—no small feat given the number of mask shops that have cropped up since *Carnevale* was reinstated in 1980. The artisan produces a variety of papier-mâché commedia dell'arte characters, as well as court jesters and more contemporary fantasy masks, but their common characteristic is the artistry with which they are lovingly created. ♦ Daily (no midday closing). Ruga degli Orefici 80 (between Ponte di Rialto and Campo San Giacomo). 5223857. *Vaporetto* stop: Rialto

17 Ponte di Rialto (Rialto Bridge)

Built at the end of the 16th century, this stone bridge replaced a wooden drawbridge that was too low for ships' masts to pass under. Until the middle of the 19th century, it was the only passage across the Canal Grande and the only link between the three city districts *de citra* ("on this side") and the three *de ultra* ("on that side"). Appropriately enough, the architect's name was **Antonio da Ponte** (no relation of the painter better known as Bassano). Competition for the bridge commission was fierce; proposals by **Michelangelo**, **Andrea Palladio**, and **Jacopo Sansovino** were all rejected in favor of da Ponte's arcaded design. Perhaps one reason his plan was preferred was his inclusion of shops lining the interior of the bridge. After all, the Rialto was the mercantile center of the city. Today these small stores sell everything from fine gold to not so fine machine made masks. The down stream façade of the bridge is decorated with a high relief of the *Annunciation* by Agostino Rubini. The buildings on the San Marco side, now owned by the city bishopry, are rented as apartments to a few lucky Venetians—lucky because the rental prices are established by a national law, which does not take into account such things as views. On the San Paolo side are two Renaissance palazzi; the building to the right (north) is the 16th-century **Palazzo dei Camerlenghi** (Finance Ministry), the ground floor of which once served as a prison. The palazzo to the left (south) housed the **Dieci Savi**, the 10 magistrates in charge of collecting taxes. ♦ Between Riva del Ferro and Fondamenta del Vin. *Vaporetto* stop: Rialto

18 Archivio di Stato (State Archives)

The **Frari** church opens onto a small square along a canal appropriately called Rio dei Frari. The building to your left as you exit, once part of the large Franciscan monastery attached to the church, has two charming cloisters, one of which is attributed to Jacopo Sansovino. Today the building houses what remains of the Venetian Republic, one of the richest, best organized archives in the world. The doges very carefully conserved all kinds of documents related to the city's government. Some 15 million files—some as much as 10 inches thick—are stored along many miles of shelves. They tell the story of Venice month by month and often even day by day. Ambassadors' letters and international files in the archives have proved invaluable in the study of the history of Europe. A competent and kind staff welcomes dozens of scholars from all over the world every day. ♦ Campo dei Frari 3002 (at Rio dei Frari). *Vaporetto* stop: San Tomà

19 Scuola Grande di San Rocco (Great School of St. Roch)

Most of the great Renaissance architects of Venice contributed to this remarkable building that epitomizes the stylistic trends of that period: The ground floor was started in 1516 by **Bartolomeo Bon**, the middle and top floors were added by **Sante Lombardo** and **Scarpagnino**, and the final touches were contributed by **Gian Giacomo dei Grigi**. Like its neighboring rival at **St. John the Evangelist** (see page 228), the brotherhood of St. Roch was a powerful association of merchants, storekeepers, and other members of the Venetian bourgeoisie, whose purposes ranged from assisting the poor to redeeming sinners and helping the sick during times of plague.

St. Roch himself was born in Montpelier in France in 1295 and spent his life from the age of 20 helping plague victims in southern France and Italy. After his death a cult grew up around him, and his body was taken to Venice in 1485 in the belief that it would ward off the plague; when the brotherhood commissioned Jacopo Tintoretto to decorate the interior of the building, it tied its name forever to one of the most extraordinary cycles of paintings in the history of Venice.

Start your visit on the second floor. A large door on the left side of the **Salone Maggiore** (to be visited later) leads to the **Sala dell'Albergo**, the first room decorated by Tintoretto in 1565. A majestic *Crucifixion* on the back wall sets the tone for the artist's amazing exploits in the composition of figures, in the use of light, and in surprising perspectives. On the ceiling, Tintoretto painted *St. Roch in Glory,* the sample work that helped him win the commission for the whole cycle (among the painters he competed against was Veronese). On the other walls of the room are *Christ in Front of Pilate*, *Ecce Homo*, and *Christ Carrying the Cross*. Back in the Salone Maggiore, the painting immediately to the right of the door is a Tintoretto portrait said by some to be of the artist himself. The ceiling here consists of 21 canvases on which the artist depicted stories of the Old Testament; the New Testament was illustrated in the large paintings on the walls. On the long wall in front of the staircase are *The Nativity*, *The Baptism*, *The Resurrection*, *The Agony in the Garden*, and *The Last Supper*; in front of the altar are *St. Sebastian* and *St. Roch*; on the entrance wall are *The Temptation of Christ*, *The Pool of Bathsheba*, *The Ascension*, *The Resurrection of Lazarus*, and *The Miracle of the Loaves and Fishes*. The altarpiece, also by Tintoretto, represents *St. Roch in Glory*. Standing on easels on the sides of the altar are an *Annunciation* by Titian and a *Visitation* by Tintoretto; in front of the banisters, also on easels, are two youthful paintings by Giambattista Tiepolo: *Abraham with Angels* and *Hagar Abandoned*. The cycle continues with eight large canvases in the ground-floor hall (**Salone Terreno**) that tell stories from the life of the Virgin Mary. These were the last works Tintoretto executed for the brotherhood and were completed when the painter was nearly 70. They are, starting from the left side: *The Annunciation*, *The Epiphany*, *The Flight into Egypt*, *The Slaughter of the Innocents*, *St. Mary Magdalen*, *St. Mary of Egypt*, *The Circumcision*, and *The Assumption*. ♦ Admission. Daily. Campo San Rocco 3054 (at Calle della Scuola). 5234864. *Vaporetto* stop: San Tomà

Andàr ombrizando in Venetian dialect labels the enjoyable pastime of going from _osteria_ to _osteria_ drinking little glasses (_ombre_) of wine.

20 Santa Maria Gloriosa dei Frari (Frari)

Frari is a local word for friars: monks of a mendicant order, and in particular Franciscans. The Franciscans were a more popular order than their rivals, the Dominicans. Their emphasis was on prayer and poverty, while the Dominicans specialized in learning and education. In Venice the two orders tried to outdo each other in the size and elaborateness of their main churches. While the Dominicans were building their grandiose **Santi Giovanni e Paolo** (see page 263), the Franciscans vastly enlarged the old chapel in their monastery, spending decades in the 14th century integrating the entire old church into the transept of the new one. At the time, the Franciscans owned all of San Paolo island, which was then mostly marshland, and the order laboriously filled in the marsh to make it buildable over the course of centuries. Today the order owns only a small part of the area, while the rest is covered with houses, streets, and squares.

The exterior of the church they built is sober and mostly unadorned. The most attractive parts are the apses and the campanile, the second highest in Venice after the one in **Piazza San Marco**. The interior, on the other hand, is awe-inspiring—in spite of its vast size, it maintains a sense of perfect unity. Like the Dominicans' Santi Giovanni e Paolo, this church is a kind of Venetian Pantheon, thickly adorned with the tombs of prominent citizens and masterworks by the best Venetian artists.

A visit should start with a walk from the back door through the magnificent 15th-century carved wood choir [1] (numbers refer to floor plan, page 233) to the main altar [2], above

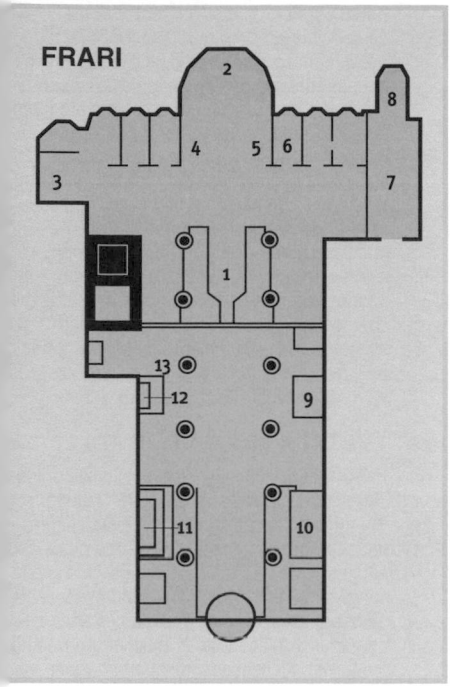

which hangs one of the masterworks of all time: Titian's *Assumption of the Virgin,* painted in 1516-1518, when the artist was in his late 20s. Surpassing Giovanni Bellini, Titian introduced new concepts in composition (such as the space division in horizontal layers, with the emphatic hands and uptilted faces of the people pointing to the Virgin) and in the use of color. Titian's contemporaries were struck by the realism of the work: The Virgin "really seems to fly upwards" and the Apostles "show marvel and happiness as if they were alive," noted Ludovico Dolce in 1577. "All painters," Dolce continued, "tried to imitate this new way, but as they embarked on this totally new territory, they were immediately lost."

The altarpiece in the **Corner Chapel** [3], *St. Mark Enthroned* (1474), is one of the last masterworks of Bartolomeo Vivarini. A comparison with the nearby *Assumption* by Titian shows the dramatic changes that occurred in Venetian painting during the 42 years that separate the two works.

The chancel contains two important monuments. The *Tomb of Doge Niccolò Tron* [4], on the left wall, was completed by Antonio Rizzo in 1476 and is considered one of the best examples of Venetian Renaissance sculpture. The doge is portrayed standing in the central niche, with Charity and Prudence on either side; he is also sculpted lying on top of his cinerary urn, under a lunette with bas-reliefs of *Christ with God the Father* and *The Annunciation*. Across the chancel is Antonio Bregno's *Monument to Doge Francesco Foscari* [5], one of the greatest Venetian leaders. Completed 20 years before the Tron monument, this work mixes the old Venetian Gothic style with influences of the Renaissance from central Italy.

The first chapel at the right of the altar [6] contains a marvelous wood sculpture of *St. John the Baptist* by Donatello.

The **Sacristy** [7] was built in the 15th century with donations from the wealthy Pesaro family, one of the most prominent families in Venetian history. The monument on top of the Sacristy door represents Benedetto Pesaro, an admiral in the Venetian navy. The altarpiece in the small chapel off the Sacristy is decorated with one of the best paintings by Giovanni Bellini, *Madonna and Child with Four Saints* [8], in the original carved wood frame.

Return through the choir screen to the nave of the church. The statue of *St. Jerome* [9] in the right aisle is one of the best works of Alessandro Vittoria, a 16th-century sculptor who is abundantly represented in Venetian churches. Farther down the aisle is a 19th-century *Monument to Titian* by Luigi and Pietro Zandomeneghi [10]. Titian died during a plague and was probably buried here. The monument was first commissioned from Antonio Canova, but was built by the Zandomeneghi, Canova's pupils, after the master's death. It is one of the latest examples of neoclassical sculpture in Venice.

In 1827, Canova's plans for the Titian monument were used by a team of his pupils, including the Zandomeneghi, for a monument to Canova himself [11]. The statues on the sides of the pyramid's open door represent *The Arts, St. Mark's Lion,* and *Genius*. Although Canova's body is elsewhere, his heart is inside the pyramid in a vase of porphyry. This entire corner of the nave is occupied by an imposing Baroque *Monument to Doge Giovanni Pesaro,* based on plans by Baldassare Longhena.

The *Pesaro Madonna* [12] was painted by Titian in 1526. Here again the artist broke with some of the most venerated rules in composition and the use of color. The striking perspective of the painting is explained by Titian's attempt to attract the eyes of visitors walking up the aisle from the church's main door; the two gigantic columns in the painting are an ideal continuation of the real columns supporting the church's roof. Nearby is the burial place of yet another member of the Pesaro family, Bishop Jacopo Pesaro [13]. ♦ Admission. M-Sa, 9AM-6PM; Su, 1PM-6PM. Campo dei Frari (between Rio dei Frari and

Salizzada San Rocco). 5222637. *Vaporetto* stop: San Tomà

21 Giberto Penzo

This little shop was opened in the late 1980s by a young artist in love with all kinds of Venetian boats, both ancient and contemporary. The astonishing variety of hulls and shapes adapted to different purposes is reproduced here in wood models and drawings. Some of the posters on sale are popular because they represent the dozen or so lagoon craft that are still in wide use and recognizable in the canals. ♦ M-Sa. Calle Seconda dei Saoneri 2681 (between Calle dei Saoneri and Rio Terrà). 719372. *Vaporetto* stop: San Tomà

22 San Paolo

The rather odd orientation of this church, with the apse facing the square and the entrance cut into one of the sides, is due to the changes the area has undergone through the centuries. The façade originally opened onto a canal. The church has been modified many times since construction on it began in the ninth century: The rose window is Gothic, and the exterior is neoclassical. Inside is calm and dim. Some of the masterpieces hanging here have little buttons that you press to get the light to come on for a while, the better to see works like Tintoretto's *Last Supper* and Giambattista Tiepolo's The *Virgin Appearing to St. John Nepomuk.* The highlight of the church is, however, in the little **Oratorio del Crocefisso**. This is a small chapel holding, hung round the walls, Giandomenico Tiepolo's *Via Crucis*—13 paintings depicting the Stations of the Cross. Wonderful paintings, wonderfully preserved. If you are feeling emotionally drained by the time you get to the end, look up at the ceiling for the "happy ending," Tiepolo's paintings of the Resurrection. ♦ M-Sa, 10AM-5PM; Su, 1PM-5PM. Campo San Paolo (at Salizzada San Paolo). *Vaporetto* stops: San Tomà, San Silvestro

23 Campo San Paolo

When the weather is nice, this square fairly brims with neighborhood life (children, mothers, and senior citizens relaxing on the benches in the sun). The curved eastern wall was built in the 15th century along the banks of a canal that was later filled. Looming over the wall are the 15th-century Gothic **Palazzi Soranzo** (**Nos. 2169-71**), and dominating the other side of the square is the **Palazzo Corner Mocenigo** (**No. 2128**), designed by **Michele Sanmichele** in 1543. For centuries the *campo* was used for fairs, outdoor theater performances, and even bullfights. Today, on hot summer evenings it becomes an open-air movie theater. Eight hundred chairs are fitted around an enormous screen, and people whose windows happen to open onto the square have no choice but to watch with any Venetians who have not fled to the seaside (and a few tourists interested in Italian-language films). The San Paolo summer movies have quickly become a tradition, with people lingering after the shows, enjoying the cozy feeling of belonging to a small and special community. ♦ At Calle Madonnetta, Salizzada San Paolo, and Calle Corner. *Vaporetto* stops: San Tomà, San Silvestro

Venice was divided into six *sestieri* (districts) for the purpose of taxation in the 12th century; the number of districts remains the same today.

24 I Vetri a Lume di Amadi

This tiny shop, fittingly, sells tiny things. A lone glass craftsman creates a world in miniature. But a most unusual world. There are cherries and red currants, gooseberries, pod peas, and all manner of beans. There are delicate glass sprigs of mistletoe and sprays of flowers. And there are animals and birds—turtles and tiny quarter-inch elephants, 2-millimeter pigs, and the tiniest dachshunds imaginable. There are little ladybirds for luck and all the fish and crustacea of the lagoon. An extraordinary little shop. ♦ M-Sa. Calle dei Saoneri 2747. 5238089. *Vaporetto* stop: San Tomà

25 Trattoria da Ignazio

★★$$$ Ignazio buys the freshest fish and vegetables at the market, and his wife, Ada, prepares them in basic, no-frills ways—poached, baked, or grilled, all very simple and good. The fresh vegetables and polenta, which also come grilled, are excellent too. The restaurant does get very busy, and service can suffer. Your bill comes with a "sweetener" of a tiny, chocolate-coated ice cream. ♦ M-F, Su, lunch and dinner. Calle dei Saoneri 2749 (between Rio di San Paolo and Rio Terrà dei Nomboli). 5234852. *Vaporetto* stop: San Tomà

26 Casa di Goldoni

The great Venetian playwright Carlo Goldoni was born here in 1707. The small palazzo now houses the **Istituto di Studi Teatrali** (Institute for Theatrical Studies), with a small museum and a **Theater Library** open to students and scholars. ♦ M-Sa, 10AM-4PM. Theater Studies Center: Tu, Th, 8:30AM-5PM; M, W, F, 8:30AM-1PM. Calle dei Nomboli 2793 (at Ramo Pisani). 5236353. *Vaporetto* stop: San Tomà

26 Tragicomica

As you probably will have seen by now, Venice is up to her glorious armpits in shops selling *Carnevale* masks. But not shops like this. Here they make them and display and

The Best

Amabel Grant

Management Consultant

Drinking your first ever Spritz con Aperol at the **Fiori** in Calle delle Botteghe under the slightly disapproving look of the bar staff, then knowing you are off the hook when you receive a big smile from them.

Wandering through the ghetto at dusk.

The best collection of Renaissance art that exists in the world, at the **Galleria dell'Accademia**.

Caffè Corretto. With grappa, of course.

Buying the most beautiful pair of handmade shoes that you have ever owned.

The view from the top of the **Campanile**.

Christmas Day in Venice: a long lunch at **Harry's Bar** with Venice artist Geoffrey Humphries and family, followed by feeding the pigeons their Christmas lunch in **St. Mark's Square** and then sipping cocktails in the **Danieli**, lounging next to the Christmas tree.

Cicchetti–sarde in saor at **Alla Vedova**, oysters at **La Cantina**, *polpette* at the **Fiori**, and watching your lover eat *nervetti* at the **Diavolo e l'Aqua Santa** even if you can't quite pluck up the courage to try this Venetian specialty for yourself!

The bridge position: take your lover, stand on a bridge with him/her–any bridge–and look down the canal. Your arm will automatically slip around him/her, his/her head will automatically rest on your shoulder. You will know when you have the position just right. And you will find it only happens on bridges!

Leaving Venice in a water taxi early in the morning in brilliant sunshine with intense turquoise blue skies, knowing you are coming back again soon.

sell them. Along with wonderful commedia dell'arte-themed puppets, fat golden cherubs that hang above you, are tiny scale-model theaters in a variety of sizes and a wonderful selection of beautiful walking sticks with figured tops in silver, ceramic, or carved wood. They also–should you be here in February–make *Carnevale* costumes. Just when you thought you were sick of masks, this place makes them magical again! ♦ Daily, 10AM-7PM. Calle dei Nomboli 2800 (opposite Casa di Goldoni). 721102. www.tragicomica.it. *Vaporetto* stop: San Tomà

27 Campo San Tomà

This is an understated little *campo*–as Venetian *campos* go–but one with plenty to offer . . . At No. 2867 there is **Cicogna**, home to some of the most over-the-top reproduction work in Venice. If you are looking for a life-size black-faced Moorish slave-shaped candleholder, then this would be where to come–it's camp, kitsch, and fabulously politically incorrect (M-F, 3861946). Next door, at No. 2868, **Lucatello** makes wonderful chairs and sofas–classy, comfortable, and classic. Across the square at No. 2849, **Mario Sfriso** has a shop selling his marvelous silver creations (M-Sa). Dying for a pizza? **Ostaria San Tomà** offers a great selection, plus a choice of what they call "spaghettimania." Just look out for the graduation parties they hold on request; they can get loud (lunch and dinner; closed Tu).

28 Vizio Virtu

Apologies to any diabetics reading this guide, but this shop had to go in. It is not just a shop but an artist's studio and workshop. This artist works in chocolate. Giovanna Mariangela is the *cioccolatiere* in question, and she creates all the gorgeous things you see and smell here. She began learning about chocolate–how and where the beans grow, the different types of beans and chocolates, how they are processed–and now chocolate is her life. She is a tiny slim creature with perfect skin, so perhaps hers is magic chocolate! It comes as hearts and boxes, spoons and chocolate alphabets in a bag; it comes as buttons and shavings and bars and, of course, filled chocolates. But these fillings are like nothing you have ever tasted. Each was created and developed by Giovanna herself. There are chocolates filled with creams flavored with fine red wines and dessert wines, grappa, and even balsamic vinegar. There is a ganache made with olive oil and fillings flavored with star anise, thyme, chamomile, wild fennel, and green tea. There are honey-filled chocolates, and chocolates scented with peperoncino or cinnamon. I have practically eaten my own weight in the chocolate she fills with soft caramel and studs with Scottish rock salt. Sip a tiny cup of dense, intense hot chocolate while making up your mind what to buy. Diet tomorrow. ♦ Daily, 10AM-7:30PM. Calle del Campanile 2898/A. 2750149. www.viziovirtu.com

SANTA CROCE

Santa Croce is a wonderful, quiet area of lazy backwater canals, crisscrossed by little bridges and a meandering maze of tiny alleyways and gently bustling streets. There can be no other city in the world offering such charm in the area that surrounds the main bus station. But two minutes from the **Piazzale Roma** and you are in the heart of neighborhood Venice. Here are little boutiques and workshops, low-key local restaurants, and laid-back bars. This is one area that will make you forget you are a tourist and make you feel like a traveler.

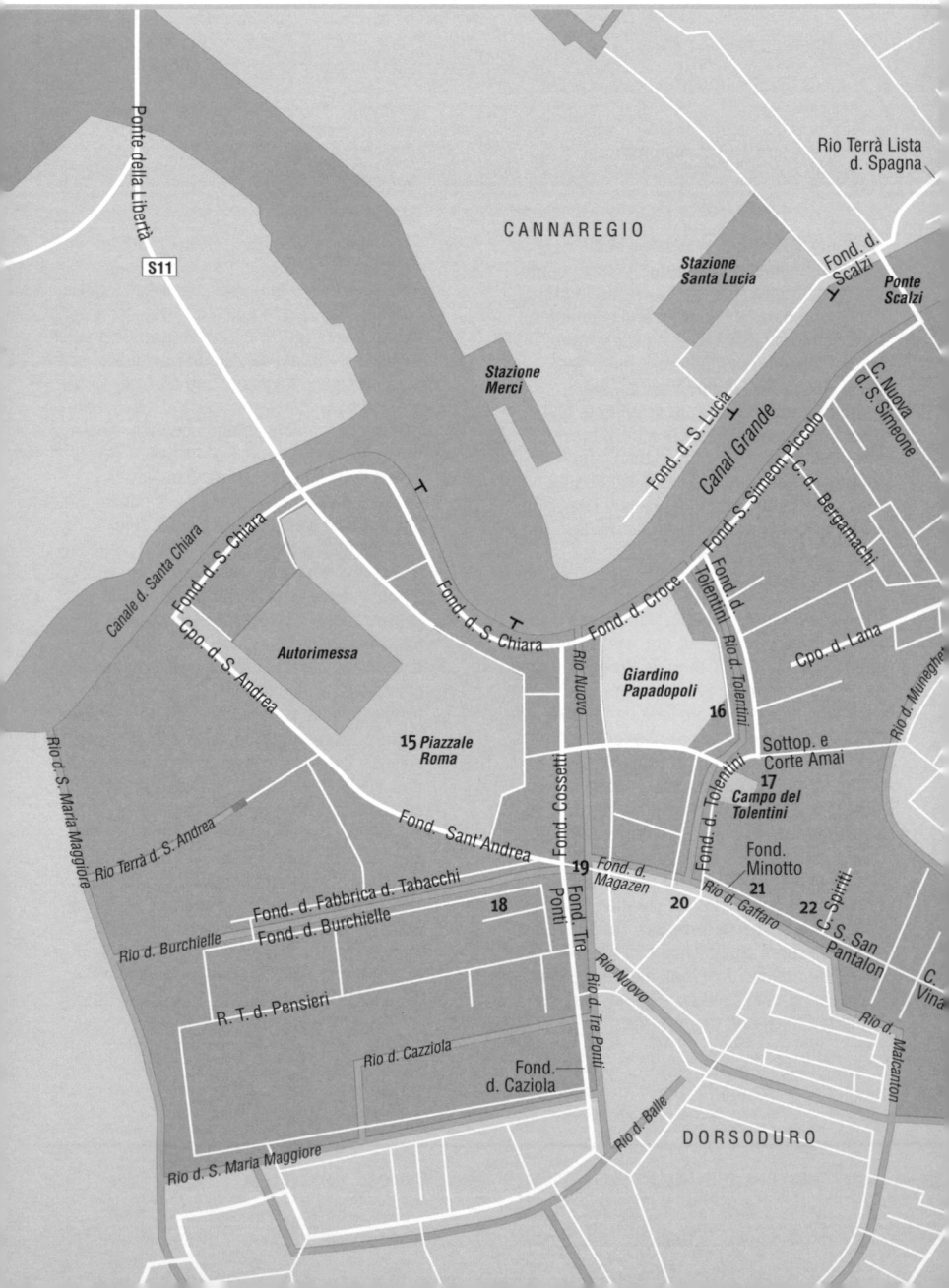

1 Museo di Storia Naturale (Museum of Natural History)

The **Fondaco dei Turchi**, the palazzo housing this museum, is one of the oldest and most unusual in Venice. The best way to appreciate its splendid façade is from the Canal Grande or from the opposite bank. The museum includes the usual exhibitions of animals, plants, and fossils. The highlights are a large dinosaur skeleton found in the Sahara desert in 1973 (the digging was financed and directed by a wealthy Venetian entrepreneur) and the rooms showing animal life in the Venice lagoon. ♦ Admission. Tu-Su. Salizzada del Fondaco dei Turchi 1730 (between Ramo del Megio and Canal Grande). 5240885. *Vaporetto* stops: Riva di Biasio, San Stae

2 Campo San Zan Degolà

There is a magical beauty to this secret spot frequented by locals. The small square, flanked by a narrow canal and adorned with a 10th-century church (the façade was redone in the 18th century), offers escape from the bustle of the city. ♦ At Rio di San Zan Degolà. *Vaporetto* stop: Riva di Biasio

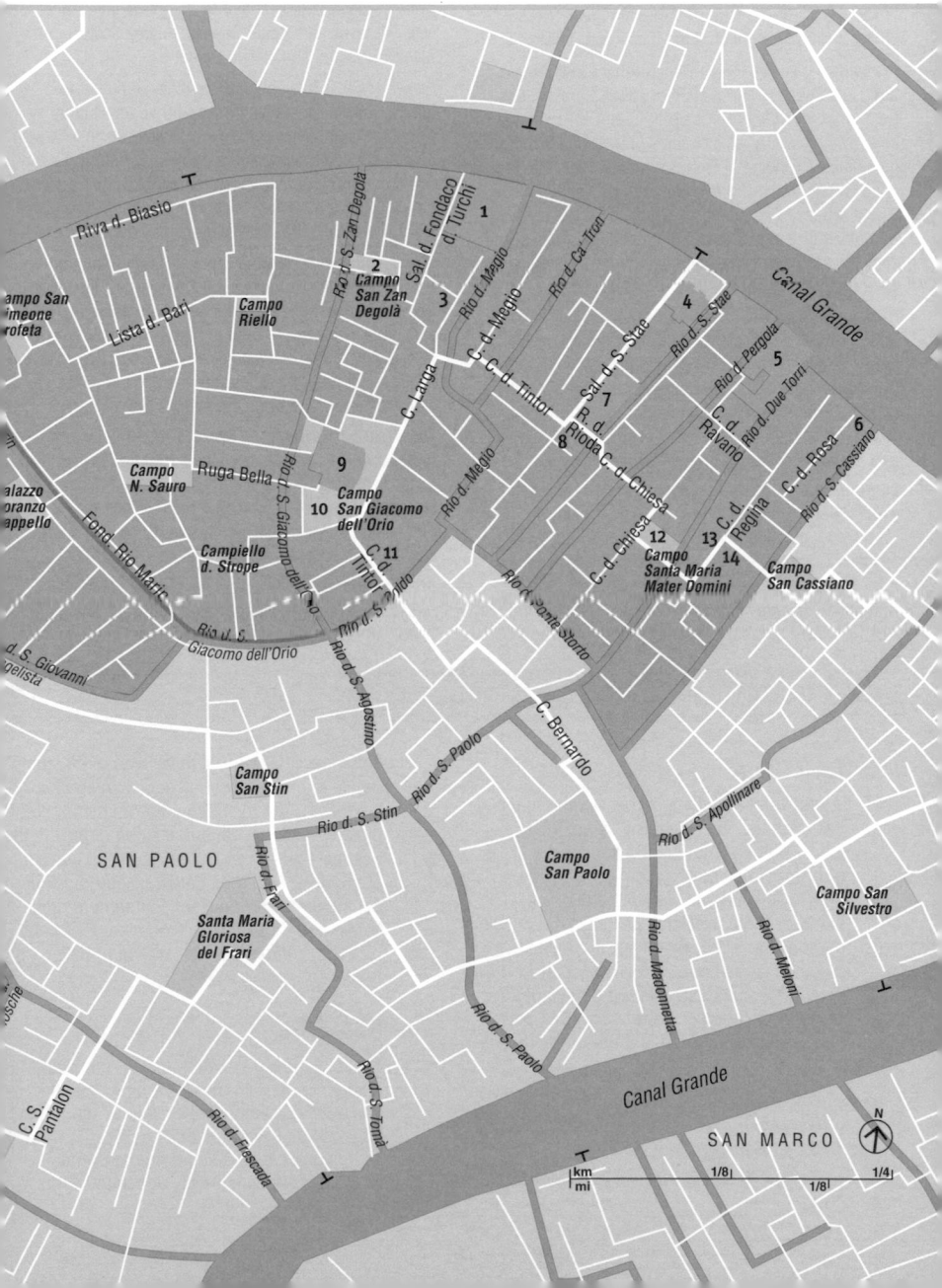

Lights, Camera, Action

Whether they were searching for an airy Renaissance light or brooding Gothic menace, movie directors have long turned to Florence and Venice and the neighboring countryside for inspiration. Among the films to take advantage of the unique settings in these two cities and in Tuscany and the Veneto are the following:

Florence

Paisan (1946) This early Roberto Rossellini and Federico Fellini classic uses six vignettes to depict life in Italy during World War II. The best has an American nurse (Harriet White) searching for her lover in battle-torn Florence.

Portrait of a Lady (1996) Filmed mostly in Florence and Lucca under the direction of Jane Campion, this adaptation of Henry James's late-19th-century novel shows us the stuffy social circles of British/American high society residing in Florence at that time. The focus is on Isabel (played by Nicole Kidman), the vivacious young American innocent who plans a life of freedom and adventure only to become entangled in the web of sophisticated admirers, particularly John Malkovich and John Gielgud.

A Room with a View (1986) This elegant and witty adaptation of the E. M. Forster novel about English mores brings to life an innocent girl (Helena Bonham Carter), who arrives in Florence with her chaperone (Maggie Smith) to spend time in the city. The well-reared Edwardian girl has her eyes opened to real life and romance, falling in love in the process.

La Sindrome di Stendhal (*Stendhal's Syndrome*; 1996) This bizarre thriller was directed by Dario Argento and stars his daughter Asia Argento as a policewoman trying to capture a serial rapist and killer. She suffers from Stendhal's Syndrome, a psychosomatic disease that makes people dizzy and prone to hallucinations when exposed to artistic masterpieces in great number. The maniac lures her into a trap inside Florence's **Uffizi**, where her troubles only begin.

Tuscany

The English Patient (1996) A dying unidentified soldier is brought to a makeshift hospital in Tuscany after World War II. The complex story, told in flashbacks, is of three relationships, one adulterous, one interracial, and the third between a nurse and her patient. Filmed near **Pienza** south of **Siena** and in northern Africa, this Academy Award–winning adaptation of Michael Ondaatje's prize-winning novel stars Ralph Fiennes, Kristen Scott Thomas, Juliette Binoche, and Willem Dafoe.

Fiorile (1993) Two children are told the story of a family curse that has lasted for 200 years. During Napoleon's presence in Tuscany, a girl falls in love with a French soldier. Directed by Paolo and Vittorio Taviani, this complex story line traces the curse to the present day, leaving the audience wondering until the very end if it will be passed on to this youngest generation.

Much Ado About Nothing (1993) Directed by and starring Kenneth Branagh, this film tells the tale of Benedick (Branagh) and Beatrice (Emma Thompson), who have sworn never to marry but are tricked into falling in love with each other anyway. This lively version of Shakespeare's witty and romantic comedy is set and shot entirely in and around a villa in Tuscany.

The Night of the Shooting Stars (1982) The Taviani brothers again turn their directorial attention to their home region in this movie about a group of Tuscan villagers during World War II in the final days before liberation by the Americans. In Italian folklore, the night of the shooting stars (of San Lorenzo) is when dreams come true.

Stealing Beauty (1996) After her mother commits suicide, a young American woman comes to visit friends of her parents at their home in the Tuscan countryside

3 La Zucca

★★$$ Opened by a group of women in the early 1970s, "The Pumpkin" is an informal eatery that has maintained a relaxed, simple atmosphere all these years. The emphasis here is still on good vegetarian cooking, although there are some delicious-sounding meat dishes such as *coniglie al prosecco con polenta* (rabbit cooked in Prosecco served on polenta). You can start with a tangy appetizer of *pepperoni al aceto balsamico* (bell peppers roasted and marinated in a dressing of aged balsamic vinegar) and finish with a refreshing *fragile al prosecco* (strawberries in sparkling Prosecco). The menu changes as the market dictates, but you can be assured of having the best of what the day offers. ♦ M-Sa, lunch and dinner. No credit cards accepted. Ramo del Megio 1762 (between Fondamenta del Megio and Salizzada del Fondaco dei Turchi). 5241570. *Vaporetto* stops: Riva di Biasio, San Stae

Ernest Hemingway said the following about Burano: ". . . an overcrowded little island where the women make splendid lace and the men make children."

4 San Stae

The name is old Venetian dialect for *Sant' Eustachio*. As with most Venetian churches, this one was remodeled at various times—the original building dates back to the 12th century. As can be seen from the Canal Grande, the façade, richly decorated with nd discovers family secrets and her own sexuality. ilmed around Siena, the scenery steals much of the nunder from an international cast of actors, including inead Cusack, Lucy Harmon, Jeremy Irons, and Liv Tyler.

nder the Tuscan Sun (2003) Superschmaltz set in uscany. Girl loses boy, girl finds Tuscany, and then girl nds another boy. All quirky locals, glorious countryside, omedy, domestic disasters, and a dream lifestyle nded by an unexplained level of private income.

enice

asanova (2005) Well, where else would it be filmed? eath Ledger, latest in a long, long line of Casanovas, t least gets to frolic through the real Venice. Even if he oesn't seem much like the real Casanova.

he Comfort of Strangers (1990) Natasha Richardson nd Rupert Everett star in this bleak and icy tale about conventional couple on vacation in Venice, where ney become involved with mysterious locals (Christo- her Walken and Helen Mirren).

eath In Venice (1971) Thomas Mann's slow-moving lassic is brought to the screen by director Luchino isconti. An artist (Dirk Bogarde) is caught up in his fe, his loves, his homosexuality, and a continuous earch for everlasting beauty. The musical score is by ustav Mahler, whom Bogarde is made up to esemble.

on't Look Now (1973) An arty, gripping Daphne du laurier occult thriller follows the parents (Julie Christie nd Donald Sutherland) of a drowned child through neir horror-laden visit to Venice.

rom Russia with Love (1963) Starring Sean Connery, ne second James Bond film is one of the best. In true 007 style, a highly charged boat chase, with plenty of uspense and action, winds through the waterways of enice.

Italian for Beginners (2001) This lovely little romantic comedy is about a class of Italian students in Copenhagen who go to Venice to hone their language skills.

Summertime (1955) David Lean directs this lilting film about an American spinster (Katharine Hepburn) vacationing in Venice and falling in love with a married man (Rossano Brazzi).

The Talented Mr. Ripley (1999) Anthony Minghella's follow-up to *The English Patient,* based on Patricia Highsmith's novel, features glorious views of Italy in the service of a plot that finds Matt Damon as a psychopathic killer enamored of Jude Law. The incandescent Cate Blanchett far outstrips everyone else—particularly a simpering Gwyneth Paltrow—in this stylish but ultimately empty cinematic treat.

Venice/Venice (1992) Director Henry Jaglom pretentiously parodies himself, playing a "maverick" American filmmaker at the Venice Film Festival, where a French journalist (Nelly Alard) becomes involved with him. The title refers to Venice, Italy, and Venice, California, where the director also is shown to have a coterie of admirers.

The Wings of the Dove (1997) Helena Bonham Carter gives the performance of her young career in this evocative tale of lust, greed, and their heartbreaking consequences. Henry James's novel is portrayed in all its Venetian splendor (with particular help from gorgeous costumes by Sandy Powell); the *gondolieri*'s songs provide the perfect lament to all that could have been—if only.

The Veneto

Romeo and Juliet (1968) The world's most famous love story, set in what Shakespeare fondly called "fair Verona," finds the perfect modern spirit in director Franco Zefferelli. His adaptation faithfully re-creates Italian medieval life, with dusty piazze and battlemented walls, but imbues the film with a lusty sense of young love.

statues, is one of the finest examples of Venetian Baroque. The interior is particularly interesting for art historians because it includes a wealth of paintings from the first half of the 18th century. The artists are not among the most famous (Camerata, Pittoni, Bambini, Balestra), but their work illustrates the process that produced painters like Tiepolo and Piazzetta. Piazzetta himself is represented here on the lower left of the chancel (*The Martyrdom of St. James*), and there is a youthful Tiepolo on the lower right (*The Martyrdom of St. Bartholomew*). Next to the Piazzetta is *St. Peter Freed from Prison* by Sebastiano Ricci, who also painted the chancel's ceiling. Ricci was one of the painters most influential in merging the new trends developed by the Roman Baroque painters with the Venetian tradition of Veronese, thus opening the way to the last great season of painting in Venice. The most significant of his paintings are in the churches of **Carmini** and **San Rocco**, and the **Accademia**. **San Stae** is a frequent venue for concerts of Baroque chamber music. ♦ Campo San Stae (between Rio di San Stae and Salizzada di San Stae). *Vaporetto* stop: San Stae

5 Ca' Pesaro

Early in the 17th century, the wealthy Pesaro family acquired three adjacent buildings on

Dolci Veneziani

Venetian sweets run the gamut from plain sugar cookies to extravagantly adorned biscuits slathered with all manner of toppings. These delights are sold in *scaletèri* (pastry shops) throughout the city, and are a conglomeration of flour, sugar, chocolate, nuts, glazed fruit, and raisins. They are the perfect complement to the sweet *vin santo,* various liqueurs, coffee, or hot chocolate in which they are dipped at the end of a meal. So important is this ritual of dipping and dunking *alla Veneziana* that Pietro Longhi (1702-1785), a painter famous for his renderings of contemporary life, commemorated it in several of his works.

Look for *scaletèri* that advertise *I Dolci Veneziani*. Some of these delectable sweets are summed up in the following list:

Baícoli Hands down, these small, thin wafers are the most popular cookies to be found in the *calli* (streets) of Venice. Dunked into coffee or milk, or spread with mascarpone or *mostarda* (a spicy purée of fruit pickled with mustard seed), they are a real taste treat. *Baícoli* make great presents, too, as they are packaged in beautiful tins.

Buranelli Either "s"-shaped (*essi*), or round (*bussolà*), these sugar cookies are most often enjoyed with a liqueur after a meal.

Cacao This chocolate delight is an offshoot of *pan dei dogi* (see opposite), sprinkled with chocolate slivers.

Dogaressa The "doge's wife" is, in fact, a close relative of the *pan dei dogi* (see opposite). Although not quite as stout as her husband, this round cake is a mixture o honey, rum, raisins, and nuts.

Focaccine Veneziana Another dunking cake, these savory delights resemble a round bun and are leavenec with beer.

Golosesso/Golosoni Depending on which pastry shop you go to, these variations on the basic dough are made with chocolate or pistachios.

Mori These vanilla and chocolate swirls are sweeter an more delicate than some of the others and will be sure to win your heart.

Moro A more fanciful version of *cacao* (see opposite), this wonder has big almonds plastered into the top.

Nosea Hazelnuts strewn on top, this is a chocolate version of *vini* (see below).

Pan dei Dogi The colorful "bread of the doges" are sturdy biscuits made of white wine, candied fruit, and raisins, and are usually topped with whole or splintered almonds.

Vini This confection boasts Prosecco wine, almonds, and dried figs, sprinkled with pine nuts.

Zaleti Second in popularity to *baícoli* are these cornmeal-and-raisin sweets, which are pronounced *zaeti* in the local dialect.

the Canal Grande and asked the fashionable architect **Baldassare Longhena** to create an imposing palazzo. The result is probably the most successful among the Baroque palazzi in Venice. The façade must be seen from the Canal Grande if you are to appreciate its grandeur and elegance. The building changed hands a few times, until Duchess Bevilacqua La Masa, the last owner, donated it to the city in 1889. The water entrance, now little used, is marked by stairs. ♦ Fondamenta Pesaro 2076 (just north of Calle del Ravano). 5240695. *Vaporetto* stop: San Stae

Within Ca' Pesaro:

Museo d'Arte Moderna Ca' Pesaro

The street entrance of this palazzo leads to a Baroque courtyard and an 18th-century staircase. The museum occupies the first two floors of the palazzo. The bulk of the collection consists of paintings and other works of art chosen from those exhibited at the Venice *Biennale* since its opening in 1895. It's hard to come up with well-known European-centered 20th-century painters who are not represented in this rich collection (although not always by their best works): Vedova, Morandi, Boccioni, de Chirico, Sironi, and Rosai are just a few of the Italians, while painters from other countries include Chagall, Dufy, Kandinsky, Klee, Ernst, and Klimt. At press time the museum had been closed for restoration for some time, with reopening dates constantly changing. ♦ Admission. Tu-Su. 5240695

Museo d'Arte Orientale (Museum of Eastern Art)

This museum was built around the collection of Duke Henry of Bourbon, a tireless traveler and acquirer of Oriental objects. It specializes in Japanese art (particularly armor and swords), but also includes rooms devoted to India, China, and Indonesia. ♦ Admission. Tu Su. 5241173

6 Hotel San Cassiano

$$$ In the second half of the 19th century, painter Giacomo Favretto owned this small,

handsome 14th-century palazzo, elements of which date back to the 11th century. His house has been remodeled into a hotel—one of the few in the neighborhood—though most of the features of the palazzo were lost in the process. The interior now looks more like a comfortable, old-fashioned hotel than an ancient palazzo. A few of the 35 rooms have beautiful Gothic windows overlooking the Canal Grande. All have air conditioning, minibar, hair dryer, TV, and fax service. There is a bar with canal terrace but no restaurant. ♦ Calle della Rosa 2232 (at Canal Grande). 5241768; fax 721033. *Vaporetto* stop: San Stae

7 Centro degli Studi di Storia dei Tessuto e dei Costume (Center for the Study of Textile and Clothing History)

This unusual center has a large collection of original textiles from the 16th, 17th, and 18th centuries, together with a library that specializes in textiles and antique prints. Scholars and students can identify the material in the library's files and ask for samples to be brought to their tables. Also housed here is the recently opened **Museo di Palazzo Mocenigo**, featuring a collection of furniture, frescoes, and paintings that are examples from the most important Venetian houses of the second half of the 18th century. These rooms also exhibit rotating shows of clothes, accessories, and fabric from the center. **Palazzo Mocenigo** also houses the library of **Casa di Goldoni** while the latter is being restored. ♦ Center: free; museum: admission. Library: Tu, W; museum: Tu-Su. Salizzada di San Stae 1992 (at Ramo de Rioda). 721798. *Vaporetto* stop: San Stae

8 El Canapon

This interesting little shop sells a selection of surprisingly well-cut shirts and dresses, jackets and sweaters, plus purses and knapsacks and little slippers and hats, all in restful natural creams and beiges. There is a cosmetic line too—everything from hair conditioner to anti-wrinkle cream. What makes it interesting is that it is the Veneto's first hemp store—absolutely everything here is from organically grown, Italian cannabis! Don't worry, the one thing the shop doesn't sell is the smokeable stuff! ♦ Daily, 10:30AM-1:30PM and 4PM-7:30PM. 1906 Salizzada de San Stae. 2440247. e-mail: elcanapon@katamail.com

9 San Giacomo dell'Orio

The handsome exterior of this 10th-century church, surrounded by the square on all sides, provides passersby with a variety of views. The main entrance is on the façade along the canal (important worshippers used to arrive by gondola); the bell tower dates from the 13th century, as does the main apse visible at the back; the other entrance was redone in the 14th century. The interior is characterized by a 14th-century wood ceiling that is often noted as an exemplar of ancient building techniques: It was built like an inverted ship hull, a familiar process for Venetian carpenters who built more ships than churches. The golden *Crucifix* hanging in front of the main altar is by Paolo Veneziano. A sweet and rather rare work by Lorenzo Lotto—*Madonna col Bambino e Santi* (Madonna with Child and Saints)—is on the back wall of the central apse. ♦ M-Sa, 10AM-5PM; Su, 1PM-5PM. Campiello del Piovan (just east of Rio di San Giacomo dell'Orio). *Vaporetto* stops: Riva di Biasio, San Stae

10 Campo San Giacomo dell'Orio

Venetians call this *campo* "Da L'Orio" after a laurel tree (*alloro* or *lorio*) that supposedly once stood in the square. Daily life in the Santa Croce neighborhood revolves around the *campo* and the nearby **Campo San Zan Degolà**. The local church is run by an active and popular parish priest, who frequently organizes dances, picnics, and other events here. ♦ Between Calle del Tintor and Rio di San Giacomo dell'Orio. *Vaporetto* stops: Riva di Biasio, San Stae

On Campo San Giacomo dell'Orio:

Il Refolo

★★$ A *refolo* is a gentle breeze, and that is exactly what you get eating at one of the tables in the tiny "*campo* off a *campo*" that is the outdoor dining space at this interesting young restaurant. Interesting in many ways, the first of which is that it has a tiny but amazingly wide-ranging menu along with its main fare, which is pizza (more of which anon). Incredibly, this tiny hole-in-the-wall place offers a half dozen *fines de claires* oysters to start with, served *au naturelle*. It offers a very well-executed *salatone* (or composed salad), full of herbs and interesting leaves alongside mozzarella, artichoke hearts, tuna, and tomatoes. There are lamb cutlets oven roasted with herbed potatoes and a *coppa de crema al mascarpone* (a delicious and frequently hard-to-find ice cream made with mascarpone). All very sophisticated stuff for a pizza joint. The pizzas are interesting too—the dough is made twice daily and left to proof for 18 hours, giving their pizzas an ultra-thin but deliciously chewy crust. Toppings are generous and intelligent. When you discover that the place is owned by the same man who owns **Da Fiore**—the only Michelin-starred restaurant in Venice's culinary firmament—all is clear. *Il faut le détour* ("The trip must be made," as they say in the Michelin guide). ♦ W-Su, lunch and dinner; Tu, dinner. Closed Nov-Mar. Campo San Giacomo dell'Orio. 1459. 5240016

11 Pizzeria Ae Oche

★★$ This spot boasts 90 varieties of pizza and a very un-Venetian choice of main-course salads. Be ready to wait for a table inside or out, either in the rear garden or the small space in front. A choice of 30 beers will make it worth your while. ♦ Daily, lunch and dinner. Calle del Tintor 1552B (between Rio di San Boldo and Campo San Giacomo dell'Orio). 5241161. *Vaporetto* stops: Riva di Biasio, San Stae

12 Campo Santa Maria Mater Domini

This delightful little *campo* is bounded on one side by a canal and on the other three sides by small Gothic palazzi that are among the most charming in Venice. **Casa Zane** (**No. 2172**), in Veneto-Byzantine style, dates back to the 13th century; across from it is **Casa Barbaro** (**No. 2173**), about a century younger; on the fourth side is **Palazzo Viaro-Zane** (**No. 2123**), built early in the 14th century (the third floor, in Renaissance style, was added later). The *campo* gives you a glimpse of Venice as it was before the introduction of the Florentine and Roman Renaissance: smaller and more intimate buildings, grace and lightness instead of majestic corpulence. The blacksmith near the bridge works outdoors in the summer; his ancestors are the cause of the smoky grayness of the stones around his shop. ♦ At Rio delle Due Torri and Calle della Chiesa. *Vaporetto* stop: San Stae

Sixteenth-century correspondence from the Venetian ambassador, Gian Francesco Morosini, to Constantinople makes mention of "boiling black water": Coffee was introduced to Europe thanks to *La Serenissima*'s first shipments from Turkey in the 17th century.

The last private gondola in Venice was owned by the eccentric American art collector Peggy Guggenheim, whose gondola rides with her beloved dogs earned her the affectionate epithet *la dogaressa* (lady doge). Her boat is now in the Museo Storico Navale.

On Campo Santa Maria Mater Domini:

Cartavenezia

If you think you might have a love letter left in you to write, this would be the place to get the paper. Every individual sheet is created by hand and each envelope folded from the sheets by renowned artisan Fernando Masone—notepaper, notelets, envelopes, diaries, albums, and book jackets, all pressed by hand from cotton while you watch. Just to feel paper like this makes you want to create poetry . . . but to touch anything in the shop you are asked to put on one of the pairs of white gloves that hang by the door. Reliefs and designs are stamped into the paper, and lampshades, bookmarks, and even pairs of slippers are created from it (by Masone's partner Zelda Rocchi). Murano glass or quaint bamboo pens and richly colored inks are there to buy. This shop offers a wonderful chance to see a master craftsman at work in light, airy surroundings where you can purchase his creations. ♦ Tu-Su. Calle della Chiesa 2125 (at Campo Santa Maria Mater Domini). Tel/fax 5241238. e-mail: cartavenezia@libero.it

13 Vecio Fritolin

★★$ Try the wonderful homemade pastas or *pesce fritto con polenta* (fried fish with polenta). They are good on seasonal treats, like *canoche* (langoustine) and *bruscandoli* (young field asparagus). The food, service, and ambience are amazing at this sort of price. ♦ M, lunch; Tu-Sa, lunch and dinner. Calle della Regina 2262 (between Ramo Regina and Calle del Ravano). 5222881. *Vaporetto* stop: San Stae

14 Osteria Al Nono Risorto

★★$$ This old wine shop was bought and remodeled by the son of Dino Boscarato, one of Venice's great restaurateurs. In keeping with the shop's tradition, the restaurant is very informal, even slightly bohemian, attracting a youthful crowd with its pizza. But class with a capital C is evident in the quality of both the food and service. The *frittura mista con polenta* (assortment of flash-fried seafood and vegetables served with polenta) is wonderfully fresh, and all the pastas are freshly prepared and delicious. The side garden is heaven in the summer, when it is scented with the perfume of a large wisteria tree. ♦ M-Tu, Th-Su, lunch and dinner. Sotto-portico della Croce 2338 (between Rio di San Cassiano and Calle della Regina). 5241169. *Vaporetto* stop: San Stae

15 Piazzale Roma

Built in the 1930s when the bridge across the lagoon from the mainland to the city was enlarged to take cars as well as trains, the

VENEZIA DI NOTTE: SAN MARCO

Venice has recently undergone something of a late-night revolution. Many bars now stay open later, and something of a new generation of "cool" eateries and drinking places has opened up.

You should know that this is probably the safest you will ever feel in a city center. In all the years I have spent here, I have never been threatened by, seen, or heard of any violence in Venice. Have confidence—walking Venice by night is like being wrapped in velvet.

Centrale (see San Marco) is probably the coolest bar—and the most expensive. Open till 2AM, it does great cocktails, perfectly okay food, and great lounge and chill music. Seriously 21st-century Venice! Also in the San Marco area is the equally new and chic **Cavatappi.** Small but delightful, it offers fantastic wines by the glass, seriously good food, and a not-too-achingly hip atmosphere until closing time at midnight. Less cool, but a terrific place to end your evening, is the **Bistrot de Venise**. Again, there are great wines by the bottle or glass, the best-made spritz in town (to say nothing of one of the most gorgeous barmen), and a nice sort of Venetian-Bohemian atmosphere. Check their brochure and come along on one of the nights when they have good live music playing till 1AM. If jazz is your thing, then the **Bácaro Jazz** is open till 4AM and plays good (albeit not live) jazz. It can be a fun place, and the nibbles are good! If pubs are more your style, the **Olandese Volante** is open till after midnight, as is the **Devil's Forest Pub** (just around the corner on Calle degli Stagneri), which has darts and backgammon and is open from 8AM till midnight. San Marco's most famous nightclub is the Antico Martini—it is open till late and can be fun, but be prepared to enter a time warp! And if you would like to end your day more traditionally, the **Enoteca al Volto** is always welcoming, bursting with interesting wine choices and open till late (albeit precise closing times rather depend on how many customers roll up!).

Piazzale Roma is the farthest a car can enter the city. The square is all you might expect of a bus station, which is its main function. The absolutely best thing about it is that it is so incredibly quick to get out of, by foot or by *vaporetto*. ♦ Bounded by Fondamenta Cossetti, Fondamenta Sant'Andrea, and Ponte della Libertà. *Vaporetto* stop: Piazzale Roma

16 SOFITEL VENEZIA

$$$$ This is so much better than your run-of-the-mill Sofitel. OK, it's still just part of a chain, but it is really rather gorgeous. And literally a stone's throw from the Piazzale Roma and the train station, though you'd never know it. The hotel sits behind a lovely garden, beside the quiet Canal Tolentini, overlooking a sweet neighborhood *campo*. You would swear you were miles from the center, when in fact you're in it. There are 100 rooms and 5 suites, each decorated in the style of 18th-century Venice but with 21st-century amenities. Rooms have multimedia centers and full Internet access. There are 16 rooms on the top floor with their own terraces looking over the nearby church, the square, and the canal. There is a marvelously lush interior garden that boasts exotic and subtropical plants. The hotel organizes intelligent tours in some of the less well-known areas of Venice, trips to the islands, and *Carnevale* parties. The charming gentleman at the desk was at pains to point out that all manner of "special rates" are available at the Sofitel . . . so don't assume the list price is the only one. ♦ Fondamenta Condulmer 245 (at Fondamenta Monastero). 710400; fax 710394. Restaurant, 720924. e-mail: sofitel.venezia@accor-hotels.it. *Vaporetto* stop: Piazzale Roma

Within Sofitel Venezia:

CAFEBAR LA BIBLIOTHÈQUE

The elegant bar has had a library added to it, dedicated to cartoon strips and the arts. There, while sipping an aperitif, you can also enjoy evenings with well known authors reading their works, artists talking about their work, and live music, such as classical harp. There are also frequent art and photography exhibitions. ♦ Daily

PAPADOPOLI RESTAURANT

★$$$ Gorgeously situated among the blooms and the greenery of the interior garden, the restaurant offers traditional Venetian specialties alongside a wider menu. You can book anything from a working lunch to a banquet for 100 people. The hotel organizes tutored wine tastings and gastronomic evenings here. ♦ Daily, breakfast, lunch, and dinner. Fondamenta Condulmer 245. 710400; fax 710394. www.sofitel.com

17 SAN NICOLA DI TOLENTINO

Even if you are in Venice only for the afternoon, you can see this gem because it is five minutes from the train station and two from the bus

The Best

Holly Snapp

(Owner of Gallery Holly Snapp)

I love walking through the streets in the early morning when everyone is going to work . . . people sing in the streets here!

The **Giudecca**, where I live, is wonderful . . . a real neighborhood and, because it is separated from the main islands by its very own canal, it never gets the crowds other places do. We have our own little stores, restaurants . . . hey, we have the **Cipriani**!

Coin—our department store. It is wonderful. The Rialto branch is terrific for all your household stuff: I have all my bed linen from there—it is deep crimson satinized cotton. Stunning, very sexy, and I have never seen anything like it anywhere else.

The art. Well, the colors, really. Venice is a fabulous subject to paint, and wherever you go in the city you will find someone with brushes and a canvas. Over the years, many people have captured it so beautifully. One of the painters whose works I exhibit at the gallery is an English guy called Geoffrey Humphries. When I look at his watercolors of Venice, I get goosebumps!

And I love my gallery. It is in a great position, we have a marvelous little restaurant opposite us and a terrific coffee shop on the corner, and I get to spend the day surrounded by wonderful paintings and lovely people!

station. The church, more commonly known as **I Tolenti**, was started by **Scamozzi** in the 16th century. What strikes you first, however, is the fantastic, eight-columned Corinthian portico added by **Andrea Tirali** in the early 1700s. The interior is even more striking. Use of black marble means that the overall impression is of startling monochrome—a sort of "Baroque meets Art Deco" feast for the eyes. The nave is flanked by eight chapels including the extravagantly impressive **Capella dei Grimani,** mainly the work of **J. Palma il Giovane** (the Younger). It is all fabulously Baroque, from Guisto le Court's fat angels making life-size candle holders in one chapel to the marvelously dramatic *Martyrdom of St. Cecilia* by Camillo Procaccini in another. And this church has one of those wonderful effects created by strategic placement of windows in the cupola. As the sun streams in, it creates fabulously dramatic shafts of light cutting a swath through the quiet air of the interior. Every so often as you walk about the church you are touched by one of these beams of light . . . it's enough to turn Darwin into a believer. ♦ M-Sa, 9:30AM-noon and 4PM-6PM; Su, afternoon only. Campo dei Tolentini. 710806. *Vaporetto* stop: Piazzale Roma

18 Trattoria alle Burchielle

★★$$ The tables along the canal make this restaurant one of the most pleasant in the area around **Piazzale Roma**. Bruno, the owner, knows how to select his fish at the morning market, one reason the place is a preferred lunch spot of gondoliers and water taxi drivers. Stick to the dishes of the day, including fish appetizers and the spaghetti with seafood. ♦ Tu-Su, lunch and dinner. Fondamenta delle Burchielle 393 (between Calle Bernardo and Calle dei Pensieri). 710342. *Vaporetto* stop: Piazzale Roma

19 Tre Ponti

This bridge—actually a group of three bridges—is one of the most complex and interesting in Venice. It was completed in 1938, when the opening of **Piazzale Roma** made it necessary to dig a new canal to join the Cana Grande with the square's automobile terminal. Although young, Rio Nuovo, as the new waterway is called, is among the most battered and fragile canals in the city. The relentless traffic of taxis and *motoscafi* (water buses) constantly erodes the building foundations along the banks. Since 1991 long stretches of the canal have been closed to traffic, allowing for the urgent repairs to underwater banks in a frustrating fight against the laws of physics. ♦ Rio Nuovo and Rio delle Burchielle. *Vaporetto* stop: Piazzale Roma

20 Il Grifone

What a marvelous perfume of quality leather hits you when you walk in from the quiet canalside to this workshop/boutique! Beautiful bags—shoulder bags and briefcases, elegant handbags, wallets and purses—are what line the shelves here, along with what the Italians call a *marsupio* (a fannypack), leather-bound diaries and photo albums, key rings and card holders. The charming craftsman/owner is happy to have you look around at his work—probably because he knows it is so lovely you'll want to buy. ♦ Tu-Sa, 10AM-1PM and 4PM-7:30PM. Fondamenta del Gaffaro. 5229452

21 Locanda Salieri

$ The quiet, neighborhood feel of this newly renovated hotel belies its location, less than five minutes from Piazzale Roma. There are 11 freshly decorated bedrooms, all with bath/shower, TV, air conditioning, and hair dryer. Four of them have a canal view. The hotel has no restaurant of its own, but the restaurant next door is part of the same building and the two establishments have a "special relationship." This is a nice, quiet relaxing base for any visitor to Venice.

Venetian Streets

"Wonderful city, streets full of water, please advise," is what humorist Robert Benchley is said to have cabled home on his first visit to Venice. A waterway in Venice is called a *rio,* but even for those streets that are not full of water the visitor to this wonderful city needs some advice, since the names are mostly in dialect and you won't find translations for them in any dictionary. A *calle* is a street. A *stretto* is a narrow passageway. A *sottoportego* is a passageway or a covered street. A *ruga* (from the French *rue*) is a street originally running next to a shop or residence, while a *fondamenta* runs alongside a canal, and a *riva* is an important *fondamenta.* A *lista* is a street that runs in front of a former embassy of the Republic and was once a place of diplomatic immunity. A *salizzada* was one of the first paved streets in a parish, while a *rio terrà* is a filled-in canal. A *piscina* is a small, filled-in basin, now acting as a small piazza. The only piazza in Venice is **Piazza San Marco**; what would be called a piazza elsewhere in Italy is known locally as a *campo* or *campiello,* and often has a well in the center. Venice's wells have long since been covered.

♦ Fondamenta Minotto 160. 710035. www.hotelsalieri.com

21 Ribo

★★★$$$ A calm, well-mannered little place with immaculately dressed young men offering well-mannered service. The food is well-mannered too—no huge robust flavors, but good pastas and risotto, lots of seafood, and a cheese board that makes it worth eating there even if you don't order anything else on the menu! ♦ Th-Tu, lunch and dinner. Fondamenta Minotto 158. 5242486. www.ristoranteribo.com

21 Venier Roberto

A lovely little glass shop owned by a charming bearded man who was thrilled to be included in this guide. He creates not just the usual colored glasses and figures, animals and flowers, but a whole range of martini glasses and champagne flutes, the bowls of which are held up by an extraordinary menagerie of glass creatures. Some ride on the backs of gold-tipped swans, some on tall pink flamingos. A cute green octopus, a fat penguin, a rotund elephant, and a fluttering finch will all bear the weight of your drinks in a fun way. The temptation is to buy the whole collection! Especially as the prices here are extraordinarily reasonable. Your purchases will even be individually boxed for you. Pop in and have a look—the shop is just minutes from Piazzale Roma. ♦ M-Sa, 9AM-1PM and 3PM-8PM. Salizzada San Pantalon 47. 5244147

21 Ca' Malcanton

$$ This is a stately home version of a B&B, within the stunning 15th-century Venice home of the charming, urbane Englishman who is your host. There are five lovely double rooms, each with its own bathroom. The vast sitting room, with its twin pillars and old wood ceiling, is classily comfortable—all cushy sofas, intelligently collected antiques, and silk wall hangings. One wall has several huge windows along its length, with tiny squares of stained glass so the room is bathed in a warm, rosy glow most of the day. Breakfast is included with your room and in good weather, you might feel moved to take it in the house's exquisite garden, which lies on the banks of a pretty canal. The Ca' Malcanton is in one of those locations you imagine exist only in movies or dreams, so perfect is it. You would never guess you were five minutes from the Piazzale Roma, but you are—behind a tiny bridge on the quiet corner of a gentle little boat-lined canal. Your host is a great source of advice on where and when to do what in Venice. This place is a real find. ♦ Salizzada San Pantalon 49. 710931 www.venice4you.co.uk

22 Hotel Al Sole

$$ On the quiet Fondamenta Minotto, this hotel is housed in the 16th-century Palazzo Marcello. It is incredibly impressive for a hotel in this price range. Currently undergoing extensive renovations, when done the hotel will have about 75 rooms with bath and/or shower, minbar, air conditioning, color television, and views over either the canal or the hotel's lovely internal garden. There is a little restaurant where the Sole's generous buffet breakfast is served. ♦ Fondamenta Minotto 134/136. 2440328. www.veniceby.com/alsole/index.htm *Vaporetto* stop: Piazzale Roma

Cannaregio

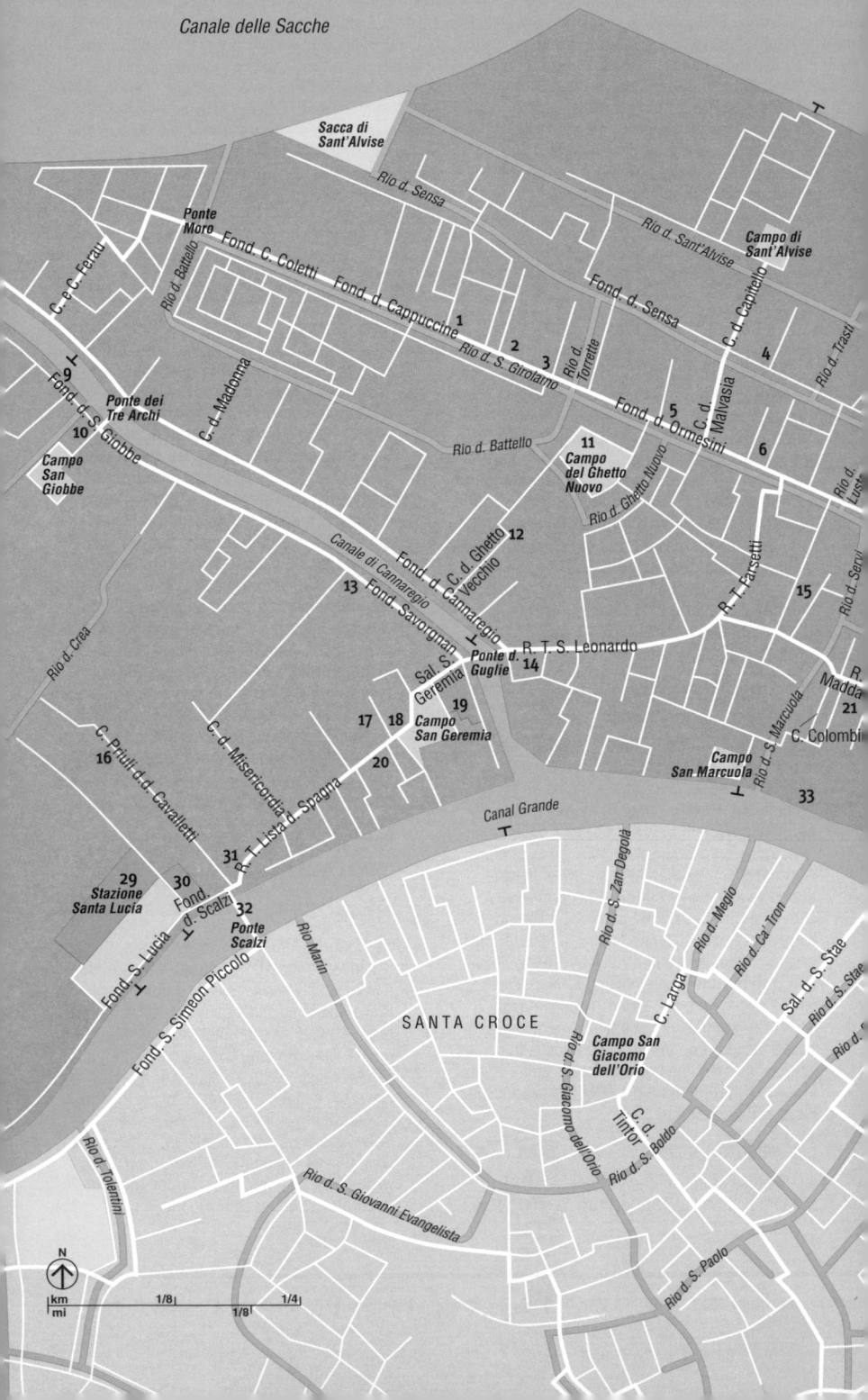
Canale delle Sacche
Sacca di Sant'Alvise
Rio d. Sensa
Rio d. Sant'Alvise
Campo di Sant'Alvise
Ponte Moro
Fond. C. Coletti
Fond. d. Cappuccine
Rio d. Battello
C. e C. Farau
Fond. d. Sensa
C. d. Capitello
Rio d. S. Girolamo
Rio d. Torrette
Rio d. Trasti
Fond. d. Ormesini
C. d. Malvasia
Ponte dei Tre Archi
C. d. Madonna
Fond. d. S. Giobbe
Campo San Giobbe
Rio d. Battello
Campo del Ghetto Nuovo
Rio d. Ghetto Nuovo
Canale di Cannaregio
Fond. d. C. d. Ghetto Vecchio
Fond. d. Cannaregio
Fond. Savorgnan
R. T. Farsetti
Rio d. Serv
Rio d. Crea
Ponte d. Guglie
R. T. S. Leonardo
Sal. S. Geremia
Campo San Geremia
R. Madda
C. Colombi
C. d. Misericordia
C. Priuli d. d. Cavalletti
R. T. Lista d. Spagna
Campo San Marcuola
Rio d. S. Marcuola
Canal Grande
Stazione Santa Lucia
Fond. d. Scalzi
Ponte Scalzi
Fond. S. Lucia
Fond. S. Simeon Piccolo
Rio Marin
Rio d. S. Zan Degolà
Rio d. Megio
Rio d. Ca' Tron
C. Larga
Sal. d. S. Stae
SANTA CROCE
Campo San Giacomo dell'Orio
Rio d. S. Giacomo dell'Orio
C. d. Tintor
Rio d. S. Boldo
Rio d. Tolentini
Rio d. S. Giovanni Evangelista
Rio d. S. Paolo
N
km
mi
1/8
1/8
1/4

Canale delle Navi
Madonna dell'Orto
Rio Braso
Campo dei Mori
Rio Madonna dell'Orto
Rio d. Mutti
Sacca della Misericordia
Fond. Nuove
C. Lunga S. Caterina
Rio d. Misericordia
Rio d. Ca' Moro
Rio d. Misericordia
Rio d. Sensa
Canale della Misericordia
Rio d. Trapolin Grimani
Rio d. S. Caterina
Strada Nuova
Rio d. Racchetta
Rio d. Racchetta
Rio d. S. Andrea
Ponte Casualunga
Rio d. S. Felice
C. Larga Doge Priuli
Rio d. S. Sofia
Rio d. Ca' Dolce
Rio d. Sartori
Rio di Noale
Ponte S. Felice
C. d. Pistor
C. d. Ca'd'Oro
Strada Nuova
Rio d. S.S. Apostoli
Rio d. Ca' Widman
Campo Santa Maria Nova
Sal. S. Canciano
Rio d. S. Giovanni Grisostomo
Sal. S. Giovanni Grisostomo
Rio d. S. Marina
Rio d. S. Lio
Rio Fontego
Ponte di Rialto
Ruga d. Orefici
Rio d. Beccarie
SAN PAOLO
CASTELLO
Rio d. Gesuiti
Fond. Nuove
Rio d. Panada
Rio d. Mendicanti
Fond. d. Mendicanti
Campo Santi Giovanni e Paolo
C. L. G. Gallina
7
8
22
23
24
25
26
27
28
34
35
36
37
38
39
40
41
42
43
44
45
46
47
48
49
50
51

CANNAREGIO

Except for the **Ghetto** and the bustling **Strada Nuova**, Cannaregio is largely unknown to the average visitor. This may be why the *sestiere* (district) has preserved its ancient characteristics—and characters. Parallel to the lagoon border on the north side are three small canals, and it is hard to decide which is more charming or typically Venetian. Houses along them are usually no higher than three stories, bridges are tiny and often made of wood, and life goes on largely oblivious to the activity on Strada Nuova. The canals here run east-west, making them a wonderful place for a stroll at sunset, when a golden light seems to fill the houses, the bridges, the water, and the old wooden boats tied along the banks. Be sure to walk past the church of **Madonna dell'Orto** at sunset, continuing on to the *vaporetto* stop of the same name. It is a lonely stop, with few if any waiting passengers. It sits on the bank of the open lagoon, with **Murano** in front, **Burano** and the terra firma in the distance. The sun sets over the lagoon to the left, and a light sea breeze usually ripples the water. On clear days even the local commuters can't stop gazing at the sight—the most spectacular sunset in Venice.

1 Osteria Bea Vita

★★$ Another new favorite place the Venetian locals are taking to their hearts. Three enterprising young men with trendily short haircuts have opened this little *osteria* offering *cicchetti*, a reasonable selection of wines, and a menu based on "what is good from the Rialto market." And it is pretty good. The menu changes, but you will always find a good risotto (if it is on the menu, try the one with Prosecco and seafood—it is very good) and plenty of smart ways with fish and crustaceans (like *scorfano battuto di zenzara fresca*—scorpion fish scented with fresh ginger). In good weather, when tables spill outside, there are many, many worse places to dine than on this quiet Fondamenta. ♦ Daily, 9AM-11PM. Fondamenta delle Cappuccine 3028. 2759347

2 Profondo Rosso

★★★$ A truly extraordinary little place, this is Venice's only "spritz bar." Tiny and as yet unvisited by the interior design fairy, it has a few little slot machines, a small bar, standing room only, and a list of 11 spritzes ranging from No. 1—white wine and fizzy water—and working up to potency No. 11—the Spritz Profondo Rosso, described as "*una fantasia.*" And it is. What kind of *fantasia* can be judged from the fact that even No. 10 comprises martini bianco, martini rosso, and gin! Dangerously, there is a Spritz Hour from 7 to 8 each evening. The genial owner, Fabrizio, offers a small but decent range of *cicchetti* and *tramezzini* (little half sandwiches) to soak up your spritz. An oddity, but a delightful one. ♦ Daily, 8AM-2AM. Fondamenta degli Ormesini 2839. 3333037205

3 Osteria Al Bacco

★★★$$$ At the end of the handsome Fondamenta degli Ormesini (where it becomes Fondamenta delle Cappuccine) is a former wine shop that is now a well-respected *ristorante*. The atmosphere is still that of an old *osteria,* with uncovered wood tables and wood panels on the walls, but the food (fish and original pasta dishes are the specialties here) is superior. Try the *spaghetti al tonno* (with tuna) or *tagliatelle cape sante* (with scallops), followed by *grigliata mista* (mixed grilled fish). After dinner, take a walk along the canal all the way to **La Misericordia**: The street is quiet—almost deserted—with long rows of boats tied along the canal and frequent bridges. A small detour will take you to splendid sites such as **Madonna dell'Orto** and the church of **Santa Maria Valverde**. ♦ Tu-Sa, lunch and dinner; Su, dinner. No credit cards accepted. Fondamenta delle Cappuccine 3054 (between Calle del Magazen and Calle dello Squero). 717493. *Vaporetto* stops: Sant'Alvise, Guglie

4 Hotel Ai Mori D'Oriente

$$$ A charming new hotel on a lovely, serene stretch of canal just five minutes from the bustle of the Strada Nuova, and yet perfectly quiet. The hotel takes its name from the Turkish merchants who lived here in the days when the Silk Route was as busy as Fifth Avenue is today. Right next door you will find the Campo dei Mori, and just across the canal, the famous Ghetto. If only cohabitation were as easy today! The rooms are for lovers of colors, decorated as they are in wonderfully vibrant hues. They have marble bathrooms and all the modern conveniences you could want, including Internet connection, in-room movies,

and a personal safe. Rooms come as singles, doubles, triples, and a Junior Suite overlooking the canal. The breakfast room is done out in lovely green, and the hotel also offers a reading room that overlooks the Sensa Canal. ♦ Fondamenta della Sensa 3319. 711001; fax 714209. www.hotelaimoridoriente.it

5 Trattoria "Antica Mola"

★★$ A *mola* is a millstone or a grindstone, but it is definitely not a grind to spend some time here, on the banks of a quiet canal close to the Ghetto Nuovo. The Antica Mola was turned from a wine shop into a trattoria in the 1980s, but has always kept its genuine neighborhood feel. Have a look at the walls—the trattoria is almost a shrine to Renato Bona, a legendary gondolier whose family lived close by and who was "almost like family." There are trophies and photos, poems and eulogies, newspaper clippings and silver plaques. This is one of the few restaurants that would be worth visiting to just look around. It is also worth coming to eat. Antonietta, who is in the kitchen, is the subject of poems herself, being dubbed "queen of the kitchen" in one. She turns out good, basic fare at incredibly loiw prices. *Gamberetti in pinzimonio* is a simple plate of tiny boiled shrimp served with lemon; *gnochetti alla granseola* dresses tiny dumplings with a fresh crab sauce. There is all manner of seafood, grilled and fried, and a tasty, if somewhat stewlike, *fegato alla veneziana* (calves' liver with onion). The house wine is perfectly fine, although a good list is available. Don't leave without having strawberries, with which you will be offered cream, lemon, or wine. Choose wine and get a *coppa* dish brimming with strawberries in *fragolino rosso* (a sweetish wine). No mixologist on the planet could do better. You will not be rushed . . . you may just want to sit for a bit with a cup of coffee, either inside or outside along the canal or in their sweet internal garden. Enjoy. ♦ M, Tu, Th-Su. Fondamenta degli Ormesini 2800 (between Calle della Malvasia and Corte Zappa). 717492. *Vaporetto* stops: Sant'Alvise, Guglie

6 Osteria da Aldo

A great little dark hole-in-the-wall on a quiet canalside. If you are longing for a taste of home—wherever home might be—then Aldo is your man. He sells 80 to 90 different bottled beers from all over the world and offers Beck's and Guinness on tap. There is also a surprisingly good wine list, a choice of premium spirits, and a classically served, rocket-fuel-strength absinthe. The sandwiches and panini are fresh and generously filled, so don't fear there is nothing to line your stomach. And there is even a small selection of snacks like Pringles and M&Ms for those longing for the comforts of home. Ask to try Aldo's personally designed approach to the "whiskey shot and a beer chaser" that is so popular in some countries. He has created a goldfish-bowl-sized glass with its own shot glass in the center of it! (For port and Prosecco, he beams.) *Benvenuto in Italia!* ♦ Daily, 11AM-5PM and 7PM-2AM Fondamenta dei Ormesini 2710

7 Madonna dell'Orto

This most sober yet pleasing Gothic church opens onto a lovely, well-proportioned square along a quiet canal with the same name. The statues in the beautiful niches over the sides represent the 12 Apostles. The five statues at the very top represent the Virgin Mary and the four Evangelists. Inside this unpretentious 15th-century church is a surprising wealth of first-class paintings painstakingly restored after severe damage by the 1966 floods. At the first altar on the right is one of the most beautiful paintings by Cima da Conegliano, *St. John the Baptist Among the Four Saints,* in which the 34-year-old artist, just after his arrival in Venice from his native village of Conegliano, dared to replace the traditional gold background—and the more recent perspectives of classical buildings—with a landscape of the beautiful hills where he had grown up. The first altar on the left contains a jewel by Giovanni Bellini, a *Virgin Mary with Child,* which epitomizes Bellini's craft in the painting of Madonnas. On the apse and behind the altar is a group of large canvases by Jacopo Tintoretto, who lived near the church (at **No. 3399** on Fondamenta dei Mori) and is buried inside it, in the last chapel on the right. On the left wall of the chancel is Tintoretto's gigantic *Adoration of the Golden Calf,* a painting strangely and dramatically divided into three horizontal sections. Behind the altar, Tintoretto painted *The Martyrdom of St. Christopher* and *The Apparition of the Holy Cross to St. Peter.* On the right wall is another huge canvas, *The Last Judgment,* with Christ and the Virgin Mary surrounded by angels and saints while a stormy whirlpool carries away the damned souls, with Charon's boat appearing on a background of fire. Tintoretto's *Presentation of the Virgin,* on the right side over the door to the last chapel before the chancel, is also dramatically beautiful. ♦ M-Sa, 10AM-5PM; Su, 1PM-5PM. Campo Madonna dell'Orto (between Fondamenta Gasparo Contarini and Fondamenta Madonna dell'Orto). *Vaporetto* stop: Madonna dell'Orto

8 Campo dei Mori and Palazzo Mastelli

According to Venetian tradition, the "Mori" in question were three brothers, silk merchants by the name of Mastelli who came to Venice about 1112 from Morea in the Peloponnesus. They built the Palazzo Mastelli, recognizable by the still impressive camel bas-relief on the side that faces the Rio Madonna dell'Orto, which then backed onto the square. Another odd thing about the palazzo is that it seems to have reversed history in that a Gothic balcony on the same façade as the camel sits on top of a Renaissance first floor. Intriguing for future archeologists when Venice does finally sink! The three brothers are still with us—albeit only in stone on the eastern side of the *campo*, along with "Signor Antonio Rioba," who is the guy with the metal nose and was a famous figure in Venetian satire. The figure with the turban, facing the canal, is on the façade of a house once occupied by the painter Tintoretto. ♦ *Vaporetto* stop: Madonna dell'Orto

9 Osteria ai Cannottieri

★★$$ A very welcoming place, mainly thanks to its two friendly owners, Christina and Fabio. It is a classic *osteria*—all marble floors and dark wood paneling and tables. You know you're not in Kansas anymore, as the saying goes. The food is good, honest stuff, mainly fishy, including a terrific *pasticcio di pesce con pasta fatta in casa* (a homemade seafood lasagna), *gnocchi di zucca con scampi e rucola* (little dumplings made with pumpkin in a scampi and arugula sauce), and *moscardini al torcellana* (baby octopus in a spicy pepper and tomato sauce). The *aperitivi* are well made, the wine list is decent, and all in all this is a comfortable place to spend some time. ♦ Closed Su, M evening. Fondamenta del Macello 690. 717999.

10 Trattoria da Marisa

★★★$$ Some of the most wonderful things about Venice never change. San Marco in the moonlight . . . the lagoon at sunset . . . the Grand Canal at dawn. And Marisa. Close your eyes and picture the paradigmatic Italian Mama: This is Marisa. Eating at her legendary trattoria is not so much like dining out as like being temporarily adopted by a vast and very noisy Italian family. It is an experience that warms your heart as it fills your stomach. This is real, unreconstructed *cucina casalinga* at its best, and in the kind of portions that only a real mama will serve up. One of Marisa's gorgeous helpers will walk you through the options, course by course. Plates hurtle out of the kitchen overflowing with pasta *al ragu*, *al anitra* (with duck), or *al tonno* (with a delicious sauce of tuna, olives, and capers). The plates of *pasta e fagioli* are vast, and just the thing when the weather is cold. Then there might be a *bollito misto* (mixed boiled meats served with *mostarda* and *salsa verde*), *museto* (boiled sausage served with mustard), *trippa* (tripe), or a gamey *salmi de cervo e capriolo* (a stew of mixed venisons). All are served with Marisa's choice of seasonal vegetables. As people arrive, they frequently pop into the kitchen at the back to greet the *regina della cucina* before squeezing around a table. In good weather there are tables out on the Fondamenta too, but even then, a table at Marisa's is like a four-leaf clover. If you manage to get one, you will be very, very lucky. ♦ Closed Su, M, and Wed PM. Fondamenta San d. Giobbe 652(b). 720211

11 The Ghetto

In 1516, the Council of Ten decreed that the Jews of Venice were to be confined on one island in Cannaregio. This island was cut off by wide canals and the water gates built at the ends of the bridges were manned by Christian guards. The gates opened at dawn and closed at sunset. Traces of the hinges can still be seen The name "ghetto" was derived from the Venetian dialect for a foundry—*geto*—for that was what had formerly occupied the site. The name spread across the world, identifying Jewish settlements everywhere, and then became a general term for areas of specifically ethnic or poor habitation. The occupants were allowed into the rest of Venice during the day but had to wear identifying badges and caps. Jews of many nationalities moved to this area, particularly after they were banished from Spain in 1492. They spoke German, Spanish, Italian, and a variety of Asian languages. They were accepted as permanent residents, but were often subjected to a series of hard conditions and were under constant threat of expulsion. They could not own land or buildings; they could not practice any professions (except to sell used clothes and objects, and at times to practice medicine). They were obliged to run three pawn shops at impossibly low interest rates—an absolute requirement in order to avoid expulsion and keep the economy of the Republic afloat. The pawn shops took heavy losses, and Jewish communities from all over Europe had to cover their debts to keep them open. The houses on the small island were built around a central square that once housed no fewer than 60 tailors' shops and three moneylenders' offices. As new families came in, extra floors were added to the buildings (some apartment ceiling heights are under six feet!). These "Venetian skyscrapers," some seven, eight, or even nine stories high (and without elevators), can still be seen today. In 1541 the original ghetto spread to the **Ghetto Vecchio** and then, as more and more people arrived, into the **Ghetto Novissimo** in 1633. By the mid-17th century the Jewish population had risen to over 5,000. The ghetto gates were finally opened permanently when the young Napoleon Bonaparte conquered the Republic in 1797.

11 Campo del Ghetto Nuovo

Today the square is a wide and peaceful space, ideal for neighborhood children to play in while mothers watch from their apartment windows. Although a handful of Jewish families still live in the ghetto, only a kosher baker and a couple of souvenir shops remain from the colorful mixture of languages and nationalities that once filled this area. ♦ Entrances on Rio dei Ghetto Nuovo. *Vaporetto* stops: San Marcuola, Guglie

On Campo del Ghetto Nuovo:

Casa di Riposa Israelitica

This enormous building—a rest home—is now home to just ten people, although the Jewish community uses it to welcome groups of travelers and occasionally to provide kosher meals.

Monumento di Arbit Blatas

On the wall opposite the museum you will find the **Holocaust Memorial**, created by Arbit Blatas. During World War II, the *campo* was used as a collecting point for people being sent to the concentration camps. The bronze plaque on the memorial depicts "The Last Train." ♦ Entrances on Rio dei Ghetto Nuovo. *Vaporetto* stops: San Marcuola, Guglie

On Campo del Ghetto Nuovo:

Locanda del Ghetto

$$ New and situated in a building dating from 1400, which became a synagogue in the 1500s, this nine-room *locanda* is Italy's only hotel with a certificate from the rabbinical authorities as to its kosher status. Rooms feature marble bathrooms, air conditioning, TV, minibar, and even a timer for those guests who wish it for the Sabbath. A couple have terraces overlooking the square. Breakfast is included and is kosher. The staff are lovely, and there is Internet access and a landing stage for water taxis. This little hotel is unique. ♦ No. 2893. 2759292; fax 2757987. e-mail: ghetto@veneziahotels.com. www.veneziahotels.com

Museo Ebraico (Jewish Museum)

Four centuries of Jewish life in the Venice ghetto, including precious books, tapestries, jewels, and sacred articles, are displayed in this small museum. The Ghetto's five synagogues can be visited only on a guided tour that leaves the museum every hour, beginning at 10:30AM. ♦ Admission. M-F, Su; closed on Jewish holidays. No. 2902B. 715359

Synagogues on the Campo del Ghetto Nuovo

Of the five remaining synagogues in this area (there were nine in Napoleon's day), three—dating from the 16th century—opened directly onto this square. Their names reflected the diversity of the population: the **Scuola Grande Tedesca** (Great German Synagogue); the **Scuola del Canton** (Synagogue of the Corner), so-called probably because of its location; and the **Scuola Italiana** (Italian Synagogue). They can be visited during museum hours (see **Museo Ebraico**, opposite), with a guide provided by the museum. ♦ Information on services: 715012

12 Ghetto Vecchio

This long, narrow area stretches down to the Fondamenta Cannaregio. Many of the buildings that hold *Bet Midhrash*—or studying houses—on their upper floors are characteristically high. The Ghetto Vecchio opens out just once into the Campiello delle Scuole. It is here you will find the two remaining synagogues, built so there is nothing between the congregation and God.

Within the Ghetto Vecchio:

Scuola Levantina (Eastern Mediterranean Synagogue)

This Sephardic synagogue is on a little square outside the original island of the Ghetto. The exterior was designed in the 17th century, probably by **Baldassare Longhena**. The interior was decorated with astonishingly beautiful wood carvings by Andrea Brustolon, the finest Venetian cabinetmaker of the 18th century. Visits must be arranged at the **Museo Ebraico** (see opposite) ♦ Campiello delle Scuole 1228 (at Calle Ghetto Vecchio). *Vaporetto* stop: Guglie

Scuola Spagnola (Spanish Synagogue)

This is the largest of the Ghetto's houses of worship. It was built in 1550 and redesigned by **Baldassare Longhena** in the 17th century, although the interior decorations are mainly 18th-century. It is thought to be the only place where services have been held continuously from 1550 until the present day. Services are held nowadays from Passover until the high holiday season. Visits can be arranged through the Museo Ebraico. ♦ Campiello delle Scuole 1146 (at Calle Ghetto Vecchio). *Vaporetto* stop: Guglie

Ristorante Gam Gam

★$ The first kosher restaurant in modern times in Venice is owned by Orthodox Jews from New York and conveniently located between Ponte Guglie and the Ghetto for the reported 24,000 people who make the pilgrimage here yearly. Gefilte fish, couscous, and a range of imaginatively cooked vegetables are choices for the main course, while such *dolcetti ebraici* (Jewish sweets) as hamantaschen add the finishing touch. There is a small selection of kosher wines from Israel, and the restaurant offers Shabbat meals on booking. ♦ M-Th, Su, lunch and dinner; F, lunch. Fondamenta di Cannaregio 1122 (between Sottoportico Campiello Pozzo and Calle Ghetto Vecchio). 717538. www.jewishvenice.org. *Vaporetto* stop: Guglie

13 Hotel Hesperia

$$ This romantic, 20-room hotel would cost far more if it were closer to the city's hub; the location on a lazy little canal only enhances its charm. Rooms are of average size, but the décor is thoughtfully done, and private, spacious baths are a plus. ♦ Calle Riello 459 (at Fondamenta Savorgnan). 715251, 716001; fax 715112. e-mail Hesperia@shineline.it. *Vaporetto* stops: Guglie, Ferrovia

14 Da Luca e Fred

★★★$ Throw away your diet books, count cholesterol tomorrow, and come inside this fantastic, friendly little *cichetteria* and treat your tummy to some fun. A lunchtime here is an education in the traditional idiosyncrasies of Venetian snack food. And the food is very good here—all of it. Down one side of the small, wood-paneled space runs the glass-topped bar, full to bursting with Venetian specialties. Choose from the huge selection of *spiedini* (brochettes)—there are prawns and calamari rings, stuffed olives and crab croquettes, all dipped in a light batter and deep fried. There is the Venetian equivalent of the French *croque monsieur*—a little sandwich of mozzarella and anchovy or tomato, also sealed in batter and fried. There are tiny tasty meatballs and tuna croquettes, batter-shrouded soft-shell crabs, sardines, and baby octopus. There are rolls of marinated eggplant wrapped around taste-bomb stuffings (before, of course, being dipped in batter and deep fried). Daily specials are announced at 11:30AM and at 7:30PM. There is a good range of beers, including Heineken and the excellent Moretti Rosso. The bar also serves good wines and a top-of-the-range Prosecco. Service is warm, friendly, and helpful. ♦ M, Tu-Su. Rio Terrà San Leonardo 1518 (at Ponte delle Guglie). 716170. *Vaporetto* stop: Guglie

15 Angolo di Tanit

★★★$$ A little corner of Sicily in Venice. And if all the food in Sicily is like this, I'll book my flight now! Allow the goateed Sicilian owner to guide you through the menu. He will make you, in the nicest possible way, some offers you can't refuse! Like the *caponata*, which comes not as a stew, but as silky eggplant rolled around pepperoni, tomato, and other ingredients. Delicious. The pasta dishes will live in your taste memory forever. Spaghetti comes with sardines and wild fennel, and the *busiati ribusiati* (little horns of pasta in a sauce of garlic, almonds, and Pecorino) is probably the best pasta dish I have eaten in my entire life. The *secondi* are just as delicious. If you like squid, you will never like it more than you will here—stuffed with a sweet-and-sour mix featuring tomatoes, raisins, and caper berries. I cannot imagine Sicily will ever have a better ambassador than the chef here. If you wish to take what you've tasted with you, the restaurant has a deli opposite stocking many Sicilian specialties and a good selection of wines and liqueurs. ♦ W-M, lunch and dinner. Calle dell'Aseo 1885. 720504

16 Hotel Abbazia

$$ This really lovely, calm, spacious hotel belies its position practically on top of the main railway station. The name means "abbey," and indeed it was—for the monks of the Scalzi order, "the Barefoot Carmelite Friars of Venice." Much of it has been recently renovated and the newer rooms are absolutely lovely, many looking onto the charming inner garden. Of the 50 rooms, there are some non-smoking and some with polished wooden floors for anyone sensitive to dust from carpets. There is a breakfast room and a beautiful bar in a long, marble-floored hall that still has the pulpit of the abbey high on the wall. A genuine find! ♦ Calle Priuli dei Cavaletti 68. 717333. www.abbaziahotel.com. *Vaporetto* stop: Ferrona

17 Hotel Rossi

$ There are rooms in this hotel in a quiet little offshoot of the Rio Terrà Lista di Spagna. It's almost always full, so it must be doing something right! Ten of the rooms have baths, and all have air conditioning but no TV or minibar. ♦ Lista di Spagna (actually Calle de le Procuratie) 262. 715164; fax 717784. e-mail: rossihotel@interfree.it

18 Hotel Amadeus

$$$$ This handsome hotel is located just 300 yards from the train station. The 63 rooms, some with small terraces, are large and decorated with 18th-century-style furniture. The hotel also has a small private garden. Oddly enough, it has a Japanese sushi restaurant, open for dinner only. ♦ Rio Terrà Lista di Spagna 227 (at Campo San Geremia). 715610; fax 2204040. *Vaporetto* stop: Guglie

19 Palazzo Labia

Built by **Andrea Cominelli** in 1720 for the wealthy Labia family, this sumptuous home has three façades: one overlooking the Canal Grande, one on the Canale di Cannaregio, and a third on the **Campo San Geremia**. Legend has it that when the palazzo opened, Signore Labia stood at a balcony and threw precious pieces of silverware into the canal one by one and said,

"L'abbia o non l'abbia, saro sempre un Labia." ("Have it or not, I will always be a Labia.") The legend continues that he had ordered sunken nets to be spread underwater, which were later hoisted up to retrieve the family valuables. The interior salons were frescoed by Giambattista Tiepolo. In all, 13 rooms of the *piano nobile* (second floor) can be visited upon request.

Today the palace is the Venice headquarters of **RAI**, the Italian radio and television network. Production studios as well as offices were installed in the countless rooms, while the Tiepolo halls are frequently used for meetings and conferences—often with protests from the Art Conservation Department. ♦ Tiepolo room, free; admission for all others. W-F, 3PM-4PM; call to confirm. Campo San Geremia 275 (at Salizzada San Geremia). 5242812. *Vaporetto* stop: Guglie

20 Rio Terrà Lista di Spagna

In the time of the Serene Republic, the Spanish embassy was on this street (hence its name), at No. 168. Like most embassies, it was far from the city's center, as though to keep foreigners away from the Republic's heart (members of the Venetian nobility were forbidden even to talk to representatives of foreign powers, except in an official capacity; in the theaters and casinos, government spies would denounce patricians simply for greeting or nodding to foreign ministers). The Lista is the most un-Venetian of Venetian streets. It is the only part of town where neon signs are allowed, and its proximity to the train station has turned parts of it into a bazaar for cheap souvenirs. ♦ Between Campo San Geremia and Fondamenta dei Scalzi. *Vaporetto* stops: Guglie, Ferrovia

21 Il Gelatone

Before you came to Italy, did you dream about what it would be like? And about how delicious your first taste of real Italian ice cream would be? Well, this place will be a dream come true. It's a tiny hole-in-the-wall on the side of the Rio Terrà della Maddalena with just the counter and the ices. But what ices! For a mouthful of luxury, try the mascarpone ice cream. Very few places make it at all, but the Gelatone makes it brilliantly. The *meringata* is vanilla packed with crunchy, melt-in-the-mouth chunks of homemade meringue. Feeling virtuous? This is the place for you, because their frozen yogurt will change your life—or it will if you try it with honey and sesame-seed ice. There is pistachio and *frutta di bosca* (forest fruits), rich chocolate and tangy lemon. And three big scoops will set you back just two dollars! All the ice creams are made fresh each day using whole milk and cream. Go with your dreams and come to Il Gelatone! ♦ Daily. Rio Terrà della Maddalena 2063. 720631

22 Scuola Vecchia della Misericordia

A charitable association of laymen (connected to the abbey of the same name) was housed in this 15th-century *scuola* (school) along the canal called Rio della Sensa. The late-Gothic façade of the *scuola,* at right angles with the Baroque church of **Santa Maria Valverde**, completes one of the most pleasant little squares in Venice. Today the *scuola* and abbey belong to the city and house one of the most advanced centers for stone restoration in the world. Peep through the small door on the Rio della Sensa to see the large garden, behind which are the sophisticated laboratories where international experts examine stones and marbles from monuments all over the world, studying their composition and figuring out how to preserve them. ♦ Campo dell'Abbazia 3551 (at Fondamenta dell'Abbazia). *Vaporetto* stops: Ca' d'Oro, Fondamenta Nuove, Madonna dell'Orto

23 Santa Maria Valverde

The name of this 14th-century church, which means Santa Maria of the Green Valley, was derived from the original landscape of the area, which was probably once covered with vegetable gardens. Secluded as it seems to be on the water's edge, with canals in front and on the right side, this small, delightful church used to be the main chapel for the friars of the abbey of the nearby **Scuola Vecchia della Misericordia**. The façade, designed by **Clemente Moli**, is a remarkable example of elegant, surprisingly sober Baroque architecture. The statue over the portal is not, as one would expect, the portrait of a saint but a monument to Gaspare Moro, the patrician who financed the works on the façade. ♦ Campo dell'Abbazia and Fondamenta dell'Abbazia. *Vaporetto* stops: Ca' d'Oro, Fondamenta Nuove, Madonna dell'Orto

24 Fondamenta della Misericordia

The name of this canal bank changes five times before ending in the northwest area called Sant'Alvise. A walk along this stretch offers a glimpse of the quiet, old-fashioned charm of the area. ♦ Between Rio della Misericordia and Rio della Sensa. *Vaporetto* stops: Ca' d'Oro, Fondamenta Nuove, Madonna dell'Orto

On Fondamenta della Misericordia:

Scuola Nuova della Misericordia

The building, unusually tall for this part of town, was designed in 1583 by **Jacopo Sansovino** for a local charitable brotherhood and was never completed. The interior, also by Sansovino, has been neglected by the city. For 50 years, until 1990, the hall on the second floor was used as a stadium, with seats for hundreds of spectators right under the decaying 16th-century frescoes. A *fondamenta* along the building's east side leads to the Ponte dell'Abbazia, which has a charming view over the Canale della Misericordia to the open lagoon. ♦ No. 3599

25 Algiubagio

★★★$$ Tired of fish? Can't face another *risotto nero*? This is the place for you. Young, new, sexy, and on the windswept Fondamenta Nuove, this place really manages to be most things to most people. It is a café and bar in front, with a good list of wines by the glass and three terrific Belgian beers on tap. There are pizzas and pastries, snacks and salads. The coffee is good and the barmen friendly. A cigarette and candy desk is available should you need anything from M&Ms to B&H. Behind this is a large and airy restaurant with lots of exposed brick and wooden beams. The menu teases you with its starter of *fritelle sorpresa con menta*, and comes with a little surprise from the chef. I can't reveal what it is—you'll have to come here and find out for yourself. The menu is very unusual for Venice, spearheaded by a raft of steaks like Aberdeen angus served up in a variety of delicious-sounding and innovative ways. It comes with a Guinness sauce, a piccante sauce, with *erbette* (sweet herbs), and with pink peppercorns. And, believe it or not, the guest book is more or less a verbal standing ovation for the chef's most daring innovation—steak with apple and chocolate. Yup, you read it here first! Apart from this there is wild duck with mango salad, carpaccio of reindeer, a good choice of *salatone* (composed salads), and a truly mouth-watering selection of 12 regional cheeses. For dessert, you can do a lot worse than their fried strawberries with vanilla cream. So you see, carnivores can be happy in Venice! Algiubagio also does a very good breakfast. ♦ W-M, 6:30AM-midnight. Fondamente Nuove 5039. 5236084. www.algiubagio.net

26 Oratorio dei Crociferi

The Crociferi were a monastic order that once owned this entire area, including the square in front of the oratory, the church, and the large building at the church's right (originally their monastery). The oratory was an extra chapel. Restored in the 1980s, it contains a cycle of paintings by Palma il Giovane, who is considered the heir of Titian and the best painter of Venetian Mannerism. Palma's works, which mark the passage between the late-Renaissance and Baroque periods, are found throughout Venice. ♦ Admission. Daily; call 5200633 to confirm schedule. Campo dei Gesuiti 4903-5 (between Calle delle Candele and Calle dei Crociferi). *Vaporetto* stop: Fondamente Nuove

27 Santa Maria Assunta (Gesuiti)

When it was readmitted to Venice after a 50-year banishment in 1657, the Jesuit order took over this church, which overlooks the beautiful lagoon toward the cemetery and Murano. The Jesuits then proceeded to rebuild the 13th-century church—according to their well-established standards of grandeur—in the international Baroque style they had successfully experimented with in Rome (Chiesa del Gesù), Paris (St. Paul), and all over Europe. The façade is tall and emphatic, with the Jesuit trademark of columns on two levels. It is topped by Baroque statues with limbs reaching skyward in typical Baroque poses. But the real magnificence is in the interior, which is decorated with a stunning wealth of marble carved to imitate damasks and draperies. White-and-green marble covers most of the walls, falling in rich folds like real drapery material and creating an effect that, depending on the viewer's taste, could be thought of as marvelous or kitsch. The canvas on the first altar at the right is *The Martyrdom of Saint Lawrence,* a masterwork painted by Titian on his return from Rome (which might explain the classical architecture in the background, not characteristic of Titian). The painting immediately became famous. Titian himself made a copy of it for Philip II of Spain, and a popular engraving, based on the painting and approved by Titian, soon circulated all over Europe. A cleaning performed for the Titian exhibition in Venice and Washington, DC, in 1990 brought out the fine details of this nighttime scene, where the only sources of light are the burning coals under the martyr's body and the divine rays breaking through thick, black clouds in the sky. ♦ Campo dei Gesuiti and Salizzada dei Specchieri (closed for renovation). *Vaporetto* stop: Fondamente Nuove

28 Fondamente Nuove

The word *fondamente* is used in Venice for the paved banks of the canals and of the open lagoon. The borders of the natural islands were—and still are—reinforced with foundations made of wood poles and stone to prevent erosion by the waves and tides. The long banks called *Fondamente Nuove* were built in the 16th century as part of a reclamation effort that involved the whole northeastern part of the city.

Far from the typical tourist tracks (except for the small part used by *vaporetti* to and from Murano, Torcello, and other islands), they constitute a splendid, although somewhat melancholy, walk, particularly during the long summer evenings. The nearest island visible from here, recognizable by its cypress trees, is San Michele, site of the Venice cemetery. Beyond that is Murano and, in the distance, the slanted bell tower of Burano. On a clear day it is not unusual to see all the way to the mainland and the snow-capped mountains of the Alps. There is a channel along the Fondamente for boat traffic. Beyond the channel, marked by the typical wood poles called *bricole,* the lagoon is not deeper than 3 feet, and motorboats can cross it only at high tide. An hour's walk along the Fondamente is a romantic experience and a way to see the daily rituals of Venetian life—on weekdays, heavy boats pass by, carrying goods to be distributed all over town, while on Sunday and in the evening, a surprising number of rowboats cross the area, with Venetians doing their equivalent of logging. Flat-bottomed sailboats, old-fashioned craft with balanced lug sails that are ideal for the flat lagoon waters, are enjoying a renaissance among Venetians, who now shun polluting powerboats. ♦ Between Rio di Santa Giustina and Sacca della Misericordia. *Vaporetto* stops: Fondamente Nuove, Ospedale Civile

29 Stazione Ferroviaria (Train Station)

The present structure was erected in 1954 to replace the original station, built under Austrian domination in 1841. Officially called the **Stazione Santa Lucia**, it carries the name of the Renaissance church that was demolished to make room for it. A pier where all the main *vaporetto* lines converge is conveniently located down the steps from the station. ♦ Fondamenta Santa Lucia. *Vaporetto* stop: Ferrovia

30 Scalzi

The Scalzi (barefoot monks) are a monastic order, an ultrastrict offshoot of the Carmelites, that settled in Venice in the 17th century. This church was designed by **Baldassare Longhena** for them in a style reminiscent of Roman Baroque; the façade was added by **Giuseppe Sardi** in 1680. The main altar is a Baroque masterpiece, also of Roman inspiration, by Giuseppe Pozzo; the ceiling was originally frescoed by Giambattista Tiepolo, but was destroyed by an Austrian bomb in 1915. A Tiepolo fresco remains in the vault in the second chapel on the right (*St. Teresa in Glory*), and two more, of lesser importance, are in the vault in the first chapel on the left. ♦ Fondamenta dei Scalzi and Fondamenta Santa Lucia. *Vaporetto* stop: Ferrovia

31 Hotel Bellini

$$$$ Its location just a stone's throw from the railroad station will strike you either as a plus or a minus. But this 97-room hotel is pretty attractive for a "station" hotel, with antique furnishings, silk damask wall covering and draperies, and Murano chandeliers. It also has a sundeck overlooking the Canal Grande, a breakfast room, and a pleasant bar. ♦ Rio Terrà Lista di Spagna 116 (between Calle della Misericordia and Calle Priuli della dei Cavalletti). 5242488; fax 715193. *Vaporetto* stop: Ferrovia

32 Ponte Scalzi

When the trains started to arrive in Venice in 1841 during the Austrian occupation, a bridge over the Canal Grande across from the station became a necessity. **A.E. Neville**, a noted builder of iron bridges and the designer of the Ponte dell'Accademia, produced another of his striking creations: a suspended iron bridge (it was his 38th), preceding such structures as the Eiffel Tower and the Brooklyn Bridge. It contrasted sharply with the Venetian aesthetic, and in 1934 the city decided to demolish it (together with the Accademia Bridge), replacing it with the present stone structure by Italian architect **Eugenio Miozzi**. ♦ Between Fondamenta San Simeon Piccolo and Fondamenta dei Scalzi. *Vaporetto* stop: Ferrovia

33 Palazzo Vendramin Calergi

The façade of this 15th-century palazzo facing the Canal Grande was the first great achievement of **Mauro Codussi**, the artist who changed Venetian architecture by abandoning the Gothic tradition for the new Renaissance style popular in Florence and Rome. Richard Wagner lived in this palazzo and died here in 1883. Today it belongs to the city of Venice and is used in the winter for the **Casino**, whose summer home is in a far less impressive modern location on the Lido. From October to early May, gamblers flock to the Casino, one of only four allowed on national territory by Italian legislation. A couple of dozen roulette tables are installed in the Renaissance rooms, with bets taken from 9 euros up; baccarat and blackjack tables are also available. A few water taxis are always at the door at night, ready to take the winners to their hotels or to their cars parked on Piazzale Roma—the losers can walk. ♦ Casino: daily, 2:45PM-2:30AM. Calle Larga Vendramin 2400 (off Rio Terrà della Maddalena, between Calle Vendramin and Calle Colombina). 5297111. *Vaporetto* stop: San Marcuola

34 Vini da Gigio

★★$$ This restaurant has the kind of tucked-away location, on the side of a baby canal, that allows you to regard it as your "discovery." It is typically Venetian, dark and friendly. Interesting *primi piatti* (first courses) include *ravioli di raddichio con zabaione di taleggio* (ravioli with raddichio sauced with a light mousse of taleggio cheese) and *penne al Gorgonzola e pistacchi* (pasta quills with Gorgonzola and pistachio). Main courses include *anguilla alla griglia* (good, chunky grilled eel) on the fishy front and a tasty stuffed rabbit for those who prefer meat. The wine list is typically enticing and equally typically almost all Italian. Service is helpful and efficient. ♦ Tu-Su, lunch and dinner. Fondamenta San Felice 3628A (between Strada Nuova and Calle della Stua). 5285140. *Vaporetto* stop: Ca' d'Oro

35 La Cantina

★★★★$$ This is the kind of place you come to Italy to find. Wine barrels guard the entrance to this low, dark little bar. There is an old piano in the corner and a huge bottle of red being decanted on the bar. Then you see the piles of oysters and local scallops nestling on hills of ice. You read the menu pinned up on the wall and it says "plates of cheese, *salume*, seafood." And you stay. The platters are a revelation. Interesting seasonal cheeses in peak condition are served perhaps with a little *miele di castagna* or *mostarda*. An aromatic plate of mixed sausage, salamis, and hams comes with a mound of delicious salad in the middle. The mixed seafood platter is a revelation. Little local clams are lightly marinated, and tuna sashimi and deliciously marinated salmon burst with freshness on your tongue. And the tiny mound of salad in the center of the platter is a perfect accompaniment. "Sometimes there will be perhaps not much fish," apologizes Andrea, the owner, "if there is bad weather, or if the fish is not good." If only more restaurants were so choosy about the freshness and quality of their ingredients! "Then," he suggests, "you must just eat more salami." There is an impressive wine list, but you won't go wrong with a glass from that big decanter on the bar. In fact, it is difficult to go wrong in here at all. ♦ Tu-Sa, 11AM-midnight. Strada Nuova 3689. 5228258

36 San Felice

Not famous, but a lovely old church, built originally in the 10th century and then rebuilt in the 16th century. If you find yourself at the end of the Strada Nuova and feeling frazzled, this is one place to find a little peace and thinking space. You can also admire the church's Tintoretto! ♦ Strada Nuova (at Ponte San Felice). Daily, 4:30PM-7PM

37 Osteria dalla Vedova

★★$$ Old bare wooden tables, antique furniture, and total informality characterize this most venerable of Venetian *bacari* (wine bars). The owners have retained the original atmosphere, with ready-made food available at the counter to accompany the drinks. An eclectic group of wealthy Venetians, gondoliers, and hard hats frequent the place. Upon entering, check the counter for the choice of food, but ask about what's cooking as well—it may be worth sipping your wine for a few minutes while the risottos, spaghetti, or *pasta e fagioli* (pasta and beans) receive their final touches. The official name of the place, written on top of the door, is **Trattoria Ca' d'Oro**, but all Venice knows it as *"dalla Vedova"* ("at the widow's"). ♦ M-W, F, Sa, lunch and dinner; Su, dinner. Closed August. Reservations required. No credit cards accepted. Ramo di Ca' d'Oro 3912-3952 (between Strada Nuova and Calle del Pistor). 5285324. *Vaporetto* stop: Ca' d'Oro

38 Ca' d'Oro

The façade of this splendid 15th-century building by **Matteo Raverti**, universally considered a masterwork of Venetian Gothic, should be seen from the Canal Grande. In striking contrast with medieval building principles, the Venetian palazzi have light façades made of carved stone, with ample loggias and open spaces between slender columns. Nothing could be further from the austere, almost hostile, appearance of the medieval and Renaissance palazzi of Florence, but the leading Florentine families were constantly fighting each other and needed to build their homes like fortresses, while the Venetian constitution guaranteed peace within the city limits (there are no examples of armed feuds among leading families nor of any popular insurrection during the millennium of the Republic's life). Hence the open loggias, the ample windows, and the very fragility of the Venetian façade—perhaps more an act of faith in the Serene Republic than an aesthetic choice.

The central part of the magnificent, restored façade in this building can be seen as a unique window, made precious by the lacework applied to the stones. Originally the façade was decorated in red and blue and trimmed with gold leaf, which gave the palazzo its name, "House of Gold." Ironically, the name no longer fits. The restoration stripped the marble of all its gilt work, as well as the red and blue embellishment. The building changed hands a number of times after it was built in 1440, until it was acquired by a Russian prince who presented it to an Italian ballerina in 1840. Later it passed on to Baron Giorgio Franchetti, who restored it and bequeathed it to the city of Venice. ♦ M, 8:15AM-2PM; Tu-Su, 8:15AM-7:15PM. Calle della Ca' d'Oro 3932 (at Canal Grande). 5238790. *Vaporetto* stop: Ca' d'Oro

Within Ca' d'Oro:

Galleria Franchetti

This gallery was built around a core collection bequeathed to the city by Giorgio Franchetti and reorganized in 1984. On the second floor is an extraordinary collection of early Venetian and Byzantine bas-reliefs in stone, dating from the 11th to 13th centuries. They were used to decorate the façades of public and private buildings, and they exhibit a delightful sense of symmetry and grace. A niche in **Room 1** contains a famous *Saint Sebastian* by Andrea Mantegna. Through the splendid, sunlit ballroom, one can reach the loggia on the Canal Grande and enjoy the view over a long stretch of the canal and of the **Pescheria** (Fish Market) on the other side. **Room 3** contains medals and bronzes of the Renaissance, and **Room 6** has a fine collection of minor Italian painters, mostly Tuscans. On the third floor, **Room 9** contains *Venus at the Mirror* by Titian, and two remarkable portraits of gentlemen, one by Tintoretto and one by Anthony Van Dyck. Collected in **Room 16** are the few remnants of the frescoes that used to cover the **Fondaco dei Tedeschi** (Germans' Warehouse) on the Canal Grande. Although barely recognizable, they have an emotional impact on art lovers because they are by Giorgione and Titian, who worked almost shoulder to shoulder on the same façade. Other items of interest on this floor include Bernini's preparatory work for his famous fountain on Piazza Navona in Rome, and two *Views of Venice* by Francesco Guardi. ♦ Admission. Daily

39 Osteria al Bomba

One of the loveliest sights in Cannaregio greets you as you come through the door of this friendly little place: their lavish counter of *cicchetti* (bar snacks). They have one of the best selections in the city. It runs the gamut of all the usual: *sarde in saor* (sardines in sauce), *polpette* (little fried patties of meat or tuna), *baccalà* (salt cod) either whipped to a creamy mousse or chopped with onion and parsley. The *baccalà* mousse can be spun into balls and deep fried, and the tangy *saor* marinade is applied to scampi as well as sardines. There are sea snails and huge prawns and all manner of delicious snacks for you to point at and try. Just around the corner of the bar is a long, long table with a gondola ax at the end where the main menu is served, offering terrific freshly made gnocchi with sea bream and green beans (in season), tagliatelle with scampi tails and fresh asparagus, a superb (and generous) *grigliata mista* (mixed grill of seafood), and an inventive dish of fresh tuna served in thin slices garnished with sesame seeds. The wine list is impressive (including many New World wines), and the list of grappas even more so. Service is incredibly friendly, and the very local clientele quickly make you one of their own. ♦ Daily. Calle Dell'Oca 4297/8. 5205175. www.osteriaalbomba.it

40 Peter's Teahouse

Very new, and a godsend to anyone in Venice who likes to drink good tea, this oasis of calm and quiet near the start of the bustling Strada Nuova offers over 250 varieties of tea from all over the world—black tea and white tea, green tea and spiced teas, herbal, ayurvedic, and fruit teas. They come as single varieties or blends. And the Teahouse sells you everything you need to brew and drink them in style. To say nothing of a few choice nibbles to accompany them. The gently spoken owners look—if they don't mind my saying so—like good tea drinkers. Welcome to their world. ♦ Tu-Sa, 10AM-12:30PM and 3:30PM-7:30PM; and M PM. Salizzada del Pistor 4553(a) (at Santi Apostoli).

41 Locanda ai Santi Apostoli

$$$ The Bianchi-Michiel family has lovingly restored its patrician home (parts of it dating to the 15th century) on the Canal Grande and made the third floor into a small and very special hotel. The 10 rooms are tastefully decorated with a choice selection of the family's elegant antiques. Request **Room 8** or **9**—the only two directly on the canal; the view is well worth the additional cost. The second floor is an apartment that can also be rented. ♦ Strada Nuova 4391 (between Calle del Duca and Calle del Pegola). 5212612; fax 5212611. *Vaporetto* stop: Ca' d'Oro

42 Strada Nuova

The **Campo dei Santissimi Apostoli** marks the beginning of this long, wide (for Venice), and unusually straight street. The Strada Nuova runs parallel to the Canal Grande from **Santissimi Apostoli** to Rio della Maddalena, crossing two canals and continuing with the relatively wide Rio Terrà della Maddalena and Rio Terrà San Leonardo before leading into the Rio Terrà Lista di Spagna, which terminates at the train station. The street was designed and built in the 19th century, and it represents one of the few attempts to accommodate pedestrian traffic in Venice. It addressed the problem of connecting the central Rialto and St. Mark's areas with the new train station, which had joined Venice to the mainland for the first time in the city's history. Among the many proposals, the one that was finally chosen was probably the least damaging to the existing urban structure, but it destroyed a large, ancient neighborhood, characterized by tiny alleys and teeming daily life. All buildings that stood in the way of the new thoroughfare were destroyed, and new façades were erected along its perfectly straight, totally un-Venetian sides. The residents showed their disapproval by refusing to call the new street by the name proposed by its builders, calling it Strada Nuova instead, making this the only *strada* (street) in Venice (as opposed to all the ones called *calle* and *rio terrà*). Today the steady flow of day-trippers arriving by train use the route extensively. The Strada has a proliferation of *pasticcerie*, so if you have a sweet tooth or find yourself longing for a serious carbohydrate fix, come here. It also boasts a surprising number of cosmetic shops, some seriously upmarket. There is even a Body Shop and a branch of Lush, the handmade cosmetics chain. At various times of the year, street stalls spring up selling scarves and gloves and hats. Don't ignore them; they are not the rip-off you might think. The best thing about the Strada Nuova is **La Cantina**, sitting at the end closest to the station. ♦ Between Campo dei Santissimi Apostoli and Rio della Maddalena. *Vaporetto* stop: Ca' d'Oro

43 Santissimi Apostoli

The relatively high banks of the islands in this part of Venice made them desirable for early settlers. The foundations of this church date back to the seventh century; however, its present shape is due to a radical renovation in the 17th century. Inside, the first chapel at the right is the **Cappella Corner**, attributed to **Mauro Codussi** and adorned with *The Communion of St. Lucy,* one of Giambattista Tiepolo's best paintings. ♦ Campo dei Santissimi Apostoli (at Salizzada del Pistor). *Vaporetto* stop: Ca' d'Oro

44 Osteria da Alberto

★★★$$ Alberto moved to this new and larger place to accommodate the huge crowds that flock here for the delicious *cicchetti* (finger food) and wines. The array of snacks at the front counter are beyond anything else in Venice and include various cheeses, *olive ascolani* (stuffed, deep-fried olives), breaded and fried vegetables, and troughs of out-of-this-world seafood including the best fried sardines in the city. Also ask about what hot pasta Alberto is whipping up that day in the kitchen. Even though there are twice as many tables and twice the room of his last *bacaro* (wine bar), it is best to book ahead since all the tables inevitably have *riservato* signs on them. ♦ M-Sa, lunch and dinner. Reservations recommended. Calle Larga Giacinto Gallina 5401 (between Rio della Panada and Rio di Ca' Widman). 5238153. *Vaporetto* stop: Rialto

45 Un Mondo diVino

★★★$ Not so long ago this was an old-fashioned *macelleria* (butcher shop)—and you will still find excellent *salume*, *nerveti* (calves' cartilage cooked with onions and served with olive oil and vinegar—superb!), and hot *musetto* (a boiled pork sausage, traditionally made from the *muso*—the snout—of a pig). But now they also offer one of Venice's nicest selections of *cicchetti*. There is a good selection of cheeses, a marvelous array of all things fishy and seafoody (including oysters each Friday in season), and everything you can think of preserved—salted, in oil, or lightly pickled. You could very nicely nibble your way to a very full stomach. There are about 40 wines available by the glass, and the couple behind the bar are always glad to advise and encourage. They are incredibly enthusiastic about their wines, and the enthusiasm is catching. You could do worse than start off with their house *aperitivo—frutto di bosco* and *brachetto*—a huge goblet that has a goodly portion of fruits of the forest spooned in, then topped up with a delicious fizz and served to you with a smile and a spoon. It could push spritz off the drinks list! ♦ Daily, 8:30AM-3PM and 5:30PM-9:30PM. Salizzada San Canziano 5984(a). 5211093

46 Santa Maria dei Miracoli

This is one of the most charming and surprising churches in Venice. **Pietro Lombardo**, one of the fathers of the Venetian Renaissance, created it (with, it is rumored, a little help from **Mauro Condussi**) as a wonderful giant mosaic of precious polychromatic marbles. The first stone was laid in 1480, and the church was consecrated in 1489. The most recent renovation, which cleaned all the marble and restored the exterior to its full glory, was started in 1991 and finished in 1998 and was funded by the marvelous Save Venice fund. The two porphyry carvings at the front are lovely—*Dio Padre e due Angeli* at the top and a *Madonna and Child* by Pyrgoteles (Giovanne Giorgio Lascaris, an Italian sculptor of Greek origin who died in 1531). The church has a single nave with walls in slabs of more of the polychromatic marble. It is quite strange, but lovely. The beautifully gilded wooden ceiling is stunning. It features 50 square paintings, arranged in 10 rows of five, depicting prophets, saints, and other religious figures. The main altar is on what can only be described as a great high stage at the far end of the church, reached by a central flight of stairs. Few priests in all of Catholicism can have such a place to preach. ♦ Daily. Rio dei Miracoli (at Calle Castelli). *Vaporetto* stop: Rialto

47 Fiaschetteria Toscana

★★★$$$$ Don't let the name ("Tuscan wine shop") fool you. This place demonstrates much of what is best about Venice. Although it is fairly formal, the welcome is warm and you will always be made to feel like a valued guest. The Fiaschetteria's owner, Albino Busato, has been head of the association of Venetian restaurateurs, and you can see why. Allow one of his wonderful waiters to help you through the men

And consider yourself to have won the jackpot if you are attended by Roberto, a multilingual master of food, wine, and charm. He knows everything the restaurant has to offer, even if it is not on the menu or the wine list. And he will make sure you have the best time you possibly can. The wine list is a tome. It should win awards. The menu is admirably concise and changes, of course, with season and market. Even the bread is excellent—your basket offers a choice including the flat, crunchy variety Italy does so well. To begin, fat spears of white asparagus, in season, are served under a crispy topping of Parmesan or with first-class prosciutto. Pastas include an aromatic spaghetti with scampi and asparagus and an unctuous and totally delicious *bigoli in salsa* (fat spaghetti in a tangy anchovy-and-onion salsa). For the main course, sea bass fillet is pearly white under its browning from the grill, *fegato alla veneziana* (calves' liver Venetian-style) comes in a mounded tangle of slim slices in an oniony sauce, and grilled eel is meaty, chewy, and delicious. Accompanying vegetables and salads are fresh and generously served. Desserts include a delicious honey-hazelnut parfait, and the cheese selection is probably unrivaled in Venice. Again, tell Roberto what you want and he will make it appear. An evening—or indeed a lunch—here is one of the memories you will treasure from your time in Venice. Reservations recommended. ♦ W-Su, lunch and dinner; M, dinner. Salizzada San Giovanni Grisostomo 5719 (at Campo San Giovanni Grisostomo). 5285281. www.fiaschetteriatoscana.it. *Vaporetto* stop: Rialto

48 San Giovanni Grisostomo

This late-15th-century church by **Mauro Codussi** lies at the center of a small island defined by the Canal Grande on the west and by three tiny, charming canals on the other sides. This was one of the first areas settled by the founders of the city and one that still maintains traces of its original Byzantine character. The church, however, is pure Venetian Renaissance; the original structure was destroyed by a fire and entirely rebuilt by Codussi, the Lombard-born master who changed the face of Venetian architecture by introducing Renaissance models to replace the late-Gothic tradition (see **San Michele**, **San Zaccaria**, and **Santa Maria Formosa**). The façade has the typical Codussi design—a full, round arch on the top with two half-arches on the sides. Codussi's interior is a masterpiece of clarity and simplicity. On the first altar at the right is one of the last and best paintings by Giovanni Bellini: *St. Christopher with St. Jerome and St. Augustine*. The canvas on the main altar is *St. John Chrysostomos with Other Saints* by Sebastiano del Piombo, painted by the artist when he was 25 and just before the pope summoned him to Rome and launched his brilliant career. ♦ Salizzada San Giovanni Grisostomo and Campo San Giovanni Grisostomo. *Vaporetto* stop: Rialto

49 Corti del Milion

The *Milion* in the name comes from the popular nickname of Marco Polo's memoirs, which contained a million wonders according to his admirers—detractors said it was a million lies. In the maze of alleys just east of **Campo San Giovanni Grisostomo**, at **No. 5845** in the **Corte Seconda dei Milion**, is where the famous explorer was probably born in 1254. The house has been modified many times over the centuries, but like the others in this little square, it preserves an unmistakably Byzantine character. Some of the window frames and columns and all of the round bas-reliefs date back to the 11th and 12th centuries. ♦ Between Rio di San Lio and Campo San Giovanni Grisostomo. *Vaporetto* stop: Rialto

50 Giacomo Rizzo

A terrific deli, and very much the place to come if you are suffering withdrawal symptoms from anything from peanut butter to cookie mixes. What they are best known for (besides stocking Oreos and Vegemite) is their pasta, which they have been making for four generations. It comes in a bewildering variety of flavors (including cuttlefish, bilberry, and bitter cocoa) and a startling selection of colors (including curaçao blue, the colors of the Italian flag, and several soccer team colors). This is a great place to shop, to eat or to give. ♦ Daily. San Giovanni Grisostomo 5778. 5222824

51 Coin

The name is that of a family of entrepreneurs who expanded out of the Venice area to conquer national and international markets. The Cannaregio branch specializes in clothing and beauty and fashion accessories, and is probably the most elegant of all the store's branches. Venetians are fond of it, and visitors might want to explore it to get an idea of the quality and prices of goods in a middle-to-high-end Italian department store. The third-floor housewares department is particularly worth a peek. There is another, really well-laid-out branch, specializing in beauty products (and it has them *all*, from Mac to Dior) and underwear, in Campo San Lucca. ♦ M-Sa, 9:30AM-7:30PM; Su, 11:30AM-7:30PM. Salizzada San Giovanni Grisostomo 5787 (at the top of Rio del Fontego dei Tedeschi). 5203581. *Vaporetto* stop: Rialto. Also at Campo San Lucca (at Calle San Lucca). 5238444. www.coin.it

Castello

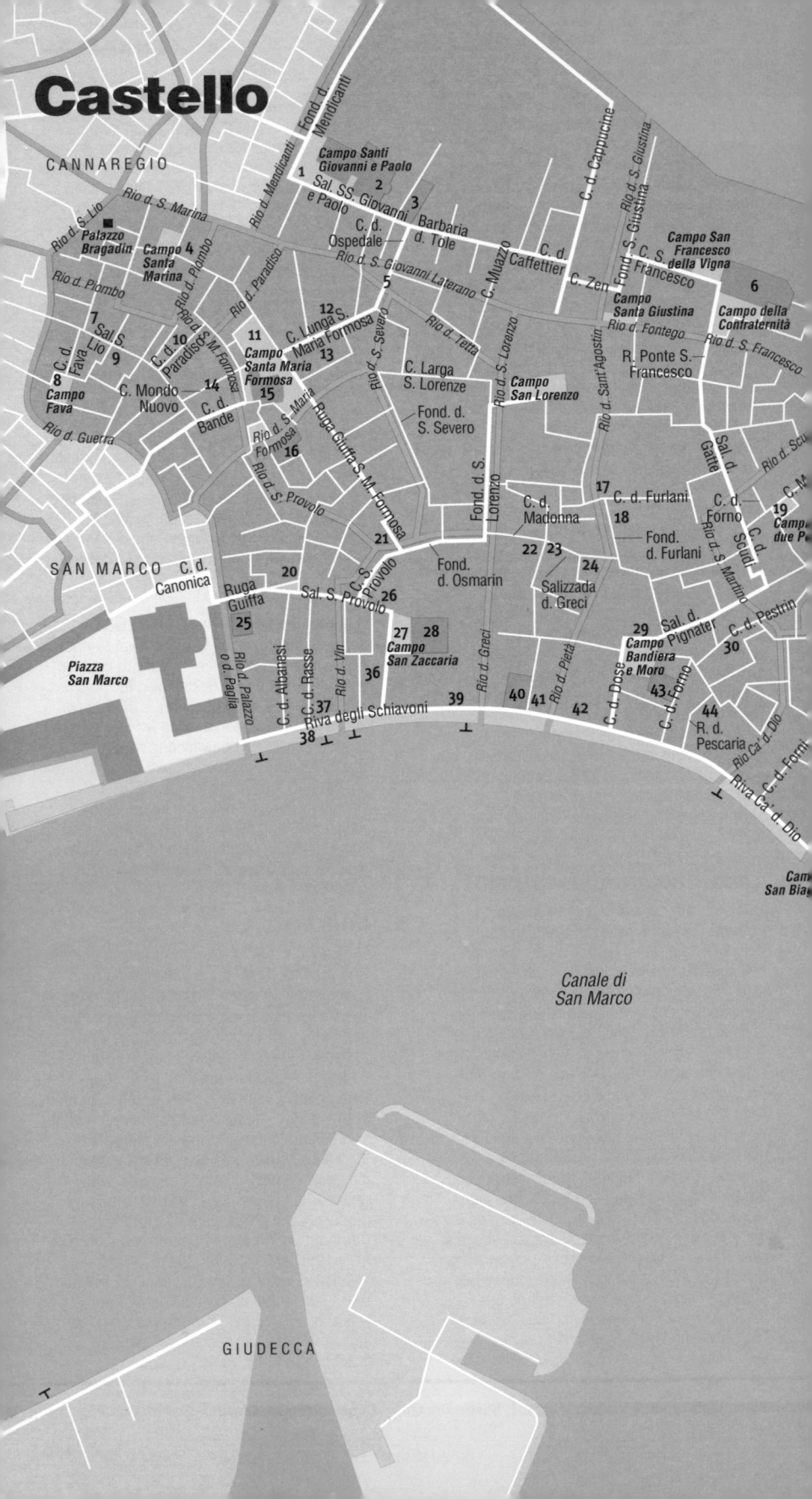
CANNAREGIO
SAN MARCO
GIUDECCA
Canale di San Marco
Piazza San Marco
Palazzo Bragadin
Campo Santa Marina
Campo Fava
Campo Santi Giovanni e Paolo
Campo Santa Maria Formosa
Campo San Lorenzo
Campo San Zaccaria
Campo Santa Giustina
Campo San Francesco della Vigna
Campo della Confraternità
Campo Bandiera e Moro
Campo Pignatei
Riva degli Schiavoni
Riva Ca' d. Dio
Rio d. S. Marina
Rio d. S. Lio
Rio d. Piombo
Rio d. Paradiso
Rio d. Guerra
Rio d. Mendicanti
Rio d. S. Giovanni Laterano
Rio d. Tetta
Rio d. S. Lorenzo
Rio d. Sant'Agostin
Rio d. Fontego
Rio d. S. Francesco
Rio d. S. Giustina
Rio d. S. Provolo
Rio d. S. Martino
Rio d. Pietà
Rio d. Greci
Rio d. Palazzo o d. Paglia
Rio d. Vin
Rio Ca' d. Dio
Fond. d. Mendicanti
Sal. SS. Giovanni e Paolo
C. d. Ospedale
Barbaria d. Tole
C. d. Cappuccina
C. d. Caffettier
C. Zen
C. S. Francesco
C. Muazzo
C. Lunga S. Maria Formosa
C. Larga S. Lorenze
Fond. d. S. Severo
Fond. d. S. Lorenzo
R. Ponte S. Francesco
Sal. d. Gatte
C. d. Furlani
Fond. d. Furlani
C. d. Madonna
C. d. Forno
C. d. Scudi
C. d. Pestrin
Sal. d. Pignatei
Salizzada d. Greci
Fond. d. Osmarin
C. d. Canonica
Ruga Giuffa
Sal. S. Provolo
C. d. Albanesi
C. d. Rasse
C. d. Dose
C. d. Forno
R. d. Pescaria
C. d. Forni
C. d. Fava
C. Mondo Nuovo
C. d. Bande
Sal. S. Lio
Ruga Giuffa S. M. Formosa
1 2 3 4 5 6 7 8 9 10 11 12 13 14 15 16 17 18 19 20 21 22 23 24 25 26 27 28 29 30 36 37 38 39 40 41 42 43 44

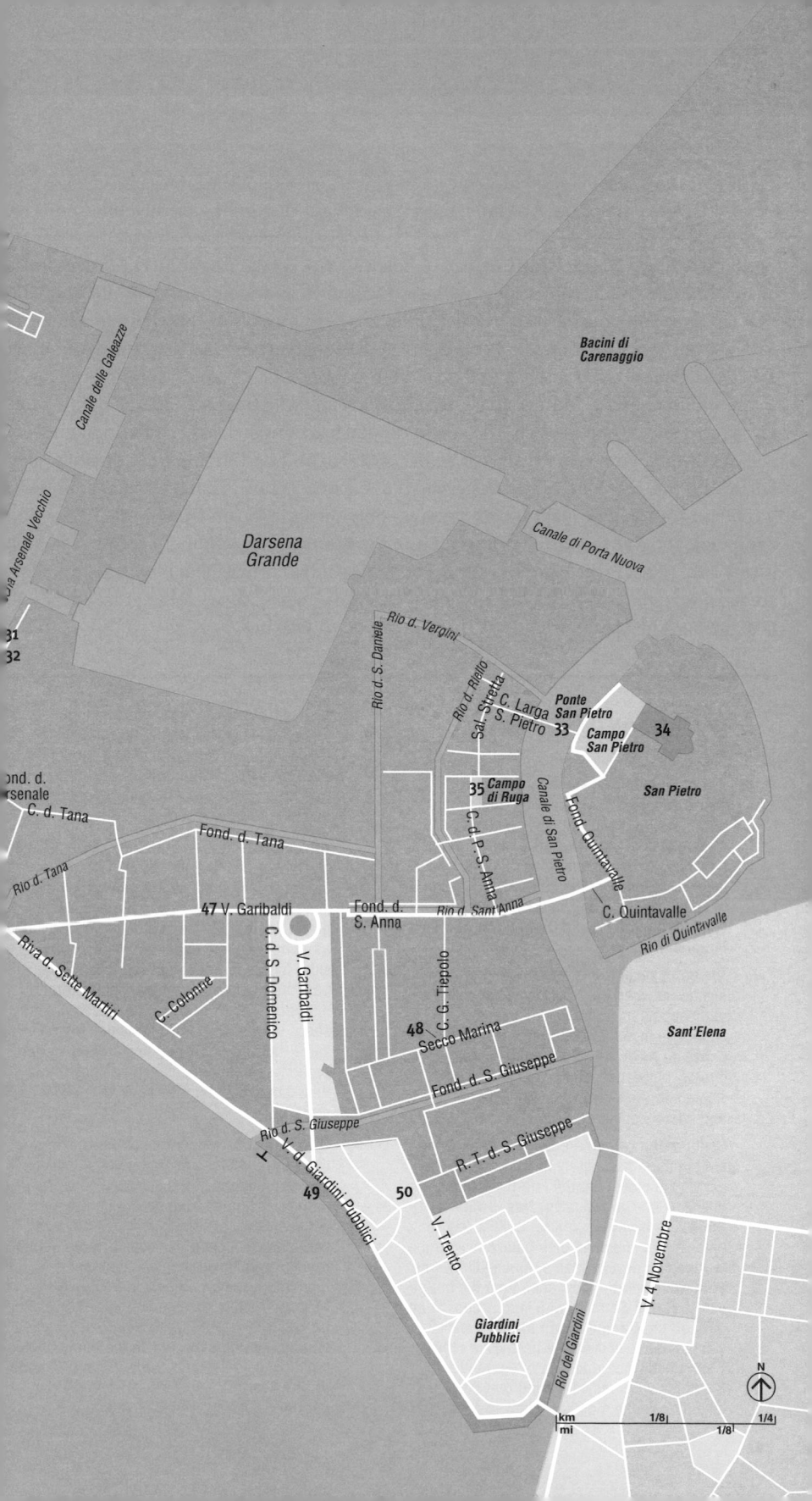
Bacini di Carenaggio
Canale delle Galeazze
Darsena Grande
Canale di Porta Nuova
Rio d. Vergini
Rio d. S. Daniele
Rio d. Riello
Sal. Stretta
C. Larga S. Pietro
Ponte San Pietro
33
Campo San Pietro
34
San Pietro
35
Campo di Ruga
Canale di San Pietro
Fond. Quintavalle
C. d. P. S. Anna
C. Quintavalle
Rio di Quintavalle
Fond. d. Tana
C. d. Tana
Rio d. Tana
47 V. Garibaldi
Fond. d. S. Anna
Rio d. Sant'Anna
Riva d. Sette Martiri
C. Colonne
C. d. S. Domenico
V. Garibaldi
C. G. Tiepolo
48
Secco Marina
Sant'Elena
Fond. d. S. Giuseppe
Rio d. S. Giuseppe
V. d. Giardini Pubblici
R. T. d. S. Giuseppe
49
50
V. Trento
Giardini Pubblici
Rio dei Giardini
V. 4 Novembre
N
km
mi
1/8
1/8
1/4

CASTELLO

The oldest *sestiere* (district) in Venice, Castello is also one of the largest. More than half of it is taken up by the **Arsenale**, the vast shipyard that once was the main source of the Republic's wealth and military power. The densely populated area around the Arsenale was largely built by the old aristocracy to house its workers and sailors. The orderly rows of small homes, often embellished with Gothic arches and windows, around **Campiello Due Pozzi** and on both sides of **Via Garibaldi** are examples of farsighted urban planning dating from the 13th century. People on the eastern part of Castello still live a quiet existence. Bakeries, fish stores, and vegetable stands have yet to disappear in favor of shops selling masks or Murano glass, primarily because the train station and parking lots are at the opposite end of town. The neighborhood has nonetheless become an interesting area for dining, with unobtrusive spots like **Al Covo** and **La Corte Sconta** drawing food fans away from San Marco. The western part of Castello is rich in palazzi and monuments. It centers around three magnificent squares—**San Zaccaria, Santi Giovanni e Paolo (San Zanipolo)**, and **Santa Maria Formosa**. From the narrow midsection of central Castello it is very easy to reach the lagoon to the north or the south. Perhaps that is why the residents are passionate boat lovers, crowding both banks of the canals with their craft, ready to take them to the lagoon islands of **Torcello** and **Sant'Erasmo**.

1 Campo Santi Giovanni e Paolo

This *campo*, known in the local dialect as **San Zanipolo**, is the center of an old and active part of the city. It was an important crossroads between the large island to which it belongs (extending northward toward the lagoon, visible from the *campo*) and a group of busy, densely populated islands to the south (centered around **Campo Santa Maria Formosa**).

The north section was reclaimed from the lagoon between the 13th and 15th centuries and used as a site for convents and charitable institutions. Today it is wholly occupied by the Venice hospital, a maze of streets, pavilions, churches, and cloisters where citizens as well as newly hired nurses and doctors easily get lost.

South of the *campo* are blocks of homes built in the 13th century for low-income residents (the oldest are the late-Byzantine buildings on Calle Muazzo, **Nos. 6450-6504**). As always in Venice, quite a few patrician families had their palazzi next to the low-income developments. Among them was **Palazzo Bragadin**, best seen from the bridge across **Rio di San Lio**, with land access in an alley off the **Campo Santa Maria**. Here young Casanova lived the best years of his youth under the protection of old Matteo Bragadin, who was convinced that the charming young man knew how to consult the spirits in order to forecast the future. Casanova played a similar trick in Paris on the Marquise d'Urfé, who in turn supported the Venetian adventurer for years, until she was rudely awakened by being conned into a mock death-and-resurrection ritual.

The *campo* is still an important center of local life, with a constant flow of Venetians crossing it in all directions, while in the two spacious cafés groups of old men kill time playing card games and sipping wine in the afternoon. On the canal at the hospital's side, frequent ambulance launches carry patients to and from the hospital's water entrance. The **Rosa Salva** *pasticceria* (pastry shop) in the *campo* has remained intact since the turn of the century, and the owners proudly serve old-fashioned pastries (most Venetians like the green ones, with pistachio nuts).

The equestrian monument at the center of the *campo* represents Bartolomeo Colleoni, one of the greatest Renaissance *condottieri*, or military heroes, who served Venice for decades until his death in 1475. Colleoni bequeathed most of his considerable wealth to the Republic on the condition that a monument to him be built in front of **San Marco**. The city government agreed, but after his death decided that this *campo* was good enough, perhaps playing on the name of the building at the church's side (**Scuola Grande di San Marco**). While the city fathers may not have done right by Colleoni on the location, they could not have chosen a better sculptor for the commission: The monument was entrusted to Andrea Verrocchio, who honored the old warrior with one of the most admired monuments in Italy (the statue was cast by his pupil Alessandro Leopardi).

The building at the left of the church and along the canal is the hospital's entrance. Originally it was the entrance of the Scuola Grande di San Marco. The 15th-century façade was designed by **Mauro Codussi** and sculpted by Pietro Lombardo with his sons Tullio and Antonio. The splendid trompe l'oeil marble statues represent *St. Mark's Lion* (left side) and two episodes from the life of St. Mark (right side). The 15th-century statue by Bartolomeo Bon over the portal represents *Charity,* while the winged lion under the top arch was added in the 19th century to replace the original one, destroyed after the French conquest (1797) along with countless similar mementos of the very antirevolutionary Republic. You can visit the large hall within the building and—among a crowd of patients and their visitors—study the exhibition of photographs representing the interior of the compound before and after the restorations. You can also explore the compound, but don't be surprised to see patients in pajamas.

For visits to the interior of the *scuola* (whose 16th-century halls are decorated with paintings by Palma il Giovane, Palma il Vecchio, and Jacopo Tintoretto's son Domenico) and to the attached convent, ask the hospital doorman. ♦ *Vaporetto* stops: Rialto, Ospedale Civile

2 Santi Giovanni e Paolo (San Zanipolo)

Owned and run by the Dominican order, this church is one of the largest in Venice, and undoubtedly one of the most beautiful. Built in the 13th and 14th centuries, it can properly be called the Pantheon of Venice, because, from the 15th century on, the funerals of the doges were held here, and no fewer than 25 doges were buried here. On the façade, never completed with the planned marble covering, are some of the oldest tombs. Inside the arches on the left side are those of the 13th-century doge Jacopo Tiepolo and of his son, Doge Lorenzo Tiepolo. The portal was designed by **Bartolomeo Bon** in the second half of the 15th century. The interior of the church is filled with chapels and monuments, and a walk through it is equal to a course in Venetian political and artistic history.

Just inside the entrance to the right is the *Monument to Doge Pietro Mocenigo* by Pietro Lombardo, one of the greatest representatives of the early Renaissance in Venice. In this monument, the warlike attributes of the doge are exalted: Six young warriors stand inside the niches, while the bas-reliefs on the sarcophagus illustrate two of his victorious expeditions. The Latin inscription means "the money for this monument came from booty of war." On top of the sarcophagus, Mocenigo appears in full battle dress. This monument is clearly as grandiose as the one erected in honor of Doge Niccolò Tron at the **Frari** church.

Nearby is the *Monument to Marcantonio Bragadin,* attributed to Vincenzo Scamozzi. Inside the urn is the skin of General Bragadin, who was flayed alive by the Turks on the island of Cyprus in 1571 after negotiating the free exit of his army. The Turks kept the skin in Constantinople, whence the Venetians stole it. The treacherous flaying is represented in the fresco surrounding the statue.

On the second altar in the right aisle is the recently and beautifully restored *Polyptych of St. Vincent Ferrer* (ca. 1465), attributed (incorrectly according to some) to a young Giovanni Bellini. **St. Dominic's Chapel**, by **Andrea Tirali**, contains *The Glory of St. Dominic,* a masterwork by the 18th-century painter Giovanni Battista Piazzetta. The narrative stained-glass window in the right transept was laboriously manufactured in Murano over a period of 50 years (1470-1520) by various master artists, including Cima da Conegliano (who did the Virgin, the Baptist, and St. Peter). The painting on the right side of the back wall of the transept, *St. Antonio Pierozzi Giving Alms,* is one of the few works by Lorenzo Lotto in Venice. The painting reflects Lotto's great interest in the world of the underprivileged; St. Antonio, a Dominican, worked on behalf of the poor in Florence in the 15th century. The social content in the painting is rare in 16th-century Venetian art: Like most of Lotto's paintings, it stands in sharp contrast to the celebrative, grandiose paintings of his contemporaries.

The high altar in the chancel is attributed to **Baldassare Longhena**. Left of the altar is *The Monument to Doge Andrea Vendramin,* a collective work of the Lombardo family and one of the best funerary monuments of its period. The top frame is missing, and the two *Holy Women* at the sides are replacements for statues of Adam and Eve.

The **Cappella del Rosario** (Rosary Chapel, through a glass door in the left transept) was destroyed by a fire in 1867 that also claimed a masterwork by Titian (*St. Peter Martyr*) and a *Crucifixion* by Tintoretto (a copy of the former can be seen on the second altar in the

An Affair of the Art

The world-renowned Venice *Biennale* came about as a way to celebrate the 1893 silver wedding anniversary of King Umberto of Italy and his wife, Margherita of Savoy. The city's original intention was to institute "a biannual national artistic exhibition." But it was soon suggested that the exhibition become international, and the inauguration of the First International Exposition of Art of the City of Venice was held on 30 April 1895 and attended by the king and queen. Thereafter held from June through September in even years only, the *Biennale* was permanently shifted to odd years in 1993 in order to appropriately celebrate these two inaugural dates.

From the beginning, the *Biennale* has chosen to put forward an unedited and innovative view of art. Among its list of strict regulations, it was decided that no artist would be able to present more than two works, and more important, that these works were not to have been shown before in Italy. Since its early years, international relations have been one of the *Biennale*'s priorities, resulting in the increase of its permanent pavilions in and around the **Giardini Pubblici** (Public Gardens) from seven in 1914 to 28 today—accommodating the work of artists from more than 50 countries. The international aspect of the Venice *Biennale* remains one of its greatest strengths.

In the 1930s, the well-known Venetian Count Giuseppe Volpi di Misurata dominated the *Biennale*. Through his impetus, the *Biennale* grew and expanded into the multidisciplinary organization that it remains today. The Music Festival (today called the **Festival of Contemporary Music**) was founded in 1930; it has premiered the music of Gershwin, Stravinsky, and Cage. The **International Film Festival** (the most important today after Cannes) was also founded under Volpi's aegis in 1932, and became an annual event in 1934. The **International Theatre Festival**, first held in 1934, has been suspended, while the popular **Architecture Biennale** was added in 1980 as an autonomous section.

Things change considerably when the *Biennale* is in town. Locals can tell you how the "art" crowd is noticeably different from the "film" crowd. Regardless, a flurry of press and international celebs—all of whom seem to know one another and live for these reunions—fill all the right hotels and restaurants. If you don't have an embossed invitation and won't be going to any black-tie galas, cheer up. The tourist information office in **Palazzetto Selva** (5226356) can give you all the information you need about how to get to the *Biennale* as well as the fringe exhibitions, installations, and performances organized primarily during the opening weeks.

Offshoots of the Art *Biennale,* such as the *Aperto* show, have drawn a growing following by offering the excitement of younger, less-established artists—in a manner, according to many, reminiscent of the *Biennale* before it became what some think is a jaded marketplace for mega-dealers. The ***Biennale* Archives** are open to the public in the **Palazzo Corner della Regina**, which is conveniently located very near the **Ca' Pesaro**'s **Museum of Modern Art** (both are directly on the **Canal Grande**). The museum's small but very selective collection of paintings has been chosen from the *Biennale* since its opening; the host of Italian and international artists represented includes De Chirico, Chagall, Kandinsky, and Klimt.

The ***Biennale* Organization** is permanently located in **Ca' Giustinian** on Calle XIII Martiri, south of Campo San Moisè (5218711).

church's left aisle). On the ceiling, rebuilt in 1932, there are now three canvases by Paolo Veronese (*Annunciation*, *Assumption*, and *Adoration of the Shepherds*) that were previously in another church and are a highlight of a visit here. ♦ M-Sa, 7:30AM-12:30PM and 3:30PM-7:30PM; Su, 3PM-6PM. Campo Santi Giovanni e Paolo (between Salizzada Santi Giovanni e Paolo and Fondamenta dei Mendicanti). *Vaporetto* stops: Rialto, Ospedale Civile

3 Santa Maria dei Derelitti

The unusual façade of this church was built between 1670 and 1674 by **Baldassare Longhena** as an answer to the equally curious façade built by a rival architect at **San Moisè**. The redundant Baroque decorations were meant as a monument to the wealthy donor, Bartolomeo Cargnoni. The church was connected to the nearby **Ospedaletto** (**No. 6691**), one of the four orphanages in town where children were given a musical education. (The most famous is **Santa Maria della Pietà**, where Vivaldi worked as choirmaster.) Pasquale Anfossi, the author of countless operas in the 18th century, was a music teacher here, as were Niccolò Porpora and Domenico Cimarosa. Concerts, considered among the best in Europe, were performed in an elegant 18th-century music hall, now part of a home for senior citizens (ask the doorman at the hall next door to the church for permission to visit). ♦ Th-Sa, 3:30PM-6:30PM. Salizzada Santi Giovanni e Paolo 6990 (at Calle Torelli). 2702464. *Vaporetto* stop: Ospedale Civile

4 Il Milione

You don't need a guidebook to tell you to stop at this little shop; you'd stop anyway. Beautiful, handmade silk lampshades in the style of Fortuny are sold here. Glowing colored silks, figured in gold and hung on silken ropes, fill the window. The two artists, Daniele Zampedri and Marco Zerbin, use techniques developed at the beginning of the century. They also produce bespoke lampshades and will have them delivered anywhere in the world. In addition, the artists sell their paintings—scenes of Venice in oils. The little postcard-sized ones would make a hugely impressive alternative to the usual cardboard version! ♦ M-Sa, 10AM-12:30PM and 3PM-7PM. Campo Santa Marina 6025. 2410722. *Vaporetto* stop: San Zaccaria

4 Hotel Santa Marina

$$ A lovely hotel in one of those *campos* that seems off the beaten track while actually being almost upon it. The Campo Santa Marina is quiet, and the hotel is a pleasant surprise. It is more glamorous than its unassuming exterior would suggest. Formerly a convent, it now offers guests pleasantly Venetian surroundings. All the rooms have been recently renovated and have private bath or shower, TV, radio, air conditioning, minibar, and safe. The public rooms have lots of polished wood and Venetian colors. There is a breakfast room, a relaxing lounge in which to flick through your *Access* guide, and a terrace. ♦ Campo Santa Marina 6068. 5239202. www.hotelsantamarina.it

5 Ponte dei Conzafelzi

The small island this bridge crosses ends at a house surrounded by water on three sides. Most of the rest of the island is occupied by a former convent, designed by **Andrea Tirali** in 1731 and now used as a high school. It is located at the eastern end next to the handsome 15th century Venetian Gothic **Palazzo Cappello**, once famous for its glorious receptions. The façade of the palazzo is visible only from the canals. ♦ *Vaporetto* stop: Ospedale Civile

6 San Francesco della Vigna

This Renaissance church is located in an extremely quiet neighborhood, where Venetians go about their daily activity seemingly unaware of being in the middle of a hectic tourist town. The whole area was redesigned from 1525 to 1540 through an ambitious project by Doge Andrea Gritti and architect **Jacopo Sansovino**. It represents a rare example of ancient urban planning. Around the grandiose church, the Gritti residence (**No. 2785**) was rebuilt and later used as the residence of the pope's ambassador; small houses were demolished to create the **Campo della Confraternità** (right side of the church) and a bell tower similar to the one in **Piazza San Marco** was added. The heavy loggia across the *campo* is a 19th-century addition. The church was carefully designed by Sansovino according to rigorous Neoplatonic geometry. The façade was designed by **Andrea Palladio** after Sansovino's death. The interior, sober and solemn, was designed by Sansovino, in collaboration with Doge Gritti and an erudite monk, as an embodiment in stone of the *Harmonia mundi* (the order and proportion found by the Humanists in God's planning of the world), and based on multiples of the number three. In 1535 the side chapels were sold to families of the Venetian nobility, such as Bragadin, Badoer, and Contarini, who vied to tie their names to this monument of Renaissance craft and thought. ♦ Daily, 8AM-12:30PM and 3PM-7PM. Campo San Francesco della Vigna (between Campo della Confraternità and Calle San Francesco). *Vaporetto* stop: Celestia

7 Giovanna Zanella

This talented and vibrantly charming young designer is one of the new wave of creative talent that is remaking Venice as an artistic mecca. Her handmade shoes, slippers, and clogs are a delight. Each pair is unique, and can be made to measure and to your exact specification. The designs range from the elegant and 1950s-influenced to the fun and the quirky. The shop also sells the gorgeous leather handbags designed by Barbara Taboni, and designer jewelry in state-of-the-art plastics and in ceramics by Marina Zaffalona and by Raku. Giovanna also designs fabulous hats from felt, leather, and thick open-weave, hand-knit yarn. Each hat is numbered and absolutely unique. Giovanna keeps a book with pictures of her work and the name and address of the person who bought each item. This woman is the Venice of the future, and it is a delight to have her in the present. ♦ Daily, 9:30AM-1PM and 3PM-7PM. Calle Carminati 5641. 5235500. *Vaporetto* stop: San Zaccaria

8 Santa Maria della Fava

The name of this church may derive from an ancient food vendor, now long gone, specializing in beans (*fave*), or from the last name of a wealthy family living nearby. The building is a fine example of Venetian architecture of the 18th century, a time when, in spite of political and economic decay, the Republic was still investing enormous funds in public and private buildings. At least 49 new churches were built in the 18th century, while many others were restored and modified, most often through private contributions by wealthy families. The final plans for this church were drawn by **Giorgio Massari**, the architect of the **Gesuati** and **Santa Maria della Pietà** churches. The church contains two masterworks of 18th-century painting: *Madonna with St. Filippo Neri* (1727) by Giambattista Piazzetta (second altar on the left) and *Virgin as a Child with St. Anne and St. Joachim* (1732) by Giambattista Tiepolo (first altar on the right). The former is a product of Piazzetta in his full maturity; the latter is one of the first great works by the young Tiepolo. Together they represent the last great flourishing of Venetian painting. The beautiful 18th-century organ is used every Sunday at 10:30AM to accompany the Mass service with Baroque music. ♦ Campo Fava and Calle della Fava. *Vaporetto* stop: Rialto

9 Salizzada San Lio

The narrow façade next to the arch at **Nos. 5691-5705** is an intact house dating from the 13th or 14th century; and the small palazzo at **Nos. 5662-72** is from the 13th century (the second-floor window to the right of the arch may belong to the 12th century). Each of the buildings may have consisted of two turretlike dwellings united by a pointed arch. The original windows in both buildings have the typical Byzantine shape (round arches pointed at the top and elongated at the base)—a shape that could naturally evolve into the Gothic arch. ♦ *Vaporetto* stop: Rialto

On Salizzada San Lio:

Silvia

The elegant Signora Silvia and her daughter Francesca discerningly edit the collections of such designer names as Desmo, Missoni, Genny, and Cerrutti to offer a representative assortment of handbags from the season's best. You can rely on the owners' on-the-mark judgment for the best in leather goods from these Italian fashion houses, with a smaller collection of shoes and accessories to complete the fashionable picture. ♦ M-Sa. No. 5540 (between Calle San Antonio and Calle del Caffettier). 5238568

If you lined up all the files in the *Archivio di Stato* (State Archives) side by side, they would extend 78 kilometers (48 miles).

Altane, covered wooden or metal decks atop the roofs of houses, were originally constructed for privacy and because no alterations were allowed to be made to a building's façade. They were used to dry clothes, and in Renaissance times courtesans used *altane* to sun-bleach their hair. Such a scene is wonderfully depicted by Carpaccio in his painting (*The Courtesans*) of two women in the Museo Correr.

10 Calle del Paradiso

Here is an example of 15th-century urban planning, where grace and functionalism didn't seem to be at odds with each other. The two rows of houses here still have shops on the ground floor. To make the upstairs apartments a bit larger, and to protect the street from rain, the top floors were made to protrude with a typical Venetian feature called a *barbacano*; the ones on this street are original. The Gothic archways at both ends of the street date from the 14th century, and the house on the canal side features Byzantine windows from the 12th century. ♦ *Vaporetto* stop: Rialto

On Calle del Paradiso:

Ristorante Ai Barbacani

★★$$$ This restaurant sits quietly on the Rio di Santa Maria Formosa just under the 14th-century, carved *Arco del Paradiso*. Inside an intimate, elegant ambience features starched white cloths and fresh flowers on the tables, and wood buttresses that support marble columns. Seafood is the main offering here, taking such forms as *cocktail di gamberetti* (shrimp cocktail), *spaghetti alla granseola* (with spider crabs), and *coda di rospo* (angler fish grilled in a sauce of oil, parsley, and lemon). ♦ Tu-Su, lunch and dinner. No. 5746. 5204691, 5210234

11 Campo Santa Maria Formosa

This square, one of the most spacious in Venice, is a real anthology of architectural styles and periods. **Palazzo Vitturi** (**No. 5246**) is one of the best examples of 13th-century Byzantine architecture; the **Palazzi Donà** (**Nos. 6123-26**) include two fine Gothic buildings dating from the 14th century; **Casa Venier** (**No 6129**) is a delightful Gothic home from the end of the 15th century; and **Palazzo Ruzzini-Priuli** (**No. 5866**) is 16th-century Renaissance. Radial streets connect this pivotal square to key neighborhoods in the city, such as Rialto and San Marco. It is therefore a busy square, even in the afternoons when the small fruit-and-vegetable market has closed for the day. ♦ *Vaporetto* stops: San Zaccaria, Rialto

12 Enoteca La Caneva Dae Tose

A veritable Aladdin's cave—if Aladdin were a gourmet, that is. This little shop is stuffed with what the sign sweetly and rightly calls *"Cose rare, sfiziose . . . e mai viste"* (rare things, things you fancy . . . and almost never see). There are hand-picked, cold-pressed olive oils from the Frantoio di Santa Tea, grape preserves from Calabria, gorgeous pickles and preserves from Monteglio (the one called L'Orto a Tavola—the kitchen garden at your table—is a delicious mix of garden vegetables that would pep up any plate of salami or cheese), and jars containing the imaginative notion of bottling pepperoni in a *bagna cauda*. There are good pastas and a marvelous selection of organic wines, delicious dessert wines, and liqueurs. It is almost impossible to come out without buying a little taste adventure to take home. ♦ 11AM-2PM; 5PM-9PM. Closed W. Calle Lunga Santa Maria Formosa 6251

12 Al Mascareta

★★★$$ The same passion for good food that drives the *Enoteca La Caneva* drives the Mascareta. Mauro Lorenzon, now in charge here, is evangelistic about really good prosciutto and cheeses *in stagione* (seasonal), the freshest seafoods, game in season, and unfiltered wines. And so on the menu here you will find much that the average *osteria* doesn't offer: a generous selection of fine Champagnes, over 100 labels on the wine list (many unfiltered), foie gras, and oysters. Alongside the platters and glasses (as *all* the wines are available by the glass) of the aforementioned delights, the small but taste bud-tingling menu of main dishes includes guinea fowl, quail, and duck. And for the simpler tastes in colder weather, Mascareta offers steaming bowls of homemade soup—bean, fish, or onion. It is fast becoming recognized as a place to enjoy the good things in life. ♦ W-M, 7PM-2AM (and occasionally Sunday lunchtime). Calle Lunga Santa Maria Formosa

13 Osteria al Mascaron

★★$$$ This place has changed over the years—you can no longer stand at the glass-topped bar and enjoy a plate of the wonders they spread there. But the food at this classic *osteria* is good stuff. There will always be the Mascaron's wonderful *antipasto misto pesce*, and it is always worth ordering for a little taste of almost everything the lagoon and waters beyond have to offer. The pastas are good—the lobster is terrific if you fancy a bit of luxury! There are a good many decent *vini sfusi*—wines by the jug—as well as bottles. ♦ M-Sa, lunch and dinner. Reservations recommended. Calle Lunga Santa Maria Formosa 5225 (between Calle dei Orbi and Campo Santa Maria Formosa). 5225995. *Vaporetto* stops: Rialto, San Zaccaria

14 Alle Testiere

★★★$$$ Another of Venice's small but perfectly formed restaurants, this place is elegant—from the simple, classic design, through the sparkling, generous goblets that await your choice from the impressive wine list (albeit the house wines are perfect for the food you are about to eat), to the utterly charming, patient, well-informed, and multilingual staff. And the food might be described as elegant too. A well-groomed young man will trot you through the all-fishy options that range from classic to classic with a twist. Their antipasto of scallops scented with licorice is delicious, and their steaming bowls of mixed shellfish in a fresh ginger broth pull discerning diners from across the city. There are generally about three options for each course. I enjoyed a tagliatelle made with beetroot and delicately sauced with scampi. These are sophisticated flavors in a sophisticated setting. ♦ Bookings definitely advised. Tu-Sa, lunch and dinner. Calle del Mundo Nuovo 5801. 5227220

15 Santa Maria Formosa

Formosa means "good-looking," with connotations of Junoesque plumpness, as was the Virgin Mary who appeared to a Venetian bishop in AD 639, ordering him to have a church built in her name. The present shape of the church is due to **Mauro Codussi**, the great early-Renaissance architect. It is surprising that there are no saints or prophets on the façade; instead there are statues of gentlemen, obviously not dressed as religious leaders. They are members of the powerful Cappello family, who financed the building of the church. The habit of adorning churches with portraits of donors was common in Venice, contributing to the puzzling mixture of sacred and profane elements so typical all over town. The church's interior, after some modifications in the 19th century, was restored in 1921 according to Codussi's plans. ♦ Campo Santa Maria Formosa and Rio di Santa Maria Formosa. *Vaporetto* stops: San Zaccaria, Rialto

16 Biblioteca Querini Stampalia (Querini Stampalia Library)

The Querini family was one of the oldest and most powerful in Venice. In 1207 they became lords of Stampalia, an island on the Aegean Sea they conquered for Venice. Among the many branches of the family, the one residing in this early-16th-century palazzo was the richest, although they never provided the city with a doge. The last scion of the family, Count Giovanni Querini, bequeathed the building to the city in 1869 to be used as a public library and art gallery. Between 1959 and 1963, the ground floor was redesigned by the brilliant Venetian architect **Carlo Scarpa**. The second floor is taken up by the library, an extremely important Venetian institution and the only library in the city open in the evening. Generations of college students

PARLA ITALIANO?

Relax. Italians don't assume that Americans speak their language. Most are very patient with your possibly flawed attempts, and are generally pleased that you've tried. Here are some basics to get you started. *Buon viaggio!* (Have a good trip!)

Hello, Good-Bye, and Other Basics

Good morning. ..... *Buongiorno.*
Good afternoon/evening. ..... *Buona sera.*
Good night. ..... *Buona notte.*
How are you? ..... *Come sta?*
Good-bye. ..... *Arrivederci.*
yes ..... *sì*
no ..... *no*
please ..... *per favore, per piacere*
Thank you. ..... *Grazie.*
You're welcome. ..... *Prego.*
Excuse me. ..... *Permesso.*
(in crowds) ..... *Mi scusi.*
I'm sorry. ..... *Mi dispiace.*
I don't speak Italian. ..... *Non parlo italiano.*
Do you speak English? ..... *Parla inglese?*
I don't understand. ..... *Non capisco.*
Do you understand? ..... *Capisce?*
More slowly, please. ..... *Più lentamente per favore.*
I don't know. ..... *Non lo so.*
My name is . . . . *Mi chiamo . . .*
What is your name? ..... *Come si chiama?*
miss ..... *signorina*
madame, ma'am ..... *signora*
mister ..... *signor/e*
good ..... *buono/a*
bad ..... *cattivo/a*
open ..... *aperto/a*
closed ..... *chiuso/a*
entrance ..... *entrata*
exit ..... *uscita*
push ..... *spingere*
pull ..... *tirare*
What time does it open/close? ..... *A che ora opre/chiude?*
today ..... *oggi*
tomorrow ..... *domani*
yesterday ..... *ieri*
week ..... *settiman*
month ..... *mes*
year ..... *anne*

Hotel Talk

I have a reservation. ..... *Ho una prenotazione*
I would like . . . . *Vorrei . .*
a double room ..... *una camera doppi*
with twin beds ..... *con due letti singo*
with a double bed ..... *con letto matrimonial*
a quiet room ..... *una camera tranquill*
with (private) bath ..... *con bagno (privato*
with air conditioning ..... *con aria condizionat*
Does that price include . . . . *Il prezzo comprende . .*
breakfast? ..... *la prima colazione?*
taxes? ..... *le tasse?*
Do you accept traveler's checks? ..... *Accettate i traveler's checks?*
Do you accept credit cards? ..... *Accettate le carte di credito?*

Restaurant Repartee

Waiter! ..... *Cameriere*
menu ..... *lista, menu*
I would like . . . . *Vorrei . .*
a glass of . . . . *un bicchiere di . .*
a bottle of . . . . *una bottiglia di . .*
a liter of . . . . *un litro di . .*
The check, please. ..... *Il conto per favore*
Is the service charge included? ..... *Il servizio è incluso?*
I think there is a mistake in the bill. ..... *Credo che ci sia uno sbaglio nel mio conto*
lunch ..... *pranze*
dinner ..... *cena*
tip ..... *mancia*
bread ..... *pane*
butter ..... *burro*
pepper ..... *pepe*
salt ..... *sale*
sugar ..... *zucchero*
soup ..... *zuppa*
salad ..... *insalata*
vegetables ..... *verdure, contorn*
cheese ..... *formaggio*

gg ..... *uova*
acon ..... *pancetta*
melette ..... *frittata*
neat ..... *carne*
hicken ..... *pollo*
eal ..... *vitello*
sh ..... *pesce*
eafood, shellfish ..... *frutta di mare*
ork ..... *maiale*
am ..... *prosciutto*
hops/pork chops ..... *costoletta/braciola*
essert ..... *dolce*

s You Like It

old ..... *freddo/a*
ot ..... *caldo/a*
weet ..... *dolce*
very) dry ..... *(molto) secco*
grilled ..... *alla griglia*
aked ..... *al forno*
oiled ..... *bollito/a*
ried ..... *fritto/a*
aw ..... *crudo/a*
are ..... *poco cotto/a*
well-done ..... *ben cotto/a*
spicy ..... *piccante*

hirsty No More

hot chocolate (cocoa) ..... *cioccolata calda*
black coffee ..... *un caffè*
coffee with steamed milk ..... *cappuccino, caffè latte*
milk ..... *latte*
tea ..... *tè*
fruit juice ..... *succo di frutta*
water ..... *acqua*
mineral water ..... *acqua minerale*
carbonated ..... *gassata*
noncarbonated ..... *non gassata*
ice ..... *ghiaccio*
without ice ..... *senza ghiaccio*
beer ..... *birra*
red wine ..... *vino rosso*
white wine ..... *vino bianco*

Sizing It Up

How much does this cost? ..... *Quanto costa?*
inexpensive ..... *a buon mercato*
expensive ..... *caro/a*
large ..... *grande*
small ..... *piccolo/a*
long ..... *lungo/a*
short ..... *corto/a*
old ..... *vecchio/a*
new ..... *nuovo/a*
used ..... *usato/a*
this one ..... *questo/a*
that one ..... *quello/a*
a little ..... *un poco*
a lot ..... *molto*

On the Move

north ..... *nord*
south ..... *sud*
east ..... *est*
west ..... *ovest*
right ..... *destra*
left ..... *sinistra*
highway ..... *autostrada*
street ..... *strada*
gas station ..... *stazione di benzina, distributore di benzina*
straight ahead ..... *sempre diritto*
here ..... *qui*
there ..... *là, lì*
bus stop ..... *fermata dell'autobus*
bus station ..... *stazione degli autobus*
train station ..... *stazione ferroviaria*
subway ..... *metropolitana*
airport ..... *aeroporto*
tourist information ..... *informazione turistica*
city map ..... *pianta*
one-way ticket ..... *biglietto di solo andata*
round-trip ticket ..... *biglietto di andata e ritorno*
first class ..... *prima classe*
second class ..... *seconda classe*
smoking ..... *fumare*
no smoking ..... *non fumare*
Does this train go to . . . ? ..... *Questo treno va a . . . ?*

Does this bus go to . . . ? .....*Quest'autobus va a . . . ?*
Where is/are . . . ? .....*Dov'è/Dove sono . . . ?*
How far is it from
here to . . . ? ....*Quanti chilometri sono da qui a . . . ?*

The Bare Necessities

aspirin .....*aspirina*
Band-Aids.....*cerotti*
barbershop/hairdresser .....*barbiere/parucchiere*
condom .....*profilattico*
dry cleaner.....*tintoria*
laundromat/
laundry.....*lavanderia automatica/lavanderia*
letter.....*lettera*
post office.....*ufficio postale*
postage stamp .....*francobollo*
postcard.....*carta postale*
sanitary napkins .....*assorbenti igienici*
shampoo .....*shampoo*
shaving cream .....*schiuma da barba*
soap .....*sapone*
tampons .....*assorbenti interni*
tissues .....*fazzoletti di carta*
toilet paper .....*carta igienica*
toothpaste.....*dentifricio*

Where is the bathroom/
toilet? .....*Dov'è il bagno/la toiletta*
men's room .....*signori, uomin*
women's room .....*signore, donn*

Days of the Week (lowercased in Italian)

Monday.....*luned*
Tuesday .....*martedì*
Wednesday .....*mercoled*
Thursday .....*giovedì*
Friday .....*venerd*
Saturday .....*sabat*
Sunday .....*domenica*

Numbers

zero .....*zero*
one.....*un*
two .....*due*
three .....*tre*
four .....*quattro*
five.....*cinque*
six .....*se*
seven .....*sette*
eight.....*otto*
nine.....*nove*
ten .....*dieci*

have prepared for their examinations here, sitting at the ancient tables, ignoring the squeaky floors, the gloomy mythological paintings on the walls, and the sounds, drifting in through the giant windows, of gondoliers serenading tourists.

On the second floor is a *pinacoteca* (art collection) specializing mostly in minor Venetian painters. It contains a series of paintings by Gabriele Bella (1730-1799) entitled *Scene de Vita Veneziana* (Scenes of Venetian Life), a room devoted to the work of Pietro Longhi, an interesting collection of traditional Venetian furniture with its characteristic engraved and lacquered wood with painted floral motifs, and Giovanni Bellini's *Presentazione di Gesu al Tempio* (Presentation of Jesus at the Temple). ♦ Gallery: admission. Library: M-Sa. Gallery: Tu-Su. Calle Querini 4778 (at Rio di Santa Maria Formosa). 2711411. *Vaporetto* stop: San Zaccaria

17 Scuola di San Giorgio degli Schiavoni

The building may look like a church, but it was actually the seat of the confraternity of the Dalmatian community, also known as Slavonians or *Schiavoni*. It contains nine masterworks by Vittore Carpaccio, himself of Dalmatian descent, painted between 1501 and 1511 to decorate the hall of the building. St. George was the chosen patron of the charitable association; therefore one of the paintings represents *St. George Killing the Dragon*. Two versions of the same scene are sculpted in stone outside the *scuola*: The one on the façade was sculpted in 1552, and the one on the canal side of the building in 1574. (St. George, one of the preferred patrons of warriors, has been removed from the list of Catholic saints because there is no proof he existed.) Two more Carpaccio paintings illustrate episodes from the legend of St. George:

the *Triumph of St. George* (second on the left wall) and *St. George Baptizing the King of Libya* (front wall, left side of the altar). An episode from the life of St. Tryphon, the second patron of the Slavonians, is painted on the other side of the altar (also by Carpaccio). On the right wall are two episodes from the Gospel and three from the life of the third Slavonic patron, St. Jerome (*The Taming of the Lion*, *St. Jerome's Funeral*, and *St. Jerome in His Study*, also called the *Vision of St. Augustine*, all by Carpaccio). For the first time in Italy, Carpaccio depicted religious and mystical subjects in a real, down-to-earth way (note the animals, the trees, and the clothes on the people). This reflected a giant step toward the independence of art from religion, which was possible in a city like Venice, run as it was by active, shrewd, and earth-oriented merchants. ♦ Admission. Tu-Sa, 9:30AM-12:30PM and 3:30PM-6:30PM; Su, 9:30AM-12:30PM. Calle dei Furlani and Rio di Sant'Agostin. 5228828. *Vaporetto* stop: San Zaccaria

18 Vino E... Vini

The name–"Wine and . . . Wines"–tells you most of what you need to know about this wonderful wine-lover's chunk of heaven. It offers hundreds of wines, hand-picked by the owner, from the top of the oeneological tree to everyday gluggable but gorgeous stuff. The wines come from all over the world but, of course, mainly from Italy. This is a real thinking drinker's paradise, selling good wine at a good price. There is a whole shelf of Barolo, two shelves of the Grand Tuscans, and another of Amarone. There is a glittering row of Prosecci and other sparkling Italians (genuinely worth exploring–these are not all sweeties for the girls, you know). There is also a mind-boggling choice of grappas–about 80. They include single varietals and caramel-colored, aged grappa–a bottle from the 1978 vintage sits on a central table. One can only imagine how fabulous its contents must be. There are another 70 bottles and half bottles of dessert wines. This is not just a wine shop, but a potable encyclopedia of wine. There is also top-of-the-line glassware on sale–you don't want to drink a really great wine out of a glass that won't do it justice! There are corkscrews and gadgets, a terrific range of oils and outrageously exclusive balsamics, as well as lesser vinegars and pickles, jams, and a delicious range of biscuits and cakes (including panettone) made with Prosecco. Each wine is priced where you can see it, obviating the frequent practice of "one price for the locals and another for tourists." A local restaurateur described this shop as *"appassionata"*–passionate–about wine. It is. You will be too, by the time you leave. ♦ Daily, 9AM-1PM and 5PM-8PM. Fondamenta dei Furlani 3301. 5210184. *Vaporetto* stop: San Zaccaria

19 Campiello Due Pozzi

Planned and built in the 14th century as the center of an island surrounded by four canals and adjacent to the **Arsenale**, this *campiello* represents small-scale Venice. The island was inhabited by the shipyard's workers, a group of choice craftspeople. All of the houses on the *campiello,* except for the one on the south side (rebuilt in 1613), belong to the 14th century; particularly interesting is **Palazzo Malipiero** (**Nos. 2684-89**). The wellhead (*pozzo*) at the center was sculpted in 1530 with the figure of St. Martin and gave the square its name. ♦ *Vaporetto* stops: Arsenale, Celestia

On Campiello Due Pozzi:

Osteria ai Forneri

★$ Just in case you are fading, revive yourself with a beer from the selection at this friendly neighborhood bar. There are also snacks and ice creams, decent wine, and very good coffee. ♦ Daily, 5PM-11PM. Campiello Due Pozzi 2613

20 Trattoria Aciugheta

★★$$ There is always a good and interesting selection of regional and local wines and *cicchetti* (finger food), like tiny pizzas or marinated anchovies (for which the *bacaro* is named). At dinnertime attention shifts to the indoor/outdoor seating area of the trattoria, where the menu is pretty standard Venetian. Expect decent interpretations of such specialties as *sarde in saor* (sardines in a subtly sour sauce) and *spaghetti alla bottarga* (with caviar-type eggs of tuna, garlic, olive oil, and a hint of chili). For the less adventurous, fresh fish baked with potatoes and rosemary will suffice. Ask Gianni, the ever-present owner, for a wine suggestion. ♦ Daily, 8AM-midnight. Campo Santissimi Filippo e Giacomo 4357 (between Calle della Chiesa and Calle della Malvasia). 5224292. *Vaporetto* stop: San Zaccaria

20 Conca D'Oro

★$ Right next door to the Aciugheta you will find the Conca D'Oro, a pizzeria that has been here since 1947 and claims to be Venice's first. It has had something of a serious make-over since then. Now nicely modern, it serves a variety of what it calls "old recipes" (lasagna, carbonara, amatriciana) alongside what it calls "new recipes" (octopus carpaccio with paprika and lemon, for example, or tuna carpaccio with mint) alongside those pizzas. The owner offers a selection of body warmers and rugs during chilly weather, and if you come inside between 6 and 9PM you'll find complimentary snacks with your drink. ♦ W-M, 11AM-11:30PM. Campo Santi Filippo and Giacomo 4338. 5229293. www.concadorovenice.com

21 Paolo Brandolisio

If you've succumbed to the magic of the gondola, you'll agree that its wooden *forcola* (oarlock) is sculpture. Its smooth twists and turns, each with a different use for propelling and steering the boat, are unique. In the workshop of Paolo Brandolisio, this everyday Venetian object becomes nothing less than modern art. The young, congenial Paolo, for years the apprentice and protégé of the late master Giuseppe Carli, is the artisan of choice of Venice's most demanding gondoliers. He mounts a small number of his oarlocks to be sold as unique mementos of Venice. ♦ M-Sa. No credit cards accepted. Ruga Giuffa Santa Maria Formosa 4725 (between Rio di San Provolo and Calle del Corona). 5224155. *Vaporetto* stop: San Zaccaria

22 Collegio Greco e Chiesa dei Greci

This area is the property of the Greek community in Venice, as it has been since 1526. It is the city's largest foreign community and one of its richest. Even today the compound is a small island of Greek civilization in the middle of Venice. Separated from the rest of the town by a grille and a canal, it is quiet and off the tourist track, although no more than five minutes from **Piazza San Marco**. The compound includes the **Museo delle Icone Bizantini e Postbizantini** (Museum of Byzantine and Post-Byzantine Icons), built by **Baldassare Longhena** in 1578. It is one of the largest collections of Byzantine icons in Western Europe, and the only museum in Europe devoted to this haunting art. The museum includes the actual letter from Doge Leonardo Loredan that granted permission for the Greeks to build their church. There are two 14th-century Byzantine icons, one representing Christ in Glory and the other, the Virgin Mary with Child and Apostles. The interior of the church of San Giorgio dei Greci itself (1539-1561) is a real triumph of late-Byzantine painting, with gold backgrounds. The bell tower (1592) is currently, remarkably and dangerously, leaning. ♦ Museum-admission. Church: M, W-Sa, 9AM-1PM and 3PM-4:30PM; Su, 9AM-1PM. Museum: M-Sa, 9AM-12:30PM and 2PM-4:30PM; Su, 10AM-5PM. Salizzada dei Greci 3412 (at Calle Bosello). 5226581. *Vaporetto* stop: San Zaccaria

Around 1750, Venice experienced its first *acqua alta*, or flooding of the canals and the lagoon (the low area around Piazza San Marco is especially afflicted). Over time, the frequency of these ephemeral floods has increased drastically; according to current accounts it is now approaching 50 times a year. The worst flood by far was in 1966, the same year Florence was devastated by water, when the tide rose nearly 6.5 feet above normal sea level and deluged the city.

23 Liassidi Palace

$$$ A very new hotel in a very old palace. The 26 classily decorated rooms are housed in a 14th-century palazzo originally owned by the Zorzi family. The hotel is a member of the Small Luxury Hotels of the World, and it's easy to see why. The walled courtyard is a perfect place to drink or have breakfast in good weather, while the second-floor salon and bar are stunning places to enjoy the same when the weather is less than fine. Décor is modern (but, I am urged to point out, not minimalist!) Yes, there are chandeliers, but no, there are not piles of reproduction 17th-century Venetian kitsch. Bathrooms are stunning (and have Jacuzzi tubs) and the public areas aptly palatial. There are 10 doubles, 12 junior suites (5 with canal view), and 4 suites (2 with canal view). All rooms have cable (including CNN), safe, minibar, hair dryer, air conditioning, bathrobes, and Internet access. If you want a little exclusivity with your stay, this would be a good place to come. ♦ Ponte dei Greci 3405. 5205658. www.liassidipalacehotel.com. *Vaporetto* stop: San Zaccaria

24 Osteria Oliva Nera

★★★$$ Though just four years old, this place has such an air of relaxed friendliness that you'd swear it had been here for generations. The husband and wife who own and run it are a great team. Their original chef came to them from the Cipriani and personally trained their present chef, who is in fact Japanese—but has the soul of an Italian, if the food here is anything to judge by. The restaurant has a *degustazione* menu at lunchtime, offering two courses from the menu accompanied by wine. Should you wish to venture on to the main menu, you will not be disappointed. It is traditional but with intelligent twists: The homemade *straccetti* ("rags" of pasta) come with a deliciously rich sauce of lamb flavored with thyme, the *sarde in saor* (sardines in a tangy, oniony marinade) come with polenta, and the carpaccio of salmon and turbot is accompanied by a perfectly judged basil sauce. Even better, the restaurant uses organic products wherever it can, as in the *bigoli* (fat spaghetti) that come with the traditional Venetian anchovy *salsa* and its absolutely stunning olive oils. Yes, oils. Plural. You are given, generally, a choice of at least three. I guarantee that at least one of them will be the best you have ever tasted. They come from a producer called Salvagno in Verona. The restaurant also gives you the sheer joy that is proper, aged balsamic vinegar—a thrill for your taste buds. This is the only restaurant that has ever offered me 12-year-old balsamic on my salad. Ah yes, the salad. It ranks among the top mixed salads in the world, in my opinion. A small thing—but aren't the details what make a restaurant great? And they get them all right here: great bread, excellent mineral water, a bowl of delicious olives (black, of course) to eat while you decide. And finally, a dessert worth getting on a plane *now* to enjoy. The panna cotta here comes with a light white chocolate sauce cut with a tangy purée of fresh strawberries that's worth forsaking any diet for. This place is a must for the visitor to Venice. ♦ M, Tu, F-Su. Salizzada dei Greci 3417/8. 5222170. *Vaporetto* stop: San Zaccaria

25 Sant'Apollonia Monastery

The gem of this compound, a former Benedictine monastery, is the 13th-century cloister, restored in 1969. Its Romanesque style is rare in Venice. The stones around the cloister are mostly fragments of decorations from the original **San Marco** basilica (9th-11th centuries). On the second floor, the **Museo Diocesano d'Arte Sacra** (Museum of Sacred Art) houses a collection of paintings and objects from churches now closed or destroyed. ♦ Free. M-Sa. Fondamenta Sant'Apollonia (just south of Ruga Guiffa). 5529166. *Vaporetto* stop: San Zaccaria

26 Anticlea Antiquariato

The city is awash with "Venetian pearls," colorful glass beads of all sizes, colors, shapes—and costs. Gianna and her daughter Elena have the best antique collection in this tiny shop, with drawers and drawers arranged according to color, shape, and value. Pick and choose and take them home to string them yourself, or have the owners do it for you. Some of the 18th-century beads were used for trade as far away as Turkey and Africa and have found their way back home. ♦ Daily, 10AM-8PM (no midday closing). Campo San Provolo 4719A (between Salizzada San Provolo and Calle San Provolo). 5286946. *Vaporetto* stop: San Zaccaria

27 Campo San Zaccaria

The church on this typical Venetian square used to belong to one of the richest convents in town, founded in the ninth century. It was the preferred nunnery for noble families with more daughters than they could conveniently marry off, to park the extra girls in. The doge used to visit it once a year, on Easter, to commemorate the 12th-century donation by the nuns of a large piece of property to enlarge **Piazza San Marco**. Eight early doges are buried inside. To the right of the church is the façade of an older chapel and the entrance to the monastery, now the headquarters of the Venice *Carabinieri* (police). The beautiful 15th-century building at the left has been spoiled by the addition of shops on the ground floor. ♦ *Vaporetto* stop: San Zaccaria

28 San Zaccaria

The splendid façade of this church was designed by **Mauro Codussi** between 1480 and 1500. Codussi was one of the first architects to break with Gothic tradition in Venice; his façades, widely imitated later, are characterized by a large round arch at the top, supported by two half-arches at the sides. His were among the first arches to be seen in Venice, which in the late 15th century was still attached to the ogee arches of the Gothic tradition. Codussi brilliantly covered the existing ninth century Gothic structure a central nave with two small side aisles—with a set of stone and marble decorations in pure Renaissance style. The façades of the **Frari** and **Santi Giovanni e Paolo**—which were never finished—give an idea of what **San Zaccaria** looked like before Codussi's intervention.

The interior marks an important moment in Venice's art history. It is in this church that Renaissance painting made its first appearance in the city, 100 years after the great Tuscan masters had introduced it to Florence and to the world. To see this groundbreaking work, walk along the right aisle and enter the **Cappella di San Tarasio** (Chapel of Saint Tarasius). The paintings in question are the frescoes on the chapel's apse, painted by Andrea del Castagno, a Florentine master. Their innovative character is made evident by a simple comparison with three polyptychs painted just a year later in the same chapel by Venetian masters (Giovanni and Antonio da Murano, with help from Antonio Vivarini), located at the altar and on the two side walls. Notice how old-fashioned they seem next to Castagno's frescoes.

In 1505, more than 60 years after Castagno created his frescoes, Giovanni Bellini painted one of his best-known altarpieces for San Zaccaria: a *Madonna and Child with Saints* on the second altar in the left aisle. This restored painting marks a further transition between early Venetian style and the new trends that were to emerge with Giorgione and Titian.

Off to the right is the **Cappella di Sant'Atanasio**, which holds works by Tintoretto and Tiepolo as well as some lovely, beautifully crafted choir stalls. ♦ Daily, 10AM-12 noon and 4PM-6PM (admission charged to Cappella di Sant'Atanasio). Campo San Zaccaria (east of Salizzada San Provolo). *Vaporetto* stop: San Zaccaria

29 Hotel La Residenza

$ Housed in the **Palazzo dei Badoari-Partecipazi** on the lovely, quiet **Campo Bandiera e Moro**, this hotel is a find. It has only 15 rooms, decorated in simple Venetian style during the hotel's 2001 refurbishment. All have a private bathroom with shower, telephone, color TV, safe, minibar, and air conditioning. The hotel's big selling point is the main reception hall, which is fabulous—all original 17th-century stuccos and paintings. It runs the full depth of the palazzo. Few hotels offer more splendid surroundings in which to breakfast. There is a boudoir grand piano in the window, should you feel moved to make music. The palazzo dates from the 15th century, as discerning guests will know from its Gothic frontage. Some of the Byzantine sculptures at the tops of the front windows date back as far as the 10th century. It was originally owned by the Gritti family, then passed on by marriage to the Morosinis in 1591 and then the Badoari. Around the middle of the 19th century it was bought by the Marquis Saibante, and it became a hotel in the 1990s. ♦ Campo Bandiera e Moro 3608 (at Salizzada del Pignater). 5285315; fax 5238859. www.venicelaresidenza.com. *Vaporetto* stops: San Zaccaria, Arsenale

30 La Corte Sconta

★★★$$$ Book now for a table for lunch or dinner at this place—it is that busy, and rightly so. Claudio, Lucia, and Rita run their family business like a finely oiled machine, up a tiny alleyway. True to its name, it has its own charming inner courtyard (*corte sconta* means "hidden courtyard") where summer dining is an added joy. The quality of the cooking needs no additions, however. Fish is the order of the day, and it *is* ordered every day. There is a satisfying selection of pastas, risotti, and gnocchi, all homemade freshly every day. Everything that swims can be served up to you hot from the restaurant's charcoal grill, but save a little room for dessert, because the caramel basket filled with lemon sorbet drizzled with a fresh strawberry purée is sublime. The wine list is extensive, intelligent, and fairly priced, but the house Prosecco—gently sparkling and available by the jug—cannot be recommended too highly. This is genuine Venetian cuisine served up by genuine Venetians. ♦ Tu-Sa, lunch and dinner. Calle del Pestrin 3886 (between Rio di San Martino and Calle Crosera). 5227024; fax 5227513. *Vaporetto* stop: Arsenale

31 Arsenale

Two elegant towers (rebuilt in 1686) mark the water entrance to this astonishingly large compound, the pride of the former Republic and the source of its maritime power. The Arsenale's origins date back to the 12th century, and its fame was already high at the end of the 13th century, when Dante described its activity in a famous simile in the *Inferno*: The damned souls of corrupt politicians were tormented in Hell by immersion in a lake of boiling pitch, with the devils moving about with pointed forks just like those used by Venetian workers to caulk the hulls of their ships. It occupies one-fifth of the city's total acreage and is completely surrounded by crenellated walls. It is now a military zone and can be visited only by appointment, with a waiting period of two to three weeks.

Over the centuries the Arsenale has been enlarged many times with named extensions: La Tana in 1303, Arsenale Nuovo (New Arsenal) in 1325, and Arsenale Nuovissimo (Very New Arsenal) in 1473. In its heyday it covered 46 hectares, housed 300 shipping companies, and employed 16,000 workers (known as *arsenaloti*).

Among the precious remnants of the ancient activities are the **sail factory** (16th century); the **Bucintoro boathouse** (16th century—the *Bucintoro* was the ship used by the doge for public ceremonies); the slips for construction and maintenance of war galleys (16th century); the **smithies** (ca. 1390); and the astonishing **Corderie** buildings (14th and 16th centuries), which were more than 300 yards long in order to allow the twining of one piece ropes.

Jobs here were coveted and hereditary; the pay was good, and the city provided housing for the workers in the surrounding neighborhood. Most of the small homes around the shipyard date back to the 13th and 14th centuries, although many have been modified countless times since.

The land entrance, on the side of the left tower, provides access through a flat bridge over a small canal. The majestic **Portal**, based on a drawing by Jacopo Bellini and built in 1460 by **Antonio Gambello**, is the first example of the Renaissance arch in Venice. The 15th-century winged lion over the arch is attributed to Bartolomeo Bon. The two *Winged Victories* were added in commemoration of a great naval victory over the Turks in the Battle of Lepanto in 1571. Four ancient lions flank the door; the one on the left was taken after a naval victory in Athens at Piraeus in 1687 (on its breast, sides, and back it carries a Viking inscription, decoded in the 15th century). The first lion on the right was also taken from Athens the same year. The smaller one on its right, with its elongated body, was taken from the island of Delos and dates back to the sixth century BC. Little is known about the last and smallest of the lions. The *No. 52 vaporetto,* which continues on to the cemetery island of San Michele and to Murano, passes through the compound, offering a rare glimpse into its backyard. ♦ Campo Arsenale. *Vaporetto* stops: Arsenale, Tana, Celestia

32 Trattoria Pizzeria da Paolo

★★$$ Few restaurants in Venice can boast a better space for outdoor dining than this informal, unpretentious neighborhood eatery. The **Arsenale** gateway is right in front and the quiet Rio dell'Arsenale flows nearby. The place fills up on summer evenings with savvy tourists and colorful residents from this popular neighborhood. The trattoria is run by the absolutely charming Paolo out front (*"simpatico e bello"* is how he describes himself, and I can't imagine anyone quibbling) and his *"tesoro"* (treasure) of a wife in the kitchen. Now his equally treasure-like daughter helps look after the customers, too. The food is good, basic, gutsy, tasty stuff—the spaghetti with clams is good, and the pizzas are freshly made, crispy, and generous. The wines are friendly, the house Prosecco well above average, and the little *baccalà* (mousse of salt cod) appetizers are delicious and light as a feather. This is the kind of place that makes you glad to be alive. And glad you found it! ♦ Tu-Su, lunch and dinner. Campo Arsenale 2389 (at Rio dell'Arsenale). 5210660. www.dapaoloarsenale.it. *Vaporetto* stops: Tana, Arsenale

33 Ponte San Pietro

Many iron bridges similar to this one were built in Venice in the second half of the 19th century. Flat and unattractive, they were in contrast to those in the rest of the city, and many were later demolished (including the Ponte dell'Accademia and Ponte Scalzi).

The small lagoon boats, double- and triple-parked along the canal, are witness to the strong ties still existing between the Venetians and the lagoon: Almost every family owns a boat, which it uses almost purely for pleasure—especially on holidays—to go fishing or to reach the popular restaurants that have sprung up on the lagoon islands. ♦ Between Campo San Pietro and Calle Larga San Pietro. *Vaporetto* stops: Arsenale, Tana, Giardini

34 San Pietro di Castello

The castle (*castello*) that once occupied this island gave its name to the whole *sestiere.* This island was the first to be inhabited when ancient settlers moved from the lagoon island of Torcello to the present Venice in the sixth century, and the church was Venice's cathedral until 1807 (when the title was passed to the **San Marco**). The island is like a country village; the families that live in the small houses on the side of the church are undisturbed by the hectic life of the city.

The bell tower, now dangerously leaning, was reconstructed in 1596 to plans by **Andrea Palladio**. The interior was totally rebuilt in the 17th century according to Palladian principles. An interesting curiosity is *St. Peter's Chair,* on the right aisle. It was created around the 13th century from an Arab stone; the original inscriptions from the Koran are still visible on the chair's back. ♦ M-Sa, 10AM-5PM; Su, 1PM-5PM. Campo San Pietro. *Vaporetto* stops: Arsenale, Tana, Giardini

35 Campo di Ruga

Since the 10th century, this *campo* has been the center of a densely populated area. The residential neighborhood of today was constructed in the 14th and 15th centuries. The structures at **Nos. 327** and **329** were rebuilt in the 17th century, and they were probably the homes of well-to-do merchants. The wellhead belongs to the 15th century. ♦ *Vaporetto* stops: Arsenale, Tana, Giardini

36 Campiello

$$ This family-run hotel sits in a tiny piazza (*campiello*) off the prestigious Riva degli Schiavoni. Its 16 rooms are always in demand—air conditioning, tasteful furnishings, and an English-speaking staff explain why. Breakfast only is served in the restaurant. ♦ Calle del Vin 4647 (between Riva degli Schiavoni and Corte Nuova). 5205764, 5239682; fax 5205798. *Vaporetto* stop: San Zaccaria

37 Hotel Danieli

$$$$ Set in the 14th-century Palazzo Dandolo, this 233-room hotel is one of the most illustrious in Venice. Since its opening in 1822 it has played host to countless celebrities, including Honoré de Balzac, Charles Dickens, Gabriele d'Annunzio, Richard Wagner, and French author George Sand, who started an affair there with an Italian physician by stroking his foot while Alfred de Musset, her lover at the time, wasn't looking. In 1948 a plain modern annex was added to the hotel, something many Venetians still cannot accept. The suites are opulent, and the comfortable waterfront rooms are obviously at a premium. The dramatic ground-floor hall is 19th-century neo-Gothic, a

curious feature in Venice. At Christmas it has the most famous Christmas tree in Italy, each branch outlined in tiny white star-lights. There is a piano bar open to nonguests from 10PM to 2AM. Dining or relaxing with a drink at the rooftop restaurant **Terrazza Danieli** is delightful. ♦ Riva degli Schiavoni 4196 (between Rio del Vin and Calle delle Rasse). 5226480, in the US 800/325.3589; fax 5200208. *Vaporetto* stop: San Zaccaria

38 Riva degli Schiavoni and Riva dei Sette Martiri

It changes names several times, but by any name this broad walkway is the most splendid embankment in town. The *riva* (bank) extends from **Piazza San Marco** all the way to the eastern end of Venice. On this bank the Slavonians (*Schiavoni*) were allowed to tie their commercial boats (the *Sette Martiri,* or Seven Martyrs, stretch derives its name from an episode of the anti-Fascist civil war, when seven partisans were captured and executed by the Germans). There is no better way to experience the peculiar nature of Venice than by taking this 20-minute walk at sunset. Tourists rarely wander beyond the first 300 or 400 yards of the walk; after that, only locals populate the wide banks along the lagoon. Water buses, private boats, and enormous cruise ships share the water space. At sunset, lights come on atop the wood poles that mark the deep canals in the lagoon flats, while the sun sets magnificently behind **La Salute** church at the Canal Grande's entrance. ♦ Between Rio dei Giardini and Molo di San Marco. *Vaporetto* stops: San Zaccaria, Arsenale, Giardini

39 Pensione Wildner

$$ This small, comfortable hotel has simply furnished front rooms with a great view of the island of San Giorgio. Back rooms are on the floor above. All 16 rooms have air conditioning. The hotel's restaurant is a convenient spot for a simple meal or snack when tables move outdoors in warm weather. ♦ Riva degli Schiavoni 4161 (between Rio dei Greci and Sottoportico e Calle San Zaccaria). 5227463; fax 5265615 (attn: Wildner). *Vaporetto* stop: San Zaccaria

40 Santa Maria della Pietà

Designed by **Giorgio Massari**, this 18th-century church was built for the nearby orphanage (the façade was added in 1906). For centuries, abandoned children were raised in four such institutions in town: La Pietà, I Mendicanti, Gli Incurabili, and L'Ospedaletto, where they were taught various professions, among the most important of which was music (the word *conservatory* originally meant "place where abandoned children are kept"). Soon the children of these institutions became famous throughout Europe for their musical talents, and their concerts were one of the main reasons foreigners visited the city. Many of the great singers of the 17th century were raised in such institutions. Among them was the soprano Adriana Ferrarese del Bene, the first Fiordiligi in Mozart's *Così fan tutte* and the lover of Mozart's librettist, the Venetian Lorenzo da Ponte. Ferrarese was brought up at **I Mendicanti**, but she eloped in 1780 to marry a young man from Rome and start a glorious singing career. The young singers and players would perform behind a grille, which made them invisible to the audience. In the 1740s, Jean-Jacques Rousseau obtained permission to visit them in the parlor and was bitterly disappointed by the plain looks of these girls who could sing so celestially. On the tiny alley at the right side of the church was the entrance to the orphanage and the spot where children were abandoned. An inscription in stone, still visible in the alley, promised revenge from earth and heaven against parents who abandoned their children. In the first half of the 18th century, the music teacher at **La Pietà** was the Baroque composer and priest Antonio Vivaldi. He died before construction of the church—therefore the popular appellation "Vivaldi's church" is not appropriate.

The interior, beautifully restored in 1988 with international funds, was conceived more as a concert hall than as a church. The oval shape, designed with acoustics in mind, encloses an elegant space, with two gilt-iron grilles on the walls. The ceiling is a masterwork by Tiepolo, the *Triumph of Faith*. Baroque music concerts are performed inside the church throughout the year, but particularly from May through September. Tickets are available in the church foyer, at the **Metropole Hotel** next door, and at a number of travel agencies around town. ♦ Daily. Riva degli Schiavoni 4150 (at Calle della Pietà). *Vaporetto* stop: San Zaccaria

41 Hotel Metropole

$$$$ This is the kind of hotel that—in a world of Starwood and Westin Excelsior clones—restores your faith in hotels and hoteliers. Owned by a marvelous man by the name of Signor Beggiato, this hotel is his love child. Signor Beggiato is a collector—and what a collector! The hotel holds over 2,000 pieces of lovingly collected memorabilia, including antique fans and glass bead evening purses, card cases and 16th-century locks, and one of Italy's most extensive and important collections of crucifixes. It is located on the waterfront that runs along San Marco, in a building dating back to the 15th century. In 1686 a chapel was built on the current site of the Metropole, and here Antonio Vivaldi composed the *Four Seasons* and gave music

lessons. In 1735 the entire area was rebuilt to accommodate a much bigger church, and the existing **Santa Maria della Pietà** was built alongside the hotel. The Metropole, of course, wasn't a hotel until 1880, when it started to attract guests like Sigmund Freud (in 1895). For a short period after 1939, foreign names were not allowed and the hotel became the Metropole!

This is the kind of place you never forget. When you tell your friends about your stay here, you will remember in detail the sumptuous ground-floor salon with its squashily comfortable chairs and sofas, its wine-and-pomegranate color scheme, its drapes, its perfume of incense, and its antique mirrored ceiling. You may even have enjoyed the afternoon tea always on offer here . . . dozens of types of teas from which you can take your pick, accompanied by a delicious torte. You will undoubtedly have enjoyed the nightly live music and perhaps the ultracool Lounge Music evening every Thursday. You will remember the tiny, atmospheric **Zodiac Bar** and the hotel's garden restaurant, with its 17th-century well and 21st-century candlelit nights (the hotel goes through 80 candles every night to create its intimate atmosphere!). The Metropole is one of the "Romantic Hotels of the World," and it is easy to see why. There are 70 rooms—53 doubles, 20 junior suites, 4 suites, and 3 single rooms, each unique. Apart from the usual satellite TV, air conditioning, hair dryer, and minibar, these rooms have some of the most wonderful furnishings and core schemes in Venice. A couple of the suites on the top floor have fabulous roof terraces; Suite 251 has its bed on a platform, flanked by barley sugar-twist pillars and tended by a host of chubby guardian cherubs. Another suite is a vision in papal reds. All the furniture is antique and individually collected by Signor Beggiato. A generous buffet breakfast is served in the private dining room in very grand style. And even if you are not staying at the hotel, you can breakfast there. It is highly recommended! ♦ Riva degli Schiavoni 4149 (at Calle della Pietà). 5205044; fax 5223679. *Vaporetto* stop: San Zaccaria

Within the Hotel Metropole:

Met Restaurant

★★★$$$ Enzo is the chef here, straight from the Cipriani and giving an interesting Eastern/Asian twist to some very Italian cuisine. On the Italian side, pastas include tortellini stuffed with goose liver in an artichoke sauce with walnut oil. One of Enzo's "twists" might be his cod served with mussels and clams in a broth flavored with star anise. He also has created a rare black rice soup—this is inventive stuff! Desserts include a light and refreshing coconut milk with mixed fruit and delicious poached strawberries in maple syrup. And of course the excellent cheese selection is all Italian. The restaurant is housed in a 17th-century chapel . . . until the good weather, when it moves to the hotel's gorgeous private garden. ♦ Daily, lunch and dinner. Riva degli Schiavoni 4149. 5205044. www.hotelmetropole.com

42 Casa di Petrarca (Petrarch's House)

This small Gothic building was given by the Republic as residence to the Tuscan poet Francesco Petrarca, who lived here with his daughter from 1362 until 1367, when he moved to Arquà, a country village in the Venetian hills. In exchange, he promised to leave to the Republic his rare collection of manuscripts, which became the core of the **Biblioteca Marciana**. The view from the Gothic balcony must have been quite exciting in Petrarch's time: The merchant ships coming from abroad would stop right in front for a salute to the city and for customs duties. The house is closed to the public. ♦ Riva degli Schiavoni 4146 (between Calle del Dose and Rio della Pietà). *Vaporetto* stop: San Zaccaria

43 San Giovanni in Bragora

Antonio Vivaldi, born in one of the houses on this charming *campo*, was baptized in this eighth-century (rebuilt in 1505) church in 1678. The main altarpiece (*The Baptism of Christ,* 1494) is a masterwork of Cima da Conegliano, one of the first Venetian painters to introduce landscape as a background to figures, thereby breaking with earlier tradition (gold background) and with more recent trends (open loggiae or small tempiet, as in the Bellini at **San Zaccaria**). Cima's birthplace was in the beautiful Venetian hills, which he portrayed, not accidentally, in his paintings, much like his contemporary Giorgione, also a native of that area. ♦ Campo Bandiera e Moro (between Calle del Dose and Calle dei Preti). *Vaporetto* stops: San Zaccaria, Arsenale

44 Al Covo

★★$$$ Thanks to the combined talents of chef Cesare Benelli and his Texan wife, Diane, this is one of the best restaurants in town. Cesare's passion is for cooking; hers is for entertaining, pleasing guests, and running a smooth operation. The menu covers traditional Venetian dishes and more inventive "new wave" Italian dishes such as pasta with lamb and thyme ragout, marinated anchovies with eggplant cubes and wild fennel, and Cesare's "sashimi-style" fish starter. At lunchtime the place becomes more of a trattoria, with a set menu and no cover charge. As is pointed out on the menu, the fruit and vegetables are local, they use no frozen ingredients, and their fish is all wild and not farmed. ♦ M, Tu, F-Su, lunch and dinner. No credit cards accepted. Campiello della Pescaria 3698 (at Ramo della Pescaria). 5223812. *Vaporetto* stop: Arsenale

45 Museo Storico Navale (Naval Museum)

Dating from the 16th century, the building that houses this museum was originally used by the Republic as a granary. The exhibits include some 25,000 items related to the history of the Italian Navy since unification (1861), as well as material collected from the ancient history of the Venetian fleets. There is a large collection of naval cannons beginning with the 16th century. **Room No. 8** contains interesting models of 18th-century Venetian ships and one of a *fusta,* a 15th-century warship with 224 oars. **Room No. 9** has a splendid model of the last *bucintoro,* the ceremonial ship used by the doge. The third floor covers the history and construction of gondolas and other lagoon boats. The underwater craft from World War I on the ground floor is fascinating to see, and the monument to Admiral Angelo Enio is quite possibly the campiest thing in naval history. There is an admission fee of $1.55, which goes to a fund providing help for the orphans of sailors who have died in service. ♦ M-Sa, 9AM-1PM. Campo San Biagio 2148 (at Fondamenta dell'Arsenale). 5200276. *Vaporetto* stops: Arsenale, Tana

46 Hotel Bucintoro

$$ Most of the 28 rooms in this *pensione*-style hotel enjoy a lovely view of the lagoon, with the **Giardini Pubblici** (Public Gardens) to the east and **Piazza San Marco** to the west. Service is friendly, the rooms are plain and simply furnished, and breakfast and dinner are served in a functional dining room. There is no elevator, but the stairs are not too steep, so the hike up isn't too taxing. It's well worth reserving in advance in order to get one of the corner rooms. And this hotel's location on Riva San Biagio can't be beat. ♦ Closed December and January. No credit cards accepted. Riva San Biagio 2135 (between Rio della Tana and Campo San Biagio). 5223240; fax 5235224. *Vaporetto* stops: Arsenale, Tana

The dizzying array of inverted bell pots at the tops of chimneys that decorate Venice's skyline have a practical as well as a picturesque function: They were designed to trap the sparks from household fires, thereby reducing the risk of flames spreading to adjoining buildings.

47 Via Garibaldi

This is one of the few areas in Venice where neighborhood life is as it was before the city became a major tourist center. In the morning, a small fruit-and-vegetable market and a few fish stands are bustling with local shoppers. This colorful street was built by filling a canal, which still flows under its pavement. The whole operation was part of an ambitious project conceived by Napoleon's urban planners during the French occupation (1800-1814): They imagined a large and perfectly straight avenue that, like a Paris boulevard, would connect Venice to the mainland, leading right to **La Salute** church. Fortunately for Venetians and visitors alike, the plan was abandoned with the passage of Venice to Austrian domination (1814-1861). It is well worth a trip along here to see a very different Venice. This is a real neighborhood and, should you need to do some "normal" shopping—for shoes, household goods, haberdashery, supermarket stuff—then this is your street. There are some terrific delis, a street market, and loads of inviting-looking cafés and *gelaterias* to relax at while watching the world go by. A walk up here will let you feel you've really been to Venice. One of the entrances to the **Giardini Pubblici** is here, and just inside is a monument to Garibaldi himself, standing on a rocky island surrounded by a pool and accompanied (you will see once you go around the island) by a foot soldier who stands guard. ♦ Between Rio di Sant'Anna and Riva dei Sette Martiri. *Vaporetto* stops: Arsenale, Tana, Giardini

On the Via Garibaldi:

Fondamenta Sant' Anna

At the top of Via Garibaldi, the road divides along two sides of a sweet little canal. On the right-hand side runs the Fondamenta Sant'Anna and, should you be thinking about eating in in Venice and want to do your grocery shopping in the loveliest possible setting, come here. Along this tiny *fondamenta*, you find little sparrows at your feet instead of great fat pigeons, and have everything you could want. At **No. 100½** is **Melita**, a *pasticceria* that attracts customers from all over the city for its delicious cakes and pastries (closed Monday). At **No. 996 (a)** is a deli/grocery store jam packed with salamis and cheeses, giant tins of preserved artichoke hearts, and all the basic necessities of dining. At **No. 997(a)** you will find a butcher with a window full of everything meaty, from lean cuts of veal to fresh sausages and *nervetti* (cartilage) for stewing. At **No. 1131** there is a fantastic fish shop with a great selection of spankingly fresh fish and shellfish. Moored right outside is a barge weighed down with the most gorgeous selection of fresh fruit and vegetables. Having bought everything you need, at the highest quality and finest freshness from charming people, expert in their fields, situated within 50 yards of each other, why not sit at the **Trattoria alla Pampa del Piave (No. 1133)** and ponder why we bother with the horror of plastic-wrapped supermarket foods?

Le Spighe

When people who care about really good food start handing out medals, Doriana, the passionate proprietrix of this place, should be up there with the best of them. Doriana makes pasta. But she makes pasta like Coco Chanel made perfume. Only the finest, purest ingredients are used. And in the case of Doriana and her pasta, she eschews expensive ingredients like truffle and salmon, and instead uses fresh, local flavors in her beloved tagliatelles—beetroot, octopus, parsley, peperoncini, and even cinnamon color and flavor her pasta. And only those things. No artificial anything. She uses extra-virgin olive oil and only Parmesan that has been aged for two and a half years. She makes and stuffs all her pastas by hand and absolutely refuses to get bigger or to mechanize any part of the process, because she feels it would compromise quality. And that quality is recognized by the many five-star hotels and award-winning restaurants who owe their plaudits at least in part to Doriana's pasta. The shop also sells an enticing array of organic produce from small producers. Go to learn, to be inspired, to buy, and to eat the best pasta you will ever have tasted. ♦ Closed Sunday and Wednesday afternoon. Via Garibaldi 1341. 5238173

San Francesco di Paola

Another of Venice's friendly working parish churches, as lovely as you could wish. Built in the 14th century and rebuilt in the 16th, it boasts works by Palma il Giovane, Schiavoni, and Tiepolo.

48 Trattoria dai Tosi

★$$ This is a great spot, full of local cheer, to rest and discuss a visit to **San Pietro di Castello**. Have a pizza if you're in the mood for something quick, or a leisurely three-course Italian meal sitting outside at one of the tables. Even if the place is at full capacity, the kind staff can usually arrange to bring out another table and put it in a spare corner.
♦ Tu-Su, 6:30PM-11:30PM. Secco Marina 738 (between Calle Giambattista Tiepolo and Calle Correra). 5237102. *Vaporetto* stop: Giardini

49 Monumento alla Partigiana (Monument to the Partisan Woman)

Venetian architect **Carlo Scarpa** designed this unusual, highly moving monument to resistance against Mussolini's Fascism in 1964. It was completed with a bronze statue by contemporary sculptor Augusto Murer. The monument is set on the lagoon's bank at mid-tide level, so that its steps and the statue itself are sometimes immersed at high tide.
♦ Viale dei Giardini Pubblici (between Rio dei Giardini and Rio di San Giuseppe). *Vaporetto* stop: Giardini

50 Giardini Pubblici (Public Gardens)

These gardens at the eastern tip of town were designed by Napoleon, who drained a section of marshland to create Venice's favorite park. They're great places to walk and spot the statues and busts of famous composers and artists. A stroll along the fondamenta that borders the gardens is wonderful, with a hard-to-beat view, although watch out that you don't get run down by jogging Venetians! In 1895 the gardens were designated the home of the Venice Biennial (*Biennale Internazionale d'Arte*), a large art show planned every second year with the purpose of exhibiting contemporary art from all over the world. Twenty-eight pavilions are now scattered throughout the gardens, representing more than 50 nations. Artists are chosen by committees from their own countries. The *Biennale* is often controversial—and is certainly meant to be so—and always memorable. ♦ June-Sept, odd years. Viale dei Giardini Pubblici. 5289327. *Vaporetto* stop: Giardini

GIUDECCA

The **Canale della Giudecca**, the canal that separates Giudecca from the rest of Venice is only 1,000 feet wide, but it is enough to make this island a distinctly autonomou community of some 8,000 residents. There are no bridges over the canal, but *vaporett* service is regular. Things get a bit complicated in winter, when a thick fog may settle i for hours, making it nearly impossible to get here. The island is named for the Jews o Venice, who mostly lived here from the 12th century until 1516, when they were confine by the Republic to the **Ghetto** on **Cannaregio**. Since then it has served mainly as a poo community of fishermen and shipyard workers, with modest but welcoming homes o the days of old; here also, however, is the most expensive luxury hotel in Venice—th **Albergo Cipriani**. A walk along the Giudecca canal bank provides one of the mos rewarding experiences you can have in Venice—a panoramic view of the city's profil from **Dorsoduro** to **San Marco** is yours for the taking. At night, after a fine dinner at local restaurant, even waiting for a *vaporetto* to take you back across the beautiful lagoo to **Piazza San Marco** is a delightful experience.

---

1 Molino Stucky

You cannot help but notice the huge, imposing building at the northern end of the island—it is the **Molino Stucky**, once a flour mill, then a wreck, and soon to be reborn, after years of more reconstruction work than Joan Rivers, as part apartment block, part office suite, part hotel. ♦ Fondamenta San Biagio. *Vaporetto* stop: Sant'Eufemia

2 Harry's Dolci

★★$$$ Arrigo Cipriani, owner of the famous (and more expensive) **Harry's Bar**, opened this annex in the early 1980s. It was supposed to specialize in desserts (*dolci*), but it quickly became one of the town's favorite restaurants—offering Harry's Bar class, complete with white-jacketed waiters, at slightly more affordable prices. It offers a restaurant menu, with *caffè* additions like club sandwiches. The eponymous *dolci* are wonderful. The *meringata alla crema* is a huge cloud of sweetened whipped cream encased in a soft meringue coating—one of the times you think "I'll never eat all that" and then do. Lose weight tomorrow! The canopies along the Canale della Giudecca

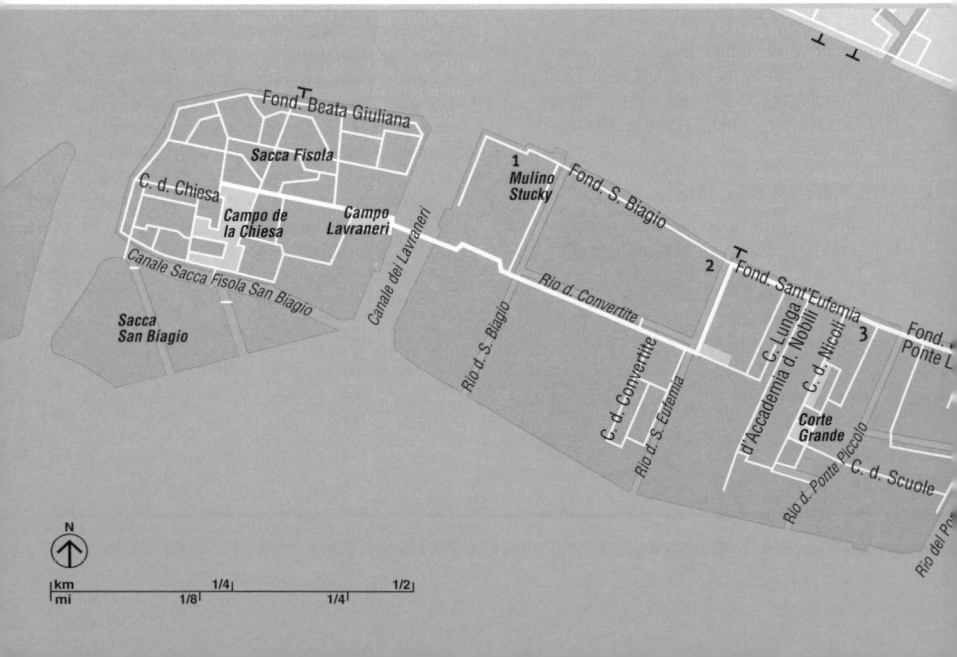

create a beautiful space for dining outdoors, the real reason to come. ♦ M, W-Su, lunch and dinner Mar-Nov. Fondamenta San Biagio 773 (near Campo Sant'Eufemia). 5224844. www.cipriani.com. *Vaporetto* stop: Sant'Eufemia

3 Trattoria Do Mori

★★$$ This really friendly place is right on the bank of the Giudecca Canal, so dining outside in good weather is a joy. Dining inside is no trial either, as the food is good, fresh, and homemade. The fish antipasto is a generous plateful, and the chef managed the real coup of getting the *seppie* (cuttlefish) actually to taste of something. Pastas come with the usual sauces, but the *ravioli al ricotta e rucola* (ravioli with a stuffing of ricotta and peppery arugula) is a wonderful summer lunch. The ever-present owner spent 15 years at Harry's Bar, so knows something about the restaurant business. He was born and raised on the Giudecca, son of a gondolier, so knows everything about Venice. He is a terrific host. ♦ M-F, lunch and dinner. Fondamenta Sant'Eufemia 588 (between Rio del Ponte Piccolo and Calle del Forno). 5225452. *Vaporetto* stop: Palanca

3 Osteria Ae Botti

★$ Should you want to experience genuine local life, there is no better place. Here on the Giudecca, you are off the beaten tourist track anyway, and this little bar-*cum*-restaurant is really only frequented by locals. Drink and snack out front and you will get a more-than-decent glass of house wine, a good Prosecco, or good coffee to accompany your homemade (and absolutely delicious) *polpette*, bruschette with fresh cherry tomato and mozzarella, or grilled vegetables. Opt for something more substantial and you will be taken through the daily offerings by a charming waiter—there is no menu—which change daily but usually include a spaghetti with cream, ham, and pepperoni or simple tomato sauce or *ragu*, and main courses that run from roast chicken to brochettes of lamb and maybe a special like *trippa alla parmigiana* (tripe in a cheese-and-tomato sauce). Vegetable or salad accompaniment is included. Bread is good. There is a better-than-average house wine, and desserts are simple but good. This is also a nice place to start the day, with a brioche and a macchiatto at a table outside on the Canale Giudecca. ♦ M-Sa. Fondamenta Sant'Eufemia 609. 5238214

4 Al Cacciatore

★★$ This new venture on the Giudecca run by two young brothers, with Mama in the kitchen, is friendly and old-fashioned in a very positive way. As at many places on the island, most of the customers are locals frequently discussing football. The bar is zinc-topped, and beside it runs the traditional *bancone* with its selections of daily offerings. There is all manner of grilled fish, fat grilled prawns, *sarde fritti* (filleted sardines lightly battered and fried), *sarde in saor* (in a tangy onion-based marinade), freshly made *polpette* (little meat rissoles), *uove asciughate* (anchovy stuffed eggs), and—the night I was there—a big bowl of steamed *garusoli* (sea snails—delicious if you can get them freshly done like this). There are tables in the bar or in a little room at the back, should you feel like ordering one of Mama's excellent pasta dishes. According to Mama, the menu changes daily. The glassware is beautiful. This

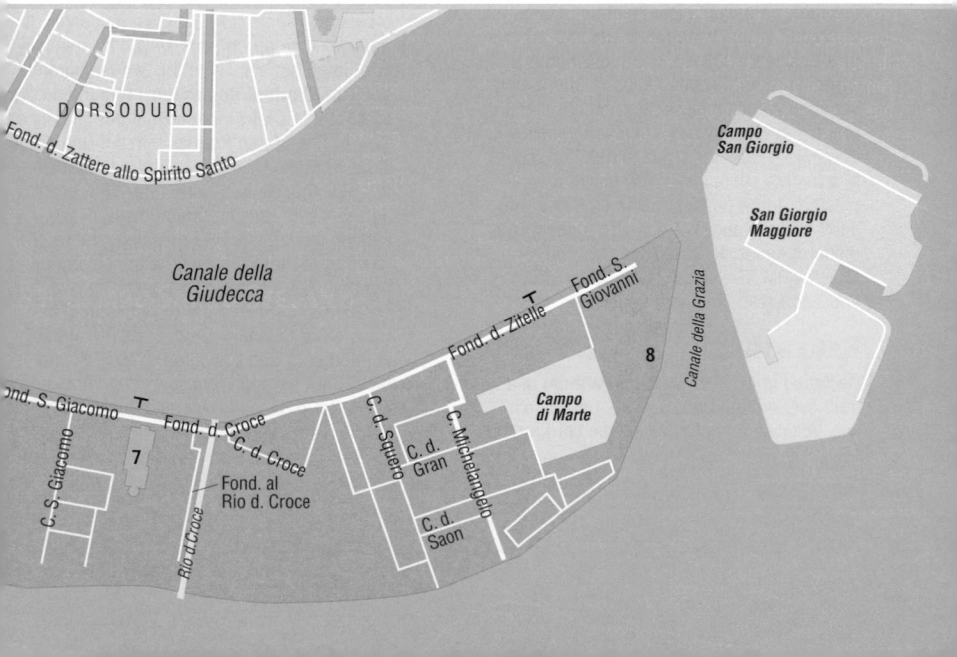

may seem like a small thing, but in most bars in Venice you drink from little round goblets or even tumblers. Here they have lovely, long-stemmed, generously sized, fine crystal glasses, and I do believe they make the wine taste better! The other thing I noticed was the sparkling cleanliness of the place—especially the rest rooms. Which was in stark contrast to the bar at the Hotel Danieli, from which I had just come, where the rest rooms were a disgrace. ♦ Tu-Su, 7AM-11PM. Fondamendante Piccolo 320. 5285849

5 Ristorante all'Altanella

★★$$ A fourth generation of the Penzo family is continuing a tradition of hospitality that began in 1889. But hope that father Gianni doesn't retire too soon . . . it would be a loss. The terrace on the canal is lovely, and the room inside is relaxed and friendly. The food is fish-biased, but if you don't want to eat the house special *gnocchi al seppie* (little feather-light dumplings sauced black with cuttlefish) then you can have the gnocchi with a fresh tomato sauce instead. The *fritto misto* is squeaky fresh, the *fegato alla veneziana* (sauted calves' liver) at a premium, and the desserts homemade by Mama. Good stuff! ♦ W-Su, lunch and dinner. Reservations required. No credit cards accepted. Calle delle Erbe 270 (between Rio della Palada and Fondamenta del Ponte Lungo). 5227780. *Vaporetto* stop: Giudecca

6 Mistra

★★$$$ Possibly the most intriguingly located restaurant in all Venice. Walk along the Giudecca canalfront and turn into what looks like a boatyard. That is because it *is* a boatyard. But the sign says Ristorante Mistra, and Mistra there is: Right at the very back of the yard, up a flight of wrought-iron stairs, on the top floor of a warehouse building overlooking the lagoon, is a bright sunlit (usually) room. The food is basic and mainly Venetian (which means fishy), with a menu that changes every day. There is frequently a delicious salad of octopus and potato, squid in a tomato sauce, fresh fish grilled or roasted, and a pasta in pesto for those who don't like seafood. There is also a cheap set menu at lunch. ♦ Closed Tuesday and Monday PM. Giudecca 212a. 5220743. *Vaporetto* stop: Palanca, Redentore

7 Redentore

Designed in 1577 by **Andrea Palladio** and built over a period of 15 years, this church was Venice's way of thanking the Lord for the end of a plague, an event that is still celebrated every year on the second Saturday in July and is called the *Festa del Redentore*. A temporary bridge of linked boats is built over the Canale della Giudecca to allow the traditional pilgrimage to the church. At night, an hour of fireworks over the lagoon attracts enormous crowds from the mainland, while Venetians watch from their boats. The rigorous, classical harmony of the church's façade was one of Palladio's best inventions and was imitated countless times in Venice and all over Europe. The paintings in the interior chapels illustrate episodes from the life of Jesus, from his birth (first chapel on the right) to the *Crucifixion* (main altar) and the *Resurrection* (on top of the dome). ♦ Campo del Redentore (between Fondamenta della Croce and Fondamenta San Giacomo). *Vaporetto* stop: Redentore.

8 Albergo Cipriani

$$$$ Located at the end of the Giudecca, this legendary hotel exists almost in a world of its own, surrounded as it is on one side by its private, extensive, and absolutely immaculate gardens and on the other by the lagoon. It oozes *richesse* and exclusivity. It has the only hotel swimming pool in Venice except for the Lido, tennis courts, and a private motorboat service to and from San Marco. Rooms—with every facility you could imagine—are regularly refurbished under the guidance of Countess Isabelle de Borchegrave. The new Palladio Suite is the work of the Countess and two architects valued by the Cipriani. It has a 180-degree vista over the lagoon, its own butler, a motorlaunch, garden, and whirlpool. The **Palazzo Vendramin dei Cipriani**, an extension of the hotel, is in an aristocratic 15th-century building where some suites enjoy a splendid view over St. Mark's basin; others open onto large wooden balconies. It includes nine apartments served by specially appointed butlers. There are two restaurants, one (the **Cipriani Restaurant**) formal and the other (**Cip's Club**) more casual but offering a view of San Marco from its terrace. One of the most wonderful things about the Cipriani is the **San Giorgio** bar, open from 7PM and to nonresidents—beside the fountain, overlooking the lagoon, and presided over for 25 years by Walter Bolzonella, a prince among barmen. Ask him for a Canaletto, his own creation and much more delicious than a Harry's Bar Bellini. ♦ Giudecca 10 (south of Fondamenta San Giovanni). 5207744; fax 5203930. www.cipriani.com. *Vaporetto* stop: Zitelle (or private motorlaunch from San Marco if you are a guest)

San Giorgio Maggiore

The solemn, triumphant sea entrance to the Canal Grande is defined by the **Palazzo Ducale**, **La Salute** church, and the island of San Giorgio Maggiore. The trio creates a majestic stage setting that seems to float on the waters of the lagoon. Architect **Andrea Palladio** was well aware of the overall effect he was creating when he designed the church that is the centerpiece of the island of San Giorgio.

The island was the property of a Benedictine abbey in the 10th century. The monks still occupy a large part of it, sharing the rest with the Fondazione Giorgio Cini, established in 1951 by wealthy Count Vittorio Cini in memory of his son Giorgio, who died in an airplane crash. The foundation (the entrance is near the church, by the boat landing) is one of the most active cultural institutions in Italy. It organizes symposia and conferences and runs three specialized libraries around two splendid cloisters, one of which was designed by Palladio. The main staircase was designed by **Baldassare Longhena** in 1644. The libraries—which are open to the public, well staffed, and never too crowded—are a pleasure to use.

The church of **San Giorgio Maggiore** (founded in the 10th century and reconstructed to Palladio's design beginning 1565) faces **Piazza San Marco** and the Canal Grande entrance. Palladio is at his best in this church—the message is one of quiet, powerful harmony, based on classical models yet still highly original. The interior contains two paintings by Jacopo Tintoretto, probably his last works: *The Last Supper* (right wall of chancel) and *The Gathering of the Manna* (left wall of chancel).

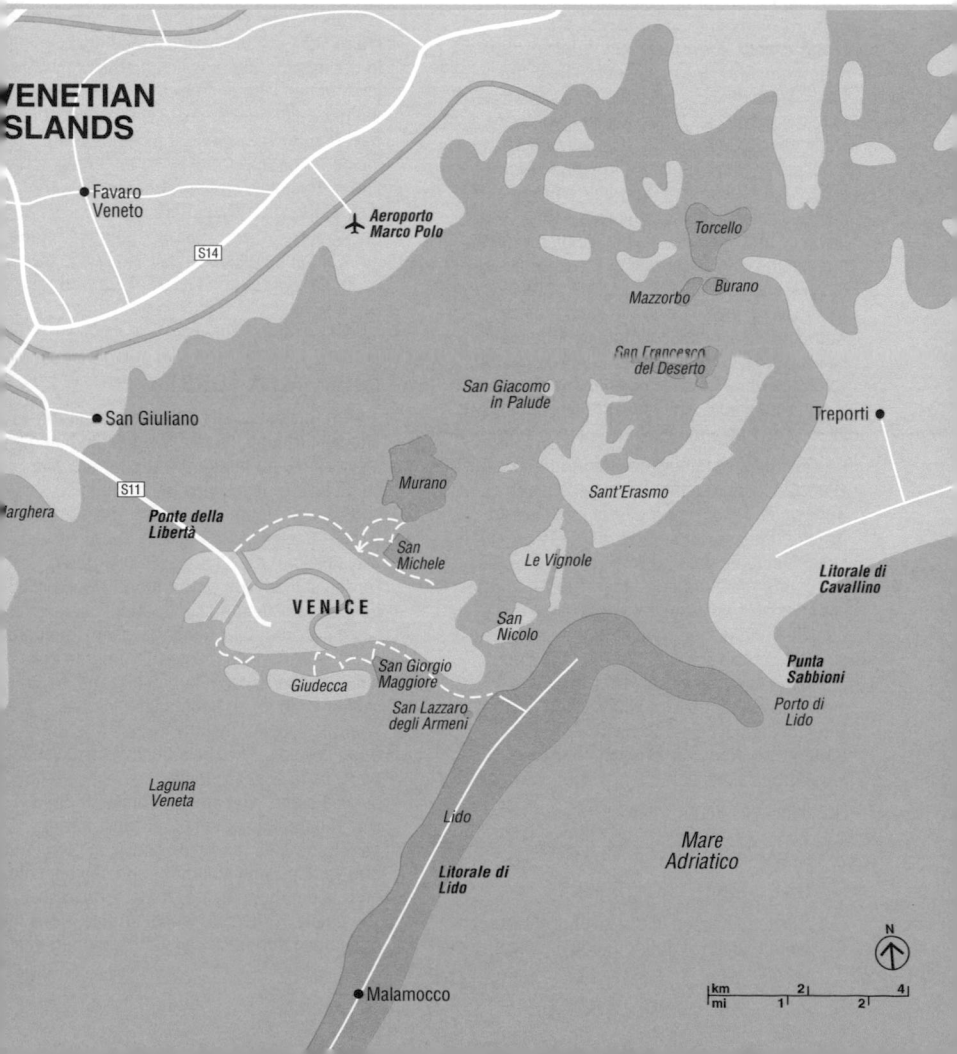

The impressive bronze above the main altar represents *God the Father over the World Supported by the Four Evangelists,* a work by Girolamo Campagna. At the right of the chancel is the entrance to the **Cappella dei Morti** (Chapel of the Dead), with a *Deposition* by Tintoretto. A spiral staircase leads from the chancel to the **Coro Invernale** (winter choir), with *Saint George and the Dragon* by Vittore Carpaccio, painted by the master eight years after his similar work in **San Giorgio degli Schiavoni**. A few of the remaining Benedictine monks meet in the chapel every Sunday at 11AM to sing a Mass in Gregorian chant. The general public is welcome. The San Giorgio campanile, much less crowded than **St. Mark**'s, offers sweeping vistas of the city and the surrounding lagoon. The elevator entrance is in the church's chancel. ♦ Campanile: admission; daily. Campo San Giorgio. 5289900. *Vaporetto* stop: San Giorgio.

MURANO

Less than a mile of water separates Murano from the northern shore of Venice (**Fondamente Nuove**), yet the island seems light-years away. The *vaporetti* will take you from the Fondamente Nuove on the short trip to Murano. You can get on earlier if you want a waterborne tour of the city . . . try boarding at the Piazzale Roma, because the trip to Murano (about a half hour from Piazzale Roma) includes some beautiful stretches of the lagoon. From the *piazzale*, the *vaporetto* runs through the colorful **Canale di Cannaregio** to reach the open lagoon at **Sant'Alvise**; then it coasts along the banks to the Fondamente Nuove, where it heads for Murano. Murano is known as "Glass Island" and as you approach, you'll see why. Glass factories and workshops line the waterfront, and glass shops are absolutely everywhere you go.

In 1291 the city fathers decided to move all glass production to the island because they were worried production on the main island posed a fire risk. In the 16th and 17th centuries, more than 30,000 people lived there; now there are fewer than 5,000. All the factories and workshops do tours and demonstrations, and no matter how tacky the odd little horses and gondolas they turn out, to see a Muranese glassblower at work is a marvelous thing, so be a tourist, and go see. The main furnaces are **Barovier & Toso**, **Cenendese**, **Nason & Moretti**, and **Toso.** All have shops attached.

Highlights on Murano include:

MUSEO DELL'ARTE VETRARIA (MUSEUM OF GLASS ART)

The museum, housed in the lovely **Palazzo Giustinian**, features an exhibition on glass-making technology curated by the island's Stazione Sperimentale (Experimental Station), an archeological section including a cup used, according to legend, by Jason and the Argonauts 3,000 years ago; and glass objects produced in Murano from way back in the 10th century until the present (a collection of 20th-century art glass is in the palazzo's former ballroom). The 16th-century collection is particularly rich in precious goblets, lovely drinking glasses, and painted dishes; the 18th-century section includes some remarkable mirrors. ♦ Admission. M-Tu, Th-Su, 10AM-4PM. Fondamenta Giustinian 8 (just north of Fondamenta Cavour). 739586. *Vaporetto* stops: Colonna, Museo

SANTA MARIA E SAN DONATO

A different Murano from the tourist-oriented glass bazaar awaits you on this corner, just a few steps from the **Museo dell'Arte Vetraria**. The apse of this church, beautifully oriented toward a canal, is a masterwork of Venetian medieval art—a simple, handsome Romanesque building with subtle Byzantine influences. The grassy square in front of the church adds to the magical medieval feeling. In the interior, the mosaics on the floor date back to the 12th century and have figures of animals, as in the floors of the basilica of **San Marco**. The splendid mosaic on the inside of the apse, similar to the one you'll find in Torcello's cathedral, represents the Virgin Mary on a Byzantine-inspired background of gold. The first painting on the left wall represents San Donato and is signed by Paolo Veneziano (1310). ♦ Campo San Donato and Calle San Donato. *Vaporetto* stops: Colonna, Museo

BUSA-ALLA-TORRE

★★$$ This amazingly genuine restaurant offers good food, reasonable prices, friendly service, and an omnipresent *padrone* ever helpful with suggestions as to what you should choose from his menu. The seafood is terrific—pastas include a truly excellent (and very unusual) *ravioli di pesce alla Busa* (ravioli stuffed with seafood and served in a delicious fresh crab sauce). Main courses cover just about anything that swims prepared on the restaurant's masterfully utilized grill, although there are grilled steaks and grilled veal or lamb as an alternative. Ask the *padrone*—or your friendly waiter—about the day's specials, like the stunningly delicious *moleche in saor* (certainly the best soft-shelled crabs I've eaten in Venice, topped with the traditional Venetian *saor*—a tangy, sweet-and-sour marinade heavy on onions and studded with sultanas—and served, cold, on a bed of hot polenta. A masterful dish.). The house *fritto misto* is lighter than air—a mix of seafood and fresh vegetables dipped in a

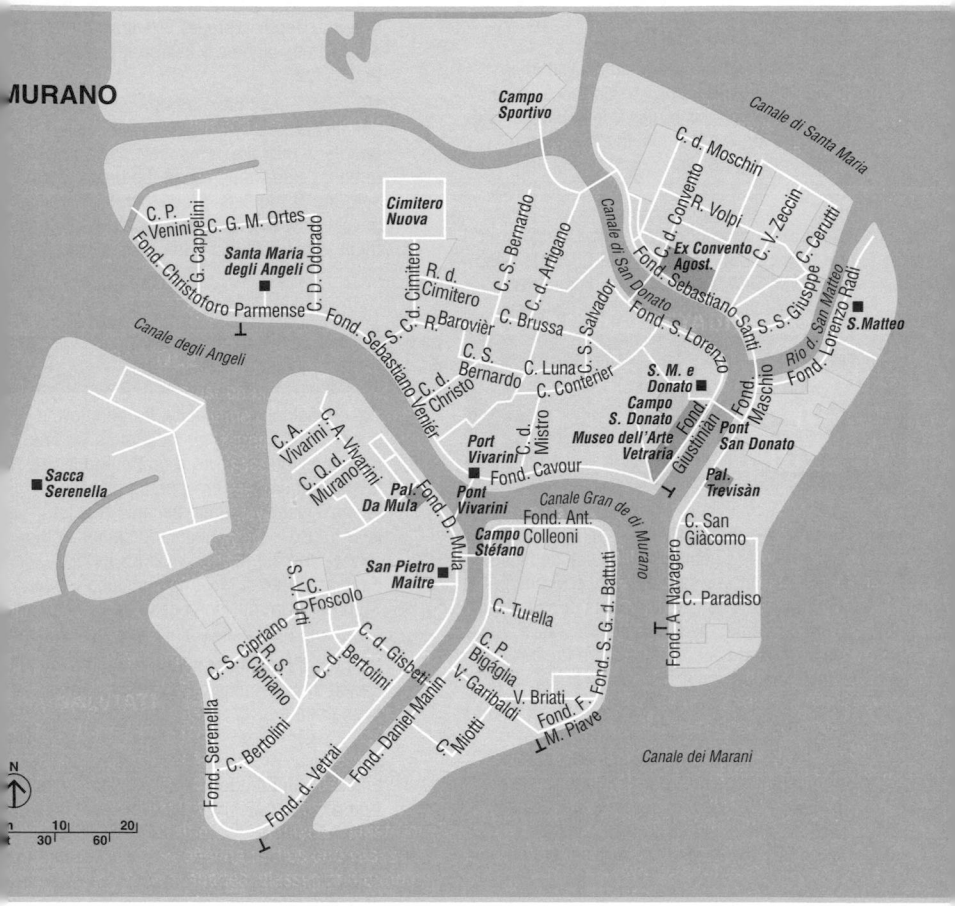

feathery batter and fried. Forgo dessert in favor of a selection of biscotti and you will enjoy *Busola Forte* (like the best Christmas cake you have ever eaten compressed to the texture of a pancake and studded with chocolate chunks!) among other biscuity deliciousness. ♦ Daily, lunch. Campo Santo Stefano (at Fondamenta Daniel Manin). 739662. *Vaporetto* stops: Colonna, Faro

Ferro & Lazzarini

The glass-master heavyweights have been manufacturing on Murano for centuries. But if their prices and over-the-top designs are out of your league, and the alternative—choosing from among a plethora of poor-quality shops—is overwhelming, where do you go? A good bet is this well-known furnace and retail store owned by the Ferro and Lazzarini families since 1927. The shop certainly has its share of touristy trinkets, but it also has a wide selection of good-quality, moderately priced glassware ranging from the traditional to the contemporary. Lighting fixtures, tabletop "art" glass, drinking glasses, paperweights, and Christmas ornaments can become works of art once rescued from their kitsch-laden environment and safely shipped home, where uniqueness is more apparent. ♦ Daily (no midday closing). Fondamenta Andrea Navagero 75 (near the *vaporetto* stop). 739299. *Vaporetto* stop: Navagero

Laboratorio di Raffaela Lamberti

The wares of this young, fun, female glass artist may be a bit tacky, but among all the standard figurines and fruit, she creates glass cartoon soccer players! In their numbered strips. They are both fun and funny, and who would have thought that Murano glass would have developed a sense of humor! She also makes sweet little glass Vespa scooters. ♦ Daily. Fondamenta Manin 70. 5274443

San Pietro Martire

Where else will you see a church with the nave hung with eight ornate glass chandeliers? From the outside this church is fairly unassuming, but there are two Bellinis and a Tintoretto inside, along with works by J. Palma the Younger and a lovely *Via Crucis* (Stations of the Cross). It is an airy, peaceful place and well worth the wander across the bridge from the **Campo San Stefano**. ♦ M-Sa, 9AM-noon and 3PM-6PM; Su, 3PM-6PM. Fondamenta dei Vetrai. *Vaporetto* stops: Faro, Colonna

Burano/San Francesco del Deserto/ Mazzorbo/Torcello

A trip to these four islands is an opportunity to spend a few hours on the quiet landscapes of the lagoon, a totally different environment from the open sea. Public boats depart about every hour from the **Fondamente Nuove**. They are large and comfortable, but in the busy tourist season you should come in the early morning and leave in the early afternoon to avoid the crowds.

This part of the lagoon is at its best at sunset in the summer—though everyone else seems to know this, too. The lagoon is surprisingly shallow; one could easily walk through it if it weren't for the mud at the bottom. At mid-tide, the depth averages 3 feet; with the tides it can go as high as 5 feet or as low as less than 1 foot.

The large public boats run through natural canals marked by the wood poles called *bricole*; a mistake of maneuvering a few yards to either side would cause the boats to run aground in the flats. Smaller craft, however, travel freely, as they have flat bottoms that allow them to move in just a few inches of water.

Spritz is the traditional Venetian aperitif and dates back to the time of the Austrian occupation of Italy in the 19th century. The Austrian soldiers found the Italian wines too strong for them and diluted them with fizzy water (*spritzen*). Ever creative, the Venetians "improved" on what the Austrians had done to their wine. They added bitters, to make a tangy, refreshing (and stronger) aperitif. Spritz now comes in a variety of forms. The exact proportions are somewhat altered to taste, but you could start with one third bitters, one third white wine, and one third fizzy water. Tweak to taste. Now then, the bitters. Spritz comes in four main forms: with Campari (*con bitters*), with Select (redder and slightly sweeter), with Aperol (more orangy, lighter and slightly medicinal), and with Cynar (darker, and bitterest of all). Each gets an olive and Aperol gets a slice of orange, while the rest get lemon. Some places (the B Bar at the Bauer Hotel, for example) like to make their spritzes with bitters and Prosecco. And it should be tried—it is really rather good. But whatever your choice, order it specifically to sound like a Venetian. And stand at the bar to drink it, to look like one! *Cin cin*!

Burano

Once a fishing community, Burano now depends on tourism for most of its income. Lace making was revived on Burano in the 19th century and has turned it into "Lace Island," just as Murano became "Glass Island." Countless shops and stands in the streets and alleys offer all kinds of lace-decorated items. Most are machine-made in Spain or Asia, but don't despair; you can still find some handmade, albeit very costly, items.

In spite of the tourist boom, Burano has maintained the charming character of a small island community. The canals are lined with small lagoon boats, used for fishing and pleasure. It was on one of these boats that the English writer Frederic W. Rolfe, known as Baron Corvo, spent the last years of his life in the early 1900s working on his novel *The Desire and the Pursuit of the Whole*. Burano's houses were typically painted in a spectrum of bright colors, apparently to make them easy to identify by fishermen returning home; today the local administration contributes to the painting by providing guidelines and funding. The best way to enjoy a visit here is to walk along the main street, **Via Baldassare Galuppi** (named after an 18th-century composer who was born on Burano), taking a few random detours along the side canals—who knows what you'll find.

Highlights on Burano include:

Ristorante da Romano

★★★$$$ This seafood restaurant at the center of Via Galuppi has a large outdoor dining area. The walls inside are hung with a serious collection of works by artists who have passed through Burano over the years. The kitchen specializes in fresh fish dishes and fish-based risotto and pasta. Before sitting down to dinner, ask about the boat schedule for your return to the city—the trip back to Venice at night is a memorable experience, but departures are infrequent. ♦ M, W-Sa, lunch and dinner; Su, lunch. Via Baldassare Galuppi 221 (just northwest of Piazza Baldassare Galuppi). 730030. *Vaporetto* stop: Burano

Museo di Merletto

A sweet little museum with a display of historic and contemporary lace designs, traditional lace-making implements, and, if you are lucky, occasionally the lace-makers themselves. ♦ Admission. W-M, 10AM-5PM. Piazza Baldassare Galuppi and Via di Vigna. 730034. *Vaporetto* stop: Burano

Panificio Pasticceria Palmisano Luigi

Great fresh bread, wonderful pastries, fresh savories (like little *pizzette*), traditional lovelies like *pinza* (a kind of dense, moist fruitcake gently scented with fennel seed), dark *croccante* (almond brittle), the whole gamut of biscotti loose or in shiny bags, and, in season, all the wonderful Venetian sweet things with which saints' days and holidays are celebrated. If you are lucky enough to be around at *Carnevale*, the *frittelle* (light, sugar-dusted dough fritters filled with zabaglione or cream, or flavored with lemon and raisins) are worth going up a size for. You will never touch a Krispy Kreme again! The back of the shop has a well-stocked deli counter with salamis and cheeses. This shop has been baking slices of Buranese and Venetian life since 1926, so you are getting an edible history lesson. Go on. Educate yourself! ♦ Daily. Via Galuppi 670. 730060

Emilia

It has always been a niggling worry for me when visiting Burano that there is so much machine-made or hand-finished (but not hand *made*) lace around (and lace is around everywhere on Burano). I know so little about lace making and have never known where to find "the real thing"—or even what it looks like. Now I know.

At Emilia, the fourth generation of the Ammendola family are carrying on a tradition begun by the formidable lady whose portrait hangs in the upstairs mini-museum and gallery of this glorious treasure trove of a shop. As well as the items for sale, there are examples of exquisite lace the family firm has produced over the decades—fans and handkerchiefs, umbrellas and a tiny grand piano, tablecloths and even a lovely, gossamer-fine lace wedding dress. The present torchbearer of the family art and craft is Lorenzo, an entrancing, dapper, passionate young man who not only designs a new generation of lace but is responsible for everything else made under the Emilia label in the shop. He and Giuseppe—his proud and equally passionate father—took me on a tour of the lacey treasures the two-story store holds. They unrolled lace that is decades old, huge expanses of beautiful, intricate work made in dozens of small pieces. Each piece of lace is only as big as the cylindrical cushions the lace-makers work them around. They showed me an exquisite tablecloth that took six *years* to make, and a circular mat about the size of a saucer that is an exact replica of a window in the Ca d'Oro that took a full twelve months to create. I begin to understand the price this work commands. Every piece of handmade lace is made not just of art and skill and finely spun cotton thread but of that most precious commodity of all—time. Weeks . . . months . . . years. Each piece has a part of someone's lifetime in it. Several lifetimes, in fact, because, as Lorenzo explains, each lace-maker does only one of the many individual stitches in the pattern and then passes the piece on to the next worker, so lace making is the ultimate in team arts. One mistake by the lady who stitches the base pattern over Lorenzo's drawing and everything has to be thrown away and started over. Everything is an area of expertise—there are two ladies engaged purely for their skill in washing old lace without damaging it. Once you have been privileged to see a few examples of the real thing, you realize it is easy to tell the difference between hand- and machine-made. On the stairway is the pattern for a piece Lorenzo designed for the Sultan of Brunei; a thank-you note from Johnny Depp, who is both a fan and a customer; and another from Julia Roberts, who also has Emilia lace in her home. Lorenzo also designed and made the lace-edged towels and bathrobes for the new Palladio Suite at the Cipriani, and has even made lace for the Vatican. Alongside his passion for lace making, Lorenzo designs most of the other beautiful things in the shop—stunning Fortuny-style wraps and throws; beautiful, delicate silk evening dresses in deep jewel colors; fragile, old-world nightgowns, and lovely, flatteringly feminine underwear in silk and, of course, lace. Emilia is just full of things that will make your life more beautiful. And gentlemen . . . of anywhere in Venice that I might recommend for a romantic gift to give, Emilia's is probably the place. ♦ Daily. Piazza Galuppi 205. 735299

Riva Rosa

★★★★$$$ This is without a doubt the loveliest and most romantic little restaurant on the lagoon. Everything about it has been done with love. From the fragile, elegant glassware to the likeable maître d', everything has been chosen with thought, with style, and with care. And its eye-mistingly lovely views makes eating in this tiny treasure one of my favorite memories of Venice. Riva Rosa

The Best

Louise Berndt

Owner, Galleria San Nicolò

Just walking around the *sestiere* (neighborhoods) away from the **San Marco–Rialto** axis.

The view of the city from the *campanile* (bell tower) on **Isola San Giorgio**.

The **Museo Storico Navale** (Naval Museum) at the **Arsenale** boat stop—the easiest and most entertaining way to understand the basis of Venice's wealth and splendor. Then walk by the Arsenale itself and think of this area filled with the largest wage-labor industrial workforce in Europe in the 13th century, making rope and the ships to fit it in.

San Pietro di Castello– This church was the patriarch's seat when San Marco was just the doge's private chapel.

The *Festa del Redentore*—All Venice takes to the water in decorated boats for the world's best fireworks show. Then the party on land that goes on until dawn on the **Giudecca** at the **Redentore** church.

The *Festa della Salute* (21 November)—All of Venice makes the pilgrimage to **Santa Maria della Salute** to light votive candles for good health during the coming year—health for one's self, family, dog, business—one candle each category. Then proceed to taste all sorts of candies made on the spot before eating the traditional meal of *castradina* (spiced leg of lamb) and cabbage.

Lunch or twilight dinner at **Harry's Dolci**.

A gondola ride at twilight with a bottle of Prosecco and three glasses—one for the *gondoliere*.

Anything on the water. Little-known fact: One can rent a small motorboat and spend Saturday or Sunday exploring the lagoon with a picnic lunch. Pick up a liter or so of local wine from one vendor and grilled meat, fish, and vegetables from another, and eat and drink alfresco at picnic tables surrounded by green.

A day on the outer islands—**Murano**, **Torcello**, **Burano**. Sunday is best. Leave early and visit Murano first—go to the **Museo dell'Arte Vetraria** (Museum of Glass Art), which is housed in a splendid palace, and visit the nearby church of **Santa Maria e San Donato** to see its mosaic floor. Don't miss the hourly boat to Burano and Torcello. In Burano, witness the Sunday *passeggiato* (families out for a stroll). Torcello's cathedral boasts some of the earliest and finest mosaic work in Italy, and a late afternoon drink at the **Locanda Cipriani** caps the day.

The monastery island, **San Francesco del Deserto**, can be visited by appointment. Near Burano in the far lagoon, it is a haven of peace and beauty, and the only place in Venice where there is absolutely nothing for sale! The monks also offer the possibility for individuals and families to stay with them for a few days or weeks on a spiritual retreat.

Fragolino, both red and white, is a local specialty wine that should be drunk as an aperitif.

The cloisters at **Sant'Apollonia Monastery** are well worth visiting, even if lately it's been housing either a show or leftover pieces by Dalí or Picasso.

For lunch on Murano see Lele at **Busa alla Torre**, and follow this Venetian Viking's suggestion for the catch of the day. If you happen to be in Venice during the *mocche* (soft-shell crab) season—spring and fall—indulge in these coin-size fried treats.

When you visit **San Marco** be sure to see the *Pala d'Oro* and visit the **Tesoro** (treasury)—more visual proof of Venice's ties with the Orient.

Any local neighborhood *festa* (party) for good, cheap eats and fun. Two of the best are the *Festa dell' Unità* on Murano in July and in **Campo Santa Margherita** in early September—traditional food, drink, and dancing in the open air.

is simply a joy. The walls are exposed brick and the ceiling is exposed old wooden beams treated to a light but deft-handed wash of white, giving them a sophisticated bleached look. The walls are white and the place bathes in light. The ground floor is an *enoteca*, so you can just pop in for coffee, a glass of wine, or a light bite. There are smart white linen-draped tables under parasols (they are too chic to call umbrellas) outside facing the canal for dining in the sun. The first floor, holding maybe a half dozen tables, looks out over canals on two sides and right across the lagoon on one. But the place that makes you catch your breath is the top floor. Nestled under the white-dragged beams are just two tiny tables in the front and one at the back. You can see right across the lagoon to Venice from the room's windows. It is the most romantic eating place in the Veneto. And just when you think you can't get closer to heaven, you find there is a tiny roof terrace! Even the restrooms are perfectly presented in Italy's top-of-the-line Bizzaza mosaic in burnished chestnut. It comes as no real surprise to learn the restaurant was created by Lorenzo Ammendola, fourth generation of a family of Buranese lace-makers. He wanted a museum for his beautiful lace collection, and somewhere along the line he joined up the Buranese traditions of fine lace, fine food, and fine wine.

And the food and the wine here is fine! Allow Andrea, a man who beams bonhomie, to guide you and you won't go wrong. The *antipasto de pesce* is a lovely mix, with some creative tastes (marinated salmon with a salsa of fresh tomato and pink peppercorn, for example), but you could opt for the *saltata di vongole con l'aqua di mare* (steamed clams finished with just a hint of seawater). As a main course, the *fritto misto mare* contains the sweetest prawns and the tiniest, cutest squid imaginable. There are feather-light pumpkin gnocchi sauced with prawn, leek, and balsamic, and meat eaters will love the meltingly tender *tagliata di manzo con rucola* (thin slices of beef served on arugula). If you have room for cheese or dessert (and I advise both!), the cheese selection is well informed and interesting, and the chocolate souffle on vanilla cream a joy to devour. The wine list is very, very good (again, let Andrea advise you and you won't go wrong), and there are pages and pages of fine Champagne, Prosecco, and other *frizzante* wines—ideal for that romantic meal this place is so perfect for. ♦ Daily, 11AM until dinner. ♦ Via San Mauro 296. 730850

San Francesco Del Deserto

Near the church of **San Martino** on Burano you will find a small private boat service to this ancient monastery island. Traces recovered from the subsoil here suggest it was visited by the Romans, and there are artifacts discovered from the fourth and fifth centuries AD. Its name comes from the first half of the 15th century, when the island was abandoned for over 20 years because the rancid state of the lagoon made it uninhabitable. The Franciscan connection begins in 1220, when St. Francis is alleged to have stopped there on his way back from the Holy Land. The island was donated to the Order in 1223 by Jacopo Michiel, a relative of the then Doge. At that time there were two churches on the island. Now there is just the monastery, but it is lovely. Its gardens, chapels, and 13th-century cloisters are looked after by gently accommodating monks who do guided tours. It is a fascinating place, with, it seems, a little something lovely added almost every century since it was originally built. ♦ W-M, 9AM-11AM and 3PM-5PM. 5286863. www.isola-sanfrancescodeldeserto.it

Panificio al Garbo

Walk along the narrow canalside in the morning, past this old family *pasticceria,* and give your nose a thrill. Let the sweet scent of the newly baked biscuits and cookies draw you inside and give your taste buds an even bigger thrill. Once you have tasted these traditional Venetian cookies warm from the oven, you will never want to eat them any other way. *Torta alla mandorla* (with almonds) and *torta al coco* (with chocolate) are crumbly slices of generously filled open tart; *busilai di Burano* and the famous *essi di Burano* are absolutely delicious traditional cookies. The charming baker is the second generation of the family who have baked here for a quarter of a century. ♦ Daily, 9AM-1PM and 4PM-7PM. Fondamenta San Mauro 336

Chiesa di San Martino

Built in the 16th century, San Martino is designed in the old Latin Cross form. The bell tower was added in the 18th century, designed by **Tirali** and yes, you might have had that extra glass of house red with lunch, but the tower *is* actually leaning quite obviously, though it has recently been reinforced so it will be here for a good while. Inside, the church has the rows of glass chandeliers typical of island churches and huge, beautiful floral arrangements all around. There is an interesting mix of artworks, from the 12-foot crucifix by Pino Signoretto, covered in giant drops of clear glass that look like huge tears, to the Tiepolo *Crucifixion.* There is a handsome trilogy by Giacomo Mansueli: *The Adoration of the Magi, The Betrothal of the Virgin,* and *The Flight into Egypt.* There is a lovely Fondebasso, *The Adoration of the Shepherds,* and a gorgeous, brilliantly colored 14th-century Russian icon, the *Madonna de Kazan.* In the left-hand altar lie the remains of three saints, and in a separate part of the building is the sweet **Capella di Santa Barbara.** ♦ Daily. Piazza Baldassare Galuppi

Restaurant Galuppi

★★$$ This is not just a restaurant, but also an art gallery crammed from floor to ceiling with the works of the genial restaurant owner. The menu covers most of the Venetian specialties, which means lots of fish. The *antipasti di pesce* (seafood antipasto) is the usual mix, but the scallops with butter and herbs are huge, meaty, and absolutely delicious. The house special *risotto di pesce* (seafood risotto) is delicate in flavor and generous in its prawn and scampi content. Tagliatelli with scampi is rich, creamy, and gorgeous, and the *fritto misto* (mixed seafood grill) is light as a feather. Don't worry about the whole sea bass that arrives at your table: Your waiter will skin and fillet it for you. Service is wholly charming, the wine list is good, and the grappas are not to be missed. Check out Gianmario's enormous visitor's book and see how much many people have enjoyed this place. Then add your own comment. ♦ Daily, lunch and dinner. Via Baldessare Galuppi 468. 730081

Don't Leave Venice Without . . .

1. Getting truly lost at least once. It is the only real way to get to know the city and make it feel like your own. The places you will remember are the ones you discover for yourself.
2. Walking through **St. Mark's Square** at night when the lights are on and the orchestras are playing.
3. Taking the last *traghetto*—any of them—across the **Grand Canal** when darkness has fallen. It is an extraordinary, memorable experience and will cost you just 50 cents.
4. Taking the No. 1 or the No. 82 *vaporetto* right up the Grand Canal. Sit outside. Be careful you don't dislocate your jaw as it drops at the sheer magical beauty of this city.
5. Going to one of Venice's little hole-in-the wall *enoteche* and having one of everything on the *bancone*. Be adventurous. Just close your eyes and open your mind with your mouth. Have some local red. Love life.
6. Finding your favorite *fondamenta*, *campo*, or terrace and sitting on it at sunset with a spritz and a contented sigh. Take tissues; you may cry.
7. Trying the pistachio ice cream at **Lo Squero**. It may change your life.
8. Visiting as many Venetian churches as you can and deciding which is your favorite.
9. Visiting as many Venetian restaurants as you can and deciding which is your favorite.
10. Making a contribution to the Venice in Peril Fund.

Dal Baffo

★★$ Probably the most "real" of the restaurants along this busiest of roads in Burano, this place is tiny inside but with tables outside in good weather. It does terrific traditional stuff. Buranese specials include *anguilla e fagioli* (grilled eel with beans—delicious, and especially good when the cold winds are blowing over the lagoon), *caparossi al pomodoro* (tiny clams in a tomatoey sauce), and *risi e bisi* (rice and peas). Desserts are local cookie-based and very nice with a glass of sweet wine. The wine list is local and fairly priced (especially the Prosecco) and all in all, this is an amazingly genuine place in a street of tourist magnets. ♦ M,Tu, Th-Su, lunch and dinner. Via Baldessare Galuppi 359. 730108

Mazzorbo

A long wooden bridge separates Mazzorbo from Burano. You'll find it just to the right of the Burano boat stop. Mazzorbo also has its own boat stop, on the LN line from Fondamenta Nova. This is known as the "vegetable garden of Venice," as the island is characterized by greenery and gardens. It is nice to wander here on a sunny afternoon and give your credit card a little rest.

Unusually, the most impressive thing to see on Mazzorbo is not 14th- or 16th- but 20th-century architecture. If you are at all interested in architecture or urban planning—or even seeing how council estate living *could* be—check out the *case soziale* designed by **Giancarlo De Carlo** and built between 1979 and 1986. There is also the medieval **Chiesa di Santa Caterina**.

Once you have worked up an appetite, there is a good little trattoria right by the boat stop, **Alla Maddelena** (★★$$, closed Tuesday, dinner by reservation only). It has a lovely garden for summer dining and offers a mainly fish-based menu, although in the hunting season they have game birds from around the lagoon.

Torcello

From the boat stop at Burano, a traghetto service (a boat that just goes back and forth across one stretch of water, not the large gondola type of traghetti you get in Venice) will take you to Torcello. The stop for this is right beside the boat stop from Venice. The trip takes 5 minutes.

Torcello was the first lagoon island where the mainland population found refuge from barbarian invasions in the fifth century. Although other lagoon areas were sparsely populated at the time, it was with this core of settlers that the city of Venice originated—in the following centuries the Torcello people expanded their settlement to the Rialto area and to the islands around it, gradually abandoning Torcello. It was a long process, and in the meantime this small island had become the civic and religious center of the entire lagoon. The remnants of that period still attract a great number of visitors. Two splendid churches stand side by side on the low, grassy land, surrounded by the lagoon and vegetable gardens of the small community that lives here year-round. The churches date back to the beginning of Venice, exhibiting a remarkable mixture of Byzantine sumptuousness and naive, almost primitive, imagery. When the area is not filled with tourists, a majestic silence reigns over it—a reminder of the beauty and frailty of all things human. A short walk from the public boat landing along a canal flanked by fields leads to the tiny former main square of Torcello.

Highlights on Torcello include:

Ristorante Al Trono di Attila

★$$ Although the well-known **Osteria al Ponte del Diavolo** and **Locanda Cipriani** are nearby, you pay dearly to dine there. At this jewel, home-style cooking is served with love, without fuss, and at a reasonable price. The *gnocchetti con rucola e scampi* (tiny dumplings with arugula and shrimp) is deliciously light, and the *fritto misto* (fried seafood) is modest but always good, as is the *cotoletto milanese* (deep-fried breaded veal cutlet). A large outdoor patio is flanked by the lazy green canal on one side and an amiable backyard garden full of flowers on the other. ♦ Tu-Su, lunch. Dinner is available, but you need to book ahead. Fondamenta Borgognoni 7A. 730094. *Vaporetto* stop: Torcello

Osteria al Ponte del Diavolo

★★$$$ Halfway between the *vaporetto* landing and the cathedral, this cozy spot with outdoor garden seating is run by a former manager of the **Locanda Cipriani**. Specialties of this excellent restaurant include dishes prepared with fresh fish and local vegetables. You'll be taken for a regular if you start with the warm *insalata di frutti di mare* (fresh seafood salad). ♦ M-W, F-Su, lunch. Closed January and February. Via Chiesa 10-11. 730401. *Vaporetto* stop: Torcello

Torcello Cathedral

This is the oldest cathedral around the lagoon, and opens onto a grassy space that used to be the busy center of town, when Torcello had 20,000 residents (today only a few dozen people are permanent residents). An excavation in front of the church shows the foundation of the ancient **Baptistry**, while behind the church stands the 11th-century bell tower, which is sometimes visible from the distant mainland. The cathedral, begun in the seventh century, was reconstructed in 1008 upon the existing structure. Some of the material used in the reconstruction was brought over from early Christian buildings abandoned on the mainland when the barbarians invaded. The interior is reminiscent of the great Byzantine churches of Ravenna. The original 11th-century parts include the capitals, the floor, and the four splendid marble bas-reliefs in the iconostasis. The mosaic *Madonna and Child* in the apse is a masterwork of the 13th century. Of the same period is the famous mosaic on the interior façade, a *Last Judgment* drawn with medieval realism (notice the scene of the *Resurrection of the Dead* and, at the bottom, the *Blessed and the Damned*). Concerts are often held in the cathedral. ♦ Admission. Daily. Piazza del Duomo. 730084. *Vaporetto* stop: Torcello

Museo di Torcello (Torcello Museum)

Across the small grassy square from the cathedral and the church of **Santa Fosca**, with its arched medieval porch, is a museum containing archeological material documenting the Roman presence in the mainland communities bordering the lagoon, as well as artifacts from the early Christian period. ♦ Admission. Tu-Sa. Piazza del Duomo. 730761. *Vaporetto* stop: Torcello

Locanda Cipriani

★★$$$$ Arrigo Cipriani, the founder of **Harry's Bar**, opened this restaurant and tiny hotel in 1946 in a restored 17th-century villa (the operation has since been sold to relatives). His idea was to create a place for a wealthy clientele to spend a restful day or two in total isolation, surrounded by the absolute beauty of Torcello. The large garden and outdoor dining area offer a view of the apse of **Santa Fosca**, and the food and service are very good. You can even have a look, if you ask nicely, at the room where Ernest Hemingway worked on *Across the River and into the Trees*, although they don't rent out rooms anymore. ♦ Su-M, W-F, lunch and dinner; closed Tuesday; Sa, dinner only. Closed November through February. Reservations recommended. 730150; fax 735433. *Vaporetto* stop: Torcello

San Lazzaro degli Armeni

This tiny island was given to a group of Armenian monks early in the 17th century. They installed a printing press that became famous throughout the Western world for the quality of its prints. It has been producing works in 36 languages for over 200 years. The press and the monastery still run, although only eight elderly monks remain.

The most famous thing on the island is the monastery library. It contains over 150,000 volumes, including an ancient Megillah (which is the story of Esther), a very old copy of the Koran, and the only remaining Armenian-language version of a history of Alexander the Great. Beside the library and press there is a well-preserved Egyptian mummy and sarcophagus, a beautiful inlaid Indian throne, a wonderful collection of porcelain, a Canova bust of Napoleon's son, and a fabulous Tiepolo painted panel of *Peace and Justice*.

Close to the boat stop there is a large plaque in memory of Lord Byron, who was a frequent visitor here. Byron was so entranced with the library that he actually learned the notoriously difficult language of Armenian and translated several gospels from the original himself. Many of his possessions and his portrait were donated to the monastery and are on exhibition here.

The island was originally a leper colony run by Benedictine monks, but it was abandoned after all the lepers died. St. Lazarus is the patron saint of lepers (not a very cheery job!), hence the name of the island. The island was given to Manul di Pietro by Venice in 1717, and he formed an order apart from both the Catholic and Eastern Orthodox churches. ♦ Monastery: admission. Daily, 3PM-5PM. There is only one boat a day—the No. 20—and it leaves from San Zaccaria at 3:10PM and returns at 7:25PM. 5260104

THE LIDO

Nine miles long and less than a half-mile wide, the Lido is one of two thin, fragile islands that separate the lagoon from the open sea. The other island is called **Peliestrina** and is a continuation of the Lido all the way to the mainland at **Chioggia**. On the side facing the sea, the Lido is an uninterrupted stretch of wide beaches covered with fair-colored sand. For this reason, and because of its proximity to Venice, it became one of the preferred seaside resorts for the European upper classes, beginning in the 17th century. Some of the most luxurious hotels in Italy were built along its shores and are still in business, while the narrow land was built up with villas surrounded by gardens. A special feature of the Lido is that cars are allowed on the limited number of roads, which makes the hotels attractive to visitors who have lots of luggage and prefer to travel by car. A frequent ferry service carries automobiles to and from the **Tronchetto** terminal, near **Piazzale Roma**, while **Piazza San Marco** is a beautiful 15-minute *vaporetto* (no cars allowed) ride away.

Changing into a bathing suit is not permitted in the open on the Lido beaches; you must rent a cabin for a day or a half-day. The least expensive area to do this is the **Zona A**, at the immediate left of the **Gran Viale** (very crowded and often noisy). Much more chic—and proportionately more expensive—are the luxury cabins of **Hotel Des Bains** (to the immediate right of the Gran Viale) and of **Hotel Excelsior** (at the end of the seaside walk). Other beach areas offer intermediate prices.

Highlights on the Lido include:

GRAN VIALE

The main street on the Lido, this colorful boulevard is the way to reach the beaches on foot from the *vaporetto* landings (a 10-minute walk). Most of the outdoor restaurants on both sides of the boulevard cater to tourists looking for a quick bite of pizza and such. There are also a number of places to rent bicycles. Don't miss the wonderful mosaic façade of the **Hotel Hungaria** (on the right, halfway along the Viale), built in 1906. ♦ Between Piazzale Bucintoro and Piazzale Santa Maria Elisabetta. *Vaporetto* stop: Lido

On Gran Viale:

CRISTALLO

$$ This family-run hotel has 24 clean and simply decorated rooms with air conditioning, color TVs, and modern bathrooms. Breakfast is included. Parking is available. ♦ Closed December through February (except Christmas and *Carnevale*). No. 51. 5265293; fax 5265615 (attn: Cristallo). www.veneziahotels.com

HUNGARIA PALACE HOTEL

$$$ It is hard to miss this astonishing building as you walk down the Gran Viale. Its undulating Art Nouveau exterior, covered in intricately figured majolica tiles, is the most eye-catching thing on the island. Built at the beginning of the 20th century, it went into decline in the 1960s, but after massive renovation work it now offers 81 rooms and suites in gloriously Art Nouveau style, with absolutely all amenities plus 24-hour room service. It has its own extensive grounds and free parking. ♦ Gran Viale Santa Maria Elisabetta 28. 2420060. fax 5264111. e-mail: info@hungaria.it. www.hungaria.it. *Vaporetto* stop: Lido

HOTEL DES BAINS

$$$$ Built in 1900 for the European aristocracy, this 191-room hotel was made even more famous by Visconti's movie *Death in Venice,* based on Thomas Mann's novella. The interior still has the original fixtures. The hotel is surrounded by a large park and has a private beach, heated swimming pool, and gymnasium. Restaurants are **Thomas Mann** (formal) and **Liberty and Pagoda** (less formal). ♦ Open March-November. Lungomare Guglielmo Marconi 17 (between Via Bragadin and Gran Viale). 5265921, 800/325.3589; fax 5260113. *Vaporetto* stop: Lido

Quattro Fontane

$$$ This is a delightful hotel in a villa surrounded by a flower-filled garden, owned by two sisters, who treat the premises like their own home and the guests like personal friends. All 59 rooms have been recently refurbished and decorated with antique furniture and brand new Internet access. Public rooms especially benefit from the sisters' penchant for collecting fascinating works of art from all over the world. The "La Barchessa" section of the hotel offers rooms in true Riviera style, most with terrace and all unique. There are sun beds in the garden, a private tennis court, and parking.

Within Quattro Fontane:

Ristorante Quattro Fontane

$$ Eat in the wonderfully atmospheric restaurant or outside in the lovely garden. The menu is an intelligent take on traditional dishes, with *scampi in saor* (Dublin Bay prawns in a tangy marinade) and *pesce spada marinato al limone e aneto* (swordfish in a lemon marinade), or beef fillet in green peppercorn sauce if you feel meaty. The Quattro Fontane also offers a fruit trolley. ♦ Via Quattro Fontane 16 (between Lungomare Guglielmo Marconi and Via Sandro Gallo). 5260227; fax 5260726. e-mail: quafonve@tin.it. *Vaporetto* stops: Lido, Casino (summer only)

Hotel Excelsior

$$$$ A mix of Moorish, Gothic, and Byzantine styles, this elegant hotel was built at the turn of the century for the posh clientele of the Lido. It is still the most lavish beachfront hotel in Venice, with a striking fountain in the main hall and the best of the rooms directly overlooking the beach. In late August and early September it becomes the headquarters of the jury for the annual Venice Film Festival (held across the street), and the list of movie stars who have stayed in its suites is long and dazzling. ♦ Closed mid-November–mid-March. Lungomare Guglielmo Marconi 41 (just south of Piazzale del Casino). 5260201, 800/325.3589; fax 5267276. *Vaporetto* stops: Lido, Casino (summer only)

Murazzi

The name means "rough walls" and refers to the huge stone-and-concrete boulders that strengthen the median part of the Lido to protect against erosion. At the end of Lungomare Marconi and just after the **Hotel Excelsior** is this lonely and, in its way, fascinating part of the Lido, a half hour on foot from the main *vaporetto* landing (also accessible by bus). Venetians come here to bathe away from the crowds without having to rent a cabin. Sunset is strikingly beautiful here, as is the walk back to the *vaporetto* if you decide to cross the Lido and walk on the lagoon side. ♦ *Vaporetto* stops: Lido (take bus line *A* or *B*), Casino (summer only)

San Michele

Just opposite the Fondamenta Nuova, this tiny island has only one *vaporetto* stop and it is called **Cimitero.** Which is what the island is. They say see Naples and die, but with a last resting place like this, Venice is the place you should go.

Although it is a cemetery, it is very far from morbid. Beautiful is one word that springs to mind. And peaceful. A redbrick wall runs around the entire island, with a line of cypress trees behind it. This sight is the inspiration for Böcklin's painting *Island of the Dead.*

The island's main church is the wonderfully decayed **San Michele in Isola**, Venice's first Renaissance church designed by **Mauro Codussi** in the 1460s in white Istrian stone. It is huge and spare and gray inside and wears its five-and-a-half centuries more obviously than some.

The cloisters are among the most peaceful places I have ever found in Venice. The grounds of the Franciscan monastery (now restored) that extended behind the church began to be used as a burial ground in Napoleonic times, in an effort to stop people from simply digging up the nearest *campo* to their parish church to bury loved ones. The island filled up a long time ago, and nowadays bodies are allowed to lie for a decent length of time before the bones are dug up and taken to an ossuary on another island. But the famous bones get to stay! Those of Sergei Diaghilev and Igor Stravinsky and his wife are in the Greek and Russian Orthodox section, and Ezra Pound and Joseph Brodsky are to be found in the Protestant section. There is also a children's area and an entire section dedicated to gondoliers. ♦ 7:30AM-4PM Oct-Mar; 7:30AM-6PM Apr-Sept; 7:30AM-noon Christmas Day, New Year's Day, Easter. *Vaporetto* stop: Cimitero

VENICE DAY TRIPS: VISIONS OF THE VENETO

Venturing onto the mainland from Venice may provide an escape from marble and bridges, but it is in no way a retreat from the glories of *La Serenissima* (Most Serene Republic). Veneto today comprises the land acquired by Venice in the 14th and 15th centuries, and the visitor is reminded at every turn of the importance the Republic had in the region surrounding the city. Flying the banner of St. Mark from rooftops and carving the lion and book on façades—all symbols of *La Serenissima*—was a welcome privilege for these communities set among the many warring factions in Northern Italy. The 12th-century political union formed by **Treviso**, **Padua**, **Vicenza**, and **Verona** for protection against invasion by the Holy Roman Emperor was scant assurance of stability. And while the tyrannical families who next ruled the region—Da Camino in Treviso, Carrara in Vicenza and Padua, Scala in Verona—enhanced the beauty of the cities and created an atmosphere for art to flourish, they weren't always there to defend them against outsiders. It would take the ambitions of the Venetian Republic to unite these dominions in a 300-year pact, destroyed only by Napoleon in 1797.

The attractions of this area have been obvious to travelers ever since the Romans first saw Verona as a perfect spot to rest before crossing the Alps. Since then, visitors have continued to explore the region on their way to the busier destinations of Venice, Florence, and Rome. This almost way-station attitude of tourists has resulted in making the Veneto one of the least spoiled and most enjoyable regions of Italy. Capped by the dramatic **Dolomiti** (Dolomite Mountains) to the north, with their attractive foothills covered with vineyards and orchards, and fertilized by rivers and streams that turn into enchanting canals in the towns, the Veneto combines the pleasures of nature with the sophistication of wealthy cities.

Its appeal is further enhanced by the mild weather. Spared the scorching heat of the south and the grim winters over the Alps, the Veneto is a delightful place in any season. Another attraction here is the region's particularly varied and rich cuisine. From the mountains come game birds and sausages, such sturdy cheeses as asiago and montasio, dozens of varieties of mushrooms, the love of polenta, and

strudel-like desserts. The foothills produce the famous wines of Valpolicella, Bardolino, Breganze, Soave, and Prosecco—each with endless tasting opportunities on the various *strade dei vini* (wine roads). The plains offer excellent vegetables in all seasons, highlighted by the four local red chicories used for salads or in cooking and the asparagus in numerous colors and sizes. The rivers yield excellent fish and freshwater shrimp.

Luckily, the Veneto offers ample occasions for walking off these marvelous meals. After only a short hike or drive up into the Dolomiti, you'll find crystalline lakes, alpine wildflowers, chestnut forests, and torrential mountain-fed rivers—usually accompanied by a *rifugio* (refuge) offering its own delicious country-style meals. The **Colli Euganei** (Euganean Hills) are filled with delightful walks, and views have changed little since the early 19th century, when the poet Shelley gazed down and saw a region "Bounded by the vaporous air,/Islanded by cities fair."

Andrea Palladio, who succeeded **Sansovino** as the chief architect of the Venetian Republic in 1529, made his mark in the Veneto. He was influenced by the first-century

BC architect **Vitruvius** and his treatise *De Architectura*. Palladio embellished the province with dignified civic buildings, and his trademarks include the rigorous adhesion to the progression of the classical orders from Doric to Ionic to Corinthian, intermixed with porches, columns, and gables, that produced a style referred to today as Palladianism. The *Naviglio Brenta* (Brenta Canal), in particular, is lined with his villas, some of which are open to the public.

But it is to "cities fair" that the traveler is most often destined: Treviso returns the imagination to the Middle Ages; Verona retains the glory of each of her epochs—Roman, medieval, Renaissance; Vicenza has many of Palladio's jewels; and Padua is still alive with intellectual energy that reminds us of Giotto's greatness. The smaller towns charm in their own ways: **Asolo** with its unmatched hilltop setting and centuries of the grace wealth affords; **Bassano** sitting astride its powerful river crowned by Palladio's bridge; and the medieval towns of **Este**, **Monselice**, and **Montagnana**, commanded by their perfectly preserved fortifications. Throughout the Veneto, a tempting range of possibilities await the visitor unhurried by crowds and open to the richness of Northern Italian life.

Some basic information: If possible, avoid taking a trip on the weekend, especially during the summer and on holidays. Traffic is heavier during these times, as Venetians go away on Friday evening and come back on Sunday night. Rent a car before leaving the US—rates are considerably lower than last-minute bookings made in Venice. If you'll be relying on public transportation, look into train and bus schedules before setting off, to avoid getting stranded. For train information, contact the **Santa Lucia** railway station (Fondamenta Santa Lucia, 715555). Buses leave from the station at **Piazzale Roma** (5287886).

Asolo and Maser

From **Mestre** head northwest 36 kilometers (22 miles) on **S245** to **Castelfranco**, then take **S307** 20 kilometers (12 miles) north to **Caerano di San Marco**. Turn left (west) onto **S248** and drive 6 kilometers (4 miles) to the cutoff for Asolo. Head north 3 kilometers (2 miles) to Asolo. To get to Maser, return to the cutoff and go east 6 kilometers (4 miles). Or take the **Venice-Udine** train to **Treviso** and change for a train to **Montebelluna**. A 20-minute bus ride—14 kilometers (9 miles)—from here brings you to Asolo.

The expatriate English poet Robert Browning begins his volume of verse *Asolando* with an enchanting description of the 16th-century verb *asolare*; "to disport in the open air, amuse oneself at random." And with this attitude the traveler approaches one of Northern Italy's most exquisite cities, an apt inspiration for both the verb and the poetry. Set on a hilly landscape enhanced by charming old houses, shops, and restaurants with views from every prospect, the town continues to delight after more than 500 years of exalted residents. It all really started with Queen Caterina Cornaro of Cyprus, who allowed Venice to take over the rule of Cyprus in exchange for getting this tiny spot as her nominal (but only nominal) kingdom from 1489 to 1509. She needed a better real-estate agent, obviously, but it is a lovely spot, known as "the pearl of Marca Trevigna." Her palace is still open to the public from time to time. In Caterina's wake (although not ceding entire kingdoms to do so) came the rich and the famous, the artistic great and good. Actress Eleonora Duse and explorer Freya Stark had homes here, as well as Robert Browning, and the holiday homes of many artists and composers, writers and musicians are still to be found here.

One of the places not to miss (it is pretty as well as fascinating) is Asolo's **Piazza Garibaldi**, where the fountain in the center is powered by an antique Roman aqueduct. The Antiques Market, which takes place the second Sunday of every month (except July and August) in **Piazza Brugnoi**, is a good place to pick up jewelry, silver-embossed mirrors and frames, gold-leaf angels, figurines, and medallions. The tiny **Museo Civico** (Via Regina Cornaro, 0423/952313) highlights items commemorating Asolo's most famous residents—Browning's manuscripts, for example—plus various paintings and archeological finds. It is open Tuesday-Sunday; there's an admission charge. The **Duomo** (Piazza del Duomo) has an early *Assumption* by Lorenzo Lotto (1506) that features a powerful landscape of the nearby hills.

Asolo's narrow, winding streets offer numerous first-class *gastronomie* (gourmet shops), none better than **Ennio** (Via Browning 151, 0423/529109). An excellent place to stock up for a picnic, the store is filled with possibly the best fruit-and-nut breads in Italy; cases of cheeses, hams, and sausages; giant white pots of *mostardo* (a spicy purée of fruit pickled with mustard seed), and other regional relishes. Every type of grappa is sold here—Picolit, Chardonnay, even "Carmina Burana" for opera lovers, as well as other beautifully labeled wines and liquors. The shop is open daily. Nearby on the same street is **Enoteca in Asolo** (Via Browning 185, 0423/952070). Tastefully rustic, it is a fine place to relax with a glass of Prosecco from the region or sample a grappa and have some snacks. The wine cellar is open Tuesday-Sunday.

A more formal dining spot is the renowned **Hotel Villa Cipriani** (Via Canova 298, 0423/523411), with its combination of sophisticated luxury and country-inn charm. Its main claim to historical fame is that is was once owned by Robert Browning. Enjoy such dishes as *carpaccio de salmone con finocchio crocante* (thin-sliced raw salmon with crisp-fried fennel wedges) or the creamy *risotto con sogliola e basilico* (with fresh sole and basil) on the splendid garden terrace with views of the valley or in the elegant candlelit dining room. The hotel features 31 guest rooms for those wanting to spend the night. The restaurant is open daily, lunch and dinner.

Less famous (and less expensive) but sharing the same vistas from its terrace is **Ristorante Due Mori** within the **Hotel Duse** (Piazza di Annunzio 5, 0423/952256). Walk past the huge open grill and sit either on the awninged balcony or in the spacious dining rooms with beamed copper pot-hung ceilings. The specialties here are seasonal, and the chef uses ingredients and recipes rarely found in restaurants. Charming and friendly, the English-speaking owner Gabriela and her son Alessandro guide guests through the menu, encouraging them to try dishes based on wild herbs from the hills, white asparagus from Bassano, or radicchio from Treviso. Don't miss the autumn *sopa coada* (roosting soup)—a delicate chicken broth with a pressed "sandwich" of bread, slivered chicken, and cheese floating in the middle. Follow with perfectly grilled meats and polenta, a mélange of seasonal vegetables, and delicious Cabernet wine, and finish with a grappa. The restaurant is open Monday-Tuesday, Thursday-Sunday, lunch and dinner.

Maser boasts one of the most beautiful villas of the Veneto—**Villa Barbaro** (Via Cornuda 2, 0423/923004). **Palladio** built it (illustrated below) in 1560 for the Barbaro family, and Veronese did the frescoes. The main **Salone dell'Olimpo** (Hall of Olympus), the most extravagant of the decorated spaces, has rooms extending to either side. The right wing passes through several doorways, at the end of which we see Veronese surrounded by a trompe l'oeil doorway. He enters the house with his hunting hounds, bringing with him the light and feeling of nature created by the luminous landscape in the background. This is a unique integration of illusionistic interior and exterior. Here Veronese introduced a felicitous combination that dominated decoration throughout the 16th century and influenced many of Tiepolo's major projects. Wander the rooms, imagining that you are a guest here, as the great art critic Bernard Berenson was so often. Mix company with the allegorical figures overhead and praise Bacchus teaching the glories of the grape; wonder what tasks the mistress of the villa is assigning as she leans over the balustrade; and amuse yourself with the monkeys, parrots, dogs, and children that so comfortably crowd the house in the frescoes. The villa is open Tuesday, Saturday,

Villa Barbaro, Maser

and Sunday, 3PM-6PM March through October; Saturday, Sunday, 2:30PM-5PM November through February. There's an admission charge.

Asolo's tourist office (Piazza di Annunzio 2, 0423/529046; fax 0423/524137) is open Monday and Saturday morning, and Tuesday-Friday.

Bassano del Grappa

Travel northwest 52 kilometers (32 miles) on **S245** from **Mestre** to **Rosà**; turn right onto **S47** to drive the final 5 kilometers (3 miles) to Bassano. From Bassano there is a bus line (**Marostica**) that frequently makes the 7-kilometer (4-mile) run to **Marostica**; another (**Schio**) travels 20 kilometers (12 miles) to **Breganze**. Or take the direct train (**Venezia-Trento** line) from **Piazzale Roma**.

This delightful little town on the banks of the **Fiume Brenta** (Brenta River) is filled with medieval and Renaissance streets, arcades, and houses with painted façades. The river bisects the city: There are charming arcaded piazzas on one side and streets lined with the famous ceramics from nearby **Nove** on the other.

Bassano is famous for **Ponte degli Alpini**, a wooden covered pedestrian bridge designed by **Palladio** in 1669 and immortalized in an immensely popular song of World War I, when the town was at the center of fierce fighting between the Austrian and Italian armies. First built between 1156 and 1209, the bridge collapsed from treacherous high waters in 1450 and periodically afterward. The latest rebuilding took place in 1966. Since Palladio stepped in, the bridge has retained the original layout and majesty that he alone could grant a wooden structure. Today it is still a meeting place for locals who congregate at the colorful *grapperie* (grappa bars) on either side. The most atmospheric is **Grapperia Nardini** (0424/227741), housed in a 1769 distillery, complete with beamed ceilings and handsome metal pots. It's the perfect spot to sample one of Bassano's claims to fame—grappa, a fiery clear distilled liquor that seems to be made from endless materials, even bilberry. Grappa is noted for its range of flavors and matchless designs for bottling. The Grapperia is open Tuesday-Sunday.

The redesigned, century-old distillery of Jacopo Poli—now the **Poli Museo della Grappa**—located just off the main square (Via Gamba 6, 0424/524426. museo@poligrappa.com)—features giant copper equipment and a museum of bottle styles that offer a unique opportunity to study this liquor further. Should you feel like doing some homework, there is plenty on sale. It is open daily.

The **Museo Civico**, located in the former monastery of the church of **San Francesco** (Piazza Garibaldi, 0424/522235), is dominated by the paintings of the Bassano family—primarily works of Jacopo da Ponte (1510-1592). With his Titian-influenced style da Ponte displays a decided affection for his mountainous landscape. The museum also houses an important library and over 8,000 prints and drawings on the history of European painting. There is an entire section devoted to the sculptor Antonio Canova, with his letters, drawings, and plaster casts. The museum is open Tuesday-Saturday and Sunday afternoon; admission is charged.

Below the bridge is the **Ostaria Ca' Brando** (Via Pusterla 52, 0424/522541). The cheery interior of this wine bar features wall paintings of folk scenes and proverbs, and there's a spectacular view of Ponte degli Alpini's wooden supports from its riverside terrace. At press time, snacks and drinks were being offered Friday, Saturday, and Sunday, 6PM-2AM. At **Al Ponte-Da Renzo** (Via Volpato 60, 0424/503055), enjoy wide views of the Ponte degli Alpini and the **Old Town**, from either the windowed dining room or the shaded terrace. In addition to fish dishes, regional seasonal specialties are offered, including Italy's most sought-after white asparagus from the area. It is open Monday, lunch, and Wednesday-Sunday, lunch and dinner; closed in January.

Bassano's tourist office (Largo Corona d'Italia 35, 0424/524351; fax 0424/525301) is open Monday-Friday, Saturday, 9AM-12:30PM.

Seven kilometers (4 miles) west of Bassano on **S248** is Marostica, the celebrated home of a restaged medieval chess game featuring 32 players in period dress. The *Partita a Scacchi* takes place the second weekend in September in even-numbered years at the **Piazza degli Scacchi**. The match originated in 1454, when Taddeo Parisio, the lord of the castle in Marostica, was faced with a dilemma: His beautiful daughter Lionora had two noblemen who sought her hand in marriage. Taddeo encouraged the two suitors to settle this question of love in a chess game instead of fighting the customary duel. Living pieces acted out the game on a huge board painted in **Piazza Castello**. Lionora, who had a preference for one suitor, told the locals that if her choice was the victor, white lights would shine from the **Castello Inferiore** (Lower Castle), also known as "La Rocca," so everyone could partake in their happiness. He won; the lights shone; and the event is repeated today with all the magnificent costumes, banners, and elegance. "La Rocca" is open to the public daily; there's an admis-

THE "GRAND TOUR" OF THE VENETO

The journey running parallel to the Alps to the flat, green plains of the **Po River** across the Veneto has held a peculiar and wide-ranging fascination for travelers from northern Europe ever since young Thomas Coryat walked the route and wrote about his new adventures in *Poor Tom's Crudities* in 1608. Once he regaled his British readers with visions of romantic **Verona**, stories of pistachio tasting in **Padua**, and images of the famed Venetian *cortigiane* (courtesans), the exodus began, and it continued into the 18th century, when the Napoleonic Wars isolated Great Britain from the European continent.

Every "milord" (the number of ladies experiencing this phenomenon was minimal), as the Italians nicknamed the first "Grand Tourists," found it a necessary adjunct to his education to visit the Mediterranean and claim some shared heritage. Surviving the grueling trip over the Alps, these visitors headed first for Verona, where they examined Roman architectural grandeur at the **Arena** while being amused by the recently revived "entertainments" of bear baiting and goose strangling. Here they also began a Shakespearean pilgrimage dear to British travelers—the Veneto was the setting of at least seven of the Bard's plays. They could imagine Romeo's fights, Juliet's balcony, and the comic antics of the "Two Gentlemen."

A short stagecoach ride away was "fair Padua, nursery of the arts," and where the British had a presence at Europe's most prestigious medical school. Its "anatomies," held at midnight to avoid the prying eyes of the medieval church's spies, had offered William Harvey his first glimpses into the circulation of blood. But the 18th-century tourists, while they might share the shade of a 200-year-old tree with the recently arrived Goethe pausing on his "race to Rome," were bent on a broader education. They knew Dante and found his presence everywhere; they admired the churches and the sculptures, sought out the three-dimensional frescoes of the famous Florentine painter Giotto, and wondered about the "Shrew" and the man who had tamed her in Padua.

Yet all this was a prelude to their eager goal—**Venice**! Coryat's delicious details of courtesans with bared breasts dusted in gold gave them hopes for a further "education," where *Carnevale* often lasted six months. They could purchase the *vedute* (views) of Venice by Canaletto and Guardi to grace their manors back home.

The 19th century ushered in a new kind of traveler—the expatriate. Both British and Americans began arriving in large numbers to visit, to stay, to record, and to experience life. The mentor-guided Grand Tour developed into the longer residence. Aided by strong foreign currencies and the rapidly declining fortunes of the Veronese aristocracy, these new visitors could afford to rent portions of Palladian villas and balconied rooms on the **Canal Grande** in Venice.

Emigration appealed especially to artists and writers. Shelley wrote and hiked in the **Colli Euganei**; William Dean Howells complained of too many hours spent at **Caffè Pedrocchi** in Padua, yet set many of his novels in the region; Lord Byron scandalized Venice from his rented **Palazzo Mocenigo** while adding to *Childe Harold's Pilgrimage*; Browning wrote, lived, and died at the **Ca' Rezzonico** in Venice; Henry James found himself in a "perpetual love affair," longing to put his "ever-cautious arms" around Venice; Bernard Berenson made the Venetian painters his "first love"; Turner captured the sunsets, Whistler the misty views, and Sargent the portraits.

From the impact of the 18th century's "Grand Tourists" to today's Junior-Year-Abroad students, the Veneto has always drawn international seekers of learning and beauty. Their diaries, travel essays, novels, and paintings endure, ensuring that their descendants will return.

sion charge. Although the chess game is the city's main draw, this colorful fortified town also has medieval ramparts, 14th-century crenellated castles, and the arcaded Piazza Castello with its many cafés.

A finer chance to enjoy *un ombra* (a glass of wine) is in **Breganze**, 10 kilometers (6 miles) southwest of Marostica. Seven *D.O.C. (Denominazione di Origine Controllata)* wines, from fresh whites to a rich Cabernet, are produced in vineyards in the area around this small town. (*D.O.C.* means the wine has met certain quality requirements and comes from an officially recognized wine-producing area.) Various wine-tasting and buying emporia dot its streets, and the asiago cheese available here is excellent. **Cittadella** (13 kilometers—8 miles—south of Bassano on S47) is a circular town with walls 40 feet high. Defended by thirty-two 13th-century towers and four main portals, the city acted as a buffer to assaults on Padua by its northern neighbors. Its ramparts circling the town cover about one mile and provide a charming walk.

A trip to Bassano from Venice inevitably passes **Castelfranco Veneto** (45 kilometers—28 miles—northwest of Venice on S245), a town surrounded by a moat and a crenellated brick wall built in 1199. It is the birthplace of one of Renaissance art's favorite sons—the 16th-century painter Giorgione (ca. 1477-1510). **Casa di Giorgione** (Piazza del Duomo) claims a series of still lifes executed in his hand, but the treasure awaiting the viewer is

The Best

Robert Wilk

Culinary Entrepreneur

Venice in winter. When it's quiet, romantic, and sexy. When it's sunny, a lunch on the sun-warmed terrace of the **Hotel Monaco and Grand Canal** is utter bliss. When it's foggy, it's magnificently mysterious, and the echoes of footsteps late at night are pure Orson Welles. To be absolutely *alone* in the center of **Piazza San Marco** after a late dinner is *unforgettable*.

The *bacari*. The uniquely Venetian, cozy, friendly wine cafés for an aperitif or lunch, with the wonderful Venetian *cicchetti* (finger food). Always run by a "character" and lots of fun. The *most* Venetian of culinary experiences.

Le Zattere. An early-morning or late-evening walk on this stretch along the **Giudecca Canal**, down to the **Punta della Dogana** (Customs Point) in the middle of the basin, with glorious views of **San Marco**, the **Grand Canal**, and the Palladian church of the **Redentore**. Breathtaking and inspiring.

Lido. The beach of Venice, which few people ever think of. It's very Venetian, with lots of families doing their thing. My favorite spot is in front of the **Hotel des Bains**, where *Death in Venice* was filmed. A pleasant antipasto buffet lunch on the upper terrace is a little-known great value.

Torcello. The original island of Venice, with a glorious sixth-century cathedral and the wonderful trattoria **Osteria al Ponte del Diavolo**. A nice day's outing to get away from the richness of Venice.

Pescheria. An early-morning visit (except Monday, when there's no fish) is exciting and fun, with the amusing, carnival atmosphere. Include a Prosecco (the delightful Veneto sparkling wine) at a *bacaro* with a *cicchetto* or two.

Traghetti, the gondolas that ply back and forth between the two sides of the Grand Canal at regular intervals, since there are only three bridges along the entire length of the Canal. At about 50 cents a crossing, it's also the cheapest experience in Venice!

Concerts at **San Rocco**. Regular concerts are held in many churches and *scuole*, attached to churches. The best is the **Scuola di San Rocco**, where besides a feast for the ears, a feast for the eyes includes being surrounded by great paintings of Tiziano, Tiepolo, and Giorgione, with an intermission viewing upstairs of the unbelievable ceiling of Tintoretto.

Al Covo. Have lunch at this relaxed and superb fish restaurant, owned by chef Cesare Benelli and his wife, Diane, a super-energized Texan, who does the desserts, like brownies.

Giudecca. The long, narrow island across from **San Marco**, where the **Albergo Cipriani** is located. A terrific pizza at **Do Mori**, a family-style trattoria, at canalside with a view across the canal to **San Marco**, is something those who stick to the center of Venice never see.

Trattoria Montin. One of my favorite lunch places in the world is the garden here. Dining under the sun-dappled, vine-covered pergola will keep you here all afternoon. There's good, no-nonsense family food with Papa Giuliano here to greet you. Don't miss the *sassolini* (baked spinach and ricotta gnocchi), usually on Thursday. Divine.

Campo Santa Margherita. The *campo* (Venetian for piazza) is alive with farmers' markets and fishmongers doing their thing. Young and lively atmosphere with the university nearby.

Grand Canal. Early in the morning or late at night, the most glorious ride in the world is to take the *vaporetto* the length of the Grand Canal and back. It's particularly wonderful at *Carnevale*, when masked balls are taking place in various palazzi. Magic.

the **Duomo**'s *Castelfranco Madonna* (1504). Located to the right of the choir, the altarpiece demands a strong upward gaze with the Madonna seated high above the two saints, who seem strangely isolated from the scene. The deftly painted natural background evoking the familiar landscape of the Veneto reminds the traveler of the richness of this region.

Brenta Riviera

The best way to see the villas on the **Naviglio Brenta** is by taking a leisurely boat ride, such as the excursion offered on *Il Burchiello*. It leaves from **Piazza San Marco** on Tuesday, Thursday, and Saturday, making the voyage as the nobles of yesteryear did; or from **Padua** on Wednesday, Friday, and Sunday, traveling the canal in reverse. In Venice, contact the tourist office (041/5226356) for more information; in Padua, call **Siamic Express** (049/660944).

In the 15th century, when Venice acquired *terra ferma* (mainland) areas, the Naviglio Brenta—which linked *La Serenissima* with Padua—became the holiday resort for wealthy Venetians. Sumptuous villas sprang up along this canal among trees, fields, and rivers, serving as cool summer estates for well-heeled lords and their ladies escaping the heat of the city. When Napoleon arrived in 1797 there were about 40 of these waterside palaces; in the surrounding Veneto region, over 3,000 were built between 1400 and 1900!

During the canal's heyday, affluent nobles boarded the cozy boats known as *burchielli* to be rowed from **Piazza San Marco** through the lagoon to **Fusina**, where the boats were then tethered to horses and pulled along the Brenta Riviera to Padua. Aboard the *burchiello* were artists, comedians, and various merrymakers, to ensure that travelers had a pleasant trip.

Instead of the performers of yore, today's modern boats feature armchairs, a bar, and a guide lecturing in several languages about the magnificent villas that the vessel visits. The **Villa Malcontenta** is one of **Palladio**'s masterpieces. He began it in about 1560 for Nicolò and Luigi Foscari (the villa is also known as "Palazzo Foscari"), and it is a typical Palladian structure. Set grandly among weeping willow trees, the villa boasts a *pronaos* (a portico), which supports a pediment with Ionic columns. Inside are wonderful frescoes by Giambattista Zelotti (1526-1578) depicting various mythological scenes. Next, the modern-day *burchiello* cruises by several villas at **Oriago** and *il termine*, the ancient boundary marker in the form of a column separating Padua and Venice. A congregation of villas abound along the route at nearby **Mira**, the finest being **Villa Wildmann**. An impressive park envelops this 18th-century Rococo summer estate. **Villa Corner** reportedly hosted parties that lasted over eight days, while **Villa Foscarini** entertained Lord Byron from 1817 to 1818. Lovely views that were probably painted by Canaletto, Guardi, and Bellotto abound between Mira and **Dolo**.

Past Fiesso and near **Strà**, where the Naviglio Brenta meets the **Brenta**, is **Villa Pisani**, or "La Barbariga" (or any of several other modest aliases, including *"La Nazionale," "Palazzo Reale," "La Perla della Riviera," "La Magnifica,"* and *"La Divina"*), set within an enormous green park. Inside are some stupendous frescoes by Tiepolo on the ballroom ceiling that depict the Pisani family; others appear in the room of Bacco del Guarana and in the Pompeiana hall. The villa has a long history of both famous and infamous occupants: Doge Alvise had this palace built when he came to power in 1735, Napoleon bought it in 1807, and Mussolini and Hitler met here for the first time in 1934.

The **Villa Grimani Valmarana** is located at **Noventa Padovan**, where passengers (and merchandise) in the canal's heyday disembarked from the *burchielli* and continued their trip to Padua by horse. (The **Canale Piovego** is now open, allowing boats to make the journey all the way to Padua.) It was built atop a 13th-century castle ruin and frescoed within by the Venetian painter Andrea Urbani. Also here is **Villa Giovannelli**, aloof in its splendor, with high Corinthian columns, tympanums, and statues.

Monselice, Este, and Montagnana

Monselice is 63 kilometers (39 miles) or an hour from Venice by autostrada **A4**. Exit the highway at **Padova Est**, and take autostrada **A13** in the direction of Bologna for about 29 kilometers (18 miles) to the Monselice exit. Este is 9 kilometers (6 miles) west along **S10**, and Montagnana is another 16 kilometers (10 miles) west along the same road. A direct train on the **Venice-Bologna** line stops at Monselice a few times a day; otherwise, a change in Padua is required (the same goes for Este and Montagnana). If traveling by bus, transfer at Padua for all three towns.

A trip to these three towns offers a visit back through the centuries to when Doge Dandolo was making his profitable agreements for the Fourth Crusade in the 1200s—an era of castles, moats, and crenellated walls.

Built on the picturesque side of a hill, Monselice boasts a main square (**Piazza Mazzini**) that features the **Torre Civica**, built in the 1240s. Also noteworthy here are castles enclosed by medieval crenellated walls at various spots on the climb up the hill, the **Duomo Vecchio**—a 13th-century Gothic church—and wonderful views. Monselice is that perfect, brief escape into another world and another age—small, excellently sited, and peaceful.

The pleasant town of Este—formerly **Ateste**—most probably took its name from the river **L'Atesis** (today the **Adige**), which flowed through the city until its course changed in the sixth century. It was an important commercial site for the Etruscans until it became Roman, between 49 and 42 BC. The city slowly declined in importance over the next centuries, but finally came back to life and took its new name in the 11th century. The Este family, later to become the Dukes of Ferrara—made infamous through Robert Browning's poem "My Last Duchess"—increased the city's grandeur.

Este retains its centuries-long charm today, with a 14th-century castle and finely preserved walls enclosing a public park. A visit to the **Museo Nazionale Atestino** (049/8751608) in the beautiful **Palazzo Mocenigo**, built on the ruins of a castle, brings the town's history to life. Past Giulio Carpioni's 17th-century frescoes on the second floor is a walk through the history of Este. You'll saunter past Etruscan vases and bronze figures, glass from the Roman period, and ceramics from the ninth to the 20th century. The museum is open daily (no midday closing); there's an admission charge.

WHAT A GIRL WANTS . . .

Stefania Prestigiacomo, Minister for Equal Opportunities in the Italian government, created a furor recently among Italy's feminists by publishing her "Ten Commandments" for female happiness . . .

1. Consider motherhood a value—it is the greatest experience for women.
2. Follow your childhood dream.
3. Keep falling in love.
4. Buy something useless every once in a while.
5. Take pride in your own beauty.
6. Do not be upset if your man doesn't notice you have been to the hairdresser—it is he who loses, not you.
7. Do not be envious of important people; they, too, often spend evenings just watching television.
8. Travel to broaden your mind.
9. Defend other women.
10. Smile.

Girls . . . what do we think?

The walls encircling the city start just at the exit of the museum. Before a brief walk to the center, the literary pilgrim might want to go behind the castle to the **Villa De Kunkler**, where Byron lived (1817-1818) and Shelley wrote "Lines Written Among the Euganean Hills." The **Duomo** (Piazza Santa Tecla) houses a stunning Tiepolo canvas (1759) over the main altarpiece that displays the flamboyant artist's ability to capture grand tragedy in the figure of St. Tecla as she attempts to rescue Este from the plague.

Este's tourist office (Piazza Maggiore 9, 0429/3635; fax 0429/3635) is open Monday-Friday, Saturday morning.

Montagnana has the most perfectly preserved fortified walls in Europe (1200-1400), 24 towers, and four elaborate city gates. The 15th-century **Duomo** juts out into the spacious **Piazza Maggiore**, which is encircled by architecture depicting all the styles of the various "visitors": painted beamed arcades; arches—round, Gothic, and Moorish; and chimneys resembling harlequin hats. Just outside **Porta Padova** is the **Villa Pisani**, constructed about 1560 following plans by **Palladio**.

Stop for lunch at the nearby **Ristorante Aldo Moro** (Via Marconi 27, 0429/81351). Start with the *gamberoni all'aceto balsamico* (jumbo shrimp in balsamic vinegar) for an antipasto, followed by *tagliolini alle erbe in crema di zucca, porcini, e fegatini* (wide noodles with herbs in a pumpkin, wild mushroom, and chicken-liver cream sauce). The *grigliata mista di carne e verdure* (grilled meat with vegetables) makes an excellent entrée. The desserts focus on tarts made from fruit from the surrounding hillsides and wild berries in season with various creams. It's open Tuesday-Sunday, lunch and dinner.

Steeped now in a time past, you may resist the hasty autostrada route back to Venice and make one more stop at **Arquà Petrarca** (7 kilometers—4 miles—northwest of Monselice). Here the famed poet Petrarch, weary from the labors of humanism and the intellectual demands of Padua, retired and built a small retreat in which to read and write in his last days (1370-1374). The guest book is signed by Byron, and a charming stone plaque reads loosely, "If thou art stirred by love of country, bow to these walls, whence passed the great soul, the singer of Scipios and of Laura." The nearby church contains his simple sarcophagus, with his own epitaph.

TREVISO

To get to Treviso by car, take autostrada **A27** 13 kilometers (8 miles) north for about 30 minutes. Exit at **Treviso Sud** and follow the *centro* signs to the heart of the city. Trains run about every 45 minutes to Treviso on the **Udine** line. Alternatively, you may choose to take a four-hour boat ride back to Venice along the **Fiume Sile** (Sile River). It runs March through October (Treviso-Venice only); call 0422/788663, 0422/788671 for more information.

"Treviso, the Painted Town" is the apt description the tourist board gives this unusually friendly and attractive city. Here the visitor begins to appreciate an age when the delicate, colorful decorating of house exteriors often excelled the interiors.

Interestingly, Treviso's most famous son these days is Luciano Benetton, founder of the "United Colors of Benetton" clothing firm. There is, of course, a huge Benetton store in the center of the town.

Strolling under arcades along the unspoiled streets, peeking into the courtyards of the splendid villas the wealthy locals built, and traversing the numerous canals that vein the city offer a perfect escape from tourism into a native world that has retained its hold on *la dolce vita*.

From the train station, a short walk up the **Corso del Popolo** leads to the **Piazza dei Signori**, which is surrounded by porticoed streets filled with shops and dominated by café terraces. The **Palazzo del Trecento** (1217) occupies one side, and the crenellated walls above create a sense of medieval life. It is not open to the public. **Caffè La Pace** next door (0422/50047) provides delicious sandwiches, drinks, and the opportunity to sit and peruse the map. It is open Monday-Wednesday, Friday-Sunday, 7AM-2AM. While Treviso has medieval houses that are mini-museums, the main attractions are the **Duomo** (Piazza Duomo), the **Museo Civico** (Borgo Cavour 24, at Via A. Caccianiga, 0422/658442), and the church of **San Nicolò** (Via San Nicolò and Piazzetta Benedetto XI).

The seven-domed **Duomo** was founded in the 12th century, but repeatedly restored. It houses an early Titian *Annunciation* (1520) with that rare occurrence in Renaissance art—the angel on the right. The chapel itself (to the right of the choir) is decorated with frescoes by Pordenone. It is open Monday-Friday, 7:30AM-noon and 3:30PM-7PM; Saturday, Sunday 7:30AM-1PM and 3:30PM-8PM.

The **Museo Civico** contains bronze swords over 2,000 years old that were supposedly tossed into the nearby **Botteniga** and Sile Rivers by ancient soldiers paying homage to the deities who were believed to reside there. Paintings by Bellini, Titian, Bassano, Pordenone, Cima, Tiepolo, Longhi, and Rosalba Carriera, among others, offer a fine opportunity to continue the exploration of Northern Italian painting begun at the **Accademia** in Venice. Pictures of special note are a haunting Lorenzo Lotto portrait of a Dominican, a delicious Guardi view of Venice's island of San Giorgio, and an unusual portrait of the sculptor Canova by Thomas Lawrence. Stop in the room dedicated to various views of the city itself and then visit the wing of charming pictures by local artists. The museum is open Tuesday-Sunday; admission is charged.

The 13th-century Dominican church of **San Nicolò** is the finest spot in Italy to see the frescoes of Tommaso da Modena, a gifted follower of Giotto. The massive columns of the church display his frescoes of saints, and the adjacent seminary contains 40 Dominican portraits (1352) that secured his reputation for realism, not only through the detailed personalities revealed, but also by one of Western art's first depictions of someone wearing glasses!

Stop in the Romanesque-Gothic church of **San Francesco** (Piazza San Francesco and Viale San Antonio da Padova) and visit the tombs of the daughters of Dante and Petrarch. Look at the **Ponte De Pria** to see where the Botteniga reaches the town and divides into three canals. From here, walk along the inside of the 16th-century city walls around the northwest perimeter, past the **Museo Civico** to **Viale Cesare Battisti**, where you can exit and retrace your path, this time on the outside of the walls. In the summer you can take a boat cruise down to the Venetian lagoon and back. By reservation only. Ask at the tourist office, or call 0422/788663 or 788671.

The food in Treviso is worth the trip even if frescoes and Benetton aren't enough of a draw. This is the hometown of that fabulous long red and white radicchio—not the ball variety we get in salads, but the stuff with bitter, fleshy white ribs fringed with a maroon leaf. It comes prepared all ways, but should at least once be tasted in the *risotto al radicchio*. The local specialty of *sopa cauda*—a soup made with pigeon meat—is a real winter warmer. Risotto or polenta is the thing here, rather than pasta. This (which may come as a relief to those of you who are "all fished out" after time in Venice) is meat country. The meat is prepared in slabs, on skewers, roasted, grilled—every which way. There is also a local sauce called *peverada*, made from liver and spices, which is a real taste bomb. The local dessert seems to be tiramisù. Cheeses are an adventure and come with names like *bastardo di grappa* (many of the cheeses, like this one, are marinated or aged in some form of alcohol). During the fall, this is major mushroom country. And all year round wash it down with Prosecco. This is its home.

Northeast of **Piazza dei Signori** at **Porta San Tomaso** is the main extension of the food market. Before getting there, stroll past stalls filled with bargain clothing and leather goods, as well as gift items at prices lower than in Venice. One irresistible spot to watch the bustling shoppers is at **Al Bottegon** (Viale B. Burchiellati 7, just west of Borgo Mazzini, 0422/548345). Have a snack and an aperitif or glass of wine here, and choose a reasonably priced bottle to take back to Venice. It's open Monday-Friday; Saturday, 8:15AM-2:30PM.

For a full meal, try **Antico Ristorante Beccherie** (Piazza Ancilotto 10, at Piazza Monte di Pietà, 0422/56601). Its stunning interior of ceramics, wood carvings, and dazzling copper pieces is matched only by the exquisitely prepared dishes. The antipasto selections are well balanced: *baccalà mantecato* (puréed salt cod on toast), *petta d'oca* (thin-sliced smoked breast of goose), and

The Best

John Julius Norwich

Writer/Historian of Venice

Dinner at my favorite restaurant, **Al Covo**, in **Castello**.

The top of the campanile of **San Giorgio Maggiore** at sunset.

A private gondola at night, exploring the swank canals only.

The Carpaccio paintings in the **Scuola di San Giorgio degli Schiavoni**.

The Bellini altarpiece in **San Zaccaria**.

The Virgin behind the altar at **Torcello**.

A drink (or dinner) on the **Hotel Gritti** raft, watching the **Grand Canal**.

vegetables in season. The first and second courses reflect the same range and attention to the market produce: *ravioli di zucca* (pasta stuffed with pumpkin), *risotto di primavera* (with spring vegetables), and *carello del bollito* (several boiled meats with green sauce chosen at the table). It's open Tuesday-Saturday, lunch and dinner; Sunday, lunch.

Al Bersagliere (Via Barberia 21, at Vicolo San Gregorio, 0422/541988), conveniently located near the Duomo, also has a seasonal focus. Try the *carpaccio con salsa di rucola* (thin-sliced raw beef sauced with arugula purée) or *pesce spada affumicato* (smoked swordfish) to start, followed by *tagliolini al tartufo* (thin noodles with shaved white truffles). Any appetite remaining can be appeased by the specialty of Treviso—*petto di faraona in pevarada con polenta* (roast guinea hen breast with a sauce of chicken livers, anchovy, oil, and lemon, served with polenta). The restaurant is open Monday-Friday, lunch and dinner; Saturday, lunch.

A place filled with color and a rustic interior that complements the fine Prosecco wine and excellent food is **Toni del Spin** (Via Inferiore 7, just west of Piazza San Vito, 0422/543829). Also conveniently located near the main piazza, its chalkboard full of wines by the glass invites a linger at the bar before heading into the dining room. An overhead board lists the day's offerings: *zuppa di carciofi* (artichoke soup), *pasta con cavolfiori o asparagi* (with cauliflower or asparagus, depending on season), *trippa in salsa* (tripe in tomato sauce), plus other fish and meat dishes typical of Northern cuisine. Many dishes are served with *polenta morbida* (soft polenta) on the side, and the dessert cart is especially seductive. It is open Monday, dinner; Tuesday-Saturday, lunch and dinner.

For picnic lovers, there are two noteworthy gourmet shops: **Danesin** (Corso del Popolo 28, at Viale Cadorna, 0422/540625) and **Cacciolato**, situated two streets behind the Duomo (Via Ortazzo 25, 0422/545971). They are both open Monday-Tuesday, Thursday-Saturday; on Wednesday, 8:30AM-1PM only.

Treviso's tourist information center (Piazza Monte di Pietà, 0422/547632) is open Monday-Saturday.

The Teatro Olimpico in Vicenza was the first roofed indoor theater in the world.

Pietro Bembo (1470-1547), besides being a leading Venetian humanist and sitting for three portraits by his friend Titian, gave the Renaissance one of its loveliest discourses on love—*Gli Asolani*, set in the gardens of Caterina Comaro in Asolo.

No reproductions of Palladio's designs give an adequate idea of the harmony of their dimensions; they must be seen in their actual perspective.

—Goethe, *Italian Journey*

Vicenza

Take autostrada **A4** 49 kilometers (30 miles) west and exit at **Vicenza Est**. Follow the *centro* signs to the downtown area. Trains leave for Vicenza every half hour on the **Venezia/Milano/Torino** line.

After a long and tumultuous history starting with the Romans, Vicenza became part of Venice's mainland possessions in 1404. It was an artistic center under the flag of San Marco up until 1797, when Napoleon ended the Republic. Today Vicenza's renown is attributed mostly to the great 16th-century architect **Andrea Palladio**.

From the train station, walk along **Viale Roma** and turn right at the **Giardini Salvi**, past **Porta Castello** (a fragment of the old city wall), where the wonderful **Corso Andrea Palladio** awaits you. The responsibility for erecting the first building on the left—**Palazzo Thiene Bonin Longare**—on the corner of **Contrà Motton** was transferred to **Vincenzo Scamozzi** after Palladio's death in 1567. Construction on the palazzo continued into the 18th century. The ground floor, consisting of eight Corinthian semi-columns, supports the upper floor, which mirrors the first with seven windows. The small **Palazzo Capra** is directly across the Corso on **Piazza del Castello** and is one of Palladio's early works, from the first half of the 1540s. The entrance, framed by two fluted Ionic pilasters, supports a balcony off the second floor. Here four elegant Corinthian pilasters bolster a triangular gable.

Farther down the Corso is the **Duomo**, one block off to the right on Stradella Loschi, with its 15th-century patterned marble façade. The dome was designed by Palladio in 1565 to resemble the Pantheon in Rome. **Lorenzo da Bologna** and **Rocco da Vicenza** constructed the apse in the beginning of the 16th century where a shining Lorenzo Veneziano polyptych now hangs. Continue down the Corso to the 1561 **Palazzo Pojana** and its arch constructed across Contrà Do Rode to join two buildings. Although the ground-floor façade is not symmetrical, the six huge Corinthian pilasters on the next floor steal all the attention. Five square upper windows top off the building. It is believed to have been designed by Palladio.

Off the Corso is the stupendous **Piazza dei Signori** and the *Loggia del Capitaniato,* now the **Municipal Council** building. Designed by Palladio in 1571 to replace the former residence of Capitiano, the highest Venetian authority in Vicenza, the building boasts four large semi-columns crowned with Corinthian capitals perched above the second floor and grandly supporting a somewhat out-of-proportion top floor and balcony. The ground floor is divided into three bays, and the interior is a harmonious area of columns and niches. The **Basilica Palladiana**, made of white Piovene stone, stands on the south side of the piazza. Two older buildings, the **Palatium Vetus** and the **Palatium Communis**, were joined in the mid-1400s and loggias added at the end of the century for the nearby markets. **Tommaso Formenton** planned and built these covered spaces, but they collapsed two years after they were finished. Fifty years elapsed and many great artists were consulted before Palladio's plans were finally accepted to rebuild the now double order of white loggias topped with statues.

The recently restored **Palazzo Corto-Barbaran** (Contrà Porti and Contrà Riale, no phone at press time) was designed by Palladio and now houses a museum devoted to the architect. A series of small pilasters and square windows look out peacefully over a row of Corinthian-capped columns that sit gracefully on a sober row of Ionic-capitaled columns below. Contact the tourist office (see page 303) for schedule and admission charge.

Palazzo Thiene, now the Banca Popolare Vicentina, occupies the corner of the parallel street one block away (Contrà San Gaetano and Stradella Banca Populare). The ground floor is defined by rusticated stone, while the second alternates between windows and thin Corinthian pilasters.

The **San Corona** church (Contrà San Corona and Corso Andrea Palladio) houses the *Adoration of the Magi* by Paolo Veronese and the superb *Baptism of Christ*, with the blue Dolomiti rising in the background, by Giovanni Bellini. Look closely at the high altar: Even though it looks rather fussy, the inlaid marble and mother-of-pearl friezes and still lifes of houses, towns, angels, and fruit are innocently naive and wonderfully simple. The wood intarsia choir stalls behind the altar are filled with steep city vistas and realistic still lifes.

At the end of Corso Andrea Palladio is the **Museo di Palazzo Chiericati** (Corso degli Angeli and Piazza Matteotti, 0444/321348), housed in what is considered to be one of the finest of Palladio's achievements of his initial period—the façade is gracefully proportioned, with subtle light and shade. Walk through the richly frescoed rooms on the ground floor to get an idea of the palazzo's grandeur. Move on to the upper floor, where the golden *Dormitio Virginis* (*Sleeping Virgin*) by Paolo Veneziano and a range of international Gothic paintings by Battista da Vicenza are found in the first few rooms. Hans Memling's *The Crucifixion with Madonna* shines in all its glory of Flemish folds in **Room 5**. An excellent sweep of Vicenza's most eminent painter—Bartolomeo Montagna—encompasses Madonnas posing with various saints and Christ carrying the cross in **Rooms 7-9**. Mixed in with these paintings is *The Madonna Enthroned* by Cima da Conegliano. While the Dutch painter Lambert Sustris was working in Venice with Titian he produced the *Rest during the Flight to Egypt*, which now can be admired in **Room 10**. The next chamber belongs to such greats as Lorenzo Lotto, Paolo Veronese, Jacopo Tintoretto, and Jacopo Bassano, and Anthony Van Dyck's *The Three Ages of Man*—a masterpiece of the Italian period—hangs in **Room 13**. In the last 10 rooms are works by Francesco Maffei, Giulio Carponi, Piazzetta, and others, ending with two masterful paintings by Giambattista Tiepolo—the *Immaculata* and *Time Discovering Truth and Chasing Falsehood*. The museum is open Tuesday-Saturday; Sunday morning; there's an admission charge.

Diagonally across the Corso Andrea Palladio is the **Teatro Olimpico** (Piazza Matteotti and Strada Teatro Olimpico, 0444/323781). Palladio died a few months after work began; **Vincenzo Scamozzi** completed the project in

Basilica Palladiana, Vicenza

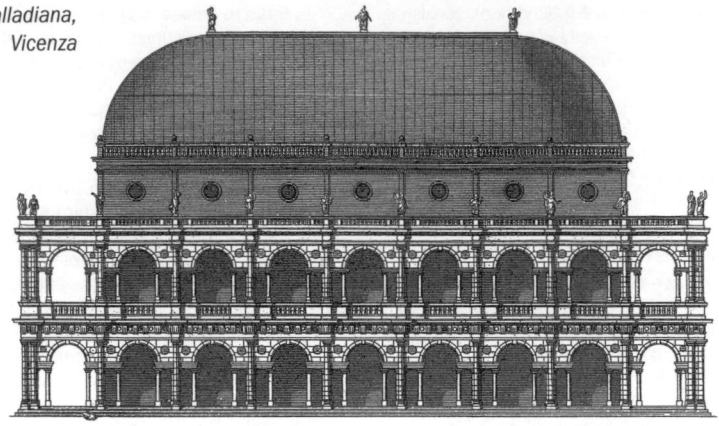

1585. The impressive stage is in the form of a triumphal arch that mirrors the tripartite form of Palladian palaces. Completely round columns on the ground level support the next layer, where they reappear as semi-columns and vanish completely in the attic. The theater is open to visitors Monday-Saturday when there are no performances; admission is charged.

Ristorante Pizzeria Zi'Teresa (Contada San Antonio 1, 0444/321411) is great for pizza, and decent for anything more complicated (pastas and game dishes are always on offer). Wash it all down with one of the wines from the vast list. The restaurant is open Tuesday-Sunday, lunch and dinner. **Bar Enoteca** (Piazza delle Erbe, just west of Piazza Biade o della Biava, 0444/320138), also known as *"Al Grottino,"* has an enchanting location next to the small flower market, a country interior, and friendly family service. It's just the spot for a sandwich and a glass of wine. It's open Monday-Saturday, 10AM-2PM and 4PM-2AM. **Antica Casa della Malvasia** (Contrà San Antonio 5, 0444/543704) has been open since 1200 and was originally the local center for importing Malvasia wine from Greece. Drinking is still the best thing to do here—they offer 80 different wines by the glass and over 100 grappas. With a knowledgeable and friendly staff, it is an education in liquid Italy. It's open Tuesday-Saturday.

If you are in a do-it-yourself mood where food is concerned, there is a terrific produce market each Tuesday and Thursday in the Piazza delle Erbe.

For those who aren't yet satiated with Palladio, two more of his villas are within walking distance of the center of town. **Villa Valmara al Nani** (Via San Bastiano 8, 0444/321803) is about a mile from Vicenza on the road to Este. Giambattista Tiepolo and his son Giandomenico covered the inside walls of the villa with a fantastic series of frescoes that depict a mythological world. It is open Tuesday afternoon, Wednesday-Thursday, Friday-Sunday morning 15 March-15 November. There's an admission charge.

Continue walking along Via San Bastiano for several hundred yards to the most famous of Palladio's villas—**La Rotonda** (Via della Rotonda 29, 0444/321793). This 16th-century palazzo with its identical four façades of Ionic hexastyle *pronaos* (a portico) looks out on a quiet hill. Jefferson's Monticello was based on this building. The interior semispherical ceiling is decorated with frescoes by Alessandro Maganza. It is open Tuesday-Saturday for external visits; Monday, Tuesday, Thursday-Sunday April-October for internal visits. There's an admission charge. Vicenza's tourist office (Piazza Matteotti 12, at Corso Andrea Palladio, 0444/320854; fax 0444/320854) is open Monday-Saturday; Sunday 9AM-12:30PM.

PADUA

Padua is 44 kilometers (27 miles) from Venice. Take the autostrada **A4**, exit at **Padova Ovest**, and follow the signs to the *centro*. Trains (**Venezia/Firenze/Roma** line) leave twice every hour; the trip takes 20 to 30 minutes.

The historian Livy (59 BC–AD 18) claims that the Trojan warrior Antenor was the founder of this fascinating city. Even without such dubious Homeric lineage, Padua retains much of its ancient and medieval character and grandeur. From the earliest Roman recognitio of its importance in 89 BC to the founding of its great university in 1222 to the city's eventual domination by the Venetian state in 1405, and the surge of travelers stopping here while making the Grand Tour in the late 19th century, Padua has long been a unique place.

Stroll the dim arcaded streets haunted by ghosts of its famed university—Dante, Petrarch, Galileo, plus legions of English students—where there's still a strong sense of intellectual openness. It was, after all, in Padua where Giotto created his greatest fresco cycle, and where Donatello ignored medieval prohibition and cast the *Gattamelata*—the first equestrian statue in a thousand years. Padua is also an easy and enchanting city to explore by foot, with delightful market squares and smart pedestrian shopping streets.

Start your tour at the train station (parking is available nearby). A 10-minute walk down the **Corso del Popolo** leads to a beautifully kept open garden accented by ruins of a Roman amphitheater and to Padua's most famous site—the **Cappella degli Scrovegni** (Scrovegni Chapel; Corso Garibaldi, between Riviera dei Ponti Romani and Via Trieste). Here Giotto's frescoes (1303-1305) narrate the story of Christian salvation in a triple band that covers the entire interior. Certainly Enrico Scrovegni chose well when he selected Giotto as the artist to help expiate the shame heaped on his father's usury by Dante in *The Inferno*. With a revolutionary imagination, Giotto made centuries of Byzantine flatness, frontality, and otherworldly gold disappear as he redeemed *this* world, filling it with solid bodies and backs, real architecture, blue skies, frolicking animals, and passion. Hampered by the chapel's small size and asymmetry, Giotto painted in architecture and sculpture to create a feigned world that both enlarges the space and provides air. The viewer is startled to find bas-reliefs, cornices, and dados (the lower part of the wall is decorated differently from the upper), which are all illusions on a flat surface.

The story of Christ begins with *The Annunciation* over the chancel arch and ends with the enormous *Last Judgment* surrounding the entry. Two tiers of framed tales on the walls relate the major events of Christ's life and death. In each panel the new use of realistic colors, believable groupings, humorous minor figures, and a single dramatic focus all combine to create a surprisingly unified effect. Giotto further brought into this world a *tour de force* painting of two simple interiors on the face of the chancel arch.

It is necessary to book a tour of the frescoes (049/2010020; afternoons are easier for getting through). Twenty-five people at a time are allowed through, and the rather scary doors are opened and closed only once during the course of each tour in order to preserve the special atmospheric conditions created for the preservation of the frescoes. If you miss the door, you miss the tour.

Be sure to visit the newly restored **Museo Civico agli Eremitani** (Municipal Gallery), with archeological pieces from various eras beginning with the Roman period; 14th-18th-century paintings; and tapestries, sculptures, ceramics, and furniture. It also has a comfortable and excellent bookstore. The chapel and museum (049/8204550) are open Tuesday-Sunday; one admission ticket is good for both.

Next door to the gardens lies the reconstructed church of **Eremitani**. Originally built in the 13th century, it was destroyed by bombs in 1944 and is considered to be World War II's greatest single loss to Italian art. Despite the damage, the church still houses the exquisite fresco remains of the **Capella del Mantegna** to the right of the apse. The splendid *Martyrdom of St. Christopher* and the fragmentary *Martyrdom of St. James* in the chapel both exhibit the young Andrea Mantegna's stellar contributions to 15th-century painting. In these biblical tales, the classical world and the Renaissance unite with marble architecture, stone reliefs, armored figures, and dramatic steep perspectives. Goethe claimed it was through the 23-year-old Mantegna that "genius and energy were able to rise above the earth and create heavenly forms which are still real."

Corso Garibaldi continues through **Piazza Cavour**. Just off the *corso* on the piazza is the **Caffè Pedrocchi** (049/8205007), with its neoclassical porticoes. It was the hotbed of liberal political discussion in the 19th century.

At the nearby **Piazza della Frutta** and **Piazza delle Erbe** are two markets—one featuring fruit, the other vegetables. Both are riots of color and activity, perfect spots to sit at a café and observe the social life that circles around any Italian outdoor market.

To the east of the markets resides the famed university, with its legendary honor roll of students and professors (Palazzo Centrale, Via VIII Febbraio, between Via San Canziano and Piazza Cavour, 049/8209711). Guided tours (some in English) are given Tuesday and Thursday at 9, 10, and 11AM; Wednesday-Friday at 3, 4, and 5PM. Open to visitors is the **Teatro Anatomico**, Europe's oldest (1594) anatomical theater, which was finely built of various woods in perfect scale. Here William Harvey stood watching secret dissections hidden from the Inquisatorial police and probably made his first discoveries into the circulation of blood. Also here is Galileo's battered desk where he taught for 18 years (1592-1610), plus numerous highlights from the school's prestigious history.

If you find that the inner traveler is in need, try a coffee and a pastry in the **Caffè Pedrocchi**, just off Via VIII Febbraio—it was one of Stendhal's favorite haunts.

For something more substantial try the **Ostaria dei Fabbri** (Via dei Fabbri 13, 049/650336), where they do a delicious *ravioloni de magro* (a large but light ravioli served in butter and sage sauce); it's open Monday-Saturday. **La Vecchia Enoteca** (Via San Martino e Solferino 32, 049/8752856) is expensive, but worth it. Try the *arrosto di salmone* (roasted salmon served with a creamy sauce). It's open Tuesday-Saturday, lunch and dinner; Monday, dinner. **Enoteca la Corte dei Leoni** (Via Pietro d'Abano 1, 049/8750083) has good food (if slightly small portions) and fantastic wine. In the summer they have occasional jazz concerts in their courtyard. It's open Tuesday-Saturday. Another choice is **Antica Trattoria dei Paccagnella** (Via dei Santo 113, 049/8750549), an elegant spot that serves delicious *baccalà* (salt cod), *tagliolini ai porcini* (wide noodles with porcini mushrooms), and *tagliata di petto d'anatra all'aceto balsamico* (duck breast with balsamic vinegar—the house special). A wide selection of local and national wines is available. It's open Monday-Saturday, lunch and dinner.

At the basilica of **Sant'Antonio** (known locally as *"Il Santo"*; Piazza del Santo), completed in the 14th century, visitors coming from Venice feel the presence of the East once again. Under the Oriental domes and minaret-looking bell towers is a magnificent collection of Western art. Don't miss the **Cappella di Sant'Antonio** in the north transept, ornamented with relief works by some of the finest 16th-century Northern Italian sculptors—Sansovino, Tullio Lombardo, Aspetti, and others. The saint's tomb is covered with small oval photographs of people praying for *Il Santo*'s help. The Baroque tomb of Caterina Cornaro (1674) invites homage to that former queen who created such a cultured world in Asolo (see page 296), and the Rococo chapel at the back of the basilica contains over 100 relics. The altar (ask a custodian to unlock the gates) sculpted by Donatello in 1445-1450 is further complemented by reliefs executed by Ricci and crowned with his towering bronze Easter candlesticks. To the right of the altar is the lovely chapel frescoed by Altichiero (ca. 1330-1395), a devoted follower of Giotto. With its pageantlike *Crucifixion* and glory of color, it marks the end of early Paduan art and prepares for the worldlier Renaissance to come. Stop in the chapel on the left and take a look at the recent paintings by Annigoni—a haunting Crucifixion and two side murals of St. Anthony.

The south side of **Piazza del Santo** offers further opportunities to explore Paduan painting with the **Oratorio di San Giorgio** and the **Scuola del Santo** (School of St. Anthony). Completely frescoed by Altichiero and Avanzo (1378-1384), the **Oratorio** depicts the lives of three saints—Lucy, Catherine, and George. The Scuola focuses on the life of St. Anthony, with three of the cycles painted by the young Titian (1511). Both are open daily, and there's one admission ticket. But the piazza's major claim is Donatello's *Gattamelata* (1453), a revolutionary equestrian statue of the Venetian *condottiere* (military commander) Erasmo da Narni. Nicknamed the "cat on horseback," da Narni was famed for his mainland victories and acquisitions of territory for *La Serenissima*. Lounge under the 400-year-old trees and look at ancient hothouse plants in the **Orto Botanico** (Via Orto Botanico, east of Via Belludi, 049/656614), Europe's first botanical garden, just as Goethe did. It is open Monday-Saturday.

VERONA

Take autostrada **A4** 103 kilometers (64 miles) to Verona, exit at **Verona Est**, and follow the *centro* signs. The train takes about 90 minutes on the **Venezia/Milano/Torino** line.

Second only to Venice in popularity in Northern Italy, the charming city of Verona offers travelers abundant reasons to stroll and absorb. Its strategic location on the broad, winding **Fiume Adige** (Adige River) made the city an important place in its early days, and throughout Verona is an architectural layering of the numerous settlers who established themselves here over the centuries.

First colonized by Euganean tribes, the site developed into an important Roman colony by 89 BC. The city was, in the days of the Roman Empire, known as *piccola Roma* (little Rome) because of its importance. Whether or not the city was actually planned by the great architect **Vitruvius** as some claim, it was certainly elevated into prominence during Roman times, and the remains of that period's magnificence decorate the piazzas and portals. In the Middle Ages (1260-1387), the Scala family brought Verona renewed glory by building many monuments and imparting a strong cultural awareness on the city. The family's most famous leader, Cangrande I della Scala, offered Dante refuge after he was exiled from Florence. In appreciation, the grateful poet dedicated his *Paradiso* to him. During the Renaissance writers and artists continued to be lured here, and Shakespeare's immortal tale of star-crossed love based on a local family feud guaranteed "fair Verona" a lion's share of future pilgrims.

Renaissance Painters of the Veneto

While Venice's passion for celebrating and embellishing *La Serenissima* ("The Most Serene") in canvases, frescoes, mosaics, and stone was primarily centered in the capital, the city's artistic influences also spread throughout the surrounding area. Painters from such towns as **Verona**, **Vicenza**, **Padua**, **Treviso**, **Bassano del Grappa**, and others went to Venice to study, often returning to ornament their places of origin with works that incorporated holy subjects in pastoral countryside scenes. Many of these towns preserve the houses and studios of their native sons as small museums open to the public, as well as showing their paintings in churches and other sites accessible to visitors.

To the north of Venice is **Conegliano**, birthplace of Cima da Conegliano (1460-1518). A pretty little town on the main train to Udine, Conegliano affords marvelous views from its hilltop castle of the surrounding vineyards. It is also the starting place for the **Strada del Vino Bianco** and **Strada del Prosecco** wine-tasting routes, both interesting side trips for visitors. More important, it gives the viewer already familiar with Cima's numerous altarpieces in Venice a glimpse of the **Dolomiti** and lower hills that he used as background for his religious works. Pious Madonnas sit on ground speckled with wildflowers and tame wandering birds that seem to have just flown down from the sky. The city maintains the **Casa di Cima** (Via Cima 24, 0438/22660), which features reproductions of his work and archives. It is open Tuesday-Saturday; there's an admission charge. The **Duomo** (Via XX Settembre) contains Cima's altarpiece of *Madonna and Saints* (1492), which shows his love of native detail.

Giorgione (ca. 1477-1510), born in **Castelfranco** west of Venice, lived too short a time to include much of the charm of this walled city in his work, but the **Casa di Giorgione** (Piazza del Duomo, 0423/491240) shows his gift for nature in a frieze of still lifes (1500). It is open Tuesday-Sunday; admission is charged. The **Duomo** houses his haunting—some might say disturbing—*Castelfranco Madonna* (1504) in the chapel to the right of the altar. Despite the Madonna's chilly gaze, the altarpiece is softened by the exquisite range of hills in the landscape background.

Titian (ca. 1490-1576), though an urbanized Venetian throughout most of his life, never forgot his origins in Pieve di Cadore, north of Belluno. Like other sons of the countryside (although Titian's hometown is just outside the Veneto), the great painter maintained his love of the landscape on a grand scale.

Jacopo da Ponte (1510-1592), generally known as Bassano, resisted Venice's lure and maintained his residence in his hometown of Bassano. He did develop a patronage in the capital, however, and by the end of the 16th century had achieved an international acclaim. Yet there is always the feel of his local affections in his work. The paintings in the **Museo Civico**'s picture gallery in Bassano (see page 298) display figures more swathed in their mountain finery than robed in Venetian elegance. Amid the satin are far fewer gems and dressed heads; the backs seem stronger than the profiles. The viewer instinctively feels they have ridden in more carts than gondolas, an indication of their countryside background. The artist's works are known for his contrasts of light and dark.

But one son of the Veneto dazzles us with his urban sophistication and charms with his sense of landscape—Verona's famed Veronese (1528-1588). By the end of the 16th century his salon-size paintings emblemized the elegance of Venetian life—both in the lagoon and the countryside. The subjects of his portraits brought their elegant and sophisticated urban style to their villas on the **Brenta** (see page 300), offering the painter a stage large enough to encompass both worlds.

By the end of the glorious 16th century, the regions under the dominion of St. Mark were permeated with the works of some of Venice's greatest Renaissance artists. And today nearly every church in Venice is graced with exquisite altarpieces that glorify the lushness and light that surround the stone-filled city.

Eminently walkable, the city center is accessible from the train station by foot in 15 minutes or by taking bus *No. 5*. **Corsa Porta Nuova** leads into **Piazza Bra** through **Portoni della Bra** (1380s) in the old walls. Here in the pedestrian-only piazza filled with trees and fountains is the famed pink marble **Arena** (045/8003204), the world's oldest (first century AD) entertainment site still in use. It is the third largest amphitheater in existence and can seat about 20,000 spectators. It is in tremendously good condition despite an earthquake in the 12th century that destroyed much of the outer wall. No recent earthquakes have been reported, and the Arena is internationally famous as a venue for opera and theater during the summer months. The Arena charges admission; it is open Tuesday-Sunday, till 6:30PM (3:30PM during opera season).

The stylish **Via Mazzini** (also closed to traffic) is the artery between the Arena and **Piazza delle Erbe** and **Piazza dei Signori** at its other end. Lined with attractive shops and filled with equally attractive people, Via Mazzini is the place to observe the wealthy Veronesi taking their *passeggiata* (stroll). At the end of the street, turn right onto **Via Cappello** and the **Casa di Giulietta** at **No. 23** (045/8034303). This restored 13th-century inn claims to be the residence of the original Capulets, and offers thousands of smitten lovers the chance to be photographed on Juliet's "balcony" (which was actually added in the 1920s). The house is open Tuesday-Sunday; admission is charged.

If you are not smitten, but desperate, then there is a tradition that if you approach the bronze statue of Juliet in the house and rub her right breast, you will find a new lover. Many who visit the house also leave their personal love graffiti on the house walls.

If you really like the Shakespearean thing, the *Tomba di Giulietta* (Juliet's Tomb) is at Via del Pontiere 5 (045/8000361). Admission is charged, and it is open Tuesday-Saturday.

Continue on Via Cappello to Fiume Adige and **Porta Leona** (first century AD). This interesting gate shows a rare example of how the increased importance of an outpost inspired the Romans to camouflage the earlier humble brick with elaborately carved and inscribed marble. Sitting discreetly back from the gate is the 36-room **Hotel All'Antica Porta Leona** (Corticella Leoni 3, 045/595499; fax 045/595214), a perfect place to stay the night for those already under Verona's spell. There's no restaurant.

Back on Via Cappello, the street enters the Piazza delle Erbe, now a picturesque, parasoled market but originally the Roman forum. The **Hotel Aurora** (Piazza delle Erbe 2, at Piazza XIV Novembre, 045/594717; fax 045/8010860) boasts a friendly staff and excellent buffet breakfast (but no restaurant). Request one of the top-floor rooms (especially **No. 24**) with slanted ceilings and delightful views over the market. The north side of the piazza has numerous cafés with outside terraces, perfect for watching the activity at the daily market or the locals out on a quiet Sunday morning. The piazza is ringed with buildings from each of Verona's illustrious ages, but especially charming is the **Casa Mazzanti**, former residence of the Scala family, which displays the exterior frescoes so fancied by the Veneto architects.

Leave the piazza through the largest of the arches, the **Arco della Costa**, to enter another, grander space—the Piazza dei Signori. Immediately to the right is the 12th-century **Torre dei Lamberti**, set in a charming Romanesque courtyard embellished by a grand exterior pink marble staircase (1450). Climb to the top of the tower (or take the elevator) and enjoy spectacular views of the city. The tower is open Tuesday-Sunday (no midday closing); there's an admission charge. The piazza itself is a palimpsest of Verona's 2,000-year history. The recently excavated Roman pavings and mosaic flooring were probably in place as early as the first century BC. The medieval buildings enclosing the space were built between 1100 and 1400, and the graceful **Loggia del Consiglio** in the 1490s. Scanning the piazza's architecture, the visitor gets an immediate sense of the life that dominated each age: the scale, material, and majesty of the Romans; the threatened citadel mentality of the Middle Ages with crenellated and high unapproachable windows; and the ease and confidence of the Renaissance, with open porches and delicate carvings. An excellent spot to contemplate such a rare combination is the **Caffè Dante** (Piazza dei Signori 2, 045/592249), named after the poet's statue that presides over the square. The café invites a leisurely stay, from either its elegant salons with their silk-shaded lamps and white-coated waiters or from the terrace out into the piazza, where concerts are often held in warm weather. In addition to café fare, a full restaurant menu is offered. It's open daily, 9AM-1AM; closed Monday in winter.

Abutting the 11th-century church of **Santa Maria Antica** are the **Arche Scaligere** (Scaligere Arches; at Via Arche Scaligere), five tombs and three statues of the leaders of the Scala family. The majority are enclosed in a tiny corner cemetery with masterfully worked iron fences depicting the Scala (ladder) emblem. Most notable is the equestrian statue of *Cangrande I* that sits atop the church entry (the original is in the **Museo Castelvecchio**, see page 311). The statue's engaging smile seems proof of his joyful spirit. The tombs are open Tuesday-Sunday. Around the right corner is a plaque celebrating the 13th-century Gothic **Casa di Romeo**.

The **Corso Sant'Anastasia** is lined with excellent antiques and carpet shops. Almost at the river is the church of **Sant'Anastasia**. Its unadorned 14th-century Gothic façade is complemented by exquisitely carved wooden doors. Just inside are two holy water fonts supported by hunchbacks known locally as the *Gobbi*. The sacristy at the back left contains the famous fresco by Pisanello of *St. George at Trebizond*, with its bizarre combina-

While he was in Vicenza, Francesco of Bologna invented italic type.

The Arco dell'Orologio in Padua was the first clock in Italy. Made in 1344, it displays the time, day of the month, phase of the moon, signs of the zodiac, and motion of the sun and the planets.

I have now packed my bags once more. Tomorrow morning I am going to travel on the Brenta by boat. It rained today but it is now clear again, and I hope to see the lagoons in brilliant sunshine and send greetings to my friends from the embrace of the Queen Bride of the sea.

—Goethe, *Italian Journey*

VENETIAN VICTUALS

Venice, the city that brought pepper and coffee to the West and such civilized eating utensils as the fork and glassware to the table, has a distinguished culinary tradition. Today, the main legacy that lives on in Venice's restaurants is the sea.

A full Venetian meal begins with a selection of seafood antipasto, bits of *seppia* (cuttlefish), *scampi* (shrimp), *bottarga* (tuna eggs), or *ostriche alla veneziana* (oysters with caviar). Even risotto dishes have a special sealike texture in Venice. Locals like them *ondoso*—literally "wavy," meaning creamier than you'll encounter in other parts of Italy. One of the most unusual risotto dishes is the black *risotto di seppie* or *risotto nero,* which gets its color from the ink of the cuttlefish.

The best-known *secondo piatto* (main course) in Venice is *fegato alla veneziana,* liver and onions, prepared with a delicacy matched nowhere else and often accompanied by pale polenta from the nearby Friuli region. Carpaccio is another popular dish. As served at **Harry's Bar** (proprietor Arrigo Cipriani claims to have invented it), the dish is thinly sliced raw beef topped with Parmesan cheese, though variations made with fish and other ingredients have sprung up all over. Of course, seafood is a natural choice in Venice, and local restaurants do wonders with the humble dried salt cod called *baccalà*. *Alla veneziana* is made with onions and anchovies, *alla vicentina* adds milk and Parmesan cheese, and *mantecata* is made with olive oil and parsley. *Seppie alla veneziana* is cuttlefish cooked in white wine and its own black ink; *bisato* is eel, served *alla veneziana* (sautéed in olive oil with bay leaves and vinegar) or *sull'ara* (baked with bay leaves). There are also seemingly endless local fish, all with unfathomable dialect names. Among the most popular are *bransin* (or *branzino*, a type of sea bass) and the tiny soft-shell crabs called *moleche*.

The most popular wines in Venice are the white Pinot Blanco and Pinot Grigio, which make excellent accompaniments for the seafood, and the dry red Merlot, which goes well with meat dishes. Before, during, and after meals, however, most Venetians sip Prosecco—a light, sparkling white. Meals are often finished with a grappa (the Italian aquavit) or *sgroppino*, a refreshing combination of lemon ice cream, vodka, and Prosecco wine.

Inexpensive eating options are the taverns known as *bacari*, which serve a wine pick-me-up called an *ombra*, along with *cicchetti,* or finger food. These little plates of seafood, vegetables, cheese, and prosciutto are filling, and *bacari* can be great places to meet the locals.

tion of elegant costumes, exotic animals, and hanging criminals.

The nearby **Bar La Cappa** (Piazzetta Molinari Bra 1, 045/8004516) features an attractive garden terrace that provides excellent views over the **Ponte di Pietra** to the **Teatro Romano**, built in the first century BC. Charmingly banked on the slopes of the Colle di San Pietro, the café reminds the viewer how elegant ancient life was here when strollers could amble from the Arena to the smaller theater for an evening's entertainment. It's open Monday-Saturday, 11AM-2AM.

The nearby 12th-century **Duomo** (Piazza Duomo) is an intriguing combination of Romanesque and Gothic elements. From the lion-guarded porch and comical animal capitals to the wide-staring statues on the façade, the cathedral reminds one of an age when every Crusade introduced new ideas and new images into architecture. The interior atmosphere of light provides an appropriate setting for Titian's dynamic *Assumption* (1530s) in the chapel to the left of the entrance.

A southward jog back toward Piazza dei Signori leads past **Porta Borsari**, the original toll entry to Roman Verona, and to the **Castelvecchio** (Corso Cavour and Rigaste San Zeno), built in the 1300s. Here again is the sense of medieval times. Built as an important fortress for the Scaligeri, the castle is now a restored museum that houses an impressive Gothic sculpture collection, as well as paintings by such masters as Pisanello, Jacopo and Giovanni Bellini, Mantegna, Veronese, Tintoretto, Bassano, Lotto, and others. The museum is open Tuesday-Sunday (no midday closing); there's an admission charge.

One of the loveliest Romanesque churches in Northern Italy, **San Zeno** (Piazza San Zeno), was founded in 1120. The stunning reliefs on the right façade by Nicolò from the Old Testament portray an Eve confronting God with a look full of accusation and disappointment, while the reliefs to the left by Guglielmo are peculiarly secular. Yet nothing matches the vigorous charm of the justly famed bronze doors! A combination of childlike innocence and imagination makes the 48 panels so appealing that replicas have been created for tourist stores throughout the town. The spacious church interior, with its ship's-keel wooden ceiling built originally by local bargemen, continues the delight begun outside. Romanesque capitals with fabulous beasts and distorted figures display the medieval mind, while the main altarpiece by Mantegna (1457) ushers in the finest sense of Renaissance order.

While there are numerous fine restaurants in Verona, none surpasses **Ristorante 12**

The Best

Gregory Dowling

Novelist/Professor, Venice University

Santa Maria dei Miracoli—A church that is one single work of art. It's become a cliché to describe it as a jewel, but that's what it is: tiny, precious, and beautifully chiseled. (Often chosen for fashionable weddings.)

Cima da Conegliano—A painter usually seen as a minor follower of Bellini's, but Bellini's *Baptism of Christ* in Vicenza came after Cima's *Baptism* in the church of **San Giovanni in Bragora**. Look out for his paintings in the churches of **Madonna dell'Orto** and **Carmini**. Rapt but solid figures against enchanting backgrounds recall the hills around his own hometown.

Via Garibaldi—At any time of day, but particularly around 7PM. It's a long, wide, and bustling street that also serves as a market, children's play area, and general meeting place. It helps to clear the mind of all clichés about melancholy, dying Venice.

Campo Arsenale—The magnificent entrance to Venice's former shipyards, guarded by great stone lions, plundered from Greece. Two bars with tables outside provide a good place for musing on the changes of history—or just for enjoying the best *tramezzini* (half sandwiches) in Venice (the bar by the canal).

Calle Varisco—The narrowest alley in Venice. I won't say where it is: the fun lies entirely in the search.

Apostoli (Corticelle San Marco 5, off Corso Porto Borsari, 045/596999). The theatrical entrance of frescoed vaulted ceilings, linen-draped tables, and silk-softened lamps creates a modern equivalent of ancient sophistication. The entrance is flanked by a staggering display of cheeses, complemented by a table of various antipasti. It is open Tuesday-Saturday, lunch and dinner; Sunday, lunch. Reservations are recommended for dinner. www.12apostoli.it

Another taste treat awaits at **Il Desco** (Via Dietro San Sebastiano 7, between Via Leoni and Via Nizza, 045/595358). The restaurant was recently awarded two Michelin stars. The ambience here artfully combines the old and the new: enormous Murano chandeliers, glazed terra-cotta walls, beamed ceilings, and gilded mirrors, complemented with contemporary paintings and glamorous table settings that include orchids and lilies. The menu (helpfully printed in English) is another blend of tradition and innovation. Extensive antipasti lead to *primi piatti* (first courses) such as *gnocchetti* (little dumplings) with basil and a seafood sauce, ravioli with beans and (unusually) fried bresaola, and fillet of John Dory with asparagus, artichoke, and pistachio. The wine cellar features important Italian and French vintages. The restaurant is open Monday-Saturday, lunch and dinner; it is closed the last two weeks in June. Reservations are required.

At the delightful **La Torretta** (Piazza Broilo 1, between Ponte di Pietra and Vicolo Broilo, 045/592752), a meal begins with an enormous antipasto buffet from which you can select endless versions of local vegetables, *salumi* (cold meats), and cheeses. Follow with a vegetable pasta, such as *pasta di zucca con burro e salvia* (ravioli with pumpkin, butter, and sage) or *penne con carote e panna* (with grated carrots and cream). Both second courses and desserts vary with the season, but are not confined to specialties of the Veneto. In summer, the modern art-filled interior extends out into the piazza with huge white umbrella-covered tables and small lanterns. The restaurant is open Monday-Saturday, lunch and dinner.

Osteria dal Duca (Via Arche Scaligere 2, at Via Nizza, 045/594474) is situated in the building known as Casa di Romeo (Romeo's House), which is in fact the former home of the Montecchi family. Unbelievably inexpensive, with a rustic charm emanating both from the beamed ceilings and the family owners' affection, this eatery offers a lengthy quasi-traditional menu including various dishes involving horsemeat and the favorite dish cooked at home by Italian late-night diners, *spaghetti aglio, olio, e pepperoncini* (pasta with garlic, oil, and red pepper flakes). The desserts follow the seasons, focusing on fruit-and-ricotta tarts, and the delightful white wine from the region, Bianco di Custoza, is the house offering. There is a set menu, which is usually to be trusted. Dal Duca is open

One of the oldest Italian drinking toasts can be attributed to the Venetians:

"Che ben beve ben dorme;

Chi ben dorme mal no pensa;

Chi mal no pensa mal no fa;

Chi mal no fa in Paradiso va;

Ora ben beve che Paradiso avere."

(He who drinks well, sleeps well; He who sleeps well does not think bad thoughts; He who does not think bad thoughts does not act badly; He who does not act badly will go to heaven; Since you are going to heaven, drink up.)

Aspects of Venice

Prosecco
Light and refreshing, Prosecco is Italy's gift to lovers of bubbles everywhere. From the area around Conegliano (no coincidence, home of Italy's greatest wine school), this delicious fizz comes *frizzante* or *spumante* (semi or fully sparkling) and *secco* or *amabile*. A single grape creates the wine (Prosecco, oddly enough), and one of its great joys is its simple purity of taste. It makes wonderful cocktails, most famous of which is the Harry's Bar Bellini, made with Prosecco and fresh peach purée (and therefore available only at reputable bars in the summer). There are variations, such as the Mimosa (with orange juice) and the Tiziano (red grape juice). But Walter, barman at the Cipriani, has created the Canaletto, which combines Prosecco with fresh raspberry purée. Heavenly! There is also a nonsparkling version of Prosecco (*prosecco spento*), and the grape does give a lovely, fairly dry grappa. All bars will sell you Prosecco by the flute for a risibly small sum. Go on . . . effervesce!

Chorus
This is a program for the preservation of the artistic heritage within Venice's churches. It covers 13 churches, and the Churches of Venice Association, which runs it, organizes the tours. The churches covered are Santa Maria del Giglio, Santo Stefano, Santa Maria Formosa, Santa Maria Miracoli, Santa Maria Gloriosa Frari, San Paolo, San Giacomo dell'Orio, San Stae, Sant'Alvise, Madonna dell'Orto, San Pietro di Castello, Redentore, and San Sebastiano. Tours: M-Sa, 10AM-5PM; Su, 1PM-5PM. Tickets are available for a single church or as a "Chorus Pass"—one of the great bargains of Venice—which gets you into all 13 churches. Information and reservations: 2750462; fax 2750494. www.chorus-ve.org

Wells
In almost all of the squares and *campos* that you visit, you will see little stone turrets. These are the wells of Venice. In times long past, it was necessary for each neighborhood to have its own water supply. And what a supply! The wells are an ingenious method of getting fresh drinking water to a population surrounded by undrinkable water. Each well is surrounded by four depressions about 4 meters (12 feet) away from it. These depressions collected the rainwater as it fell, which then drained into a cistern below. Sand within the cistern acted as a filter and then the well itself, a brick cylinder, stretched down, down, down. The lot was sealed with impenetrable clay to keep out the salt water. When running water was introduced to the city, the wells were sealed—hence the stout metal caps on them.

Pigeons
Many people in Venice are right with Tom Lehrer when he sings of "Poisoning Pigeons in the Park." Officials in Venice estimate the pigeon population at around 100,000. And cute as they might look fluttering around St. Mark's Square, they are seriously antisocial little creatures, as you know if you are one of the many unfortunates to have become a walking pigeon depository! The authorities have tried banning the feeding of pigeons (it carries a fine of about $50) to absolutely no effect, as well as sterilizing the birds with chemically treated birdseed (which they did not swallow). Should you be tempted to feed them anyway, remember that about 15% are infected with salmonella (and can infect you too!) and that that seed you feed them will become acid droppings, which eat away at the very stone of Venice itself, undoing much of the restoration work that is under way. Don't feed the pigeons!

Monday-Saturday, lunch and dinner.

Another restaurant where location is all is the **Ristorante Maffei**, situated in the Grand Palazzo Maffei (Piazza delle Erbe 38, 045/8010015). In the summer, the central courtyard is a wonderfully elegant place for dinner.

Any stroll through Verona offers a delightful chance to sample the wines of the region. As the Veneto has seventeen *D.O.C.* zones, and Verona hosts Italy's largest wine fair—the *Vinital*—in April each year, the selection in both bars and restaurants exceeds what the traveler normally expects. The reds from Bardolino, Valpolicella, and Breganze, the whites from Soave and Custoza, and the sparkling Prosecco from near Treviso provide a fine sampling of wines.

Verona's tourist office in **Palazzo Municipio** (Piazza Bra, between Via Pallone and the Arena, 045/592828) is open Monday-Friday.

Soave invites a leisurely stop for lunch on the trip back to Venice (take autostrada **A4** 13 kilometers—8 miles—east from Verona, and exit at Soave). With its dramatic 14th-century fortified walls and castle, plus numerous Gothic buildings, it is the sort of town harried travelers long for: close to the road, unspoiled, with an exalted history under the Scaligeri of Verona and a fine restaurant in a 14th-century palazzo. The **Ristorante Bruna & Gerry** (Via Roma 15, 045/7680337) serves all house-made pasta with original sauces in two small vaulted and columned dining rooms. It is open Monday, Wednesday-Sunday, lunch and dinner.

HISTORY

2000 BC The Etruscans build **Faesulae**, today's **Fiesole**.

205 BC Etruscans fall to Roman rule.

59 BC The town of Roman **Florentia** is founded.

AD 405 Roman troops defend Florence from an Ostrogoth siege in their last successful attempt to ward off the barbarian onslaught and the ensuing Dark Ages.

421 Venice's official founding, as the mainland peoples flee into the lagoon to escape the barbarian invasions.

532 The Byzantine Empire acknowledges early Venice's commerce and sea power.

639 The first basilica is erected on **Torcello**; it would be rebuilt in 864 and 1008.

697 Venice selects her first doge, initiating an 1,100-year tradition.

800 Charlemagne is crowned first Holy Roman Emperor by Pope Leo III. This act served to usher in the violent wars between forces of the pope and those loyal to the emperor for the ensuing centuries, often with Florence as the battleground.

810 Pépin, second son of Charlemagne, invades the lagoon in a failed attempt to force the Venetians to ally themselves with his father's empire and abandon their allegiance to Byzantium. Their spirited defense unites the islanders and confirms their invulnerability.

828 Two Venetians steal the body of St. Mark from Egypt, hiding it in a barrel of pork to discourage inspection by the Muslims. St. Mark becomes the patron saint of *La Serenissima* (Most Serene Republic).

832 The first church of **San Marco** is consecrated to hold the saint's remains.

976 The great fire that destroyed over 300 houses also burns the basilica of San Marco.

1013 Work on the monastery of **San Miniato al Monte** in Florence begins under the sponsorship of Bishop Hildebrand.

1025 Guido d'Arezzo of Tuscany invents the musical scale.

1062 After a victorious battle with Sicily, the Maritime Republic of **Pisa** fights with Venice for control of the Mediterranean.

1076 Matilda reigns as Countess of Tuscany. Creating a cultural center in her castle at Canossa in Emilia-Romagna, she gives support to artists from both Italy and the north, initiating a tradition of Tuscan and Florentine patronage.

1078 The population inside Florence's new walls reaches 20,000, demonstrating the increasing health and wealth of the citizenry, whose numbers had become as few as 1,000 in the sixth century after the collapse of the Roman Empire.

1094 The rebuilding and consecration of the basilica of San Marco makes it the most sumptuous church in the Western world.

1096 The Crusades begin with their reliance on Venice for transport; they will later prove both a highly profitable and shameful experience for Venice.

1104 Venice's famed **Arsenale** is constructed; it will be repeatedly enlarged.

1125 With Florence's trade and security at risk from the towns of Tuscany, she attacks various neighbors, finally capturing and destroying neighboring Fiesole.

1143 Venice engages her first battle on land, but the fighting is done by mercenaries.

1152 San Marco's campanile is completed 250 years after its founding stone was laid.

1170 With its population at over 30,000, Florence erects more extensive walls, complete with guarded gates and watchtowers.

1177 The Congress of Venice brings together Pope Alexander III, Emperor Barbarossa, and Doge Sebastiano Ziani for the meeting commemorated in many paintings.

1204 The infamous Fourth Crusade culminates in Venice's sack of Constantinople, an event that would enrich the city beyond measure and make the Republic ruler of "a quarter and a half of the Eastern Empire."

1216 The Guelphs, supporters of the pope, and the Ghibellines, followers of the emperor, begin their long-sustained quarrel that will divide Florence for generations.

1228 The new preaching order of the Franciscans establishes its presence just outside the walls of Florence with the building of the church of **Santa Croce**.

1230 The Dominicans and Franciscans start preaching in Venice.

1246 The Dominicans quickly follow the Franciscans in Florence with the construction of the church of **Santa Maria Novella** beyond the western gates.

1252 Florence mints the first floral-decorated *florin* and establishes its own emblems of a red lily on a white ground and the Marzocco lion.

1255 The Florentine government of the Guelphs initiates the building of the **Palazzo del Popolo**, later called the **Bargello**.

1257 Venice begins the first of a long series of wars with the Republic of Genoa over land and maritime trade.

1260 The Sienese defeat the Florentines at Montaperti, and the Ghibellines return to power in Florence—with the customary architectural destruction—for the final time.

1261 Marco Polo and his two uncles leave for their journey to the East, which would last 25 years and result in the famous *Travels of Marco Polo*.

1265 Dante Alighieri, Florence's most famous son, is born.

1267 The Guelphs retake Florence and retain control, paving streets, establishing merchant guilds, and ushering in a period of peace and prosperity.

1284 Venice begins to mint the *zecchino* (gold ducat), which will last until 1797.

1296 **Arnolfo di Cambio** begins the construction of a new cathedral, **Santa Maria del Fiore** (the **Duomo**) in Florence.

1299 **The Palazzo Vecchio**, Florence's civic center, is begun.

1302 Dante is exiled from Florence for political "intrigue" and monetary malfeasance. His continued writing in the Tuscan vernacular promoted the notion that Italian was suitable for literary works (prior to this, Latin was used). Dante begins *The Divine Comedy*.

1305 Cimabue dies. He is later described in *Lives of the Artists* by art historian Giorgio Vasari as the genius who began the rebirth, or *rinascimento*, of Italian painting.

1310 After a failed conspiracy to depose Doge Pietro Gradenigo, the Council of Ten is established to prevent future organized unrest.

1321 The death of Dante in Ravenna, in Emilia-Romagna.

1333 Florence is inundated by her first disastrous flood; destroying bridges, palaces, and lives, it plants an enduring fear of the **Arno**'s ravages.

1334 With **Giotto** as the head of the building of Florence's cathedral, work proceeds to make **Santa Maria del Fiore** a suitable landmark.

1339 **Treviso** becomes the first city of the **Veneto** under Venetian domination.

1345 The second **Ponte Vecchio** is completed by **Taddeo Gaddi** after the 12th-century bridge was swept away in a flood. The second floor of this two-story, arched bridge today connects the **Palazzo Pitti**, **Galleria degli Uffizi**, and numerous other palazzi.

1348 After a Venetian ship brings back bubonic plague from the East, three-fifths of Venice's population dies within 18 months.

1348-1393 The Black Plague decimates Florence, reducing the population by 50 percent to 50,000 people.

1350 Boccaccio creates the 100 stories that constitute the *Decameron*. Pisa's leaning **Torre** (tower) is completed.

1355 Doge Marino Falier is beheaded for conspiracy; his portrait in the **Palazzo Ducale** is the only one covered with a black cloth.

1378 The revolt of the *ciompi* (woolworkers) demonstrates the force of the guilds and the populace in demanding a voice in the operation of Florence.

1386 After 50 years of expansion in the Mediterranean, Venice occupies the island of Corfu, retaining it until the fall of the Republic.

1402 In Florence, **Ghiberti** defeats **Brunelleschi** in competition for the **Baptistry**'s north doors.

1404 **Vicenza**, **Belluno**, and **Bassano** come under the banner of *La Serenissima*, followed by **Padua** and **Verona**.

1420 The conquest of Udine and the regaining of Dalmatia increase Venice's power.

1425 Venice embarks on a disastrous series of wars over Lombardy, lasting nearly 30 years.

1425-1427 Masaccio's revolutionary painting of *The Trinity* at Florence's Santa Maria Novella employs the new discoveries by

Brunelleschi of the laws of perspective. He dies one year later, at age 27.

1432 The Sienese are defeated at the Battle of San Romano, celebrated in Uccello's three panels painted for the Medici.

1434 Cosimo de' Medici survives his family's political ousting and returns to Florence.

1436 The Duomo is finally completed by Brunelleschi and inaugurated with a grand ceremony.

1440 Florence is full of artists working under Medici patronage: Fra Filippo Lippi, Fra Angelico, and Donatello.

1452 Ghiberti installs the east doors—the "Gates of Paradise"—of Florence's Baptistry.

1453 The Ottoman Turks take Constantinople, ending the Byzantine Empire of the East and escalating their war against Venice for control of the Mediterranean.

1454 Piero della Francesca begins the fresco cycle *The Legend of the True Cross* in **Arezzo**'s **San Francesco** church.

1457 Cosimo de' Medici initiates construction of the Palazzo Pitti, ushering in a boom in palazzo-building.

1464 The death of Cosimo de' Medici the Elder places his politically untalented son, Piero, as head of the family and businesses. Under Piero, the Medici continue their artistic patronage: Gozzoli decorates the chapel of the **Palazzo Medici-Riccardi**; Pollaiuolo executes numerous commissions; and Botticelli puts various Medici members in his grand canvases.

1469 On the death of his father, Piero, 20-year-old Lorenzo de' Medici becomes the leader of Florence.

1473 After losing most of its Mediterranean territories to the Turks, Venice solidifies its acquisition of Cyprus.

1475 Venice's most valued *condottiere* (mercenary), Bartolomeo Colleoni, dies, leaving the city his enormous private fortune.

1478 The bloody Pazzi Conspiracy that attempted to assassinate Lorenzo de' Medici, and succeeded in murdering Giuliano, creates new fears for the future peace of Florence.

1481 Savonarola comes to Florence and begins his residence at the monastery of **San Marco** just when Florentine paintings are becoming more secular. This results in the monk giving even more fiery sermons.

1489 Queen Caterina Cornaro of Cyprus abdicates, ceding her powers to Venice in exchange for rule in Asolo.

1490 The young Michelangelo is invited to reside at the Palazzo Medici-Riccardi.

1492 The death of Lorenzo de' Medici places his lazy and incompetent son, Piero, in the thankless position of facing an inflamed citizenry as well as defending the city against troops from France and much of the peninsula.

1494 Florence's governors exile the Medici from the city "in perpetuity." King Charles VIII of France takes over the city and declares it a republic, while the Florentines loot and destroy much of the Medici's personal artistic legacy.

1497 Savonarola, put in charge of Florence by King Charles, initiates his "Bonfire of the Vanities" by piling mountains of luxury items in a pyre lit and celebrated by the "pious."

1498 After being excommunicated, tried, and tortured for heresy, Savonarola is burned at the stake in **Piazza della Signoria**.

1499 Portuguese explorer Vasco da Gama returns from his successful trip around the Cape of Good Hope, ending Venice's monopoly of the Mediterranean trade route to the East.

1504 Michelangelo completes the *David*, which is later transported with great ceremony into Piazza della Signoria after much discussion of where it might best issue its warning against tyranny.

1508 Venice's major enemies—the emperor, the pope, Spain, France, and Hungary—join forces in the League of Cambrai, with wars and deals that further doom Venice.

1512 After French forces leave Italy, the Medici return to Florence in triumph.

1513 Machiavelli, retired from the Florentine militia and resident of the nearby countryside, writes *The Prince*, his treatise of advice to rulers.

1520 **Michelangelo** begins architectural commissions for Florence that will continue throughout the decade, including the **Sacrestia Nuova** in the **Cappelle Medicee** and the staircase to the **Biblioteca Medicea-Laurenziana**.

1527 The appalling sack of Rome by Emperor Charles V, causing the fall of the

Medici Pope Clement VII, sends Florence into a renewed anti-Medici foment. To escape with their lives, Alessandro and Ippolito leave the city.

1530 With the pope's acceptance of imperial authority in Italy under Charles V, Florence surrenders after undergoing 10 months of starvation and disease. The Medici return.

1531 The impetuous and imperious Alessandro de' Medici becomes first Duke of Tuscany, angering the city with his tyrannical laws and appropriations of property.

1537 Alessandro is murdered by his companion and cousin Lorenzino de' Medici. The city selects 17-year-old Cosimo de' Medici to rule. He continues the Medici tradition with patronage of such major artists as Pontormo, Bronzino, Bandinelli, Giambologna, Ammannati, and Cellini.

1538 Venice loses the battle of Prevesa (Préveza in today's Greece); control of the seas passes to the Turks.

1560 Vasari, appointed as Cosimo de' Medici's architect for the reconstruction of the Palazzo Vecchio, executes his designs for the Galleria degli Uffizi.

1570 After establishing political unity throughout Tuscany for the first time, Cosimo de' Medici is granted the title of Grand Duke of Tuscany.

1571 The battle of Lepanto, fought with the combined forces of Venice and Spain, is the West's first decisive victory over the Turks and ends Ottoman control of the Mediterranean.

1574 Medici heir Francesco I succeeds his father and continues the family's art patronage. He commissions **Buontalenti** to build **La Tribuna**, the octagonal room in the Galleria degli Uffizi that now houses portraits.

1574 Venice hosts the young King Henry III of France in a series of splendid festivities so spectacular that they often appear on lists of the Republic's most important events.

1575 The plague once again reduces Venice's population to under 50,000, counting the painter Titian among its victims.

1577 Fire destroys the main halls of Venice's Palazzo Ducale, including many precious paintings.

1587 Ferdinando I succeeds his brother and enlarges the Medici's traditional concerns to include vast programs to help the poor. Construction of **Forte di Belvedere** begins.

1605 Venice is excommunicated by the pope and defended by Friar Paolo Sarpi.

1609 Cosimo II succeeds Ferdinando I for a brief, inauspicious reign.

1621 The near 50-year reign of Cosimo II's son, Ferdinando II, begins another of the depressing, though popular, rules that seem to plague the last Medici years.

1645 The 22-year Turkish siege of Candia, Crete, and final conquest further reduce Venice's power at sea.

1670 Ferdinando II's son Cosimo III succeeds his father and imprints his excessively pious stamp on the city, waging war on heresy and decadence with equal fervor.

1723 At age 52, Gian Gastone inherits the reign from his father, Cosimo III, ultimately ending his own rule in drunken lechery.

1733 Venice continues to decline in military and economic influence. She loses most of her remaining ports in the Mediterranean and much of her trade on land.

1737 After half the powers of Europe lay claim to the Tuscan Succession—the Medici dynasty nearly defunct—Francis, the Austrian Duke of Lorraine, takes over as Grand Duke. The House of Lorraine and its imperial Habsburg in-laws remain in power—except for the Napoleonic era—until 1860.

1743 The last Medici, Anna Maria Lodovica, dies. Her will requires that all family treasures remain within the borders of Tuscany.

1744 The Venetian Republic embarks on her last important public building—the sea walls. For nearly 40 years, the construction of protecting walls between Pellestrina and Chioggia on the mainland continues as Venice commits all her resources to this final defense of the lagoon.

1789 The first non-Venetian doge in over 1,000 years, and the last to wear the ducal bonnet, is elected—Lodovico Manin from northern Friuli.

1791 **La Fenice** opera house is built in Venice and named after the mythological phoenix.

1797 The world's longest-lived republic capitulates without resistance to the demands of Napoleon, who claims he will "be an Attila to the state of Venice."

1798 Venice is ceded to Austria.

1801 Napoleon appropriates Tuscany, eventually naming his pleasure-loving sister Elisa Grand Duchess.

1805-1814 Venice is removed from Austrian rule and comes under French dominion. Napoleon transforms the Italian Republic into a kingdom and crowns himself King and Emperor of Italy.

1814 Tuscany returns to Florentine hands with Grand Duke Ferdinand III.

1815 Venice is once again ceded to Austria. The four gilded bronze horses that Napoleon had removed from the basilica of San Marco are returned.

1837 After a fire destroys La Fenice, the opera house reopens, fulfilling the prophecy of the bird rising from its own ashes.

1846 A railway causeway is built, making Venice more accessible to outsiders.

1851 John Ruskin publishes his three volumes of *The Stones of Venice,* creating an even larger foreign audience than ever for the city.

1860 Tuscany votes to unite with Victor Emmanuel II's government. The king moves into the Palazzo Pitti.

1861 Italy becomes a united kingdom.

1865 Italy welcomes Florence as its new capital.

1866 Venice joins the new Italian state.

1870 The final unification of Italy. The capital transfers to Rome. Increasing numbers of Americans join British expatriates in Florence.

1895 The first art *Biennale* is held in Venice.

1896 The first performance of *La Bohème,* written by Tuscany's most beloved composer, Giacomo Puccini, takes place.

1902 Venice's **Campanile di San Marco** collapses on 14 July, filling the piazza with tons of debris but mercifully sparing the major buildings.

1912 The rebuilt campanile is inaugurated on 25 April, the Feast of St. Mark.

1915 Italy enters World War I on the side of the Allies.

1922-1926 Benito Mussolini rises to the helm of the country's first Fascist regime.

1930 Over 100,000 people hear Mussolini speak in the Piazza della Signoria in Florence.

1931 A causeway is built from Mestre to Venice, opening the edge of the city up to vehicular traffic.

1932 The *Biennale di Venezia* for theater, music, and cinema is established, enhancing the city's international reputation as a thriving arts center. The festival continues to this day.

1938 Hitler joins Mussolini in a parade through Florence.

1940 Italy enters World War II against Great Britain and France.

1943 The Germans take control of Florence. Mussolini is arrested by Italian partisans.

1944 Florence is freed by the Allies and Italian partisans after the Germans destroy all of the city's bridges except the Ponte Vecchio.

1945 British armed forces enter Venice. Mussolini is executed.

1946 The first Italian Republic is proclaimed.

1966 The worst flood in Florence's history, on 4 November, decimates irreplaceable artworks and damages architecture. Within 10 years most of the restoration is completed, thanks to a commitment from Florence's government and the assistance of other countries.

Coincidentally, November sees the most catastrophic downpour in Venice's history. The city's dangerous situation is taken seriously and the Venice in Peril Committee begins its work.

1973 Venice seals off the artesian wells at industrial Marghera, west of the Mestre causeway, to protect the city from further sinking.

1984 The most splendid of the Gothic palaces on the Canal Grande, the **Ca' d'Oro**, is reopened after a 15-year restoration. Fiat (the automobile manufacturer) buys the **Palazzo Grassi** and establishes a new center for art on the canal.

1990 Masaccio's (and Lippi's) frescoes in the **Brancacci Chapel** in Florence's **Santa Maria del Carmine** are restored.

1993 The Galleria degli Uffizi in Florence is damaged by a terrorist bomb and five people are killed. Most of the artwork is miraculously spared.

1995 After a 15-year restoration, the frescoes in the cupola of Florence's Duomo are once again visible to the public.

1996 La Fenice burns down a second time, although the façade remains intact.

1997 Venice dredges its canals for the first time in 50 years, returning to a tradition that dates back centuries.

2002 In September, Venetian authorities crack down on boats plying the Grand Canal and its tributaries, turning the area into a veritable speed trap. Officials say big waves caused by reckless navigation have had corrosive effects on the foundations of historic buildings and also endangered gondolas.

More than 10,000 anti-globalization protestors gather in Florence in November for a meeting that culminates in an antiwar demonstration. Unable to get the venue for the European Social Forum changed, local officials have no choice but to build scaffolding around treasured sculptures.

2003 Officials in Venice declare that "tourism is killing the city" and set out a ten-point "code of conduct" to be observed by visitors. Instructions range from keeping to the right when walking along Venice streets and alleyways to the correct way to register a complaint.

2005 The Palazzo Zorzi hosts the launch of an important new work of research: "The Science of Saving Venice," an in-depth look at how science and scientists can help prevent Venice sinking forever.

Smoking is no longer allowed inside public places.

2006 Italy gives Italian citizens living abroad (including 3 million in the United States) the right to vote in the General Election.

INDEX

A

Abbate, Enrica **174** (bests)
Abbazia di San Gregorio **181**
Abbazia di Sant'Antimo **150**
Accademia Bridge (Ponte dell'Accademia) **180, 216**
Accommodations (Florence) **15**
Accommodations (Venice) **173**
Acqua al Due ***$ **113**
Acquacotta **$$ **107**
Additional Florence Highlights **130** (chapter)
Addresses **15**
Aeroporto Amerigo Vespucci **13**
Aeroporto Amerigo Vespucci, ground transportation **13**
Aeroporto Galileo Galilei **13**
Aeroporto Galileo Galilei, ground transportation **13**
Aeroporto Marco Polo **168**
Aeroporto Marco Polo, ground transportation **170**
An Affair of the Art **264**
Airlines (Aeroporto Amerigo Vespucci) **13**
Airlines (Aeroporto Galileo Galilei) **13**
Airlines (Aeroporto Marco Polo) **170**
Airlines (Italy) **3**
Airport services (Aeroporto Amerigo Vespucci) **13**
Airport services (Aeroporto Galileo Galilei) **13**
Airport services (Aeroporto Marco Polo) **168**
Airports (Florence) **13**
Airport (Venice) **168**
Al Bacareto ***$$ **188**
Albergaccio **142**
Albergo ai Do Mori $$ **190**
Albergo Cipriani $$$$ **282**
Albergo Firenze $ **29**
Albergo San Zulian $$ **186**
Al Bersagliere **304**
Alberti, Leon Battista **68, 80, 82**
Al Bottegon **303**
Albrici e Paderni **127**
Al Cacciatore **$ **281**
Al Covo **$$$ **277**
Alessandro Bizzari **36**
Alessandro Dari **58**
Alessi **25**
Alfredo Laggia **202**
Algiubagio ***$$ **254**
Al Grottino (Bar Enoteca) **306**
Alice's Masks Art Studio **94**
Alimentari Orizi **84**
Alinari Museum of the History of Photography (Museo di Storia della Fotografia Alinari) **82**
Aliseda **152**
All Antico Vinaio **$ **119**
Alla Vecchia Bettola **$$ **128**
Alle Murate ***$$$ **115**
Alle Testiere ***$$$ **267**
Al Lume di Candela **$$$ **87**
Al Marsili **164**
Al Mascareta ***$$ **267**
Al Ponte-Da Renzo **298**
Al Portico **38**
Ammannati, Bartolommeo **55, 86, 87, 96, 102, 103, 104**
Amon **$ **75**
Ando, Tadao **187**
Anfiteatro Romano **146**
Angela Caputi **126**
Angels **32**
Angolo di Tanit ***$$ **252**
Annalena $$ **59**
Antica Drogheria **141**
Antica Farmacia del Cinghiale **33**
Antica Farmacia di San Marco **91**
Antica Legatoria Piazzesi **203**
Antica Locanda Montín $ **216**
Antica Osteria l'Agania **138**
Antica Trattoria "da Bruno," 154
Antica Trattoria dei Paccagnella **308**
Antica Trattoria La Furatola ***$$$ **214**
Antica Trattoria Papei **164**
Antica Trattoria Poste Vecie ***$$$ **227**
Antiche Carampane **$$ **228**
Antichità V. Trois **202**
Anticlea Antiquariato **273**
Antico Caffè del Moro **82**
Antico Caffè Di Simo **144**
Antico Fattore **$$ **42**
Antico Locanda Al Gambero $$ **186**
Antico Martini **$$$ **195**
Antico Ristorante Beccherie **303**
Antico Ristoro di Cambi **$$ **123**
Antico Setificio Fiorentino **123**
Antinori, Piero **152** (bests)
Antiquità M **196**
Antiquus **188**
Antonio Frilli **79**
Aprile $$ **72**
Archbishop's Palace (Palazzo Arcivescovile) **19**
Arche Scaligere (Scaligere Arches) **310**
Archivio di Stato (State Archives) **231**
Arciconfraternità della Misericordia **20**
Arena **309**
Arezzo, Sansepolcro, and Cortona **136**
Arredamenti Castorina **125**
Arsenale **274**
Arte & Mestieri **53**
Arte Creta **25**
Arte del Mosaico **117**
Arte di Gioire **123**
Artigianato Veneziano **188**
Asolo and Maser **296**
Aspects of Venice **313**
Assolibri **79**
Atelier Nube **188**
Aulenti, Gae **67, 187**
Avignonesi/Classica **152**
Avventurino **216**

B

Bacaro **$$$ **196**
Bácaro Jazz **$$ **183**
Bacino Orseolo **194**
Badia a Coltibuono **143**
Badia Fiorentina (Florentine Abbey) **36**
Baldini ***$$ **66**
Baldini (metal workshop) **68**
Baldovino *$$ **118**
Banchi Lamberto **125**
Bapistry of San Giovanni (Battistero di San Giovanni) **24**
Bar All'Angolo **201**
Bar Belle Donna **84**
Bar Enoteca (Al Grottino) **306**
Bargello **36**
Baroni, Nello **67**
Bartolozzi e Maioli **126**
Basilica di San Domenico **162**
Basilica di San Francesco **137**
Basilica Palladiana **305**
Bassano del Grappa **298**
Battistero (Volterra) **166**
Battistero di San Giovanni (Baptistery of San Giovanni) **24**

Battistero di San Giovanni (Siena) **161**
Bazzani, Cesare **121**
Bazzani Camilla **211**
Bar **205**
Beacci Tornabuoni $$ **85**
Beccofino *$$$ **124**
Beggiato, P. L. **202** (bests)
Bellettini $ **71**
Belluomini, Alfredo **165**
Beltrami **82**
Bene Vobis **127**
Berardi, Piero **67**
Bergamasco, Guglielmo **179**
Berndt, Louise **288** (bests)
Biblioteca Correr (Correr Library) **198**
Biblioteca del Conservatorio di Musica Luigi Cherubini (Library of the Luigi Cherubini Conservatory of Music) **99**
Biblioteca Marucelliana (Marucelli Library) **94**
Biblioteca Nazionale (National Library) **121**
Biblioteca Nazionale Marciana (St. Mark's Library) **197**
Biblioteca Querini Stampalia (Querini Stampalia Library) **267**
Bicycles, Florence **14**
Bistrot de Venise ***$$$ **186**
BM Bookshop **81**
Boats **170**
Boboli Gardens (Giardino di Boboli) **60** (map)
Bojola **75**
Bon, Bartolomeo **197, 218, 232, 263**
Bondiuti, Telemaco **00, 00**
Borghese Palace Art Hotel $$ **112**
Borgo Antico (Greve) **142**
Borgo Antico (Oltrarno) *$$ **128**
Borgo di San Frediano **124**
Borgo San Lorenzo **104**
Borsalino **33**
Boschetti, Lorenzo **213, 219**
Boscolo Hotel Astoria $$$$ **70**
Bosio, Giovanni Antonio **84**
Bottega d'Arte Favelli **19**
Bottega del Rame **152**
Botteganova **164**
Bowden, John-Henry **230** (bests)
Bracchetti, Fra Giovanni **70**
Breganze **299**
Brenta Riviera **300**
Bridge of Sighs (Ponte dei Sospiri) **201**
Bridges of Venice **217**
Brioni **30**
Brunelleschi, Filippo **12, 20, 24, 38, 52, 55, 70, 75, 77, 97, 102, 103, 120, 128**
Brunellesco **102**
Brunello Restaurant and Bar **$$$ **41**
Buca di Sant'Antonio **146**
Buca Lapi *$$ **76**
Buca Mario **$$ **78**
Bulgarella, Mary Westerman **105** (bests)
Buontalenti, Bernardo **19, 29, 43, 44, 47, 60, 61, 74, 83, 86, 91, 105, 128, 148**
Burano/San Francesco del Deserto/Mazzorbo/Torcello **286**
Busa-alla-Torre **$$ **284**
Buses (Florence) **13, 14**
Buses (Italy) **3, 13**
Buses (Venice) **170**
Bus station (Long-Distance) (Florence) **14**
Bus Station (Long-Distance) (Venice) **170**

C

Caccini, Giovanni Battista **29**
Cacciolato **304**
Ca' da Mosto **179**
Ca' d'Oro (Canal Grande) **179**
Ca' d'Oro (Cannaregio) **256**
Cafaggi **$$ **93**
Cafebar La Bibliothèque **243**
Caffè Chioggia **$$ **155**
Caffè delle Carrozze *$ **47**
Caffè Fiaschetteria Italiana **150**
Caffè Florian **$$$ **198**
Caffè Italiano **$ **33**
Caffè La Posta *$ **33**
Caffè Lavena **$$$ **194**
Caffè Pedrocchi **307**
Caffè Pitti **$ **54**
Caffè Poliziano **152**
Caffè Quadri **$$$ **195**
Caffè Rossa **210**
Caffè Santa Trinità *$ **126**
Ca' Foscari (Canal Grande) **180**
Ca' Foscari (Dorsoduro) **210**
Ca' Giustinian **180**
Calle delle Botteghe **188**
Calle delle Mende **223**
Calle del Paradiso **266**
Calle Larga XXII Marzo **204**
Calzoleria Bologna **23**
Ca' Malcanton $$ **245**
Ca' Maria Adele $$$ **223**
Camiceria San Marco **206**
Cammillo **$$ **126**
Campanile **23**
Campanile di San Marco (St. Mark's Bell Tower) **197**
Campiello $$ **275**
Campiello Barbaro **219**
Campiello Due Pozzi **271**
Campo Beccarie **227**
Campo dei Mori **249**
Campo del Ghetto Nuovo **250**
Campo di Ruga **275**
Campo San Bartolomeo **184**
Campo San Giacomo **231**
Campo San Giacomo dell'Orio **241**
Campo San Gregorio **219**
Campo San Luca **185**
Campo San Paolo **234**
Campo Santa Margherita **210**
Campo Santa Maria Formosa **266**
Campo Santa Maria Mater Domini **242**
Campo Sant'Angelo (or Sant'Anzolo) **189**
Campo Santi Giovanni e Paolo **262**
Campo San Tomà **235**
Campo Santo Stefano **201**
Campo San Zaccaria **273**
Campo San Zan Degolà **237**
Campo San Zanipolo (Campo Santi Giovanni e Paolo) **262**
Canal Grande **176** (chapter and map)
Cannaregio **246** (chapter and map)
Cantina Do Mori ***$$ **229**
Cantina Do Spade **$$ **229**
Cantinetta Antinori **$$$ **76**
Cantinetta da Verrazzano *$ **30**
Capella delle Volte **163**
Capella di Piazza (Chapel of the Square) **161**
Ca' Pesaro (Canal Grande) **178**
Ca' Pesaro (Santa Croce) **239**
Ca' Pisani Hotel $$$$ **223**
Capocaccia *$$ **87**
Cappella degli Scrovegni (Scrovegni Chapel) **307**
Cappella di Santa Fina **155**
Cappella Pazzi and Museo dell'Opera di Santa Croce (Pazzi Chapel and Santa Croce Museum) **120**
Cappella Rucellai (Rucellai Chapel) (Santa Maria Novella) **80**

Cappelle Medicee (Medici Chapels) **103**
Cappelli-Croce di Savoia **144**
Ca' Rezzonico **180**
Ca' Rezzonico—Museo del Settecento Veneziano (Museum of the Venetian 17th Century) **213**
Cartavenezia **242**
Caruso Jazz Internet Cafe **$$ **42**
Casa Artigiana dell'Orafo **47**
Casa Buonarroti (Michelangelo Museum) **115**
Casa di Bianca Cappello **128**
Casa di Galileo Galilei **57**
Casa di Giacomo Puccini **165**
Casa di Giulietta **309**
Casa di Goldoni **234**
Casa di Petrarca (Petrarch's House) **277**
Casa di Riposa Israelitica **251**
Casa e Museo di Dante (Dante House and Museum) **32**
Casa Guidi **54**
Casa Mazzanti **310**
Casa-Torre degli Amadei **42**
Casa-Torre dei Buondelmonti **87**
Casci $ **99**
Casino di San Marco **91**
Cassetti **49**
Castellina in Chianti **141**
Castello **260** (chapter and map)
Castello di Spaltenna **143**
Castello di Uzzano **142**
Castello di Vicchiomaggio **141**
Castello Inferiore (Lower Castle) **298**
Castelvecchio **311**
Cathedral of Santa Maria del Fiore (Duomo) **20**
Cavalier **202**
Cavatappi **$$ **186**
Celestino **$$ **53**
Cellerini **78**
Cellerini—Forniture per Orafi **48**
Cenacoli (Last Suppers) **132**
Cenacolo di Fuligno **91**
Cenacolo di San Salvi **131**
Cenacolo di Sant'Appollonia **91**
Cenedese **198**
Centrale (San Lorenzo) $ **102**
Centrale (San Marco) **$$$ **193**
Central Market (Mercato Centrale) **94**
Centro degli Studi di Storia dei Tessuto e dei Costume (Center for the Study of Textile and Clothing History) **241**
Centro Di **57**
Centro Storico **17** (chapter), **18** (map)
Cerrutti, Giulio **124**
Certosa di Maggiano **163**
A Challenge . . . **23**
Chianti Classico Country **141**
Chiesa dei Scalzi **178**
Chiesa dell'Angelo Raffaele **214**
Chiesa di San Martino **289**
Child's Play **203**
Chini, Galileo **165**
Chiostri di Santa Maria Novella (Cloisters of Santa Maria Novella) **70**
Chiostro del Convento di Santa Trinità (Cloister of the Convent of the Holy Trinity) **83**
Chiostro dello Scalzo **91**
Chiostro di San Lorenzo (Cloister of San Lorenzo) **104**
Chiusarelli **163**
Cibrèo ****$$$ **111**
Cibrèo: Teatro del Sale ****$$ **111**
Cigoli, Ludovico Cardi da **29, 52**
Cimitero degli Inglesi (English Cemetery) **106**
Cinema Odeon **83**
Cirri **42**
City maps **4**
Climate (Florence) **15**
Climate (Italy) **4**
Climate (Venice) **173**
Clock Tower (Torre dell'Orologio) **191**
Cloister of the Convent of the Holy Trinity (Chiostro del Convento di Santa Trinità) **83**
Cloister of San Lorenzo (Chiostro di San Lorenzo) **104**
Cloisters of Santa Maria Novella (Chiostri di Santa Maria Novella) **70**
Coco Lezzone **$$ **83**
Codussi, Mauro **178, 180, 191, 194, 228, 255, 258, 259, 263, 267, 273, 293**
Cohen, Suzanne B. **159** (bests)
C.O.I. (Commercio Oreficeria Italiana) **39**
Coin (Venice) **259**
Collegio Greco e Chiesa dei Greci **272**
Collezione Peggy Guggenheim (Peggy Guggenheim Collection) **219**
Colli **50** (chapter and map)
Collodi **143**
Colomba $$ **99**
Colombini, Donatella Cinelli **142** (bests)
Colonna della Giustizia **86**
Cominelli, Andrea **252**
Commercio Oreficeria Italiana (C.O.I.) **39**
Conca D'Oro *$ **271**
Conservatorio di Musica Benedetto Marcello **207**
Consulates (Florence) **15**
Consulates (Venice) **173**
Contini Galleria d'Arte **202**
Convento di San Francesco **158**
Corbellini, Carlo **179**
Correr Library (Biblioteca Correr) **198**
Corso Andrea Palladio **304**
Corti del Milion **259**
Cortona **136**
Cose Così **112**
Crafts, Florentine **26**
Cristallo $$ **292**
Croce al Trebbio **75**
Cucciolo **30**
Customs **4**
Customs Point (Punta della Dogana **181, 222**

D

10 Ala Napoleonica **196**
Da Benvenuto *$ **119**
da Bologna, Lorenzo **305**
da Como, Guidetto **145**
Da Ganino **$$ **31**
d'Agnolo, Baccio **20, 62, 86, 102, 116, 129**
Dal Baffo **$ **290**
Dal Falco **151**
Da Luca e Fred ***$ **252**
da Maiano, Benedetto **83**
da Maiano, Giuliano **30, 76, 83**
Danesin **304**
Daniela Ghezzo **192**
Danny Rock *$$ **112**
Da Noi *$ **108**
Dante House and Museum (Casa e Museo di Dante) **32**
Dante's Church—Santa Margherita dei Cerchi **29**
da Ponte, Antonio **179, 231**
da Sangallo, Antonio **38, 65, 106, 152, 166**
da Sangallo, Aristotele **90**

da Sangallo, Francesco **62**
da Sangallo, Giuliano **38, 70, 106, 116, 128, 148**
da Vicenza, Rocco **305**
De Carlo, Giancarlo **290**
dei Grigi, Gian Giacomo **179, 232**
dei Rosso, Zanobi **29**
Del Carmine **$$ **124**
del Mozzi, Andrea **62**
del Rosso, Zanobi **60**
Del Secco **51**
del Tasso, Giovanni Battista **37**
De' Medici *$$ **70**
Denker, Eric **175** (bests)
De Pisis Restaurant ***$$$$ **205**
Desmo **82**
Desserts **240**
di Barsento, Puccio Pucci **155** (bests)
di Cambio, Arnolfo **20, 40, 117**
di Cione, Benci **30, 40**
di Fioravante, Neri **30, 86**
Diladdarno **$$ **129**
Diletti, Stefano **20**
Dino ***$$ **116**
Dino Bartolini **104**
Diva e Maceo **152**
di Zanobi, Mariotto **38**
Doges' Palace (Palazzo Ducale) **199**
Dolce Vita **125**
Dolci Veneziani **240**
Don Chisclotte ***$$$ **89**
Donnini *$ **28**
Don't Leave Florence Without . . . **78**
Don't Leave Venice Without . . . **290**
Dorando **158**
Dorsoduro **208** (chapter and map)
Dosio, Giovanni Antonio **19**
Dowling Gregory **312** (bests)
Drinking **4**
Driving (Florence) **13, 14**
Driving (Italy) **3**
Driving (Venice) **170**
Drugs **4**
Duomo (Asolo) **297**
Duomo (Cathedral of Santa Maria del Fiore) **20**
Duomo (Este) **302**
Duomo (Montagnana) **302**
Duomo (Sansepolcro) **140**
Duomo (Siena) **161**
Duomo (Treviso) **303**
Duomo (Verona) **311**
Duomo (Vicenza) **305**
Duomo (Volterra) **166**
Duomo Museum (Museo dell'Opera del Duomo) **21**
Duomo Vecchio **301**

E

Eastern Mediterranean Synagogue (Scuola Levantina) **251**
Eat, Drink, and Be Merry at Florence's Wine Bars **74**
El Canapon **241**
Elite **191**
Elto *$$ **119**
Embassies (Florence) **15**
Embassies (Venice) **173**
Emergencies (Florence) **15**
Emergencies (Venice) **172**
Emilia **287**
Emilio **154**
Emilio Pucci (Santa Maria Novello) **85**
Emporio Pettenello **210**
Emporium **52**
English Cemetery (Cimitero degli Inglesi) **106**
Ennio **297**
Enoteca Al Volto ***$ **185**
Enoteca in Asolo **297**
Enoteca Bar FuoriPorta **$ **59**
Enoteca Italiana **163**
Enoteca La Caneva Dae Tose **266**
Enoteca Romano Gambi **42**
Erboristeria Inglese (at the Officina de' Tornabuoni) **84**
Erboristeria Palazzo Vecchio **40**
Eremitani **307**
Ermenegildo Zegna **82**
Este **301**
Etiquette **4**
Evoè **152**

F

Fabbri, Elisabetta **193**
Fabbriche Nuove di Rialto **179**
Fabbriche Vecchie di Rialto **179**
Falcini, Mariano **58, 109**
Falconieri, Paolo **104**
Fallani Best **58**
Fancelli, Luca **55**
Fanciulla del West **144**
Fantoni Libri Arte **185**
Farmacia Molteni **33**
Fattoria dei Barbi **151**
Fattoria Pulcino **153**
Fattoria Querce Sola **142**
Fattoria Vignale **143**
Ferri, Antonio Maria **22, 86, 123**
Ferri, Ciro **123**
Ferro & Lazzarini **285**
Fiaschetteria Nuvoli **$ **19**
Fiaschetteria Toscana ***$$$$ **258**
Fiaschetteria Vecchio Casentino *$ **120**
Fiaschetteria Zanobini **100**
Ficaibi & Balloni **62**
Fiesole: A Jewel in the Florentine Hills **96**
Films **238**
Fiore ***$$ **189**
Fiorella Gallery **201**
Firenze of Papier Mâché **55**
Fish Market (Pescheria) (Canal Grande) **179**
Fish Market (Pescheria) (San Paolo) **227**
Florence **11** (map)
Florence Area **130** (map)
Florence Day Trips-The Treasures of Tuscany **136** (chapter)
Florence Orientation **11** (chapter)
Florentine Abbey (Badia Fiorentina) **36**
Florentine Crafts **26**
Foggini, Gian Battista **57, 123**
Fondaco dei Tedeschi (Germans' Warehouse) **179, 183**
Fondaco dei Turchi (Turks' Warehouse) **178**
Fondamenta della Misericordia **253**
Fondamenta del Soccorso **212**
Fondamenta San Sebastiano **212**
Fondamenta Sant' Anna **278**
Fondamente Nuove **254**
Fondazione Accademia Musicale Chigiana **163**
Fondazione Salvatore Romano **128**
Fonte dei Dolci **93**
Fonte Gaia **161**
Fonterutoli **142**
Food, Tuscan **114**
Food, Venetian **311**
Formenton, Tommaso **305**
Forte dei Marmi **164**
Forte di Belvedere **61**
Fortezza (Volterra) **167**
Fortezza da Basso **65**
Fortezza Medicea **163**
Foscari, Antonio **187**
Fountain **66**
Fra Angelico Museum (Museo dell'Angelico) **92**
Franceschi **129**
Francesco **124**
Francesco, Giovanni **90**
Franchetti, Amerigo **148** (bests)

Franco Maria Ricci **76**
Frari (Santa Maria Gloriosa dei Frari) **232**
Fratelli Piccini **49**
Fratelli Poli **$$ **31**
Frette (Florence) **101**
Frette (Venice) **204**
Frezzeria **194**
From the Grapevine **156**
Fujiyama $ **214**
Fusion Bar **$$$ **46**

G

G (Gaggio) **189**
Gaddi, Taddeo **48**
Gaiole in Chianti **141**
Galleria Corsini **83**
Galleria d'Arte l'Occhio **220**
Galleria degli Uffizi (Uffizi Gallery) **43**
Galleria dell'Accademia (Florence) **94**
Galleria dell'Accademia (Venice) **216**
Galleria di Palazzo Cini **218**
Galleria Franchetti **257**
Galleria Marina Barovier **188**
Gallery Holly Snapp **188**
Gallery Hotel Art $$$$ **46**
Gambello, Antonio **274**
Gamberini, Italo **67**
Garga **$$$ **80**
Gelateria dei Neri **120**
Gelateria Frilli **59**
Gelateria Michelangiolo *$ **61**
Germans' Warehouse (Fondaco dei Tedeschi) **179, 183**
Gesuati (Santa Maria del Rosario) **224**
Gesuiti (Santa Maria Assunta) **254**
Getting around Florence **14**
Getting around Italy **3**
Getting around Venice **170**
Getting to Florence **13**
Getting to and from Aeroporto Amerigo Vespucci **13**
Getting to and from Aeroporto Galileo Galilei **13**
Getting to and from Aeroporto Marco Polo **170**
Getting to Italy **3**
Getting to Venice **168**
The Ghetto **250**
Ghetto Vecchio **251**
Ghiberti, Lorenzo **24, 69**
Ghini, Lapo **20**
Giacomo Rizzo **259**
Giannini, Enrico **165** (bests)
Giardini ex Reali **206**
Giardini Pubblici (Public Gardens) **279**
Giardino **150**
Giardino di Boboli (Boboli Gardens) **60** (map)
Giberto Penzo **234**
Giglio **150**
Gilli **$$ **27**
Giorgio Armani **82**
Giotto **20, 23, 24**
Giotti Bottega Veneta **76**
Giovanna Zanella **265**
Giovanni da Verrazzano **142**
Gipsoteca dell'Istituto d'Arte **62**
Giubbe Rosse *$$ **28**
Giudecca **280** (chapter and map)
Giulio Giannini & Figlio **54**
Gondola, Gondola, Gondola **221**
Gondolas, Venice **170**
Gourmet **144**
Granaio di Cosimo III **123**
Grand Hotel $$$$ **77**
Grand Hotel Cavour $$$ **32**
Grand Hotel Duomo **155**
Grand Hotel e La Pace **144**
Grand Hotel Minerva $$$$ **72**
Grand Hotel Villa Cora $$$$ **63**
Grand Hotel Villa Medici $$$$ **68**
The "Grand Tour" of the Veneto **299**
Grant, Amabel **235** (bests)
Gran Viale **292**
Great School of the Carmelites (Scuola Grande dei Carmini) **211**
Great School of St. John the Avangelist (Scuola Grande di San Giovanni Evangelista) **228**
Great School of St. Roch (Scuola Grande di San Rocco) **232**
Greve **142**
Gritti Palace $$$$ **207**
Grom **25**
Gualti **212**
Guarnieri, Baldassare **67**
Gucci **84**
Guido Bartolozzi **126**
Guido Longhinotto **51**
GustaVino **35**

H

Harry's Bar (Florence) **$$$ **81**
Harry's Bar (Venice) ***$$$$ **206**
Harry's Dolci **$$$ **280**
Hazan, Marcella **63** (bests)
Healing with Herbs: Florence's *Erboristerie* **66**
Herb shops **66**
History **314**
Holidays (Florence) **15**
Holidays (Italy) **5**
Holidays (Venice) **173**
Hong Kong *$$ **104**
Hotel Abbazia $$ **252**
Hotel Ai Mori D'Oriente $$$ **248**
Hotel Ala $$ **207**
Hotel Albani $$$$ **66**
Hotel All'Antica Porta Leona **310**
Hotel Al Sole $$ **245**
Hotel Amadeus $$$$ **252**
Hotel American $$ **218**
Hotel and Restaurant Bel Soggiorno **158**
Hotel Aurora **310**
Hotel Balestri $$$ **120**
Hotel Bauer $$$$ **205**
Hotel Belle Arti $$ **223**
Hotel Bellini $$$$ **255**
Hotel Berchielli $$$$ **87**
Hotel Bernini Palace $$$$ **41**
Hotel Brunelleschi $$$$ **25**
Hotel Bucintoro $$ **278**
Hotel Calzaiuoli $$$ **29**
Hotel Cellai $$ **90**
Hotel Cimabue $ **90**
Hotel Croce di Malta $$$ **75**
Hotel Danieli $$$$ **275**
Hotel Dèco $$ **71**
Hotel de la Ville $$$$ **84**
Hotel delle Tele $$ **71**
Hotel des Bains $$$$ **292**
Hotel Excelsior $$$$ **293**
Hotel Flora $$$ **204**
Hotel Galleria $ **218**
Hotel Genesio $ **90**
Hotel Helvetia & Bristol $$$$ **80**
Hotel Heperia $$ **252**
Hotel Hermitage $$ **47**
Hotel J & J $$$$ **109**
Hotel Kraft $$$ **68**
Hotel La Fenice et des Artistes $$$ **193**
Hotel La Residenza (Castello) $ **274**
Hotel La Residenza (Santa Maria Novella) $$ **85**
Hotel Liana $ **106**
Hotel Lungarno $$$$ **126**
Hotel Majestic $$$$ **70**
Hotel Mario's $$ **65**
Hotel Metropole $$$$ **276**

Hotel Monaco and Grand Canal $$$$ **206**
Hotel Monna Lisa $$$$ **108**
Hotel Montecarlo $$$ **190**
Hotel Nuova Italia $$ **94**
Hotel Paris $$ **74**
Hotel Pescille **159**
Hotel Pierre $$$$ **33**
Hotel Porta Faenza $$ **65**
Hotel Porta Rossa $$ **86**
Hotel Principe $$$$ **71**
Hotel Regency $$$$ **106**
Hotel Rialto $$$ **183**
Hotel Rossi $ **252**
Hotels, rating **3**
Hotel San Cassiano $$$ **240**
Hotel San Lino **167**
Hotel San Stefano $$ **201**
Hotel Santa Maria Novella $$$$ **73**
Hotel Santa Marina $$ **265**
Hotel Sofitel $$$$ **74**
Hotel Torre Guelfa $$ **41**
Hotel Unicorno $$ **79**
Hotel Villa Cipriani **297**
Hours (Florence) **15**
Hours (Italy) **5**
Hours (Venice) **173**
Hungaria Palace Hotel $$$ **292**

I

I Carmini (Santa Maria del Carmelo) **212**
I Ghibellini **$ **110**
Il Bisonte **83**
Il Cantinone *$$ **125**
Il Cavallino **$$ **38**
Il Cesello **36**
Il Cestello ***$$$ **78**
Il Contadino *$ **71**
Il Cronaca (Simone Pollaiuolo) **83, 120, 129**
Il Desco **312**
Il Falconiere **141**
Il Gelatone **253**
Il Gourmet **$$ **67**
Il Grifone **244**
Il Guelfo Bianco $$$ **99**
Il Latini ****$$ **81**
Il Milione **264**
Il Pallottino **$$ **113**
Il Pizziuolo **$ **111**
Il Prato (Calle delle Ostreghe) **204**
Il Profeta **$$ **71**
Il Refolo **$ **241**
Il Torchio **57**
Il Triangolo delle Bermude **93**
Il Tribolo **148**
Immigration **4**
Information, essential (Florence) **15**
Information, essential (Italy) **4**
Information, essential (Venice) **173**
Istituto e Museo di Storia della Scienza **47**
Italian phrases **268**
Italy *see inside front cover* (map)
i'Toscano *$$ **91**
I Vetri a Lume di Amadi **234**

J

Jewish Museum (Museo Ebraico) **251**
Jewish Temple (Tempio Israelitico) **108**
JK Place $$$$ **72**
J. Palma il Giovane (the Younger) **244**

K

Kartell **77**
Ken's Art Gallery **42**
Kleine Galleria **188**
Kramer, Laura **140** (bests)

L

La Baraonda ***$$$ **116**
La Baruciola *$$ **129**
La Beppa **$$ **61**
La Biscotteria **92**
Laboratoria di Raffaela Lamberti **285**
La Bottega dei Mascareri **231**
La Bottega dell'Olio **87**
La Bottega Veneta **206**
La Buca di San Francesco **138**
La Calcina $$ **225**
La Cantina ****$$ **256**
La Capannina da Sante **$$ **131**
La Carabaccia *$$ **68**
La Casalinga ***$ **129**
La Chiusa **153**
La Cisterna **158**
La Collegiata **155**
La Corte Sconta ***$$$ **274**
La Coupole **205**
La Cucina di Edgardo **150**
La Ghiacciaia **143**
La Loggia **$$$ **61**
La Macelleria **$ **89**
La Maremma **$$ **116**
La Mescita *$ **99**
La Mora **147**
La Mora a Moriano **146**
La Nina **144**
La Norcineria **98**
La Piscina **$$ **225**
La Porcellana Bianca **52**
La Rinascente **28**
La Rivista ***$$$ **223**
La Rocca (Castello Inferiore) **298**
La Rotonda **306**
La Salute (Santa Maria della Salute) **181, 220**
La Saracina **151**
Last Suppers (*Cenacoli*) **132**
La Terrazza **152**
La Torretta **312**
La Zucca **$$ **238**
l'Bambino **$$$ **68**
Le Barrique *$$ **127**
Le Cascine **131**
Le Cernacchie **142**
Le Due Fontane $$$ **97**
Le Fonticine ***$$ **93**
Legal emergencies **173**
L'Enoteca Pinchiorri **$$$$ **114**
Leo in Santa Croce **$$ **116**
Le Spighe **279**
Le Tastevin **138**
Le Terrazze **158**
L'Etruria **167**
Le Volpi e L'Uva **$ **53**
Le Zattere **224**
Liassidi Palace $$$ **272**
Library of the Luigi Cherubini Conservatory of Music (Biblioteca del Conservatorio di Musica Luigi Cherubini) **99**
Libreria del Porcellino **37**
Libreria del Sansovino **194**
Libreria EPT **34**
Libreria Feltrinelli **74**
Libreria Linea d'Aqua **189**
Libreria Piccolomini **161**
Libreria Studium **191**
Libreria Toletta **215**
Liceo Marco Polo **216**
The Lido **292**
Lights, Camera, Action **238**
Literary Italy **8**
Lobs **$ **94**
Locanda ai Santi Apostoli $$$ **257**
Locanda Cipriani **$$$$ **291**

Locanda del Ghetto $$ **251**
Locanda l'Elisa **147**
Locanda Ovidius $$ **230**
Locanda Poste Vecie $ **227**
Locanda Salieri $ **244**
Locanda Sturion $$$ **229**
Loggetta di San Marco **198**
Loggia dei Lanzi **40**
Loggia dei Rucellai **82**
Loggia del Consiglio **310**
Loggia del Grano **48**
Loggia di San Paolo **75**
Loggia di San Pier Maggiore **110**
Loggia di Santa Maria del Bigallo **23**
Loggiato dei Serviti $$$ **95**
Lombardo, Pietro **181, 228, 258**
Lombardo, Sante **232**
Longhena, Baldassare **178, 180, 181, 198, 213, 220, 222, 240, 251, 255, 263, 264, 272, 283**
Longo **184**
Loretta Caponi **76**
Loris Marazzi **210**
Lo Squero **216**
L'Osteria di Giovanni **$$$ **79**
Lower Castle (Castello Inferiore) **298**
Lucca **143**
Luciano Ugolini **127**
Lucolena **142**
Luisa Via Roma **23**
Luna Hotel Baglioni $$$$ **206**
Lusanna, Leonardo **67**

M

McCobb, Donald and Jessie **160** (bests)
McRae Books **119**
Madonna dell'Orto **249**
Madova **51**
Maggio Musicale **24**
Magic's in the Air **211**
Mago Merlin Tea House **$ **108**
The Main Events **6**
Maledetti Toscana **152**
Mamma Gina *$$$ **127**
Mandarina Duck **42**
Manetti, Antonio **103**
Mannaioni, Giulio **105, 127**
Map key **3**
Marangon da Soaze **220**
Marcellini, Carlo Andrea **78**
Margerie **203**
Marino **124**
Marione **$ **80**
Mariotti **125**
Marucelli Library (Biblioteca Marucelliana) **94**
Maser **296**
MA Sfilio **29**
Masks, Glass, and Old Lace **172**
Massari, Giorgio **180, 187, 213, 224, 225, 228, 265, 276**
Matas, Niccolò **117**
Matassini **42**
Mazzoni, Sebastiano **180**
Mazzorbo **286, 290**
Medical care **5**
Medical emergencies (Florence) **16**
Medical emergencies (Venice) **173**
Medici Chapels (Cappelle Medicee) **103**
Medici Villas **147**
Mengoni, Giuseppe **94**
Mercato Centrale (Central Market) **94**
Mercato della Frutta (Produce Market) **231**
Mercato di San Lorenzo (San Lorenzo Market) **101**
Mercato di Sant'Ambrogio **112**
Mercato Nuovo (New Market) **37**
Met Restaurant ***$$$ **277**
Michelangelo **38, 62, 91, 103, 104**
Michelangelo in Florence **34**
Michelangelo Museum (Casa Buonarroti) **115**
Michelazzi, Giovanni **77**
Micheli, Vincenzo **109**
Michelozzo **54, 62, 80, 83, 88, 92, 95, 101, 152**
Michelucci, Giovanni **67**
Migliori **119**
Miozzi, Eugenio **255**
Miró $$ **91**
Missiaglia **195**
Missoni **205**
Mistra **$$$ **282**
Moli, Clemente **253**
Molino Stucky **280**
Molo di San Marco **207**
Momoyama **$$ **124**
Monastero di Sant'Appollonia **91**
Mondonovo Maschere **212**
Money (Florence) **16**
Money (Italy) **5**
Money (Venice) **173**
Monopola, Bartolomeo **199**
Monselice, Este, and Montagnana **301**
Montagnana **301**
Montagnaro, Ennio **195** (bests)
Montalcino, Pienza, and Montepulciano **149**
Montana, Umberto **117** (bests)
Montecarlo **143**
Montecatini Golf Club **144**
Montecatini Terme, Collodi, Montecarlo, and Lucca **143**
Montepulciano **149**
Monterchi **138**
Monumento alla Partigiana (Monument to the Partisan Woman) **279**
Monumento di Arbit Blatas **251**
Mopeds, Florence **14**
Morandi alla Crocetta $$ **98**
Motoscafi, Venice **170**
Mr. Jimmy's Dolci **54**
Municipal Gallery (Museo Civico agli Eremitani) **307**
Munstermann of Florence **81**
Murano **284, 285** (map)
Murazzi **293**
Museo Accademia Etrusca **140**
Museo Archeologico (Florence) **98**
Museo Archeologico Mecenate **137**
Museo Archeologico Nazionale **197**
Museo Camposanto Monumentale **154**
Museo Civico (Asolo) **297**
Museo Civico (Bassano del Grappa) **298**
Museo Civico (San Gimignano) **156**
Museo Civico (Sansepolcro) **139**
Museo Civico (Treviso) **303**
Museo Civico agli Eremitani (Municipal Gallery) **307**
Museo Correr **196**
Museo d'Arte Moderna Ca' Pesaro **240**
Museo d'Arte Orientale (Museum of Eastern Art) **240**
Museo d'Arte Sacra **167**
Museo dell'Angelico (Fra Angelico Museum) **92**
Museo dell'Arte Vetraria (Museum of Glass Art) **284**
Museo della Tortura **157**
Museo delle Sinopie **154**
Museo dell'Opera (Palazzo Ducale) **199**
Museo dell'Opera del Duomo (Duomo Museum) (Centro Storico) **21**
Museo dell'Opera del Duomo (Duomo Museum) (Pisa) **154**
Museo dell'Opera del Duomo (Siena) **161**

Museo dell'Opera di Santa Croce (Santa Croce Museum) **120**
Museo dell'Opera di Santa Maria del Fiore **21**
Museo del Settecento Veneziano (Museum of the Venetian 17th Century) **213**
Museo di Firenze Com'Era **105**
Museo di Leonardo **102**
Museo di Merletto **287**
Museo Diocesano **140**
Museo di Palazzo Chiericati **305**
Museo di San Marco (San Marco Museum) **92**
Museo di Storia della Fotografia Alinari (Alinari Museum of the History of Photography) **82**
Museo di Storia Naturale (Museum of Natural History) **237**
Museo di Torcello (Torcello Museum) **291**
Museo Ebraico (Jewish Museum) **251**
Museo Etrusco Guarnacci **167**
Museo Fortuny **185**
Museo Horne **120**
Museo La Specola **60**
Museo Marino Marini **79**
Museo Nazionale Atestino **301**
Museo Salvatore Ferragamo **85**
Museo Stibbert **130**
Museo Storico Navale (Naval Museum) **278**
Museum of Eastern Art (Museo d'Arte Orientale) **240**
Museum of Glass Art (Museo dell'Arte Vetraria) **284**
Museum of Natural History (Museo di Storia Naturale) **237**
Museum of the Venetian 17th Century (Ca' Rezzonico-Museo del Settecento Veneziano) **213**

N

Nardi **198**
National Library (Biblioteca Nazionale) **121**
Nava & Nencini **128**
Naval Museum (Museo Storico Navale) **278**
Negroni *$ **57**
Nerbone *$ **95**
NERI **53**
Nervi, Pier Luigi **131**
Neville, A. E. **178, 216, 255**
New Market (Mercato Nuovo) **37**
Newsstand **39**
Nigetti, Matteo **76, 79, 103, 110**
Nightlife (Venice) **243**
Noferi, Andrea **67**
Northern Italy Orientation **2** (chapter)
Norwich, John Julius **304** (bests)
Novecento $$$ **207**
Nuti *$ **104**

O

869 **216**
Officina Profumo-Farmaceutica di Santa Maria Novella **72**
Ognissanti **76**
Old England Stores **23**
Old Palace or Palazzo della Signoria (Palazzo Vecchio) **40**
Olio & Convivium **$$ **125**
Olive Oil: Liquid Gold **138**
Olive Tree **43**
Oliviero ***$$$ **87**
Oltrarno **122** (chapter and map)
Omero **$$ **131**
Opificio delle Pietre Dure **99**
Oratorio dei Buonomini di San Martino **31**
Oratorio dei Crociferi **254**
Oratorio di San Giorgio **308**
Orsanmichele **30**
Oscuro Medioevo Fiorentino **100**
Ospedale degli Incurabili **225**
Ospedale degli Innocenti **97**
Ospedale di San Giovanni di Dio **78**
Ospedale di Santa Maria Nuova **105**
Ostaria al 4 Ferri ***$$ **214**
Ostaria al Diavolo e l'Aquasanta **$ **230**
Ostaria Antico Dolo **$$ **229**
Ostaria Ca' Brando **298**
Ostaria dei Centopoveri ***$$ **75**
Osteria Ae Botti *$ **281**
Osteria ai Cannottieri **$$ **250**
Osteria ai Forneri *$ **271**
Osteria Al Bacco ***$$$ **248**
Osteria al Bomba **257**
Osteria al Mascaron **$$ **267**
Osteria Al Nono Risorto **$$ **242**
Osteria al Ponte del Diavolo **$$$ **291**
Osteria Antica Mescita San Niccolò ***$ **59**
Osteria Bea Vita **$ **248**
Osteria da Alberto ***$$ **258**
Osteria da Aldo **249**
Osteria da Codroma **$ **210**
Osteria da Fiore ****$$$$ **228**
Osteria dal Duca **312**
Osteria dalla Vedova **$$ **256**
Osteria del Caffè Italiano ***$$ **113**
Osteria Oliva Nera ***$$ **272**
Osteria Vasari **$ **53**
Otello **$$ **67**
Ottica, Danilo Carraro **189**
The Outlets **139**

P

Pacini, Michele **104**
Padlocks **49**
Padua **306**
Painters **309**
Palace Bonvecchiati $$$ **186**
Palace Hotel **165**
Palatium Communis **305**
Palatium Vetus **305**
Palazzi dei Mozzi **58**
Palazzi Mocenigo **180**
Palazzi Pucci **104**
Palazzo alla Rovescia **81**
Palazzo Altoviti **109**
Palazzo Antellesi **163**
Palazzo Antinori **76**
Palazzo Arcivescovile (Archbishop's Palace) **19**
Palazzo Avignonese **151**
Palazzo Balbi **180**
Palazzo Barbarigo **180**
Palazzo Bartolini Salimbeni **86**
Palazzo Bembo **179**
Palazzo Bencl $$$ **100**
Palazzo Buonsignori **162**
Palazzo Capra **305**
Palazzo Chigi-Saracini **159**
Palazzo Cocconi **152**
Palazzo Comunale (Cortona) **140**
Palazzo Comunale (Montepulciano) **151**
Palazzo Comunale (Siena) **159**
Palazzo Contarini-Fasan **180**
Palazzo Corner della Ca' Grande **180**
Palazzo Corner-Spinelli **180**
Palazzo Corsini (Santa Maria Novella) **86**
Palazzo Corsi (Santa Maria Novella) **80**
Palazzo Corto-Barbaran **305**

Palazzo Dario **181**
Palazzo degli Affari **65**
Palazzo degli Albizi **109**
Palazzo degli Alessandri **110**
Palazzo dei Camerlenghi **179**
Palazzo dei Congressi **65**
Palazzo dei Frescobaldi **126**
Palazzo dei Priori **166**
Palazzo della Fraternità dei Laici (Palace of the Lay Fraternity) **137**
Palazzo dell'Antella **117**
Palazzo della Regione (Palazzo Riccardi-Mannelli) **96**
Palazzo della Stufa **101**
Palazzo delle Laudi **139**
Palazzo delle Logge **137**
Palazzo delle Poste e Telegrafi **32**
Palazzo dello Strozzino **83**
Palazzo del Podestà **142**
Palazzo del Popolo **156**
Palazzo de Priori **166**
Palazzo Dolfin Manin **179**
Palazzo Ducale (Doges' Palace) **199**
Palazzo Foscari (Villa Malcontenta) **301**
Palazzo Franchetti **180**
Palazzo Garzoni **180**
Palazzo Giugni **102**
Palazzo Gondi **38**
Palazzo Grassi **180, 187**
Palazzo Grimani **180**
Palazzo Gritti **180**
Palazzo Guicciardini **52**
Palazzo Inghiarini **101**
Palazzo Labia **252**
Palazzo Lenzi **76**
Palazzo Liberty **77**
Palazzo Loredan **179**
Palazzo Marucelli **91**
Palazzo Mastelli **249**
Palazzo Medici-Riccardi **101**
Palazzo Moro-Lin **180**
Palazzo Niccolini **102**
Palazzo Nonfinito (Unfinished Palace) **29**
Palazzo Orlandini del Beccuto **22**
Palazzo Panclatichi Ximenes **106**
Palazzo Pandolfini **90**
Palazzo Papadopoli **179**
Palazzo Pazzi-Quaratesi **30**
Palazzo Piccolomini **151**
Palazzo Pisani-Moretta **180**
Palazzo Pitti (Colli) **55**
Palazzo Pitti (Santa Maria Novella) **75**
Palazzo Pojana **305**
Palazzo Pretorio **140**
Palazzo Quaratesi **113**
Palazzo Ravizza **163**
Palazzo Ricasoli **83**
Palazzo Riccardi-Mannelli (Palazzo della Regione) (Via dei Servi) **96**
Palazzo Riccardi-Mannelli (Via Faenza) **100**
Palazzo Rucellai **82**
Palazzo Salviati **29**
Palazzo Sansedoni **159, 161**
Palazzo Serristori (Colli) **58**
Palazzo Serristori (Santa Croce) **116**
Palazzo Spinelli-Rasponi **120**
Palazzo Spini-Ferroni **85**
Palazzo Strozzi **83**
Palazzo Thiene **305**
Palazzo Thiene Bonin Longare **304**
Palazzo Uguccioni **38**
Palazzo Vecchio (Old Palace or Palazzo della Signoria) **40**
Palazzo Vendramin Calergi **178, 255**
Palazzo Venier dei Leoni **181**
Palazzo Zaguri **202**
Palladio, Andrea **148, 265, 275, 282, 283, 295, 296, 297, 298, 302, 304, 305**
Palle d'Oro **$ **98**
Pane & Co **38**
Pane Vino e San Daniele ***$$ **215**
Panificio al Garbo **289**
Panificio Pasticceria Palmisano Luigi **287**
Paoli **$$ **31**
Paolo Brandolisio **272**
Paolo Romano Antichità **81**
Papadopoli Restaurant *$$$ **243**
Paperback Exchange **25**
Parco degli Stabilimenti **144**
Parco di Pinocchio **144**
Parenti **126**
Parigi, Alfonso **20, 83**
Parigi, Alfonso, the Younger **55, 101**
Parigi, Giulio **48, 55, 117**
Parking (Florence) **14**
Park Palace Hotel **164**
Parla Italiano? **268**
Passamaneria Toscana **101**
Passamaneria Valmar **33**
Passeggio del Prato **137**
Pasticceria Maioli **$ **52**
Paszkowski *$$ **27**
Paulin **201**
Pauly & C. **198**
Pazzi Chapel and Santa Croce Museum (Cappella Pazzi and Museo dell'Opera di Santa Croce) **120**
Peggy Guggenheim Collection (Collezione Peggy Guggenheim) **219**
Pelliceria Caberlotto **184**
Pendini $$ **28**
Pensieri **190**
Pensione Accademia–Villa Meravege $$ **215**
Pensione Seguso $$ **224**
Pensione Sorelle Bandini $$ **129**
Pensione Wildner $$ **276**
Pentola dell'Oro ***$ **109**
Perchè No! **31**
Per Modo di Dire **51**
Perseus Restoration (Restauro del Perseo) **46**
Personal safety (Florence) **16**
Personal safety (Venice) **173**
Peruzzi **117**
Peruzzi, Baldassare **164**
Pescheria (Fish Market) (Canal Grande) **179**
Pescheria (Fish Market) (San Paolo) **227**
Peter Bazzanti & Son **86**
Peter's Teahouse **257**
Petrarch's House (Casa di Petrarca) **277**
Pettirossi, Bartolomeo **76**
Pharmacies (Florence) **16**
Pharmacies (Venice) **174**
Piazza dei Ciompi **111**
Piazza dei Miracoli **153**
Piazza dei Peruzzi **119**
Piazza dei Signori **309**
Piazza del Duomo (San Gimignano) **155**
Piazza della Cisterna **155**
Piazza della Frutta **307**
Piazza della Repubblica **26**
Piazza della Santissima Annunziata **96**
Piazza della Signoria **39**
Piazza delle Erbe (Padua) **3**
Piazza delle Erbe (Verona) **309**
Piazza di Parte Guelfa **38**
Piazza Grande **137**
Piazzale Michelangiolo **61**
Piazzale Roma **242**
Piazza Matteotti **142**
Piazza Napoleone **145**
Piazza Nicola Demidoff **58**
Piazza San Marco (Florence) **92**
Piazza San Marco (Venice) **197**
Piazza Santa Croce **117**
Piazza Santa Maria Novella **72**
Piazza Santo Spirito **129**
Piazza Torre di Berta **139**

Piazzetta San Marco **199**
Piccolo Hotel Etruria **163**
Piccolo Puccini **146**
Piccolo Slam **120**
Pienza **149**
Pietrasanta **166**
Pieve di Santa Maria **137**
Pinacoteca Nazionale **162**
Pincenti, Kirsten Aachengreen **163** (bests)
Pineider 1774 **38**
Pinoteca **166**
Pisa **153**
Pisano, Andrea **23, 24, 123**
Pisano, Giovanni **153, 154, 161**
Pisano, Nicola **153, 161**
Pisano, Nino **154**
Piscina San Samuele **187**
Pitti Gola e Cantina **53**
Pitti Mosaici **54**
Pitti Palace $$ **128**
Pizzeria Ae Oche **$ **242**
Planet Earth **210**
Plaza Hotel Lucchesi $$$$ **121**
Poggi, Giuseppe **61, 65**
Poggio Antico **150**
Pollaiuolo, Simone (Il Cronaca) **83, 120, 129**
Ponte alla Carraia **85**
Ponte dei Conzafelzi **265**
Ponte dei Pugni **213**
Ponte dei Sospiri (Bridge of Sighs) **201**
Ponte dell'Accademia (Accademia Bridge) **180, 216**
Ponte della Donna Onesta **209**
Ponte De Pria **303**
Ponte di Rialto (Rialto Bridge) **179, 231**
Ponte San Pietro **275**
Ponte Santa Trinità **87**
Ponte Scalzi **178, 255**
Ponte Vecchio **48**
Porta al Prato **66**
Porta di San Miniato **59**
Porta Romana **62**
Porta San Frediano **123**
Porta San Niccolò **59**
Postal service (Florence) **16**
Postal service (Italy) **5**
Postal service (Venice) **174**
Preludio **141**
Prezzemolo **129**
Procacci *** **80**
Procuratie Nuove **198**
Procuratie Vecchie **194**
Produce Market (Mercato della Frutta) **231**
Profondo Rosso ***$ **248**
Profumerie Aline **28**
Pronti, Giocchino **92**
Publications (Florence) **16**
Publications (Italy) **8**
Publications (Venice) **174**
Public Gardens (Giardini Pubblici) **279**
Pulcino **152**
Punta della Dogana (Customs Point) **181, 222**

Q

Quattro Fontane $$$ **293**
Querini Stampalia Library (Biblioteca Querini Stampalia) **267**

R

Radda in Chianti **141**
Rafanelli **79**
Raffaello Romanelli **41**
Raspini **22**
Raverti, Matteo **179, 256**
Redentore **282**
Refettorio della Chiesa di Ognissanti (Refectory of the Church of Ognissanti) **76**
Relais Il Chiostro di Pienza **151**
Relais La Suvera **164**
Relais Le Jardin ***$$$ **106**
Relais Santa Chiara **158**
Relais Uffizi $$ **42**
Relais Vignale **143**
Renaissance Painters of the Veneto **309**
Rental cars (Florence) **13, 14**
Rental cars (Venice) **170**
Residenza Johanna Uno $ **89**
Residenze Johlea I and Johlea II $$ **90**
Restaurant Galuppi **$$ **289**
Restaurants, rating **3**
Restaurants (Florence) **16**
Restaurants (Italy) **8**
Restaurants (Venice) **174**
Restauro del Perseo (Perseus Restoration) **46**
Rialto Biocenter **227**
Rialto Bridge (Ponte di Rialto) **179, 231**
Ribo ***$$$ **245**
Riccardo Mazzanti, Marani and Carrère **67**
Richard Ginori **75**
Ricordi **25**
Rigattieri **189**
Rio Terrà Antonio Foscarini **222**
Rio Terrà dei Saloni **225**
Rio Terrà Lista di Spagna **253**
Ristorante ai Barbacani **$$$ **266**
Ristorante Aldo Moro **302**
Ristorante all'Altanella **$$ **282**
Ristorante Alle Zattere **$$ **224**
Ristorante al Teatro **$$ **193**
Ristorante Al Trono di Attila *$$ **291**
Ristorante Bruna & Gerry **313**
Ristorante da Romano (Burano) ***$$$ **286**
Ristorante da Romano (Viareggio) **165**
Ristorante Due Mori **297**
Ristorante Gam Gam *$ **251**
Ristorante La Caravella **$$$$ **204**
Ristorante Pizzeria Zi'Teresa **306**
Ristorante Quattro Fontane $$ **293**
Ristorante Riviera **$$ **222**
Ristoteca Oniga **$$ **213**
Riva degli Schiavoni and Riva dei Sette Martiri **276**
Riva del Carbon **184**
Riva Rosa ****$$$ **287**
Rivoire **$$ **39**
Roberto Tolin **209**
Robiglio **100**
Rocca (Montalcino) **150**
Rosselli, Jacopo **83**
Rossellino, Bernardo **82, 151**
Rossi, Domenico **178**
Rosticceria San Bartolomeo **$ **184**
Rotonda di Brunelleschi **102**
Rucellai Chapel (Cappella Rucellai) (Santa Maria Novella) **80**
Ruga Rialto **$ **229**
Ruga Vecchia San Giovanni **229**
Ruggero **$$ **132**
Ruggieri, Ferdinando **52, 103**
Ruggieri, Giuseppe **127**
Ruggini **119**
Ruth's *$$ **108**

S

Sabatini, Rodrigo **32**
Sabatini ***$$$$ **70**

Safety, personal (Florence) **16**
Safety, personal (Venice) **173**
St. Georges **219**
St. James **67**
St. Mark's Bell Tower (Campanile di San Marco) **197**
St. Mark's Library (Biblioteca Nazionale Marciana) **197**
St. Moses (San Moisè) **205**
Salimbeni **113**
Salizzada San Lio **266**
Saloni or Magazzini dei Sale (Salt Warehouses) **225**
Salvatore Ferragamo **85**
Salviati **205**
Sam's Market **113**
San Barnaba **213**
San Carlo dei Lombardi **33**
San Corona **305**
San Domenico **137**
San Felice (Cannaregio) **256**
San Felice (Colli) **54**
San Filippo Neri and San Firenze **38**
San Francesco **298**
San Francesco del Deserto **286, 289**
San Francesco della Vigna **265**
San Francesco di Paola **279**
San Frediano (Lucca) **146**
San Frediano in Cestello **123**
San Gaetano **79**
San Giacometto **231**
San Giacomo dell'Orio **241**
San Gimignano **155**
San Giorgio Maggiore **283**
San Giovanni in Bragora **277**
San Giovanni Evangelista **101**
San Giovanni Grisostomo **259**
San Lazzaro degli Armeni **291**
San Leonardo **62**
San Lorenzo **88** (chapter and map), **103**
San Lorenzo Market (Marcato di San Lorenzo) **101**
San Marco **182** (chapter and map), **191**
San Marco Museum (Museo di San Marco) **92**
San Maurizio **202**
San Michele **293**
San Michele in Foro (St. Michael in the Forum) **146**
Sanmicheli, Michele **180, 234**
San Michelino **104**
San Miniato al Monte **62**
San Moisè (St. Moses) **205**
San Niccolò sopr'Arno **58**
San Nicola di Tolentino **243**
San Nicolò **303**
San Nicolò dei Mendicoli **212**
San Paolo **226** (chapter and map), **234**
San Paulo a Ripa d'Arno **154**
San Pietro di Castello **275**
San Pietro Martire **286**
San Remigio **119**
San Salvador **184**
San Salvatore al Monte **62**
San Salvatore al Vescovo **19**
San Sebastiano **215**
Sansepolcro **136**
San Simone **113**
Sansovino, Jacopo **179, 180, 184, 194, 197, 198, 254, 265, 295**
San Stae **178, 238**
Santa Croce (Florence) **106** (chapter), **107** (map), **117**
Santa Croce (Venice) **236** (chapter and map)
Santa Croce Museum (Museo dell'Opera di Santa Croce) **120**
Santa Felicità **52**
Sant'Agostino (Montepulciano) **152**
Sant'Agostino (San Gimignano) **156**
Santa Margherita dei Cerchi—Dante's Church **29**
Santa Margherita in Santa Maria de' Ricci **29**
Santa Maria Antica **310**
Santa Maria Assunta (Gesuiti) **254**
Santa Maria dei Derelitti **264**
Santa Maria dei Miracoli **258**
Santa Maria del Carmelo (I Carmini) **212**
Santa Maria del Carmine **127**
Santa Maria del Giglio **203**
Santa Maria della Fava **265**
Santa Maria della Pietà **276**
Santa Maria della Salute (La Salute) **181, 220**
Santa Maria della Scala **162**
Santa Maria della Spina **154**
Santa Maria e San Donato **284**
Santa Maria Formosa **267**
Santa Maria Gloriosa dei Frari (Frari) **232**
Santa Maria Maddalena de' Pazzi **106**
Santa Maria Maggiore **19**
Santa Maria Novella **64** (chapter and map), **69** (map), **73** (map)
Santa Maria Valverde **253**
Sant'Ambrogio **111**
Sant'Anastasia **310**
Sant'Antonio **308**
Sant'Apollonia Monastery **273**
Santa Trinità **86**
Santi Apostoli **87**
Santi Geremia and Lucia Church **179**
Santi Giovanni e Paolo (San Zanipolo) **263**
Santissima Annunziata **95**
Santissimi Apostoli **258**
Santo Spirito **128**
Santo Stefano **192**
Santo Stefano al Ponte **47**
Santuario Cateriniano **163**
San Zaccaria **273**
San Zanipolo (Santi Giovanni e Paolo) **263**
San Zeno **311**
Sardi, Giuseppe **178, 184, 203, 212, 255**
Savoy $$$$ **28**
Sbigoli Terrecotte **109**
Scala del Bovolo **190**
Scaligere Arches (Arche Scaligere) **310**
Scalzi **255**
Scamozzi, Vincenzo **29, 197, 198, 244, 304, 305**
Scarpa, Carlo **72, 267, 279**
Scarpagnino, Antonio **179, 183, 215, 232**
School of St. Anthony (Scuola del Santo) **308**
School of St. Theodore (Scuola di San Teodoro) **184**
Scrovegni Chapel (Cappella degli Scrovegni) **307**
Scudieri **19**
Scuola del Cuoio **118**
Scuola del Santo (School of St. Anthony) **308**
Scuola di San Giorgio degli Schiavoni **270**
Scuola di San Teodoro (School of St. Theodore) **184**
Scuola Grande dei Carmini (Great School of the Carmelites) **211**
Scuola Grande di San Giovanni Evangelista (Great School of St. John the Evangelist) **228**
Scuola Grande di San Rocco (Great School of St. Roch) **232**
Scuola Levantina (Eastern Mediterranean Synagogue) **251**
Scuola Nuova della Misericordia **254**
Scuola Spagnola (Spanish Synagogue) **251**

cuola Vecchia della Misericordia **253**
ebasti, Lorenza **146** (bests)
elva, Giannantonio **202**
eminario Patriarcale **222**
eravezza **166**
ergio *$ **101**
ervizio Noleggio Biciclette **147**
hopping (Florence) **16**
hopping (Venice) **174**
iena **159**
iena: The Palio **149**
ieni **98**
illa *$ **57**
ilvani, Gherardo **29, 52, 79, 91, 106, 109, 113**
ilvani, Pier Francesco **79, 86**
ilvia **266**
moking **9**
napp, Holly **244** (bests)
oave **313**
ofitel Venezia $$$$ **243**
olferino **146**
oli, Giuseppe Maria **196**
ostanza ***$$ **77**
padolini, Pierluigi **65**
panish Synagogue (Scuola Spagnola) **251**
pavento, Giorgio **184**
pecial events **6**
pirito Santo **57**
quero di San Trovaso **222**
tadio Comunale **131**
tand **111**
tate Archives (Archivio di Stato) **231**
tazione Centrale di Santa Maria Novella **67**
tazione Ferroviaria (Train Station) **255**
tefano ***$$ **133**
trada Nuova **257**
treet plan (Florence) **16**
treet plan (Venice) **174**
ynagogues on the Campo del Ghetto Nuovo **251**

T

abasco **39**
acca, Ferdinando **47, 105**
addei **29**
alenti, Fra Jacopo **68, 70**
alenti, Francesco **20, 23, 30**
alenti, Simone di Francesco **40**
aste of Tuscany **114**
Taverna da Baffo *$ **228**
Taverna dei Barbi **151**
Taverna del Bronzino ***$$$ **90**
Taxes **9**
Taxi Acqueo **172**
Taxis (Florence) **13, 14**
Taxis (Venice) **170**
Teatro Anatomico **307**
Teatro Comunale **68**
Teatro della Pergola **105**
Teatro dell'Oriuolo **105**
Teatro Goldoni **185**
Teatro La Fenice **193**
Teatro Niccolini **105**
Teatro Olimpico **305**
Teatro Verdi **113**
Telephone numbers, essential (Florence) **15**
Telephone numbers, essential (Venice) **172**
Telephones (Florence) **16**
Telephones (Italy) **9**
Telephones (Venice) **175**
Tempio di San Biagio **152**
Tempio Israelitico (Jewish Temple) **108**
Tenuta di San Rossore **154**
Time zone **10**
Tipping **10**
Tirali, Andrea **216, 244, 263, 265, 289**
Tognetti, Vittorio **32**
Toilets **10**
Toni del Spin **304**
Toraldo di Francia, Cristiano **67**
Torcello **286, 290**
Torcello Cathedral **291**
Torcello Museum (Museo di Torcello) **291**
Torre Civica **301**
Torre degli Adimali **25**
Torre dei Donati Consorti **47**
Torre dei Lamberti **310**
Torre della Castagna **32**
Torre del Lago Puccini **164**
Torre dell'Orologio (Clock Tower) **191**
Torre del Mangia **161**
Torre di Bellosguardo $$$ **131**
Torre di Pisa **153**
Torre Grossa **156**
Torrini **19**
Tours (Florence) **14**
Tours (Venice) **172**
Tozzi **49**
Traghetti **170**
Traghetto to Santa Maria del Giglio **219**
Tragicomica **234**
Trains (Florence) **13**
Trains (Italy) **4, 14**
Train Station (Long-Distance) (Florence) **14**
Train Station (Long-Distance) (Venice) **170**
Train Station (Stazione Ferroviaria) **255**
Transportation (Florence) **13**
Transportation (Italy) **3**
Transportation (Venice) **168**
Trattoria Aciugheta **$$ **271**
Trattoria Alla Madonna **$$ **230**
Trattoria alle Burchielle **$$ **244**
Trattoria Antellesi **$$ **100**
Trattoria "Antica Mola" **$ **249**
Trattoria da Arturo ****$$$ **190**
Trattoria da Ignazio **$$$ **234**
Trattoria dai Tosi *$$ **279**
Trattoria da Marisa ***$$ **250**
Trattoria da Montín *$$ **216**
Trattoria della Donna Onesta *$$ **210**
Trattoria Do Mori **$$ **281**
Trattoria Garibardi **98**
Trattoria Pizzeria da Paolo **$$ **275**
Trattoria San Martino **166**
Trattoria Sant'Omobono **155**
Tremignon, Alessandro **205**
Tre Ponti **244**
Treves, Marco **109**
Treviso **302**
Tripperia **31**
Tripperie **123**
T. Ristori **49**
Turks' Warehouse (Fondaco dei Turchi) **178**
Tuscany **134** (map)

U

Uffizi Gallery (Galleria degli Uffizi) **43**
U. Gherardi **49**
Ugolini (Oltrarno) **124**
Unfinished Palace (Palazzo Nonfinito) **29**
Un Mondo diVino ***$ **258**

V

Valese **190**
Valli **26**

Valori, Baccio **109**
Vaporetti, Venice **170**
Vaporetto stops, Venice **171** (map), *see also inside back cover* (map)
Vasari, Giorgio **38, 43, 60, 69, 103, 104, 117, 137, 148**
The Vasari Corridor **46**
Vecio Fritolin **$ **242**
Venetian Islands **283** (chapter and map)
Venetian Streets **245**
Venetian Victuals **311**
Venetia Stadium **204**
Venezia di Notte: San Marco **243**
Venice **169** (map)
Venice Day Trips: Visions of the Veneto **294** (chapter and map)
Venice Orientation **168** (chapter)
Venice Vaporetto Stops **171** (map); *see also inside back cover* (map)
Venier Roberto **245**
Venini **191**
Verona **308**
Verrocchia, Janice **71** (bests)
Verrocchio, Andrea **20**
Vestri **110**
Via dei Fossi **79**
Via dei Tornabuoni **84**
Via del Corso **29**
Via delle Volte **142**
Via de San Salvatore al Monte **61**
Via Fillungo **146**
Via Garibaldi **278**
Via Giucciardini **51**
Via Guinigi **146**
Viareggio, Forte dei Marmi, and Torre del Lago Puccini **164**
Vicenza **304**
Viceversa **102**
Vignola, Giacomo **151**
Villa Banfi **151**
Villa Barbaro **297**
Villa Carlotta $$$ **63**
Villa Corner **301**
Villa De Kunkler **302**
Villa della Petraia **147**
Villa Demidoff **148**
Villa di Castello **148**
Villa di Poggio a Caiano **148**
Villa Foscarini **301**
Villa Franceschi **166**
Villa Giovannelli **301**
Villa Grimani Valmarana **301**
Villa Kinzica **155**
Villa la Principessa **147**
Villa Malcontenta (Palazzo Foscari) **301**
Villa Mansi **147**
Villa Nencini **167**
Villa Pisani (Brenta Riviera) **301**
Villa Pisani (Montagnana) **302**
Villa Reale di Marlia **147**
Villa Rosa **143**
Villa Torrigiani **147**
Villa Valmara ai Nani **306**
Villa Wildmann **301**
Vini Da Gigio **$$ **256**
Vini dei Chianti **33**
Vino E . . . Vini **271**
VinOlio *$ **90**
Vino Olio **128**
Vino Vino **$$ **195**
Virgo Fidelis **89**
Visitors' information (Florence) **15, 16**
Visitors' information (Venice) **172, 175**
Vitruvius **296, 308**
Vivoli **113**
Vizio Virtu **235**
Vogini **198**
Volterra **166**

W

Walking (Florence) **15**
Walking (Venice) **173**
Waterline **126**
The Westin Europa & Regina $$$$ **207**
Westin Excelsior $$$$ **77**
What a Girl Wants **302**
Wilk, Robert **300** (bests)
Willinger, Faith **110** (bests)
Wine **156**
Wine bars **74**

Z

Zaguri, Pietro **202**
Zecchi **26**

RESTAURANTS

Only restaurants with star ratings are listed below. All restaurants are listed alphabetically in the main (preceding) index. Always call in advance to ensure a restaurant has not closed, changed its hours, or booked its tables for a private party. The restaurant price ratings are based on the average cost of an entrée for one person, excluding tax and tip.

**** An Extraordinary Experience
*** Excellent
** Very Good
* Good

$$$$ Big Bucks ($70 and up)
$$$ Expensive ($45-$70)
$$ Reasonable ($25-$45)
$ The Price is Right (less than $25)

★★★★

Cibrèo $$$ **111**
Cibrèo: Teatro del Sale $$ **111**
Il Latini $$ **81**
La Cantina $$ **256**
Osteria da Fiore $$$$ **228**
Riva Rosa $$$ **287**
Trattoria da Arturo $$$ **190**

★★★

Acqua al Due $ **113**
Al Bacareto $$ **188**
Algiubagio $$ **254**
Alle Murate $$$ **115**
Alle Testiere $$$ **267**
Al Mascareta $$ **267**
Angolo di Tanit $$ **252**
Antica Trattoria La Furatola $$$ **214**
Antica Trattoria Poste Vecie $$$ **227**
Baldini $$ **66**
Bistrot de Venise $$$ **186**
Cantina Do Mori $$ **229**
Da Luca e Fred $ **252**
De Pisis Restaurant $$$$ **205**
Dino $$ **116**
Don Chisclotte $$$ **89**
Enoteca Al Volto $ **185**
Fiaschetteria Toscana $$$$ **258**
Fiore $$ **189**
Harry's Bar (Venice) $$$$ **206**
Il Cestello $$$ **78**
La Baraonda $$$ **116**

a Casalinga $ **129**
a Corte Sconta $$$ **274**
a Rivista $$$ **223**
e Fonticine $$ **93**
'et Restaurant $$$ **277**
liviero $$$ **87**
staria al 4 Feri $$ **214**
staria dei Centopoveri $$ **75**
steria Al Bacco $$$ **248**
steria Antica Mescita San Niccolò $ **59**
steria da Alberto $$ **258**
steria del Caffè Italiano $$ **113**
steria Oliva Nera $$ **272**
ane Vino e San Daniele $$ **215**
entola dell'Oro $ **109**
rocacci **80**
rofondo Rosso $ **248**
elais Le Jardin $$$ **106**
.bo $$$ **245**
istorante da Romano (Burano) $$$ **286**
abatini $$$$ **70**
ostanza $$ **77**
tefano $$ **133**
averna del Bronzino $$$ **90**
rattoria da Marisa $$ **250**
n Mondo diVino $ **258**

★

cquacotta $$ **107**
l Cacciatore $ **281**
l Covo $$$ **277**
ll Antico Vinaio $ **119**
lla Vecchia Bettola $$ **128**
l Lume di Candela $$$ **87**
mon $ **75**
ntiche Carampane $$ **228**
ntico Fattore $$ **42**
ntico Martini $$$ **195**
ntico Ristoro di Cambi $$ **123**
acaro $$$ **196**
ácaro Jazz $$ **183**
runello Restaurant and Bar $$$ **41**
uca Mario $$ **78**
usa-alla-Torre $$ **284**
afaggi $$ **93**
affè Florian $$$ **198**
affè Italiano $ **33**
affè Lavena $$$ **194**
affè Pitti $ **54**
affè Quadri $$$ **195**
ammillo $$ **126**
antina Do Spade $$ **229**
Cantinetta Antinori $$$ **76**
Caruso Jazz Internet Cafe $$ **42**
Cavatappi $$ **186**
Celestino $$ **53**
Centrale (San Marco) $$$ **193**
Coco Lezzone $$ **83**
Da Ganino $$ **31**
Dal Baffo $ **290**
Del Carmine $$ **124**
Diladdarno $$ **129**
Enoteca Bar FuoriPorta $ **59**
Fiaschetteria Nuvoli $ **19**
Fratelli Poli $$ **31**
Fusion Bar $$$ **46**
Garga $$$ **80**
Gilli $$ **27**
Harry's Bar (Florence) $$$ **81**
Harry's Dolci $$$ **280**
I Ghibellini $ **110**
Il Cavallino $$ **38**
Il Gourmet $$ **67**
Il Pallottino $$ **113**
Il Pizziuolo $ **111**
Il Profeta $$ **71**
Il Refolo $ **241**
La Beppa $$ **61**
La Capannina da Sante $$ **131**
La Loggia $$$ **61**
La Macelleria $ **89**
La Maremma $$ **116**
La Piscina $$ **225**
La Zucca $$ **238**
l'Bambino $$$ **68**
L'Enoteca Pinchiorri $$$$ **114**
Leo in Santa Croce $$ **116**
Le Volpi e L'Uva $ **53**
Lobs $ **94**
Locanda Cipriani $$$$ **291**
L'Osteria di Giovanni $$$ **79**
Mago Merlin Tea House $ **108**
Marione $ **80**
Mistra $$$ **282**
Momoyama $$ **124**
Olio & Convivium $$ **125**
Omero $$ **131**
Ostaria al Diavo'lo e l'Aquasanta $ **230**
Ostaria Antico Dolo $$ **229**
Osteria ai Cannottieri $$ **250**
Osteria al Mascaron $$ **267**
Osteria Al Nono Risorto $$ **242**
Osteria al Ponte del Diavolo $$$ **291**
Osteria Bea Vita $ **248**
Osteria da Codroma $ **210**
Osteria dalla Vedova $$ **256**
Osteria Vasari $ **53**
Otello $$ **67**
Palle d'Oro $ **98**
Paoli $$ **31**
Pasticceria Maioli $ **52**
Pizzeria Ae Oche $ **242**
Restaurant Galuppi $$ **289**
Ristorante ai Barbacani $$$ **266**
Ristorante all'Altanella $$ **282**
Ristorante Alle Zattere $$ **224**
Ristorante al Teatro $$ **193**
Ristorante La Caravella $$$$ **204**
Ristorante Riviera $$ **222**
Ristoteca Oniga $$ **213**
Rivoire $$ **39**
Rosticceria San Bartolomeo $ **184**
Ruga Rialto $ **229**
Ruggero $$ **132**
Trattoria Aciugheta $$ **271**
Trattoria Alla Madonna $$ **230**
Trattoria alle Burchielle $$ **244**
Trattoria Antellesi $$ **100**
Trattoria "Antica Mola" $ **249**
Trattoria da Ignazio $$$ **234**
Trattoria Do Mori $$ **281**
Trattoria Pizzeria da Paolo $$ **275**
Vecio Fritolin $ **242**
Vini Da Gigio $$ **256**
Vino Vino $$ **195**

★

Baldovino $$ **118**
Beccofino $$$ **124**
2Borgo Antico (Oltrarno) $$ **128**
Buca Lapi $$ **76**
Caffè Chioggia $$ **199**
Caffè delle Carrozze $ **47**
Caffè La Posta $ **33**
Caffè Santa Trinità $ **126**
Cantinetta da Verrazzano $ **30**
Capocaccia $$ **87**
Conca D'Oro $ **271**
Da Benvenuto $ **119**
Danny Rock $$ **112**
Da Noi $ **108**
De' Medici $$ **70**
Donnini $ **28**
Elto $$ **119**
Fiaschetteria Vecchio Casentino $ **120**
Gelateria Michelangiolo $ **61**
Giubbe Rosse $$ **28**
Hong Kong $$ **104**
Il Cantinone $$ **125**
Il Contadino $ **71**
i'Toscano $$ **91**
La Baruciola $$ **129**

La Carabaccia $$ **68**
La Mescita $ **99**
Le Barrique $$ **127**
Mamma Gina $$$ **127**
Negroni $ **57**
Nerbone $ **95**
Nuti $ **104**
Osteria Ae Botti $ **281**
Osteria ai Forneri $ **271**
Papadopoli Restaurant $$$ **243**
Paszkowski $$ **27**
Ristorante Al Trono di Attila $$ **291**
Ristorante Gam Gam $ **251**
Ruth's $$ **108**
Sergio $ **101**
Silla $ **57**
Taverna da Baffo $ **228**
Trattoria dai Tosi $$ **279**
Trattoria da Montín $$ **216**
Trattoria della Donna Onesta $$ **210**
VinOlio $ **90**

HOTELS

The hotels listed below are grouped according to their price ratings; they are also listed in the main index. The hotel price ratings reflect the base price of a standard room for two people for one night during the peak season.

$$$$ Big Bucks ($250 and way up)
$$$ Expensive ($175-$250)
$$ Reasonable ($125-$175)
$ The Price is Right (less than $125)

$$$$

Albergo Cipriani **282**
Boscolo Hotel Astoria **70**
Ca' Pisani Hotel **223**
Gallery Hotel Art **46**
Grand Hotel **77**
Grand Hotel Minerva **72**
Grand Hotel Villa Cora **63**
Grand Hotel Villa Medici **68**
Gritti Palace **207**
Hotel Albani **66**
Hotel Amadeus **252**
Hotel Bauer **205**
Hotel Bellini **255**
Hotel Berchielli **87**
Hotel Bernini Palace **41**
Hotel Brunelleschi **25**
Hotel Danieli **275**
Hotel de la Ville **84**
Hotel des Bains **292**
Hotel Excelsior **293**
Hotel Helvetia & Bristol **80**
Hotel J & J **109**
Hotel Lungarno **126**
Hotel Majestic **70**
Hotel Metropole **276**
Hotel Monaco and Grand Canal **206**
Hotel Monna Lisa **108**
Hotel Pierre **33**
Hotel Principe **71**
Hotel Regency **106**
Hotel Santa Maria Novella **73**
Hotel Sofitel **74**
JK Place **72**
Luna Hotel Baglioni **206**
Plaza Hotel Lucchesi **121**
Savoy **28**
Sofitel Venezia **243**
The Westin Europa & Regina **207**
Westin Excelsior **77**

$$$

Ca' Maria Adele **223**
Grand Hotel Cavour **32**
Hotel Ai Mori D'Oriente **248**
Hotel Balestri **120**
Hotel Calzaiuoli **29**
Hotel Croce di Malta **75**
Hotel Flora **204**
Hotel Kraft **68**
Hotel La Fenice et des Artistes **193**
Hotel Montecarlo **190**
Hotel Rialto **183**
Hotel San Cassiano **240**
Hungaria Palace Hotel **292**
Il Guelfo Bianco **99**
Le Due Fontane **97**
Liassidi Palace **272**
Locanda ai Santi Apostoli **257**
Locanda Sturion **229**
Loggiato dei Serviti **95**
Novecento **207**
Palace Bonvecchiati **186**
Palazzo Benci **100**
Quattro Fontane **293**
Torre di Bellosguardo **131**
Villa Carlotta **63**

$$

Albergo ai Do Mori **190**
Albergo San Zulian **186**
Annalena **59**
Antico Locanda Al Gambero **186**
Aprile **72**
Beacci Tornabuoni **85**
Borghese Palace Art Hotel **112**
Ca' Malcanton **245**
Campiello **275**
Colomba **99**
Cristallo **292**
Hotel Abbazia **252**
Hotel Ala **207**
Hotel Al Sole **245**
Hotel American **218**
Hotel Belle Arti **223**
Hotel Bucintoro **278**
Hotel Cellai **90**
Hotel Dèco **71**
Hotel delle Tele **71**
Hotel Heperia **252**
Hotel Hermitage **47**
Hotel La Residenza (Santa Maria Novella) **85**
Hotel Mario's **65**
Hotel Nuova Italia **94**
Hotel Paris **74**
Hotel Porta Faenza **65**
Hotel Porta Rossa **86**
Hotel San Stefano **201**
Hotel Santa Marina **265**
Hotel Torre Guelfa **41**
Hotel Unicorno **79**
La Calcina **225**
Locanda del Ghetto **251**
Locanda Ovidius **230**
Miró **91**
Morandi alla Crocetta **98**
Pendini **28**
Pensione Accademia–Villa Meravege **215**
Pensione Seguso **224**
Pensione Sorelle Bandini **129**
Pensione Wildner **276**
Pitti Palace **128**
Relais Uffizi **42**
Residenze Johlea I and Johlea II **90**
Ristorante Quattro Fontane **293**

$

Albergo Firenze **29**
Antica Locanda Montín **216**
Bellettini **71**

asci **99**
entrale (San Lorenzo) **102**
ujiyama **214**
otel Cimabue **90**
otel Galleria **218**
otel Genesio **90**
otel La Residenza (Castello) **274**
otel Liana **106**
otel Rossi **252**
ocanda Poste Vecie **227**
ocanda Salieri **244**
esidenza Johanna Uno **89**

EATURES

n Affair of the Art **264**
spects of Venice **313**
ridges of Venice **217**
enacoli (Last Suppers) **132**
Challenge . . . **23**
hild's Play **203**
olci Veneziani **240**
on't Leave Florence Without . . . **78**
on't Leave Venice Without . . . **290**
at, Drink, and Be Merry at Florence's Wine Bars **74**
iesole: A Jewel in the Florentine Hills **96**
lorentine Crafts **26**
rom the Grapevine **156**
ondola, Gondola, Gondola **221**
he "Grand Tour" of the Veneto **299**
ealing with Herbs: Florence's *Erboristerie* **66**
ights, Camera, Action **238**
iterary Italy **8**
Maggio Musicale **24**
Magic's in the Air **211**
The Main Events **6**
Masks, Glass, and Old Lace **172**
Michelangelo in Florence **34**
Olive Oil: Liquid Gold **138**
The Outlets **139**
Parla Italiano? **268**
Renaissance Painters of the Veneto **309**
Siena: The Palio **149**
Taste of Tuscany **114**
Venetian Streets **245**
Venetian Victuals **311**
Venezia di Notte: San Marco **243**
What a Girl Wants **302**

BESTS

Abbate, Enrica **174**
Antinori, Piero **152**
Beggiato, P. L. **202**
Berndt, Louise **288**
Bowden, John-Henry **230**
Bulgarella, Mary Westerman **105**
Cohen, Suzanne B. **159**
Colombini, Donatella Cinelli **142**
Denker, Eric **175**
di Barsento, Puccio Pucci **155**
Dowling, Gregory **312**
Franchetti, Amerigo **148**
Giannini, Enrico **165**
Grant, Amabel **235**
Hazan, Marcella **63**
Kramer, Laura **140**
McCobb, Donald and Jessie **160**
Montagnaro, Ennio **195**
Montana, Umberto **117**
Norwich, John Julius **304**
Pincenti, Kirsten Aachengreen **163**
Sebasti, Lorenza **146**
Snapp, Holly **244**
Verrocchia, Janice **71**
Wilk, Robert **300**
Willinger, Faith **110**

MAPS

Canal Grande **176**
Cannaregio **246**
Castello **260**
Centro Storico **18**
Colli **50**
Dorsoduro **208**
Florence **11**
Florence Area **130**
Giardino di Boboli (Boboli Gardens) **60**
Giudecca **280**
Italy *see inside front cover*
Map key **3**
Murano **285**
Oltrarno **122**
San Lorenzo **88**
San Marco **182**
San Paolo **226**
Santa Croce (Florence) **107**
Santa Croce (Venice) **236**
Santa Maria Novella **64, 69, 73**
Tuscany **134**
Vaporetto stops, Venice **171,** *see also inside back cover*
Venetian Islands **283**
Venice **169**
Venice Day Trips: Visions of the Veneto **294**
Venice Vaporetto Stops **171;** *see also inside back cover*

CREDITS

Writer and Researcher for the Eighth Edition
Kate Copstick

Editorial Supervisor
Lyndee Stalter

Jacket Design
Chin-Yee Lai

Design Director
Leah Carlson-Stanisic

Map Designer
Patricia Keelin

Associate Director of Production
Dianne Pinkowitz

Senior Production Editor
Helen Song

The publisher and authors assume neither legal responsibility for the completeness or accuracy of the contents of this book nor any legal responsibility for the appreciation or depreciation in the value of any premises, commercial or otherwise, by reason of inclusion in or exclusion from this book. All contents are based on information available at the time o publication. Some of the maps are diagrammatic and may be selective of street inclusion.

ACCESS®PRESS does not solicit individuals, organizations, or businesses for inclusion in our books, nor do we accept payment for inclusion. We welcome, however, information from our readers, including comments, criticisms, and suggestions for new listings. Send all correspondence to: ACCESS®PRESS, 10 East 53rd Street, New York, NY 10022

PRINTED IN HONG KONG

Look for these other Access Guides at your local bookstore:

ACCESS Boston
ACCESS California Wine Country
ACCESS Chicago
ACCESS London
ACCESS Los Angeles
ACCESS Montreal & Quebec City
ACCESS New Orleans
ACCESS New York City
ACCESS Paris
ACCESS Philadelphia
ACCESS Rome
ACCESS San Diego
ACCESS San Francisco
ACCESS Seattle
ACCESS Sydney
ACCESS Washington, DC